Information Modeling and Relational Databases

From Conceptual Analysis to Logical Design

The Morgan Kaufmann Series in Data Management Systems

Series Editor: Jim Gray, Microsoft Research

Information Modeling and Relational Databases

From Conceptual Analysis to Logical Design

Terry Halpin

Microsoft Corporation

MORGAN KAUFMANN PUBLISHERS

AN IMPRINT OF ACADEMIC PRESS

A Harcourt Science and Technology Company

SAN FRANCISCO   SAN DIEGO   NEW YORK   BOSTON
LONDON   SYDNEY   TOKYO

Executive Editor	Diane D. Cerra
Publishing Services Manager	Scott Norton
Senior Production Editor	Cheri Palmer
Assistant Editor	Belinda Breyer
Editorial Assistant	Mona Buehler
Cover Design	Ross Carron Design
Cover Image	© Leslie Harris/PictureQuest
Text Design	Mark Ong, Side by Side Studios
Copyeditor	Ken DellaPenta
Proofreader	Jennifer McClain
Composition/Illustration	Technologies 'N Typography
Indexer	Ty Koontz
Printer	Courier Corporation

Designations used by companies to distinguish their products are often claimed as trademarks or registered trademarks. In all instances in which Morgan Kaufmann Publishers is aware of a claim, the product names appear in initial capital or all capital letters. However, readers should contact the appropriate companies for more complete information regarding trademarks and registration.

Morgan Kaufmann Publishers
340 Pine Street, Sixth Floor, San Francisco, CA 94104-3205, USA
http://www.mkp.com

ACADEMIC PRESS
A Harcourt Science and Technology Company
525 B Street, Suite 1900, San Diego, CA 92101-4495, USA
http://www.academicpress.com

Academic Press
Harcourt Place, 32 Jamestown Road, London, NW1 7BY, United Kingdom
http://www.academicpress.com

Library of Congress Cataloging-in-Publication Data

Halpin, T. A.
   Information modeling and relational databases : from conceptual analysis to logical
   design / Terry Halpin.
      p.   cm.
   Includes bibliographical references and index.
   ISBN 1-55860-672-6
   1. Database design.   2. Relational databases.   I. Title.
QA76.9.D26 H355 2001
005.75'6—dc21   00-053468

This book is printed on acid-free paper.

To Norma, my wonderful wife.
Here's to another 30 years!
—Terry Halpin

Contents

Foreword

by John Zachman, Founder and President
Zachman International

I have known Terry Halpin for many years, and I have known *about* Terry Halpin for many more years than I have actually known him personally. His reputation precedes him, and—take it from me—he is one of those people who is bigger than his reputation and far more humble than his contribution warrants.

When Terry asked me to write the industrial foreword to his book, my first reaction was, "Good night! Am I qualified to write a foreword for a Terry Halpin book"? I suggested that he send me the manuscript, and I would decide whether I could write the foreword for him or not. Once I received the book, my next problem was, I couldn't put it down! Can you imagine that? A technical book that keeps you wanting to read the next page?

Yes, it is a technical book, a *very* technical book in that Terry goes into great detail about how to produce graphic models that exquisitely and rigorously capture the semantic nuances of an information system. But it is also an easy-to-ready book because it spells out clearly, concisely, and simply the complexities of logic that provide any enterprise and any natural language with its capacity for nuance of expression and richness of description. For every step in his logic, Terry provides an illustration and a test for your comprehension. There are hosts of models of real cases, none so contrived or so convoluted that it takes more energy to understand the case than to get the point.

Yes, Terry uses Object-Role Modeling (ORM) for his illustrations, not simply because he virtually "wrote the book" on modern ORM, but because of ORM's incomparable ability to capture semantic intent and unambiguously express it graphically. And, yes, Terry discusses ORM modeling in sufficient detail for modelers to acquire ORM language capability. But the cases and illustrations are rich with analysis that can help even modelers unfamiliar with ORM to accurately extract the precise semantics of a "universe of discourse".

But to me, all of these features are not the true strength of this book. The enduring strength of the book is two-fold. First, this text is a very clear and vivid demonstration of the incredible complexities of accurately discerning and capturing the intentions of an enterprise and transforming them into the realities of an implementation. There is little wonder why the systems we have been implementing for the last 50 years (i.e., the entire history of "data processing") are so inflexible, unadaptable, misaligned, disintegrated, unresponsive, expensive, unmaintainable, and frustrating to management. We never bothered to produce an accurate conceptual model! If you don't rigorously describe an enterprise to begin with, why would anybody expect to be able to produce a relevant design and implementation that reflected the enterprise's reality or intent, or could be adapted over time to accommodate its changes?

Tragically, few general managers would normally consider reading so technical a book as *Information Modeling and Relational Databases.* But *all* general managers ought to read this book to get some perspective on the semantic complexity of their own enterprises, of the challenges of accurately capturing that complexity, of the necessity of their own participation in conceptual modeling, of the sophistication of the engineering that is required to produce quality and flexible implementations—of the fact that systems are not magic, they are logic and good judgment and engineering and a lot of hard work.

In fact, every data modeler, regardless of his or her syntactic specialty—whether it be Chen, Barker, Finkelstein, IDEF1X, IDEF1x(Object), UML, XML, or XYZ—ought to read this book for the same reasons. In fact, modelers of all kinds ought to read the book. In fact, every *programmer* ought to read the book. In fact, anyone who has anything to do with information or information systems ought to read the book!

The second strength of this book lies in the derivations from the high standard of semantic expression established by employing Object-Role Modeling. Once one has demonstrated that it is possible to be rigorous and graphic in capturing precise semantic intent, it is very straightforward to evaluate all other graphic modeling notations in terms of their ability to duplicate that expression. Terry compares every other modeling notation that I have ever heard of, including those I've just mentioned. Terry is apologetic about appearing to be critical of other languages, but my observation is that his comparison is the most dispassionate, precise, and objective discussion I have every encountered. Terry even points out the strengths of these other notations and how and where in the overall process they can be used effectively. How's that for objectivity?! And who else but Terry Halpin could produce a complex conceptual model in ORM, Chen, Barker (Oracle), Finkelstein, IDEF1X, UML, and so on, for comparative purposes? Good night! Most of us spend a lifetime getting conversant with a single notation.

There is one more interesting dimension of these rigorous, precise semantic models—they have to be transformed into databases. Terry describes in detail and by illustration the transformation from conceptual models to logical models, to physical database design, and to implementation. In this context, it is easy to evaluate and compare the various database implementation possibilities including relational databases, object-oriented databases, object-relational databases, and declarative databases; and he throws in star schemas and temporal and spatial databases for good measure! Once again, I cannot remember seeing so dispassionate and objective an evaluation and comparison of the various database structures. Within this context, it is a straightforward task to make a considered and realistic projection of database technology trends into the foreseeable future.

This is a book that is going to sit on my bookshelf forever. I would consider it a candidate to be one of the few classics in our rather young, 50-year-old discipline of information management. I hope I have the personal discipline to pick it up about once a year and refresh my understanding of the challenges and the possibilities of the information profession. I am confident you will find *Information Modeling and Relational Databases* as useful and enlightening as I have.

Foreword

by Professor Dr. Robert Meersman, Director
Laboratory for Systems Technology and Applications Research
Computer Science Department, Vrije Universiteit Brussel, Belgium

As in a previous book by Dr. Halpin, it is again my distinct pleasure to introduce you to this wonderfully useful work—fundamentally reworked and updated in many places. As with the earlier book, which I adopted for many years as a one-semester course text on information systems as part of the computer science curriculum at the Vrije Universiteit Brussel, I am sure *Information Modeling and Relational Databases* will prove equally useful as a teaching tool and support and be enjoyed by staff and students alike.

As with all good reference works, this book provides a solid, formal, and, therefore, authoritative basis for the study, as well as the application in practice, of the ORM methodology. The science and techniques behind this methodology, originating as "NIAM" in the 1970s, went far too long without a high-quality reference work in the literature. In a sense, this lapse has delayed the acceptance of ORM and its tools by the DP and IT communities as well as, unfortunately, by the database and information systems research communities. In a way, the NIAM/ORM method quite literally was ahead of its time; in Flemish we have an elegant expression, "de remmende voorsprong", literally "the restraining lead", which certainly applies to the concepts underlying this method of database design.

As I had the very good fortune, together with many others, to participate in the inception of this methodology in Nijssen's research lab in Brussels, the above may be seen as not a little bit of self-praise. However, the emphasis very clearly must be on the "many others": all good methodologies are like good wine—the result of a long maturation process, much experimentation, and filtering through the intellects of many practitioners. But to take the wine metaphor one step further, only a really creative cellar master can produce a truly great wine. The result is in front of you, bottled by the master himself. As Terry Halpin uniquely combines excellent academic research skills with an unmistakable talent for the business of providing useful tools to database practitioners, it should not be a surprise that he is now widely considered to be the world's top expert on Object-Role Modeling in all its facets. (By the way, for those interested in historical tidbits and other trivia, this book contains many lesser-known and never-before-published facts about the origins and development of NIAM and ORM.)

Finally, there may still be some poetic justice resulting from the "restraining lead", as one sees that competing but less rigorous methods such as EER and UML have cornered the easy "methodology markets" for prosaic database design. Recent research indeed indicates that the much greater attention to matters semantical in NIAM/ORM could make it a more sophisticated candidate for the specification of new types of computerized repositories of semantics, so-called *ontologies,* while other methods may be doomed to syntactical insignificance.

I wish you an enjoyable study of ORM and many productive applications of it.

Foreword

by Gordon Everest, Professor of MIS and DBMS
Carlson School of Management, University of Minnesota

I am delighted and honored to write a foreword to this book. It gives me one more opportunity to convince those in the world of data modeling that there is a better way. I am absolutely convinced that Object-Role Modeling (ORM) is a better way to do data modeling. My underlying motive in this foreword is to peak your interest sufficiently to study ORM seriously . . . and this book is the best resource available to you.

Data modeling is the foundation of information systems development B: If you don't get the database design "right", then the systems you build will be like a house of cards, collapsing under the weight of inevitable future forces for revision, enhancement, integration, and quality improvement. Therefore, we need a scheme to guide our data modeling efforts that will help produce data models that are a clear and accurate representation of the users' domain of discourse and that will facilitate human communication, understanding, and validation.

I have long been a student and advocate of "recordless" data modeling, ever since sharing the lectern with Sjir Nijssen, Michael Senko, and Eckhard Falkenberg in Freudenstadt, Germany, in 1975. Upon my return, I began teaching "binary modeling" in my advanced database course, which is taken by most of our MBA and Ph.D. students majoring in MIS, along with many of our undergraduate majors. In those formative years, teaching NIAM was difficult because we lacked good written materials and an affordable software tool. Then by 1990, we had an earlier version of this book from Halpin and Nijssen, followed by InfoDesigner (later VisioModeler), a viable computer-based tool to support ORM. Today we offer three sections of the advanced database design course, servicing upward of 100 students each year. Students have consistently rated this book as the best of the materials used in the course. They find it well written and clearly understandable.

This book is a must for anyone who is serious about data modeling, but with a caution: You must devote enough time and effort to really understand ORM. Fortunately, I have my students as a captive audience for a whole semester—long enough for them to learn and practice ORM and become convinced that it is a better way. This book builds on its predecessor with more exercises to sharpen your data modeling skills and help you understand ORM. ORM is quite different from traditional data modeling, which is based on records representing entities—Chen's Entity-Relationship (ER) diagrams and their many variations, Teorey's Extended ER, Finkelstein's Information Engineering (IE, and adapted by Martin), Appleton's IDEF1X (U.S. Government; Bruce), Ullman's Semantic Data Model (SDM), Kroenke's Semantic Object Model (SOM), UML class diagrams, and Codd's relations in the relational model. Many CASE software tools today embody these data modeling schemes. Such record-based modeling schemes use three constructs: entity, attribute, and relationship. It is the clustering of attributes into entity records that is the root of many of our problems in data modeling. Normalization is the test to see if we clustered too much, and record decomposition is *always* the remedy to correct a violation of the normal forms. If you fully decompose a record-based design, such that every record has at most one nonkey domain, then you end up with an ORM design in which each "record" corresponds to a predicate, that is, a relationship.

Normalization is the Achilles' heel of data modeling. Oh, to be able to avoid normalization altogether! The mere suggestion is intriguing to students and practitioners of data modeling. Well, with ORM you can. The problem stems from the lack of clear definition of relationships when we throw stuff into a record, so that the intrarecord structure is implicitly defined or assumed. ORM forces you to consider and define separately all relevant relationships and constraints among the object domains in your universe.

ORM is actually based on only two constructs: objects and relationships (which correspond to the concepts of nouns as subject or object and verbs as predicates in sentences). Both entities and attributes are treated as objects in ORM (not to be confused with objects in object-oriented technology). Objects play roles in relationships with other objects. Entities or objects have attributes or descriptors by virtue of the roles they play in relationships with other objects. When the ORM model is a valid representation of the world being modeled, the functional dependencies are explicitly defined, and the generation of "records" (in a relational table diagram) can be automated with a guaranteed result that is fully normalized (to 5NF). That's good news for data modelers.

ORM does not supplant ER diagrams or relational database designs; rather, it is a stage before. Thus, we call it conceptual modeling, which comes before the "logical" modeling in which we build records, often in a relational database structure. The formation of records is actually more for system efficiency than for human convenience or comprehension. The premature notion of a record (a cluster of attribute domains along with an identifier to represent an entity) actually gets in the way of data modeling.

ORM is also a richer and more expressive data modeling scheme, in both its diagrams and its verbalizations, than any record-based scheme could be. ORM can capture and directly represent more semantics, (e.g., many-to-many relationships, ternary and higher-order relationships, and mixed interentity constraints), and it does so directly, without introducing artificial or spurious constructs such as intersection entities or foreign keys, which are undesirable and confusing to the user domain specialists who must understand and validate our data models.

Well, is that sufficient to peak your interest in learning more about ORM for data modeling? If you are a would-be student of ORM and you take data modeling seriously, I encourage you to invest some time in reading this book. You won't regret it. You will grow to appreciate ORM and will become a better data modeler for it. In order to develop effective and maintainable information systems we need good data models, and for that we need a good data modeling scheme. ORM allows us to develop database designs at the highest conceptual level, unencumbered by things that are not of primary concern to user domain specialists. My deep desire is to see more and more database designers using ORM. The systems we build and the world we live in will be better for it. Join me in this journey and enjoy the adventure.

Preface

This book is about information systems, focusing on information modeling and relational database systems. It is written primarily for database practitioners as well as students of computer science or information management. It should also be useful to anyone wishing to formulate the information structure of applications in a way readily understood by humans yet easily implemented on computers. In addition, it provides a simple conceptual framework for understanding what database systems really are and a thorough introduction to SQL.

A major part of this book deals with Object-Role Modeling (ORM), a conceptual modeling approach that views the world in terms of objects and the roles they play. ORM originated in Europe, where it is often known by other names such as NIAM (natural-language information analysis method) or FCO-IM (Fully Communication Oriented Information Modeling). The version of ORM described in this book is based on extensions to NIAM and has tool support from Microsoft Corporation.

Two other popular notations for information modeling are Entity-Relationship (ER) diagrams and Unified Modeling Language (UML) class diagrams. For conceptual information analysis, the ORM method has several advantages over the ER and UML approaches. For example, ORM models can be easily verbalized and populated for validation with domain experts, they are more stable under changes to the application domain, and they typically capture more business rules in diagram form. However, ER diagrams and UML class diagrams are good for compact summaries. Their structures are closer to the final database implementation, so they also have value. Hence, the coverage includes chapters on data modeling in ER and UML and indicates how ER and UML data models can be easily abstracted from ORM models.

To make the text more approachable to the general reader with an interest in databases, the language is kept simple, and a formalized, mathematical treatment is deliberately avoided. Where necessary, relevant concepts from elementary logic and set theory are discussed prior to their application. Most of the material in this book has been class tested in courses for both industry and academia, and the basic ORM method has been taught successfully for many years at the high school level. The content is modularized, so that instructors wishing to omit some material may make an appropriate selection for their courses.

The first chapter motivates the study of conceptual modeling and briefly compares the ORM, ER, and UML approaches. It also includes an historical and structural overview of information systems. Chapter 2 provides a structural background, explaining the conceptual architecture of, and development frameworks for, information systems. It introduces a number of key concepts that are dealt with more thoroughly in later chapters and should be read in full by the reader with little or no database experience.

Chapter 3 is fundamental. Following an overview of conceptual modeling language criteria and the ORM conceptual design procedure (CSDP), it covers the first three steps of the CSDP. The first step (verbalizing familiar examples in terms of elementary facts) may seem trivial, but it should not be rushed, as it provides the foundation for the model. The rest of this chapter covers the basic graphical notation for fact types and then offers guidance on how to classify objects into types and identify information that can be arithmetically derived.

Chapter 4 begins the task of specifying constraints on the populations of fact types. The most important kind of constraint (the uniqueness constraint) is considered in detail. Then some checks on the elementarity of the fact types are discussed. This chapter also introduces the join and projection operations at the conceptual level—the relational version of these operations is important in the later work on relational databases.

Chapter 5 covers mandatory role constraints, including a check for detecting information that can be logically derived. Reference schemes are then examined in some depth. Some of the more complex reference schemes considered here could be skipped in a short course. The CSDP steps covered so far are then reviewed by applying them in a case study.

Chapter 6 covers value, set comparison (subset, equality, and exclusion), and subtyping constraints. Section 6.6 deals with advanced aspects of subtyping. Though important in practice, the material in this section could be skimmed over in a first reading.

Chapter 7 deals with the final step of the conceptual schema design procedure. Less common constraints are considered (e.g., occurrence frequencies and ring constraints), and final checks are made on the design. Sections 7.3–7.5 are somewhat advanced and could be skipped in a short course.

Chapter 8 discusses the Entity-Relationship (ER) approach, starting with Chen's original notation then moving on to the three most popular notations in current use: the Barker ER notation supported by Oracle Corporation, the Information Engineering notation, and the IDEF1X notation, which is actually a hybrid of ER and relational notations. Comparisons with ORM are included along the way.

Chapter 9 examines the use of UML class diagrams for data modeling, including a detailed comparison with ORM. Business rule constructs in ORM with no graphic counterpart in UML are identified, then captured in UML, using user-defined constraints or notes.

Chapter 10 describes how a conceptual model may be implemented in a relational database system. The first three sections are fundamental to understanding how a conceptual schema may be mapped to a relational schema. Section 10.4 considers advanced mapping aspects and could be omitted in an introductory course.

Chapter 11 examines some query languages for relational databases. Section 11.1 covers relational algebra; although not used as a practical query language, the algebra is important for understanding the basic relational operations supported by SQL. Section 11.2 provides an overview of how the relational model of data compares with data models adopted by some relational database management systems. Sections 11.3–11.4 cover the main features of SQL, with attention to the SQL-89, SQL-92, and SQL:1999 standards and some popular dialects.

Chapter 12 discusses how and when to transform one schema into another schema at the same level (conceptual or logical). Sections 12.1–12.4 examine the notion of conceptual schema equivalence and ways in which conceptual schemas may be reshaped. As one application of this theory, Section 12.5 specifies a procedure for optimizing a database design by performing conceptual transformations before mapping. Section 12.6 provides a concise coverage of normalization theory. Section 12.7 briefly considers denormalization and low-level optimization. Section 12.8 illustrates the role of conceptual optimization in database reengineering. Sections 12.4, 12.5, 12.7, and 12.8 are of an advanced nature and may be skipped in a short course. In a very short course, the whole chapter could be skipped.

Chapter 13 examines other modeling issues, methods, and trends. Topics covered include data warehousing, conceptual query languages, schema abstraction mechanisms, process modeling (e.g., UML use cases and activity diagrams, data flow diagrams), postrelational databases (e.g., object databases and object-relational databases), and metamodeling. Though these topics are important and interesting, they could be omitted in a short course.

In line with the ORM method, this text adopts a "cookbook" approach, with plenty of diagrams and examples. Each chapter begins with a brief overview and ends with a chapter summary of the major points covered, with chapter notes to provide fine points and further references. One of the major features of the book is its large number of carefully graded exercises, which have been thoroughly class-tested. A bibliography of all cited references is included at the end of the book, where you will also find glossaries of technical symbols and terms for ORM, ER, and UML (class diagrams only). A comprehensive index provides easy access to explanations of technical topics.

Online Resources

To reduce the size and, hence, cost of the book, a significant amount of supplementary material has been made available online at the publisher's Web site (www.mkp.com/

imrd/) for downloading. There are three appendices. Appendix A provides an overview of the evolution of computer hardware and software. Appendix B discusses two kinds of subtype matrix that can be used to determine subtype graphs from significant populations. Appendix C discusses advanced aspects of SQL, focusing on set-comparison queries and group extrema queries.

The answers to the exercises are contained in two files: one for the odd-numbered questions and one for the even-numbered questions. The answers to the odd-numbered questions are openly accessible, but the answers to the even-numbered questions are password-protected in order to provide classroom instructors with a range of exercises for classroom discussion. Additional material on ORM is available from the author's Web site at *www.orm.net.*

Electronic versions of the figures, as well as further exercises and related pedagogic material, are included in an accompanying Instructor's Guide. This guide and a password for exercise answers are available to classroom instructors by contacting their reps as listed at *www.mkp.com/academic/rep_locator.asp.*

ORM Software

ORM is supported by a variety of modeling tools from Microsoft Corporation and other companies. A discontinued ORM modeling tool known as VisioModeler is freely available as a download from Microsoft's MSDN Web site. Although no technical support is available for this download and the product is somewhat outdated in its database driver support, it is fine for learning ORM, and it does allow you to create ORM models and map them to a range of database systems. To access this download (25 MB), point your browser at *http://download.microsoft.com/,* and then do a keyword search for VisioModeler.

At the time of writing, a basic ORM modeling solution is available in Microsoft's Visio Enterprise 2000 product. This provides better driver support than VisioModeler and includes support for views and code editing, but it has very limited ability to display ORM constraints. Future versions of Visio will support ORM diagramming but not mapping.

A substantially improved version of the Visio-based ORM modeling solution will appear in Visual Studio.net, which is scheduled for release in the second half of 2001. As well as displaying all ORM constraints, this solution includes many improvements for specifying and mapping logical database models. This solution will first appear in Beta 2 of Visual Studio.net. Further details about Microsoft Visual Studio are accessible from *http://msdn.microsoft.com/vstudio/.*

Acknowledgments

At Morgan Kaufmann, the editorial work of Diane Cerra, Belinda Breyer, Cheri Palmer, and Scott Norton has been first class. I've never worked with a publishing team as good as this before. Several passages in the book have benefited from feedback from the following reviewers: Scot Becker, Dave Brumbaugh, Dr. Earl F. Ecklund Jr., Pat Hallock, and Dr. Arthur ter Hofstede. Frank Pellow was kind enough to review the SQL chapter, and Dr. Gordon Everest offered useful suggestions on the early chapters. Advice on early versions of various sections was also received from the following academic colleagues: Dr. Erik Proper, Professor Maria Orlowska, Professor Bernhard Thalheim, and Dr. Millist Vincent. Any remaining mistakes are, of course, my own.

Some of this book's content is based on articles I wrote for the *Journal of Conceptual Modeling* and material from editions of my earlier book, *Conceptual Schema and Relational Database Design,* previously published by Prentice Hall Australia and WytLytPub. The first edition of that book was coauthored by Dr. Sjir Nijssen, who wrote the final four chapters (since replaced). For readers familiar with my earlier book, the major differences are now summarized. The content has been essentially rewritten from scratch, so the changes are significant. While new chapters have been added (e.g., ER and UML), there are many new topics (e.g., data warehousing and conceptual queries), several topics are covered in much greater depth (e.g., SQL), and there are many new exercises. The conceptual schema design procedure has been refined, the ORM notation has been brought more into line with that supported by Microsoft tools, and the treatment of all topics has been improved and updated. The new content has led to a much larger book, even after moving the answers to the Web.

The version of Object-Role Modeling discussed in this book is largely based on my revisions and extensions to the NIAM method, which was largely developed in its original form by Dr. Eckhard Falkenberg, Dr. Sjir Nijssen, and Dr. Robert Meersman, with other contributions from several researchers including Professor Dirk Vermeir, Mr. Frans van Assche, and Dr. Olga de Troyer. Many other researchers in the 1970s made significant contributions to the semantic data modeling movement (e.g., Mr. William Kent and Dr. Michael Senko) that gave birth to the fact-based, object-role modeling approach.

It is a pleasure to acknowledge my debt to these people for their pioneering work and for the fruitful discussions I have had with many of them. In particular I would like to express my gratitude to Sjir Nijssen for introducing me to conceptual modeling and for demonstrating the communicative power of examples and intuitive diagrams. In more recent years, other ORM researchers such as Dr. Anthony Bloesch, Dr. Arthur ter Hofstede, Dr. Erik Proper, Dr. Linda Bird, Dr. Peter Ritson, Dr. Theo van der Weide, and Dr. Andrew Goodchild have all made valuable contributions to extending ORM.

Some of the work discussed in this book was developed jointly with three of my former Ph.D. students: Dr. Anthony Bloesch and I developed the architecture and mapping algorithms for the ConQuer conceptual query language; Dr. Linda Bird (neé Campbell) worked with me on schema abstraction and reengineering; and Dr. Peter Ritson worked with me on disjunctive reference, relative closure, and extensions to the relational mapping procedure. It has been a pleasure working with these colleagues, as well as with the many hundreds of students and practitioners with whom trial versions of the material in this book were tested. I also gratefully acknowledge permission by the Computer Science and Electrical Engineering Department at the University of Queensland to include a selection of past assessment questions of mine within the exercises.

A modeling method as good as ORM deserves a good CASE tool. Over the last decade, talented staff at ServerWare, Asymetrix Corporation, InfoModelers Incorporated,

Visio Corporation, and, finally, Microsoft Corporation, have worked to develop state-of-the-art CASE tools to support the specific ORM method discussed in this book. The following four key developers currently working on ORM at Microsoft deserve special mention: Anthony Bloesch, Ross Grayum, Mike Ishimitsu, and Chang Oh. Three other developers, Jed Derickson, Charlotte Fallarme, and Pat Tseng, have also made valuable contributions to the logical and physical side of the database modeling solution. I'm also grateful to Jim Harding for initiating the ORM tool project at ServerWare and to Lance Delano for his continued management support.

Finally I thank my wife, Norma, for being so understanding and supportive while I was busily occupied in the writing task.

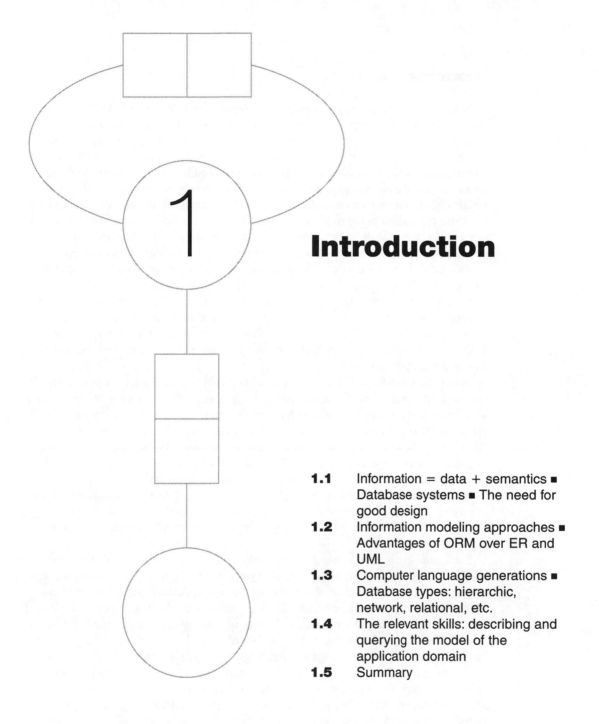

Introduction

1.1   Information Modeling

Do you remember the news flashes back in September 1999 when NASA's Mars Climate Orbiter was lost in space? Apparently, errors in its course settings caused the $125 million craft to burn up in the Martian atmosphere. Embarrassingly, the likely cause of this demise was the failure to make a simple conversion from the U.S. customary system of measurement to metric units. One team worked in customary units and sent its data to a second team working in metric, but no conversion was made. If I tell you that I weigh 180, do I need to go on a drastic diet? No if I mean 180 lb, but yes if I mean 180 kg. *Data* by itself is not enough—what we really need is *information,* the meaning or semantics behind the data. Since computers lack common sense, we need to pay especial attention to semantics when we use computers to model some aspect of reality.

This book provides a modern introduction to database systems, with the emphasis on information modeling. At its heart is a very high level semantic approach that is *fact-oriented* in nature. If you model databases using either traditional or object-oriented approaches, you'll find that fact orientation lifts your thinking to a higher level, illuminating your current way of doing things. Even if you're a programmer rather than a database modeler, this semantic approach provides a natural and powerful way to design your data structures.

A **database** is basically a collection of related data (e.g., a company's personnel records or a bus timetable). When interpreted by humans, a database may be viewed as a set of related *facts*—an *information base.* In the context of our semantic approach, I'll often use the popular term "database" instead of the more technical "information base". Discovering the kinds of facts that underlie an application area, and the rules that apply to them, is interesting and revealing. The quality of the database *design* used for these facts and rules is critical. Just as a house built from a good architectural plan is more likely to be safe and convenient for living, a well-designed database simplifies the task of ensuring that its facts are correct and easy to get at. Let's review some basic ideas about database systems, and then see how things can go wrong if the database design is poor.

Each database is used to model some application domain, typically a part of the real world. Consider a library database. As changes occur in the library (e.g., a book is borrowed or a new book is purchased), the database is updated to reflect these changes. This task could be performed manually (e.g., using a card catalog) or be automated (e.g., an online catalog) or both. We focus our attention on automated databases. Sometimes these are implemented by means of special-purpose computer programs, coded in a general-purpose programming language (e.g., C#). More often, database applications are developed using a **database management system** (DBMS). This is a software system for maintaining databases and answering queries about them (e.g., Microsoft Access, DB2, Oracle, SQL Server). The same DBMS may handle many different databases. Although the design methods we discuss are relevant to special-purpose database programs, our implementation focus is on DBMSs.

If an application requires maintenance and retrieval of large amounts of data, a DBMS offers many advantages over manual record-keeping systems. Data may be quickly processed and stored compactly on disk, and many data errors can be avoided by automatic integrity checking. With multiuser systems, access rights to data can be enforced by the system. People can spend more time on creative design rather than on routine tasks more suited to computers. Convenient interfaces are easily supported (e.g., form-based data entry and graphical output). Finally, the development of the application software and its documentation can be facilitated by use of *computer-assisted software engineering* (CASE) tool support.

In terms of the dominant employment group, the Agricultural Age was supplanted late in the 19th century by the Industrial Age, which is now replaced by the Information Age. The ongoing information explosion and mechanization of industrial processes indicate that the proportion of information workers will steadily rise in the foreseeable future. Most businesses can achieve significant productivity gains by exploiting information technology. Imagine how long a newspaper firm would last if it returned to the methods used before word processing and computerized typesetting. Apart from direct employment opportunities, the ability to interact efficiently with information systems empowers us to exploit the information they contain.

Although most employees need to be familiar with information technology, there are vast differences in the amount and complexity of information management tasks required of these workers. Originally, most technical computer work was performed by computer specialists such as programmers and systems analysts. However, the advent of user-friendly software and powerful, inexpensive personal computers led to a redistribution of computing power. End users now commonly perform many information management tasks, such as spreadsheeting, with minimal reliance on professional computer experts.

This trend toward more users "driving" their own computer systems rather than relying on expert "chauffeurs" does not eliminate the need for computer specialists. There is still a lot of programming going on in languages like C and COBOL. However, there is an increasing demand for high-level skills such as modeling complex information systems. The general area of *information systems engineering* includes many subdisciplines such as requirements analysis, database design, user interface design, and report writing. In one way or another, all these subareas deal with information. Since the database design phase selects the underlying structures for capturing the relevant information, it is of central importance.

To highlight **the need for good database design,** let's consider the task of designing a database to store the movie details shown in Table 1.1 (some data are fictitious). The *header* of this table is shaded, to help distinguish it from the *rows of data*. Even if the header is not shaded, we do not count it as a table row.

We interpret the data in terms of facts. For example, the movie *Awakenings* was released in 1991, was directed by Penny Marshall, and starred Robert De Niro and Robin Williams. The movie *Cosmology* had no stars (it might be a documentary). The table is an example of an *output report*. It provides one convenient way of viewing the information. How the information is actually stored in a database depends on the kind of database used.

In Table 1.1 each *cell* (row-column slot) may contain many values. For example, *Awakenings* has two stars recorded in the row 1, column 4 cell. Some database systems allow a cell to contain many values like this, but in a *relational* database each table cell

Table 1.1 An output report about some motion pictures.

Movie	Year	Director	Stars
Awakenings	1991	Penny Marshall	Robert De Niro Robin Williams
Backdraft	1991	Ron Howard	William Baldwin Robert De Niro Kurt Russell
Cosmology	1994	Terry Harding	
Dances with Wolves	1990	Kevin Costner	Kevin Costner Mary McDonnell

Table 1.2 A badly designed relational database table.

Movie:

movieName	releaseYr	director	star
Awakenings	1991	Penny Marshall	Robert De Niro
Awakenings	1991	Penny Marshall	Robin Williams
Backdraft	1991	Ron Howard	William Baldwin
Backdraft	1991	Ron Howard	Robert De Niro
Backdraft	1991	Ron Howard	Kurt Russell
Cosmology	1994	Terry Harding	?
Dances with Wolves	1990	Kevin Costner	Kevin Costner
Dances with Wolves	1990	Kevin Costner	Mary McDonnell

may hold at most one value. Hence the data cannot be stored like this in a relational database. Since relational database systems are dominant in the industry, our implementation discussion focuses on them. How can we design a relational database to store these facts?

Suppose we use the structure shown in Table 1.2. This has only one entry in each cell. The "?" denotes a "null value" (no actual star is recorded for *Cosmology*). To help distinguish the rows, I've included lines between them. But from now on, I'll adopt the normal practice of omitting lines between rows. Each relational table must be named—here we called the table "Movie". Can you see some problems with this design?

Notice that the table contains redundant information. For example, the facts that *Backdraft* was released in 1991 and directed by Ron Howard are shown three times (once for each star of that movie). We might try to fix this by deleting the extra copies in the releaseYr and director columns, but this artificially makes some rows special and also introduces problems with null values.

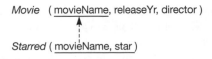

Movie (movieName, releaseYr, director)

Starred (movieName, star)

Movie:

movieName	releaseYr	director
Awakenings	1991	Penny Marshall
Backdraft	1991	Ron Howard
Cosmology	1994	Terry Harding
Dances with Wolves	1990	Kevin Costner

Starred:

movieName	star
Awakenings	Robert De Niro
Awakenings	Robin Williams
Backdraft	William Baldwin
Backdraft	Robert De Niro
Backdraft	Kurt Russell
Dances with Wolves	Kevin Costner
Dances with Wolves	Mary McDonnell

Figure 1.1 A relational database representation of Table 1.1.

Besides wasting space, the Table 1.2 design can lead to errors. For example, there is nothing to stop us adding a row for *Backdraft* with a different release year (1994, say) and a different director (Peter Weir, say). Our database would then be inconsistent with the real world, where a movie can have only one release year and director.

To correct the design, we use two relational tables named "Movie" and "Starred" (Figure 1.1). The design of these tables is shown in schematic form above the populated tables. The constraints that each movie has only one release year and director are enforced by checking that each movie occurs only once in the Movie table (shown by underlining the movieName column).

The constraints that each movie must have a release year and director are enforced by checking that all movies occur in the Movie table and that null values are excluded from the releaseYr and director columns. In the schema, this is captured by the dotted arrow (indicating that if a movie is listed in the Starred table, it must be listed in the Movie table) and by not marking any columns as optional. These concepts and notations are fully explained later in the book. Even with this simple example, care is needed for database design. With complex cases, the design problem is much more challenging. The rest of this book is largely concerned with helping you to meet such challenges.

Designing databases is both a science and an art. When supported by a good method, this design process is a stimulating and intellectually satisfying activity, with tangible benefits gained from the quality of the database applications produced. The next section explains why Object-Role Modeling has been chosen as our main modeling method. Later sections provide historical background and then highlight the two essential communication skills. The chapter concludes with a summary and supplementary notes, including references for further reading.

1.2   Modeling Approaches

When we design a database for a particular application, we create a model of the application area. Technically, the application area being modeled is called the **universe of discourse** (UoD), since it is the world (or universe) that we are interested in talking (or discoursing) about. The UoD is also called "the application domain" and typically is "part" of the "real world". To build a good model requires a good understanding of the world we are modeling, and hence is a task ideally suited to people rather than machines. The main challenge is to describe the UoD clearly and precisely. Great care is required here, since errors introduced at this stage filter through to later stages in software development, and the later the errors are detected, the more expensive they are to remove.

A person responsible for modeling the UoD is called a *modeler.* If we are familiar with the application area, we may do the modeling ourselves. If not, we should consult with others who, at least collectively, understand the application domain—these people are called *domain experts,* subject matter experts, or UoD experts. Modeling thus is a collaborative activity between the modeler and the domain expert. Since people naturally communicate (to themselves or others) with words, pictures, and examples, the best way to arrive at a clear description of the UoD is to make extensive use of *natural language, intuitive diagrams,* and *examples.* And as a safety measure, it makes sense to simplify the modeling task by examining the information in the smallest units possible: *one fact at a time.*

Hence the model should first be expressed at the *conceptual* level, in concepts that people find easy to work with. Figure 1.1 depicted a model in terms of relational database structures. This is too far removed from natural language to be called conceptual. Instead, relational database structures are at the level of a *logical* data model. Other logical data models exist (e.g., network, hierarchic, and various object-oriented approaches), and each DBMS is aligned with one of these. However, in specifying a draft conceptual design, the modeler should be free of implementation concerns. It is a hard enough job already to develop an accurate model of the UoD without having to worry at the same time about how to translate the model into data structures specific to a chosen DBMS.

Implementation concerns are of course important, but should be ignored in the early stages of modeling. Once an initial conceptual design has been constructed, it can be mapped down to a logical design in any data model we like. This added flexibility also makes it easier to implement and maintain the same application on more than one kind of DBMS.

Although most applications involve processes as well as data, I'll focus on the information (and hence data) because this perspective is more stable, and all processes are contingent on the underlying data. Three information modeling approaches are discussed: Entity-Relationship modeling, fact-oriented modeling, and object-oriented modeling.

Any modeling method comprises a notation as well as a procedure for using the notation to construct models. To seed the data model in a scientific way, we need examples of the kinds of data that the system is expected to manage. I call these examples *data use cases,* since they are cases of data being used by the system. They can be output reports, input screens, or forms, and they can present information in many ways (tables, forms, graphs, etc.). Such examples may already exist as manual or computer records. Sometimes the application is brand-new, or an improved solution or adaptation is required. If needed, the modeler constructs new examples by discussing the application with the domain expert.

As a simple example, suppose our information system has to output room schedules like that shown in Table 1.3. Let's look at some different approaches to modeling this. It is not important that you understand details of the different approaches at this stage because the concepts are fully explained in later chapters.

Entity-Relationship modeling (ER) was introduced by Peter Chen in 1976 and is still the most widely used approach for data modeling. It pictures the world in terms of entities that have attributes and participate in relationships. Over time, many different versions of ER arose, and today, there is no standard ER notation. Different versions of ER may support different concepts and may use different symbols for the same concept. Figure 1.2 uses a popular ER notation long supported by CASE tools from Oracle Corporation. Here, entity types are shown as named, soft rectangles (rounded corners). Attributes are listed below the entity type names. An octothorpe "#" indicates the attribute is a component of the primary identifier for the entity type, and an asterisk "*" means the attribute is mandatory. Here, an ellipsis "..." indicates other attributes exist but their display is suppressed.

Relationships are depicted as named lines connecting entity types. Only binary relationships are allowed, and each half of the relationship is shown either as a solid line (mandatory) or broken line (optional). For example, each RoomTimeSlot must have a Room, but it is optional whether a Room is involved in a RoomTimeSlot. A bar across one end of a relationship indicates that the relationship is a component of the primary

Table 1.3 A simple data use case for room scheduling.

Room	Time	ActivityCode	ActivityName
20	Mon 9 a.m.	VMC	VisioModeler class
20	Tue 2 p.m.	VMC	VisioModeler class
33	Mon 9 a.m.	AQD	ActiveQuery demo
33	Fri 5 p.m.	SP	Staff party
...	...	...	...

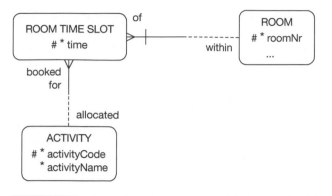

Figure 1.2 An ER diagram for room scheduling.

identifier for the entity type at that end. For example, RoomTimeSlot is identified by combining its time and room. Room is identified by its room number, and Activity by its activity code.

A fork or "crow's foot" at one end of a relationship indicates that many instances of the entity type at that end may be associated (via that relationship) with the same entity instance at the other end of the relationship. The lack of a crow's foot indicates that at most one entity instance at that end is associated with any given entity instance at the other end. For example, an Activity may be allocated many RoomTimeSlots, but each RoomTimeSlot is booked for at most one Activity.

To its credit, this ER diagram portrays the domain in a way that is independent of the target software platform. For example, classifying a relationship end as mandatory is a conceptual issue. There is no attempt to specify here how this constraint is implemented (e.g., using mandatory columns, foreign key references, or object references). However, the ER diagram is incomplete (can you spot any missing constraints?). Moreover, the notation is less than ideal for validating the model with the domain expert, and the conceptual step from the data use case to the model is less than obvious.

Let's see if fact-oriented modeling can improve the situation. Our treatment of fact orientation focuses on **Object-Role Modeling** (ORM), since this is the only fact-oriented method with significant support in industry. ORM began in the early 1970s as a semantic modeling approach that views the world simply in terms of objects playing *roles* (parts in relationships). For example, you are now playing the role of reading this book, and the book is playing the role of being read. ORM has appeared in a variety of forms such as the natural-language information analysis method (NIAM). The version discussed in this book is based on extensions to NIAM and is supported by industrial software tools.

Whatever the appearance of the data use cases, a domain expert familiar with their meaning should be able to verbalize their information content in terms of natural-language sentences. It is the modeler's responsibility to transform that informal verbalization into a formal yet natural verbalization that is clearly understood by the domain expert. These two verbalizations, one by the domain expert transformed into one by the modeler, comprise steps 1a and 1b of ORM's conceptual analysis procedure. Here we verbalize sample data as fact instances that are then abstracted to fact types. Constraints and perhaps derivation rules are then added and themselves validated by verbalization and sample fact populations.

To get a feeling of how this works in ORM, suppose that our system is required to output reports like Table 1.3. We ask the domain expert to read off the information contained in the table, and then we rephrase this in formal English. For example, the subject matter expert might read off the facts on the top row of the table as follows: Room 20 at 9 a.m. Monday is booked for the activity 'VMC' which has the name 'VisioModeler class'.

As modelers, we rephrase this into two elementary sentences, identifying each object by a definite description: the Room numbered '20' at the Time with day-hour-code 'Mon 9 a.m.' is booked for the Activity coded 'VMC'; the Activity coded 'VMC' has the ActivityName 'VisioModeler class'. Once the domain expert agrees with this verbalization, we abstract from the fact instances to the *fact types* (i.e., the types or kinds of fact). We might then depict this structure on an ORM diagram and populate it with sample data as shown in Figure 1.3.

Entity types are shown in ORM as named ellipses and must have a reference scheme, that is, a way for humans to refer to instances of that type. Simple reference schemes may be shown in parentheses (e.g., "(nr)"), as an abbreviation of the relevant association (e.g., Room has RoomNr). Value types such as character strings need no reference scheme and are shown as named, dashed ellipses (e.g., ActivityName). In ORM, a role is a part played in a relationship or association. A relationship is shown as a named sequence of one or more role boxes, each connected to the object type that plays it. Here we have one ternary (three-role) association, Room at Time is booked for Activity, and one binary association, Activity has ActivityName.

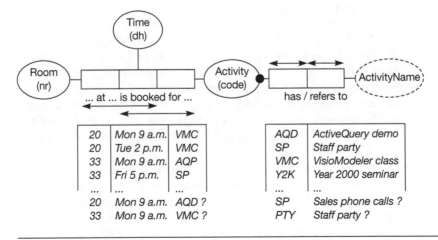

Figure 1.3 An ORM diagram for room scheduling, with sample and counter data.

Unlike ER, ORM makes no use of attributes in its base models. All facts are represented in terms of objects (entities or values) playing roles. Although this leads to larger diagrams, an attribute-free approach has many advantages for conceptual analysis, including simplicity, stability, and ease of validation. If you are used to modeling in ER, this approach may seem strange at first, but please keep an open mind about it.

ORM allows associations of any *arity* (number of roles). Each *n*-ary association (*n* > 0) may be given *n* readings, one starting at each role. For a binary association, forward and inverse predicates may be shown separated by a slash "/". As in logic, a predicate is a sentence with object holes in it. Mixfix notation is used, so the object terms may be mixed in with the predicate at various positions (as required in many languages such as Japanese). An object placeholder is explicitly indicated by an ellipsis (three dots). To save space, especially on diagrams, and to emphasize that it is a placeholder for a single object term, a compact ellipsis "..." is normally used instead of a standard ellipsis ". . .". For instance the ternary predicate shown is "... at ... is booked for ...". For unary postfix predicates (e.g., "... smokes") or binary infix predicates (e.g., "... has ..."), the ellipses may be omitted.

For each association, or fact type, a fact table may be added with a sample population to help validate the constraints. Each column in a fact table is associated with one role. The arrow-tipped bars are internal *uniqueness constraints,* indicating which roles or role combinations must have unique entries.

ORM schemas can be represented in either diagrammatic or textual form, and some ORM tools can automatically transform between the two representations. Models are *validated* with domain experts in two main ways: *verbalization* and *population.* For example, the uniqueness constraints on the ternary association verbalize as **the same** Room at **the same** Time is booked for **at most one** Activity; **at most one** Room at **the same** Time is booked for **the same** Activity. The ternary fact table provides a satisfying population (each Room-Time combination is unique, and each Time-Activity combination is unique). The uniqueness constraints on the binary verbalize as **each** Activity has **at most one** ActivityName; **each** ActivityName refers to **at most one** Activity. The 1:1 nature of this association is illustrated by the population, where each column is unique.

The black dot on Activity is a *mandatory role* constraint, indicating that each instance in the population of Activity must play that role. This verbalizes as **each** Activity has **at least one** ActivityName. A role that is not mandatory is *optional.* Since sample data are not always significant, additional data (like Y2K in the binary fact type) may be needed to illustrate some rules. The optionality of the other role played by Activity is shown by the absence of Y2K in its population. Since ORM schemas can be specified in unambiguous sentences backed up by illustrative examples, it is not necessary for domain experts to understand the diagram notation at all. Modelers, however, find diagrams very useful for thinking about the universe of discourse.

To double-check a constraint, a *counterexample* to the constraint being investigated may be presented. The counter-rows marked "?" below the fact tables test the uniqueness constraints. For instance, the first row and counter-row of the ternary indicate that room 20 at 9 a.m. Monday is booked for both the VMC and AQD activities. This challenges the constraint that **the same** Room at **the same** Time is booked for **at most one** Activity. This constraint may be recast in negative form as **it is impossible that the same** Room at

the same Time is booked for **more than one** Activity. The counterexample provides a test case to see if this situation is actually possible. Concrete examples make it easier for many domain experts to decide whether something really is a rule. This additional validation step is especially useful in cases where the domain expert's command of language suffers from imprecise or even incorrect use of logical terms (e.g., "each", "at least", "at most", "exactly", "the same", "more than", "if", "possible").

To challenge the constraint that at most one room at the same time is booked for the same activity, the first row and second counter-row of the ternary fact table in Figure 1.3 indicate that both room 20 and room 33 are used at 9 a.m. Monday for the VMC activity. Is this kind of thing possible? If it is (and for some application domains it would be), then this constraint is not a rule, in which case the constraint should be dropped and the counter-row added to the sample data. On the other hand, if our business does not allow two rooms to be used at the same time for the same activity, then the constraint is validated and the counterexample is rejected (though it can be retained merely as an illustrative counterexample).

Compare Figure 1.2 with Figure 1.3. Though useful for compact overviews, ER models suffer a number of defects in comparison with ORM models. To begin with, they are *further removed from natural language,* and hence harder for the domain expert to conceptualize. In this case, it was more natural to verbalize the first schedule fact as a ternary, but all popular ER notations with industrial support are restricted to binary (two-role) relationships. Being only binary does not make a language less expressive, since an *n*-ary association can always be transformed into binaries by coreferencing or nesting (e.g., see Section 12.3). However, such a transformation may introduce an object type that appears artificial to the domain expert, which can hinder communication. Wherever possible, we should try to formulate the model in a way that appears natural to the domain expert.

Another problem with ER notation is that is far *less expressive* than ORM for capturing constraints or business rules. For example, the ER notation used for Figure 1.2 was unable to express the constraint that activity names are unique, or the constraint that it is impossible that more than one room at the same time is booked for the same activity.

A third problem with ER is that it encourages decisions about relative importance at the conceptual analysis stage. For example, instead of using RoomTimeSlot in Figure 1.2, we could model the room schedule information using ActivityTimeSlot. Which of these choices is preferable may depend on what other kind of information we might want to record. But we have been forced to make a decision about this without even knowing what other facts need to be recorded, so we may need to change this part of the model later. In general, if you model a feature as an attribute and find out later that you need to record something about it, you are typically forced to remodel it as an entity type or relationship. For instance, suppose we record phone as an attribute of Room, then later discover that we want to know which phones support voice mail. Since you almost never know what all the future information requirements will be, an attribute-based model is inherently *unstable*. Even worse, applications using the model often need to be recoded when a model feature is changed. Since ORM is essentially immune to changes like this, it offers greater *semantic stability*.

We have already seen that ORM models are designed to facilitate validation by both verbalization and population. Attributes make it very awkward to use sample data populations. Moreover, populating optional attributes introduces null values, which are often a source of confusion to nontechnical people. In sum, ORM's fact-oriented approach offers many advantages over ER modeling for conceptual analysis. Now let's consider a third approach to modeling to see if it does any better.

Object-oriented modeling is an approach that encapsulates both data and behavior within objects. Although it is used mainly for designing code for object-oriented programs, it can also be used for database design. Dozens of object-oriented approaches exist, but by far the most influential is the **Unified Modeling Language** (UML), which has been adopted by the Object Management Group (OMG). Among its many diagram types, UML includes class diagrams to specify static data structures. Class diagrams may be used to specify operations as well as low-level design decisions specific to object-oriented code (e.g., visibility of attributes and navigability of associations). When stripped of such implementation detail, UML class diagrams may be regarded as an extended version of ER.

A UML class diagram for our example is shown in Figure 1.4. To overcome some of the problems mentioned for the ER solution, a ternary association is used for the schedule information. Because of its object-oriented focus, UML does not require conceptual identification schemes for its classes. Instead, entity instances are assumed to be identified by internal object identifiers (oids).

Currently, UML does not include a standard notation to signify that attribute values must be unique for their class. However, UML does allow user-defined constraints to be added in braces or notes in whatever language users wish. So I've added {P} to denote primary uniqueness and {U1} for an alternate uniqueness—these symbols are not standard and hence not portable. The uniqueness constraints on the ternary are captured by the two 0..1 (at most one) multiplicity constraints. The "*" means "0 or more". Attributes are mandatory by default.

How well does this UML model support validation with the domain expert? Let's start with verbalization. Although often less than ideal, implicit use of "has" could be used to form binary sentences from the attributes. But what about the ternary? About the best we can do is something like "Booking involves Room and Time and Activity"—which is pretty useless. What if we replaced the association name with a mixfix predicate, as we did in ORM, for example, "... at ... is booked for ..."? This is no use,

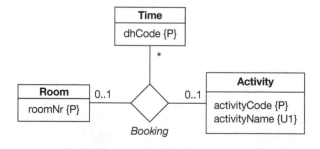

Figure 1.4 A UML class diagram for room scheduling.

because UML association roles (or association ends as they are now called) are not ordered. So formally we can't know if we should read the sentence type as "Room at Time is booked for Activity", or "Activity at Time is booked for Room", and so on. This gets worse if the same class plays more than one role in the association (e.g., Person introduced Person to Person).

UML does allow association roles to have names (ORM allows this also, although the role names are not normally displayed on the diagram), but this doesn't help either because role names don't form sentences, which are always ordered in natural language. UML's weakness with regard to verbalization of facts carries over into its verbalization of constraints and derivation rules. It does suggest that Object Constraint Language (OCL) be used for formal expression of such rules, but despite its claims, OCL is simply too mathematical in nature to be used for validation by nontechnical domain experts.

Since verbalization in UML has inadequate support, let's try validation with sample populations. Not much luck here either. To begin with, attribute-based notations are almost useless for multiple instantiation, and they introduce null values into base populations, along with all their confusing properties. UML does provide object diagrams that enable you to talk about attributed single instances of classes, but that doesn't help with multiple instantiation. For example, the 1:1 nature of the association between activity codes and names is transparent in the ORM fact table in Figure 1.3, but is much harder to see by scanning several activity objects.

In principle, we could introduce fact tables to multiply instantiate binary associations in UML, but this wouldn't work for ternary and longer associations. Why not? Because in UML you cannot specify a reading direction for an association unless it's a binary. So there is no obvious connection between an association role and a fact column as there is in ORM. The best we can do is to name each role, and then use role names as headers to the fact table. The visual connection of the fact columns to the class diagram would be weak because of the nonlinear layout of the association roles, and the higher the arity of the association, the worse it gets. However, this technique would allow us to make some use of sample populations in UML.

In spite of its simplicity, the ORM notation is significantly richer than ER or UML in its capacity to express constraints in a conceptual data model, as well as being far more orthogonal and less impacted by change. As a simple example, consider the output report of Table 1.4. You might like to try modeling this yourself before reading on.

One way of modeling this in UML is shown in Figure 1.5. Here movies are identified by a movie number. Although the population of the sample report suggested that movie titles are unique and that a person can direct only one movie, let's assume that the domain expert confirms that this is not the case. We should adapt our sample population to illustrate this (e.g., add a new movie 4 with the same title *Star Peace* directed by Ron Howard). Assuming people are identified simply by their name, Movie and Person classes may be used as shown.

Instead of naming the associations between Movie and Person, the role names "director" and "reviewer" are used here to distinguish the two roles played by Person. Association names may be used as well as, or instead of, role names if desired.

Unlike Chen's original ER notation, UML binary associations are depicted by lines without a diamond. While this is convenient, the use of diamonds in longer associations

Table 1.4 Another sample output report about movies.

	Movie	Director		Reviewers	
Nr	Title	Name	Born	Name	Born
1	Backdraft	Ron Howard	US	Fred Bloggs	US
				Ann Green	US
2	Crocodile Dundee	Peter Faiman	AU	Ann Green	US
				Ima Viewer	GB
				Tom Sawme	AU
3	Star Peace	Ann Green	US	?	?
...	...		...	...	

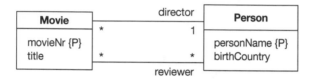

Figure 1.5 A UML class diagram for Table 1.4.

is somewhat inconsistent, and the avoidance of unary associations is unnatural. In contrast, ORM's depiction of associations as a sequence of one or more roles, where each role is associated with a fact table column, provides a uniform, general notation that facilitates validation by both verbalization and sample populations.

The multiplicity constraints indicate that each movie has exactly one director but may have many reviewers, and that a person may direct or review many movies. But there is still a missing business rule. Can you spot it?

Figure 1.6 indicates how the same domain might be modeled in ORM. The rule missing from the UML model is captured graphically here by the circled "X" constraint between the role pairs making up the directed and reviewed associations. This is called an *exclusion constraint,* and verbalizes as **no** Person directed **and** reviewed **the same** Movie. Or reading it the other way: **no** Movie was directed by **and** was reviewed by **the same** Person.

To validate this rule with the domain expert, you should verbalize the rule and also provide a counterexample. For example, is it possible for movie 1 to be directed by Ron Howard and also reviewed by Ron Howard? Figure 1.6 includes this counterexample. If the exclusion constraint really does apply, at least one of those two facts must be wrong.

Some domain experts are happy to work with diagrams and some are not. Some are good at understanding rules in natural language and some are not. But all domain experts are good at working with concrete examples. Although it is not necessary for the domain expert to see the diagram, being able to instantiate any role directly on the diagram makes it easy for you as a modeler to think clearly about the rules.

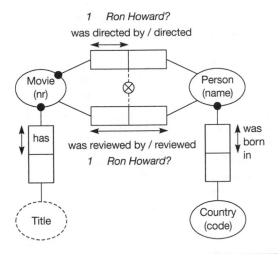

Figure 1.6 ORM model for Table 1.4, with counterexample for exclusion constraint.

Although UML has no graphic notation for general exclusion constraints, it does allow you to document other constraints in a note attached to the relevant model elements. Although this is useful, there is no guarantee that a software tool will be able to make any sense of the note, other than as a comment. *If a concept is already part of your modeling language, it's easier to think of it.* Since the exclusion constraint notation is not built into the UML language, it is easy to miss the constraint in developing the model. The same thing goes for ER. In contrast, the ORM modeling procedure prompts you to consider such a constraint and allows you to visualize and capture the rule formally. An ORM tool can then map the constraint automatically into executable code to ensure the rule is enforced at the implementation level.

ER diagrams, and to some extent UML diagrams, tend to *hide attribute domains.* For example, the birthCountry attribute in Figure 1.5 should be based on the *semantic domain* Country, but this is not represented visually. In ER, attribute domains can be listed in another document, and in UML they may be listed in the class diagram after the attribute name (though this is usually avoided, to save space). All too often in practice, only *syntactic,* or value, domains are specified. For example, if birthCountry and title are both given the "domain" varchar(20), the semantic distinction between countries and movie titles is lost.

An ER diagram might show population and elevation as attributes of City, and an associated table might list the domains of these attributes simply as Integer, despite the fact that it is nonsense to equate a population with an elevation. Conceptual object types, or semantic domains, provide the conceptual "glue" that binds the various components in the application model into a coherent picture. Even at the lower level of the relational data model, E. F. Codd, the founder of the relational model, argues that "domains are the glue that holds a relational database together" (Codd 1990, p. 45). The object types in ORM diagrams are the semantic domains, so the *connectedness* of a model is transparent. This property of ORM also has significant advantages for conceptual queries, since a user can query the conceptual model directly by navigating through its object types to establish the relevant connections—this notion is elaborated further in Sections 4.4 and 13.3.

ER and UML diagrams often fail to express relevant *constraints on, or between, attributes.* Figure 1.7 provides a simple example. Notice the circled black dot over an "X" in the ORM model in Figure 1.7(a). This specifies two constraints: the dot is a mandatory constraint over the disjunction of the two roles (each truck is either bought or leased); the "X" indicates the roles are exclusive (no truck is both bought and leased). The two constraints collectively provide an XOR (exclusive-or) constraint (each truck plays exactly one of the roles). Unlike ER, UML does provide an XOR constraint, but only between association roles. Since the UML model in Figure 1.7(b) models these two fact types as attributes instead of associations, it cannot capture the constraint graphically (other than adding a note). The "[0..1]" indicates an attribute is optional and single-valued. Notice also how the ORM diagram reveals the semantic domains. For instance, tare may be meaningfully compared with maximum load (both are masses) but not with length. In UML this can be made explicit by appending domain names to the attributes. At various stages in the modeling process it is helpful for the modeler to see all the relevant information in one place.

Another feature of ORM is the flexible way in which *subtyping,* including multiple inheritance, is supported based on formal subtype definitions. For example, the subtype LargeUSCity may be defined as a City that is in Country 'USA' and has a Population > 1,000,000. As discussed in Chapter 6, subtype definitions provide stronger constraints than simple declarations about whether subtypes are exclusive or exhaustive.

In principle, there are infinitely many kinds of constraints. So a textual notation in some formal language is often required for completeness to supplement the diagram. This is true for ER, ORM, and UML models. However, the failure of ER and UML diagrams to include standard notations for many important ORM constraints

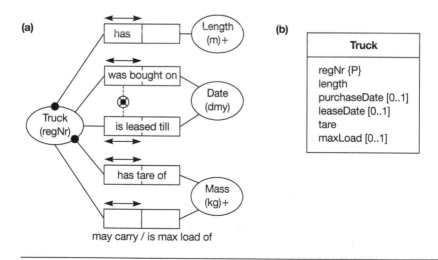

Figure 1.7 (a) ORM model. (b) UML model revealing less detail.

makes it harder to develop a comprehensive model or to perform *transformations* on the model.

For example, suppose that in any movie an actor may have a starring role or a supporting role but not both. This can be modeled by two fact types: *Actor* has starring role in *Movie; Actor* has supporting role in *Movie*. The "but not both" condition is expressed in ORM as a pair-exclusion constraint between the fact types. Alternatively, these fact types may be replaced by a single longer fact type: *Actor* in *Movie* has role of *RoleKind* {star, support}. Transformations are rigorously controlled in ORM to ensure that constraints in one model are captured in the alternative. For instance, the pair-exclusion constraint is transformed into the constraint that each Actor-Movie pair has only one RoleKind. The formal theory behind such transformations is much easier to apply when the relevant constraints can be visualized.

Unlike UML and ER, ORM was built from a linguistic basis. If you want to reap the benefits of verbalization and population for communication with, and validation by, domain experts, it's better to use a language that was designed with this in mind. The ORM notation is simple and can be learned in a fraction of the time it takes to master just a part of UML.

I'm not arguing here that ER and UML have no value. They do. I'm just suggesting that you consider using ORM for your original conceptual analysis before you move to an attribute-based notation such as that of ER, UML, or relational tables. Once you have validated the conceptual model with the domain expert, you need to map it to a DBMS or program code for implementation. At this lower level, you will want to use an attribute-based model, so you have a compact picture of how facts are grouped into implementation structures. For database applications, you will typically want to see the table structures, foreign key relationships, and so on. Here a relational or object-relational model offers a nice compact view, similar to an ER or UML model.

ORM models often take up much more space than an attribute-based model, since they show each attribute as a relationship. This is ideal for conceptual analysis, where we should validate one fact type at a time. But for logical design, we typically group facts into attribute-based structures such as tables or classes. At the logical design stage, attribute-based models are more useful than ORM models. UML is well suited for the logical and physical design of object-oriented code, since it allows implementation detail on the data model (e.g., attribute visibility and association navigation) and can be used to model behavior and deployment.

Having used ER, ORM, and UML in practice, I've found that time and again ORM makes it easier to get the model right in the first place, and to change the model as the business domain evolves. I believe in the method so strongly that I've made it the basis for most of the modeling discussion in this book. After devoting my doctoral thesis to formalizing ORM and helping to design industrial ORM tools, could I be biased on this topic? You can decide for yourself. Arguments about modeling approaches can take on the character of religious debates, and certainly not everyone is as convinced of the virtues of ORM as I am. All I ask is that you look objectively at the ideas presented in this book and consider making use of whatever you find helpful.

Although the book focuses on ORM, it also covers data modeling in other popular notations (ER, IDEF1X, UML, and relational). These other notations have value too. Even if you decide to stay with ER or UML as your conceptual analysis approach, an insight into ORM should make you a better modeler regardless of which method(s) you use.

1.3   Some Historical Background

This section briefly overviews the evolution of computing languages for information systems, then outlines the historical development of the main kinds of logical data structures used in database systems.

Table 1.5 summarizes how **five generations of computing languages** might be used to request a computer to list the name, mass, and moons (if any) of each planet, assuming the information is stored in an astronomical database. The higher the generation, the closer to natural language, and usually the less you have to say.

Nowadays nobody uses machine code or assembler to access databases. Most database applications are coded using fourth-generation languages (4GLs), perhaps in combination with third-generation languages (3GLs). Third-generation languages, such as C# and COBOL, are *procedural,* emphasizing the procedures used to carry out the task. With 3GLs we need to specify how to access information in a database one record at a time. Fourth-generation languages, such as SQL and QBE, are primarily *declarative* in nature: the programmer essentially declares *what* has to be done rather than *how* to do it. With a 4GL, a single statement can be used to perform operations on whole tables, or sets of rows, at once. Hence 4GLs are *set oriented* rather than record oriented.

Fifth-generation languages (5GLs), such as ConQuer (an ORM query language) allow you to specify queries naturally, without knowing the underlying data structures used to store the information. The widespread use of fifth-generation languages is still in the future.

Table 1.5 Five generations of computer languages.

Generation	Language example	Sample code for same task
5	ConQuer	✓ Planet **that** has ✓ Mass **and possibly** is orbited by ✓Moon
4	SQL	**select** X1.planetName, X1.mass, X2.moonName **from** Planet **as** X1 **left outer join** Moon **as** X2 **on** X1.planetName = X2.planetName
3	Pascal	Two pages of instructions like **for** i := 1 **to** n **do begin** write (planetName[i], mass[i]);
2	8086 assembler	Many pages of instructions like ADDI AX, 1
1	8086 machine code	Many pages of instructions like 00000101 00000001 00000000

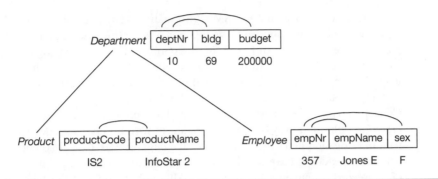

Figure 1.8 A hierarchic database schema with sample data and fact arcs.

The first database management systems were developed in the early 1960s, starting with simple file managers. From that time, various **logical data architectures** have been proposed as a basis for specifying the structure of databases. In the *hierarchic data model,* the database schema is basically a tree of linked record types, where each record type has a different structure (unlike many trees where each node is of the same type). Records may include one or more fields, each of which can hold only a single value. Record types are related by parent-child links (e.g., using pointers), where a parent may have many children but each child has only one parent. Hence the type structure is that of a tree, or hierarchy.

For example, in Figure 1.8 the parent record type Department has two child record types: Product and Employee. Each record type contains a sequence of named fields, shown here as boxes, and the parent-child links are shown as connecting lines. For discussion purposes, one record instance has been added below each record type. As an exercise, try reading off all the facts that are contained in this database before reading on.

To begin with, there are five facts stored in the record instances. To make these facts more obvious, the figure includes arcs connecting the relevant fields, one arc for each fact. Although these arcs are a useful annotation, they are not part of the schema notation. If we are familiar with the application, we can verbalize these arcs into relationships. For example, we might verbalize the five facts as

Department 10 is located in Building 69.
Department 10 has Budget 200000 USD.
Product 'IS2' has ProductName 'InfoStar 2'.
Employee 357 has EmployeeName 'Jones E'.
Employee 357 is of Sex 'F'.

Are there any more facts? Yes! The parent-child links encode the following two facts:

Department 10 develops Product 'IS2'.
Department 10 employs Employee 357.

Hierarchic DBMSs such as IBM's Information Management System (IMS) are very efficient at handling applications with a hierarchic structure (e.g., a computer's file directory system) and are still used for that purpose. However, having to explicitly navigate over predefined record links to get at the facts you want can be somewhat challenging. The complexity rapidly rises if the application is not hierarchic in nature.

Suppose that the same product may be developed by more than one department. Conceptually, the Department develops Product association is now many:many. Since parent-child links are always 1:many, an inelegant workaround is needed to handle this situation. For example, to record the facts that departments 10 and 20 both develop product 'IS2', we could have the two department record instances point to separate copies of the record instance for product 'IS2'. Although the type and instance link structures are still trees, the fact that product 'IS2' has the product name 'InfoStar 2' now appears twice in the database. So we need to worry about controlling this redundancy. Moreover, while retrieving products developed by a given department is easy, retrieving all the departments who developed a product is not so easy.

The *network data model* was developed by the Conference on Data Systems and Languages (CODASYL) Database Task Group. This model is more complex than the hierarchic model. Most of the data is stored in records, a single field of which may contain a single value, a set of values, or even a set of value groups. Record types are related by owner-member links, and the graph of these connections may be a network: a record type may have many owners as well as owning many record types. As in the hierarchic model, facts are stored either in records or as record links. An owner-member link between record types is restricted to a 1:many association. To handle a many:many association like the case discussed earlier, we might introduce a new record type (e.g., Development) with many:1 associations to the other record types (in this case, Department and Product).

In general, encoding of facts in access paths such as interrecord links complicates the management of the application and makes it less flexible. For example, some new queries will have to wait until access paths have been added for them, and internal optimization efforts can be easily undone as the application structure evolves.

Partly to address such problems, Dr. Edgar ("Ted") Codd introduced an even simpler model: the *relational data model*. A year after his original 1969 IBM research report on the subject, Codd published a revised version for a wider audience (Codd 1970) where he first argued that relations should be normalized so that each data entry should be atomic—we now call this first normal form. Other normal forms were defined later (see Chapter 12).

The most significant feature of the relational model is that *all the facts are stored in tables,* which are treated as mathematical relations. For example, Figure 1.9 shows the relational database for our sample application. Again, the database has been annotated with arcs corresponding to the facts stored. Notice the extra deptNr columns in the Employee and Product tables. The facts that Department 10 employs Employee 357 and develops product 'IS2' are stored in the table rows themselves. Access paths between tables are not used to specify facts (as allowed in the hierarchic and network models).

To specify queries and constraints, table columns may be associated by name. This allows *ad hoc* queries to be specified at will and simplifies management of the application. Note that constraints specified between tables are not the same as access paths.

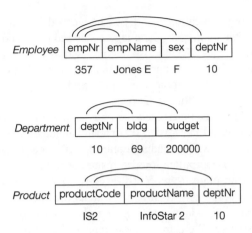

Figure 1.9 All the facts in a relational database are stored in the tables themselves.

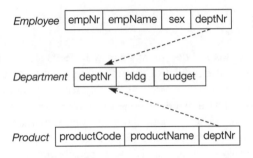

Figure 1.10 "Links" between tables express constraints, not facts.

For example, in Figure 1.10 arrows are shown "linking" the deptNr column of the Employee and Product tables to the deptNr column of the Department table. However these "links" merely express the constraints that any value in the deptNr column of the Employee and Product tables must also occur as a value in the deptNr column of the Department table. These constraints do not express employment and product development facts.

The relational model is logically cleaner than the network and hierarchic models, but it initially suffered from performance problems, which led to its slow acceptance. However, by the late 1980s efficient relational systems had become commonplace. Although many network and hierarchic database systems are in use today, relational DBMSs are now the preferred choice for developing most new database applications.

A DBMS should ideally provide an integrated data dictionary, dynamic optimization, data security, automatic recovery, and a user-friendly interface. The main query languages used with relational databases are SQL (informally known as "Structured Query Language") and QBE (Query By Example). Many systems support both of these. SQL has long been accepted as a standard at the international level and is now the common language for communication of queries between different database systems. For this reason, SQL is the main query language discussed in this book. Recently, the eXtensible Markup Language (XML) has also become widely used for communication between different systems, but this is currently focused on sharing data structures and content for purposes such as electronic commerce and Web publication. Many SQL-based DBMSs now support mapping to XML.

Newer data architectures have been proposed for *object-oriented databases* and *deductive databases,* but these have a long way to go in terms of standardization and maturity before they have a chance of widespread acceptance. Although relational systems give adequate performance for most applications, they are inefficient for some applications involving complex data structures (e.g., VLSI design).

To overcome such difficulties, many relational systems are being enhanced with object-oriented features, leading to *object-relational database systems.* It appears that such extended relational systems will ensure the dominance of relational databases for the near future, with object-oriented databases being their main competitor. A discussion of postrelational databases and future trends is included in the final chapter.

1.4   The Relevant Skills

Since relational database systems are dominant, they will be the focus of our implementation discussion. Although conceptual or semantic interfaces to database systems are still in their infancy, developing our models at this higher level is more productive and avoids wasting time acquiring knowledge and skills that will rapidly become obsolete. Consider the impact of the electronic calculator on school mathematics curricula (e.g., the removal of the general square root algorithm).

Fundamentally, there are two skills that will always be relevant to interacting with an information system. Both of these skills relate to *communicating* with the system about our particular application area. Recall that the application domain is technically known as the *universe of discourse* (UoD). The two requirements are to

- **describe** the universe of discourse
- **query** the system about the universe of discourse

The first skill entails describing the *structure* or *design* of the UoD, and describing its *content* or *population;* the structural aspect is the only challenging part of this. Obviously, the ability to clearly describe the application domain is critical if you wish to add a model to the system. Complex models should normally be prepared by expert modelers working with domain experts. The main aim of this text is to introduce you to the fundamentals of information modeling. If you master the methods discussed, you will be well on your way to becoming an expert in modeling information systems.

Issuing queries is often easy using a 4GL, but the formulation of complex queries can still be difficult. Occasionally, the ability to understand some answers given by the system requires knowledge about how the system works, especially its limitations. This book provides a conceptual basis for understanding relational structures and queries, explains the algebra behind relational query languages, and includes a solid introduction to SQL.

No matter how sophisticated the information system, if we give it the wrong picture of our UoD to start with, we can't expect to get much sense out of it. This is one aspect of the GIGO (garbage in, garbage out) principle. Most of the problems with database applications can be traced to bad database design. This text shows how to model information at a very high level using natural concepts. While covering popular data modeling approaches such as ER and UML, its focus is on the higher-level ORM approach.

For immediate use, conceptual schemas can be mapped onto the lower-level structures used by today's database systems. This mapping can be performed automatically using an appropriate CASE tool or manually using an appropriate procedure. The book discusses how to map a conceptual model to a relational database system, and how query languages may be used to retrieve data from such systems. It also provides an overview of other related methods and modern trends.

1.5   Summary

This chapter provided a motivation for studying conceptual modeling techniques and presented a brief historical and structural overview of information systems.

Database management systems are widely used and are a major productivity tool for businesses that are information oriented. For a database to be used effectively, its data should be correct, complete, and efficiently accessed. This requires that the database be well designed. Designing a database involves building a formal model of the application domain or universe of discourse (UoD). To do this properly requires a good understanding of the UoD and a means of specifying this understanding in a clear, unambiguous way.

Object-Role Modeling (ORM) simplifies the analysis and design process by using natural language, intuitive diagrams, and examples, and by examining the information in terms of simple or *elementary facts.* By expressing the model in terms of natural concepts, like *objects* and *roles,* this fact-oriented method provides a truly *conceptual* approach to modeling. Other modeling approaches include Entity-Relationship (ER) modeling and object-oriented modeling. While many popular versions of ER exist, the Unified Modeling Language (UML) is by far the most influential object-oriented approach.

Although ER and UML models are typically more compact than ORM models, they are less suitable than ORM models for the tasks of formulating, transforming, or evolving a conceptual information model. ER and UML diagrams are further removed from natural language, lack the expressibility and simplicity of a role-based notation for constraints, are less stable in the face of domain evolution, are harder to populate with fact instances, and often hide information about the semantic domains that glue the model together.

For such reasons, ORM is used as our basic conceptual modeling method. ER models and UML class diagrams are useful for providing compact summaries and are best developed as views of ORM diagrams. For database applications, conceptual models typically need to be mapped to attribute-based logical and physical models. For object-oriented applications, UML models can incorporate implementation details as well as behavior and deployment aspects.

Fourth-generation database languages like SQL are declarative in nature, enabling users to declare what has to be done without the fine detail of how to do it, and are set oriented rather than record oriented. Fifth-generation languages like ConQuer enable users to query conceptual models directly. Hierarchic and network database systems store some facts in record types and some facts in links between record types. Relational database systems store all facts in tables. No matter how "intelligent" software systems become, people are needed to describe the universe of discourse and to ask the relevant questions about it.

Chapter Notes

Since most of the topics introduced in this chapter are treated in detail in later chapters, only a few references are cited here. To obtain the full bibliographic entries for these references, please consult the Bibliography at the back of this book.

Codd (1969, 1970) introduced the relational model of data. For a historical discussion of these two papers, see Date (1998). Codd (1990) suggests future directions for the relational model. The classic paper that introduced Entity-Relationship modeling is Chen (1976). Kent (1978) is a classic that provides a clear and insightful analysis of the nature of information and data. A concise introduction to Object-Role Modeling is given in Halpin (1998b). An overview of UML can be found in Booch et al. (1999). Muller (1999) discusses how to use UML for database design. Halpin and Bloesch (1999) compares data modeling in ORM and UML. Celko (1999) provides a very readable coverage of various database topics. Date (2000) provides a clear, standard introduction to most aspects of database systems. Further background on network and hierarchic database management systems is included in Appendices C–E of Connolly et al. (1999).

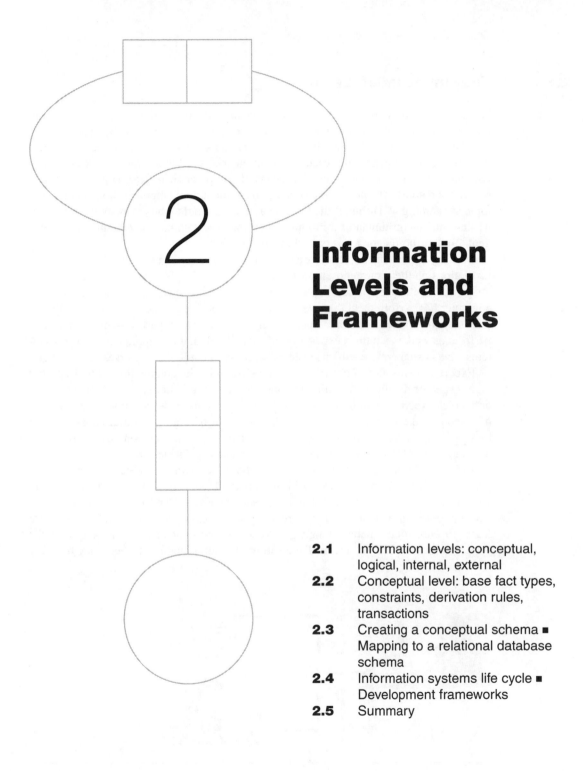

Information Levels and Frameworks

2.1   Four Information Levels

Advanced information systems are sometimes described as "intelligent". Just what intelligence is, and whether machines will ever be intelligent, are debatable questions. In the classic "Turing Test" of intelligence, an opaque screen is placed between a typical human and the object being tested for intelligence (see Figure 2.1). The human can communicate with the object only by means of computer (with keyboard for input and screen for output). The human may communicate in natural language about any desired topic. According to Turing, if the human can't tell from the object's responses whether it is an intelligent human or a machine, then the object should be classified as intelligent. To date, no machine has passed the Turing Test.

Two key conditions in the test are that natural language be used and that there be no restrictions on the topics chosen for discussion. Once we place restrictions on the language and confine the discussion to a predefined topic, we can find examples where a computer has performed at the level of a human expert (e.g., chess, diagnosis of blood diseases, mineral exploration). Such systems are called "expert systems" since they perform as well as a human expert in some specific domain of application. Expert systems have passed "restricted Turing Tests" specific to particular universes of discourse.

Expert systems use sophisticated programs, often in conjunction with large but highly specific databases. A fifth-generation information system (5GIS) is like a "user-definable" expert system in that it allows the user to enter a description of the universe of discourse and then conduct a conversation about this, all in natural language. Just how well the system handles its end of the conversation depends on how powerful its user interface, database management, and inference capabilities are.

Although desirable, it is not necessary that a 5GIS always be able to operate at expert level when we communicate with it. It must, however, allow us to communicate with it in a natural way. Natural languages such as English and Japanese are complex and subtle. It will be many years before an information system will be able to converse freely in unrestricted natural language. We should be content in the meantime if the system supports dialog in a formalized subset of natural language. There may be many

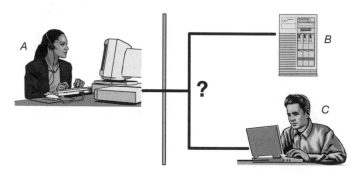

Figure 2.1 The Turing Test: can *A* distinguish between *B* and *C?*

of these "formal, natural languages", one for English, one for Japanese, and so on. A 5GIS should be able to respond in the same language used by the human.

For example, suppose we posed the query

What is the age of Selena?

and we received the reply

Nijusai.

This would not help unless we knew that this is Japanese for "20 years old". Even if we can translate from Japanese to English, we might still misinterpret the reply, because instead of assigning people an age of zero years when born, the Japanese give them an age of one year. So an age of 20 years in the Japanese system corresponds to an age of 19 years in the Western system. Besides the requirement for a *common language,* effective communication between two people requires that each assigns the *same meaning* to the words being used. To achieve this, they should (1) share the same context or universe of discourse and (2) speak in sentences that are unambiguous with respect to this UoD.

With our example, the confusion over whether Selena's age is 19 or 20 years results from different age conventions being used, one Western and one Japanese. Natural speech abounds with examples that can be disambiguated only by context. Consider this example: Pluto is owned by Mickey. This is true for the world of Walt Disney's cartoon characters. But suppose someone unfamiliar with Mickey Mouse and his dog Pluto interpreted this within an astronomical context, taking "Pluto" to refer to the planet Pluto—a drastic communication failure! It is essential to have a clear way of describing the UoD to the information system.

An information system may be viewed from four levels: *conceptual, logical, internal,* and *external.* The conceptual level is the most fundamental, portraying the application domain naturally in human concepts. At this level, the blueprint of the UoD is called the **conceptual schema.** This describes the *structure* or *grammar* of the application domain (e.g., what types of objects populate it, what roles these play, and what constraints apply).

While the conceptual schema indicates the structure of the UoD, the **conceptual database** at any given time indicates the *content* or instances populating a specific *state* of the UoD. Although the term "information base" is more appropriate (van Griethuysen 1982), since information adds meaning to the data, I'll use the briefer and more popular term "database". Conceptually, the database is a set of sentences expressing propositions asserted to be true of the UoD. Since sentences may be added to or deleted from the database, the database may undergo transitions from one state to another. However, at any particular time, the sentences populating the database must individually and collectively conform to the domain-specific grammar or design plan that is the conceptual schema. To summarize:

The conceptual schema specifies the structure for all permitted states and transitions of the conceptual database.

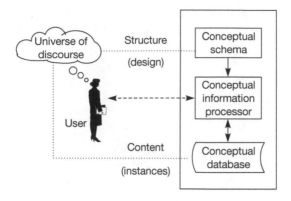

Figure 2.2 Information system: conceptual level.

To enforce this law we now introduce a third system component: the **conceptual information processor** (CIP). This supervises updates to the database by the user and answers user queries. Figure 2.2 shows the basic conceptual architecture of an information system. This diagram assumes the conceptual schema is already stored in the system. For each application area, a different conceptual schema is entered.

Although the diagram may seem to suggest that the user is interacting directly with the conceptual information processor, the user's interaction with the system is external rather than conceptual. The conceptual schema is not concerned with providing convenient interfaces for various users, or with the physical details of how the database can be efficiently maintained. These concerns are catered to by including external and internal components within the overall architecture.

When interpreted by people, the conceptual schema and database both provide knowledge about the UoD. Hence the combination of conceptual schema and (conceptual) database may be described as the *knowledge base*. The knowledge base is a formal description of the UoD, and the CIP controls the flow of information between the knowledge base and humans. Some authors use the term "knowledge base" in a more restricted sense.

Recall that the *domain expert* is a person or group of people collectively familiar with the application area. The *modeler* or conceptual designer is a person or team that specifies the conceptual schema by formalizing the domain expert's knowledge. An *end user* makes use of the implemented system. For a small system, the domain expert, modeler, and user might be the same person. A large system might have several partial domain experts, a team of analysts and designers, and thousands of end users.

The modeler inputs the conceptual schema to the system and has read/write access to it. A user who merely works with an existing schema has read-only capability for the schema, but typically has read/write access to the database. Different interfaces might be created for different users so that some users have access to only part of the knowledge base. In this case, different users may access different subschemas of the global

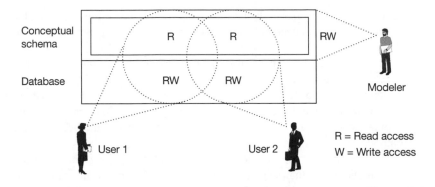

Figure 2.3 Access to the knowledge base.

conceptual schema. This situation is summarized in Figure 2.3. Some users may have read-only access to the database.

An **external schema** specifies the UoD design and operations accessible to a particular user or group of users. Here we specify *what* kind of facts may be read, added, or deleted, and *how* this is displayed. For *security* reasons, different user groups are often allocated different access rights (e.g., to ensure sensitive information is not made public). For *user convenience,* views may be constructed to hide information irrelevant to a user group, or to collect and display information more efficiently. Different interfaces may be designed to cater to users with different expertise levels even when accessing the same underlying information.

Conceptual schemas are designed for clear communication, especially between the modeler and the domain expert. While they give a clear picture of the UoD, they are usually converted to a lower-level structure for efficient implementation. For a given application, an appropriate logical data model (e.g., relational, hierarchic, object-relational) is chosen, and the conceptual schema is mapped to a **logical schema** expressed in terms of the abstract structures for data and operations supported in that data model. For example, in a relational schema facts are stored into tables, and constraints are expressed using primary and foreign key declarations and so on.

The logical schema may now be realized as an **internal schema** in a specific DBMS. For example, a relational schema might be implemented in Microsoft SQL Server or IBM's DB2. The internal schema includes all the details about the physical storage and access structures used in that system (indexes, file clustering, etc.). Different physical choices can be made for the same DBMS, and different DBMSs often differ in what choices are possible. Hence different internal schemas might be chosen for the same logical schema. Operations at the external level are converted by the system into operations at the internal level.

One advantage of the conceptual level is that it is the most *stable* of all the levels. It is unaffected by changes in user interfaces or storage and access techniques. Suppose a conceptual schema is implemented in a hierarchic DBMS, and later we wish to use a relational DBMS instead. Unless the UoD has changed, the conceptual schema can re-main the same. We need only apply a different mapping procedure and then migrate the data.

If a language is the object of study, it is said to be the *object language.* The language used to study it is then called the *metalanguage.* For example, you might use English as a metalanguage to study Japanese as an object language. An object language may be its own metalanguage; for example, English may be used to learn about English. Any conceptual schema may be expressed as a set of sentences, and hence may be viewed as a database in its own right.

This enables us to construct a **metaschema** for talking about conceptual schemas. This meta conceptual schema specifies the design rules that must be obeyed by any conceptual schema (e.g., each role is played by exactly one object type). CASE tools used to assist in designing conceptual schemas make use of such a metaschema to en-sure that schemas entered by the modeler are well formed or "grammatical".

While on the subject of grammar, let us agree to accept both "schemas" and "sche-mata" as a plural of "schema". Although "data" is the plural of "datum", I'll adopt the common practice of allowing "data" to be used in both singular and plural senses. The first exercise in the book is shown below. Answers to exercises are included in the on-line supplement.

Exercise 2.1

1. Classify each of the following as A (external), B (conceptual), or C (internal).
   (a) This level is concerned with physical details of how to efficiently store and access data.
   (b) This level is concerned with providing a convenient and authorized view of the database for an individual user.
   (c) This level is concerned with representing information in a fundamental way.

2.2   The Conceptual Level

At the conceptual level, all communication between people and the information system is handled by the conceptual information processor. This communication may be di-vided into three main stages:

1. If the conceptual schema for the UoD is not already stored, the modeler enters it. The CIP accepts the schema if and only if it is consistent with the meta con-ceptual schema.
2. The user updates the database by adding or deleting specific facts. The CIP ac-cepts an update if and only if it is consistent with the conceptual schema.
3. The user queries the system about the UoD and is answered by the CIP. The CIP can supply information about the conceptual schema or the database, provided it has stored the information or can derive it.

In these three stages, the CIP performs as a *design filter, data filter,* and *information supplier,* respectively. To process update and query requests, the CIP accesses the

| Base fact types | Constraints | Derivation rules |

Figure 2.4 The three main sections of the conceptual schema.

conceptual schema, which comprises three main sections as shown in Figure 2.4. The **base fact types** section lists the kinds of primitive sentences or *facts* that may be stored in the database. Base facts are not derived from other facts in the database. Fact types indicate what types of *objects* are permitted in the UoD (e.g., Employee, Country), how these are *referenced* by values in the database (e.g., SSN, countryCode), and their *relationships* (e.g., was born in, lives in).

The **constraints** section lists the constraints or restrictions that apply to populations of the fact types. These may be either static or dynamic. *Static constraints* apply to every state of the database. For example, suppose a database stores information about countries and their populations. Although a country's population may change over time, at any given time each country has at most one value recorded for its current population. *Dynamic constraints* exclude certain transitions between states of the database. For instance, a person may change his or her age status from child to adult, but not vice versa.

Constraints are also known as *validation rules* or *integrity rules*. A database is said to have integrity when it is consistent with the UoD being modeled. Although most database constraints can be represented graphically on conceptual schema diagrams, some constraints may need to be represented in other ways (e.g., using conceptual sentences, logical formulae, tables, graphs, or program code).

The **derivation rules** section provides a list of rules, functions, or operators that may be used to derive new facts from other facts. These may involve *mathematical calculation* or *logical inference*. In practice, many operators and functions are generic to particular data types. This permits a large variety of possible queries without the need to document each related derivation. Typical mathematical facilities include arithmetic operators, such as $+$, $-$, $*$ (multiply), and $/$ (divide); set operators such as $\cup$ (union); and functions for counting, summing, and computing averages, maxima, and minima.

In addition to such generic derivation facilities, specific *derived fact types* that are known to be required may be individually listed in the schema by means of rules. Some mathematically computed fact types and almost all logically inferred fact types fit into this category. Fact types derived by use of logical inference typically involve rules that make use of logical operators such as **if.**

Although derivable facts could be stored in the database, it is usually better to avoid this. Apart from saving storage space, the practice of omitting derived facts from the stored data usually makes it much easier to deal with updates. For instance, suppose we want to regularly obtain individual ages (in years) of students in a class, and, on occasion, the average age for the class. If we stored the average age in the database, we would have to arrange for this to be recomputed every time a student was added to or deleted from the class, as well as every time the age of any individual in the class increased.

As an improvement, we might store the number of students as well as their individual ages and have the average age derived only upon request. But this is still clumsy. Can you think of a better design?

As you probably realized, there is no need to store the number of students in a class since this can be derived using a count function. This avoids having to update the class size every time someone joins or leaves the class. Moreover, there is no need to store even the individual ages of students. Computer systems have a built-in clock that enables the current date to be accessed. If we store the birth date of the students, then we can have the system derive the age of any student upon request by using an appropriate date subtraction algorithm. This way, we don't have to worry about updating ages of students as they become a year older.

Sometimes, what is required is not the current age but the age on a certain date (e.g., entrance to schooling, age grouping for a future sports competition). In such cases where a single, stable age is required for each person, it may be appropriate to store it.

Before considering a derivation example using logical inference, note the difference between *propositions* and *sentences*. Propositions are asserted by declarative sentences and are always true or false (but not both). The same proposition may be asserted by different sentences, for example, "Paris is the capital of France" and "The French capital is Paris". While humans can deal with underlying meanings in a very sophisticated way, computers are completely literally minded: they deal in sentences rather than their meanings. If we want the computer to make connections that may be obvious to us, we have to explicitly provide it with the background or rules for making such connections.

Suppose that facts about brotherhood and parenthood are stored in the database. For simplicity, assume that the only objects we want to talk about are people who are identified by their first names. We might now set out facts as follows:

Alan is a brother of Betty.
Charles is a brother of Betty.
Betty is a parent of Fred.

You can look at these facts and readily see that both Alan and Charles are uncles of Fred. In doing so, you're using your understanding of the term "uncle". If we want a computer system to be able to make similar deductions, we need to provide it with a rule that expresses this understanding. For example:

Given any X, Z:
  X is an uncle of Z **if** there is a Y such that
    X is a brother of Y **and** Y is a parent of Z

This may be abbreviated to

X is an uncle of Z **if** X is a brother of Y **and** Y is a parent of Z.

This rule is an example of a *Horn clause*. The head of the clause on the left of the "if" is derivable from the conditions stated on the right-hand side of the "if". Horn clauses are used in languages like Prolog, and enable many derivation rules to be set out briefly.

To appreciate how the CIP works, let's look at an example. The notation is based on a textual version of an ORM language called FORML (Formal ORM Language). A more convenient graphical version is explained in later chapters. For simplicity, some constraints are omitted. The structure of the UoD is set out by means of the conceptual schema shown:

Reference schemes: Person (firstname); City (name); Year (AD)

Base fact types: F1   Person lives in City
             F2   Person was born in Year
             F3   Person is a brother of Person
             F4   Person is a parent of/is a child of Person

Constraints: C1   **each** Person lives in **some** City
            C2   **each** Person lives in **at most one** City
            C3   **each** Person was born in **at most one** Year
            C4   **no** Person is a brother of **itself**
            C5   **no** Person is a parent of **itself**

Derivation rules:
D1   Person$_1$ is an uncle of Person$_2$ **if** Person$_1$ is a brother of **some** Person$_3$
                        who is a parent of Person$_2$
D2   nrChildren(Person) ::= **count each** Person$_2$ **who** is a child of **that** Person

The *reference schemes* section declares the kinds of *objects* of interest and how they are referenced. Objects are either entities or values. *Entities* are real or abstract things we want to talk about that are referenced by relating *values* (e.g., character strings or numbers) to them in some way. Here we have three kinds of entities: Person, City, and Year. In this simple UoD, people are identified by their first name, and cities are identified by their name. Years are identified by their AD values (e.g., Einstein died in the year 1955 AD). You may find it strange to treat years as entities, but each year is a time segment.

The *fact types* section declares which kinds of facts are of interest. This indicates how object types participate in relationships. Object type names are usually highlighted by starting with a capital letter. Since database columns have attribute names like "birthYear", you may feel it is better to reword "Person was born in Year" as "Person has BirthYear". However, suppose we add another fact type "Person has DeathYear". The formal connection between BirthYear and DeathYear is now hidden. Expressing the new fact type as "Person died in Year" reveals the semantic connections to "Person was born in Year" and makes comparisons between years of birth and death meaningful (the underlying domain is Year).

Attribute names are often used in ER, UML, and relational schemas to express facts. But this way of expressing facts is often unnatural (compare "Person.deathYear" with "Person died in Year"), and it is incomplete unless domain names such as "Year" are added.

The *constraints* section declares constraints on the fact types. The examples here are all static constraints (i.e., each is true for each state of the database). Reserved words in the schema language are shown in bold. Constraint C1 means that for each person referenced in the database, we know at least one city where they live. C2 says nobody can live in more than one city (at the same time). C3 says nobody was born in more than one year; note that we might not know their year of birth. Constraint C4 says that nobody is his/her own brother, and C5 says that nobody is his/her own parent (brotherhood and parenthood is "irreflexive").

The *derivation rules* section declares a logical rule for determining uncles and a function for computing the number of children of any person. Given any person, the nrChildren function returns a count of the number of fact instances where that person appears as the parent.

At the conceptual level, each fact in the database is a simple or *elementary fact*. Basically this means it can't be split up into two or more simpler facts without loss of information. We may *add* or insert a fact into the database, and we may *delete* a fact from it. However, we may not modify or change just a part of a fact. By "fact" we mean "fact *instance*", not "fact type".

The operation of adding or deleting a single fact is an *elementary update* or *simple transaction*. In our sample conceptual query language, add and delete requests start with "**add:**" and "**del:**", and queries end with "?". The CIP either accepts updates or rejects them with an indication of the violation. The CIP answers legal queries and rejects illegal ones.

To explain the conceptual notions underlying database transactions, we now discuss some examples of CIP interactions. If this seems tedious, remember that we are talking about the conceptual level, not the *external level where the user actually interacts with the system*. At the external level, the user typically enters, deletes, or changes values in a screen version of a form or table. Conceptually, however, we may think of such an operation being translated into the appropriate delete and add operations on elementary facts before being passed on to the CIP. Suppose we now start populating our conceptual database as follows:

User:	CIP:
add: Person 'Terry' lives in City 'Seattle'.	→ accepted.

The CIP recognizes the type of this sentence and sees that no constraints are violated. So it adds it to the database and issues the reply "accepted". If an update is inconsistent with the conceptual schema, the CIP rejects it, indicating the reason for rejection. You should now be able to follow the following dialogue:

add: Person 'Norma' was born in Year 1950.	→ rejected. C1 violated.
add: Person 'Norma' lives in City 'Brisbane'.	→ accepted.
add: Person 'Norma' was born in Year 1950.	→ accepted.
add: Person 'Terry' is a brother of Person 'Paul'.	→ rejected. C1 violated.
add: Person 'Paul' lives in City 'Brisbane'.	→ accepted.
add: Person 'Terry' is a brother of Person 'Paul'.	→ accepted.
add: Person 'Paul' is a brother of Person 'Paul'.	→ rejected. C4 violated.
add: Person 'Terry' plays Sport 'judo'.	→ rejected. Unknown fact type.

For brevity, constraint numbers indicate the constraints violated. In practice, the full text description of the constraint would be displayed, to make the CIP response meaningful to humans. Now suppose that Terry moves from Seattle to Brisbane. How would we record this change? Here are two incorrect attempts:

add: Person 'Terry' lives in City 'Brisbane'.	→ rejected. C2 violated.
del: Person 'Terry' lives in City 'Seattle'.	→ rejected. C1 violated.

Is there any way to change Terry's city from Seattle to Brisbane? Yes. Sometimes it is convenient, or even necessary, to submit a bundle of elementary updates as a single group. This is referred to as a *compound transaction*. To show this, we use "**begin**" and "**end**" as brackets to open and close the transaction. With compound transactions, the CIP considers only the total or *collective effect* of the transaction on the database. It is quite possible that the CIP will accept a compound transaction even if, taken individually, some of its component simple updates would be rejected. To change Terry's location we proceed thus:

begin
  del: Person 'Terry' lives in City 'Seattle'.
  add: Person 'Terry' lives in City 'Brisbane'.
end →   accepted.

The CIP accepts a transaction if and only if its overall effect is consistent with the conceptual schema. The user entered this compound transaction as a sequence of two elementary updates. It is more natural here to specify the delete before the add operation. However, the CIP treats any compound transaction as a *set* of updates, disregarding the order of the components, and looks only at the total effect. So even if the add operation had been specified before the delete, this would have been accepted with the same result.

Note that the CIP cannot accept just part of a compound transaction: it is a case of "all or nothing". Here are a few more simple interactions:

add: Person 'Linda' lives in City 'Brisbane'.   →   accepted.
add: Person 'Selena' lives in City 'Brisbane'.   →   accepted.
add: Person 'Terry' is a parent of Person 'Linda'.   →   accepted.
add: Person 'Terry' is a parent of Person 'Selena'. →   accepted.
nrChildren(Person 'Terry')?   →   2.
what Person is a brother of Person 'Paul'?   →   Terry.
what Person lives in City 'Brisbane'?   →   Norma
                                                               Linda
                                                               Selena
                                                               Terry.
what Person is an uncle of Person 'Selena'?   →   No Person.
add: Person 'Paul' is a brother of Person 'Terry'.   →   accepted.
what Person is an uncle of Person 'Selena'?   →   Paul.
what Person is an aunt of Person 'Selena'?   →   rejected. Unknown fact type.

Now suppose the UoD is changed by adding the following constraint:

C6 **each** Person was born in **some** Year

Our current database fails to meet this constraint. Suppose we start over with an empty database and try to add the following fact. How would the CIP respond?

add: Person 'Bernard' is brother of Person 'John'.

This update request is rejected. It actually violates two constraints (C1 and C6), since all people mentioned in the database must have both their city and birth year recorded. Chapter 5 uses the terminology "mandatory roles" to describe such constraints.

In general, the order in which constraints are listed does not matter. However, if an update request violates more than one constraint, this order may determine which constraint is reported as violated. Usually, if a CIP finds a constraint violation, then it reports this and doesn't bother looking for any more violations. In this case, the CIP would respond thus to the previous request: "rejected. C1 violated". Of course, it is possible to program the CIP to report all constraint violations (e.g., "rejected. C1, C6 violated"), but this tends to be less efficient. As an exercise, convince yourself that with C6 added, the following update requests are processed as shown:

add: Person 'Jim' lives in City 'Seattle'.   → rejected. C6 violated.
begin
  add: Person 'Jim' lives in City 'Seattle'.
  add: Person 'Jim' was born in Year 1960.
end   → accepted.
add: Person 'Jim' was born in Year 1959.   → rejected. C3 violated.
begin
  del: Person 'Jim' was born in Year 1960.
  add: Person 'Jim' was born in Year 1959.
  add: Person 'Bob' lives in City 'London'.
  add: Person 'Bob' was born in Year 1970.
  add: Person 'Jim' is a brother of Person 'Bob'.
end   → accepted.

The CIP uses the conceptual schema to supervise updates of the database and to supply information in response to a question. We may think of the designer of the conceptual schema as the *"law giver"*, and the schema itself as the *"law book"* since it contains the laws or ground rules for the UoD. The CIP is the *"law enforcer"*, since it ensures these laws are adhered to whenever the user tries to update the database. Like any friendly police person, the CIP is also there to provide information on request.

Whenever we communicate to a person or an information system, we have in mind a particular universe of discourse. Typically, this concerns some small part of the real universe, such as a particular business environment. In rare cases, we might choose a fictional UoD (e.g., one populated by comic book characters) or perhaps a fantasy world we have invented for a novel that we are writing. Fictional worlds may or may not be (logically) possible.

You can often rely on your own intuitions as to what is logically possible. For instance a world in which the Moon is colored green is possible, but a world in which the Moon is simultaneously green all over and red all over is not. A possible world is said to be *consistent,* and an impossible world is *inconsistent.*

As humans, we carry prodigious amounts of information around in our minds. It is highly likely that somewhere in our personal web of beliefs some logical contradictions are lurking. In most cases it does not matter if our belief web is globally inconsistent, so long as the local portions of the web that we use to communicate about are internally consistent. When reasoning about a particular UoD, however, consistency is essential. It is easy to show that once you accept a logical inconsistency, it is possible to deduce anything (including rubbish) from it—an extreme case of the GIGO (garbage in, garbage out) principle.

There are basically two types of garbage: logical and factual. Inconsistent designs contain logical garbage. For example, we might declare two constraints that contradict one another. A good design method supported by a CASE tool that enforces metarules can help to avoid such problems. Many factual errors can be prevented by the enforcement of constraints on the database. For example, a declared constraint that "each person was born in at most one country" stops us from giving a person more than one birth country.

However, even if the schema is consistent, and the CIP checks that the database is consistent with this world design, it is still possible to add false data into the knowledge base. For example, if we tell the CIP that Einstein was born in France, it might accept this even though in the actual world Einstein was born in Germany. If we want our knowledge base to remain factually correct, it is still our responsibility to ensure that all the sentences we enter into the database express propositions that are true of the actual world.

The following exercise is designed to check your grasp of the concepts discussed in this section and to introduce some further constraint types to be treated formally later.

Exercise 2.2

1. (a) Assuming the conceptual schema is already stored, what are the two main functions of the conceptual information processor?
    (b) What are the three main components of the conceptual schema?
    (c) "The CIP will reject a compound transaction if any of its component update operations is inconsistent with the conceptual schema". True or false?

2. Assume the following conceptual schema is stored. Constraints apply to each database state. C1 means that each person referred to in the database must have his/her fitness rating recorded there. C3 says the possible fitness values are whole numbers from 1 to 10. C4 means no person can be recorded as expert at more than one sport, and C5 says a person can be recorded as being an expert at a sport only if that person is also recorded as playing the same sport.

Reference schemes:	Person (firstname); Sport (name); FitnessRating (nr)	
Base fact types:	F1	Person has FitnessRating
	F2	Person plays Sport
	F3	Person is expert at Sport
Constraints:	C1	**each** Person has **some** FitnessRating
	C2	**each** Person has **at most one** FitnessRating
	C3	FitnessRating **values are** 1..10
	C4	**each** Person is expert at **at most one** Sport
	C5	$Person_1$ is expert at $Sport_1$ **only if** $Person_1$ plays $Sport_1$
Derivation rules:	D1	Person is martial artist **if** Person plays Sport 'judo'
		or Person plays Sport 'karatedo'
	D2	nrPlayers(Sport) ::= **count each** Person who plays **that** Sport

The database is initially empty. The user now attempts the following sequence of updates and queries. For each update, circle the letter if the update is accepted. In cases of rejection supply a reason (e.g., state which part of the conceptual schema is violated). For queries supply an appropriate response from the CIP.

(a)   **add:** Person 'Ann' has FitnessRating 9.
(b)   **add:** Person 'Fred' plays Sport 'tennis'.
(c)   **add:** Person 'Bob' has FitnessRating 7.
(d)   **add**: Person 'Ann' has FitnessRating 8.
(e)   **add:** Person 'Chris' has FitnessRating 7.
(f)   **add:** Person 'Fred' has FitnessRating 15.
(g)   **add:** Person 'Ann' plays Sport 'judo'.
(h)   **add:** Person 'Bob' is expert at Sport 'soccer'.
(i)   **add:** Person 'Ann' is expert at Sport 'judo'.
(j)   **add:** Person 'Ann' programs in Language 'SQL'.
(k)   **add:** Person 'Ann' plays Sport 'soccer'.
(l)   **add:** Person 'Chris' plays Sport 'karatedo'.
(m)   **del:** Person 'Chris' has FitnessRating 7.
(n)   **begin**
    add: Person 'Bob' has FitnessRating 8;
    del: Person 'Bob' has FitnessRating 7
  end
(o)   **add:** Person 'Ann' is expert at Sport 'soccer'.
(p)   **add:** Person 'Bob' plays Sport 'soccer'.
(q)   Person 'Ann' plays Sport 'judo'?
(r)   **what** Person plays Sport 'karatedo'?
(s)   nrPlayers(Sport 'soccer')?
(t)   **what** Person is martial artist?
(u)   FitnessRating **values?**
(v)   **what** is the meaning of life?

3. The UoD design is given by the following schema. Constraints apply to the database, not necessarily to the real world being modeled. Although each student in the real world has a marital status, for this application it is optional whether a student's marital status is recorded. There may be good reasons for this, for example, to respect the wishes of particular students to keep their marital status private. Constraint C1 is a shorthand way of entering two weaker constraints, since "exactly one" means "at least one (i.e., some) and at most one".

Reference schemes: Student (firstname); Degree (code); MaritalStatus (name)

Base fact types: F1   Student is enrolled in Degree
                F2   Student has MaritalStatus

Constraints: C1   **each** Student is enrolled in **exactly one** Degree
                C2   **each** Student has **at most one** MaritalStatus
                C3   MaritalStatus **values are** 'single', 'married', 'widowed', 'divorced'
                C4   MaritalStatus **transitions:** ("1" = "allowed")

From\to	Single	Married	Widowed	Divorced
Single	0	1	0	0
Married	0	0	1	1
Widowed	0	1	0	0
Divorced	0	1	0	0

The database is initially empty. The user now attempts the following sequence of updates and queries. For each update, circle the letter if the update is accepted; in cases of rejection supply a reason. Assume questions are legal, and supply an appropriate response.

(a) **add:** Student 'Fred' is enrolled in Degree 'BSc'.

(b) **add:** Student 'Sue' has MaritalStatus 'single'.

(c) **begin**
    add: Student 'Sue' has MaritalStatus 'single'.
    add: Student 'Sue' is enrolled in Degree 'MA'.
end

(d) **add:** Student 'Fred' is enrolled in Degree 'BA'.

(e) **add:** Student 'Fred' is studying Subject 'CS112'.

(f) MaritalStatus **values?**

(g) **add:** Student 'Bob' is enrolled in Degree 'BSc'.

(h) **add:** Student 'Sue' has MaritalStatus 'married'.

(i) **begin**
    del: Student 'Sue' has MaritalStatus 'single'.
    add: Student 'Sue' has MaritalStatus 'married'.
end

(j) **add:** Student 'Bob' has MaritalStatus 'single'.

(k) **begin**
    del: Student 'Bob' has MaritalStatus 'single'.
    add: Student 'Bob' has MaritalStatus 'divorced'.
end

(l) Student 'Sue' is enrolled in Degree 'BSc'?

(m) **what** Student is enrolled in Degree 'BSc'?

(n) **what** Student is enrolled in Degree 'MA'?

(o) **add:** 3 students are enrolled in Degree 'BE'.

What is the final state of the database?

4. Assume the following conceptual schema:

Reference schemes: Person (firstname)

Base fact types: F1   Person is male
                        F2   Person is female
                        F3   Person is a parent of Person

Constraints:
    C1   **each** Person is male **or** is female
    C2   **no** Person is male **and** is female
    C3   { each person has at most 2 parents }
             each $Person_2$ **in** ($Person_1$ is a parent of $Person_2$) **occurs there at most 2 times**
    C4   **no** Person is a parent of **itself**

Derivation rules:
    D1 $Person_1$ is a grandparent of $Person_2$ **if** $Person_1$ is a parent of **some** $Person_3$ **and**
                                                     $Person_3$ is a parent of $Person_2$

Assume the database is populated with the following data.

Males: David, Paul, Terry
Females: Alice, Chris, Linda, Norma, Selena

The user now attempts the following sequence of updates and queries. Indicate the CIP's response in each case.

(a) **add:** Person 'Jim' is male.
(b) **add:** Person 'Bernie' is parent of Person 'Terry'.
(c) **begin**

       Person 'Terry' is parent of Person 'Selena'.
       Person 'Norma' is parent of Person 'Selena'.

    end
(d) **add:** Person 'David' is parent of Person 'David'.
(e) **begin**

       Person 'Norma' is parent of Person 'Paul'.
       Person 'Alice' is parent of Person 'Terry'.

    end
(f) **add:** Person 'Chris' is male.
(g) **add:** Person 'Chris' is parent of Person 'Selena'.
(h) **what** Person is grandparent of Person 'Selena'?

Formulate your own derivation rules for the following:

(i) X is father of Y
(j) X is daughter of Y
(k) X is grand_daughter of Y

5. Consider the following conceptual schema:

Reference schemes: Employee (surname); Department (name); Language (name)

Base fact types: F1   Employee works for Department
                 F2   Employee speaks Language

Constraints: C1   **each** Employee works for **some** Department
                C2   **each** Employee works for **at most one** Department
                C3   **each** Employee speaks **some** Language

(a) Provide an update sequence to add the facts that Adams and Brown, who both speak English, work for the Health department.
(b) Invent some database populations that are inconsistent with the schema.

2.3   From External to Conceptual to Relational

This section provides an overview of how conceptual schemas may be implemented in relational database systems. An example illustrates the main ideas. The topic is developed in detail in later chapters. Consider a company that is based in an English-speaking country, but carries out some of its business overseas. Some of its employees can speak languages other than English, which can be useful when dealing with foreign customers. The company wishes to move from a manual to an automated personnel record system. Prototype examples of some online personnel record forms to be kept by the company are shown in Figure 2.5. For simplicity, only a few details are recorded in our example.

To model this small domain, we should first verbalize information on these forms in English. At this stage we should ignore any user interface details such as the geometric

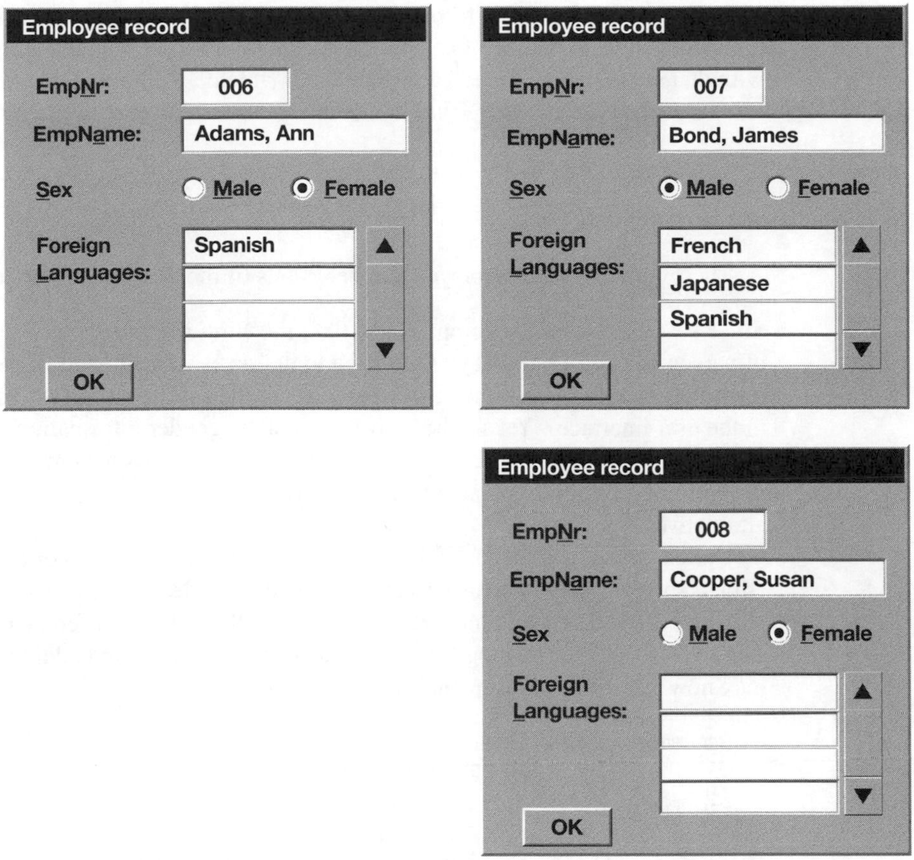

Figure 2.5 Personnel forms for three employees.

positioning of fields on the form or accelerator key choices (shown by underlined characters). Try this yourself for the first employee record before reading on.

Even at the conceptual level, there is often more than one correct way to verbalize the information. Here is one way of reading the relevant facts from the first employee record:

The Employee with employee number 006 has the EmployeeName 'Adams, Ann'.
Employee 006 is of Sex 'Female'.
Employee 006 speaks the ForeignLanguage 'Spanish'.

From the sample data, it appears that we could also identify employees by their name. However, this is usually not a good idea. To begin with, employees can change their name (e.g., on marriage). Moreover, in a large company it is often possible for two employees to have the same name. Let's suppose this possibility is confirmed by the domain expert. In this case, the sample data was not significant in this regard.

I modeled the gender information of the first employee by treating Sex as an entity type with 'Female' as one of its possible names, and associating that employee instance with that sex instance. Instead of using names ('male', 'female') for sexes, we could instead use codes (e.g., 'M', 'F'). The second fact would then read

Employee 006 is of Sex 'F'.

or more explicitly

The Employee with employee number 006 is of the Sex with sexcode 'F'.

Since sexcodes are more compact, and their meaning is obvious, let's use them instead of names as our primary way or referring to the sexes. If ever needed, we could add another two fact instances to relate the sexcodes to the full sexnames (this is actually used in the user interface). Yet another way to model the gender information is to use unaries (e.g., Employee 006 is female). Later in the book I'll discuss how to transform between different ways of conceptualizing and give you guidelines to help you choose between alternatives.

Unlike gender, the names of foreign languages have no obvious or common abbreviations, so we'll stay with using names instead of codes to identify languages. If you verbalize the other two employee records, you'll just find different instances of the same fact types. Abstracting from the instances to the types and adding constraints, we may now set out the conceptual schema as follows:

Reference schemes:	Employee (empNr); EmpName(); Sex (code); ForeignLanguage (name)
Base fact types:	F1 Employee has EmpName
	F2 Employee is of Sex
	F3 Employee speaks/is spoken by ForeignLanguage
Constraints:	C1 **each** Employee has **exactly one** EmpName
	C2 **each** Employee is of **exactly one** Sex
	C3 Sex **values are** 'M', 'F'

In setting out the reference schemes, I've abbreviated "employee number" as "empNr". I always use "Nr" to abbreviate "Number". This works well with other languages like German since the first and last letters of their word for "Number" also form "Nr". Some people use "no" from the Italian "numero", but I dislike this because it needs a dot (i.e., "no.") to distinguish it from the negative "no". Some others use "num". The choice really is up to you, and decent CASE tools allow you to declare the abbreviations you prefer to use.

Notice that I've also abbreviated "EmployeeName" to "EmpName". The empty parentheses after "EmpName" indicate that this is just a value type (in this case a character string) and hence needs no reference scheme. If there is any likelihood of confusion, you should avoid abbreviations at the conceptual level. Some modelers never abbreviate, but I often do so if the meaning is still clear. Maybe I'm just lazy.

Each of constraints C1 and C2 is actually a pair of elementary constraints. The phrase "exactly one" is shorthand for "at least one and at most one". The constraints section does not restrict the fact type Employee speaks ForeignLanguage. So some employees may speak no foreign language (e.g., Cooper), some may speak many (e.g., Bond), and many may speak the same foreign language (e.g., Spanish). This "no constraint" or *"default"* case may be explicitly declared using the following *verbalization:*

> **It is possible that the same** Employee speaks **more than one** Language **and that the same** Language is spoken by **more than one** Employee

The conceptual database for this schema contains three fact tables, one for each elementary fact type. Some important consequences of this conceptual approach are that the schema is easy to understand, it is automatically free of redundancy, and constraints are easy to specify.

Once a conceptual schema has been designed, it may be mapped to a *logical schema* that is described in terms of the generic logical data model (e.g., relational, network, or hierarchic) chosen for implementation purposes. The physical schema is then constructed by adapting the logical schema to the specific DBMS and improving performance by adding indexes, and so on. In this book, the implementation discussion focuses on relational DBMSs. A schema specified in terms of the relational data model is called a *relational database schema,* or **relational schema** for short.

Chapter 1 introduced some basic ideas about relational databases. The remainder of this section expands briefly on these ideas. A more detailed discussion of these concepts is provided in Section 10.2.

A relational database is made up of *named tables,* divided *horizontally* into *unnamed rows* and *vertically* into *named columns.* A particular row-column location is a *cell.* Each cell contains only one data *value.* Figure 2.6 shows how the information from Figure 2.5 is stored in a relational database. The Employee table has three rows and three columns. The Speaks table has four rows and two columns. The number of rows of a table increases or decreases as data are added or deleted, but the number of columns stays the same.

All tables must have different names. Within the same table, all columns must have different names. Columns are often called "fields", though this term is sometimes used for cells. Column names are also called *attribute* names. Each attribute is based on some *domain,* or pool of values from which the column values are drawn. For example, if we added a column for manager, this would have the same domain as empNr. The relational concept of domain is connected to our conceptual notion of object type, but in practice most relational DBMSs support only syntactic domains (value type declarations like smallint) rather than semantic domains.

Employee:

empNr	empName	sex
006	Adams, Ann	F
007	Bond, James	M
008	Cooper, Susan	F

Speaks:

empNr	foreignLanguage
006	Spanish
007	French
007	Japanese
007	Spanish

Figure 2.6 Relational database tables for Figure 2.5.

In contrast to a conceptual database, a relational database allows facts of different types to be grouped into the same table. For example, Figure 2.6 groups the three elementary fact types into two tables. The Employee table caters to fact types F1 and F2, while the Speaks table caters to fact type F3.

The first row of the Employee table expresses two facts: the Employee with employee number 006 has the EmployeeName 'Adams, Ann'; the Employee with employee number 006 is of the Sex with sexcode 'F'. In general, *each row of a table in a relational database contains one or more elementary facts.* Strictly speaking, a rare exception to this rule may occur when a table is used to store only a reference—let's ignore this rare case for now (we'll return to it when discussing the mapping of independent object types in Chapter 10).

With relational databases, care is needed in grouping fact types into tables. Chapter 10 provides a simple procedure for mapping a conceptual schema onto a relational schema. This procedure shows that the choice of tables in Figure 2.6 is correct. Suppose, however, that we tried to group all three fact types into just one table. This would cause problems similar to those discussed earlier with the movie star example (Table 1.2).

Relational databases are based on the relational model of data developed by E. F. Codd. In this model, the table is the only data structure. Tables that have their rows of data stored in the database are called *base tables*. Derived tables that have only their definitions stored (not their content) are called *views*. Within a base table, duplicate rows are not allowed.

The order of the rows or the columns doesn't matter. For example, in Table 2.1 the columns and the rows of the Employee table have been reordered, but the meaning is unchanged (the same six facts are present). The reason that the order of rows doesn't matter is that each fact is totally contained within a single row. The reason that the order of columns doesn't matter is that each column is named, so we know what its values mean. In a sense, the columns are "ordered by their name" rather than their position.

Although the order of rows and columns is irrelevant at the logical level, at the physical level the order does exist and needs to be taken into account when tuning the database for efficient access. The results of queries are also tables, but these are unnamed and may contain duplicate rows. When you formulate queries, you can specify whatever order you want the data to be displayed in, regardless of the actual order used to store the data in base tables.

Table 2.1 The order of columns or rows has no impact on the meaning of the data.

Employee:	*empName*	*empNr*	*sex*
	Cooper, Susan	008	F
	Bond, James	007	M
	Adams, Ann	006	F

We may treat a base table as a set of rows and each row as a sequence or *tuple* of data values (or more strictly, a tuple of attribute-value pairs). In this sense, a table is a set of tuples. Since a mathematical relation is defined as a set of tuples, each table is a *relation*—hence the name "relational database".

We have seen that conceptual facts are grouped into tables in a relational schema. What about *constraints?* Relational systems typically supply only a few built-in, declarative constraint types. Columns may be specified as *mandatory* or optional for their table. In our example all the columns of the Employee table are mandatory (each entry must be an actual value, not a "null" value). This goes part of the way toward capturing the constraints that each employee is identified by empNr and has at least one name and is of at least one sex. To complete these constraints, we demand that each employee listed in the Speaks table is also listed in the Employee table (this is a *subset* or *referential integrity* constraint).

To restrict each employee to at most one name and at most one gender, entries in the empNr column of the Employee table must be *unique* (i.e., no duplicates). This may be enforced by declaring empNr as the *primary key* for the Employee table (a key is a minimal combination of columns where no duplicates are allowed). In the relational model each table has a primary key that provides the primary way of accessing its rows. Finally, the constraint on Sex values may be enforced by a simple *check clause.*

The relational schema may be set out compactly as shown in Figure 2.7. Column names are placed in parentheses (round brackets) after the table name, and *keys are underlined.*

In this notation, columns are assumed mandatory for their table by default. The dotted arrow expresses the subset constraint mentioned earlier. The possible values for sexcodes are placed in braces (curly brackets). For simplicity, domains are omitted. This notation is logical, not physical. Precisely how the tables are defined and the constraints are declared depends on the relational database language used (often a dialect of SQL). Examples of this are provided in Chapter 11.

The process of declaring a schema is often called *data definition,* and the language component specially designed for this task is called a *data definition language* (DDL). Our example was simple enough for the relational schema to be fully specified within the DDL component of standard SQL. Often, however, some constraints have to be coded separately.

In general, a relational schema may contain table definitions, constraints, and derivation rules. Most derivation rules declared at the conceptual level may be specified in a relational DBMS by defining virtual tables (or "views") or by coding triggers or

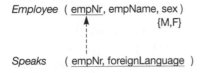

Figure 2.7 The relational schema for Figure 2.5.

stored procedures. If a query type is commonly used and requires derivation, it is explicitly included in the derivation rules section of the conceptual schema. In contrast, ad hoc queries are catered to by including derivation functions and operators in the query language itself, so that the user may express the required derivation rule within the query formulation itself.

In a relational database language like SQL, it is fairly easy to express many mathematical and logical derivation rules (e.g., averages or grandparenthood derived from parenthood). Some derivation rules that are difficult to express in SQL can be easily expressed in other languages. For example, the following Prolog rules recursively define ancestry in terms of parenthood:

X is an ancestor of Y **if** X is a parent of Y.
X is an ancestor of Y **if** X is a parent of Z **and** Z is an ancestor of Y.

Although recursive queries like these are unusual in a business application, if the need for them arises, one solution is to provide an interface between the database language (e.g., SQL) and the other language (e.g., C# or Prolog), so that the languages can "call" one another to do the tasks for which they are best suited. The SQL standard itself now supports many cases of recursion, but commercial SQL differ in their support for this feature.

Languages like Prolog are often used in artificial intelligence (AI) applications. In the past, AI systems tended to work with small populations of a large number of complex fact types, and database systems worked with large populations of fewer and simpler fact types. One of the aims of next-generation technology is to combine powerful inference capabilities with efficient database management.

Once the schema is defined, the *data manipulation* phase may begin. The tables, which are initially empty, may be populated with data (i.e., rows are *inserted*). After that, rows may be *deleted* or *modified*. A row is modified if one or more of its values is changed: this is sometimes called "update", but, when not talking specifically about SQL, I often use the term "update" generically to include insert, delete, and modify operations. Collectively, these three operations are called *data maintenance*. If the constraints have been properly specified, the DBMS will automatically enforce them whenever a maintenance operation occurs.

Note that the row modify operation of a relational DBMS can be expressed conceptually in terms of adding or deleting elementary facts. For example, changing 'Adams, Ann' to 'Smith, Ann' on the third row of the Employee table of Figure 2.6 corresponds to deleting the fact that employee 006 is named 'Adams, Ann' and adding the fact that employee 006 is named 'Smith, Ann'. Of course, at the external level, the user would simply modify values in a screen version of a form (as in Figure 2.5) or a table row (as in Figure 2.6).

Another aspect of data manipulation is *data retrieval*. This typically involves three steps: (1) the user requests information; (2) the system searches the database and/or the schema to locate the relevant information and uses this to obtain the required result; and (3) the system then outputs this result. The second stage may involve sorting data and/or deriving results (e.g., an average value). Unlike maintenance, retrieval operations leave the database unaltered.

Data presentation refers to special techniques for displaying information on the screen (screen display) or for producing formatted printed output (report writing). I use the term *output report* generically to include screen and hard copy reports. Typically, users of a relational database application do not interact directly with the relational tables in which the data is stored. Usually they enter and access the data via a *forms interface*. Issues such as design and management of screen forms, and *security* enforcement, often constitute a major part of the application development.

For reasons such as correctness, clarity, completeness, and portability, database designs should be first specified as conceptual schemas before mapping them to relational schemas. The rest of the book is largely devoted to showing how to do this in detail.

2.4   Development Frameworks

Information systems development involves at least *four worlds:* the subject world, the system world, the usage world, and the development world (Jarke et al. 1992). The *subject world* is the universe of discourse, or application domain, typically part of the real world. The *system world* is the information system's model of the UoD, and hence is a formal abstraction. The *usage world* is the organizational world in which the system is to function and includes the community of users of the system, their user interfaces to the system, associated activities, and so on. This is sometimes called the environment of discourse. The *development world* covers the environment and processes used to develop the system, including the modelers and programmers, their design methods and rationale, project schedules, and so on.

The system world is sometimes called the *information system in the narrow sense,* while the combination of the four worlds is sometimes called the *information system in the broad sense,* since it includes all related human factors. Specialists who focus on the system world are called *dry* (they deal with formal aspects), and those who focus on the other three worlds are called *wet* (they are willing to get their hands wet dealing with the informal, softer aspects). In practice, both the dry and wet approaches are needed. This book is largely concerned with the system and development worlds.

Developing an information system for a particular application is essentially a *problem-solving* process. This general process may be broken down into four main stages: (1) define the problem; (2) devise a plan; (3) execute the plan; and (4) evaluate what happened. Two of the most generally useful problem-solving strategies are to divide the problem into a number of *subproblems* and deal with these individually, and to try a *simpler* version of the problem first.

When the problem-solving process involves the development of computer software, it may be refined into the simple five-stage *software life cycle* shown in Figure 2.8: *specify* (say what we need the software to do); *design* (decide how to do it); *implement* (code it); *test* (check that it works); and *maintain* (keep it working). In the naive "waterfall" version of this process, the path through these five stages is a simple sequence. In practice, however, the process is typically *cyclic* in nature, as indicated by the dotted arrows.

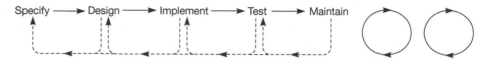

Figure 2.8 The software life cycle, with iterations.

If a need for change is detected at a later stage of the cycle, it is often necessary to return to one of the earlier stages. Moreover, large development projects are usually best divided into small projects, which can be further divided into components, each having its own cycle. The additional cycles at the right of Figure 2.8 depict further iterations, each of which can be refined into a multistage cycle as shown on the left. In this *iterative* approach to development, the more essential or critical components are often developed first, to minimize the risk of the project failing overall.

When the software to be developed is an information system, the development cycle for each component may be refined further into the following typical phases:

- Feasibility study
- Requirements analysis
- Conceptual design: data, processes
- Logical design: data, processes
- Basic internal design: data, processes
- Basic external design: data, processes
- Prototyping
- Completion of design
- Implementation of production version
- Testing and validation
- Release of software, documentation, and training
- Maintenance

In practice, these phases often overlap, feedback cycles are common, and some phases might be omitted.

A **feasibility study** identifies the main objectives of the proposed information system and determines which components may be implemented with known resources (e.g., budget allocations and staff). It examines the cost-effectiveness of alternative proposals and assigns priorities to the various system components. The cost/benefit analysis might reveal that some objectives are unrealistic, or that some of the objectives can be best achieved by improved manual procedures rather than by use of computers.

Assuming the go-ahead for the project is given, a detailed **requirements analysis** is undertaken to determine just what the system is required to do. Various components of the system are delineated, and people familiar with the relevant application areas are interviewed, including domain experts, intended users, and policy makers. Interviews may be supplemented by questionnaires. Relevant documentation is examined (e.g., forms, reports, charts, policy manuals, even code from legacy systems to be reengineered). Where no such documentation is available, the domain experts are requested to invent examples of the kind of information to be recorded. Simple diagrams are often used to clarify how the information system is to interact with the business environment. The main operations or transactions to be supported are identified and prioritized, and estimates are made of their expected data volumes, frequencies, and required response times.

The output of this requirements collection and analysis phase is a *requirements specifications* document that details functional requirements, nonfunctional requirements (e.g., performance), and maintenance information (e.g., anticipated changes). This document should be *unambiguous, complete, verifiable* (there is some way of checking whether the requirements are satisfied), *consistent* (requirements do not contradict one another), *modifiable* (changes can be made easily and safely), *traceable* (requirements can be tracked to their origins and are identifiable across different versions of the document), and *usable* (by current and future users of the document).

Various textual and graphical notations are used for different aspects of the requirements specification. Some of the process-oriented notations in use (e.g., use case diagrams, context diagrams, data flow diagrams) are discussed in Chapter 13. For large, complex projects the requirements analysis stage might take several months. As fact-oriented modeling uses verbalization of familiar examples to clarify the UoD, its conceptual design method is also useful for analysis of data requirements.

One way of measuring the overall progress of a requirements activity is to see how it lines up along the following three dimensions of requirements engineering: *specification* (opaque, fair, complete), *representation* (informal, semiformal, formal), and *agreement* (personal view, common view). The further along these dimensions, the better (Pohl 1994).

With the understanding that phases may overlap, the next stage in the information systems life cycle is **conceptual design.** This is sometimes simply called *analysis,* to distinguish it from the later stages of logical and physical design. With large applications, subproblems or components of a more manageable size might be selected, an *architecture* specified for coupling components, and a conceptual *subschema* designed for each. The various subschemas may then be *integrated* within a *global* conceptual schema. In this text, the problems discussed are small enough for us to design the whole conceptual schema without needing to first design subschemas. However, the main design process itself is broken up into various stages. For example, fact types are identified before adding constraints.

Experienced modelers often notice similarities between new applications and previous ones they have designed. In this case, significant savings in the design effort may result from judicious **reuse** of design strategies adopted in their earlier models. For example, if we have already modeled a university library system, and now have to model a videotape rental business, there are many features of the earlier model that may be reused. We might choose to identify an object type Loan in a similar way, and either adopt or adapt several fact types from the earlier application. By abstracting similar, specific concepts (e.g., "book", "videotape") to more general concepts (e.g., "rentable item"), it is easier to recognize a new application as related to earlier ones.

In recent years, a substantial and growing body of work on *design patterns* and *best practices* has been developed to facilitate reuse. Large commercial packages are available for Enterprise Resource Planning (ERP) that can be adapted to handle various functions of a business (e.g., order processing, payroll management). To widen the scope of their reuse, such packages often model practices at a very high level of abstraction, which can make them harder to apply to concrete cases.

Over the years, many dimensions or perspectives have been suggested for capturing different aspects of information systems design. One classic survey of information systems design methods identified three design perspectives: data, process, and behavior (Olle et al. 1991). The *data-oriented perspective* focuses on what kinds of data are stored in the database, what constraints apply to these data, and what kinds of data are derivable. The *process-oriented perspective* examines the processes or activities performed, to help understand the way a particular business operates. Processes are described, as well as information flows between processes and other components. Often, a complex process is refined into several subprocesses. The *behavior-oriented perspective* looks at how *events* trigger actions in the information system. Often, an activity analysis may be rephrased in terms of an event analysis, or vice versa. The distinction between "process", "behavior", and "event" is somewhat fuzzy, and different people often define these terms differently.

The most important thing is to specify the information needed and conditions sufficient for a process to execute or "fire". For example, the process of retrieving an account balance might be triggered by the event of a client requesting an account balance, and require input of information from the client (e.g., client number and account type) as well as from the relevant database tables. Since the dividing line between process and behavior is often blurred, I'll follow one common practice of bundling any discussion of processes, events, operations, activities, and so on into a single perspective that I'll feel free to call "process", "behavior", or "operations". From that viewpoint there are just two main perspectives: data and process.

Decades ago, systems were designed largely from the process perspective, but this proved to be inefficient and unreliable in many cases. The data perspective came to be the dominant one used for information systems development, since it was more fundamental and much more stable. Business processes change continually, but the underlying data tends to undergo only minor changes by comparison. More recently, object-oriented modeling has provided one way of combining the data and process perspectives, with objects encapsulating data and operations. Unfortunately, this combination is often specified at a subconceptual level, so this integration is not as rosy as it seems. This book focuses largely on the data perspective, but some aspects of the process perspective are also discussed.

If correctly designed, the conceptual schema provides a formal model of the structure of the UoD. Once this semantic modeling is completed, we select the class of DBMS to be used, and perform a *mapping* of the conceptual design to a **logical design** expressed in terms of the generic data model of the DBMS. For example, we might map a conceptual schema to a relational schema. CASE tools can perform this mapping automatically. Once the logical design is determined, a **basic internal design** can be undertaken. The logical design is adapted to the specific DBMS(s) being used, and various strategies (e.g., indexes or clustering) are specified to improve the efficiency of the physical design.

The **basic external design** of an information system involves determining which kinds of data and operations will be accessible to which user groups, and designing the appropriate human-computer interfaces for these groups. Typically, access rights tables are constructed for different user types, decisions are made about what functions to support on different screen forms, and the layout of screen forms and menus is decided. If the basic internal design is completed, the basic external design can include cross-references between the two designs (e.g., to show which forms access which tables).

Except for trivial applications, the next stage of the life cycle usually involves **prototyping.** A prototype is a simplified version of the intended product that is used to gain early feedback from users on the quality of the design. It aims to cover the major functions in the requirements specification, but usually omits most of the error checking and finer details required for the final version, and it uses only a small set of sample data. Early feedback is more important than efficiency at this stage, so the prototype might be coded in a higher-level language than the one(s) ultimately used for the product. For user interface design, the initial prototypes may simply be drawn on paper; these are called "paper prototypes". At any rate, the prototypes are demonstrated to the clients, and their feedback is used to revise the requirements and designs where necessary.

Once a prototype is accepted, the (hopefully) **final design** of the actual product or component can be completed. The **implementation** of the internal and external design is now completed by writing the actual code for the production version. The product is now subjected to extensive **testing and validation.** The software is run using carefully chosen data and operations to check that it functions as expected. Selected users might then be issued with prerelease versions (e.g., alpha and one or more betas) to help find other errors. Typically, the further advanced the prerelease version is, the wider is the audience of test users. With certain types of software (e.g., military security systems), correctness proofs may be developed to ensure the program meets its specifications. Finally the **release** version of the product is made available to the public, along with extensive *documentation* and *training.*

Software **maintenance** involves making modifications to the software after it has been initially released. This maintenance may be of three main types: *corrective* (eliminate bugs), *adaptive* (alter software to cater to changes in the environment or UoD), and *perfective* (add improvements). Maintenance continues as long as the product is available. As mentioned before, the overall development process is often *iterative,* applying the development cycle to one major component at a time rather than trying to build the whole product at once. The earlier errors are detected in the development cycle, the easier they are to fix. The cost of correcting an error at the implementation stage can be orders of magnitude greater than the cost of fixing it at the analysis stage.

In developing information systems, various factors are considered generally important. These include practicality (is use of a computer the best way to solve the problem?), correctness, clarity (designs and code should be readable and well documented), efficiency (memory requirements, speed, production costs), portability, maintainability, adaptability, user-proofing, and support.

Early in the chapter we saw how information schemas can exist at four different levels (conceptual, logical, internal, and external). The inclusion of the logical level is a refinement of the original three-schema architecture developed by an international standards group. This notion of levels provides a vertical way of partitioning an information system's architecture. It is also useful to provide a horizontal partitioning. One way of doing this is to use the "six friends" Rudyard Kipling referred to in his 1902 story "The Elephant's Child": "I keep six honest serving friends . . . Their names are What and Why and When and How and Where and Who". If we include a column for each of these six questions, and show each of the four levels as a row, we obtain a tabular, *level/focus framework* with 24 cells.

The most influential framework to incorporate both vertical and horizontal partitioning is John Zachman's framework for information systems architecture (Zachman 1987). It uses six focus columns for Kipling's interrogatives, but has five perspective rows instead of four levels. Hence the *Zachman framework* has 30 cells, as shown in Table 2.2.

Row 1 (the scope) provides a very high level, ballpark view. Row 2 (the enterprise model) corresponds roughly to the conceptual level, or "owner view". Row 3 (the system model) is basically the logical level, or "designer view". Row 4 (the technology model) corresponds to most of the internal level, or "builder view", with row 5 providing more detail in the "subcontractor" view. Aspects of the external level appear in various cells.

This book focuses on column 1 (data) of rows 2 and 3, with some discussion of column 2 (function) and row 3. In practice, different projects will involve various other cells in this framework. For example, you often need to consider where the system will be deployed, who the stakeholders are, when system components are due, and why various business rules need to be enforced (columns 3–6). Formal connections between cells should be established. For example, we should be able to map (or forward-engineer) a conceptual model to a logical model, or go back the other way (reverse-engineering). Having a framework like this helps us to evaluate how well we are catering to different aspects of an information system.

Another framework is the Framework of Information System Concepts (FRISCO), which was developed by an IFIP working group to provide a standard taxonomy of concepts used in information systems work (Falkenberg et al. 1998). Although not

Table 2.2 Zachman framework for enterprise architecture.

	Data (what)	Function (how)	Network (where)	People (who)	Time (when)	Motivation (why)
Scope						
Enterprise model						
System model						
Technology model						
Detailed representations						

widely adopted, the FRISCO report does provide useful insights into information system development.

2.5   Summary

An information system for a given application may be viewed from at least four levels: conceptual, logical, internal, and external. At each level the formal model or knowledge base comprises a *schema* that describes the structure or design of the UoD and a database that is populated with the fact instances. Each schema determines what states and transitions are permitted for its database. The *conceptual schema* does this in terms of simple, human-oriented concepts. The *logical schema* groups information into structures supported by the generic logical architecture (e.g., relational). The *internal* schema specifies the physical storage and efficient access structures (e.g., indexes) for the specific DBMS being used to implement the application. For the same global conceptual schema, different *external* schemas can be constructed for different user groups depending on what information is to be accessible and how the information is to be displayed.

A conceptual schema comprises three main sections: *base fact types, constraints,* and *derivation rules.* Base facts are primitive (i.e., they are not derived from other facts). Derived facts are computed or inferred by applying derivation rules to other facts. In specifying fact types, we indicate what kinds of *objects* there are, how these are *referenced,* and what *roles* they play. Each role in a *relationship* is played by only one object type. The simplest kind of object is a *value* (character string or number). *Entities* are real or abstract objects that are identified by their relationship to values. For example, a country might be identified by its name. *Static constraints* determine the allowable populations of fact types. *Dynamic constraints* restrict transitions between these populations. For example, each city is the capital of at most one country, and no adult may become a child.

Each fact in a conceptual database is *elementary.* The addition or deletion of a fact is a simple update. In a *compound transaction,* several simple updates may be included; in this case, constraints apply only to the net effect of the complete update sequence, not to each individual update. Updates and queries on a conceptual database or conceptual schema are responded to by the conceptual information processor (CIP).

Each DBMS conforms to a *logical* data model (e.g., network, hierarchic, or relational). If a relational DBMS is chosen for the implementation, the conceptual schema is mapped to a *relational schema,* or relational database schema. Here all the stored facts are placed in named *tables,* with named columns and unnamed rows. Each row of a relational table corresponds to one or more elementary facts. Each cell (row-column position) contains only one value. Within a table, no row may be duplicated. The population of a relational table may be changed by inserting, deleting, or modifying a row. Most conceptual constraints and derivation rules can be expressed either within the relational DBMS language or by interfacing to another language.

The *information systems life cycle* typically involves the following stages: feasibility study; requirements analysis; conceptual design of data and processes; logical design;

basic internal design; basic external design; prototyping; implementation of production version; testing and validation; release of software, documentation, and training; and maintenance. Feedback from a later stage may indicate a need to rework earlier stages. Careful attention to the earlier stages reduces the overall effort involved, as does reuse of design strategies used previously on similar applications. For large projects, an iterative approach to development is generally recommended, where the life cycle is applied to one component before moving on to another component.

Various frameworks for information system architecture exist. The Zachman framework is comprised of five rows that view the system from different perspectives (scope, enterprise model, system model, technology model, and details) and six columns with a different focus (data, function, network, people, time, and motivation).

Chapter Notes

The classic discussion of the conceptual, internal, and external schemas of an information system is given in van Griethuysen (ed. 1982). Some people who worked on this ISO standard also worked on the FRISCO report (Falkenberg et al. 1998). Along with many other authors (e.g., Elmasri and Navathe 1994), I consider the relational model of data to be a *logical* model rather than a conceptual model, mainly because it is too distant from natural language. From this viewpoint, a relational schema represents the logical portion of an internal schema (omitting details specific to the chosen DBMS, and storage and access details such as indexes). Codd (1990, pp. 33–34) proposes an alternative interpretation of the three-level architecture, in which the base relations of a relational database provide the conceptual schema and views provide an external schema.

A standard reference on requirements analysis is the ANSI/IEEE standard 830-1984. A comparative review of different approaches to information system work is given in Olle et al. (1991). An informative overview of key issues in information systems modeling is provided by Mylopoulos (1998). Pohl (1994) gives a detailed treatment of the specification, representation, and agreement dimensions of requirements engineering. Zachman (1987) introduces his architectural framework, and its use in modeling repository work is soon suggested (Matthews and McGee 1990). Zachman has a regular column on architectural issues in the *Data to Knowledge Newsletter (www.BRSolutions.com)*. The Zachman Institute for Framework Advancement is dedicated to promoting the use of the Zachman framework in industry *(www.zifa.com)*.

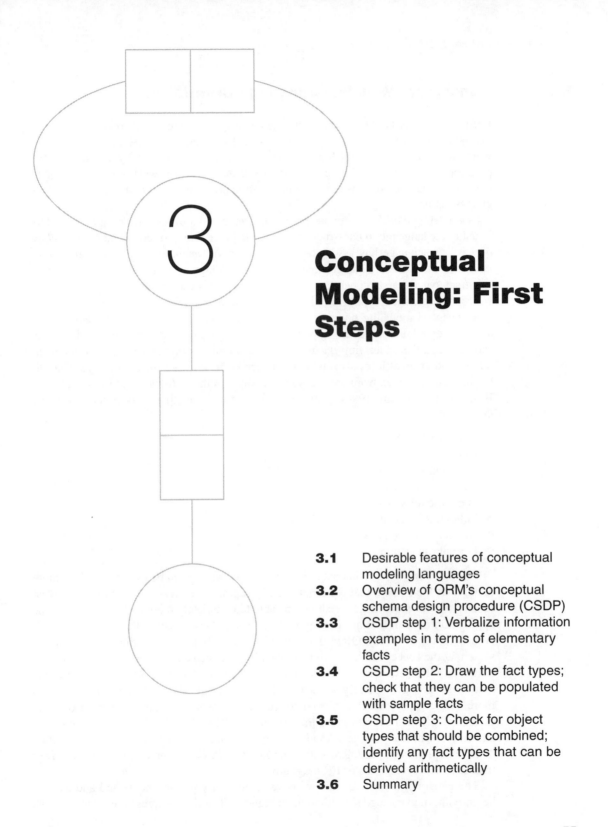

Conceptual Modeling: First Steps

3.1   Conceptual Modeling Language Criteria

Before discussing ORM's conceptual schema design procedure, let's review the fundamental design principles that underlie the ORM language itself. Some of these ideas
were mentioned before, but I'll generalize the discussion here so that you can apply the
principles to evaluate modeling languages in general. As you work your way through
the book, you should consider how these principles are realized in the various languages discussed.

A modeling *method* comprises both a *language* and a *procedure* to guide modelers
in using the language to construct models. This procedure is often called the *modeling
process*. A language has associated *syntax* (marks), *semantics* (meaning), and *prag-
matics* (use). Written languages may be graphical (diagrams) and/or textual. The terms
"abstract syntax" and "concrete syntax" are sometimes used to distinguish underlying
concepts (e.g., object type) from their representation (e.g., named ellipse).

Conceptual modeling portrays the application domain at a high level, using terms
and concepts familiar to the application users, ignoring logical- and physical-level
aspects (e.g., the underlying database or programming structures used for implementation) and external-level aspects (e.g., the screen forms used for data entry). The following criteria drawn from various sources (van Griethuysen 1982; ter Hofstede 1993;
Bloesch and Halpin 1996) provide a basis for evaluating conceptual modeling
languages:

- Expressibility
- Clarity
- Simplicity and orthogonality
- Semantic stability
- Semantic relevance
- Validation mechanisms
- Abstraction mechanisms
- Formal foundation

The *expressibility* of a language is a measure of what it can be used to say. The more
features of the domain that the language can capture, the greater its expressive power.
Ideally, a conceptual language should be able to completely model all details about the
application domain that are conceptually relevant. This is called the *100% Principle*
(van Griethuysen 1982). ORM is a method for modeling and querying an information
system at the conceptual level, and for mapping between conceptual and logical levels.
Although ORM extensions exist for process modeling, the focus of ORM is on information modeling (popularly known as data modeling), since the data perspective is
more stable and provides a formal foundation on which operations can be defined.
Overall, UML can express more than standard ORM, since UML use case, behavior,
and implementation diagrams model aspects beyond static structures. For conceptual
data modeling, however, ORM's diagram notation has much greater expressive power
than UML class diagrams or ER diagrams.

The *clarity* of a language is a measure of how easy it is to understand and use. To
begin with, the language should be unambiguous. The more expressible a language is,

the harder it is to maintain clarity. Ideally, the meaning of diagrams or textual expressions in the language should be intuitively obvious. This ideal is rarely achieved. A more realistic goal is that the language concepts and notations should be easily learned and remembered. To meet this goal, a language should exhibit *simplicity and orthogonality*. By avoiding attributes, ORM's role-based notation is simplified, yet easily understood by populating it with fact instances. Orthogonality allows use of an expression wherever its meaning or value may be used. ORM's constructs were designed from the ground up to be orthogonal. For example, ORM constraints can be used and combined whenever this is meaningful. As we will see later, this is not true of languages like UML.

Semantic stability is a measure of how well models or queries expressed in the language retain their original intent in the face of changes to the application. The more changes we are forced to make to a model or query to cope with an application change, the less stable it is. Models and queries in ORM are semantically more stable than in ER or UML since they are not impacted by changes that cause attributes to be remodeled as relationships or vice versa.

Semantic relevance requires that only conceptually relevant details need be modeled. Any aspect irrelevant to the meaning (e.g., implementation choices, machine efficiency) should be avoided. This is called the *conceptualization principle* (van Griethuysen 1982). Section 13.3 shows how conceptual queries in ORM meet this criterion better than queries based on attribute-based models.

Validation mechanisms are ways in which domain experts can check whether the model matches the application. For example, static features of a model may be checked by verbalization and multiple instantiation, and dynamic features may be checked by simulation. Unlike ER and UML, ORM models are always easily verbalized and populated.

Abstraction mechanisms allow unwanted details to be removed from immediate consideration. This is very important with large models (e.g., wall-size schema diagrams). ORM diagrams tend to be more detailed and larger than corresponding ER or UML models, so abstraction mechanisms are often used. For example, a global schema may be modularized into various scopes or views based on span or perspective (e.g., a single page of a data model or a single page of an activity model). Successive refinement may be used to decompose higher-level views into more detailed views. Though not a language issue, tools can provide additional support such as layering and object zoom (see Section 13.4). Such mechanisms can be used to hide and show just that part of the model relevant to a user's immediate needs. With minor variations, these techniques can be applied to ORM, ER, and UML. ORM also includes an attribute abstraction procedure to generate ER and UML diagrams as views.

A formal foundation is needed to ensure unambiguity and executability (e.g., to automate the storage, verification, transformation, and simulation of models) and to allow formal proofs of equivalence and implication between models. Although ORM's richer, graphical constraint notation provides a more complete diagrammatic treatment of schema transformations, use of textual constraint languages can partly offset this advantage. For their data modeling constructs, ORM, ER, and UML have an adequate formal foundation.

Bentley (1998) suggests the following alternative yardsticks for language design: orthogonality, generality, parsimony, completeness, similarity, extensibility, and openness. Some of these criteria (e.g., completeness, generality, extensibility) may be subsumed under expressibility. Parsimony may be treated as one aspect of simplicity. Another criterion sometimes mentioned is convenience (how convenient, suitable, or appropriate a language feature is to the user). We can treat convenience as another aspect of simplicity.

Language design often involves a number of *trade-offs* between competing criteria. One well-known trade-off is that between *expressibility and tractability:* the more expressive a language is, the harder it is to make it efficiently executable (Levesque 1984). Another trade-off is between *parsimony and convenience.* Although *ceteris paribus,* the fewer concepts the better (cf. Occam's razor), restricting ourselves to the minimum possible number of concepts may sometimes be too inconvenient. For example, it is possible to write computer programs in pure binary, using just strings of ones and zeros, but it's much easier to write programs in higher-level languages like C#. As an example from logic, it's more convenient to use several operators such as "not", "and", "or", and "if-then" even though we could use just one (e.g., "nand"). See the chapter notes for further discussion of this example.

One basic question relevant to the parsimony-convenience trade-off is whether to use the attribute concept as a base modeling construct. I've already argued in favor of a negative answer to this question. ORM models attributes in terms of relationships in its base model (used for capturing, validating, and evolving the conceptual schema), while still allowing attribute views to be displayed in derived models (in this case, compact views used for summary or implementation purposes). Traditional ER supports single-valued attributes, while UML supports both single-valued and multivalued attributes. Section 9.3 argues that multivalued attributes are especially bad for conceptual modeling, although they can be useful for logical and physical modeling.

The rest of this chapter provides an overview of ORM's conceptual schema design procedure and a detailed discussion of the first three steps in this procedure. The ORM approach has been used productively in industry for over 25 years; details of its history can be found in the chapter notes.

3.2   ORM's Conceptual Schema Design Procedure

When developing an information system, we first specify what is required and produce a design to meet these requirements. For reasons outlined earlier, I recommend first developing this design at the conceptual level using Object-Role Modeling. This entails describing the structure of the UoD formally in terms of an ORM conceptual schema. If an ORM context is understood, I'll often shorten "ORM conceptual schema" to just "conceptual schema".

The procedure for designing a conceptual schema that is small enough to manage as a single unit is referred to as the **conceptual schema design procedure** (CSDP). With large applications, the universe of discourse is divided into components or subsections (which may overlap). These are normally prioritized to determine which ones to develop first, and a conceptual *subschema* is designed for each. With a team of modelers, a consensus on terminology is reached, so the same names are used for the same concepts. Later the subschemas are *integrated* or merged into a global conceptual schema that covers the whole UoD. This integration is often performed iteratively. This top-down design approach can be summarized as follows:

- Divide the universe of discourse into manageable subsections.
- Apply the CSDP to each subsection.
- Integrate the subschemas into a global conceptual schema.

For each manageably sized application, the conceptual schema design is performed in **seven steps:**

1. Transform familiar information examples into elementary facts, and apply quality checks.
2. Draw the fact types, and apply a population check.
3. Check for entity types that should be combined, and note any arithmetic derivations.
4. Add uniqueness constraints, and check arity of fact types.
5. Add mandatory role constraints, and check for logical derivations.
6. Add value, set comparison, and subtyping constraints.
7. Add other constraints and perform final checks.

Often all seven steps are performed for each model component as it is discussed with the domain expert, rather than applying step 1 to all components, then step 2, and so on.

The procedure begins with the analysis of examples of information to be output by, or input to, the information system. Basically, the first three steps are concerned with identifying the fact types. In later steps we add constraints to the fact types. Throughout the procedure, checks are performed to detect derived facts and to ensure that no mistakes have been made. In the rest of this chapter we consider the first three steps in detail.

With large applications, the preliminary segmentation and final integration add two further stages, resulting in nine steps overall. Although the CSDP is best learned in the sequence of steps shown, in practice we might apply the steps somewhat differently. For example, we might add constraints as soon as the fact types are entered, rather than waiting for all the fact types to be entered before adding any constraints.

In the commercial world, there are many existing applications that have been implemented using lower-level approaches, resulting in database designs that may be inconsistent, incomplete, inefficient, or difficult to maintain. Such systems are often poorly documented. These problems can be overcome by **reengineering** the existing applications using conceptual modeling techniques. For example, sample populations from existing database tables can be used as input to the CSDP.

Even without sample populations, an existing database schema can be *reverse-engineered* to a tentative conceptual schema by using information about constraints and domains and making simplifying assumptions about use of names. The conceptual design can then be validated and completed by communicating with a domain expert. The conceptual schema can then be *forward-engineered* by applying a conceptual optimization procedure and then mapping to the target database system to provide an improved and maintainable implementation. This reengineering approach is discussed in Chapter 12.

3.3   CSDP Step 1: From Examples to Elementary Facts

To specify what is required of an information system, we need to answer the question *What sort of information do we want from the system?* Clearly, any information to be output from the system must either be stored in the system or be derivable by the system. Our first step is to begin with *familiar examples* of relevant information, and *express these in terms of elementary facts.* As a check on the quality of our work, we ask the following questions. *Are the entities well identified? Can the facts be split into smaller ones without losing information?* This constitutes step 1 of the conceptual schema design procedure.

CSDP step 1: Transform familiar examples into elementary facts, and apply quality checks.

For process modeling, it helps to begin with examples of the processes to be carried out by the system. Such process examples have long been used in industry, but in 1987 they were coined "use cases", which nicely suggests cases of the system being used, and this term has stuck. UML recommends use cases to drive the modeling process. Although use cases help with designing process models, in practice the move from use cases to data models is often somewhat arbitrary and frequently results in data models that need substantial reworking.

The solution is clear. If you want to get the data model right, start with examples of the *data* to be delivered by the system. By analogy with the UML term, I now call these "data use cases", since they are cases of data being used. However, this is just another name for the "familiar information examples" concept that was introduced in step 1 of the ORM conceptual schema design procedure back in the 1970s. If you still want to use UML's process use cases to drive the modeling process, you should at least flesh them out with associated data samples before working on the class diagrams.

If we are designing a conceptual schema for an application previously handled manually or by computer, information examples will be readily available. If not, we work with the domain expert to provide examples. Two important types of examples are output reports and input forms. These might appear as tables, forms, diagrams, or text. To verbalize such examples in terms of elementary facts, we need to understand what an **elementary fact** is.

To begin with, an elementary fact is a simple assertion, or atomic proposition, about the UoD. The word "fact" indicates that the system is to treat the assertion as being true of the UoD. Whether this is actually the case is of no concern to the system. In everyday speech, facts are true statements about the real world. However, in computing terminology we resign ourselves to the fact(!) that it is possible to have "false facts" in the database (just as we use the word "statement" for things that aren't really statements in languages like SQL).

We may think of the UoD as a set of *objects playing roles*. Elementary facts are assertions that particular objects play particular roles. The simplest kind of elementary fact asserts that a single object plays a given role. For example, consider a very small domain in which people can be identified by their first names. One fact about this domain might be

1. Ann smokes.

Here we have one object (Ann) playing a role (smokes). Strictly, we should be more precise in identifying objects (e.g., expand "Ann" to "the person with firstname 'Ann'"), but let's tidy up later. With sentences like (1), the role played by the object is sometimes called a *property* of the object. Here an elementary fact asserts that a certain object has a certain property. This is also called a *unary relationship,* since only one role is involved. Usually, however, a relationship involves at least two roles. For example:

2. Ann employs Bob.
3. Ann employs Ann.

In (2) Ann plays the role of employer and Bob plays the role of employee. In (3) Ann is self-employed and plays both roles. In general, *an elementary fact asserts that a particular object has a property, or that one or more objects participate together in a relationship.*

The adjective "elementary" indicates that the fact *cannot be "split" into smaller units of information* that collectively provide the same information as the original. Elementary facts typically do not use logical connectives (e.g., **not, and, or, if**) or logical quantifiers (e.g., **all, some**). For example, sentences (4)–(9) are not elementary facts:

4. Ann smokes **and** Bob smokes.
5. Ann smokes **or** Bob smokes.
6. Ann does **not** smoke.
7. **If** Bob smokes **then** Bob is cancer prone.
8. **All** people who smoke are cancer prone.
9. **If some** person smokes **then that** person is cancer prone.

All of these sentences express information. Proposition (4) is a logical conjunction. It should be split into two elementary facts: Ann smokes; Bob smokes. Proposition (5) is a disjunction, (6) is a negation, and (7) is a conditional fact: most database systems do not allow such information to be stored conveniently and are incapable of making relevant inferences (e.g., deducing that Bob smokes from the combination of (5) and (6)). For most commercial applications, there is no need to store such information.

Often the absence of positive information (e.g., Ann smokes) is taken to imply the negative (Ann does not smoke): this is the usual "closed-world" assumption. With an "open-world" approach, negative information can be explicitly stored using negative predicates or status object types, in conjunction with suitable constraints. For example, the roles "smokes" and "is a nonsmoker" are mutually exclusive, and the fact type Person has SmokerStatus {'S', 'NS'} requires the constraint that **each** person has **at most one** SmokerStatus. Sometimes the choice of whether to store positive or negative information depends on which occupies less space, and the borderline between positive and negative may become blurred (e.g., consider Person dislikes Food and Patient is allergic to Drug). These topics are discussed further in later chapters.

Universally quantified conditionals like (8) and (9) may be catered to either in terms of a subset constraint (see later) or by a derivation rule. Such rules can be specified readily in SQL by means of a view and are also easily coded in languages such as Prolog. For example: cancerProne(X) **if** person(X) **and** smokes(X).

Elementary facts assert that objects play roles. How are these objects and roles specified? For now we consider only basic objects: these are either *values* or *entities*. For our work it is sufficient to recognize two kinds of **values:** *character string* and *number.* These are identified by constants. Character strings are shown inside single quotes (e.g., 'USA'). Numbers are denoted without quotes, using the usual Hindu-Arabic decimal notation (e.g., 37 or 5.2). Numbers are abstract objects denoted by character strings called numerals. For example, the number 37 is denoted by the numeral '37'. We assume that any information system supports strings and numbers as built-in data types. Values are displayed textually, but are internally represented by bit strings.

Conceptually, an **entity** (e.g., a particular person or car) is referenced in an information system by means of a *definite description.* For example, kangaroos hop about on an entity identified as "the Country with name 'Australia'". Entities may also be called "described objects". Unlike values, some entities can change with time. An entity may be a tangible object (e.g., the City with name 'Paris') or an abstract object (e.g., the Subject with code 'CS114'). We consider both entities and values to be objects that exist in the UoD. Note that object-oriented approaches use the term "object" in the more restrictive sense of "entity". Usually we want to talk about just the entities, but to reference them we make use of values. Sometimes we want to talk about the values themselves. Consider the following sentences:

10. Australia has six states.
11. "Australia" has nine letters.

Here we have an illustration of what logicians call the use/mention distinction. In (10) the word "Australia" is being used as a label to reference an entity. In (11) the word "Australia" is being mentioned and refers to itself. In natural language, quotes are used to resolve this distinction. In everyday talk, entities are often referred to by a *proper name* (e.g., "Bill Clinton") or by some definite description (e.g., "the previous president of the USA" or "the president named 'Bill Clinton'"). Proper names work if we can decide what the name refers to from the context of the sentence. For example, in (10) you probably took "Australia" to refer to the country named "Australia". However, the sentence itself does not tell you this. Perhaps (10) was talking about a dog named "Australia" who has six moods (sleepy, playful, hungry, etc.).

Since humans may misinterpret, and information systems lack any creativity to add context, we play it safe by demanding that entities be clearly identified by special kinds of definite descriptions. To begin with, the description must specify the kind of entity being referred to: the **entity type.** A *type* is the set of all possible *instances.* Each entity is an instance of a particular entity type (e.g., Person, Subject). For a given UoD, the entity type Person is the set of all people we might possibly want to talk about during the lifetime of the information system. Note that some authors use the word "entity" for "entity type". I'll sometimes expand "entity" to "entity instance" to avoid any confusion. Consider the sentence

12. Lee is located in 10B.

This could be talking about a horse located in a stable, or a computer in a room, and so on. By stating the entity types involved, (13) avoids this kind of referential ambiguity. Names of object types are highlighted here by starting them with a capital letter.

13. The Patient 'Lee' is located in the Ward '10B'.

This brings to mind the old joke: "*Question:* Did you hear about the man with the wooden leg named 'Smith'? *Answer:* No—What was the name of his other leg?" Here the responder mistakenly took the label "Smith" to refer to an entity of type WoodenLeg rather than of type Man. Sometimes, even stating the entity type fails to fully clarify the situation. Consider the following sentence:

14. The Patient 'Lee' has a Temperature of 37.

Now imagine that the UoD contains two patients named "Lee Jones" and "Mary Lee". There is more than one person to which the label 'Lee' might apply. Worse still, there may be some confusion about the units being used to state the temperature: 37 degrees Celsius is normal body temperature, but 37 degrees Fahrenheit is close to freezing! We resolve this ambiguity by including the **reference mode** (i.e., the manner in which the value refers to the entity). Compare the following two sentences:

15. The Patient with surname 'Lee' has a Temperature of 37 Celsius.
16. The Patient with firstname 'Lee' has a Temperature of 37 Fahrenheit.

A more common way around the potential confusion caused by overlap of first names and surnames would be to demand that a longer name be used instead (e.g., "Lee Jones", "Mary Lee"). In some cases, however, even these names may not be unique, and another naming convention must be employed (e.g., PatientNr). To avoid confusing "No." with the word "No", I'll use "Nr" or "#" to abbreviate "Number". Most entity designators involve three components:

- *Entity type* (e.g., Patient, Temperature)
- *Reference mode* (e.g., surname, Celsius)
- *Value* (e.g., 'Lee', 37)

This is the simplest kind of entity designation scheme. I'll restrict our discussion of reference schemes to this simple case for quite some time. Composite identification schemes are considered later.

Now that we know how to specify objects, how do we specify the roles they play? We use logical **predicates.** In logic, a predicate is basically a *sentence with object holes in it.* To complete the sentence, the object holes or placeholders are filled in by *object* *terms.* Each object term refers to a single object in the UoD. Object terms are also called singular terms or object designators. For us, values are designated by constants (sometimes preceded by the value type name), and entities are designated by definite descriptions that relate values to entities. Consider the following sentence:

17. The Person with firstname 'Ann' **smokes.**

Here the object term is "The Person with firstname 'Ann'", and the predicate identifier is shown in bold. The predicate may be shown by itself as

... smokes

This is a *unary predicate,* or *sentence with one object hole* in it. It may also be called a property or a unary relationship type. A *binary predicate* is a *sentence with two object holes.* Consider this example:

18. The Person with firstname 'Ann' **employs** the Person with firstname 'Bob'.

Here the predicate may be shown as

... employs ...

Notice that the *order* in which the objects are placed here is important. For example, even though Ann employs Bob, it may be false that Bob employs Ann. A *ternary predicate* is a *sentence with three object holes.* For instance, the fact that Terry worked in the Computer Science Department for 10 years involves the predicate

... worked in ... for ...

In general, an *n-ary predicate* is a sentence with n object holes. Since the order is significant, a filled-in n-ary predicate is associated with a *sequence* of n object terms, not necessarily distinct. The value of n is the **arity,** or degree, of the predicate. Predicates of arity ≥ 2 are polyadic. An elementary fact may now be thought of as asserting a proposition of the form

$Ro_1 \ldots o_n$

where R is a predicate of arity $n,$ and $o_1 \ldots o_n$ are n object terms, not necessarily distinct. Moreover, with respect to the UoD the proposition must not be splittable into a conjunction of simpler propositions. This definition ties in with the notation of *predicate logic.*

For naturalness, we write predicates in *mixfix* (or distfix) form, where the terms may be mixed in with the predicate. For example, the following ternary fact uses the predicate "... moved to ... during ...".

19. The Scientist with surname 'Einstein' **moved to** the Country with code 'USA' **during** the Year 1933 AD.

Step 1 of the CSDP involves translating relevant information examples into sentences like this. As a simple example, consider the output report of Table 3.1. Try now to express the information in the first row in the form of elementary facts. To help with this, use the *telephone heuristic.* Imagine you have to convey the information over the

Table 3.1 Some languages and their designers.

Designer	*Language*
Wirth	Pascal
Kay	Smalltalk
Wirth	Modula-2

telephone to someone. In performing this visual-to-auditory transformation, make sure you fully specify each entity in terms of its entity type, reference mode, and value, and that you include the predicate name.

In reports like this, the column headings and table names or captions often give a clue as to the object types and predicates. The column entries provide the values. Here is one way of translating row 1 as an elementary fact:

20. The Person with surname 'Wirth' **designed** the Language named 'Pascal'.

Notice that the entity types and reference modes appear as nouns and the predicate as a verb phrase. This is fairly typical. In translating row 1 into the elementary fact (20), we read the row from left to right. If instead we read it from right to left, we might say:

21. The Language named 'Pascal' **was designed by** the Person with surname 'Wirth'.

In reversing the order of the terms, we also reversed the predicate. We speak of "was designed by" as the *inverse* of the predicate "designed". Although semantically we might regard sentences (20) and (21) as expressing the same fact, syntactically they are different. Most logicians would describe this as a case of two different sentences expressing the same proposition. Linguists like to describe this situation by saying the two sentences have different *surface structures* but the same deep structure.

For example, one linguistic analysis might portray the *deep structure* sentence as comprising a verb phrase (Design), various noun phrases (the object terms) each of which relate to the verb in a different case (e.g., agentive for Wirth and objective for Pascal), together with a modality (past tense). Different viewpoints exist as to the "correct" way to portray deep structures (e.g., what primitives to select), and the task of translation to deep structures is often complex. In practice, most information systems can be designed without delving further into such issues.

It is important not to treat sentences like (20) and (21) as different, unrelated facts. Our approach with binary fact types is to choose one standard way of stating the predicate, but optionally allow the inverse reading to be shown as well. For example:

22. The Person with surname 'Wirth' **designed / was designed by** the Language named 'Pascal'.

Here the predicate on the left of the slash "/" is used for the standard (left-to-right) reading (20). The predicate on the right of the slash is used for the inverse reading (21). The slash visually suggests jumping over the other predicate when reading left to right,

Table 3.2 An output report about marriages.

Married couples	
Adam	Eve
Jim	Mary

and jumping under the other predicate when reading right to left. Having two ways to talk about a binary fact type can help communication and can simplify constraint specification. For example, the specification "each Language was designed by some Person" is preferable to the equivalent "for each Language, some Person designed that Language". For *n*-ary fact types there are many possible orderings, but only one is displayed at a time.

Now consider Table 3.2. This is a bit harder to verbalize since the columns don't have separate names. You may assume that Adam and Jim are males and that Eve and Mary are females. As an exercise, verbalize the top row in terms of elementary facts before reading on.

Perhaps you verbalized this as shown in (23). For completeness, the inverse is included.

23. The Person with firstname 'Adam' **is married to / is married to** the Person with firstname 'Eve'.

Notice that the forward predicate is the same as the inverse. This is an example of a *symmetric* relationship. Such relationships create special problems (as discussed in Section 7.3). To help avoid such problems, at the conceptual level *no base predicate should be the same as its inverse*. You can always rephrase the fact to ensure this. For example, (24) does this by highlighting the different roles played by each partner.

24. The Person with firstname 'Adam' **is husband of / is wife of** the Person with firstname 'Eve'.

As another example, consider Table 3.3. This is like our earlier Table 3.1 but with an extra column added. Try to express the information on the first row in terms of elementary facts before reading on.

We might at first consider expressing this information as sentence (25), using the ternary predicate "... designed ... in ...". Do you see any problems with this?

25. The Person with surname 'Wirth' **designed** the Language named 'Pascal' **in** the Year 1971 AD.

Recall that an elementary fact must be simple or irreducible. It cannot be split into two or more simpler facts in the context of the UoD. The appearance of the word "and" in a sentence usually indicates that the sentence may be split into simpler facts. Here there is no "and", but "common sense" tells us that the fact can be split into the following two elementary facts with no information loss:

Table 3.3 Origin details of some programming languages.

Designer	Language	Year
Wirth	Pascal	1971
Kay	Smalltalk	1972
Wirth	Modula-2	1979

26. The Person with surname 'Wirth' designed the Language named 'Pascal'.
27. The Language named 'Pascal' was designed in the Year 1971 AD.

Here "no information loss" means that if we know (26) and (27), then we also know (25). The phrase "common sense" hides some formal ideas. In order to split (25) into (26) and (27) we probably relied on our implicit understanding that each language was designed in only one year. This constraint holds if we interpret "was designed in" to mean "had its design completed in". Let us agree with this interpretation.

If instead we meant "had work done on its design", then a language may be designed in many years. In this case, we could still justify the split if each language had only one designer or at least the same set of designers for each year. But this might not be true. For example, if we include UML as a language, it had different designers in different years. This illustrates the need to be clear about the meaning of our wording and to strive for significant sample data.

Later steps in the CSDP add formal checks to detect the relevant dependencies, so if our "common sense" fails us here, we will normally see this error at a later stage. For now, though, let's work with our intuitions. Suppose we split the ternary into the two binaries: Person designed Language; Person completed design in Year. Would this be acceptable? As an exercise, use the table's population to show that this kind of split would actually lose information.

After plenty of practice at step 1, you may wish to write the elementary facts down in abbreviated form. To start with, you can drop words such as "the" and "with" where they introduce object types and reference modes. Reference modes are placed in parentheses after the object types. Some versions of ORM append a "+" to indicate the referencing value is numeric, and hence may appear in addition (+) and other numeric operations.

You might also shorten some identifiers used for object types, reference modes, and predicates so long as the shorter names are still meaningful to you. Don't forget to start the name of object types with a capital letter. Start the name of reference modes with a small letter, unless capitals have significance (e.g., "AD"). For example, facts (26) and (27) may be set out more concisely as (26') and (27').

26'. Person (surname) 'Wirth' designed Language (name) 'Pascal'.
27'. Language (name) 'Pascal' was designed in Year (AD) 1971.

If the reference schemes for entity types are declared up front, they may be omitted in setting out the facts. For example, (26) and (27) may be specified as

Reference schemes: Person (surname); Language (name); Year (AD)

Facts: Person 'Wirth' designed Language 'Pascal'.
Language 'Pascal' was designed in Year 1971.

Even more conveniently, a fact type may be displayed in diagram form (see next section), and fact instances may be entered into the relevant fact table simply by entering values.

The task of defining a formal grammar sufficient to capture any sentence expressed in natural language is daunting, partly because of the many ways in which objects may be referenced. For example, consider the sentence: "The next person to step on my toe will cop it". Some artificial intelligence research is directed toward sorting out the semantics in sentences like this.

Fortunately for us, such sentences don't appear in database tables, where simple value-based schemes are used to reference objects. ORM is capable of formally capturing the relevant semantics of any fact that can be represented in a database table. Structured object terms and predicates provide the logical deep structure, independent of the natural language (English, Japanese, etc.) used to express the fact. By supporting ordered, mixfix predicates ORM enables this deep structure to be expressed in a surface structure in harmony with the ordered, mixfix nature of natural language. For example, consider Figure 3.1.

Here the two tables convey the same fact in different languages. The fact may be expressed in English as (28) and in Japanese as (29). The reference modes are italicized and the predicates are in bold.

28. The Employee with *employeeNr* '37' **works in** the Department with *name* 'Sales'.

29. Jugyo in *jugyo in bango* '37' **wa** 'Eigyo' to iu *namae* no Ka **ni shozoku suru.**

These are parsed into the structures shown in 28′ and 29′. They have the same deep structure. Object terms are enclosed in square brackets. The infix predicate "... works in ..." corresponds to the mixfix predicate "... wa ... ni shozoku suru".

28′. [Employee *(employeeNr)* '37'] **works in** [Department *(name)* 'Sales'].

29′. [Jugyo in *(jugyo in bango)* '37'] **wa** [Ka *(namae)* 'Eigyo'] **ni shozoku suru.**

Although ordered, mixfix predicates are preferred for naturalness, you could also treat a fact as a named set of (object, role) pairs: $F\{(o_1,r_1),...,(o_n,r_n)\}$. Here each object o_i is paired with the role r_i that it plays in the fact F. For example, (22) might be specified as Design{ (The Person with surname 'Wirth', agentive), (The Language named 'Pascal', objective) }. Instead of the case adjectives "agentive" and "objective", other role names could be used (e.g., "designer" and "language" or "designing" and "being

EmployeeNr	Department
37	Sales

Jugyo in	Ka
37	Eigyo

Figure 3.1 The same fact in English and Japanese.

designed by"). By pairing objects with their roles, the order in which the pairs are listed is irrelevant. This approach is used in RIDL (Reference and Idea Language), as discussed in Section 13.3.

Now consider the output report of Table 3.4, and try to express the information contained in its top row in terms of one or more elementary facts. Here the table itself has a name ("Result") that can help us with the interpretation.

To save writing later, let us declare the reference schemes: Student (name); Subject (code); and Rating (nr). Because this table looks similar to Table 3.3, you might have been tempted to try to split the information into two facts. For example:

30. The Student 'Bright S' **studied** the Subject 'CS112'.
31. The Student 'Bright S' **scored** the Rating 7.

This approach is incorrect because it results in loss of information. Since Bright studies more than one subject, we don't know for sure from these two facts that Bright's 7 rating is for CS112. In some cases a ternary that is not splittable into two facts may be split into three facts. Here we might try to split the information into the above two facts as well as

32. The Rating 7 **was obtained for** the Subject 'CS112'.

However, even these three facts don't guarantee that Bright got a 7 for CS112. For example, Jones studied CS112, Jones scored a 7, and a 7 was obtained for CS112, but Jones did not score a 7 in CS112. So the whole of the first row should be expressed as one elementary fact. For example, using the predicate "... for ... scored ..." we obtain

33. The Student 'Bright S' **for** the Subject 'CS112' **scored** the Rating 7.

Notice that we chose to think of a rating not as a number, but as an entity that is referenced by a number. This has two advantages. Suppose that students are rated numerically on their exam performance and are also rated numerically on their popularity. In this case we have the object types ExamRating and PopularityRating. Is an exam rating of 7 the same thing as a popularity rating of 7? I would answer, "No, only the numbers are the same".

If we treat ratings as numbers we would have to answer "Yes" to the previous question. I prefer to think of ratings as entities rather than as numbers. Another advantage of this approach is that decisions about preferred reference schemes can be delayed until

Table 3.4 A relational table for storing student results.

Result:	student	subject	rating
	Bright S	CS112	7
	Bright S	CS100	6
	Collins T	CS112	4
	Jones E	CS100	7
	Jones E	CS112	4
	Jones E	MP104	4

Table 3.5 A relational table storing facts about lecturers.

Lecturer:	*name*	*birthyear*	*age*	*degrees*
	Adams JB	1946	46	BSc, PhD
	Leung X	1960	32	BE, MSc
	O'Reilly TA	1946	46	BA, BSc, PhD

Table 3.6 An output report indicating tutorial allocations.

Tute group	*Time*	*Room*	*StudentNr*	*Student name*
A	Mon 3 p.m.	CS-718	302156	Bloggs FB
			180064	Fletcher JB
			278155	Jackson M
			334067	Jones EP
			200140	Kawamoto T
B1	Tues 2 p.m.	E-B18	266010	Anderson AB
			348112	Bloggs FB
...	...	...	...	...

the conceptual schema is to be mapped to a logical schema. For example, exam ratings are often given in both numbers and codes. A 7 might correspond to "HD" (high distinction). With the suggested approach, the same rating is involved no matter which way we reference it.

As another example, consider the report shown in Table 3.5. Try step 1 yourself on this table before reading on. One of the tricky features of this table is the final column. Entries in this column are sets of degrees, not single degrees.

You should phrase your sentences to include only one degree at a time. When applied to the first row, step 1 results in four facts that may be set out as follows.

34. The Lecturer with name 'Adams JB' **was born in** the Year 1946 AD.
35. The Lecturer with name 'Adams JB' **has** the Age 46 years.
36. The Lecturer with name 'Adams JB' **holds** the Degree with code 'BSc'.
37. The Lecturer with name 'Adams JB' **holds** the Degree with code 'PhD'.

Here the entity types and reference modes are Lecturer (name), Year (AD), Age (years), and Degree (code). There are three fact types: Lecturer **was born in** Year; Lecturer **has** Age; Lecturer **holds** Degree. The entity types Year and Age are semantically different. For example, Year involves a starting point in time, whereas Age is merely a duration of time.

A harder example is shown in Table 3.6. This is an extract of a report listing details of tutorial groups. Perform step 1 yourself before reading on.

Since verbalization of an example involves interpretation, it is important that the kind of example is *familiar* to us or another person (e.g., the domain expert) who is assisting us with step 1. Since domain experts often lack technical expertise in modeling, we should not expect them to do the whole of step 1 themselves. It is sufficient if they verbalize the information correctly in their own terms. This is **step 1a:** *Verbalize the information.* As modelers we can then refine their verbalization by ensuring the facts are elementary and the objects are well identified. This is **step 1b:** *Verbalize the information as elementary facts.* For example, a domain expert might perform step 1a by verbalizing the information on the top row of this report as

> Tute group A meets at 3 p.m. Monday in Room CS-718.
> Student 302156 belongs to group A and is named "Bloggs F".

We might then perform step 1b by refining these informal sentences into the following four elementary sentences:

38. The TuteGroup with code 'A' **meets at** the Time with dayhrcode 'Mon 3 p.m.'.
39. The TuteGroup with code 'A' **meets in** the Room with roomNr 'CS-718'.
40. The Student with studentNr 302156 **belongs to** the TuteGroup with code 'A'.
41. The Student with studentNr 302156 **has** the StudentName 'Bloggs FB'.

Many features in this example rely on interpretation. For instance, I assumed that StudentNr and StudentName refer to students, and that a student number and student name on the same row refer to the same student. I also filled in the associations as "meets at", "meets in", "belongs to", and "has". The report itself does not tell us this. We use our background familiarity with the situation to make such assumptions.

Decisions were made about entity types and reference schemes. For example, I chose to think of Time as an entity type referenced by a day-hour code rather than introducing Day and Hour as separate entity types. A similar comment applies to Room and StudentName.

StudentNr was chosen rather than StudentName to identify Student. The report helps here since StudentNr appears first (on the left) and 'Bloggs FB' appears with two different student numbers. But we are still making assumptions (e.g., that students have only one student number or that students belong to only one group). Another major assumption is that each tutorial group meets only once a week. We need to know this to justify using separate facts for the time and room (rather than verbalizing this as TuteGroup meets at Time in Room). Of course the fact that group A is not repeated in the report helps us with this decision, but this still assumes the sample is representative in this regard.

Since interpretation is always involved in the initial step, if we are not familiar with the example we should resolve any doubts by asking a person who is familiar with the UoD. Communication with domain experts should use examples familiar to them. Although we as modelers might be expert in expressing ourselves at a formal, type level, the same cannot be said of the average domain expert. By working with examples familiar to the subject matter experts, we can tap their implicit understanding of the UoD without forcing them to abstract and express, perhaps incorrectly, the structure we seek.

Sentence (41) expresses a relationship between an entity (a student) and a value (a name). When verbalizing facts in this way, the **value type** is stated just before the value (e.g., StudentName 'Bloggs FB'). Unlike entity terms, value terms do not include a

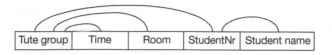

| Tute group | Time | Room | StudentNr | Student name |

Figure 3.2 Drawing connections for the verbalized relationships.

CS114 Tutorial Preferences Form

Please complete this form to assist in tutorial allocation.
Tutorials are of 1-hour duration and are available at these times:

Monday	Tuesday	Thursday
		10 a.m.
		11 a.m.
		12 noon
	2 p.m.	2 p.m.
3 p.m.		3 p.m.

Student number: _____
Student surname: _____ Initials: _____
Tutorial preference 1: _____
Tutorial preference 2: _____
Tutorial preference 3: _____

Figure 3.3 An input form for collecting tutorial preferences.

---

reference mode. The next section discusses the connection between value types and reference modes.

With many kinds of reports it is sometimes useful to draw a connection between the relevant fields as we verbalize the corresponding fact. For example, we might add links between the columns of Table 3.6 as shown in Figure 3.2. This informal summary of the fact types may help us to see if some connections have been missed (each field is normally involved in at least one connection).

Besides tables, *forms* are a common source of information examples. These are more often used for input than output, but may be used for both (e.g., the personnel forms considered in the previous chapter).

As another example, consider the input form shown in Figure 3.3. Suppose students studying the subject CS114 use this form to indicate up to three preferences regarding which tutorial time is most suitable for them. This form is used to help decide which students are assigned to which groups and which groups are eventually used. If this information is to be taken into account in determining tutorial allocations, it must be stored in the system.

Let's assume that the previous output report (Table 3.6) shows the tutorial allocations for CS114, made after all the student preferences are considered. The preference input form lacks some of the information needed for the allocation report. For example, it does not show how groups are assigned to rooms and times. This helps to prevent students from entering wrong data (they enter the times they prefer directly rather than indirectly through associated group codes) and allows flexibility in offering many tutorials at the same time.

To perform step 1 here, you should first fill out the form with some examples, as shown in Figure 3.4. These facts may now be verbalized as Student (nr) 302156 has Surname 'Jones'; Student 302156 has Initials 'ES'; Student 302156 has first preference at Time (dh) 'Mon 3 p.m.'; Student 302156 has second preference at Time 'Thurs 11 a.m.'.

Taken individually, the output report and the input form reveal only partially the kinds of information needed for the system. In combination, however, they might be enough for us to arrive at the structure of the UoD. If so, the pair of examples is said to be significant. In general, a set of examples is **significant** or adequate with respect to a specific UoD only if it illustrates all the relevant sorts of information and constraints required for that application.

With complex UoDs, significant example sets are rare. With our current application, if a student can be allocated to only one group, then Table 3.6 is significant in this respect. However, if more than one group can be held at the same time, Table 3.6 is not significant in this other respect. A further row is needed to show this possibility (e.g., a row indicating that group B2 meets at Tues 2 p.m.).

When using information examples to extract facts, we need to decide *which aspects should be modeled.* This helps to determine the scope of the UoD. A useful heuristic is to ask the question *Which parts may take on different values?* Look again at the input form in Figure 3.4. The header section contains information that we may or may not wish to model. The first item we see is "CS114". Is it possible to have other values in

---

CS114 Tutorial Preferences Form

Please complete this form to assist in tutorial allocation.
Tutorials are of 1-hour duration and are available at these times:

Monday	Tuesday		Thursday
			10 a.m.
			11 a.m.
			12 noon
	2 p.m.		2 p.m.
3 p.m.			3 p.m.

Student number: 302156

Student surname: Jones   Initials: ES

Tutorial preference 1: Mon 3 p.m.

Tutorial preference 2: Thurs 11 a.m.

Tutorial preference 3: _____

Figure 3.4 The input form populated with sample data.

place of it, within our overall application? If the only subject of interest is CS114, then the answer is "No". However, if we wish to cater to other subjects as well, we might require another form with a different value here (e.g., "CS183"). In this case we need to introduce Subject (or some equivalent term) as an object type within our UoD.

Different places use different names to refer to a unit of study in which a student may enroll. I use "Subject" for this concept, but you might prefer "Course" or "Unit" or some other term. If the domain experts all prefer the same term, you should use that. In large projects, different people might use different terms for the same concept. In that case, you should get them to agree upon a *standard term,* and also note any *synonyms* that they might still want to use.

Returning to the header of our preferences form, we see the word "Tutorial". Could this change (e.g., to "Lecture")? If we wish to capture preferences for lectures as well as tutorials, the answer is "yes" and we could model this as data. But let's assume that this is not the case. The rest of the form header contains other information (e.g., duration of tutorials), but let's assume this doesn't need to be modeled.

The middle section of the form contains information about the tutorial times. If our UoD has only one subject (CS114), we could model this information as unary facts (e.g., Time 'Mon 3 p.m.' is available). If we need to cater to other subjects as well, then we need to treat the "CS114" at the top of the form as data, and hence verbalize the schedule as binary facts (e.g., Subject 'CS114' has a tutorial slot at Time 'Mon 3 p.m.'). A completed tutorial preferences form for a different subject is shown in Figure 3.5.

Here the layout of the five weekdays into columns makes it more obvious that the times are to be treated as data. The first fact from this section reads: Subject 'CS183' has a tutorial slot at Time 'Tues 2 p.m.'. If you reformat the structure of the earlier CS114 example (Figure 3.4) to agree with this structure, and place the two forms side by side, you can see what aspects are to be modeled as data by looking at what changes between the two forms (subject code, times, student details).

CS183 Tutorial Preferences Form				
Monday	Tuesday	Wednesday	Thursday	Friday
			9 a.m.	
			11 a.m.	
	2 p.m.		2 p.m.	
	3 p.m.	3 p.m.		

Student number: 211780
Student surname: Smith   Initials: JA
Tutorial preference 1: Tues 2 p.m.
Tutorial preference 2: Thurs 11 a.m.
Tutorial preference 3: Tues 3 p.m.

Figure 3.5 A completed tutorial preferences form for a different subject.

In this larger UoD, assuming that students may enroll in many subjects, the facts about student preferences now need to take the subject into account. Instead of binaries, the preference facts are now verbalized as ternaries. For example: Student 302156 has first tutorial preference for Subject 'CS114' at Time 'Mon 3 p.m.'; Student 211780 has third tutorial preference for Subject 'CS183' at Time 'Tues 3 p.m.'. Tutorial allocations would also need to indicate the relevant subject (e.g., Table 3.6 would need a header showing the subject). Tutorial groups would then need a composite reference scheme that included both the subject code and the group code. For example, the first fact from the CS114-headed version of Table 3.6 would now read as TuteGroup 'A' of Subject 'CS114' meets at Time 'Mon 3 p.m.'. Composite reference schemes are discussed in detail later in Section 5.4.

We will see later that no set of examples can be significant with respect to derivation rules or subtype definitions. In such cases the use of a domain expert is essential. With the current application, we made no mention of the rules used to arrive at the tutorial allocations. If in addition to storing information about preferences and allocations, the information system has to compute the allocations in a nearly optimal way, respecting preferences and other practical constraints (e.g., size of groups), the design of the derivation rules becomes the challenging aspect of the schema. While this can be automated, an alternative is to divide the task between the human expert and the system. High-level languages facilitate such cooperative solutions.

Often, the information examples used for verbalization in step 1 apply to the way the business or application domain currently works. From these examples we can build the *as-is model* to reflect the current practice (as it is now). Some changes may also be needed to expand or improve the way the business operates. For example, we might have started with separate applications to administer tutorials for just one subject, and then realized it would be better to integrate these into a single application capable of handling all the subjects (as discussed above). By including examples of the new data requirements, we are then able to build the *to-be model,* which reflects the way we want the business to be in the future. A proper understanding of the as-is model is a great assistance in designing the to-be model. As you gain more experience as a modeler, you will be able to draw upon lessons learned from prior modeling projects to help spot ways to improve things on future projects. Modeling is not just a science. It's an art as well, and that makes it more fun.

A comprehensive set of output reports (covering intermediate stages) may include all the information on input forms. Output reports tend to be easier to interpret, especially if the input forms have been poorly designed. Care is needed in the design of the input forms to make them clear and simple for users.

Information can appear in lots of ways. Apart from many kinds of tables and forms, information may be expressed graphically in all kinds of *diagrams, charts, maps,* and *graphs.* Harris (1996) discusses several hundred different ways of presenting information graphically. Regardless of how it's presented, information can always be verbalized as facts. Because practice helps a lot with verbalization skills, I've included lots of varied examples in the book to prepare you for performing step 1 in practical situations. As a simple graphical example, Figure 3.6 might be used to display information about nonstop flight connections provided by a particular airline, with the arrowheads

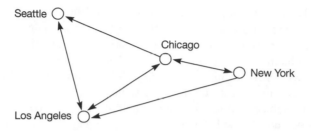

Figure 3.6 A graph showing flight connections between cities.

indicating the direction of the flights. As an exercise, perform step 1 for this graph before reading on.

How did you go? There is only one entity type: City (name). There is also only one fact type: City has a flight to City. For instance the arrow from Chicago to Seattle may be verbalized as City 'Chicago' has flight to City 'Seattle'. The "to" in the predicate is important, since it conveys direction and avoids the symmetry problem with the earlier marriage example.

In this UoD, not all the connections are two-way. If this was an as-is model, and we wanted also to talk about the flight connections or to include many airlines, we should add flight numbers to the arrows on the graph. This to-be model leads to a different verbalization, which you might like to try for yourself. A later exercise returns to this example.

By now you may have some sense of the power of verbalizing examples in terms of elementary facts. No matter what kind of example you start with, if you or an assistant understands the example, then you should be able to express the information in simple facts. This does require practice at the technique, but this is fun anyway—isn't it? If you can't do step 1, there is little point in proceeding with the design—either you don't understand the UoD or you can't communicate it clearly.

Although it might sound hard to believe, if you have performed step 1 properly, you have completed most of the "hard part" of the conceptual schema design procedure. The remaining steps consist of diagramming and constraining the fact types. Apart from the problem of detecting unusual constraints and derivation rules, once you learn the techniques you can carry out those steps almost automatically. With step 1, however, you always need to draw upon your interpretation skills.

Exercise 3.3

1. Assuming suitable entity types and reference modes are understood, which of the following sentences express exactly one elementary fact?
   (a) Adam likes Eve.
   (b) Bob does not like John.
   (c) Tom visited Los Angeles and New York.
   (d) Tom visited Los Angeles or New York.
   (e) If Tom visited Los Angeles, then he visited New York.

      (f) Sue is funny.

      (g) All people are funny.

      (h) Some people in New York have toured Australia.

      (i) Brisbane and Sydney are in Australia.

      (j) Brisbane and Sydney are in the same country.

      (k) Who does Adam like?

2. Indicate at least two different meanings for each of the following sentences, by including names for object types and reference modes.

      (a) Pluto is owned by Mickey.

      (b) Dallas is smaller than Sydney.

      (c) Arnold can lift 300.

Perform step 1 of the CSDP for the following output reports. In verbalizing the facts, you may restrict yourself to the top row of the table unless another row reveals a different kind of fact.

3.

Athlete	Height
Jones EM	166
Pie QT	166
Smith JA	175

4.

Athlete	Height
Jones EM	400
Pie QT	450
Smith JA	550

5.

Person	Height (cm)	Birth year
Jones EM	166	1955
Pie QT	160	1970
Smith JA	175	1955

6.

Person	Height (cm)	Birth year
Jones EM	160	1970
	166	1980
	166	1990

7.

Advisory panel	Internal member	External member
Databases	Codd Kowalski	Ienshtein Spock
Logic programming	Colmerauer Kowalski Spock	Robinson

8.

Parents	Children
Ann, Bill David, Fiona	Colin, David, Eve Gus

9.

Country	Friends	Enemies
Disland Hades	Oz	Oz Wundrland
Wundrland Oz	Oz Disland Wundrland	Hades Hades

10.

Apple	Australia	June, July, Aug
	America	Oct, Dec, Jan
	Ireland	Oct, Dec
Mango	Australia	Nov, Dec, Jan, Feb
Pineapple	America	June, July
	Australia	Oct, Nov, Dec, Jan

3.4   CSDP Step 2: Draw Fact Types, and Populate

Once we have translated the information examples into elementary facts and performed quality checks, we are ready for the next step in the conceptual schema design procedure. Here we *draw* a conceptual schema diagram that shows all the *fact types*. This illustrates the relevant object types, predicates, and reference schemes. Once the diagram is drawn, we check it with a *sample population*.

CSDP step 2: Draw the fact types, and apply a population check.

Consider the sample output report of Table 3.7. Let us agree that the information in this report can be expressed by the following three elementary facts, using "regNr" to abbreviate "registration number":

The Person named 'Adams B' **drives** the Car with regNr '235PZN'.
The Person named 'Jones E' **drives** the Car with regNr '235PZN'.
The Person named 'Jones E' **drives** the Car with regNr '108AAQ'.

Before looking at the relevant conceptual schema diagram, it may help to explain things if we first view an *instance diagram* for this example (see Figure 3.7). Instance diagrams illustrate particular instances of objects and relationships.

Taking advantage of the concrete nature of the entities in this example, cartoon drawings denote the actual people and cars. The values are shown as character strings. A particular fact or relationship between a person and a car is shown as a solid line. A particular reference between a value and an entity is shown as a broken line. Figure 3.8 shows a *conceptual schema diagram* for the same example.

Instance diagrams and conceptual schema diagrams depict an *entity type* as a *named, solid ellipse,* which may be a circle (the simplest form of an ellipse). A *value*

Table 3.7 A relational table indicating who drives what cars.

Drives:

person	car
Adams B	235PZN
Jones E	235PZN
Jones E	108AAQ

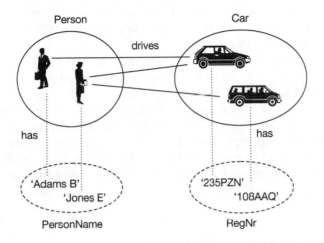

Figure 3.7 An instance diagram.

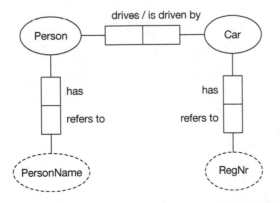

Figure 3.8 A conceptual schema diagram (constraints omitted).

type is shown as a *named, broken ellipse*. The object type's name is written inside or beside the ellipse.

On an instance diagram, individual objects of a given population are explicitly portrayed (by cartoon figures or other symbols). However, on a conceptual schema diagram, individual objects are omitted (unless we reference them in associated tables). Recalling that a type is the set of permitted instances, we may imagine that objects of a particular type are represented as points inside the ellipse.

On a conceptual schema diagram, the *roles* played by objects are explicitly shown as *boxes*. Each n-*ary predicate* ($n > 0$) is depicted as a *named, contiguous sequence of* n *role boxes* ("contiguous" means the boxes are adjacent, with no gaps in between). Predicates are ordered from one end to the other, with their name starting inside or beside their first role box (which must be an end role). For binary predicates (two roles), both forward and inverse readings may be shown. If shown combined, forward and inverse predicates are separated by a slash "/".

Each role is connected to exactly one object type by a *line,* indicating that the role is played only by objects of that type. A complete conceptual schema diagram includes the relevant constraints. We'll see how to add these later.

A relationship used to provide an identification scheme is called a *reference.* All other relationships are called *facts.* Typically, facts are relationships between entities, and references are relationships between entities and values. References provide the bridge between the world of entities and the world of values. This is clearly seen in Figure 3.9(a), where an instance has been added to populate each relationship. The

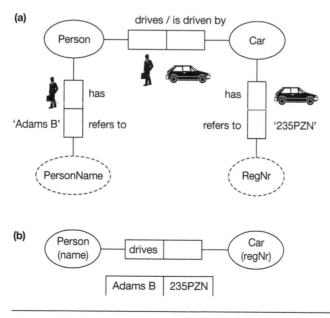

Figure 3.9 Using reference modes for 1:1 reference: (a) model; (b) abbreviation.

relationship between the person and car (depicted with icons) is a fact. The relationship between the name 'Adams B' and the person is a reference, and so is the relationship between the registration number '235PZN' and the car.

Although both reference predicates are displayed with the name "has", they are different predicates. Internally a CASE tool may identify the predicates by surrogates (e.g., "P2", "P3") or expanded names (e.g., "PersonHasPersonName", "PersonhasRegNr"). Although the predicate name "has" may also be used with fact types, it is best avoided if there is a more descriptive, natural alternative. For example, "Person drives Car", if accurate, is better than "Person has Car", which could mean many things (e.g., Person owns Car).

For this example, each person has exactly one name, and each person name refers to at most one person. Moreover, each car has exactly one registration number, and each registration number refers to at most one car. This situation is seen clearly in the earlier instance diagram (Figure 3.7). Each of the two reference types is said to provide a *simple 1:1 reference scheme*. We read "1:1" as "one to one". Later we'll see how to specify this on a conceptual schema diagram using uniqueness and mandatory role constraints.

When a simple 1:1 naming convention exists, we may indicate the *reference mode* simply by placing its name in *parentheses* next to the name of the entity type, and use the values themselves to depict entity instances in associated fact tables. Assuming appropriate constraints are added, the populated schema of Figure 3.9(a) may be displayed more concisely by Figure 3.9(b). Unless we want to illustrate the reference schemes explicitly, this concise form is preferred because it's closer to the way we verbalize facts and it simplifies the diagram. The fact table is omitted if we wish to display just the schema.

Reference modes indicate the mode or manner in which values refer to entities. Using reference modes, we rarely need to display value types explicitly on a schema diagram. However, to understand the abbreviation scheme, we need to know how to translate between reference modes and value types. Different versions of ORM have different approaches to this. One method for doing this is now outlined. Let the notation "$E\ (r) \rightarrow V$" mean "Entity type E with reference mode r generates the Value type V". Reference modes may be partitioned into three classes: popular, unit based, and general. The *popular reference modes* are *name, code, title, nr, #,* and *id*. To obtain the value type name, a popular reference mode has its first letter shifted to upper case and is then appended to the name of entity type. For example: Person (name) $\rightarrow$ PersonName; Item (code) $\rightarrow$ ItemCode; Song (title) $\rightarrow$ SongTitle; Rating (nr) $\rightarrow$ RatingNr; Room (#) $\rightarrow$ Room#; Member (id) $\rightarrow$ MemberId.

The *unit-based reference modes* include a built-in list of physical units (e.g., cm, kg, mile, Celsius), monetary units (e.g., EUR, USD), and abnormal units (e.g., AD), as well as user-defined units. Value type names are generated from unit-based reference modes by appending the word "Value". For example: kg $\rightarrow$ kgValue; USD $\rightarrow$ USDValue.

All other reference modes are called *general reference modes*. These generate value type names simply by shifting their first letter to upper case. For example: surname $\rightarrow$ Surname; empNr $\rightarrow$ EmpNr.

Commercial ORM tools may support different, more flexible schemes for mapping between the names of reference modes and corresponding value types, allowing you to choose different options, such as whether to insert underscore separators when appending.

As a check that we have drawn the diagram correctly, we should populate each fact type on the diagram with some of the original fact instances. We do this by adding a **fact table** for each fact type and entering the values in the relevant columns of this table. In ORM, a fact table is simply a table for displaying instances of an elementary fact type. The term "fact table" is used in a different sense in data warehousing (see Chapter 13). A diagram that includes both a schema and a sample database is called a *knowledge base diagram.*

Consider the output report of Table 3.8. Here "LicenseNr" refers to the person's driver's license. Performing step 1 reveals that there are two binary fact types involved (check this for yourself).

We can now draw the conceptual schema diagram. As a check, we populate it with the original data (see Figure 3.10). If desired, the inverse predicate may be included, as shown in this figure. At this stage the diagram is incomplete because constraints are not shown. At least one fact from each fact table should be verbalized to ensure the diagram makes sense. Populating the schema diagram is useful not only for detecting schema diagrams that are nonsensical, but also for clarifying constraints (as we see later).

Table 3.8 Driver details.

Person	*LicenseNr*	*Cars driven*
Adams B	A3050	235PZN
Jones E	A2245	235PZN, 108AAQ

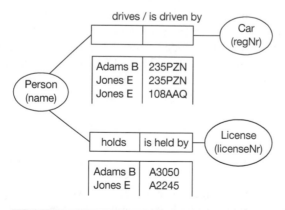

Figure 3.10 A knowledge base diagram for Table 3.8 (constraints omitted).

Table 3.9 Smokers and nonsmokers.

Smokers	Nonsmokers
Pat Lee	Norma Shir Terry

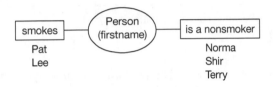

Figure 3.11 Knowledge base diagram for Table 3.9 (unary version).

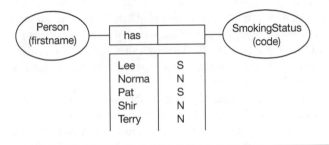

Figure 3.12 Knowledge base diagram for Table 3.9 (binary version).

Nowadays most nonsmokers prefer a smoke-free environment in which to work, travel, eat, and so on. So for some applications, a report like Table 3.9 is relevant. Please perform step 1 on this table before reading on.

One way to express the facts on row 1 is Person (firstname) 'Pat' smokes; Person (firstname) 'Norma' is a nonsmoker. Each of these facts is an instance of a different *unary fact type*. With a unary fact type, there is only one role. The knowledge base diagram is shown in Figure 3.11.

Here the two roles belong to different fact types. This is shown by separating the role boxes. If desired, the two unaries may be transformed into a single binary by introducing SmokingStatus as another entity type, with codes "S" for smoker and "N" for nonsmoker. So the first row of Table 3.9 could be rephrased as Person (firstname) 'Pat' has SmokingStatus (code) 'S'; Person (firstname) 'Norma' has SmokingStatus (code) 'N'. This approach is shown in Figure 3.12. Schema transformations are discussed in depth in Chapter 12.

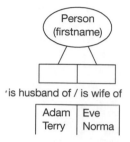

Figure 3.13 A ring fact type with sample population.

Each of the binary examples discussed had two different entity types. Fact types involving different entity types are said to be *heterogeneous fact types*. Most fact types are of this kind. However, the fact type in Figure 3.13 has one entity type—Person. If each role in a fact type is played by the same object type, we have a *homogeneous fact type*. The binary case of this is called a *ring fact type* since the path from the object type through the predicate loops back to the same object type, forming a ring.

Here both the forward predicate (is husband of) and inverse predicate (is wife of) are shown. In some versions of ORM, role names are used instead of predicates (e.g., husband, husband of, being husband of). Although this can be useful for some styles of queries, it is generally better to use full predicates, since this leads to better verbalization of both facts and constraints.

To make diagrams more compact, you may abbreviate names for predicates, object types, and reference modes if their expanded versions are obvious to users of the system. But this relaxed policy should be used with care. ORM tools often allow you to attach descriptions of model elements as notes, which can compensate for such name shortening.

Apart from communication with humans, conceptual schemas provide a formal specification of the structure of the UoD, so that the model may be processed by a computer system. Hence the schema diagrams we draw must conform to the formation rules for legal schemas. They are not just cartoons.

Now consider the output report of Table 3.10. This is similar to an example discussed previously, but to be more realistic, students are now identified by their student number. Here we have a *ternary fact type*. The object types and reference schemes are Student (nr), Subject (code), Rating (nr)+. Given this, we may express the fact on the first row as Student '1001' for Subject 'CS100' scored Rating 4.

On a conceptual schema diagram, a ternary fact type appears as a sequence of three role boxes, each of which is attached to an object type, as shown in Figure 3.14. When names for ternary and longer predicates are written on a diagram, the placeholders are included, each being depicted by an *ellipsis* "...". Figure 3.14 includes a sample population. No matter how high the arity (number of roles) of the fact type, we can easily populate it for checking purposes. Each column in the fact table is associated with one role in the predicate.

Table 3.10 A relational table storing student results.

Result:	*studentNr*	*subject*	*rating*
	1001	CS100	4
	1002	CS100	4
	1002	CS114	5

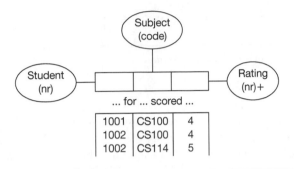

Figure 3.14 A populated ternary fact type for Table 3.10.

An earlier example transformed unaries into a binary. Another kind of schema transformation is **nesting.** *This treats a relationship between objects as an object itself.* Consider once more the top row of Table 3.10. Instead of expressing this as a single sentence, we might convey the information in the following two sentences:

Student '1001' enrolled in Subject 'CS100'.
This Enrollment resulted in Rating 4.

Here "This Enrollment" refers back to the enrollment relationship between the specific person and the specific subject mentioned in the first sentence. Any such enrollment may be treated as an object in its own right. The act of making an object out of a relationship is called *objectification* and corresponds to the linguistic act of nominalization (making a noun out of a verb phrase). An object formed by objectification is called an *objectified relationship* or a *nested object* (since other objects are nested within it). The type of object so formed is called an *objectified association,* an *objectified relationship type,* or a *nested object type.* Recall that the term "association" means the same as "relationship type".

An objectified association is depicted by a *soft rectangle* around the predicate being objectified (see Figure 3.15). Soft rectangles have rounded corners and are sometimes called frames or fillets. A name for the objectified association is added beside it, in *double quotes.* An objectified association usually has two roles, but may have more: ⊏⊏⊐. An alternative notation uses an ellipse instead of a frame.

Entries in fact columns for nested objects may be shown as bracketed pairs (triples, etc.) of values. For example, the enrollment of student 1001 in CS100 appears as

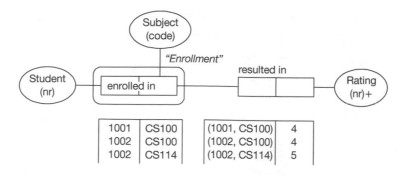

Figure 3.15 Knowledge base for Table 3.10 (nested version).

"(1001, CS100)" in the fact table for the resulted in predicate. Note that *nesting is not the same as splitting.* Figure 3.15 does not show two independent binaries. The resulted in predicate cannot be shown without including the enrolled in predicate. So the ternary in Figure 3.14 is still elementary. Figure 3.14 is said to be the *flattened,* or *unnested,* version.

Chapter 12 deals with the notion of schema equivalence in detail. The nested and flattened versions are not equivalent unless the role played by the objectified association is mandatory. With our current example, this means that a rating must be known for each enrollment. In this case the flattened version is preferred, since it is simpler to diagram and populate. As discussed later, nesting is often preferred if the nested object type has an optional role or more than one role to play. For example, suppose we widen the UoD to include information about when the enrollments occurred. With the flattened solution, we need to add another ternary: Student enrolled in Subject on Date. With the nested solution, we simply add the binary: Enrollment occurred on Date. As we'll see later, the nested solution also simplifies constraint specification in this case, and hence would now be preferred.

Now consider the travel record example depicted in Figure 3.16. Using the telephone heuristic, the modeler verbalizes the first row of data as an instance of the ternary fact type Politician visited Country in Year.

The sample data indicates that many politicians may visit many countries in many years. Because of this symmetry, there are many options for nesting. We could objectify Politician visited Country as Visit, and then add Visit occurred in Year. We might instead objectify Politician traveled in Year as Travel and then add Travel visited Country, or objectify Country was visited in Year as Visit, and add Visit was by Politician. With no strong reason for one nesting choice over the other, it is simpler to leave it as a ternary.

Although we display only one reading for ternary and longer fact types on the diagram, there are many possible readings depending on the order in which we traverse the roles. In principle, an *n*-ary predicate has *n!* (*n* factorial, i.e., $n \times (n - 1) \times ... \times 1$) readings. So a ternary has 6 possible readings, a quaternary has 24 possible readings,

Politician	Country	Year
Clinton	Australia	1994
Clinton	Italy	1994
Clinton	Australia	1995
Keating	Italy	1994

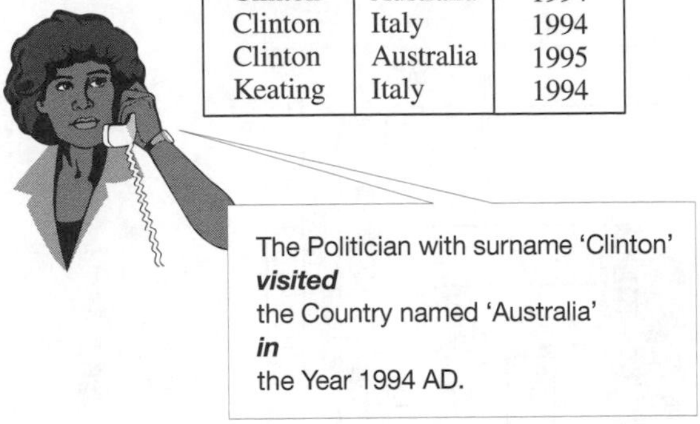

The Politician with surname 'Clinton'
visited
the Country named 'Australia'
in
the Year 1994 AD.

Figure 3.16 One way of verbalizing the first row.

and so on. For example, the ternary fact type above could be specified by any of the following six readings: Politician visited Country in Year; Politician in Year visited Country; Country was visited by Politician in Year; Country in Year was visited by Politician; Year included visit by Politician to Country; Year included visit to Country by Politician.

In practice, one reading is enough for modeling purposes. However, if we wish to query the schema directly, it is handy to be able to navigate from any given role. To cater to this we would need to supply, for each role, a reading that starts at that role (the order of the later roles doesn't matter). So we never need any more than *n* readings for any *n*-ary fact type. This is a lot fewer than *n* factorial. ORM tools usually accept *n* readings for any *n*-ary, but display only one on the diagram.

Now suppose we need to design a database for storing sales data that can be displayed graphically as shown in Figure 3.17. This three-dimensional bar chart shows the sales figures for two computer-aided drafting products code-named "ACAD" and "BCAD". As an exercise in steps 1 and 2, try to verbalize the sales information and then schematize it (on a conceptual schema diagram) before reading on.

Consider the first bar on the left of the chart. A person familiar with the application might verbalize the fact as "BCAD in the first quarter had sales of one million dollars". This completes step 1a. As modelers, we complete step 1b by refining this into one or more well-formed elementary facts. In this case, we may verbalize it as a single ternary: "The Product with code 'BCAD' in the Quarter numbered 1 had sales of MoneyAmount 1000000 USD".

I chose to identify quarters using numbers (e.g., 1) but you can use codes (e.g., 'Q1') if you like. I used the object type "MoneyAmount" instead of "Sales" because I wanted to make the underlying domain explicit. This makes it clear that we can compare sales figures with other monetary values (e.g., costs and profits). I often abbreviate this to "MoneyAmt". Assuming the chart applies to the USA, I chose USD (United States dollar) for the monetary unit. This distinguishes it from other dollars (e.g., AUD

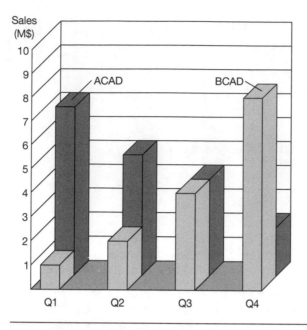

Figure 3.17 Can you verbalize this bar chart?

for Australian dollar). This is good practice, but if there is no danger of confusion, you could simply show the unit as "$".

Each remaining bar may be verbalized similarly. This completes step 1. In preparation for step 2, we could set the fact type out with reference modes in parentheses, as follows:

Product (code) in Quarter (nr) had sales of MoneyAmt (usd)+.

As a general rule, I use lower case for reference modes whenever practical; hence the "usd" instead of "USD". This is largely a matter of taste. A "+" is appended to the monetary unit to indicate that we can perform arithmetic on it. This is a minor aspect and can be ignored if at some stage you associate MoneyAmt with a system data type such as Numeric or Money that implies this—Microsoft's ORM tool actually requires you to specify an underlying numeric data type before you can use the numeric "+" marker. It is now a simple task to draw the conceptual schema diagram. As a check, we populate it with some sample fact instances (see Figure 3.18).

Another common way for presenting numeric data is the pie chart. A legend is often provided beside the chart to indicate the items denoted by each slice. Each slice of the pie indicates the portion of the whole taken up by that particular item. An example is given in Figure 3.19. Try to schematize this yourself before reading on.

Applying step 1a to the defense slice of the first pie, we could verbalize the fact represented as follows: "In 1965 defense consumed 43% of the budget". To complete step1, we may refine this to "In Year 1965 AD the BudgetItem named 'Defense'

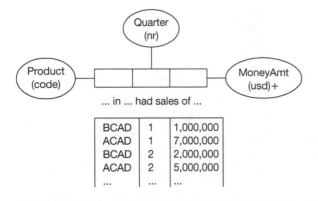

Figure 3.18 A conceptual schema for the sales data, with a sample population.

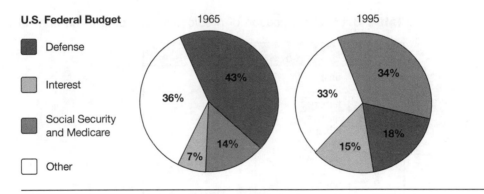

Figure 3.19 Can you schematize this pie chart?

consumed Portion 43% of the budget". All the other slices denote the same kind of fact. So we may generalize from the fact instances to the following ternary fact type:

in Year (AD) BudgetItem (name) consumed Portion (%) of the budget.

Here, the predicate "in ... ... consumed ... of the budget" has leading text and two object holes adjacent to one another. Though fairly rare, this is a legal mixfix predicate. This kind of flexibility makes verbalization easier than it would have been otherwise. To complete step 2, the resulting schema and sample data are shown in Figure 3.20.

To conclude this section, let's review some terminology. Three terms for objects have now been introduced. Entities are the objects in the UoD that we reference by means of descriptions. Values (character strings or numbers) are depicted as entries in database tables and are used to refer to entities. Finally, relationships between objects may be treated as objects themselves: these are objectified relationships (or nested objects).

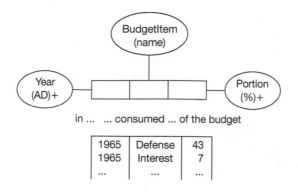

Figure 3.20 A conceptual schema for the budget data, with a sample population.

Table 3.11 Classification of predicates according to number of roles.

Nr roles	Main descriptor	Alternate descriptor
1	unary	monadic
2	binary	dyadic
3	ternary	triadic
4	quaternary	tetradic
5	quinary	...
6	senary	
7	septenary	
8	octanary	
9	nonary	

There are two commonly used notations for describing the arity or "length" of a predicate. The preferred notation, shown as the main descriptor, is set out for the first nine cases in Table 3.11. The alternate descriptor tends to be restricted to the first four cases, as shown. In practice it is extremely rare for any elementary predicate to exceed five roles.

Although we should populate conceptual schema diagrams for checking purposes, fact populations do not form part of the conceptual schema diagram itself. In the following exercise, population checks are not requested. However, I strongly suggest that you populate each fact type with at least one row as a check on your work.

Exercise 3.4

1. The names and gender of various people are indicated below:
    Male: Fred, Tom
    Female: Ann, Mary, Sue

(a) Express the information about Fred and Ann in unary facts.

(b) Draw a conceptual schema diagram based on this choice.

(c) Express the same information in terms of binary elementary facts.

(d) Draw a conceptual schema diagram based on this choice.

Note: For the rest of this exercise, avoid using unary facts.

2. Draw a conceptual schema diagram for the fact types in the following questions of Exercise 3.3:

(a) Question 3

(b) Question 4

(c) Question 5

(d) Question 6

(e) Question 7

(f) Question 8

(g) Question 9

(h) Question 10

Perform steps 1 and 2 of the CSDP for the following output reports.

3.

Retailer	Item	Quantity sold
CompuWare	SQL+	330
	Zappo Pascal	330
	WordLight	200
SoftwareLand	SQL+	330
	Zappo Pascal	251

4.

Item	Retailer	Quantity sold
SQL+	CompuWare	330
	SoftwareLand	330
Zappo Pascal	CompuWare	330
	SoftwareLand	251
WordLight	CompuWare	200

5.

Tute group	Day	Hour	Room
A	Mon	3 p.m.	69-718
B	Tue	2 p.m.	42-B18
C1	Thu	10 a.m.	69-718
C2	Thu	10 a.m.	67-103

6. *Hint:* Make use of nesting.

Subject	CreditPts	Semester	Enrollment	Lecturer
CS100	8	1	500	DBJ
CS102	8	2	500	EJS
CS114	8	1	300	TAH
CS115	8	2	270	TAH
CS383	16	1	50	RMC
CS383	16	2	45	PNC

7. Assuming appropriate names are supplied for entity types, reference modes, and predicates, and that appropriate constraints are added, which of the following conceptual schema diagrams are legal? Where illegal, briefly explain the error.

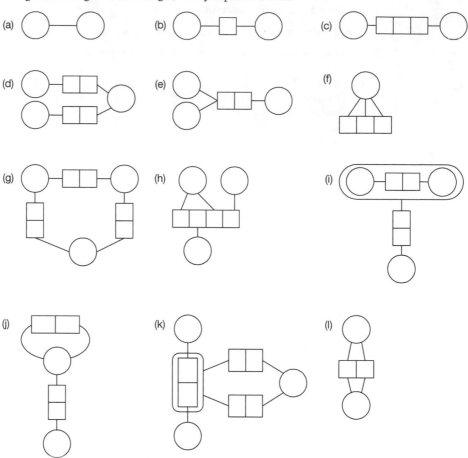

8. The following interactive voting form is used to input votes by cruise club members on various motions (proposals that have been officially moved by a club member). This example shows a screen shot of one completed form after a member has selected his/her voting choices. Although passwords are not displayed on-screen, they are captured by the information system. Perform CSDP steps 1 and 2 to schematize this UoD.

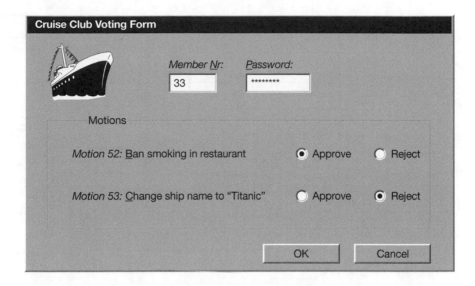

3.5 CSDP Step 3: Trim Schema; Note Basic Derivations

Having drawn the fact types and performed a population check, we now move on to step 3 of our design procedure. Here we check to see if there are some entity types that should be combined. We also check to see if some fact types can be derived from the others by arithmetic computation.

CSDP step 3: Check for entity types that should be combined; note any arithmetic derivations.

To understand the first part of this step, we need to know how the objects in the UoD are classified into types. Figure 3.21(a) shows the basic division of objects into entities (nonlexical objects) and values (lexical objects). *Entities* are identified by definite descriptions and may typically change their state, whereas *values* are simply constants (character strings or numbers). Values might include other objects directly representable on a medium (e.g., sounds), but such possibilities are ignored in this text.

Atomic entities are treated as individuals in their own right (e.g., persons, cars, engines). For modeling purposes, an atomic entity is treated as having no internal structure—any portrayal of structure must be depicted externally in terms of roles played by the entity. For example: Car (regNr) contains Engine (engineNr).

Nested entities are those relationships that we wish to think of as objects (i.e., objectified relationships; e.g., enrollments). Unlike atomic entities, nested entities are portrayed as having an internal structure (composed of the roles in the relationship). Relationships are not objects unless we think of them that way and want to talk about them.

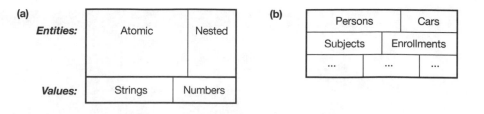

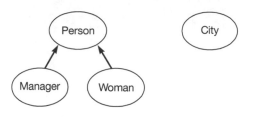

Figure 3.21 Partitioning into types of (a) objects and (b) primitive entities.

Figure 3.22 Person and City are primitive entity types and hence mutually exclusive.

These subdivisions are **mutually exclusive** (i.e., they have no instance in common). For example, no string can be an entity. The division of a whole into exclusive parts is called a **partition.** You may think of it as cutting a pie up into slices. The slices are *exclusive* (they don't overlap) and *exhaustive* (together they make up the whole pie).

Figure 3.21(b) gives an example of how the entities might be further divided into entity types for a particular UoD. Only a few entity types are listed. Which kinds of entities exist depends on the UoD. Basically, entities are grouped into the same type if we want to record similar information about them.

For any UoD, there is always a top-level partitioning of its entities into exclusive types: these are called **primitive entity types.** We may introduce *subtypes* of these primitive types, if they have some specific roles to play. In ORM, subtypes are shown connected by an arrow to their supertype. Though shown separately, it is possible that subtypes of a given entity type may overlap. However, *primitive entity types never overlap.* For example, no person can be a city. On a conceptual schema diagram, the visual separation of primitive entity types indicates that these types are mutually exclusive. The same is not true of subtypes. In Figure 3.22, for example, Person and City are mutually exclusive but Manager and Woman need not be. Subtypes are discussed in detail in Chapter 6.

Value types often overlap, but are still shown separately on a schema diagram (e.g., Figure 3.23(a)) since they are implicitly assumed to be a subtype of String or Number (e.g., Figure 3.23(b)). In this example, Surname and CityName overlap because they may have common instances (Figure 3.23(c)). Although the explicit depiction of value subtyping or value type overlap may clarify the situation, for compactness we leave this

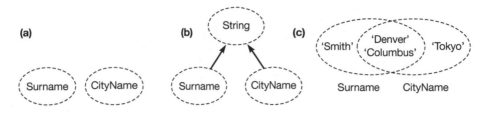

Figure 3.23 String types (a) are implicit subtypes (b) and hence may overlap (c).

Table 3.12 Some motion pictures.

Movie	Stars	Director
Awakenings	Robert De Niro, Robin Williams	Penny Marshall
Backdraft	Kurt Russell, Robert De Niro, William Baldwin	Ron Howard
Dances with Wolves	Kevin Costner, Mary McDonnell	Kevin Costner
...	...	...

implicit (as in Figure 3.23(a)). Chapter 6 discusses how to constrain value types to a specific subtype of String or Number. For example, Surname might be restricted to strings of at most 20 characters and RatingNr to integers in the range 1..7.

Step 3 of the design procedure begins with a check to see if some entity types should be combined. At this stage we are concerned only with primitive entity types, not entity subtypes. So if you spot some entity types that do overlap, you should combine them into a single entity type. For example, consider Table 3.12, which concerns the movie application discussed in Chapter 1. Suppose that as a result of applying steps 1 and 2 we arrived at the diagram shown in Figure 3.24. Do you see what's wrong with this diagram?

Figure 3.24 displays MovieStar and Director as separate, primitive entity types. This implies that these types are mutually exclusive (i.e., no movie star can be a director). But is this the case? Our sample population lists the value "Kevin Costner" in both the Stars column and the Director column. Does this refer to the same person?

If in doubt, you can ask a domain expert. In actual fact, it is the same person. So we must combine the MovieStar and Director entity types into a single entity type as shown in Figure 3.25. This shows it is possible to be both a star and a director. Of course, it does not imply that every movie star is a director. Chapter 6 discusses how to add subtypes later if necessary. For example, if some other facts are to be recorded only for directors, we form a Director subtype of Person for those additional facts.

One reason for suspecting that two entity types should be combined is if they both have the *same unit-based reference mode*. Here the entity is typically envisaged as a

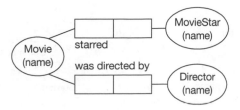

Figure 3.24 A faulty conceptual schema.

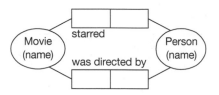

Figure 3.25 The result of applying step 3 to Figure 3.24.

Table 3.13 Monetary details about articles on sale.

Article	Wholesale price ($)	Retail price ($)	Markup ($)
A1	50	75	25
A2	80	130	50
A3	50	70	20
A4	100	130	30

quantity of so many units (e.g., kilograms or years). Let's look at a few examples. Consider the output report of Table 3.13.

At first glance, we might consider representing the design of this UoD by the diagram shown in Figure 3.26. Note however that the entity types Wholesale price, Retail price, and Markup all have the same unit-based reference mode ($). Here we assume that it is well understood which kind of dollar (AUD, USD, etc.) is denoted by "$".

In the table, $50 appears as both a wholesale price and a markup. In both cases the $50 denotes the same amount of money. This makes it even more obvious that these entity types overlap and hence should be combined. If the table population is significant, the set of retail prices does not overlap the set of markups. Nevertheless, it is *meaningful to compare* retail prices and markups since they have the same unit (dollars). For instance, article A1 has a retail price that is three times its markup. These considerations

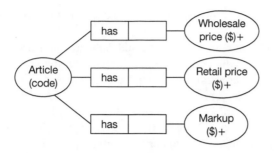

Figure 3.26 Another faulty conceptual schema.

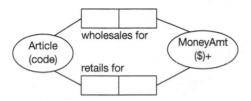

* { markup = retail price − wholesale price }

Article has markup of MoneyAmt **iff** Article retails for MoneyAmt$_1$ **and**
Article wholesales for MoneyAmt$_2$ **and**
MoneyAmt = MoneyAmt$_1$ − MoneyAmt$_2$

Figure 3.27 The result of applying step 3 to Figure 3.26.

lead us to collapse the three entity types into the concept of money amount, abbreviated here as "MoneyAmt", as shown in Figure 3.27.

There is one other point to be noted with this example. The output report satisfies the following mathematical relationship between the values in the last three columns: markup = retail price − wholesale price. Assuming this is significant, the markup value may be **derived** from the wholesale and retail values by means of this rule. To minimize the chance of human error, we have the system derive this value rather than have humans compute and store it. In this book, *derivation rules are written as text below the schema diagram.* With an ORM tool you might enter the rule in a text box or a properties sheet. If the derivation rule is captured, there is no need to include the derived fact type on the diagram itself.

An informal version of the rule may be written as a comment in braces. What about a formal version of the rule? One way of stating the derivation rule formally is shown in Figure 3.27. Here object type variables are subscripted, as in ConQuer, an ORM query language. An alternative is to introduce the variable after the type name (e.g., Article *a*).

Notice the use of "**iff**": this abbreviates "if and only if", indicating the rule is a *biconditional* (it works in both directions). From a strict conceptual viewpoint, the derivation rule merely declares a constraint between the three fact types for markup, retail price, and wholesale price. Any one of the three could be derived from knowledge of the other two. Sometimes we might wish to enter the retail and wholesale prices and have the system derive the markup. At other times, we might wish to enter the wholesale price and markup and have the system derive the retail price. It is possible to build a system that supports both these choices, and this can be quite useful in practice.

In most derivation cases, however, we usually decide beforehand that one specific fact type will always be the derived one. In this case, the derivation rule may be specified as a *definition,* where the derived fact type is defined in terms of the others. For example:

define Article has markup of MoneyAmt **as**
  Article retails for MoneyAmt$_1$ **and**
  Article wholesales for MoneyAmt$_2$ **and**
  MoneyAmt = MoneyAmt$_1$ − MoneyAmt$_2$

In such a definition, the derived fact type is said to be the *definiendum* (what is required to be defined). A fact type that is primitive (i.e., not defined in terms of others) is said to be a *base* fact type. *Derived* fact types are defined in terms of other fact types (base or derived).

All the ways discussed so far for setting out the derivation rule use the *relational style.* Here the fact types are set out fully as relationship types. Although this style is ideal for logical derivation rules (e.g., the uncle example from Chapter 2), it is awkward for arithmetical derivation rules, as in our current example. For such cases, the *attribute style* of rule is more compact and readable. If all the attributes are single valued, this is also called the *functional* style. In addition to the required predicate name, ORM allows you to optionally add a *rolename* for any individual role. Rolenames are used mainly for improving the readability of the attribute names automatically generated when mapping to attribute-based models such as ER, UML, or relational schemas. But they can also be used as attribute names in derivation rules.

In Figure 3.28 the rolenames "wholesalePrice" and "retailPrice" appear in square brackets next to their role. For binary associations, rolenames may be treated as attributes of the object type at the opposite end of the association. Using the dot naming convention, the qualified rolenames are Article.wholesalePrice and Article.retailPrice.

The derivation rule may now be formally but concisely expressed by the equation shown in Figure 3.28. Typing rules imply that the markup role is played by MoneyAmt, and the predicate name "has markup of" can be generated by default for the underlying fact type.

Most ORM tools do not yet support the square bracket notation for rolenames used in Figure 3.28. Displaying both predicate and rolenames on a diagram can lead to a cluttered appearance, so ideally you should be able to toggle their display on or off. The dot notation for attributes is used in UML and many other approaches, but if you are using the attribute style for derivation rules, a bracket notation or "of" notation may

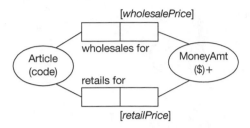

* Article.markup = Article.retailPrice − Article.wholesalePrice

Figure 3.28 Use of rolenames in an attribute style of derivation rules.

Table 3.14 Window sizes.

Window	Height (cm)	Width (cm)	Area (cm²)
1	4	5	20
2	6	20	120
3	10	15	150
4	5	5	25

be preferable for validating rules with the domain experts. For example, the rule could also be formally declared in either of the following ways:

markup(Article) = retailPrice(Article) − wholesalePrice(Article)
markup **of** Article = retailPrice **of** Article − wholesalePrice **of** Article

Let's consider now a somewhat similar example. The output report of Table 3.14 shows details about windows on a computer screen. Try to schematize this before reading on.

As you probably guessed, we can get by with fewer than four entity types here. Seeing that the values shown in the last three columns are all numbers, you may have been tempted to combine Height, Width, and Area into one entity type. You might argue that Height and Width overlap since the value 5 is common, and that Width and Area overlap since each includes the value 20. But notice that Area is measured in square centimeters, which is quite a different unit from centimeters.

Heights and widths may be meaningfully compared since both are lengths: a length of 5 cm may be an instance of a height or a width. But a length of 20 cm is not the same thing as an area of 20 cm². If our final column was headed "Perimeter (cm)", we could collapse three headings into one entity type as for the previous example. But since Area is fundamentally a different type of quantity, we must keep it separate, as shown in Figure 3.29.

Derived fact types are usually specified only as rules, to avoid cluttering up the diagram. However, it is sometimes instructive to show a derived fact type on the diagram. In this case it must be marked as being derived, to distinguish it from the base fact

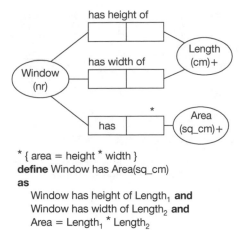

$*\ \{\ \text{area} = \text{height} * \text{width}\ \}$
define Window has Area(sq_cm)
as
    Window has height of Length_1 **and**
    Window has width of Length_2 **and**
    Area = $\text{Length}_1 * \text{Length}_2$

Figure 3.29 Schema for Table 3.14.

types. To do this in ORM, *place an **asterisk** beside any derived fact type that is included on the diagram,* as shown in Figure 3.29. Whether or not a fact type is displayed on a diagram, a rule for deriving it should be declared.

The informal rule shown for area computation uses an asterisk in a different sense (for multiplication). For the formal rule, I've decided to always make Area the derived quantity, so I've used a definitional form for the rule. In principle any one of the three quantities could be derived from the other two. In cases like this, where there really is a choice as to which is the definiendum, the decision is often based more on performance than on conceptual issues. In many cases, however, there simply is no choice. For example, facts about sums and averages are derivable from facts about individual cases, but except for trivial cases we cannot derive the individual facts from such summaries.

Using rolenames, the rule could be specified more compactly as Window.area = Window.height * Window.width. The main advantage of predicate-based notation is that it is more stable than an attribute-based notation, since it is not impacted by schema changes such as attributes being remodeled as associations. Though unlikely in this particular example, when such changes are possible the choice between the attribute style or relational style for derivation rules involves a trade-off between convenience and stability.

It is an implementation issue whether a derived fact type is *derived-on-query (lazy evaluation)* or *derived-on-update (eager evaluation)*. In the former case, the derived information is not stored, but computed only when the information is requested. For example, if our Window schema is mapped to a relational database, no column for area is included in the base table for Window. The rule for computing area may be included in a view definition or stored query, and it is invoked only when the view is queried or the stored query is executed. In most cases, lazy evaluation is preferred (e.g., computing a person's age from their birth date and current date).

Sometimes eager evaluation is chosen because it offers significantly better performance (e.g., computing account balances). In this case, the information is stored as soon as the defining facts are entered, and updated whenever they are updated. In an ORM tool, this option might be chosen by selecting "Derived and Stored" from a predicate dialog box. As a subconceptual annotation, a double asterisk "**" may be used to indicate this choice. When the schema is mapped to a relational database, a column is created for the derived fact type, and the computation rule should be included in a trigger that is fired whenever the defining columns are updated (including inserts or deletes).

Now consider Figure 3.30. This might describe part of a UoD concerning practitioners in a medical clinic. Here the entity types Doctor, Dentist, and Pharmacist have a similar reference mode (name), but this is not unit based, so this is no reason to combine the types. If somebody could hold more than one of these three jobs, then the overlap of the entity types would normally force a combination.

However, suppose that the entity types are mutually exclusive (i.e., nobody can hold more than one of these jobs). In this case we still need to consider whether the entity types should be combined, since the *same kind of information* (their sex) is recorded for each.

In such cases, we ask ourselves the following question: *Do we ever want to list the same kind of information for the different entity types in the same query?* For example, do we want to make the request "List all the practitioners and their sex"? If we do, then we should normally combine the entity types as shown in Figure 3.31. If we don't, then there may be grounds for leaving the schema unchanged. Section 6.6 examines this issue in more detail.

Even if no doctor can be a dentist, the schema of Figure 3.30 permits a doctor and a dentist to have the same name (e.g., "Jones E"). In Figure 3.31, the use of "(name)" with Practitioner implies that each instance of PractitionerName refers to only one Practitioner.

Suppose we add the constraint each Practitioner holds at most one Job. A graphical notation for this kind of constraint is discussed in the next chapter. With this constraint added, Figure 3.31 would forbid any doctor from having the same name as a dentist. If the original names did overlap, we would now need to rename some practitioners to ensure their new names are distinct (e.g., "Jones E1" and "Jones E2"). Alternatively, we might choose a new simple identification scheme (e.g., practitionerNr), or identify practitioners by the combination of their original name and job. Reference schemes are discussed in detail in Section 5.4.

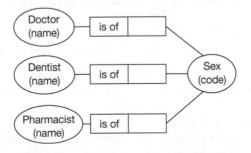

Figure 3.30 Should Doctor, Dentist, and Pharmacist be combined?

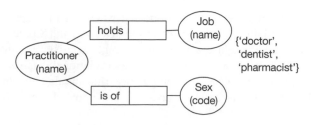

Figure 3.31 An alternative schema for the UoD of Figure 3.30.

To preserve the distinction between the different kinds of practitioners, I introduced the entity type Job, and constrained job names to the set {"doctor", "dentist", "pharmacist"}. Such "value constraints" are discussed in detail in Chapter 6. As an exercise, you might like to invent a small population for this UoD and populate both schemas.

The new schema is simpler than the old one since it replaced three binary fact types with two binaries. If we had even more kinds of practitioners (e.g., acupuncturist, herbalist), the savings would be even more worthwhile. If we have only two kinds of practitioners (e.g., doctor and pharmacist), both schemas would have the same number of fact types. But even in this case, the new version is generally favored. If additional information is required for specific kinds of practitioners, subtyping should be added, as discussed much later.

In rare cases, entity types might overlap, but we are not interested in knowing this, and collapsing the types is awkward. We may then leave the types separate so long as we declare that our model differs from the real world in this respect.

In performing step 3 of the CSDP, the relevant questions to ask ourselves may be summarized thus:

1. *Can the same entity be a member of two entity types?* If so, combine the entity types into one (unless such identities are not of interest).
2. *Can entities of two different types be meaningfully compared (e.g., to compute ratios)? Do they have the same unit or dimension?* If so, combine the entity types into one.
3. *Is the same kind of information recorded for different entity types, and will you sometimes need to list the entities together for this information?* If so, combine the entity types into one, and if necessary add another fact type to preserve the original distinction.
4. *Is a fact type arithmetically derivable from others?* If so, add a derivation rule. If you include the fact type on the diagram, mark it with an asterisk "*".

At this step, the derivation rules that concern us are of an arithmetic nature. These are usually fairly obvious. Logical derivations can be harder to spot and are considered in a later step.

Besides verbalization and population, a third way to validate a model is to see whether it enables *sample queries* to be answered, either directly from, or by derivation on, the fact populations. If you know what kinds of questions the system must be able to answer, navigate around the ORM model to see if you can answer them. If you can't, your schema is incomplete, and you should add the fact types and/or derivation rules needed to answer the queries.

Exercise 3.5

Perform steps 1–3 of the CSDP for the following output reports. In setting out derivation rules, you may use any convenient notation.

1.

Software	Distributor	Retailer
Blossom 1234	CompuWare	PCland SoftKing
SQL++	TechSource	PCland
WordLight	TechSource	CompuWare SoftKing

2.

Project	Manager	Budget	Salary	Birth year
P1	Smith J	38000	50000	1946
P2	Jones	42000	55000	1935
P3	Brown	20000	38000	1946
P4	Smith T	36000	42000	1950
P5	Collins	36000	38000	1956

3.

Dept	Budget	NrStaff	EmpNr	Salary	Salary total
Admin	80000	2	E01	40000	
			E02	25000	65000
Sales	90000	3	E03	30000	
			E04	25000	
			E05	30000	85000
Service	90000	2	E06	45000	
			E07	25000	70000

4.

Employee	Project	Hours	Expenses
E4	P8	24	200
E4	P9	26	150
E5	P8	14	100
E5	P9	16	110
E6	P8	16	120
E6	P9	14	110

5.

Female staff		Male staff	
Name	Dept	Name	Dept
Sue Bright	Admin	John Jones	Sales
Eve Jones	Admin	Bob Smith	Admin
Ann Smith	Sales		

6. The following excerpt is from the final medal tally for the 1996 Olympics. Only the top five countries are listed here.

	G	S	B	Total
United States	44	32	25	101
Germany	20	18	27	65
Russia	26	21	16	63
China	16	22	12	50
Australia	9	9	23	41
...	...	...	...	...

(a) Schematize this using binary fact types only.
(b) Schematize this using a ternary fact type.

3.6   Summary

The following criteria are desirable characteristics for any language to be used for conceptual modeling: expressibility, clarity, simplicity and orthogonality, semantic stability, semantic relevance, validation mechanisms, abstraction mechanisms, and formal foundation. Object-Role Modeling was designed with these criteria in mind. In particular, its omission of the attribute concept from base models led to greater stability and simplicity, while facilitating validation through verbalization and population.

With large-scale applications, the UoD is divided into convenient modules, the *conceptual schema design procedure* is applied to each, and the resulting subschemas are integrated into the global conceptual schema. The CSDP itself has seven steps, of which the first three were discussed in this chapter:

1a. Verbalize familiar information examples as facts (domain expert's task).
1b. Refine these into formal, elementary facts, and apply quality checks (modeler's task).
 2. Draw the fact types, and apply a population check.
 3. Check for entity types that should be combined, and note any arithmetic derivations.

Step 1 is the most important. This is seeded by *data use cases,* which are relevant information *examples* (e.g., tables, forms, diagrams) that are familiar to the domain expert. These are *verbalized in terms of elementary facts.* The domain expert should verbalize the examples informally as facts in natural-language sentences (step 1a). The modeler should complete step 1 by refining these into elementary facts (step 1b). An elementary fact is a simple assertion that an object has some property, or that one or more objects participate together in some relationship. With respect to the UoD, an elementary fact cannot be split into smaller facts without information loss.

Elementary facts are expressed as instantiated logical predicates. A logical *predicate* is a declarative sentence with object holes in it. To complete the sentence, the holes are filled in by object terms. With simple reference schemes, an entity term is a definite description that includes the name of the *entity type, reference mode,* and *value* (e.g., "the

Scientist with surname 'Einstein'"). A value term comprises the name of the value type and the value (e.g., "the Surname 'Einstein'").

Each object hole corresponds to a *role*. A predicate with one role is *unary*, with two roles is *binary*, with three roles is *ternary*, with four roles is *quaternary*, and with *n* roles is *n*-ary. The value *n* is the *arity* of the predicate.

In CSDP *step 2* we draw the fact types and apply a population check. Entity types are depicted as named, solid ellipses and value types as named, broken ellipses. An *n*-ary predicate is shown as a named, contiguous sequence of *n* role boxes. Predicates are ordered; the predicate name is placed in or beside the first role of the predicate. Each role is played by exactly one object type, as shown by a connecting line.

A *simple 1:1 reference scheme* involves a reference predicate between an entity type and a value type, where each entity is associated with exactly one value, and each value is associated with only one entity. This kind of scheme may be abbreviated by enclosing the *reference mode in parentheses* next to the entity type name. If the value type is numeric, this may be indicated by adding a "+" sign or by assigning it a numeric data type.

Once a fact type is drawn, it should be checked by populating it with at least one fact and reading it back in natural language. Each column in the associated *fact table* corresponds to a specific role.

A relationship may be thought of as an object itself, if we wish to talk about it. *Objectified associations* or *nested object types* are depicted by a soft rectangle. Figure 3.32 summarizes the graphic notations met so far. Objects are classified into three main groups: atomic entities, nested entities (objectified relationships), and values (strings or numbers).

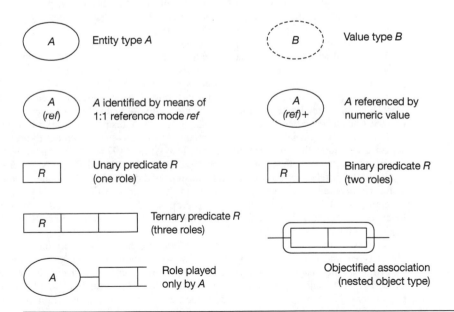

Figure 3.32 Some basic symbols used in conceptual schema diagrams.

In *step 3* of the CSDP, we check for entity types that should be combined, and note any arithmetic derivations. For any given UoD, each entity belongs to exactly one of the *primitive entity types* that have been selected (e.g., Person, Car). Hence, if we have drawn two entity types that may have a common instance, we should combine them. Even if they don't overlap, entity types that can be meaningfully compared should normally be combined; these typically have the same unit-bearing reference mode (e.g., cm). If the same kind of information is to be recorded for different entity types, these should often be combined, and if needed, a fact type should be added to preserve the original distinction.

If a fact type is arithmetically derivable from others, an appropriate derivation rule should be provided. The rule may be declared in relational style (using predicates) or in attribute style (using attributes derived from rolenames). Usually the derived fact type is omitted from the diagram, but if included, it should be marked with an asterisk.

Chapter Notes

The parsimony-convenience trade-off is nicely illustrated by two-valued propositional calculus, which allows for 4 monadic and 16 dyadic logical operators. All 20 of these operators can be expressed in terms of a single logical operator (e.g., nand, nor), but while this might be useful in building electronic components, it is simply too inconvenient for direct human communication. For example, "not p" is far more convenient than "p nand p". In practice, we use several operators (e.g., not, and, or, if-then) since the convenience of using them directly far outweighs the parsimonious benefits of having to learn only one operator such as nand. When it comes to proving metatheorems about a given logic, it is often convenient to adopt a somewhat parsimonious stance regarding the base constructs (e.g., treat "not" and "or" as the only primitive logical operators), while introducing other constructs as derived (e.g., define "if *p* then *q*" as "not *p* or *q*"). Similar considerations apply to modeling languages.

A classic paper on linguistics that influenced the early development of a number of modeling methods is Fillmore (1968). Use case specification was central to the former Objectory approach of Ivar Jacobson, one of the main contributors to UML. For a clear overview of logicians' approaches to proper names and descriptions, see Chapter 5 of Haack (1978). Some heuristics to help with step 1 in interpreting common forms used in business are discussed in Choobineh et al. (1992). In this book, the term "line" is used informally to mean "line segment" or "edge" (in geometry, lines have no beginning or end). The following notes provide a brief history of ORM.

In the 1970s, especially in Europe, substantial research was carried out to provide high-level semantics for modeling information systems. Jean Abrial (1974), Mike Senko (1975), and others discussed modeling with binary relationships. In 1973, Eckhard Falkenberg generalized their work on binary relationships to *n*-ary relationships and decided that attributes should not be used at the conceptual level because they involved "fuzzy" distinctions and they also complicated schema evolution. Later, Falkenberg (1976) proposed the fundamental ORM framework, which he called the "Object-Role Model". This framework allowed *n*-ary and nested relationships, but depicted roles with arrowed lines.

Shir Nijssen adapted this framework by introducing the now standard circle-box notation for object types and roles, and adding a linguistic orientation and design procedure to provide a modeling method called ENALIM (Evolving Natural Language Information Model) (Nijssen 1976, 1977). A major reason for the role-box notation was to facilitate validation using sample populations. Nijssen led a group of researchers at Control Data in Belgium who developed the method further, including Franz van Assche who classified object types into lexical object types (LOTs) and nonlexical object types (NOLOTs). Today, LOTs are commonly called "entity types" and NOLOTs are called "value types". Bill Kent (1977, 1978) provided several semantic insights and clarified many conceptual issues.

Robert Meersman (1982) added subtypes to the modeling framework and invented RIDL, which enabled the conceptual models to be specified, updated, and queried directly at the conceptual level. The method was renamed "aN Information Analysis Method" (NIAM) and summarized in a paper by Verheijen and van Bekkum (1982). In later years the acronym "NIAM" was given different expansions, and is now known as "Natural-language Information Analysis Method". Two matrix methods for subtypes were developed, one (the role-role matrix) by Dirk Vermeir (1983) and another by Falkenberg and others.

In the 1980s, Falkenberg and Nijssen worked jointly on the design procedure and moved to the University of Queensland, where the method was further enhanced by various academics. It was there that I provided the first full formalization of the method (Halpin 1989b), including schema equivalence proofs, and made several refinements and extensions to the method. In 1989, Nijssen and I coauthored a book on the method. Another early book on the method was written by Wintraecken (1990).

In the early 1990s I developed an extended version of NIAM called Formal ORM (FORM), initially supported in the InfoDesigner modeling tool from ServerWare. This product later evolved to InfoModeler (at Asymetrix Corp., then InfoModelers Inc.), then VisioModeler (at Visio). This ORM technology was then recoded to work on the Visio engine, first appearing in Visio Enterprise. Anthony Bloesch and I designed an associated query language called ConQuer (Bloesch and Halpin 1997), supported in the ActiveQuery tool. Microsoft acquired Visio in 2000 and is currently extending the ORM technology for use within. A number of other commercial and academic institutions have also engaged in research and development to provide CASE tool support for the Visual Studio.net method (e.g., Ascaris Software 2000).

Many researchers have contributed to the ORM method over the years, and a full history would include many not listed here. Today various versions of the method exist, but all adhere to the fundamental object-role framework. Although most ORM proponents favor n-ary relationships, some prefer Binary-Relationship Modeling (BRM), for example, Peretz Shoval (Shoval and Shreiber 1993). Henri Habrias (1993) developed an object-oriented version called MOON (Normalized Object-Oriented Method). The Predicator Set Model (PSM) was developed mainly by Arthur ter Hofstede, Erik Proper, and Theo van der Weide (ter Hofstede et al. 1993) and includes complex object constructors. Olga De Troyer and Robert Meersman (1995) developed another version with constructors called Natural Object-Relationship Model (NORM). Harm van der Lek and others (Bakema et al. 1994) allowed entity types to be treated as nested roles, to produce Fully Communication Oriented Information Modeling (FCO-IM). The term "Object-Role Modeling" (ORM), originally used by Falkenberg for his modeling framework, is now used generically to cover the various versions of the modeling approach.

Independently of the main ORM movement, Dave Embley and others decided that using attributes in conceptual modeling was a bad idea, so they developed Object-oriented Systems Analysis (OSA) that includes an attribute-free "Object-Relationship Model" component that has much in common with ORM (Embley et al. 1992; Embley 1998).

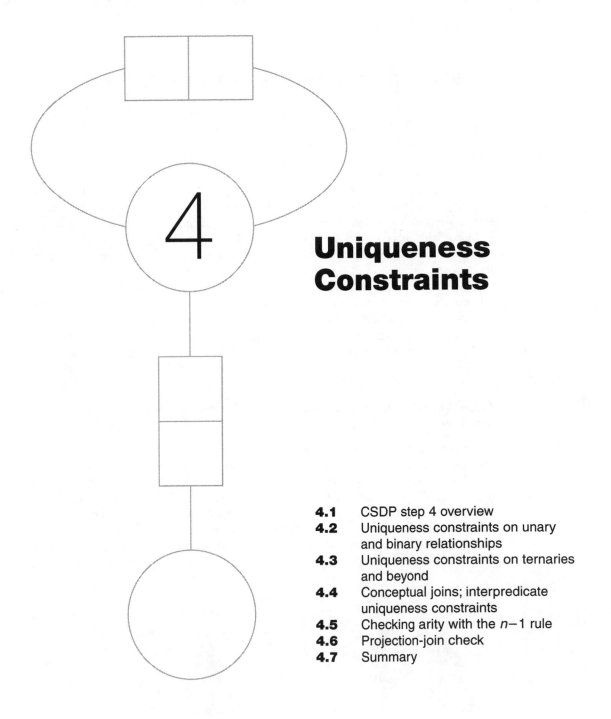

Uniqueness Constraints

4.1   CSDP Step 4: Uniqueness Constraints; Arity Check

So far, the conceptual schema design procedure has focused on specifying the elementary fact types, both base and derived. The rest of the CSDP is concerned mostly with specifying **constraints.** Constraints apply to the database and are either static or dynamic. *Static constraints* apply to each individual state of the database and may usually be specified on a conceptual schema diagram, as discussed in CSDP steps 4–7. Examples include uniqueness, mandatory role, set comparison, value, subtyping, frequency, and ring constraints. *Dynamic constraints* restrict the possible transitions between states, are often expressed in other ways (e.g., statecharts), and are considered in step 7, along with other special constraints. In practice, we usually capture all the constraints relevant to the fact types being discussed before moving on to another part of the model.

This chapter discusses **uniqueness constraints.** These play a pivotal role when the conceptual schema is later mapped onto a relational schema. Once uniqueness constraints have been added to a fact type, some further checks are made to see whether the fact type is of the right arity or length. In particular, there is a simple check based on uniqueness that shows that certain kinds of fact types are not elementary and hence should be split.

CSDP step 4: Add uniqueness constraints, and check the arity of fact types.

Static constraints are often described as being "constraints on the fact types". More accurately, *static constraints apply to every possible state of the database.* Here "every state" means *each and every state, taken one at a time.* Hence, static constraints apply to all possible *populations* of the fact types. For example, given the fact type Person (surname) has Weight (kg), let's add the constraint **each** Person has **at most one** Weight. A sample population for two different states is shown in Figure 4.1.

During the lifetime of the information system, the database goes through a sequence of states. In one of these states, Smith is recorded to weigh 95 kg, and Jones is recorded

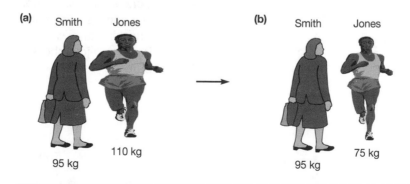

Figure 4.1   For each state taken individually, each person has at most one weight.

to weigh 110 kg (Figure 4.1(a)). In a later state, Smith is still the same weight, but Jones has lost weight by exercising (Figure 4.1(b)). Over time, Jones has two different weights. However, in each state of the database, at most one weight is recorded as the current weight for Jones. Likewise for Smith or any other person. This is how we should interpret the static constraint **each** Person has **at most one** Weight.

Fact types like Person has Weight are *snapshot fact types* since each instance of them applies to a single state, or snapshot, of the database. If we wish to record the history, one way is to use a *historical fact type* that explicitly makes reference to time (e.g., Person had Weight on Date).

This chapter discusses how to specify uniqueness constraints on a conceptual schema diagram. Each base fact type must be assigned at least one uniqueness constraint. Typically, we may ignore derived fact types in our discussion of constraints since, given the constraints on the base fact types, such "derived constraints" are typically implied by the derivation rules. For example, if a window has at most one height and at most one width, then the derivation rule "area = height * width" implies that each window has at most one area (which is the uniqueness constraint on the derived fact type Window has Area).

The rest of the chapter discusses CSDP step 4 in the following order. First we discuss how to mark uniqueness constraints on unary and binary predicates. Then we consider uniqueness constraints on longer predicates. After that, we examine external uniqueness constraints (these apply between different predicates). Finally we discuss ways of checking that our fact types have the right arity (number of roles).

4.2   Uniqueness Constraints on Unaries and Binaries

Unary fact types are the easiest, so let's look at them first. Suppose that, as part of a fitness application, we record which people are joggers. This can be handled with a unary fact type, as shown in Figure 4.2.

For simplicity, let's again assume we can identify people just by their surname. A sample population is included. From the conceptual viewpoint, the fact population is the set containing the following facts:

The Person with surname 'Adams' jogs.
The Person with surname 'Brown' jogs.
The Person with surname 'Collins' jogs.

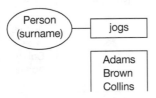

Figure 4.2 A unary fact type with sample population.

Suppose that after recording these facts, we see Adams run by again. Forgetting that we already recorded his jogging, we now try the following update:

add: The Person with surname 'Adams' jogs.

If accepted, this update may be pictured as shown in Figure 4.3. The database is a variable whose population at any state is a set of elementary facts. Since the fact that Adams jogs was already present, if this fact were added again, the population would remain unaltered because sets are insensitive to repetition. For example, the set {Adams jogs, Adams jogs} is identical to the set {Adams jogs}. Sets are defined simply by their membership and don't change if we display a member more than once (even if this is unusual). So the two fact tables shown in Figure 4.3 are equivalent if we look at each as a set of instances. From this viewpoint, there is no problem with accepting the update.

From the internal viewpoint, however, when an elementary fact is added to a database it is typically stored in a previously unallocated space. So accepting this update would mean that the fact that Adams jogs is actually stored twice, in separate locations. This is an example of **redundancy.** If redundancy occurs, the database is a *bag* of facts rather than a *set* of facts. A bag or *multiset* is just like a set, except repetition of its members is significant. For example, although the sets {1} and {1,1} are equal, the bags [1] and [1,1] are different.

Avoiding redundancy in a database helps maintain its integrity by simplifying the correct handling of update operations. For instance, suppose the fact that Adams jogs is stored twice in the database. If we later wanted to delete this fact, then we would need to take care to delete both its recorded instances. Controlling redundancy in this way can be a headache, and uncontrolled redundancy can lead to inconsistency. A second reason for avoiding redundancy is to save space (computers have finite storage capabilities).

On the other hand, to retrieve information more efficiently it is sometimes necessary to allow controlled redundancy at the *logical* schema level. However, for *conceptual* schema design we demand that *no redundancy may occur in the conceptual database.* Redundancy is simply the repetition of an elementary fact. Since each row of a conceptual fact table corresponds to one elementary fact, this means that *no row of an elementary fact table may be repeated.* This implies that the fact table in Figure 4.3(b) is illegal, since the Adams row is repeated.

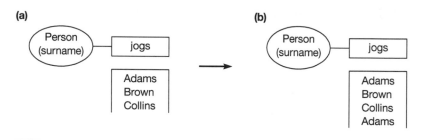

Figure 4.3 Is this update allowed?

Here, for any particular state of the database, each person is listed as a jogger at most once. In other words, each entry in the column of the fact table is unique (no duplicates may appear in this column). We may represent this uniqueness constraint explicitly by placing an arrow-tipped bar above the fact column, as in Figure 4.4.

Notice that the uniqueness constraint also appears next to the role. We can show the constraint on the conceptual schema diagram alone by placing the symbol next to the role, either below it (Figure 4.5(a)) or above it (Figure 4.5(b)). If we omit the symbol, the uniqueness constraint is implied (Figure 4.5(c)).

Every ORM fact type has an implied uniqueness constraint spanning it, since for each state of the conceptual database, each fact instance is unique. Unary predicates have just one role, so only one kind of uniqueness constraint can be applied to it. This is why the uniqueness constraint symbol for a unary is implied (and hence may be omitted). However, a binary or longer predicate has more than one role, so there is more than one kind of uniqueness constraint pattern that could apply to the predicate. Hence, for such predicates, the uniqueness constraints need to be stated explicitly.

For *binary* predicates, the most common case has a uniqueness constraint over just one role, as in Figure 4.6. This indicates that *each entry in that role's fact column must be unique.* Duplicate entries are allowed in the other column. Here the politicians of interest are identified by their surname, and countries are identified by their two-letter ISO codes (e.g., 'AU' denotes Australia). For simplicity, we ignore cases where different politicians have the same surname (e.g., 'Bush'). In the sample fact table, each value in the politician column occurs only once, but the 'US' value in the country column is repeated. The constraint indicates that for all possible populations, the values in

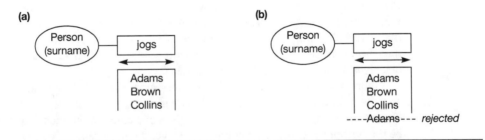

Figure 4.4 The uniqueness constraint ensures entries are unique (no duplicates).

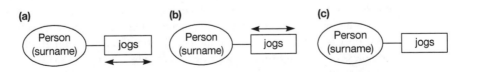

Figure 4.5 Uniqueness constraint: (a) shown below unary predicate; (b) above unary predicate; and (c) if omitted, it is implied.

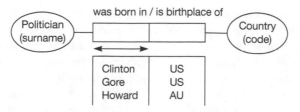

each Politician was born in **at most one** Country

Figure 4.6 Uniqueness constraint on first role: entries for that column must be unique.

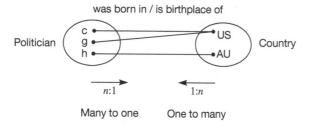

Figure 4.7 The forward predicate is n:1; the inverse predicate is 1:n.

the politician column are unique. Since each politician is referenced at most once in that column, he or she is associated with at most one country in this fact type. In other words, **each** Politician was born in **at most one** Country. This is how the constraint is formally verbalized. If desired, the absence of a uniqueness constraint on the other role may be expressed explicitly by the default verbalization: **it is possible that the same** Country is birthplace of **more than one** Politician.

Figure 4.7 is an instance diagram for the same example. Here entities are depicted as dots inside the entity types, and fact instances are shown as connecting lines. Clearly, many politicians may be born in the same country, but many countries may not be the birthplace of the same politician. Hence, the predicate "... was born in ..." is said to be *many to one* (n:1). The inverse predicate "... is birthplace of ..." is *one to many* (1:n).

Instance diagrams like Figure 4.7 are often used in logic or mathematics to discuss the theory of relations. Although instance diagrams and fact tables are useful for understanding and validating constraints, they are not part of the schema itself, which is concerned only with the structure, not the population. On a conceptual schema diagram, a uniqueness constraint over a single role is shown by placing it next to the role (on either side), as shown in Figure 4.8.

ORM's role-based notation facilitates validation with sample populations, since each role corresponds to a column in the associated fact table. The uniqueness

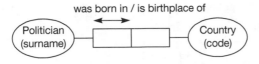

Figure 4.8 Each person was born in at most one country.

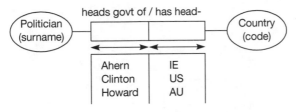

Figure 4.9 Entries in each column must be unique.

constraint on the first role means its entries must be unique. The absence of a uniqueness constraint on the second role indicates that its entries may be duplicated. Although this notation is easy to understand, and schema diagrams reveal how things are connected, the domain expert assisting you in the modeling task should not be required to master the diagram notation. To validate a constraint, it is more important to use verbalization and sample populations.

For a binary fact type, three rows are enough for a *significant population,* so long as you pick the data carefully. If a column can have duplicates, give it two values that are the same and one different. If a column is unique, make each value the same. If you look back at Figure 4.6, you'll see that its population is significant. Using a good ORM tool, you can enter sample populations like this and have them printed out along with automatic verbalizations of the constraints for the domain expert to validate.

Now consider the example shown in Figure 4.9, which concerns heads of government (e.g., presidents or prime ministers). At any point in time, a politician can head the government of at most one country, and each country can have at most one head of government. Hence the entries in the politician column must be unique, and the entries in the country column must be unique also. To indicate this, uniqueness constraints are added above each of these columns. These constraints may be verbalized as shown. The conceptual schema diagram for this fact type can be obtained by removing the fact table.

Note the use of the *hyphen* in the inverse predicate. This binds the word with the hyphen to the object type when the constraint is verbalized. So the right-hand uniqueness constraint is verbalized as "**each** Country has **at most one** head Politician", not "**each** Country

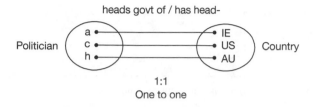

Figure 4.10 A one-to-one relation.

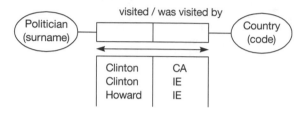

Figure 4.11 A politician may visit many countries and vice versa.

has head **at most one** Politician". Microsoft's ORM tool interprets hyphens this way when it automatically generates the constraint verbalization.

If you don't include an inverse reading, the right-hand uniqueness constraint verbalizes as "**at most one** Politician heads govt of **each** Country". Usually, a constraint on a role verbalizes better if you include a predicate reading that starts at that role. I generally recommend that you include both predicate readings for binaries, but this is especially advisable if each role has a constraint that applies just to it.

For any state of the database, any one politician can be recorded as government head of only one country and vice versa. Hence each population of this fact type is said to be a *one-to-one* (or 1:1) relation. The instance diagram of Figure 4.10 best illustrates the idea.

Now consider the populated binary fact type shown in Figure 4.11. First note that no whole row of the fact table is repeated. This must be the case, since each row corresponds to an elementary fact, and we have agreed not to repeat facts in our database.

Although each row is unique, we cannot say the same for each politician. For example, "Clinton" appears twice in the first column. Nor is the country unique. For example, "IE" (Ireland) occurs twice in the second column. For this fact type then, the only uniqueness constraint that applies to every one of its possible populations is that the *combination* of politician and country is unique. This uniqueness constraint is depicted by an arrow-tipped bar that spans both columns of the fact table. The constraint verbalizes as shown.

The sample data shows that a politician may visit many (i.e., at least two) countries, and a country may be visited by many politicians. The fact population is an example of a *many-to-many* (or *m:n*) relation. Figure 4.12 shows the instance diagram.

Simple 1:1 reference schemes are usually abbreviated by placing the name of the reference mode in parentheses. However, we may set them out fully as shown in Figure 4.13. This diagram is still incomplete; the next chapter shows how to add the constraint that each country has a country code. Here we have a *reference type* rather than a fact type. If there is only one means of referring to an entity type, the uniqueness constraints on the reference type are the responsibility of the user to enforce rather than the system. For example, we must ensure that there really is only one country with the code 'US'. If two 1:1 naming conventions are used (e.g., code or name), we choose one for our primary reference type for identification and treat the other like any other fact type.

The four possible patterns of uniqueness constraints for a binary predicate are many to many, many to one, one to many, and one to one. Each of our examples so far has involved a heterogeneous predicate (different object types). Let's look now at some ring predicates (both roles played by same object type). To clarify the different roles being played, inverse predicate names are included. Our first example concerns parenthood (see Figure 4.14). For simplicity, assume that we can identify people by their first names.

As the sample fact table in Figure 4.14 reveals, a person may have many children. Moreover, a person may have many parents. The column entries need not be unique, but the whole row must be. So the uniqueness constraint spans the whole row. Contrast this with motherhood (see Figure 4.15). Although a mother may have many children, each person has only one mother. So we mark the constraint as shown. Entries in the second column of the fact table must be unique to that column (not necessarily unique to the table; e.g., after she becomes an adult, Mary also becomes a mother).

The next example shown in Figure 4.16 is consistent with monogamy: at any time each man has at most one wife, and each woman has at most one husband. So entries in

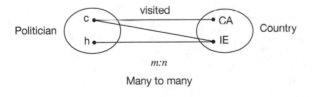

Politician   visited   CA   Country

c

h   IE

m:n

Many to many

Figure 4.12 A many-to-many relation.

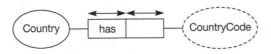

Country — has — (CountryCode)

Figure 4.13 A simple 1:1 naming convention shown explicitly.

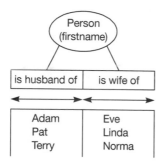

Figure 4.14 Parenthood is many to many.

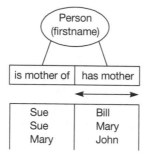

Figure 4.15 Each person has only one mother.

Figure 4.16 Monogamy is one to one.

each column must be unique. As an exercise, draw a knowledge base for the following marriage conventions: polyandry (a woman may have many husbands but not vice versa); polygyny (a man may have many wives but not vice versa); and polygamy (a man may have many wives, and a woman may have many husbands).

Uniqueness constraints are best understood in the context of a populated schema diagram, as discussed in this section. With this understanding, for any given fact type *each role is associated with a corresponding column of the fact table.*

In terms of logical predicates, the role boxes are the "object holes". For a set of relationship instances of this type, the holes expand to columns. Marking a *single role with a uniqueness bar* means that entries in the associated column must be unique to that column (i.e., *no duplicates are allowed in that column*).

A uniqueness bar that spans the whole predicate means that each whole row is unique to the table. Since we never allow whole rows to be repeated, this whole row constraint applies to any fact type that we consider. If we have a stronger uniqueness constraint, then the whole row constraint is implied by this and hence is redundant. For this reason, we never mark the whole row constraint across a fact type unless that is the only uniqueness constraint that applies.

With this understanding, we must choose exactly one of the four constraint patterns shown in Figure 4.17 for any binary predicate. For brevity, *a* and *b* denote object variables, and "*a R*'s *b*" means "*a* bears the relation *R* to *b*".

Provided a significant example is supplied, the uniqueness constraints on a predicate can be determined simply by looking for duplicates in its fact table. If we are not familiar with the application, we may be unsure as to whether the population is significant. Consider, for example, the output report of Table 4.1.

Suppose this is a sample output report for a conference management system. One task involves getting qualified people to referee (assess the suitability of) papers submitted by people who hope to present a paper at the conference. Let us agree that the information in the table may be modeled using the fact type Person(name) referees

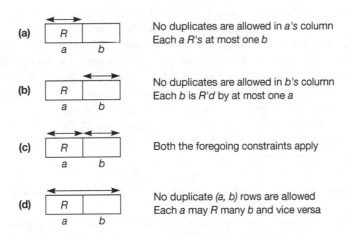

Figure 4.17 The four uniqueness constraint patterns for a binary.

Table 4.1 An output report of doubtful significance.

Referee	Paper Nr
Jones E	1
Smith JB	2

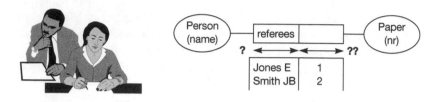

Figure 4.18 Is the population significant?

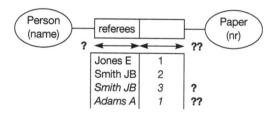

Figure 4.19 Adding counterexamples to test the constraints.

Paper(nr). Which of the four binary uniqueness constraint patterns should be specified for this fact type? If the population of Table 4.1 is significant, then we have a 1:1 situation, and constraints should be marked on each role, as shown in Figure 4.18.

This means that each person referees at most one paper (good news for the referees), and each paper is refereed by at most one person (bad news for the people submitting the papers). While this arrangement is possible, we would probably doubt whether this constraint pattern is really intended. To resolve our doubts, we should *question each constraint in English, backed up by counterexamples.* Consider the uniqueness constraint on the first column. Its positive verbalization is **each** Person referees **at most one** Paper. Its equivalent, negative verbalization is **it is impossible that the same** Person referees **more than one** Paper. To test this constraint, we ask, "Is it possible for a person to referee more than one paper? For instance, could Smith referee papers 2 and 3?" This counterexample appears as the second and third rows of the expanded fact table in Figure 4.19.

To test the uniqueness constraint on the second column, ask, "Is it possible for a paper to have more than one referee? For instance, could paper 1 be refereed by Jones and

Adams?" This counterexample appears as the first and fourth rows of the expanded fact table in Figure 4.19. If the domain expert replies "yes" to both these tests, the fact type is many to many, and we modify the constraint as shown in Figure 4.20.

If desired, a more compact population may be provided for the *m:n* case, by using the tuple ('Smith JB', 1) instead of the last two rows. This tests both constraints at once. For testing purposes, however, it's normally better to test just one constraint at a time, as discussed. If just one of the two test cases were accepted, the final constraint pattern would be *n*:1 or 1:*n*. If both test cases were rejected, we would stay with the 1:1 pattern.

Remember that all constraints on fact types are to be interpreted as applying to what is recorded in the database, not necessarily to the real world. An information system can only enforce constraints on its formal model of the application. The constraint schema for the "real world" need not be the same as for the "recorded world". For example, suppose the application model includes the schema of Figure 4.21(a). The uniqueness constraints assert that for any particular state of the database, each patient is recorded as having at most one gender and at most one phone. Now it may be the case in the real world that some patients have more than one phone (e.g., a home phone and a business phone), as shown in the "real-world schema" of Figure 4.21(b).

For some reason, the designer of the information system has decided that no patient will be recorded to have more than one phone. So the constraints in the first schema (Figure 4.21(a)) fit the intended model that is to be implemented in the information system. Unless otherwise indicated, *when we speak of a conceptual schema, we mean the recorded-world schema* of the application model.

Nevertheless, we often use our background knowledge of the "real-world schema" when designing the conceptual schema. In any case, *the uniqueness constraints should be at least as strong as those that apply in the real world.* For the case being discussed we know that in the real world each person has at most one gender. So we should

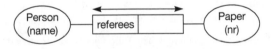

Figure 4.20 If the test examples are accepted, the predicate is many to many.

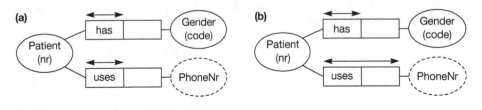

Figure 4.21 A uniqueness constraint in the application model (a) may be stronger than in the real world (b).

enforce this in our schema. With the phone fact type, we need to consciously decide whether a stronger constraint than the real-world constraint is required.

Exercise 4.2

1. For a given fact type, a sample population is significant with respect to uniqueness constraints if all the relevant uniqueness constraints can be deduced from the sample. A template is shown for a binary fact type. The names of the predicate and the reference modes are omitted for simplicity. For each of the fact tables shown, add the uniqueness constraints to the template assuming the population provided is significant.

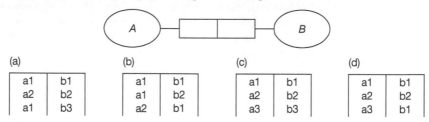

(a)			(b)			(c)			(d)	
a1	b1		a1	b1		a1	b1		a1	b1
a2	b2		a1	b2		a2	b2		a2	b2
a1	b3		a2	b1		a3	b3		a3	b1

2. In a given department, employees are identified by employee numbers "e1", "e2", and so on, and projects are identified by project numbers "p1", "p2", and so on. Draw a schema diagram for the fact type Employee works on Project, and provide populations that are significant with respect to the following constraint patterns:

   (a) 1:many   (b) many:1   (c) many:many   (d) 1:1

3. Add the relevant uniqueness constraints to the conceptual schema diagrams for the exercise questions listed below. For some of these questions, the output report provided in the question might not be significant with respect to uniqueness constraints. Using common sense, you should be able to avoid adding uniqueness constraints that are likely to be violated by a larger population.

   (a) Exercise 3.4, Question 1b   (b) Exercise 3.4, Question 1d   (c) Exercise 3.4, Question 2
   (d) Exercise 3.4, Question 5   (e) Exercise 3.5, Question 2   (f) Exercise 3.5, Question 3

4. By now you must be feeling like a challenge. The following report is an extract from an actual computer science department handbook. Verbalize this report in terms of *binaries,* draw the fact types, and add uniqueness constraints.

   The first column, headed "Subject title", actually lists the codes and titles of postgraduate topics (don't expect all the names in real-life examples to be well chosen!). A topic is not the same kind of thing as a subject. A postgraduate student first enrolls in a subject (identified by subject code, e.g., CS451), then later chooses a topic to study for this subject. Subject enrollments are not part of this question. A topic may be offered in semester 1 only, in semester 2 only, or over the whole year (at half the pace).

   The fact that different students might be enrolled in the same subject (as identified by subject code) and yet be studying different topics is a source of possible confusion. As information modelers, one of the most significant contributions we can make is to suggest improvements to the UoD itself. In this example, we might argue it would simplify things if topics were treated as subjects. The department involved eventually accepted this change. For this exercise, however, you are to model things as they were.

Postgraduate coursework topics in computer science.

Subject title	Staff	When	Prerequisites
AIT: Advanced Information Technology	MEO, PNC, TAH	1st sem	CS315
CLVS: Computational Logic and Verification Systems	JS, PJR	Year	CS260 preferred
DBMS: Advanced topics in Database Management	MEO, PNC, RC, TAH	2nd	CS315
FP: Functional Programming	EJS, PAB	Year	CS225 CS220 preferred
GA: Geometric Algorithms	PDE	1st	CS340

N.B. Topics are offered subject to the availability of staff and to there being sufficient demand for a topic. In each case the first-mentioned member of staff is lecturer-in-charge of the subject. Preferred prerequisites may become mandatory in later years.

4.3   Uniqueness Constraints on Longer Fact Types

This section shows how to specify uniqueness constraints on fact types of arity 3 and beyond, including nested versions. Let's begin with an example. Figure 4.22 shows a populated ternary fact type of the form Person scored Rating for Subject. For simplicity, assume that persons are identified just by their surname. Even if we are not familiar with the example, sample populations supplied by the domain expert can reveal that certain constraints don't apply.

Looking at the fact table, first consider each column individually. Each column has at least one value that is repeated. So no column by itself has a uniqueness constraint. As shown later, this must be true of any ternary fact type that is elementary.

Now let's look at pairs of columns. For ease of reference here, the columns are numbered 1, 2, 3 in the order shown in the diagram. Beginning with columns 1 and 2, note that the pair (Adams, 7) is repeated. With columns 1 and 3, each pair is unique. That is, each (Person, Subject) combination occurs on only one row of the table. With columns 2 and 3, the pair (7, PD102) is repeated.

There are only three ways to pair columns in a ternary. So if the population of the fact table is significant, the only pair-unique constraint is that each (Person, Subject) pair must be unique to the table. If we are familiar with the application, we can usually decide whether the population is significant in this regard simply by using common sense. With the present example, this constraint means that for each (Person, Subject) combination, at most one rating may be obtained. This agrees with our background knowledge about the UoD, and so the uniqueness constraint suggested by the table is accepted.

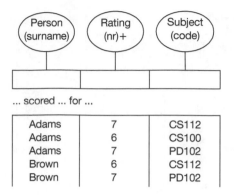

... scored ... for ...

Adams	7	CS112
Adams	6	CS100
Adams	7	PD102
Brown	6	CS112
Brown	7	PD102

Figure 4.22 What are the uniqueness constraints?

Sample fact tables may be obtained from output reports (which often represent a combination of separate fact tables) or from simple factual knowledge about the UoD. Unless the population is large or well chosen, it is unlikely to be completely significant with respect to all uniqueness constraints. For instance, suppose row 3 were deleted from the table in Figure 4.22. For the smaller sample, both the column 1-2 pair and the column 2-3 pair would then show no duplicates. The table would then suggest a uniqueness constraint for all three column pairs. Apart from *insufficient data,* a population may fail to be significant because of *bad data* (i.e., some incorrect values have mistakenly been entered as data in the example).

So we need to be wary of relying on just a sample fact table to determine uniqueness constraints. We should *ask whether any suggested constraint really makes sense.* A uniqueness constraint spanning columns 1 and 2 would mean that a (Person, Rating) combination could occur for at most one subject. This would forbid somebody obtaining the same rating for two subjects—an unrealistic restriction! Similarly, the suggested constraint on the column 2-3 pair must be rejected as unrealistic (it would prevent two people from scoring the same rating for a particular subject).

Uniqueness constraints may often be determined simply by background knowledge about how the UoD works. As seen in the previous section, real-world uniqueness constraints usually determine the weakest uniqueness constraints that may be considered for the actual database. If we know the fact table is significant, then we can always generate the constraints from it.

Usually, however, we won't know in advance that the table is significant, and we will have to use some of our background knowledge. If we lack such knowledge, we should consult the domain expert about any doubtful constraints, posing the relevant questions while adding concrete examples of facts to violate the constraints and asking whether such updates may be accepted.

With a ternary fact type, the constraint spanning all three columns is always implied, since no whole row may be repeated. This constraint should be specified if and only if no other uniqueness constraint holds.

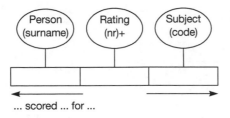

... scored ... for ...

Figure 4.23 Each (Person, Subject) combination is unique.

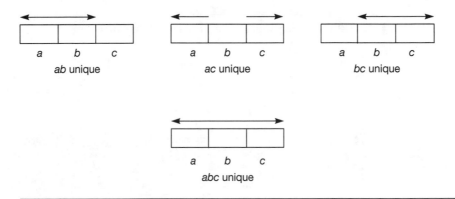

Figure 4.24 Allowed basic uniqueness constraints for a ternary.

For our current example then, we mark just the constraint for the column 1-3 pair, indicating that each (Person, Subject) pair is assigned at most one rating. Since the two role boxes involved are not adjacent, a *divided constraint bar* is used as shown in Figure 4.23. Notice that this time we *must include the arrowheads*. If we omitted them, we would interpret the bars as two separate constraints, one for each of the two columns. To avoid confusion, always include arrow tips on uniqueness constraints for any fact type longer than a binary. If we had reordered the fact type instead as Person for Subject scored Rating, there would be two contiguous roles spanned by an undivided constraint bar.

The term n-*role constraint* denotes a constraint that spans *n* roles. A uniqueness constraint that spans just one role is a **simple** uniqueness constraint. The constraint in Figure 4.23 is a two-role constraint since it spans two of the three roles involved in the fact type. A binary fact type has three basic constraints (two one-role and one two-role) that give rise to four possible cases. A later section demonstrates that *no (elementary) ternary fact type can have a simple uniqueness constraint.* So a ternary fact type has four basic uniqueness constraints to be considered: three two-role constraints and one three-role constraint, as shown in Figure 4.24.

In practice, ternaries usually have just a single uniqueness constraint either over one role pair or over all three roles. As an example of the latter, the politician travel

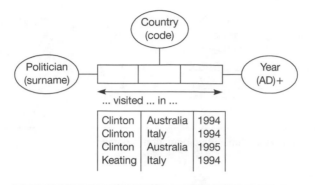

Figure 4.25 A ternary with a spanning uniqueness constraint.

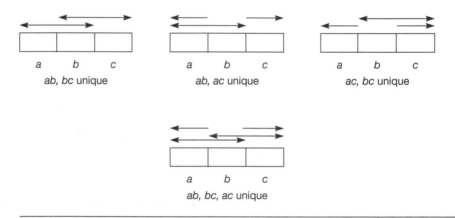

Figure 4.26 Allowed uniqueness constraint combinations for a ternary.

example from Chapter 3 is modeled in Figure 4.25. Here many politicians may visit many countries in many years. Such a fact type is said to be "many to many to many". Since no whole row can be repeated, we cannot use this fact type to record multiple visits to the same country by the same politician in the same year. If you want to record this, you should use a different model (e.g., replace Year by Date or add Quantity).

With a ternary fact type, we should systematically test each of the three two-role constraints to see which ones hold. Only if none of these hold should the three-role constraint be specified. As an exercise, check for yourself that the sample data is significant for this constraint.

For a ternary association, there is only one way to have a three-role uniqueness constraint. There are three ways of having precisely one two-role constraint and three ways of having exactly two two-role constraints. Finally there is one way of having three two-role constraints. Thus there are eight different uniqueness constraint patterns that may arise with a ternary fact type. Four of these involve just one constraint (Figure 4.24) and four involve combinations (see Figure 4.26).

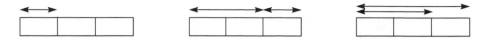

Figure 4.27 Some illegal constraint patterns.

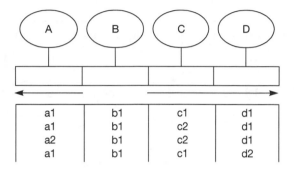

Figure 4.28 Each *acd* combination occurs on at most one row.

All other constraint patterns for a ternary are illegal (i.e., disallowed). Some examples of these are shown in Figure 4.27. The first two of these are fundamentally wrong, since a ternary fact type with a simple uniqueness constraint cannot be elementary. The third example is wrong because the three-role constraint is implied by the two-role constraint and hence should not be displayed.

This general approach for specifying uniqueness constraints applies to fact types of any arity. Figure 4.28 shows a template for a quaternary predicate with a uniqueness constraint spanning roles 1, 3, and 4. This indicates that each *acd* combination must be unique to the fact table, where *a, c,* and *d* occur in the first, third, and fourth columns on the same row of this table. A small but significant population of the fact table is shown. Verify for yourself that this is consistent with the indicated uniqueness constraint.

We will show later that any uniqueness constraints on a quaternary must span at least three roles. As an exercise, you might like to explore all the possible cases. Or maybe not! Since elementary fact types are rarely longer than quaternaries, no examples are discussed here.

To visualize the connection between roles and columns of the fact table, think of the role boxes as the holes in which the objects get placed to complete the fact. No matter what the arity of the fact type, a uniqueness constraint across a combination of role boxes means that any instance of that column combination that does appear in the table must occur on one row only, and hence can be used to identify that row.

Since a role combination governed by a uniqueness constraint thus provides a "key to unlock" any row of the fact table, this combination is sometimes referred to as a *key* for that table. This notion will be elaborated later in the context of the (often nonelementary) tables used in relational databases.

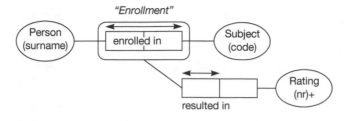

Figure 4.29   The enrollment association is objectified as a nested object type.

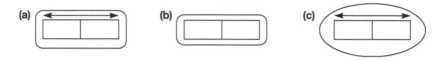

Figure 4.30   Alternative notations for nesting: (a) is preferred.

Now let's consider *nesting.* In Figure 4.23 the subject ratings example was set out in flattened form. Suppose that instead we use a nested approach as shown in Figure 4.29. Here each (Person, Subject) enrollment is treated as an object that may result in a rating. For example, the enrollment of Adams in CS112 results in a 7.

Figure 4.23 is not actually equivalent to Figure 4.29 unless a further constraint is added that a rating must be known for each enrollment (see the next chapter). However, at this stage our discussion focuses only on how to specify the uniqueness constraints.

The Enrollment entity type in Figure 4.29 may be referred to as an objectified association, an objectified relationship type, an objectified predicate, a nested entity type, or a nested object type. We will show later that if all conceptual fact types are elementary, then *each nested object type must be spanned by a uniqueness constraint* (as shown in Figure 4.29). This spanning uniqueness constraint indicates that each person may enroll in many subjects, and the same subject may be enrolled in by many people. The simple uniqueness constraint on the scored predicate indicates that each (Person, Subject) enrollment resulted in at most one rating.

If no uniqueness constraint is included on an objectified association, a spanning uniqueness constraint is assumed. To avoid any misunderstanding, however, it is best to explicitly include the uniqueness constraint. An ellipse may be used instead of a frame: in this case the uniqueness constraint must be explicitly marked. Figure 4.30 shows the three notations for nesting.

I recommend the first notation (a) since it highlights the uniqueness constraint and is more compact than the ellipse notation. Notation (a) is also the best choice if the ORM version allows nested objects without a spanning uniqueness constraint. Section 10.4 discusses such a case (nesting a 1:1 marriage association); however, such cases violate elementarity and are rarely encountered in this book.

Exercise 4.3

1. A template for a ternary fact type is shown. For each of the fact tables provided, add the uniqueness constraints, assuming that the population is significant in this regard.

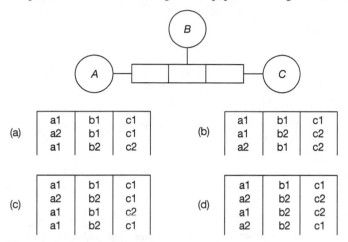

(a)	a1	b1	c1
	a2	b1	c1
	a1	b2	c2

(b)	a1	b1	c1
	a1	b2	c2
	a2	b1	c2

(c)	a1	b1	c1
	a2	b2	c1
	a1	b1	c2
	a1	b2	c1

(d)	a1	b1	c1
	a2	b2	c2
	a1	b2	c2
	a2	b2	c1

2. Verbalize and then schematize the following report, marking uniqueness constraints.

Department	Staff category	Number
CS	Professor	3
CS	Senior lecturer	6
CS	Lecturer	10
EE	Professor	3
EE	Senior lecturer	7
EE	Lecturer	7

3.

Year	Branch	Profit ($)	Total profit ($)
1987	New York	100,000	150,000
	Paris	50,000	
1988	New York	150,000	250,000
	Paris	100,000	

(a) Verbalize this report making no use of nesting, then schematize it, marking uniqueness constraints.

(b) As for (a) but instead use a nested approach.

4.4 External Uniqueness Constraints

The uniqueness constraints discussed so far are called *internal* (intrapredicate) uniqueness constraints, since each applies to one or more roles inside a single predicate. This section discusses **external** (interpredicate) **uniqueness constraints.** These *apply*

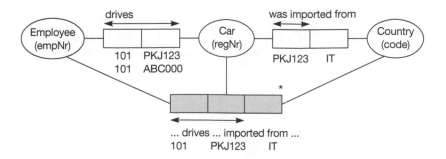

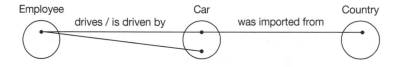

* **define** Employee drives Car imported from Country **as**
Employee drives Car **that** was imported from Country

Figure 4.31 A compound ternary derived from a conceptual (inner) join of the binaries.

Figure 4.32 An instance diagram for the model shown in Figure 4.31.

to roles from different predicates. To help understand these constraints, and in preparation for our later discussion of queries, the *conceptual join* operation is first discussed.

Consider the schema and sample population shown in Figure 4.31. The left-hand binary fact table indicates that employee 101 drives two cars, with registration numbers PKJ123 and ABC000. The right-hand binary fact table tells us that the car PKJ123 is imported from Italy. The ternary fact table indicates that employee 101 drives the car PKJ123 imported from Italy. As the definition reveals, this ternary is derived by combining the binaries, with Car as the connecting or join object type.

The defining expression "Employee drives Car **that** was imported from Country" is a formal verbalization of the conceptual path from Employee, through the drives predicate, Car type, and import predicate, to Country. The key word "**that**" declares that the driven car must be *the same* as the imported car. In other words, if an employee drives a car, to continue the path to Country we must use the very same car.

The instance diagram in Figure 4.32 may help clarify the situation. The three binary facts are shown as lines connecting two dots. The ternary fact instance corresponds to the continuous path from Employee to Country. Starting at the Car object type, this continuous path may also be verbalized as the conjunction Car is driven by Employee **and** was imported from Country.

A fact type resulting from a join is a *compound fact type,* not an elementary fact type, since it is essentially the conjunction of two or more simpler fact types. For this reason, *join fact types are normally forbidden on ORM schema diagrams.* If included for discussion purposes, they may be *shaded* as shown to indicate they are just views. Unlike elementary derived fact types, their compound nature can lead to redundancy unless each join role is covered by a simple uniqueness constraint. For example, if we add the row (102, PKJ123) to the drives table in Figure 4.31, this causes the row (102, PKJ123, IT) to be added to the ternary. The fact that car PKJ123 is imported from Italy is now contained twice in the ternary. Although join fact types are never used as base fact types, join paths are often involved in constraints and queries, as we'll discuss later.

In an ORM schema, to navigate from one predicate to another, we must pass through an object type, performing a *conceptual join* (or *object join*) on that object type. By default, the join condition is that the object instance remains the same as we pass through. This is called a *conceptual inner join.* This is similar to a relational natural inner join (see Chapter 11), except that conceptual joins require the conceptual objects to be the same, instead of simply matching attribute names and values. ORM object types are conceptual domains, not attributes. Conceptual joins still apply if we declare different rolenames (cf. attribute names) for the join roles.

In terms of the fact tables, however, the column value of the role entering the join object type must equal the column value of the role that exits the object type. Figure 4.33 depicts two predicates, *R* and *S,* sharing a common object type, *B.* From a fact table perspective, the conceptual inner join of *R* and *S* is obtained by pairing rows of *R* with rows of *S* where the *B* column values match, and arranging for the final *B* column to appear just once in the result. The dotted lines show how the rows are paired together. For example, row (a1, b1) is paired with rows (b1, c1) and (b1, c3) to give rows (a1, b1, c1) and (a1, b1, c3).

The final result of this join operation is shown in Figure 4.34. Notice that the final *B* column is the intersection of the original *B* columns. The natural inner join of any two tables *R* and *S* is denoted by "*R* ⋈ *S*" or "*R* natural join *S*". The word "inner" is often omitted and is assumed by default.

Other kinds of joins are sometimes discussed (e.g., joins based on operators other than equality, and outer joins). A left (right, full) *outer join* is obtained by adding to the

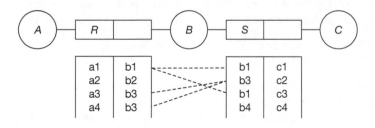

Figure 4.33 Joining on *B* requires the values in the two *B* columns to match.

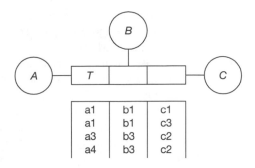

Figure 4.34 Table resulting from the natural inner join of the tables in Figure 4.33.

Table 4.2 An output report about high school students.

StudentNr	Name	Class
001	Adams J	11A
002	Brown C	12B
003	Brown C	11A

inner join those rows, if any, where the join column value occurs in just the left (just the right, just one) of the tables, and padding the missing entries of such rows with null values. For example, the left outer join of the binary fact tables in Figure 4.31 adds the row (101, ABC000, ?), where "?" denotes a null value.

As another example, the full outer join of the tables in Figure 4.33 includes the rows (a2, b2, ?) and (?, b4, c4). Since base fact types in ORM are elementary, their fact tables cannot have null values. So outer joins have little relevance to conceptual modeling, and we will ignore them for now. However, as discussed later, outer joins are often used in queries at both conceptual and relational levels.

With this background, let's consider an example with an external uniqueness constraint. An output report concerning high school students is shown in Table 4.2. As an exercise, perform step 1 for the top row of this report before reading on.

The information for row 1 may be verbalized as two elementary facts:

The Student with studentNr '001' has the StudentName 'Adams J'.
The Student with studentNr '001' is in the Class with code '11A'.

The first fact is a relationship between an entity and a value. The second fact is a relationship between two entities. In this UoD, students are identified by their student numbers. As rows 2 and 3 show, it is possible for two different students to have the same student name ("Brown C"). A populated schema diagram is shown in Figure 4.35.

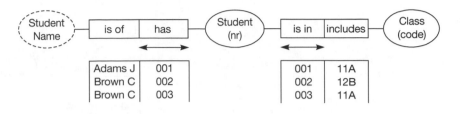

Figure 4.35 A populated schema for Table 4.2 (draft version).

Table 4.3 Uniqueness constraints added to original table.

StudentNr	Name	Class
001	Adams J	11A
002	Brown C	12B
003	Brown C	11A

Let us agree that the population supplied is significant. It follows that each student has at most one name, and each student is in at most one class. These uniqueness constraints have been captured on the schema diagram. However, there is another uniqueness constraint that is missing. What is it?

The output report is reproduced in Table 4.3, with uniqueness constraints marked above the relevant columns. Notice that the combination of name and class is unique. Let's suppose that this is significant. Although a student's name need not be unique in the high school, it is unique in the student's class. While there are two students named "Brown C", there can be only one student with this name in class 12B, and only one student with this name in class 11A. In the rare case where another student named "Brown C" joined one of these classes, at least one of the names would be modified to keep them distinct within that class. For instance, we could add extra initials or numbers (e.g., "Brown CT", "Brown C2").

Each row of the output report splits into two elementary facts, one for the name and one for the class. So to specify the name-class uniqueness constraint on the schema diagram we need to involve two fact types. The relevant role boxes to which the constraint applies are joined by dotted lines to a *circled "u"* symbol "ⓤ" as shown in Figure 4.36. The "u" stands for "unique". Because this constraint involves roles from different predicates, it is called an *external constraint* or interpredicate constraint. A uniqueness constraint on a single predicate is an *internal* or intrapredicate constraint.

In this example, the external uniqueness constraint indicates that for each student the *combination* of student name and class is unique. Given any student name and class code from the tables, there is *at most one* student who is paired with both. For instance, given 'Adams J' and '11A' there is only one studentNr sharing rows with both ('001'). Given 'Adams J' and '12B' there is no studentNr paired with both.

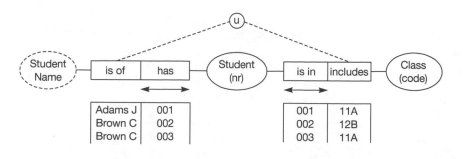

Figure 4.36 An external uniqueness constraint has been added.

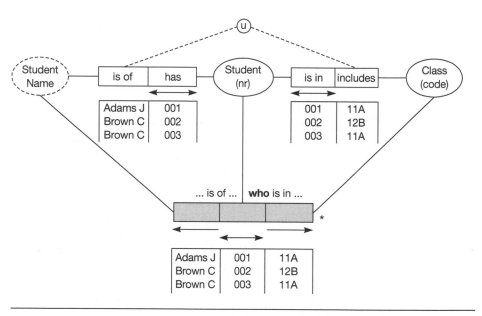

Figure 4.37 Equivalent constraints on derived, join fact type (illegal in base model).

Perhaps the easiest way to understand this constraint is to say that if we perform the conceptual (inner) *join* operation on the two fact tables, then the resulting table has a uniqueness constraint across the (name, class) column pair. Note that when we join the two fact tables, we obtain the table in the original report (Table 4.3).

The external uniqueness constraint is equivalent to an internal uniqueness constraint on the first and last roles of the derived, ternary fact type formed from the join path StudentName is of Student **who** is in Class. (See Figure 4.37.) Reading in the other direction, the path may be verbalized as Class includes Student **who** has StudentName. Because the object type Student is personal, it is better to use the personal pronoun "who" instead of "that".

(a)   (b)

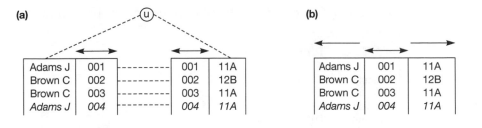

Adams J	001
Brown C	002
Brown C	003
Adams J	*004*

001	11A
002	12B
003	11A
004	*11A*

Adams J	001	11A
Brown C	002	12B
Brown C	003	11A
Adams J	*004*	*11A*

Figure 4.38 This update would violate the external uniqueness constraint.

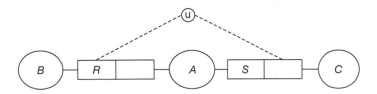

Each *b, c* combination is paired with at most one *a*

Each population of *R* **join** *S* has *bc* unique
(where "join" denotes "conceptual inner join")

Figure 4.39 External uniqueness constraint.

Notice that the middle role of the join fact type has a simple uniqueness constraint. This is equivalent to the two simple uniqueness constraints on the binaries. Although join fact types may be included on a schema diagram for discussion purposes, they are illegal in the base ORM model because they are compound, not elementary, fact types. As discussed shortly, the presence of a simple uniqueness constraint on a ternary disqualifies it from being elementary. So don't feel that it's OK to do this in your normal model.

Suppose we added the following facts to the current populations: Student '004' has StudentName 'Adams J'; Student '004' is in Class '11A'. If this update were accepted, the new populations would be shown in Figure 4.38(a). To test your understanding, explain why this would violate the external uniqueness constraint before reading on.

The extra row added to each table provides a counterexample to the constraint, since for 'Adams J' and '11A' there are two studentNr entries paired with these entries (001 and 004). This breaks the rule that student names within a given class are unique to that class. In class 11A, two students (001, 004) have the same name ('Adams J'). If we join the tables on studentNr (the dotted lines indicate the matches for the join), we obtain the ternary table shown in Figure 4.38(b), which clearly violates the equivalent compound uniqueness constraint over the StudentName and Class columns.

The general case is summarized in Figure 4.39, where *A, B,* and *C* are any object types, and *R* and *S* are predicates. External uniqueness constraints may apply to roles

Table 4.4 Student rankings within subjects (no ties allowed).

Person	Subject	Position
Adams J	CS114	3
Adams J	CS100	10
Adams J	PD102	3
Brown C	CS114	10
Brown C	PD102	5

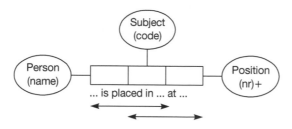

Figure 4.40 A schema for Table 4.4.

from reference types, not just fact types. This is the basis for composite reference schemes, as discussed in Section 5.4.

As a more complex case, consider a UoD in which persons enroll in subjects but are given subject positions (i.e., first, second, third, etc.) rather than subject ratings. Each person achieves at most one position in any given subject. Moreover, no ties may occur (i.e., for each position in a subject there is only one student). A sample output report for this UoD is shown in Table 4.4.

Performing step 1 on the first row, we might express the information as the ternary: Person (name) 'Adams J' is placed in Subject (code) 'CS114' at Position (nr) 3. This leads to the schema of Figure 4.40. Notice the overlapping uniqueness constraints. Check these with the population and make sure you understand them.

Now suppose we adopt a nested approach instead. For example, we might express the information on row 1 as follows: Person (name) 'Adams J' enrolled in Subject (code) 'CS114'; this Enrollment achieved Position (nr) 3. This leads to the nested version shown in Figure 4.41. Actually, for this to be equivalent to the ternary, the role played by the objectified association must be mandatory (see the next chapter).

The Enrollment predicate is many:many. With this in mind, the simple uniqueness constraint on the achievement predicate captures the uniqueness constraint spanning the first two roles in the flat (unnested) version (Figure 4.40). The external uniqueness constraint corresponds to the constraint spanning the last two roles in the flattened version—each (Subject, Position) combination is unique. In other words, if we *flatten* the nested version into a ternary, then any (Subject, Position) pair occurs on at most one row of the ternary table. To help understand this, I suggest you add the fact tables

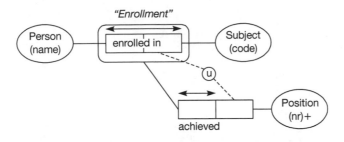

Figure 4.41 Another schema for Table 4.4 (nested version).

Table 4.5 Students are assigned ratings and positions.

Person	Subject	Rating	Position
Adams J	CS114	7	3
Adams J	CS100	6	10
Adams J	PD102	7	3
Brown C	CS114	6	10
Brown C	PD102	7	5

to the diagram. The fact table for the outer predicate effectively matches the output report.

External uniqueness constraints sometimes connect more than two roles. In all cases, however, the underlying predicates can involve at most one object type that doesn't play or include one of these roles. Otherwise the complete fact type under discussion is not elementary. Basically this means that when the fact tables are combined to produce a single table (by joining or flattening), there is at most one column not spanned by the uniqueness constraint. This rule is proven later in the chapter.

As you may have gathered from these examples, nesting tends to produce a more complex constraint picture. For this example, the flattened version is preferred. However, if the Position information is optional (e.g., to be added later), then the nested approach is preferred. Such modeling choices will be covered in more detail later.

Another reason for nesting is to avoid embedding the same association within more than one fact type. Suppose we have to record both a rating and a unique subject position for each student taking any given subject. A sample report for this situation is shown in Table 4.5. We might describe this UoD in terms of two ternaries, as shown in Figure 4.42. Note however that all (Person, Subject) combinations appearing in one fact table must also appear in the other. Section 6.4 shows how such a constraint may be added.

Alternatively, we may objectify the enrollment association between Person and Subject, and attach rating and position predicates to this (see Figure 4.43). The nested

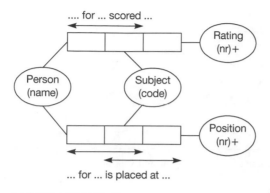

Figure 4.42 A schema for Table 4.5 (flattened version).

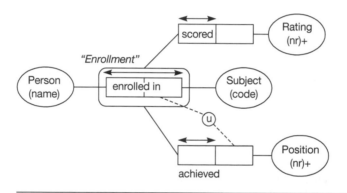

Figure 4.43 Another schema for Table 4.5 (nested version).

approach corresponds to reading the information on row 1 of the table as: Person 'Adams J' enrolled in Subject 'CS114'; this Enrollment scored Rating 7; this Enrollment achieved Position 3. To indicate that rating and position must be recorded, additional constraints are needed (see next chapter).

Note that if a role has a simple, internal uniqueness constraint, then it should not be included in an external uniqueness constraint. Even if a join path exists to enable an external uniqueness constraint to be declared, the external constraint would be implied by the stronger, simple uniqueness constraint, and it is generally preferable to omit implied constraints. As an exercise to illustrate this point, you may wish to modify Figure 4.36 so that student names are actually unique, then show that the external constraint is implied.

Before you start the section exercise, there's one point you should be clear about. When you examine an information sample, you are seeing it at the external level. *There are often many aspects of the presentation that may not be relevant to your application.* In a tabular output report, for example, the order of the columns or rows is not normally something that you need to model. If the information is presented in nontabular ways (e.g., diagrammatic), there are always topological and metric aspects, and possibly other aspects (e.g., color), that are represented along with basic data. Whether these additional aspects of the presentation need to be modeled is something that only you and the domain expert can decide. To fully appreciate this point, make sure you attempt at least Question 2 from the following exercise.

Exercise 4.4

1. Add the uniqueness constraints to the conceptual schema diagrams for
   (a) Exercise 3.4, Question 6   (b) Exercise 3.5, Question 4

2. Many manufactured products contain parts that may themselves be products of even smaller parts. The structure of one such product is shown.

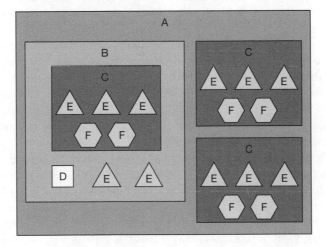

   (a) List at least three different kinds of facts that are captured in this diagram.
   (b) Assume that we are interested in modeling only containment facts. These facts may also be displayed as a labeled tree (hierarchy) as shown.

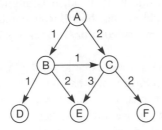

       Draw a conceptual schema diagram for this UoD, including uniqueness constraints, but make no use of nesting.
   (c) Draw an equivalent conceptual schema diagram that does make use of nesting.

3. A car dealer maintains a database on all the cars in stock. Each car is identified by the vehicle identification number (VIN) displayed on a plate attached to the car (e.g., on its

dashboard). For each car the dealer records the model (e.g., Saturn SW2), the year of manu-facture (e.g., 1998), the retail price (e.g., $17,000), and the color (e.g., dark green).

Because of space limitations the dealer will never have in stock more than one car of the same model, year, and color at the same time. The dealer also keeps figures on the number of cars of a particular model and color that are sold in any given year. For example, in 1999, five dark green Saturn SW2s were sold. Draw the conceptual schema diagram, including all uniqueness constraints.

4.5   Key Length Check

In step 1 of the CSDP we try to express information examples in terms of elementary facts. At that stage we rely on familiarity with the UoD to determine whether a fact type is simple or compound (splittable). Once uniqueness constraints have been added, a formal check can be conducted in this regard. This section discusses a check based on uniqueness constraints, and the next section discusses a projection-join check.

Until we are very experienced at conceptual schema design, we might include some fact types that are too long or too short. "Too long" means that the arity of the fact type is higher than it should be—the predicate has too many roles. In this case we must split the compound fact type into two or more simple fact types. For example, the fact type Scientist was born in Country during Year should be split into two fact types: Scientist was born in Country; Scientist was born during Year.

"Too short" means the arity of some fact types is too small, resulting in loss of infor-mation—a fact type has been split even though it was elementary. In this case, the fact types resulting from the split need to be recombined into a fact type of higher arity.

For example, suppose that scientists may lecture in many countries in the same year. It would then be wrong to split the fact type Scientist lectured in Country during Year into the fact types Scientist lectured in Country; Scientist lectured during Year. This kind of error is rare, but serious nevertheless.

For a given fact type, a minimal combination of roles spanned by a uniqueness con-straint is called a *key* for that fact type. "Minimal" means the uniqueness constraint has no smaller uniqueness constraint inside it; if it did, it is implied by the smaller (but stronger) constraint and hence should not be shown. Role combinations for such longer, implied uniqueness constraints are called *proper superkeys* and are excluded from the following discussion.

Each role is associated with a column of the fact table for the fact type. Unless the fact type is unary, it is possible for it to have more than one key. Consider the cases shown in Figure 4.44. Here the binary has two one-role keys, the middle ternary has two two-role keys, and the other ternary has one three-role key.

The first two predicates also have implied uniqueness constraints across their whole length, but these are not counted as keys for these predicates. The *length* of a role se-quence is the number of roles it contains. A key of length 1 is a *simple key*. All other keys are *composite*.

We can imagine unaries or binaries that should be split, but in practice not even a novice designer is likely to verbalize one (e.g., "The Barrister with surname 'Rumpole'

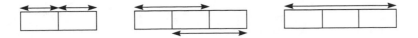

Figure 4.44 A fact type has one or more keys.

Table 4.6 Key length check for ternaries and longer fact types.

Arity of fact type	Minimum key length	Illegal key lengths
3	2	1
4	3	1, 2
5	4	1, 2, 3
⋮	⋮	⋮
n	$n-1$	$1,..., n-2$

Table 4.7 Country data.

Country	Population	Area (sq. km)
Australia	19,000,000	7,686,850
Germany	83,000,000	356,910
United States	281,000,000	9,372,610

smokes and drinks"). So the question of splittability is really an issue only with ternaries and longer fact types.

To help decide when to split in such cases, the so-called *n−1 rule* may be used: each *n*-ary fact type has a key length of at least *n*−1. If this rule is violated, the fact type is not elementary, and hence should be split. Various cases of this rule are set out in Table 4.6. A proof is sketched later in the section.

If a fact type is elementary, all its keys must be of the same length. Either there is exactly one key and this spans the whole fact type, or there are one or more keys and each is one role shorter than the fact type. So, if two or more roles in a predicate are not part of a key, the fact type is compound and must be split. To start with the simplest case, *a ternary fact type can be split if it has a simple key*. Consider the sample extract of geographic data shown in Table 4.7.

The first row of data may be verbalized thus: "The Country with name 'Australia' has a Population of 19,000,000 people and an Area of 7,686,850 square kilometers". The presence of "and" suggests that the fact is splittable. Suppose, however, that we foolishly ignore this linguistic clue and schematize the report using the ternary fact type Country has Population and Area.

Our familiarity with the UoD tells us that, at any given time, each country has at most one population and at most one area. So there is a uniqueness constraint on the

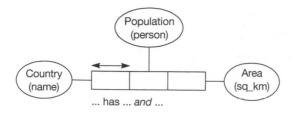

Figure 4.45 This ternary is a compound fact type, and hence splittable.

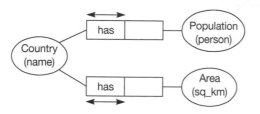

Figure 4.46 The previous ternary splits into these two elementary fact types.

Country column of the fact table. Although the populations and areas in Table 4.7 are unique, our common sense indicates this is not significant. For example, the population of India is projected to soon equal China's population, and it is certainly possible to have two countries of the same size. The combination of population and area need not be unique either. This leaves us with the simple uniqueness constraint on the Country role as shown in Figure 4.45.

Now let's apply the $n-1$ rule. Here the key has length 1, which is 2 less than the length of the fact type. So the fact type is not elementary, and must be split. But *how do we split it?* Examining our verbalization of row 1, we find a conjunction of two facts about the same country. Assuming our interpretation of the output report is correct, we must split the fact type into two fact types as shown in Figure 4.46.

Since the common entity type is Country, the original ternary fact type has been "split on Country". If we have correctly captured the semantics of the output report in step 1, then it would be wrong to split this fact type in any other way. Before considering this point further, let's see why the splittability rule works in this case.

Look back at Table 4.7. A uniqueness constraint on the Country column means that, given any state of the database, no country can be referenced more than once in this column. Each country has at most one population, and each country has at most one area. So for any given country, if we are given as separate pieces of information that country's population and that country's area, we can reconstruct that country's row in the output report. Since the ternary fact type of the output report can be split and recombined without information loss, it is not elementary.

If a fact type violates the $n-1$ rule, it is essentially a conjunction of smaller fact types even if its predicate name doesn't include a conjunctive operator such as "and".

For example, suppose we verbalized the previous ternary as Country with Population has Area. This still means the same, so is really a conjunction in disguise. In general, *if a fact type can be rephrased as a conjunction, it should be split,* since it is not elementary.

Before considering other examples, let's review some terminology commonly used in the normalization approach to database design. For a given fact table, let X denote a single column or combinations of columns, and let Y denote a single column. Then we say that Y is *functionally dependent on X* if and only if, for each value of X there is at most one value of Y. In other words, Y is a *function of X*. A function is just a many:1 relation (including 1:1 as a special case). If Y is a function of $X,$ then we say that X functionally determines $Y,$ written $X \rightarrow Y.$ This constraint is called a **functional dependency**, commonly abbreviated **FD.** Although FD arrows are not used directly in ORM schemas, the theory of FDs provides another way to understand uniqueness constraints.

Now consider the sample output report shown in Table 4.8. If this population is significant, then any functional dependencies should be exposed here. Note that Degree is functionally dependent on Person, since for any given person there is only one degree. Moreover, Gender is a function of Person since for any given person there is only one gender. But can you spot any other functional dependencies?

If the population is significant, then Gender is a function of Degree, and Degree is a function of Gender! Does this make sense? To answer this question we need to know more about the semantics of the UoD. Spotting a functional dependency within a population is a formal game. Knowing whether this dependency reflects an actual constraint in the UoD is not. To assume the population is significant begs the question. Only someone who understands the UoD, a domain expert, can resolve the issue.

If one column functionally determines another column, this reflects a many:1 association (or 1:many depending on the direction of reading) that can be given a meaningful name by the domain expert. Normally we would interpret the table in terms of degree and gender facts about specific persons. But suppose instead that the domain expert says row 1 of the output report should be read as "the Person with surname 'Adams' seeks the Degree with code 'BSc', and the Degree with code 'BSc' is sought by people of Gender with code 'M'". With this unusual interpretation, we have two facts about the same degree, and so we split on Degree rather than Person (see Figure 4.47).

If Gender really is a function of Degree, then any given degree is restricted to one gender (e.g., only males can seek a BSc). If Degree really is a function of Gender, then all people of a given gender seek the same degree (e.g., all females seek just a BA). These two FDs are captured in Figure 4.47 by the two uniqueness constraints on the relationship type between Degree and Gender.

Table 4.8 Is the population significant?

Person	*Degree*	*Gender*
Adams	BSc	M
Brown	BA	F
Collins	BSc	M

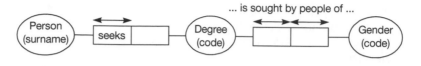

Figure 4.47 A weird UoD where Degree and Gender are functions of each other.

Table 4.9 A counterexample to any FD between degree and gender.

Person	Degree	Gender
Adams	BSc	M
Brown	BA	F
Collins	BSc	M
Davis	BSc	F

While such a UoD is possible, our knowledge about degree-awarding institutions makes this interpretation highly unlikely. To resolve our doubts, we could add test rows to the population. Although this is best done on conceptual fact tables, we could also test this example using the original output report. For example, if the domain expert accepts the population of Table 4.9 as being consistent with the UoD, then no FDs occur between Degree and Gender.

This by itself does not guarantee that Gender should be related to Person rather than Degree. For example, the schema of Figure 4.47 with the 1:1 constraint changed to a many:many constraint is still a remote possibility, but it would be silly to have a report with so much redundancy (e.g., the fact that the BSc is sought by males would be shown twice already). The only way to be sure is to perform step 1 properly, verbalizing the facts and having them confirmed by the domain expert. This avoids all the hassle.

While the notion of FD is sometimes useful, it is impractical to treat fact tables in a purely formal way, hunting for FDs. The number of dependencies to check increases very rapidly as the length of the fact type grows. Although our conceptual focus on elementary fact types constrains this length, the search for such dependencies can still be laborious. While an automated FD checker can be of use in a CASE tool, this kind of exhaustive checking is not fit for humans. We can short-circuit this work by taking advantage of human knowledge of the UoD.

As another simple example, consider the output report of Table 4.10. Suppose that, with the help of the domain expert, we express row 1 thus: the Lecturer with surname 'Halpin' works for the Department coded 'CS', which is located in the Building numbered '69'. Is this fact splittable, and if so, how?

Here the pronoun "which" introduces a nonrestrictive clause about the department that may be stated separately. So this can be rephrased as two facts about the

Table 4.10 University data.

Lecturer	Department	Building
Halpin	CS	69
Okimura	JA	1
Orlowska	CS	69
Wang	CN	1

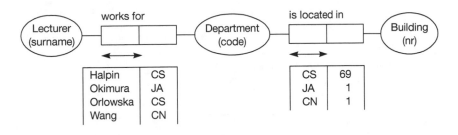

Figure 4.48 Populated conceptual schema for Table 4.10.

department: Halpin works for the CS department, and the CS department is located in building 69. So we should split on Department to get two fact types as shown in Figure 4.48.

As a challenge question, would it also be acceptable to split on Lecturer (e.g., Lecturer works for Department; Lecturer works in Building)? The logical derivation theory discussed in the next chapter shows it is unwise to split on Lecturer. If the population is significant, then each lecturer works for only one department, and each department is located in only one building. If these constraints are confirmed by the domain expert, they are added to the schema as shown.

An outline proof of the $n-1$ rule is now sketched. An n-ary fact type with a key of length less than $n-1$ has at least two columns in its fact table that are functionally dependent on this key. Split the table by pairing the key with exactly one of these columns in turn. Recombining by join on this key must generate the original table since only one combined row is possible (otherwise the common key portion would not be a key). Although the n-ary fact table thus formally splits in this way, in practice the splitting might need to be made on part of the key or even a nonkey column if an FD applies there (consider the previous examples).

As an example of a *quaternary* case, consider the report shown in Table 4.11. Suppose we did a bad job at Step 1 and schematized this situation as in Figure 4.49. Notice the uniqueness constraint. Here we have a fact type of length 4 and a key of length 2. *Since two roles are excluded from this key, we must split the fact type.* How do we split it? Each person seeks at most one degree, but this constraint is not captured by the two-role uniqueness constraint, so we split on Person. In terms of FD theory, the

Table 4.11 Student data.

Person	Degree	Subject	Rating
Adams	BSc	CS112	7
		CS110	6
		PD102	7
Brown	BA	CS112	6
		PD102	7
Collins	BSc	CS112	7

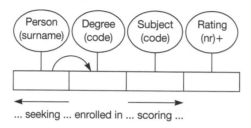

Figure 4.49 A quaternary fact type that is splittable (FD added).

Person role functionally determines the Degree role (shown in Figure 4.49 as a solid arrow).

If an FD like this is involved, splitting takes place on its source. So the quaternary splits on Person into a binary (Person seeks Degree) and a ternary (Person for Subject scored Rating). As an exercise, draw these, being sure to include all constraints. In any correct ORM schema, *all FDs should be captured by uniqueness constraints.* So FD arrows are not used on final conceptual schema diagrams. Any quaternary splits if it has a key of length 1 or 2.

Now consider the populated schema in Figure 4.50. Suppose this interpretation of the UoD is correct. For example, suppose the first row of the output report behind this schema really does express the information "the Person with surname 'Adams' seeking the Degree with code 'BSc' studies the Subject with code 'CS112'". Should the ternary be split?

Unlike the quaternary example, this ternary satisfies the $n-1$ rule. *Violating the $n-1$ rule is a sufficient condition for splittability, but it is not a necessary condition.* The ternary in this example does actually split. One way to see this is to realize that there is an *embedded FD* (i.e., an FD not captured by the uniqueness constraint(s)). In this case there is an embedded FD from the Person role to the Degree role, shown as an arrow in Figure 4.50.

But *every FD corresponds to a uniqueness constraint on some predicate,* and it is better to verbalize this. Here the fact type behind the embedded FD is Person seeks

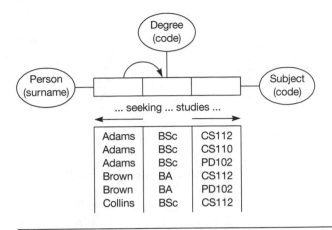

Figure 4.50 Is this ternary splittable?

Degree. The remaining information can then be expressed with another fact type: Person studies Subject.

We can achieve the same effect without talking about FDs, by simply answering the question *Can you rephrase the information in terms of a conjunction?* This approach was used earlier with the Country example. With our current example, instead of using the present participle "seeking", we can rephrase the information on the first row as

The Person with surname 'Adams' seeks the Degree with code 'BSc'
and studies the Subject with code 'CS112'

which is equivalent to

The Person with surname 'Adams' seeks the Degree with code 'BSc'
and
the Person with surname 'Adams' studies the Subject with code 'CS112'.

This is obviously a conjunction with Person common to each conjunct. So the ternary should be split on Person into two binaries (see Figure 4.51).

In general, given a significant fact table, the fact type is splittable if a column is functionally dependent on only some of the other columns. The phrase "only some" means "some but not all". This result corresponds to a basic rule in normalization theory (discussed in Section 12.6). With our present example, the Degree column is functionally dependent on the Person column only, so it should not be combined in a fact type with Subject information.

Another way to test for splittability is to *perform a redundancy check* by determining whether some fact is (unnecessarily) duplicated in the fact table. For example, in Figure 4.50 the pair (Adams, BSc) occurs three times. Using our semantic insight, we see that this pair corresponds to a fact of interest (Adams seeks a BSc degree). Since

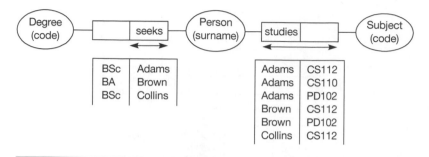

Figure 4.51   The ternary in Figure 4.50 should be split like this.

this fact has been duplicated, the ternary is not elementary. Redundancy is not a necessary requirement for splittability. For example, the ternary in Table 4.9 has no redundancy but is splittable.

Whichever method we use to spot splittability, we still need to phrase the information as a conjunction of simpler facts. Notice how the redundancy within the ternary of Figure 4.50 has been eliminated by splitting it into two binaries in Figure 4.51. Although we may allow redundancy in output reports, we should avoid redundancy in the actual tables stored in the database.

Our examples so far have avoided nested fact types. Recall that nesting is not the same as splitting. If nesting is used, the following **spanning rule** can be used to avoid splittable fact types: **the uniqueness constraint on an objectified association should span all its roles.**

This rule simply adapts earlier results to the nested case. Suppose the objectified predicate has a uniqueness constraint over only some of its roles. If an attached, outside role has a uniqueness constraint on it, when the outer predicate is flattened we have at least two roles not spanned by a uniqueness constraint.

If an attached role has no uniqueness constraint, then flattening generates a predicate with an embedded FD not expressed as a uniqueness constraint (consider the cases of Figures 4.49 and 4.50). In either case, the flattened version must split because it is not elementary. Hence the nested version must obey the spanning rule.

An exception to the spanning rule allows 1:1 binaries to be objectified (e.g., Person is husband of / is wife of Person may be objectified as "Marriage"). Although allowed for pragmatic reasons, this exception does violate elementarity and requires special treatment when mapped to logical models. Unlike ORM, many other modeling approaches allow other exceptions to the spanning rule (e.g., they allow *n*:1 associations to be objectified). The spanning rule is generally recommended because it ensures elementarity, helps to avoid some basic modeling mistakes, and simplifies the implementation of many mapping and transformation procedures.

Consider the output report of Table 4.12. Here the credit for a given subject is measured in points. The "?" on the second row is a null value, indicating that a real value is not recorded (e.g., a lecturer for CS109 might not yet have been assigned). Recall that

Table 4.12 Subject details.

Subject	Credit	Lecturer
CS100	8	DBJ
CS109	5	?
CS112	8	TAH
CS113	8	TAH

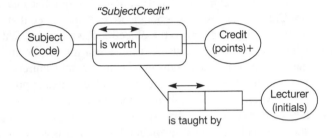

Figure 4.52 A faulty schema.

elementary fact tables can't contain null values (because you can't record half a fact). However, since output reports can group facts of different kinds in one table, they often do contain null values (indicating absence of a fact instance).

Now let's play the part of an inexperienced, and not very clever, schema designer, so that we can learn by the mistakes made. Looking just at the first row, we might be tempted to treat the information as a ternary:

Subject (code) 'CS100' worth Credit (points) 8 is taught by Lecturer (initials) 'DBJ'.

If we drew the schema diagram now and populated it, we would discover an error, since the second row doesn't fit this pattern (since we don't allow null values in our fact tables). The second row reveals the need to be able to record the credit points for a subject without indicating the lecturer. So we then rephrase the first row as follows:

Subject (code) 'CS100' is worth Credit (points) 8.
This SubjectCredit is taught by Lecturer (initials) 'DBJ'.

This overcomes the problem with the second row, since we can now express the information there simply as "Subject 'CS109' is worth Credit 5". Using this approach, we can now develop the schema shown in Figure 4.52.

Assuming the population of the output report is significant, we mark the uniqueness constraints as shown. Note that a simple uniqueness constraint has been added to the objectified association. This breaks the spanning rule: an objectified association has no key shorter than itself. So something must be wrong. Since the schema follows from our handling of step 1, this means that we must have made a mistake at step 1.

Have another look at the way we set out the information for row 1. The second sentence here is the problem. In this UoD each subject has exactly one credit point value, so this is independent of who teaches the subject. So there is no need to mention the credit point value of a subject when we indicate the lecturer. In FD terminology, the Credit column is functionally dependent on the Subject column alone. The information on the first row can be set out in terms of two simple binaries:

Subject (code) 'CS100' is worth Credit (points) 8.
Subject (code) 'CS100' is taught by Lecturer (initials) 'DBJ'.

This leads to the correct schema shown in Figure 4.53. Note that Lecturer depends only on Subject, not Credit. The nested schema incorrectly suggested that Lecturer was dependent on both, by relating Lecturer to the objectified association. With this example, Lecturer is a function of Subject, but this has no bearing on the splittability. We should use two binaries even if the same subject can have many lecturers. It is the functional dependency of Credit on Subject that disqualifies the nested approach.

In a case like this where it is difficult to come up with a natural name for the objectified association, such nesting errors are unlikely to occur in practice. When a natural name for the nested object type is available, however, it is easier to make the error. For example, we might objectify the fact type Person was born in Country as "Birth", and then add the fact type: Birth occurred on Date. Although it sounds reasonable, this nesting violates the spanning rule and should be replaced by the unnested binary Person was born on Date.

One lesson to be learned from this section is that experienced modelers should look out for uniqueness constraints even when performing step 1. Consider the output report of Table 4.13. If told the population is significant, how would you schematize this?

If you used either a ternary or a nested fact type you have made a mistake! Although similar to an earlier example, the UoD described by this table is more restricted. Given that the population is significant, the lack of duplicates in the Person column indicates that, at any given time, each person can be enrolled in only one subject. For example, these people might be your employees, and you are funding their studies and want to ensure they don't take on so much study that it interferes with their work performance.

Since we store information only about the current enrollments, and each person is enrolled in only one subject, it follows that each person can get only one rating. So if

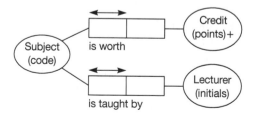

Figure 4.53 The corrected schema for Figure 4.52.

Table 4.13 Student results.

Person	Subject	Rating
Adams	CS112	7
Brown	CS112	5
Collins	PD102	5

we know the subject in which a person is enrolled and we know the rating obtained by the person, we do know the subject in which this rating is obtained by that person. To begin with, we might express the information on the first row of the table in terms of the ternary "Person (surname) 'Adams' scores Rating (nr) 7 for Subject (code) 'CS112'". However, because of the uniqueness constraint on Person we should rephrase this information as the conjunction

Person (surname) 'Adams' studies Subject (code) 'CS112'
and
Person (surname) 'Adams' scores Rating (nr) 7

leading to a conceptual schema with two binary fact types. Because of this unusual uniqueness constraint, the ternary has the same truth value as the conjunction of binaries for all possible states of this UoD.

Exercise 4.5

1. The keys for certain fact types are as shown. On this basis, which of these fact types are definitely splittable?

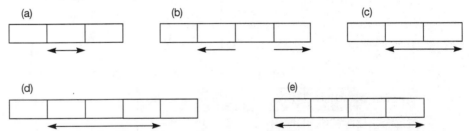

2. The following map provides information on nonstop flights between cities. The population is significant with respect to uniqueness constraints.
   (a) In step 1a of the design procedure, a domain expert verbalizes the information on the NW378 arrow as "Flight 'NW378' goes from Seattle to Chicago". Assuming this interpretation is correct, complete steps 1 and 2 to draw a schema diagram for facts of this type, and populate it with rows of data for the flights NW378, NW102, UA123, and UA246.
   (b) Now complete the first part of step 4 by adding any uniqueness constraints.
   (c) Is the fact type elementary? How do you know?
   (d) Split the fact type into elementary fact types, and populate them with the data for the same four flights mentioned earlier.

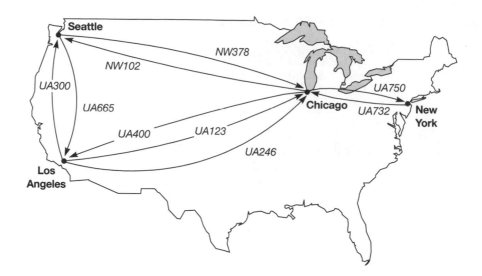

3. Executives may be contacted at work on one or more phone numbers and at home on one phone number. The following output report provides a sample population for this UoD. A novice information modeler notes that this ternary table lacks a simple key, and on this basis decides to schematize in terms of a single ternary fact type. Evaluate this approach, and draw a correct conceptual schema diagram.

Executive	Work phone	Home phone
Adams A	4235402	5837900
Adams A	4235444	
Adams S	4235444	5837900
Brown T	4235300	7578051

4. The following table contains data about some moons in our solar system.

Moon	Planet	Orbital period (days)
Callisto	Jupiter	16.7
Deimos	Mars	30.0
Phobos	Mars	0.3

(a) Schematize this as a ternary. Is this OK?
(b) Schematize this using nesting. Is this OK?
(c) Schematize this using only simple binaries. Is this OK?

5. The following table contains information about movie exports.

Movie	Origin	Export performance	
		Country	Sales level
Backdraft	US	AU	High
		NZ	Low
		GB	Medium
Crocodile Dundee	AU	NZ	Low
		US	High
Terminator 2	US	?	?

Suppose we model this using the quaternary Movie exported from Country to Country achieved SalesLevel. Draw the schema diagram for this approach. Is this acceptable? If not, explain clearly why.

4.6   Projection-Join Check

The previous section discussed two *sufficient* conditions for splitting a fact type: a fact type splits if it has two roles excluded from a key; an objectified association splits if it has a shorter key. Since these are not *necessary* conditions for splitting, in some cases further analysis is required to make a definite decision. At the heart of such an analysis is the question *Can the fact type be rephrased as a conjunction of smaller fact types?*

With a bit of experience behind us, we can usually answer this question fairly quickly. This section discusses a formal procedure for addressing this question in a systematic way. The procedure makes use of two operations, known as "projection" and "join", that are of considerable importance in relational database work. The *join* operation has already been discussed and involves combining two tables by matching values referencing the same object to form a new table (review Section 4.4).

The **projection** operation also produces a table, but it is performed on a single table. To project on one or more columns of a table, we *choose just the columns of interest* (removing all other columns) and then *ensure each row in the result appears just once* (removing any duplicates).

Notationally, the columns on which a projection is made are listed in *italic square brackets* after the table name, separated by commas. For example, *T [a, c]* is a projection on columns *a* and *c* of table *T*. Academics often write this instead as $\pi_{a,c}(T)$, where "π" (pi) is the Greek "p" (first letter of "projection"). I prefer the square bracket notation because it encourages a top-down view of the operation (first find the table, then choose the columns). Visually we can picture the operation as returning a vertical subset of the whole table (see Figure 4.54).

For example, a ternary fact type we met earlier is reproduced in Figure 4.55(a). Its fact table T1 has six rows. Projecting on the Person and Degree roles, we obtain the fact

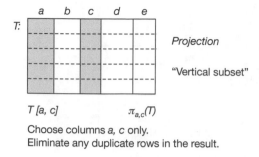

Choose columns *a, c* only.
Eliminate any duplicate rows in the result.

Figure 4.54 The projection operation.

type Person seeks Degree, with its fact table T2 as shown in Figure 4.55(b). Notice that T2 has only three rows because projection eliminates duplicates. Projecting on the Person and Subject roles yields the fact type Person studies Subject and its fact table T3. Since T3 is a projection on a key of T1, it must have the same number of rows as T1 (why?).

Since the roles on the ternary are played by different object types, by default the roles are named using lowercase versions of the object type names. Using these role names as attribute names, the fact tables may be set out in relational terms as T1 (person, degree, subject), T2 (person, degree), and T3 (person, subject). The two projections may now be expressed thus: T2 = T1[person, degree] and T3 = T1[person, subject].

In an earlier section, the ternary Person seeking Degree studies Subject was reworded as the conjunction Person seeks Degree **and** studies Subject. Here, the logical **and** operator performs a conceptual join on Person of the two binary fact types: Person seeks Degree; Person studies Subject. Since the ternary is equivalent to the conjunction of the binaries, no information is lost if we transform the ternary into the two binaries or vice versa. So no matter what the fact populations are, the ternary fact table must contain exactly the same elementary facts as the two binary fact tables collectively contain. In relational terms, the ternary relation is equal to the (natural inner) join of the two binary projections. So, T1 = T2 ⋈ T3. Check this out for yourself using the populations shown in Figure 4.55.

Conceptually, the situation is summarized by the following equivalence:

Person seeking Degree studies Subject   **iff**   Person seeks Degree
                                                     and studies Subject

Here "iff" abbreviates "if and only if". The projection corresponds to the conditional "*if* the ternary is true *then* the conjunction is true". The join corresponds to the conditional "*if* the conjunction is true *then* the ternary is true". Any compound fact can always be formulated as a logical conjunction (using "and"). In principle, if you are ever

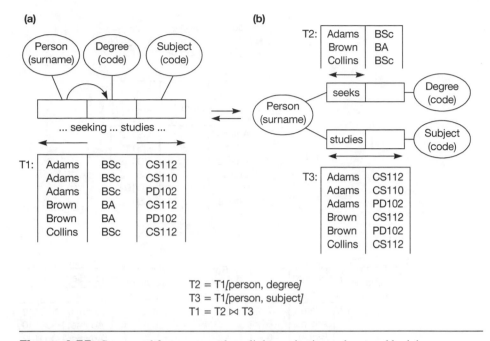

T2 = T1/person, degree/
T3 = T1/person, subject/
T1 = T2 ⋈ T3

Figure 4.55 Compound fact types can be split by projection and restored by join.

in doubt, the following *projection-join check* can be applied to test whether a fact type is compound (and hence splittable):

Provide a significant fact table for the fact type.
Split this table into two or more projections.
Recombine by natural (inner) join.
The fact type is splittable in this way **iff** the result is the same as the original.

An inner join is acceptable since the conceptual fact table (and hence its projections) cannot have null values. I chose a significant population for the ternary example just discussed, so the test confirms that ternary's splittability.

Now consider our familiar ternary example about people scoring ratings for subjects. A significant fact table is provided for it in Figure 4.56(a). Suppose we suspect that this ternary is splittable on Person. For example, we might feel that in this UoD the following equivalence holds:

Person scored Rating for Subject   **iff**   Person scored Rating
                                        and studied Subject

To test this way to split, we could form the two binary projections shown in Figure 4.56(b), and then recombine by joining on Person. The result is shown in Figure 4.56(c). As an exercise, please confirm this result. In forming the join, several new rows (marked in bold italics) appeared that were not in the original table. Any one of

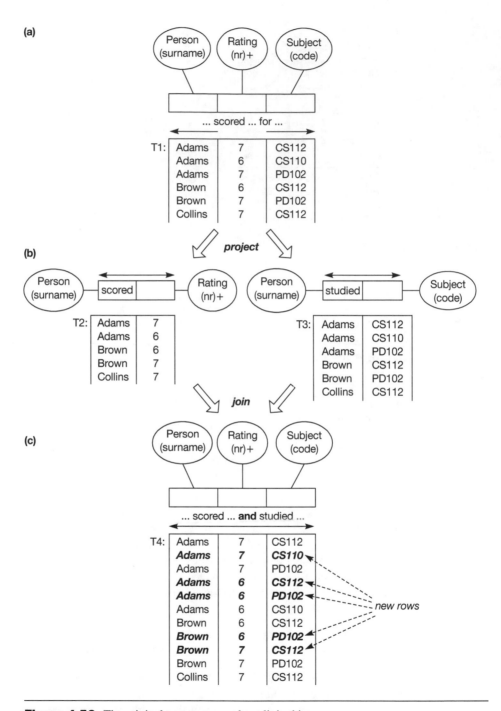

Figure 4.56 The original ternary cannot be split in this way.

these new rows is enough to prove that the fact type cannot be split this way (i.e., on Person).

Consider for instance the information on the first row of our original table: the person with surname "Adams" scored a rating of 7 for the subject CS112. We attempted to split this fact into the two separate facts: Adams scored a rating of 7; Adams studied CS112 (see first rows of the two projections). If this splitting is legitimate, the two separate facts must, in combination, be equivalent to the original fact. However, they are not. Adams can score more than one rating and study more than one subject. Knowing that Adams scored a 7 does not tell us the subject(s) for which Adams scored this rating. It could be any of Adams's subjects (CS112, CS110, or PD102).

Joining the projections causes each rating of Adams to be paired with each subject of Adams. Some of these rows were not present in the original, and the join does not tell us which ones apply to the original ternary. Since we are unable to construct the population of the original ternary from the new ternary population, information has been lost. Hence the new ternary fact type is not equivalent to the original fact type. So the original ternary fact type cannot be split in this way.

This projection-join check invalidated the proposed equivalence: Person scored Rating for Subject **iff** Person scored Rating **and** studied Subject. The forward conditional of the equivalence does hold (*if* ternary *then* conjunction). However, the backward conditional fails (it is not generally true that *if* conjunction *then* ternary). Simply understanding the English verbalization of the fact types should really be enough for us to understand that "Person scored Rating for Subject" differs in meaning from "Person scored Rating and studied Subject", so long as we take care to read "and" in a purely conjunctive sense. Another way to spot the difference is that the uniqueness constraint on the join fact type in Figure 4.56(c) is weaker than that of the original in Figure 4.56(a).

If you use some insight, it should be clear that trying to split on Subject or Rating or all three would be pointless. In this case you may conclude that the fact type is unsplittable and leave it as a ternary. If this is not clear, then you can use the algorithm to test all possible ways of splitting. You would find that none of them work.

In general, for a ternary A-B-C there are four ways in which it might split: A-B, A-C; B-A, B-C; C-A, C-B; A-B, A-C, B-C. In the fourth case the schema diagram is triangular in shape: this is referred to as three-way splitting. As an exercise, draw these four possibilities. With three-way splitting the join should be done in two stages. For example, first join A-B and A-C (with A common); then join the A-B-C result of this join with B-C (with B and C common).

A classic example of testing for three-way splitting involves the fact type Agent sells Cartype for Company. Even if the key spans the whole fact type, the fact type can be split into three binaries if a derivation rule allows the ternary to be deduced from the binaries (this kind of derivation is discussed in Section 12.6.). Such examples are very rare in practice. For an *n*-ary fact type, if the *n*-way split fails (by generating new rows in the final join), then all other ways of splitting can be ruled out too: the fact type is unsplittable.

Though useful for understanding the notion of splittability, the projection-join test is of little practical value for actually determining splittability. The problem is that it only works if the population is significant. But to know the population is significant implies that we know what all the constraints are and have crafted a population to illustrate these constraints. If we already know what the constraints are, it is obvious whether the fact type is elementary or compound, so there's no need to do any projection-join test. In Figure 4.55(a), for example, if we already know that each person seeks at most one degree then we need to separate out the underlying binary. In Figure 4.56(a) there was no similar constraint, because a person can score many ratings. Formally this is the only difference between the two cases, but it's enough for us to determine splittability without resorting to the tedious projection-join test. The best test for splittability is to work linguistically with the domain expert to see if a fact can be phrased as a conjunction, and to test this with a couple of carefully chosen instances.

In case you feel like you've just wasted a lot of time learning a projection-join check that is of theoretical interest only, please don't be angry with me for discussing the topic. It's very useful to understand what the projection and join operations are, at both conceptual and logical levels. Apart from their modeling impact, these operations are used extensively in both conceptual and relational query languages, as we'll discuss later.

Exercise 4.6

1. A template for a ternary fact type is outlined below. The population shown in the fact table is significant.

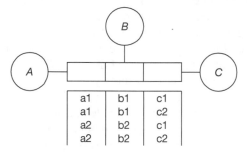

a1	b1	c1
a1	b1	c2
a2	b2	c1
a2	b2	c2

(a) Add the uniqueness constraints for this fact type.
(b) Use the projection-join test to show that this fact type cannot be split into two binaries with *C* as the common node.
(c) Use the projection-join test to show that this fact type can be split into two binaries with *B* as the common node.
(d) Draw a schema outline for this result.

4.7   Summary

This chapter discussed step 4 of the conceptual schema design procedure: *add uniqueness constraints, and check the arity of fact types.* Uniqueness constraints (UCs) come in two varieties: internal and external. An *internal* (or intrapredicate) uniqueness constraint applies to one or more roles of a single predicate. It is marked as a bar across the role(s) it constrains. Arrow tips may be added to the ends of the bar. If the roles are noncontiguous, the bar is divided, and arrow tips at the outer ends must be included.

Redundancy is repetition of an elementary fact. Since redundancy is not permitted in a conceptual fact table, each row must be unique. This is shown as a UC across the whole predicate, unless a stronger UC exists. If an internal UC spans just some of the roles spanned by another internal UC, the former UC implies the latter UC, and the implied UC should not be displayed.

Each unary predicate has a UC across its role, whether or not it is displayed. Binary predicates have four possibilities: UC on role 1 only; UC on role 2 only; UC on role 1, and another UC on role 2; one UC spanning both roles. These cases are respectively described as many to one ($n{:}1$), one to many ($1{:}n$), one to one ($1{:}1$), and many to many ($m{:}n$). For example, if each Employee works for at most one Department, but many employees may work for the same department, the predicate "works for" is many to one and has a UC across its first role. In Figure 4.57, the R predicates are $n{:}1$ and the S predicate is $m{:}n$.

Each role in a predicate is associated with a column of the predicate table. A simple UC across just one role means no duplicates are allowed in its column. A UC spanning n roles means each sequence of n entries taken from the associated columns can occur in that column sequence on only one row.

Let $a\ R\ b$ and $b\ S\ c$ be two fact instances. The conjunction of these facts ($a\ R\ b$ **and** $b\ S\ c$) is a compound fact instance ($a\ R\ b$ **that** $S\ c$) of the schema path A-R-B-S-C that is the conceptual (inner) *join* of R and S via the common object type B. The fact table for this join is obtained by pairing rows of R with rows of S where the B values match, and showing the B column(s) just once in the result. In relational terms this is a natural inner join, symbolized by "$\bowtie$". For example, $R \bowtie S$ in Figure 4.57(b) joins on A and has a table population of $\{(\,a1, b1, c1), (a1, b1, c2), (a2, b2, c2)\}$.

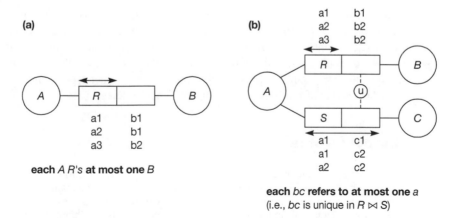

(a)

each *A R*'s **at most one** *B*

(b)

each *bc* **refers to at most one** *a*
(i.e., *bc* is unique in $R \bowtie S$)

Figure 4.57 Some uniqueness constraints.

An *external* (or interpredicate) uniqueness constraint is shown by connecting two or more roles from different predicates to the symbol "Ⓤ". This indicates that when the join operation is applied to the predicates, an internal UC spans these roles in the result. As an example of the constraints shown in Figure 4.57(b), a program may appear on at most one channel, and may appear at different time slots, but for any given channel and time slot at most one program is shown.

Uniqueness constraints apply to the recorded information and must be at least as strong as those in the real world. A combination of roles spanned by an internal UC, with no smaller UC inside it, is a *key* of its predicate. A one-role key is a *simple key*.

Because conceptual predicates are elementary, a ternary fact type cannot have a simple key. It has either a three-role UC or one or more two-role UCs. For a predicate with *n* roles, *each internal UC must span at least* n−1 *roles*. This *n*−1 rule may be applied as a *key length check*.

This rule also implies the following *spanning rule: a uniqueness constraint on an objectified association must span all its roles*. Violation of this rule is a sufficient but not necessary condition for splittability. An exception to this rule is allowed for 1:1 cases.

For a given predicate, let X denote a combination of one or more roles (or columns) and Y denote a single role (or column). We say that X *functionally determines Y*, written $X \to Y$, if and only if for each value of X there is at most one value of Y. In this case, Y is said to be *functionally dependent* on X. The term "FD" abbreviates "functional dependency". If the conceptual schema is correct, all FDs are implied by UCs. If a non-implied FD $X \to Y$ exists, the predicate should be split on the source X.

With experience, you can usually determine whether a fact type splits by using background knowledge of the UoD to answer the following questions: "Can the fact type be rephrased as a conjunction? Is information lost by splitting the fact type?" The shortest key rule and the detection of a nonimplied FD provide simple ways of checking that our intuitions are correct here.

The *projection* on columns *a, c, ...* of table *T*, written *T[a, c, ...]*, is obtained by choosing just those columns and removing any duplicate rows from the result. If we know we have a significant population for a fact type, the *projection-join check* can be used to determine its elementarity. If we suspect that a predicate might split in a certain way, we can split its significant table in this way by projection, then recombine by natural join: if new instances appear in the result, then the fact type cannot be split in this way. This test is of more theoretical than practical interest.

Chapter Notes

By depicting each role as a box associated with a table column, ORM enables uniqueness constraints to be portrayed in a natural way where the impact of the constraint on populations is immediately apparent. ER modeling and UML depict internal uniqueness constraints on associations using a variety of notations for "cardinality constraints" or "multiplicity constraints", as discussed later. ER offers support for uniqueness constraints on attributes, but UML does not. Neither ER nor UML offers any significant support for external uniqueness constraints.

Object-Role Modeling makes minimal use of the notion of functional dependency, but this notion is central to many other methods. For a clear treatment of an ER approach as well as functional dependency theory, see Elmasri and Navathe (1994).

Although it is generally wise to objectify a predicate only if it has a spanning uniqueness constraint, rare cases may arise where it may be useful to remove this restriction (e.g., the current marriage example discussed in Section 10.4.)

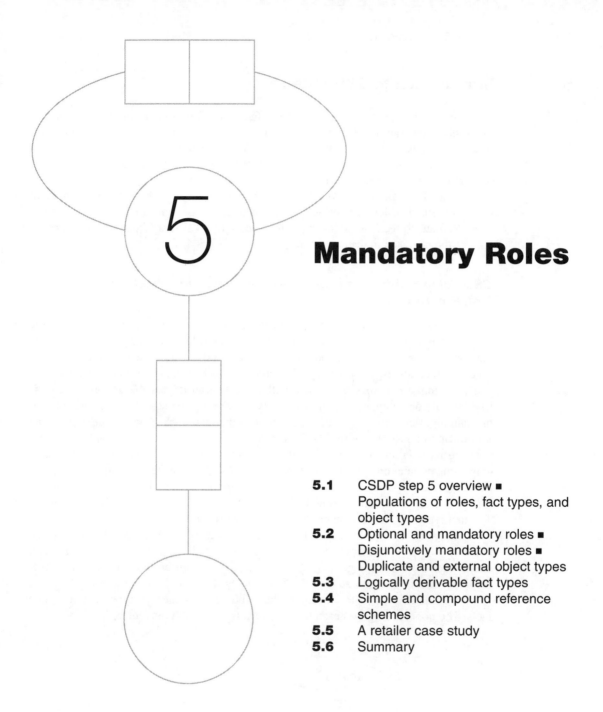

Mandatory Roles

5.1   Introduction to CSDP Step 5

So far you've learned how to proceed from familiar information examples to a conceptual schema diagram in which the elementary fact types are clearly set out, with the relevant uniqueness constraints marked on each. You also learned to perform some checks on the quality of the schemas. In practice, other kinds of constraints and checks need to be considered also. Next in importance to uniqueness constraints are *mandatory role constraints*. Basically these indicate which roles *must* be played by the population of an object type and which are optional. Once mandatory role constraints are specified, a check is made to see if some fact types may be *logically derived* from others. This constitutes the next step in the design procedure.

***CSDP step 5: Add mandatory role constraints, and check for
logical derivations.***

The next two sections cover this step in detail. The rest of this section discusses some basic concepts used in our treatment of mandatory roles and later constraints. Once mandatory roles are understood, we are in a good position to examine reference schemes in depth, especially composite reference—we do this later in the chapter.

Recall that a *type* may be equated with the set of all its possible instances. This is true for both object types and relationship types. For a given schema, types are fixed or unchanging. For a *given state* of the database and a given type T, we define *pop(T)*, the **population** of T, to be *the set of all instances of T in that state*. Let us use "{ }" to denote the *null set,* or *empty set* (i.e., the set with no members). When the database is empty, the population of each of its types = { }. As the database is updated, the population of a given type may change. For example, suppose the ternary shown in Figure 5.1 is used to store information about medals won by countries in the next Olympic Games. The fact type and roles are numbered for easy reference.

Initially the fact table for F1 is empty, since no sporting results are known, so pop(F1) = { }. Now suppose the database is to be updated after each sporting event, and in the first event the gold and bronze medals are won by the USA and the silver medal by Japan. The new state of the fact table is shown in Figure 5.2, using 'G', 'S', 'B' for gold, silver, and bronze. Now the population of the fact type contains three facts. The population grows each time the results of an event are entered.

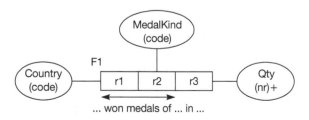

Figure 5.1 A fact type for Olympic Games results.

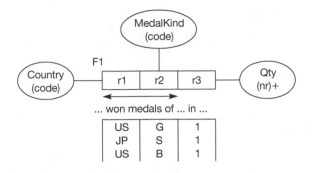

Figure 5.2 A fact type populated with results of the first event.

We may also define the *population of a role*. Each role of a fact type is associated with a column in its fact table. Values entered in the column refer to instances of the object type that plays that role. Given any role r and any state of the database:

$pop(r)$ = population of role r
= set of objects referenced in the column for r

Typically the objects referenced are entities, not values. For example, in Figure 5.2, pop(r1) = {the Country with code 'US', the Country with code 'JP'}. The *valuation* of a role r, written *val(r)*, is the set of values entered in its column. For example, in Figure 5.2, val(r1) = {'US', 'JP'}.

When there is no chance of confusion, object terms may be abbreviated to constants in listing populations. With this understanding, in Figure 5.2, pop(r1) = {US, JP}, pop(r2) = {G, S, B}, and pop(r3) = {1}. Role populations are used to determine *object type populations*. With our current example, if each country referenced in the database must play r1, then after the first event pop(Country) changes from { } to {US, JP}, and pop(CountryCode) changes from { } to {'US', 'JP'}. Assuming the application is just about the Olympics, the entity type Country is the set of all countries that might possibly compete in the Games; this set contains a large number of countries.

A predicate occurs within a fact type or reference type. Reference types are usually abbreviated as a parenthesized reference mode. Roles in a reference type are called *referential roles*. Roles in a fact type are called *fact roles*. Each entity type in a completed conceptual schema plays at least one referential role and, unless declared independent (see Section 6.3), at least one fact role. In general, the *population of an entity type equals the union of the population of its roles*. Unless the entity type is independent, its population is the union of the populations of its fact roles.

For example, the populated schema in Figure 5.3 indicates the natural gas and coal reserves of some countries (for 1982). The unit symbols "Gt" and "Gm³" stand for gigatonnes and giga cubic meters (giga = 10^9, i.e., 1,000,000,000). The Country entity *type* might include many countries (e.g., from Afghanistan to Zimbabwe), but for this state of the database, only two countries are recorded in each fact type. Each instance in the database population of Country plays the role r1 or r2 or both. So the current

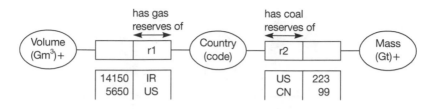

Figure 5.3 pop(Country)=pop(r1) ∪ pop(r2).

population of Country is the set of all the instances referenced in either the r1 column or the r2 column. We could set this out as

    pop(Country) = pop(r1) ∪ pop(r2)
                 = {IR, US} ∪ {US, CN}
                 = {IR, US, CN}

Here "∪" is the operator for *set union.* The union of two sets is the set of all the elements in either or both. For instance, {1, 2} ∪ {2, 3, 4} = {1, 2, 3, 4}. In the above case, the United States occurs in both role populations, while Iran and China occur in only one.

5.2   Mandatory and Optional Roles

Consider the output report of Table 5.1. The question mark "?" denotes a *null value,* indicating that an actual value is not recorded. For instance, patient 002 may actually have a phone but this information is not recorded, or the patient may simply have no phone.

Patients are identified by a patient number. Different patients may have the same name and even the same phone number, so the population of Table 5.1 is not significant. We must record each patient's name, but it is optional whether we record a phone number. Figure 5.4 shows a preliminary conceptual model for this situation. Conceptual facts are elementary, so they cannot contain null values. The null value in Table 5.1 is catered to by the absence of a fact for patient 002 in the fact type Patient has PhoneNr.

In step 5 of the design procedure, each role is classified as mandatory or optional. A **role is mandatory** if and only if, for all states of the database, the role must be played by every member of the population of its object type; otherwise the role is **optional.** A mandatory role is also called a *total role,* since it is played by the total population of its object type. Which of the four roles in Figure 5.4 are mandatory and which are optional?

If the diagram includes all the fact types for the application, and its sample population is significant, we can easily determine which roles are mandatory. In practice, however, we work most of the time with subschemas rather than the complete, or

Table 5.1 Details about hospital patients.

PatientNr	Patient name	Phone
001	Adams C	2057642
002	Brown S	?
003	Collins T	8853020

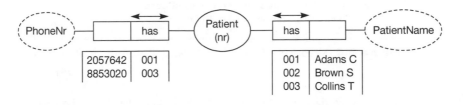

Figure 5.4 A populated schema for Table 5.1.

global, schema; and sample populations are rarely significant. In such cases we should check with the domain expert whether the relevant information must be recorded for all instances of the object type (e.g., must we record the name of each patient?).

Consider the two roles played by Patient. For the database state shown, the populations of these roles are {001, 002, 003} and {001, 003}. If these are the only roles played by Patient, then pop(Patient) = {001, 002, 003}. The first role is played by all recorded patients, and the second role is played by only some. Assuming the population is significant in this regard, the first role is mandatory and the second is optional.

To indicate explicitly that a role is mandatory, we add a **mandatory role dot** to the line that connects the role to its object type. This dot may be placed at either end of the role line. In Figure 5.5(a), the dot is placed at the object type end. This reinforces the *global* nature of the constraint in applying to the object type's population. If we add a patient instance to the population of Patient role, we must also include this instance in the population of every other role declared mandatory for Patient. In this sense, a mandatory role constraint can have an impact beyond its predicate. In contrast, a uniqueness constraint is *local* in nature, constraining just the population of its role(s), with no impact on other predicates.

In Figure 5.5(b), the mandatory dot is placed at the role end. This choice is useful when role lines attached to an object type are so close together that if we added a dot at the object type end, it would be unclear which role(s) is/are intended. This situation can arise when an object type plays a large number of roles, and we wish to see all of these on the same schema page.

In Figure 5.5 the first role of the top predicate is both mandatory and unique. The mandatory role constraint verbalizes as **each** Patient has **at least one** PatientName. This may also be phrased as **each** Patient has **some** PatientName. The uniqueness constraint verbalizes as **each** Patient has **at most one** PatientName. In combination, these constraints

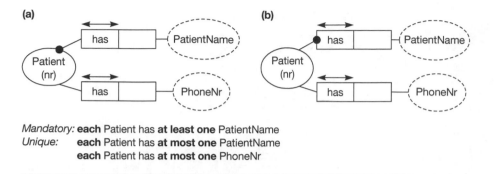

Figure 5.5 is shown here with (a) and (b) diagrams.

(a)   **(b)**

Mandatory: **each** Patient has **at least one** PatientName
Unique: **each** Patient has **at most one** PatientName
              each Patient has **at most one** PhoneNr

Figure 5.5 Mandatory role constraint shown as a black dot at either end of role line.

may be verbalized as **each** Patient has **exactly one** PatientName (i.e., each recorded patient has one and only one name recorded). In general, *at least one* + *at most one* = *exactly one*.

In a completed schema, *if two or more fact roles are played by the same object type, then individually these roles are optional unless marked mandatory.* For example, in Figure 5.5 the first role of Patient has PhoneNr is optional. This means it is possible to add a patient to the database population without adding a phone number for that patient.

What about the roles played by PatientName and PhoneNr? If these are the only roles played by these object types in the global schema, then these roles are mandatory. Unless declared independent (see Section 6.3), each primitive object must play some role, and each primitive entity must play some fact role. Hence, *by default, if a primitive object type plays only one role, or a primitive entity type plays only one fact role* (in the global schema), *this role is mandatory.* In such cases, the implied mandatory role dot is usually omitted. In Figure 5.5, if no other roles are played by PatientName and PhoneNr, their roles are mandatory by implication. In this case, although not recommended, these implied constraints could be marked explicitly as shown in Figure 5.6.

The explicit depiction of implied mandatory role constraints has several disadvantages. First, it complicates schema evolution. For example, suppose that tomorrow we decide to add the fact types Patient had previous- PatientName; Patient has secondary-PhoneNr. With the implicit approach, this is simply an addition to the current schema. But with the explicit approach, we need to delete the formerly implied mandatory role constraints and replace them with weaker constraints (e.g., each PatientName is of, or was of, at least one Patient; each PhoneNr is used by, or is a secondary number for, at least one Patient—such disjunctive mandatory constraints are discussed shortly).

Another problem with marking implied mandatory constraints is that this de-emphasizes the mandatory role constraints that are really important, that is, the ones we need to enforce (e.g., you must record a name for each patient). If you think about it, you should see that implied mandatory constraints are automatically enforced and hence have no implementation impact.

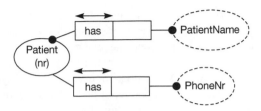

Figure 5.6 Implied mandatory role constraints specified explicitly (not recommended).

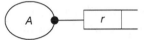

Role r is **mandatory** (for the population of A)

Each instance of type A that is recorded in the database
is also recorded to play r

pop(r) = pop(A)

Figure 5.7 The role r is mandatory.

If we demanded the explicit approach for simple mandatory constraints, we should do the same for disjunctive mandatory constraints. But if the roles involved in the disjunction occur on separate schema pages, there is no convenient way to mark the constraint between them.

Another problem with the explicit approach is that it complicates theorem specification. Later on we will consider some schema equivalence theorems. In this context, the implicit approach allows us to discuss schema fragments independently of other roles played in the global schema, but the explicit approach would forbid this, leading to extra complexity.

For such reasons, the explicit specification should be avoided unless we have some special reason for drawing the attention of a human reader to the implied constraints. As discussed in the next chapter, the rule for implicit mandatory roles does not apply to subtypes: if they play just one fact role, this is optional unless marked mandatory.

If a role is mandatory, its population always equals the total population of its attached object type. Figure 5.7 depicts the general case for an object type A and an attached role r. The role r may occur in any position in a predicate of any arity, and A may participate in other predicates as well. Mandatory role constraints are enforced on populations rather than types. If the only fact stored in the database is that patient 001 is named "Adams C", the name role played by Patient is still mandatory even though many more instances of the Patient type have yet to be added to the population.

Recall that the UoD (real-world portion of interest) is not the same thing as the recorded world or formal model of the UoD. Like other constraints, mandatory role constraints are assertions about our model and do not necessarily apply to the real world. With our current example, it is optional whether a patient has a phone. This simply means that we do not need to record a phone number for each patient. Maybe this is because in the real world not every patient has a phone, or perhaps each patient does have a phone but some patients won't supply their phone number.

The real-world schema of Figure 5.8(a) concerns applicants for an academic position. By nature, each person has exactly one sex. As a business decision, each applicant is required to have at least one degree. Applicants may or may not have a fax number. Figure 5.8(b) shows the model actually used. Here, applicants may choose whether to have their sex recorded, but must provide details about their degrees. For this model, a business decision has been made (perhaps to avoid gender bias) to remove a mandatory constraint that applies in the real world. This practice of relaxing a real-world mandatory constraint is not unusual, but it should always be a conscious decision.

Do *not* read a mandatory role constraint to mean "if an object plays that role in real life, then we must record it". The information system can work only with the model we give it of the world—it cannot enforce real-world constraints not expressed in this model.

The following checking procedure helps ensure our mandatory role constraints are correct. For each mandatory role: is it mandatory in the real world? If not, make it optional. For each optional role: is it optional in the real world? If not, what reasons are there for making it optional? We'll refine this further when we discuss subtypes.

In Figure 5.8(b) the mandatory constraint is on a nonfunctional role (i.e., a role not covered by a simple uniqueness constraint). In this case it is acceptable, since we wouldn't want to hire any academic without a degree, and we would be interested in all their degrees. In general, however, you should *be wary of adding mandatory constraints to nonfunctional roles.* Do so only if you are sure the constraint is needed. Such cases can lead to complexities (e.g., referential cycles) in the implementation, which

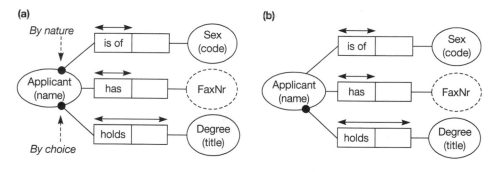

*If a role is mandatory in the real world,
it may be optional in the model.*

Figure 5.8 A conscious decision to make recording of an Applicant's sex optional: (a) real world and (b) model actually used.

are best avoided if possible. Of course if your application really requires such a constraint, then you should declare it, regardless of its implementation impact.

Novice modelers tend to be too heavy-handed with mandatory role constraints, automatically making a role mandatory if it's mandatory in the real world. In practice, however, it is often best to make some of these roles optional in the model to allow for cases where for some reason we can't obtain all the information. As a general piece of advice, *make a role mandatory if and only if you need to.*

When an object type plays more than one role, special care is needed in updating the database to take account of mandatory roles. Suppose we want to add some facts from Table 5.1 into a database constrained by the conceptual schema of Figure 5.5 (recall that it is mandatory to record a patient's name but optional to record a phone number). Assuming the database is initially empty, an untutored user might proceed as follows:

User   *CIP*

add: Patient 001 has PatientName 'Adams C'.   →   accepted.
add: Patient 001 has PhoneNr '2057642'.   →   accepted.
add: Patient 003 has PhoneNr '8853020'.   →   rejected. Violates constraint:
                                                        each Patient has **some** PatientName.

To add the third fact into the database we must either first record the fact that patient 003 has the name 'Collins T', or include this with the phone fact in a compound transaction.

Now consider the two report extracts shown in Figure 5.9. These list sample details maintained by a sporting club. Membership of this club is restricted to players and coaches. The term "D.O.B." means date of birth. On joining the club, each person is assigned to a team, in the capacity of player or coach (possibly both). Teams are identified by semantic codes (e.g., 'MR-A', 'BS-B', 'WS-A' denote the men's rugby A team, the boy's soccer B team, and the women's soccer A team), but the semantics of these codes is left implicit rather than being stored explicitly in the information system. A

Member	D.O.B.	Joined
Adams F	02/15/75	01/02/99
Anderson A	12/25/86	01/02/99
Brown C	11/02/60	11/14/92
Collins T	02/15/46	05/05/80
Crystal B	01/02/86	11/14/99
Downes S	11/02/60	06/17/95
...	...	...

Team	Pts	Coach	Players
MR-A	23	Downes S	Adams F Brown C Collins T ...
BS-B	0	Collins T	Anderson A Crystal B ...
WS-A	0	?	?
...	...	...	...

Figure 5.9 Extracts of two reports from a sporting club.

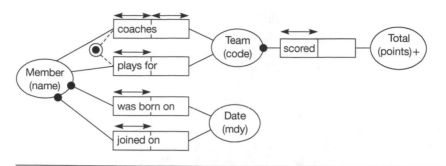

Figure 5.10 Disjunctive mandatory constraint: each member coaches or plays (or both).

record is kept of the total number of points scored by each team. Each team is initially assigned zero points, even if it doesn't yet have any members.

As an exercise, you might like to model this yourself before peeking at the solution in Figure 5.10. The uniqueness constraints assert that each member coaches at most one team, plays for at most one team, was born on at most one date, joined the club on at most one date, and each team has at most one coach and scored at most one total. The reference mode "mdy" for Date indicates that for verbalization purposes date instances are in month/day/year format—of course, this conceptual choice does not exclude other formats being specified for internal or external schemas.

The mandatory role dot on Team asserts that each team scored some total (possibly 0). The lower mandatory role dots on Member indicate that for each member we must record their birth date as well as the date they joined the club. The circled mandatory role dot is linked to two roles: this is a **disjunctive mandatory role** (or **inclusive-or**) **constraint,** indicating that the disjunction of these two roles is mandatory for Member. That is, each member *either* coaches *or* plays *(or both).* For example, Adams is a player only, Downes is a coach only, and Collins is both a player and a coach. A coach of one team may even play for the same team (although the population doesn't illustrate this).

If Figure 5.10 includes all the roles played by Date in the global schema, then the disjunction of Date's roles is also mandatory (each date is a birth date or a join date). This could be shown explicitly by linking these roles to a disjunctive mandatory role dot; however, this constraint is implicitly understood, and the explicit constraint would need to be changed if we added another fact type for Date, so it is better to leave the figure as is.

This Date example illustrates the following generalization of the rule mentioned earlier for single mandatory roles: *by default, the disjunction of roles played by a primitive object type is mandatory* (this default can be overridden by declaring the object type independent—see next chapter). If the object type is an *entity type, the disjunction of its fact roles is also mandatory by default.* Apart from highlighting the important cases where disjunctive mandatory roles need to be enforced (e.g., the coach-player disjunction), and simplifying schema evolution and theorem specification, this rule facilitates the drawing of schemas. For example, object types like Date and MoneyAmt often have several roles that are disjunctively mandatory, and to display this constraint explicitly

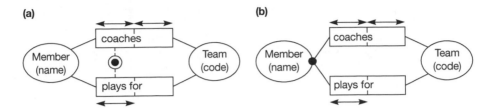

Figure 5.11 Alternative notations for disjunctive mandatory role constraint.

would be messy (or even impossible if the object type occurs on separate schema pages).

As an alternative to the circled-dot notation for disjunctive mandatory role constraints, shown in Figure 5.11(a), a dot may be placed at the junction of the lines connecting the relevant roles to their object type, as shown in Figure 5.11(b).

Although tidier, this notation has three disadvantages. First, it cannot handle the rare case where a role may belong to two disjunctive mandatory constraints. For example, suppose we later add the constraint that each member either coaches a team or takes a class on how to coach. Only the circled-dot notation can express both the disjunctive constraints on the same diagram. Second, as discussed in Section 6.4, the circled "X" notation for exclusion can be neatly superimposed on the circled-dot notation for inclusive-or to express an exclusive-or constraint. The alternative notation requires two separate constraints for this case. Finally, the alternative notation requires role lines to connect to the same point on the object type ellipse, which makes it harder to add constraints and to distinguish them when many roles are connected to the object type.

To avoid confusion, a mandatory role, or disjunctive mandatory role, should be shown *explicitly* if the object type it constrains has an explicit identification scheme or a subtype. For example, consider a global schema comprising just the coach and play fact types in Figure 5.11. If the identification scheme for Member is left implicit (i.e., the reference mode is parenthesized, as shown), then its disjunctive mandatory role constraint may be left implicit. However, if the reference type for Member is shown explicitly (Member has MemberName), the constraint that members must coach or play should be shown explicitly. Similarly, the explicit notation should be used if a Member subtype (e.g., Coach) is introduced (subtypes are discussed later).

In the case of implied (possibly disjunctive) mandatory role constraints, it is OK to *mark the constraint explicitly if it will still apply if more roles are added to the object type* (where these extra roles are excluded from the constraint). For object types like Date, this would almost never happen. But suppose you began with the two fact type schema in Figure 5.11 and felt that you would stay with the rule that members must play or coach, but allowed that you might later record some data about teams before choosing their coach or players (e.g., as in Figure 5.10). In that case, it's fine to explicitly show the disjunctive mandatory constraint on the two member roles (but not the two team roles), as in Figure 5.11.

A disjunctive mandatory role constraint, or inclusive-or constraint, indicates that each instance in the population of the object type must play at least one of the

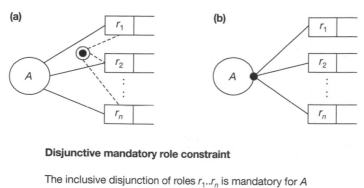

Disjunctive mandatory role constraint

The inclusive disjunction of roles $r_1..r_n$ is mandatory for A

i.e., each member of pop(A) plays r_1 **or** ... r_n (or all)

i.e., each member of pop(A) plays *at least one of* $r_1,..., r_n$

Figure 5.12 The role disjunction is mandatory (two notations).

constrained roles (and possibly all of them). Figure 5.12(a) indicates in general how to explicitly specify that a disjunction of roles r_1, r_2,..., r_n is mandatory by linking the n roles to a circled dot. The roles may occur at any position in a predicate, and the predicates need not be distinct. The alternative notation in Figure 5.12(b) may be used if each role occurs in only one such constraint. The inclusive "or" is used in the *verbalization* of the constraint. For example, the disjunctive constraint in Figure 5.11 is formally verbalized as **each** Member coaches **some** Team **or** plays for **some** team. As in logic and computing, "or" is always interpreted in the inclusive sense unless we say otherwise.

Disjunctive mandatory role constraints sometimes apply to roles in the same predicate. Figure 5.13 relates to a small UoD where people are identified by their first name. A sample population is shown for the ring binary; here each person plays one (or both) of the two roles. For instance, Terry is a child of Alice and Bernie and a parent of Selena. Since Person plays another role in the schema, the disjunctive mandatory role constraint must be depicted explicitly.

As an example involving derivation, consider Table 5.2. For simplicity, assume students are identified by their surname. Here students take a test and an exam, and their total score is computed by adding these two scores.

The schema for this, shown in Figure 5.14, includes a derived fact type. If included on the diagram, a derived fact type must be marked with an asterisk, and its constraints should be shown explicitly (even though these constraints are typically derived). The mandatory constraint on the derived fact type means the total score must be known—this does not mean that it must be stored.

If desired, the roles played by Score may be named "testScore", "examScore", and "totalScore", and the derivation rule may be specified in attribute style as **define** Student.totalScore **as** Student.testScore + Student.examScore. The uniqueness constraint on

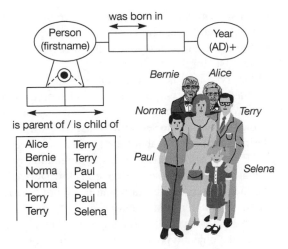

Figure 5.13 Each person is a parent or child.

Table 5.2 Student scores.

Student	Test	Exam	Total
Adams	15	60	75
Brown	10	65	75
Einstein	20	80	100

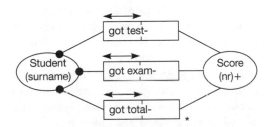

* Student got total-Score **iff**
        Student got test-Score **and** got exam-Score
        and total-Score = test-Score + exam-Score

Figure 5.14 Constraints on the derived fact type are derivable.

the total score fact type is derivable from the derivation rule and the uniqueness constraints on the other fact types (each student has only one test score and only one exam score, and the total score is the sum of these). The mandatory role on the total score fact type is derivable from the derivation rule and the other mandatory roles (each student has a test score and an exam score, and the rule then provides the total score).

By default, all constraints shown on a derived fact type are derivable. This default rule is discussed in more detail later. In very rare cases we may want to draw a derived fact type with a nonderivable constraint—in this case the fact type is marked with an "®" to indicate an extra rule exists for this predicate.

In principle, a derived fact type may be drawn with no constraints if these can be derived. Typically, however, a derived fact type is only included on the diagram for discussion purposes, and in such cases it is illuminating to show the constraints explicitly.

The term "mandatory role" is used in the sense of "must be *known*" (either by storing it or deriving it). If desired, we may talk about the population of derived fact types as well as base fact types. For a given object type *A*, the population of *A*, pop*(A)*, includes all members of *A* that play either base or derived roles. Derived roles may be optional. For example, if either the test or the exam role in Figure 5.14 is optional, the total score role is also optional (though it is still unique).

With large schemas, an object type may play so many roles that it becomes awkward to connect a single ellipse for the object type to all its roles. To solve this problem, *object types may be duplicated* on a schema as often as desired. In this case, the rule for implicit mandatory disjunctive roles applies to the union of all the duplicate ellipses for the object type. Large schemas are typically divided into pages, and the same object type might appear on many pages. In addition, an object type might be duplicated on a single page. An object type may also be *imported from an external model* where it is originally defined. Different ORM tools may use different notations to indicate such cases.

To indicate that an object type is duplicated in the same model, either on the same or a different page, the VisioModeler tool uses the arrow tip symbol "▲" (think of this as a pointer to another occurrence). If Figure 5.15 is the only diagram on a given schema page, Date is duplicated on that page and Member on another page. VisioModeler allows you to right-click an object type to navigate to its other occurrences. It also uses a double-ellipse notation to indicate an object type is *external* (imported from another model). For example, the Medication object type in Figure 5.15 is defined in another model (and hence its reference scheme is suppressed).

Microsoft's latest ORM tool uses a slash fill notation for externals, but at the time of writing had no notation for duplicate object types. For the remainder of this book, I'll use shadows for duplicates and slash fill for externals (see Figure 5.16). A shadow intuitively suggests the presence of an extra copy of the object type.

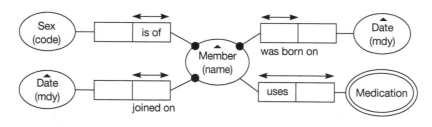

Figure 5.15 Object types may be duplicated, or imported from an external model.

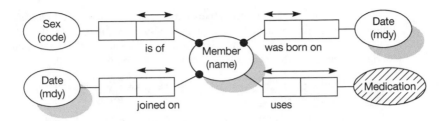

Figure 5.16 An alternative notation for duplicate and external object types.

Exercise 5.2

1. Schematize the UoD described by the following sample output report. At the time these figures were recorded, the former Commonwealth of Independent States (CIS) was treated as a single country. Include uniqueness and mandatory role constraints.

Country	Reserves (Gt)	
	Coal	Oil
CIS	233	8.6
USA	223	4.1
China	99	2.7
Germany	82	?
Australia	59	?
Saudi Arabia	0.1	23.0

2. Set out the conceptual schema for the following output report. Include uniqueness and mandatory role constraints. Identify any derived fact type(s).

Subject	Year	Enrollment	Rating	NrStudents	%	Lecturer
CS121	1982	200	7	5	2.50	P.L. Cook
			6	10	5.00	
			5	75	37.50	
			4	80	40.00	
			3	10	5.00	
			2	5	2.50	
CS123	1982	150	7	4	2.67	R.V. Green
			6	8	5.33	
			5	60	40.00	
			4	70	46.67	
			1	6	4.00	
CS121	1983	250	7	10	4.00	A.B. White
			6	30	12.00	
			5	100	40.00	
			4	80	32.00	
			3	15	6.00	

3. A cricket fan maintains a record of boundaries scored by Australia, India, and New Zealand in their competition matches. In the game of cricket a *six* is scored if the ball is hit over the field boundary on the full. If the ball reaches the boundary after landing on the ground, a *four* is scored. In either case, a *boundary* is said to have been scored.

Year	Australia			India			New Zealand		
	4s	6s	Total	4s	6s	Total	4s	6s	Total
1984	120	30	150	135	23	158	115	35	150
1985	112	33	145	110	30	140	120	25	145
1986	140	29	169	135	30	165	123	35	158

Although it is possible to score a four or six by running between the wickets, such cases do not count as boundaries and are not included in the database. A sample output report from this information system is shown. Here "4s" means "number of fours", and "6s" means "number of sixes". Schematize this UoD, including uniqueness constraints, mandatory roles, and derived fact types. Use nesting.

4. Report extracts are shown from an information system used for the 1990 Australian federal election for the House of Representatives (the main body of political government in Australia). The table lists codes and titles of political parties that fielded candidates in this election or the previous election (some parties competed in only one of these elections). For this exercise, *treat Independent as a party*.

PartyCode	Title
ALP	Australian Labor Party
AD	Australian Democrats
GRN	Greens
GRY	Grey Power
IND	Independent
LIB	Liberal Party of Australia
NDP	Nuclear Disarmament Party
NP	National Party of Australia
...	...

A snapshot of voting details is shown about two seats (i.e., voting regions) in the 1990 election. This snapshot was taken during the later stage of the vote counting. The number of votes for each politician, as well as the informal vote, is initially set to zero. During the election the voting figures are continually updated. The percentage of votes counted is calculated assuming all those on roll (that is, registered voters) actually vote. For simplicity, *assume each politician and each seat has a unique name*. Figures are maintained for all seats in all states.

An asterisk (*) preceding a politician's name indicates an incumbent, or *sitting member* (e.g., Fife is the sitting member for the seat of Hume); express this as a binary. Sitting members are recorded only if they seek reelection. Some seats may be new (these have no results for the previous election). States are identified by codes (e.g., "QLD" denotes Queensland). Each state has many seats (not shown here).

Draw a conceptual schema diagram for this UoD. Include uniqueness constraints and mandatory roles. If a fact type is derived, omit it from the diagram but include a derivation rule for it (you may specify this rule informally). Do not attempt any nesting.

QLD:

FADDEN (On roll: 69110)	
CROSS (AD)	7555
FRECKLETON (NP)	2001
JULL (LIB)	24817
HEYMANN (IND)	641
WILKINSON (ALP)	21368
Informal	1404
% counted: 84	
Previous election: AD 4065; ALP 24481; LIB 21258; NP 9581	

NSW:

HUME (On roll: 70093)	
JONES (IND)	9007
* FIFE (LIB)	29553
KIRKWOOD (IND)	507
MARTIN (ALP)	20554
ROBERTS (AD)	3889
Informal	1309
% counted: 92	
Previous election: AD 2498; ALP 24516; IND (total) 2086; LIB 33687; NDP 1105	

5.3   Logical Derivation Check

Step 3 of the design procedure included a check for basic arithmetic derivations—these are usually obvious (e.g., totals). Once uniqueness and mandatory role constraints have been specified, we are in a good position to *check for logical derivations*—these can be harder to spot, especially if some important facts were missed at step 1. As a simple example, consider the report extract shown in Table 5.3.

You may recall this table from the previous chapter, where it was correctly modeled as two binaries. I'll now deliberately model it the wrong way, to illustrate the logical derivation check. Suppose we verbalize the first row as the two facts: Lecturer (surname) 'Halpin' works for Department (code) 'CS'; Lecturer (surname) 'Halpin' works in Building (nr) '69'. Assuming the table is significant with respect to uniqueness constraints and mandatory roles, this leads to the schema shown in Figure 5.17.

To begin our logical derivation check we now ask ourselves: *Are there any other associations of interest between the object types, especially functional ones?* A binary association is *functional* if at least one of its roles has a simple uniqueness

Table 5.3 University data.

Lecturer	*Department*	*Building*
Halpin	CS	69
Okimura	JA	1
Orlowska	CS	69
Wang	CN	1

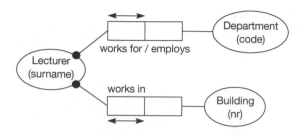

Figure 5.17 A first draft schema for Table 5.3. Any other association of interest?

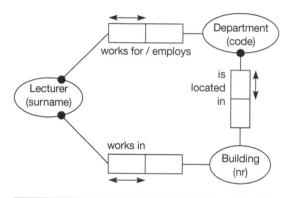

Figure 5.18 A second draft schema for Table 5.3. Which fact type is derivable?

constraint: ○—□. Each column entry for this role functionally determines the entry for the other role. Hence a role with a simple uniqueness constraint is said to be a *functional role*.

Looking at Figure 5.17, we now notice that the following fact type is also of interest: Department is located in Building. Suppose we interpret Table 5.3 as also giving us this information. For example, the first row of the table also tells us that the computer science department is located in building 69. Is the new fact type functional? From rows 2 and 3 we see that the same building may house more than one department. However, the population suggests that each department is located in only one building. Suppose the domain expert verifies that this is the case. We might now add this fact type to our schema to obtain Figure 5.18.

The optional roles of Department and Building in Figure 5.18 allow for other possibilities in the global schema (departments without lecturers or buildings without departments) not covered by Table 5.3. We now ask ourselves the following question: *Can any fact type be derived from the others?* Looking at the three binaries in Figure 5.18, you would probably suspect that one can be derived from the other two. Is this suspicion justified? If so, which binary should be derived? Is there a choice? What do you think?

Suppose we decide to make the new fact type about department location derivable, adding the following logical rule to our derivation rule section:

Department is located in Building **iff**   Department employs **a** Lecturer
who works in Building

This treats the department location fact type as a projection on Department and Building from the compound fact type that is the schema path from Department through Lecturer to Building. Suppose the domain expert agrees that this rule does apply. Is it now OK to make the department location derived? No! Why not? Recall the following design guideline: *by default, all constraints on a derived fact type are derivable.* Is this true with our choice of derived fact type?

With our example, the uniqueness constraint on the fact type Department is located in Building is not derivable. How can we know this? One way of seeing this is to provide a *counterexample*—in this case, a sample population that satisfies all constraints except the uniqueness constraint that each department is located in at most one building.

One such population is shown in Figure 5.19. If we populated the horizontal binaries as shown, the derivation rule proposed earlier generates a population for the vertical binary that locates the computer science department in two buildings.

If we derive the vertical binary, we must specify the uniqueness on it as an additional nonderived constraint to be enforced separately—that is, when one of the two horizontal binaries is updated we need to check that all lecturers working for the same department work in the same building. Sometimes a design decision like this is made in

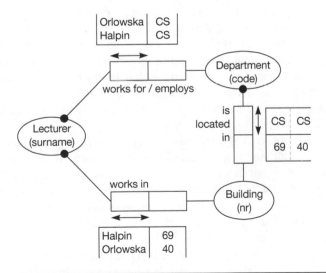

Figure 5.19 The uniqueness constraint on the vertical binary is violated.

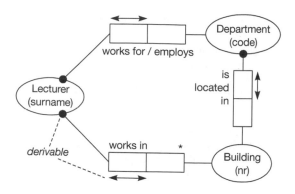

* Lecturer works in Building **iff**   Lecturer works for **a** Department
                                                    that is located in Building

Figure 5.20 If the rule applies, the constraints on the derived fact type are derivable.

order to speed up queries, even though updates become more expensive. However, the default design guideline should usually be followed, since this simplifies updates.

Another problem with deriving the department location fact type is that its mandatory role constraint can't be derived unless we add a mandatory constraint on the employs role. But perhaps some departments have no lecturers. For example, if the public relations department does not employ any lecturers, its location cannot be derived. To satisfy our default guideline, the only possible choice of derived fact type is Lecturer works in Building (see Figure 5.20).

The derived fact type is included on the diagram for discussion purposes, but would usually be omitted, with just the derivation rule being stated. If the domain expert agrees with the derivation rule shown here, it is safe to derive Lecturer works in Building because its constraints are implied by constraints on the base fact types. Since each lecturer works for exactly one department, and each department is located in exactly one building, the derivation rule implies that each lecturer works in exactly one building. So both the uniqueness and mandatory role constraints on the derived fact type are implied.

In cases like this we say the uniqueness constraint is *transitively implied.* You are probably familiar with the notion of transitive relations, where if the relation holds between each consecutive pair in a sequence, it holds between the first and last member of the sequence (e.g., if $x > y$ and $y > z$, then $x > z$). Similarly, functional determinacy is transitive: *if a chain of binaries has a uniqueness constraint on the first role of each* (○—▭), *then the binary from start to end projected from their inner join has an implied uniqueness constraint on its first role.*

In Figure 5.21, the schema is populated with the sample facts from Table 5.3, as well as the fact that the PR (public relations) department is located in building 2. A chain of two functional binaries goes from Lecturer through Department to Building, and the derivation rule defines the *[lecturer, building]* projection on the conceptual join of these

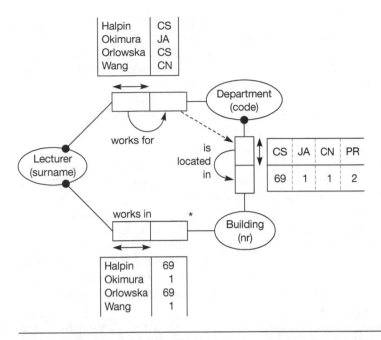

Figure 5.21 The derived association is projected from a functional chain.

two binaries. For exposition purposes, the FDs corresponding to the uniqueness constraints on the base fact types are displayed. In such cases, we may use the uniqueness constraint pattern (or FD chain) to help choose the derived fact type.

To ensure that no lecturers are lost along the chain, we also require that their departments have a location. So each department playing the employs role must also play the role of having a location. This requirement is an example of a *subset constraint* and is depicted in Figure 5.21 as a dotted arrow from the incoming role to the outgoing role of Department.

This subset constraint is implied by the mandatory constraint on Department. In combination with the base mandatory constraint on Lecturer, this subset constraint implies the mandatory constraint on the derived association. Subset constraints are discussed in detail in the next chapter.

We always need to check with the domain expert whether our derivation rule is semantically correct. The mere existence of such a constraint pattern doesn't guarantee that the other fact type is derived. There are infinitely many associations that could be specified between Lecturer and Building. The other fact type cannot be derived from the work and location fact types unless within the UoD it is logically equivalent to the /lecturer, building/ projection on their join path. So we still need to ensure the following equivalence really does apply: Lecturer works in Building **iff** Lecturer works for **a** Department **that** is located in Building. Is it possible for Okimura, say, who works in the Japanese department, located in building 1, to work instead in another building (e.g., building 5)? If the answer is "yes", then we have a counterexample to the equivalence, so we cannot derive the association Lecturer works in Building. If no such violation of the derivation rule is possible, then the association is derivable.

To clarify this point, note that the same constraint pattern may occur if we replace the derived fact type in Figure 5.21 by Lecturer has lunch in Building. In most academic domains, it is common for some lecturers to have their lunch in a building different from their work building. In such a UoD, the lunch fact type is *not* derivable since the following derivation rule does not apply: Lecturer has lunch in Building **iff** Lecturer works for **a** Department **that** is located in Building.

As an aside, the derivation rule in Figure 5.20 may also be expressed by means of a "pair-equality" constraint between the works_in predicate and the join-path projection formed by connecting the outer roles of Department's predicates. Such "join constraints" are discussed in the next chapter.

Sometimes, fact types may be derived even if they do not have a mandatory role. For example, suppose some lecturers (e.g., guest lecturers) don't work for a department and don't work in a building. So long as the derivation rule in Figure 5.20 still applies, we may still derive the fact type Lecturer works in Building. The only difference is that the two mandatory role constraints on Lecturer are removed. Of course, in the global schema Lecturer would normally play some other mandatory role, but this is irrelevant to the derivation.

Now consider the case where some lecturers don't work for a department, but all lecturers do work in a building. We might consider handling this case with a fact type that is only *partly derived,* weakening the main operator of the derivation rule from **iff** to **if**. For example: Lecturer works in Building **if** Lecturer works for **a** Department **that** is located in Building. This allows us to enter building facts directly for those lecturers without a department. In practice, such cases are usually *reformulated using a disjunction of base and fully derived predicates.*

To cater to the lecturers without a department, we use the fact type Lecturer works individually in Building. For the lecturers with a department, we use the derivation rule Lecturer works departmentally in Building **iff** Lecturer works for **a** Department **that** is located in Building. Now the overall derivation may be specified as Lecturer works in Building **iff** Lecturer works individually in Building **or** works departmentally in Building. While such cases often arise in logic programming (e.g., grandparent_of may be partly derived from parent_of and partly stored directly), they are fairly rare in business applications.

Sometimes we encounter derived associations with neither a mandatory nor a functional role. Consider the schema shown in Figure 5.22. This has two optional many:many associations. Can you see any logical derivation possibilities? This would be easier to deal with if we had an output report or sample data. At any rate, which (if any) of the associations do you consider derivable?

Knowledge about each group member is more precise than knowledge about the group as a whole. So if we are interested in the language expertise of each person, we should store this and derive the group expertise from the rule Group has expertise in Language **iff** Group includes **a** Person **who** is expert in Language. This approach requires a closed-world approach to the expert role played by Person (if a person is an expert in a language, we must record it). Section 7.4 discusses this notion of "relative closure" in

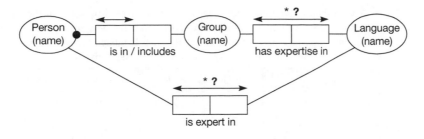

Figure 5.22 Which (if any) of the *m:n* associations is derivable?

more detail. Obviously we cannot derive the expertise of a person from that of his or her group. But what if we are not interested in each person's expertise? In this case the fact type Person is expert in Group should be deleted, and the remaining binaries would both be base fact types.

Exercise 5.3

1. In a computer company, workers are standardly identified by their initials, but also have a unique name. Each worker has access to exactly one PC, and each PC is accessed by at least one worker. For each PC a record is kept of its room location, the worker(s) who access it, and the computer language(s), if any, installed on it.

PC	Room	Workers with access		Languages installed
pc01	507	EFC	(Ed Codfish)	Pascal, Prolog, SQL
		TAH	(Terry Happy)	
pc02	507	NW	(Nancy Wirth)	Pascal, Modula-2
pc03	618	PAB	(Paul Boles)	Hope, Miranda
		JM	(Joan McCarthy)	
pc04	508	IN	(Ima Newie)	
pc05	508	PNC	(Peter Crusoe)	COBOL, SQL
...	...	...	...	...

Each computer language is one of three types (declarative, functional, or procedural), and is installed on a PC or has an expert (or both). The PC a worker accesses must be in the room in which he or she works. The next table provides a full record of the languages, their types, who are expert at each, and each expert's room.

Language	Type	Experts (rooms)
COBOL	procedural	PNC (508), REK (611)
Hope	functional	?
LISP	functional	JM (618)
Modula-2	procedural	NW (507)
Miranda	functional	PAB (618), DC (708)
Pascal	procedural	NW (507), TAH (507)
Prolog	declarative	JS (407)
SQL	declarative	EFC (507), PNC (508), TAH (507)

A workshop on computer languages is to be delivered by some of the workers. The full workshop program, shown in the final table, indicates how many hours (h) speakers talk about each language and the total hours for each language type. Schematize this UoD, including uniqueness and mandatory role constraints and derivation.

Declarative (6 h)		Functional (4 h)		Procedural (6 h)	
Prolog: SQL:	JS (3 h) PNC (1 h) TAH (2 h)	Hope: Miranda:	PAB (1 h) PAB (3 h)	Modula-2: Pascal:	NW (3 h) NW (2 h) TAH (1 h)

2. (a) The following report refers to a UoD like that discussed in this section, except that departments may be located in many buildings. Each lecturer works in exactly one building. Some departments employ no lecturers. Schematize this UoD using three binaries, and note which if any is derivable. Specify any derivation rules.

Lecturer	Dept	Building
Halpin	CS	69
Okimura	JA	1
Orlowska	CS	69
Wang	CN	1
Yamamoto	JA	3
?	PR	2

(b) Consider a UoD as in (a), except that each department employs a lecturer, so the final row of the table in (a) is illegal. Schematize this UoD including derivation.

5.4   Reference Schemes

With uniqueness and mandatory role constraints covered, it is time to consider reference schemes in more depth. With simple identification schemes, each entity is identified by associating it with a single value. For example, a country might be referenced using a code. For instance, Australia may be referenced by the definite description "The Country that has CountryCode 'AU'". We usually abbreviate simple reference schemes by parenthesizing the reference mode, or manner in which the value relates to the entity, for example, Country (code). In practice, more complex reference schemes are often encountered, and we need to deal with them even as early as step 1 of the CSDP, when we verbalize facts.

Before examining these harder cases, let's have a closer look at simple reference schemes. Table 5.4 contains data about a small UoD where people can be identified by their surnames and each city has a unique name. You might like to draw the conceptual schema for this yourself before looking at the solution (Figure 5.23). Here the reference schemes are abbreviated as reference modes in the usual way, using parentheses.

The schema is repeated in Figure 5.24, this time with the reference schemes depicted explicitly—each appears as a *mandatory, 1:1 reference type*. For example, each person has exactly one surname, and each surname refers to at most one person. Technically, this is called an *injection* (or *1:1 into* mapping) from Person to Surname. In this

Table 5.4 Personal details.

Person	City	Height (cm)	Chest (cm)	Mass (kg)	IQ
Adams	Brisbane	175	100	77	100
Brisbane	Sydney	182	91	80	120
Collins	Sydney	173	80	67	100
Darwin	Darwin	175	95	90	90

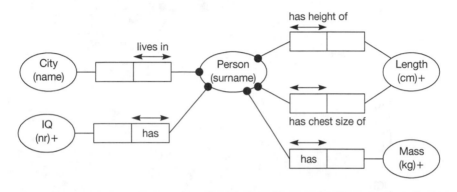

Figure 5.23 Conceptual schema for Table 5.4 (reference schemes abbreviated).

explicit version of the schema, each of the value types Surname, Cityname, IQNr, kgValue, and cmValue play just one role, so it is better not to mark this role as mandatory.

Implicitly, each value type is considered to be either identical to, or a subtype of, a primitive value type (e.g., String or Number). To help avoid cluttered diagrams, the primitive value types and their subtype graphs are not displayed. It should be remembered, however, that string value types often overlap with one another, as do numeric value types. For example, Surname and CityName are both subtypes of String; their populations do overlap here since both include the string 'Brisbane'.

Figure 5.24 also illustrates our earlier decision to indicate mandatory roles explicitly when the reference scheme is explicit. For example, the fact roles played by City, IQ, and Mass are marked mandatory, as is the disjunction of fact roles played by Length. The abbreviated version in Figure 5.23 is usually preferable. However, the explicit version is useful for clarifying the distinction between entities and the values that refer to them.

For example, assuming the population shown in Table 5.4, and an appropriate query language, consider the following dialogue between a user and the CIP.

User: Which person lives in a city with the same name as his/her surname?
CIP: Darwin.

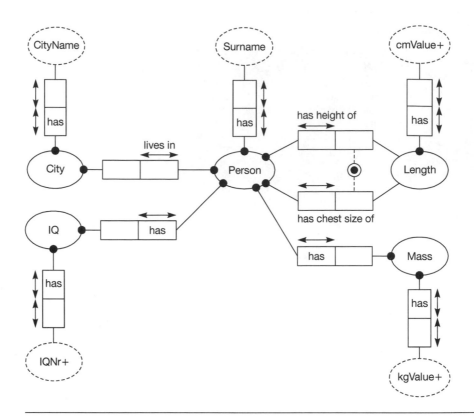

Figure 5.24 Conceptual schema for Table 5.4 (reference schemes explicated).

User: Which person is a city?
CIP: None: Entity types Person and City are mutually exclusive.

It is meaningful to compare the names for Person and City, since they are both charac-ter strings. But it is not sensible to compare persons and cities—they are completely different types of entities.

Notice that the value types for IQ, mass, and length are all numeric (as indicated by the "+" mark). However, mass and length have different units, while IQ is dimen-sionless (i.e., it has no units). Conceptually, two numerically referenced entities may be compared or added only if they have the same unit (or both have no unit). Hence the following queries do not make sense:

List persons whose mass equals their IQ.
List persons whose height is more than twice their mass.
List height + mass for each person.

Of course, the numbers themselves may always be compared. Also, height and chest size are both based on the same domain and unit, so they are compatible. So the follow-ing queries are acceptable:

List persons whose mass number equals their IQ number.
List persons whose height number is more than twice their mass number.
List height + chest size for each person.

Most current database systems provide little or no support for the distinction between entities and their values. Operations specified in queries are always interpreted as applying directly to the values. For example, assuming the data of Table 5.4 is stored in a relational database as the table *Athlete* (person, city, height, chest, mass, iq), the following SQL query is quite legal:

select person **from** Athlete
where person = city
and mass = iq **and** chest + mass > height

For the population shown, this query returns the value 'Darwin', despite the fact that taken literally the query is nonsense. Of course, the comparisons evaluated in the query are actually between values, not entities, and we could clarify what is going on by a better choice of column names (e.g., use "surname" and "cityname" instead of "person" and "city").

Values are constants with a predefined interpretation, and hence require no explicit reference scheme. For example, 'Brisbane' denotes itself (i.e., the character string 'Brisbane'), and when written without quotes the numeral '77' denotes the number 77 (Hindu-Arabic decimal notation is assumed). It is sometimes claimed that when written without quotes, a constant like 'Brisbane' is enough to identify a single entity. However, some context is always required (at least implicitly). Even in Table 5.4, 'Brisbane' is used to refer to both a person and a city.

Earlier in the book we saw that entities are referenced by means of definite descriptions (e.g., "the City with name 'Brisbane'"). Within the context of a reference type, a value may, somewhat loosely, be said to be an identifier for an entity if the value relates to only one entity of that type.

When only one value is used in a definite description, we have a simple 1:1 reference scheme. Sometimes, however, two or more values may be required. In this case we have a *compound reference scheme*. As an example, consider how computer files are identified in Table 5.5. Within a given folder, a file may be identified by its local filename (e.g., "flag.vsd"). But when many folders are involved, we need to combine the folder name with the local filename to know which file we are talking about.

To reflect the two-part naming convention suggested by the two columns for File in Table 5.5, we could model the situation as shown in Figure 5.25. The mandatory roles

Table 5.5 Details about computer files.

File		Size (kb)
Folder	Filename	
MyDocs	flag.vsd	35
MyDocs	orm1.doc	1324
OzWork	flag.vsd	40

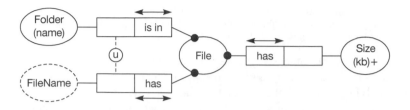

each Folder, Filename **combination refers to at most one** File

Figure 5.25 File has a compound reference scheme.

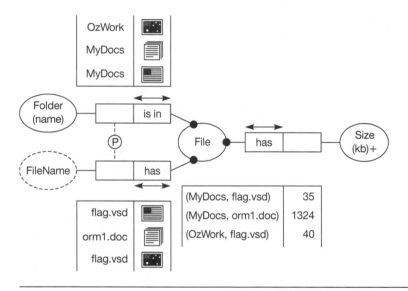

Figure 5.26 The previous schema populated with references and facts.

and internal uniqueness constraints declare that each file is in exactly one folder, has exactly one (local) filename, and has exactly one size. The external uniqueness constraint can be used to provide a compound reference scheme and may be verbalized as **each** Folder, FileName **combination refers to at most one** File.

If no other identification scheme is preferred for File, the external uniqueness constraint is the basis for the primary way in which humans communicate about the files. To emphasize this choice of *primary reference,* a circled *P* (for Primary) symbol "ⓟ" may be used instead of a circled *u,* as shown in Figure 5.26. Using icons for entities, the reference types File is in Folder and File has FileName may be populated as shown. In the fact table for File has Size, the file entries appear as value pairs. Though not apparent in the diagram, these pairs are ordered (Folder, FileName) in the same order as the reference types were added to the schema—a CASE tool can display this order on request.

If the reference predicates are included in the definite descriptions for the files, any order can be used. For example, "the File that is in Folder 'MyDocs' and has FileName 'flag.vsd'" is equivalent to "the File that has FileName 'flag.vsd' and is in Folder 'MyDocs'". In general, compound reference schemes involve a mandatory 1:1 map of objects to a tuple of two or more values.

Textually, a compound reference scheme for an object type *A* may be declared by listing the reference types, with the leading *A* removed, in parentheses after *A*. The relevant uniqueness and mandatory constraints on reference predicates are assumed, and if the reference schemes are declared first, the facts may be stated in shortened form. For example, the sample model may be specified textually as follows:

Reference schemes:	Folder (name); File (is in Folder, has FileName); Size (kb)+
Fact type:	File has Size
Constraints:	**each** File has **at most one** Size
	each File has **at least one** Size
Fact instances:	File ('MyDocs', 'flag.vsd') has Size 35
	File ('MyDocs', 'orm1.doc') has Size 1324
	File ('OzWork', 'flag.vsd') has Size 40

In principle, we could model Files using a simple reference scheme, by concatenating the folder name and local filename into one string with a separator (e.g., "\"). For example, the files may then be named simply "MyDocs\flag.vsd", "MyDocs\orm1.doc", and "OzWork\flag.vsd". This approach is normally undesirable because it requires extra derivation work to extract and group the components to produce various reports. I'll have more to say about this issue later. Indeed, if we wish to issue queries about the file extension (e.g., "vsd", "doc") as well, a three-part reference scheme is desirable (combination of folder name, simple name, and file extension).

Identification schemes are *relative* to the particular UoD. Often, a simple scheme that works in a local context fails to work in a UoD of wider scope. A simple file reference scheme used in a UoD with only one folder may need to be extended if we add other folders. This notion is important to bear in mind when merging subschemas into a larger schema. For example, suppose that within a given University department each subject offered by that department can be identified by its title. For instance, consider the output report in Table 5.6, which indicates which subjects are offered by the Physics Department in which semesters.

If designing a schema for just the Physics Department, we have a 1:1 correspondence between subjects and their titles. So this table may be schematized as the fact type Subject (title) is offered in Semester (nr). A similar schematization could be used

Table 5.6 Physics Department offerings.

Subject	Semester
Electronics	1
Mechanics	1
Optics	2

Table 5.7 Mathematics Department offerings.

Subject	Semester
Algebra	2
Calculus	1
Mechanics	1

Table 5.8 University subject offerings.

Department	Subject title	Semester
Physics	Electronics	1
	Mechanics	1
	Optics	2
Mathematics	Algebra	2
	Calculus	1
	Mechanics	1
...	...	...

for just the Mathematics Department, a sample output report for which is shown in Table 5.7.

But now suppose we need to integrate departmental schemas into an overall schema for the whole university. Our simple identification scheme for subjects will no longer work because, in this wider UoD, different subjects may have the same title. For example, the subject Mechanics offered by the Physics Department is different from the subject Mechanics offered by the Mathematics Department. A combined output report would look like Table 5.8.

The first row may be verbalized using a compound reference scheme as follows: "The Subject that is offered by the Department named 'Physics' and has the SubjectTitle 'Electronics' is offered in the Semester numbered 1". This approach is schematized in Figure 5.27. If desired, the external uniqueness constraint symbol may be replaced by ℗. However, this is not needed, since no other reference scheme exists for Subject. If an object type has only one candidate reference scheme, this must be the primary one.

Though conceptually this picture is illuminating, in practice its implementation may be somewhat awkward, with two labels (one for the department and one for the title) needed to identify a subject. In such cases, a new identification scheme is often introduced to provide simple 1:1 reference. For example, each subject may be assigned a unique subject code, as shown in Table 5.9.

In this output report there are two *candidate identifiers* for Subject. We could identify a subject by its code (e.g., 'PH102') or by combining its department and title (e.g., ('Physics', 'Mechanics')). One of these is chosen as the *primary identifier*, or standard

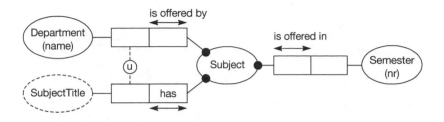

Figure 5.27 A schema for Table 5.8 using a compound reference scheme.

Table 5.9 Subject codes provide a simple reference scheme.

Subject	Title	Department	Semester
PH101	Electronics	Physics	1
PH102	Mechanics	Physics	1
PH200	Optics	Physics	2
MP104	Algebra	Mathematics	2
MP210	Calculus	Mathematics	1
MA109	Mechanics	Mathematics	1

means of referring to the entity. In this case, we would usually pick the subject code as the primary identifier. We can indicate this choice by displaying the subject code identification scheme as reference mode in parentheses (see Figure 5.28). *If a parenthesized reference mode is displayed, this is always taken to be the primary reference scheme.* In this case, the Department and SubjectTitle predicates are treated just like any other fact types; they are no longer considered to be reference types. Of course, the external uniqueness constraint between them must still be declared.

Suppose that for some strange reason you preferred to make the composite reference scheme primary even though subject codes exist. To do this you need to do two things. First, you must use ℗ for the external uniqueness constraint; second, you must display the subject code predicate explicitly, as shown in Figure 5.29.

In this case, the department and title predicates are reference types, and the subject code predicate is a fact type. Although unusual, this illustrates how you can control the choice of primary reference. The Visio Enterprise and VisioModeler tools determine the primary reference for an entity type basically as follows. If a reference mode is declared, then this is the primary reference; else if exactly one candidate reference scheme is marked ℗, then this is the primary reference; else an arbitrary choice is made from those candidate reference schemes with the fewest components (e.g., a simple reference scheme is preferred over a composite reference scheme).

Choosing one primary reference scheme from two or more existing schemes is perhaps not always a conceptual issue. At the conceptual level, its main use is to disambiguate abbreviated references that omit the reference predicate(s) (e.g., "Patient 3452

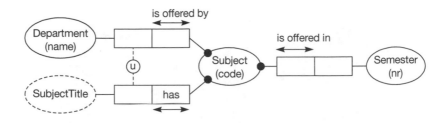

Figure 5.28 A schema for Table 5.9, using subject code as Subject's primary identifier.

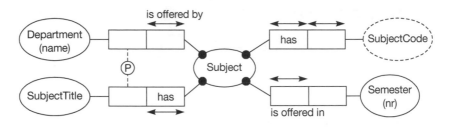

Figure 5.29 The composite reference scheme is now Subject's primary identifier.

has Temperature 37"). This is especially useful when populating fact tables with instances. At the logical level, however, the choice of primary reference typically has a major impact (e.g., determining the primary key of a table).

Here are some *guidelines for selecting a primary identifier.* First, *minimize the number of components.* A single subject code is easier to enter than two values for department and title. Moreover, a compound identifier adds extra overhead in the later database implementation (joins, indexes, and integrity checks over composite columns require more effort).

Second, favor an identifier that is *more stable.* In a university environment, the same subject may undergo some title changes throughout its history, and sometimes the department that offers a given subject changes. It is even possible for the same department-title combination to refer to different subjects at different times. On the other hand, it is extremely rare for a subject to have its code changed, and the same subject code is never reused for a different subject.

If a historical record is needed for an object, and its identifier changes through time, extra work is required to keep track of these changes so that we know when we are talking about the same object. This extra effort can be minimized by making the identifier as stable as possible. Ideally, the object has the same identifier throughout the lifetime of the application; this is known as a *rigid identifier.* Most organizations choose rigid identifiers such as employeeNr, clientNr, serialNr for their employees, clients, equipment, and so on.

To explain some basic concepts in a friendly way, I've used identifiers such as PersonName, Surname, or even Firstname in some examples. However, except for trivial applications, this kind of identification is unrealistic. Often, two people may have the same name. Moreover, people may change their name—women usually change their surname when they marry, and anyone may legally change their name for other reasons. A philosophy lecturer of mine once changed his surname to "What" and his wife changed her surname to "Who"!

A third criterion sometimes used for selecting an identifier is that it be easy for users to recognize. This criterion is mainly used to minimize errors when users enter or access artificial identifiers such as subject or stock item codes. This effectively endows codes with semantics, at least implicitly. For example, the subject code "CS114" was used in my university for a particular subject in informatics. The first two characters "CS" indicate the discipline area (Computer Science), the first digit indicates the level (first), and the last two digits merely distinguish it from other computer science subjects at the same level. Such a code is less likely to be misread than an arbitrary code (e.g., "09714").

Such "information-bearing" identifiers are sometimes called *semantic names*. They should be avoided if the semantic relationships involved are unstable, since the names would then often need changing. In the current example, however, the semantics are fairly stable—the subject discipline is unlikely ever to change, and the subject level would normally be stable too. The linking of the two letters to discipline (e.g., "MP" for pure maths and "MA" for applied maths) rather than department is better, since disciplines are more stable than departments.

If semantic names are used, we need to decide whether their semantics are to be modeled in the system or simply assumed to be understood by users. The semantics of subject codes may be modeled explicitly by including the following three binaries in the schema: Subject is in Discipline; Subject is at YearLevel; Subject has SerialNr. An external uniqueness constraint spans the roles played here by the three components. Figure 5.30(a) shows the case where subject code is the primary identifier. In this case, these three binaries would normally be derived, and appropriate derivation rules specified (e.g., the discipline code may be derived using a substring operator to select the

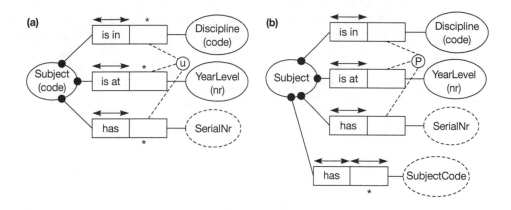

Figure 5.30 Different ways of exposing the semantics of subject codes.

first two characters of the subject code). The external uniqueness constraint is then derivable.

An alternative approach is shown in Figure 5.30(b). Here the three-part identification scheme is used for primary reference, and the subject code is derived by concatenation. The major advantage of storing the components separately like this is that it facilitates queries concerning the components. In particular, *if we wish to formulate queries **for each** instance of a reference component, then that component should be stored.* The schema in Figure 5.30(b) makes it easy to query properties for each discipline or year level (e.g., "How many subjects are offered for each discipline?"). As discussed in Section 11.10, the conceptual "for-each" construct corresponds to "group-by" in SQL. The model in Figure 5.30(a) is extremely awkward for such queries, since groups can normally only be formed from stored columns. On the other hand, a simple code is more compact and offers much better performance for relational joins than a three-part identification scheme.

Is there a way of having your cake and eating it too? Yes, at least to some extent. In Figure 5.31 the three components are both derived and stored (as shown by the "**"). This allows fast joins on the subject code and grouped queries on the components.

Semantic codes were often used in legacy systems, with no attempt to expose their semantics as separate components. If these legacy systems have to be retained in their current form, a separate system (e.g., a data warehouse) can be constructed to better support queries on the components. In copying the data from the legacy system to the new system, the codes are transformed into separate component fields.

Just how much of the semantics underlying an information-bearing name should be exposed in a conceptual schema depends on what kinds of queries we wish to issue. For example, consider the output report shown in Table 5.10. Here room numbers have the format *dd-ddd* (where *d* denotes a digit). The first two digits provide the building number for the room's building, the third digit indicates the room's floor (in this UoD no building has more than nine floors), and the last two digits comprise a serial number to distinguish rooms on the same floor.

If we never wish to query the information system about buildings or floors, it's fine to model rooms using the simple reference scheme Room(nr). Now suppose instead that we also expect the system to output reports like the extract shown in Table 5.11. Here we *are* interested in buildings, and even want to issue a query that lists the number

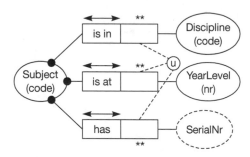

Figure 5.31 The three components are derived and stored.

Table 5.10 Employee details.

EmpNr	Employee name	Room
715	Adams A	69-301
139	Cantor G	67-301
503	Hagar TA	69-507
...	...	...

Table 5.11 Building details.

BuildingNr	Building name	Nr rooms
...	...	...
67	Priestly	100
68	Chemistry	100
69	Computer Science	150
...	...	...

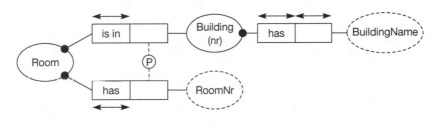

Figure 5.32 The reference scheme for Room exposes the building component.

of rooms *for each* building. In this case we must expose at least the building component of the reference scheme for buildings, as shown in Figure 5.32.

In the new model, the term "RoomNr" indicates a local room number (e.g., "301") that identifies a room within a given building. It corresponds to the last three digits in a campuswide room number such as "67-301". If we are not interested in querying the system about floors, there's no need to expose the room number semantics any further.

Now suppose that we wish to query the system about floors; for example, "How many rooms are there on floor 3 of building 67?" To facilitate this, we could expand the reference scheme to three components to expose the floor semantics. One way to model this is shown in Figure 5.33. This divides the previous room number (e.g., "301") into a FloorNr (e.g., "3") and a serial number (e.g., "01").

If we want to think about floors themselves, rather than just floor numbers, it is better to model Floor as an entity type as shown in Figure 5.34. Here Floor plays in the composite reference scheme for Room, and also has its own composite reference scheme.

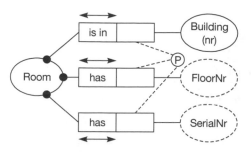

Figure 5.33 One way of exposing the three-part reference scheme for rooms.

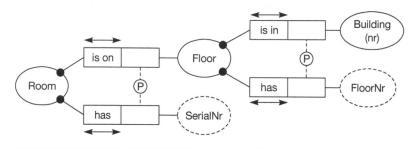

Figure 5.34 This alternative allows us to think directly about floors.

Although less convenient, it is possible to use derivation functions to formulate queries about single *instances* of a reference component, without actually storing the component. For example, to list the number of rooms on floor 3 of building 67, we could use the following SQL query: **select count(*) from** Room **where** roomNr **like** '67%' **and** roomNr **like** '%-3%'. Even though this approach is possible, I would still recommend exposing the semantics. If ever in doubt as to whether to expose some semantics, it's generally better to do so.

You should always store a reference component if you wish to query about a *group* of its instances; for example, "*For each* floor of building 67, how many rooms are there?" Using the schema of Figure 5.34, this may be formulated in ORM by selecting the path from Room to Building (i.e., Room is on **a** Floor **that** is in Building), adding the condition "= 67" for Building (implicitly applied to BuildingNr), and then requesting Floor and **count**(Room) **for each** Floor. At the relational level, the query may be formulated in SQL using a group-by clause; for example, **select** floorNr, count(*) **from** Room **where** buildingNr = 67 **group by** floorNr. The SQL language is discussed in detail in Chapter 11.

Choosing reference schemes for entity types is an important aspect of modeling. As a strict guideline, *an entity type's primary identification scheme must 1:1 map each entity of that type to a tuple of one or more values* (either directly or indirectly). So, each primary reference scheme provides an *injection* (mandatory, 1:1 mapping). For example, in Figure 5.34, each building maps directly to a unique building number, and each room maps (indirectly via the reference predicates) to a unique triple of values (building number, floor number, serial number).

In everyday life, weaker kinds of identification schemes are used in some contexts. For example, some people have identifying nicknames (e.g., "Tricky Dicky" denotes President Nixon, and "the great white shark" denotes the golfer Greg Norman). However, in a typical application not everybody will have a nickname, so nicknames are not used for primary reference (they are not mandatory).

Sometimes a 1:many reference scheme is used. For example, a plant or animal type may have more than one identifying common name. For instance, the bird species with the scientific name of *Dacelo gigas* may also be identified by any of the following common names: "kookaburra", "laughing jackass", "great brown kingfisher", or "bushman's clock". As a botanical example, "gorse" and "furze" refer to the same plant. In Figure 5.35, common names are used to provide the primary reference scheme for bird species. This choice is signified by the "P" on the uniqueness constraint symbol. A sample population is included to illustrate the 1:many nature of this reference type. Do you spot any problem with this reference scheme?

This association must not be used for primary reference, because it is not 1:1. You can imagine the problems that would arise if we used "kookaburra" to identify a bird species in one part of a database and "laughing jackass" in another part. In the absence of any standard identifier like a scientific name, how would we know that we were talking about the same bird species?

For primary reference, we must choose a mandatory, 1:1 scheme. Such a scheme may already exist (e.g., scientific name). If not, we create one with the help of the domain expert. This might be partly artificial (e.g., standard common name) or completely artificial (e.g., birdkindNr). Whatever we choose, we need to get the users of the information system to agree upon it.

The scientific name for a bird species is actually a semantic name with two components. For example, in *Dacelo gigas,* the "Dacelo" is the name of the genus, and "gigas" is a species name. By itself, a species name like "gigas" or "americana" does

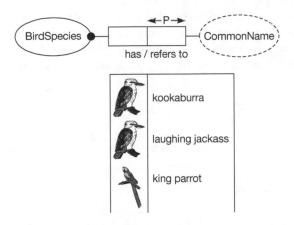

Figure 5.35 This association is not 1:1, so should *not* be used for primary reference.

not identify a species. For instance, *Certhia americana* (the brown creeper) is a different bird species from *Parula americana* (the northern parula). If we wish to query about the genus or species name, we should unpack the naming semantics into a two-part reference scheme as shown in Figure 5.36; otherwise we can use the simple reference scheme BirdSpecies (scientificName). Notice that we can still include facts about common names, because they are not used for primary reference. Once this schema is fully populated, we could let users interact with the system via the common names, still using the scientific naming convention to establish identity.

Simple 1:1 naming schemes relate entities directly to values (e.g., subjects to subject codes). In life we sometimes identify entities by 1:1 relating them to other entities (e.g., "the Olympics that was held in the Year 1992", "the Warehouse that is located in the City 'Brisbane'", "the Director who heads the Department 'Sales'"). Such identification schemes may be chosen for primary reference and depicted as mandatory 1:1 binaries (e.g., Olympics was held in Year (AD)). These binaries are then regarded as reference types, not fact types.

However, this practice is rare. Instead such binary associations are usually modeled as fact types, and other primary reference schemes are chosen (e.g., Olympics (sequenceNr), Warehouse (nr), Director (empNr)). Alternatively, the relevant entity types may be removed by using suitably descriptive predicates. For example, the assertion "The Olympics of Year 1992 was located in City 'Barcelona'" may be portrayed as a binary association between the entity types Year and City. If the original referential semantics are not needed, another alternative is to use simple value reference, but this is usually a last resort. For example, "Warehouse (name) 'Brisbane'" loses the semantics that this warehouse is located in the city Brisbane.

In compound reference schemes, each reference predicate is typically mandatory. In such cases, each entity of the same type is identified using the same number of values. In the real world, however, we sometimes encounter identification schemes where some of the reference roles are optional, but their disjunction is still mandatory. This is called *disjunctive reference*. In these cases, different entities of the same type may be referenced by different numbers of values. For example, consider the botanical identification scheme depicted in Figure 5.37.

Some kinds of plants are identified simply by a genus (e.g., *Agrostis*). Many other plant varieties are referenced by a combination of genus and species names (e.g., *Acacia interior*). Still others are identified by combining genus, species, and infraspecies, where the infraspecies itself is identified by a rank and infraname (e.g., *Eucalyptus*

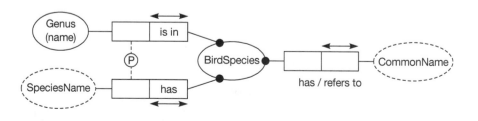

Figure 5.36 Common names may be used for alternate reference.

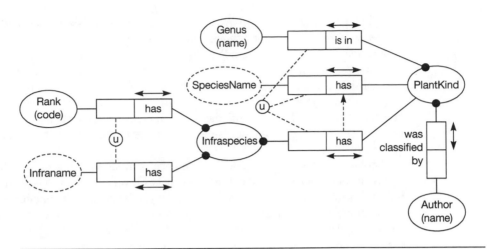

Figure 5.37 With botanical identification, some reference roles are optional.

fibrosa ssp. *nubila*). So depending on the kind of plant, there may be one, two, or four values required to identify it.

The external uniqueness constraint over three roles indicates that each subtuple of (genus, species, infraspecies) refers to at most one plant kind. The other external uniqueness constraint declares that the (rank, infraname) pair identifies infraspecies. In the reference scheme for PlantKind, only the genus is mandatory. Moreover, for each genus there is at most one plantkind with only a genus name. And for each genus-species combination there is at most one plantkind with no infraspecies. From a relational database perspective, each plantkind maps to a sequence of four values, three of which may be null, and each quadruple is unique (treating the null value just like any other value).

Years ago when Peter Ritson and I formalized disjunctive reference within ORM, we displayed it with a percentage sign next to the external uniqueness marker (e.g., "ⓤ%"). The "%" intuitively suggested that "partial" sequences of components are allowed. Nowadays, however, this notation is no longer used, and the basic external uniqueness symbol is used for both ordinary and disjunctive reference. You know the reference scheme is disjunctive if at least one reference role is optional. The minimum requirement for a legal reference scheme is that it provides a mandatory 1:1 mapping to a sequence of one or more values. So the disjunction of the reference roles must still be mandatory.

You may have noticed the dotted arrow running from the first role of Plant has Infraspecies to the first role of Plant has SpeciesName. This denotes the subset constraint that infraspecies is recorded only if species is. Subset constraints are discussed in detail in the next chapter.

Believe it or not, the reference scheme of Figure 5.37 is a simplified version of the actual identification scheme used in botany, where complications such as hybrids and cultivars also need to be catered to. Life can be messy!

In practice we should *try to avoid using a disjunctive reference scheme for primary reference.* With the current example, we should consider introducing an alternative simple identifier (e.g., plantkindNr). If the users agree to use this in their normal communication, this change can be made to the conceptual model. If not, we can still consider using it in the logical design model. Note that if we do this, we still need to model the disjunctive information as a disjunctive fact scheme (or "secondary reference" scheme). Although still messy to implement, moving the disjunction from primary to secondary reference simplifies and improves the performance for most implementations.

Another way to avoid disjunctive reference is to simply concatenate the reference components into a single name. Since this makes it very difficult to issue queries about individual components, this approach is unlikely to be viable with our current example.

Yet another way to avoid disjunctive reference is to incorporate special default values in the identification scheme. For example, if we use a symbol such as "#" or "--" for "does not exist" all the reference roles become mandatory, and this special value can be treated like any other value in enforcing uniqueness. Although this approach can work for implementing some cases, it is hardly conceptual and may be impractical if you require the user community to actually use the special values, or you need the same symbol to work with different data types (e.g., numbers as well as strings).

Sometimes reference chains can get lengthy. A value is identified by a constant. Each entity is referenced directly using a sequence of one or more objects, which in turn may be values or entities. In the latter case, the reference chain continues, recursively, until finally the referencing objects are all values. In this way, each object is ultimately referenced by one or more values that appear as entries in named columns of output reports or database tables.

Candidate identifiers for the same entity are said to be *synonyms.* In the information systems literature the term *homonym* is used for a label that refers to more than one entity. For example, the same surname "Jones" may refer to more than one person. Since "homonym" has different grammatical senses, another term such as "nonidentifying label" is preferable. At any rate, the "problem of homonyms" is solved either by augmenting the reference scheme until identification is achieved (e.g., combining surname and initials) or by using a completely different primary identification scheme (e.g., social security number).

In cases considered so far, an object's reference scheme has been the same throughout the whole schema. The next chapter examines some cases involving subtypes where this assumption is removed; this leads to *context-dependent reference.* To end this section, let's consider the case of variable reference where *different units are used for the same physical quantity* in the same application domain.

In Australia, for example, pieces of lumber have their longest length specified in meters, but their breadth and depth are measured in millimeters. Because this is a standard in the Australian building industry, an output report on lumber sizes might look like Table 5.12.

Suppose we want to compare the different linear measurements (e.g., Which sizes of lumber are 20 times as long as their breadth?) or compute volumes in standard units

Table 5.12 Lumber details.

Lumber size	Length (m)	Breadth (mm)	Depth (mm)
A4	3	100	100
B7	2	100	75
C7	5	200	100

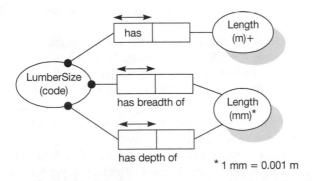

Figure 5.38 Different reference schemes for the same object type.

(e.g., What is the volume of lumber size C7 in cubic meters?). Figure 5.38 shows one way of modeling this situation. Here all three measures are based on the conceptual object type Length, used in a general sense. To indicate which units are used in which contexts, the object type is duplicated but the different units are indicated with different reference modes.

Finally, a *conversion rule* between the units is specified. Since several units might be used for the same physical quantity, we can reduce the number of conversion rules by choosing a *standard unit* and just supplying rules to convert to this standard (rather than separate conversions between each unit pair). The reference mode of the standard unit is set out in the normal way (in parentheses, with a "+"). However, in the case of a *derived unit,* an asterisk is appended. Being a kind of derivation rule, any conversion rule is written below the schema diagram. A derived unit is always placed on the left of the equals sign, as shown.

If we enforce the discipline that object types with the same unit-based reference mode are always compatible, we could model this case using the fact types: LumberSize (code) has Length (m)+; LumberSize has Breadth (mm)*; LumberSize has Depth (mm)*. The conversion rule 1 mm = 0.001 m is still needed. While this approach often leads to more natural verbalization, it makes the domain connection less obvious, and it requires care to apply the discipline. For example, if we want to include Length and Pressure in the same UoD, it would be incorrect to use the reference schemes Length (mm) and Pressure (mm) since this implies that Length and Pressure are based on the same semantic domain. To avoid this problem, we need to rename one of the reference modes, for example, Pressure (mmHg).

If we are not interested in modeling the connections between different units, then we could avoid collapsing physical quantities to the same dimension. For example, an astronomy application might have an entity type StellarDistance measured in parsecs and TelescopeDiameter measured in centimeters. What should we do here? The populations of the StellarDistance and TelescopeDiameter types would never overlap. If we never wanted to compare them, we could leave them just like this— the real-world semantic connection between these lengths is then excluded from our model.

At a more abstract level, we could model the metadata (length, etc.) as data. For instance, the lumber example could be modeled using the two fact types shown in Figure 5.39. The first fact from Table 5.12 could then be expressed by the following facts: LumberSize 'A4' has Attribute 'length' of NumericValue 3; Attribute 'length' has Unit 'm'. The unit conversion rule is still required. While this abstract approach is very powerful, it is often unnatural for most users. If used at all, it should normally be transformed into a simpler external schema for user interaction.

As a simpler example of treating different units as values, a financial application involving many currencies might model amounts of money using the compound reference scheme MoneyAmt(is in Currency(code), has NumericValue()). Demoting metadata (types) to data (values) can help to minimize structural changes to the schema over time. An abstract model like that in Figure 5.39 might be used to permit new kinds of attributes to be added without altering the database schema. For example, a medical application might use the ternary association Patient has Attribute of Value to anticipate new patient tests that might be added later. In such cases, additional associations are often needed to control the use of units within their relevant contexts.

In some cases, we may need to work with multiple unit systems. For example, we may need both metric and U.S. customary (or British imperial) nonmetric measures while users gradually move from one unit system to a newer one or during the merging of applications based on different unit systems. Besides supplying conversion rules to transform between the different readings, we must take care to expose the units to humans interacting with the system (recall the fate of the Mars Climate Orbiter).

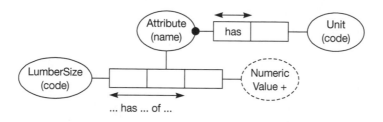

Figure 5.39 Demoting metadata to data.

Exercise 5.4

1. It is desired to identify a warehouse by its physical location. Design an appropriate identification scheme for the each of the following contexts:
   (a) UoD restricted to one suburb. The street in which the warehouse is located is identified by its name.
   (b) UoD restricted to one city. Each suburb is identified by its name.
   (c) UoD restricted to one country. Each city is a major city, so can be identified by name.
   (d) UoD restricted to planet Earth. Countries are identified by name.
   (e) UoD restricted to Milky Way galaxy. Planets are identified by name.

2. The UoD is restricted to Earth, and we wish to store facts of the form Warehouse has Floorspace; Warehouse contains Item in Quantity. Is the identification scheme discussed in Question 1(d) practical from the implementation point of view? If not, suggest a better scheme and support your scheme by comparing a sample population for the two fact types, using both approaches. Comment on the relative work needed to perform a join (conceptual or relational) between the fact types.

3. (a) A triangle ABC is formed from points in a Cartesian coordinate system. The coordinates are pure numbers (no units). You may assume that at any given time, only one shape can be displayed, and this must be a triangle. Model the information displayed here.

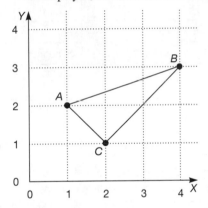

   (b) The map below indicates the approximate location of parking stations near a famous cathedral. The squares on the grid represent city blocks. Model the parking information stored on this map.

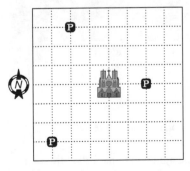

4. Members of a small social club are identified by the combination of their given names and surname. Each member has at least one and at most three given names. For example, one member is Eve Jones, another is Johann Sebastian Bach, and another is Eve Mary Elizabeth Jones. It is required that each component of their names be individually accessible. Draw a conceptual schema diagram for this situation.

5. Members of a small American gym have their weight recorded in pounds (lb). The weight that each member can bench-press is also recorded, but in kilograms (kg). It is desired to compare these two weights but retain the separate units. Specify a conceptual schema for this situation. Note that 1 lb = 0.454 kg and 1 kg = 2.205 lb.

6. The following table lists the common names by which beer drinks of various volumes may be ordered in hotels in the states of Australia. Volumes are measured in fluid ounces (oz). The sample data is significant. A double hyphen "--" indicates that beer drinks of that volume are not on sale in that state. For instance, in Queensland exactly three different beer drinks may be ordered. Schematize this UoD.

	4 oz	5 oz	6 oz	7 oz	8 oz	10 oz	15 oz	20 oz
Qld	--	Small beer	--	--	Glass	Pot	--	--
NSW	--	Pony	--	Seven	--	Middy	Schooner	Pint
Vic	--	Pony	Small	Glass	--	Pot	Schooner	--
SA	--	Pony	--	Butcher	--	Schooner	Pint	--
WA	Shetland pony	Pony	--	Glass	--	Middy	Schooner	Pot
Tas	Small beer	--	Beer or six	--	Eight	Pot or ten	--	--
NT	--	--	--	Seven	--	Handle	Schooner	--

7. The following report is an extract from an information system that records the results of driving tests for various employees. A person may take as many tests as he or she wishes, but cannot take more than one test on the same day. A minimum score of 80 is required to pass the test. Sometimes a person takes another test simply to try for a better score. Schematize this UoD.

Test	Date	Driver		Result	
		SSN	Name	Score	P/F
101	1/2/00	539-31-1234	Hagar, David Paul	75	F
102	1/2/00	438-12-3456	Jones, Selena Linda	85	P
103	1/9/00	539-31-1234	Hagar, David Paul	80	P

5.5   Case Study: A Compact Disc Retailer

The following small case study is designed to consolidate the main ideas in CSDP steps 1–5. To derive maximum benefit from it, you should attempt to solve the problem yourself before looking at the solution. The application domain concerns a compact disc retailer who uses an information system to help with account and stock control, and to provide a specialized service to customers seeking information about specific musical compositions and artists.

Figure 5.40 illustrates the kind of musical information required for compact discs (some of the data is fictitious). Each disc contains several individual musical items, referred to as "tracks". Although compact discs usually have about 20 tracks, for this example only a few tracks are listed. Before reading the next two paragraphs, try to verbalize information from Figure 5.40 as elementary facts. Pay particular attention to the reference schemes involved.

Each compact disc (CD) has a CD number as its primary identifier. Although not shown here, different discs may have the same name. Note that "CD" is used here in a generic sense, like a catalog stock item or car model. The retailer may have many copies of CD 654321-2 in stock, but for our purposes these are all treated as the same CD. In some applications (e.g., car sales) you do need to distinguish between different copies of the same model, but for our application this is not a requirement.

An artist is a person or a group of persons. For a given CD, a main artist is listed if and only if most of the tracks on the disc are by this same artist (this constraint is enforced by a data entry operator, not by the system). Assuming that each artist has an identifying name, we use the fact type CompactDisc (cdNr) has main- Artist (name). If this were not the case, we must replace Artist by the ArtistName value type thus: CompactDisc (cdNr) has ArtistName(). The record company that releases the disc must be recorded.

A challenging aspect of this application is understanding what is meant by "track" and determining its identification scheme. To clarify terms, you often need to consult the domain expert. The term "track" is commonly used in two senses: the *physical track* on a compact disc and the musical composition, or *work,* recorded on this track. Within the context of a given CD, tracks are identified by their track number, or sequential position on the disc. But there are many CDs in this domain, so we need both the CD number and the track number to identify a track. Using "track" in the physical sense, the fact involving "Maya's Dance" in the first CD report may be verbalized thus:

The Track that is on the CompactDisc with cdNr '654321-2' and has trackNr 1
stores a work with the Title 'Maya's Dance'.

This used the compound reference scheme Track (is on CompactDisc, has TrackNr). Notice that the fact predicate says "*a* work" of that title, not "*the* work". Different musical works may have the same title. Although a physical track occurs on only one CD, the same work may appear on many discs. For example, track 5 of CD 654321-1 and track 2 of CD 925838-2 hold the same title and probably the same work. There are also two tracks titled "Sultans of Swing", but they have different durations, so they are not the same work. In rare cases, two tracks with the same title can occur on the same CD (not shown here).

The previous verbalization did not include Work as an entity type. Should we include it? Do we need to know whether a work on one disc is exactly the same as a work on another disc? Only the domain expert can tell us whether he or she wants to know

cd#: 654321-2		name: Special Oldies	
artist:		record company: EMI	
track#	*title*	*duration*	*singers*
1	Maya's Dance	225	Donovan
2	Wonderful Land	200	
3	King of the Trees	340	Cat Stevens
4	Sultans of Swing	240	Mark Knopfler
5	Seven Wonders	300	Stevie Nicks
...	...	...	...

cd#: 792542-2		name: The Other Side of the Mirror	
artist: Stevie Nicks		record company: EMI	
track#	*title*	*duration*	*singers*
1	Rooms on Fire	300	Stevie Nicks
2	Two Kinds of Love	250	Bruce Hornsby, Stevie Nicks
...	...	...	...

cd#: 836419-2		name: Money for Nothing	
artist: Dire Straits		record company: Phonogram	
track#	*title*	*duration*	*singers*
1	Sultans of Swing	346	Mark Knopfler
2	Walk of Life	247	Mark Knopfler
...	...	...	...

cd#: 925838-2		name: Fleetwood Mac Greatest Hits	
artist: Fleetwood Mac		record company: Warner Bros.	
track#	*title*	*duration*	*singers*
1	Say You Love Me	200	Chris McVie, Stevie Nicks
2	Seven Wonders	300	Stevie Nicks
...	...	...	...

Figure 5.40 Musical details about four compact discs.

this. For our solution, let's assume the answer to this question is "no". However, if the answer were "yes", we would need a 1:1 identification scheme for Work. A natural scheme is hard to find (even the combination of title, artist, and duration might not be enough). We might introduce an artificial identifier (e.g., workNr), but this might be hard to enforce, since humans are responsible for enforcing the constraints in primary reference schemes.

The duration of a track is the time it takes to play. Each track has exactly one duration, measured in seconds. Most tracks have one or more singers. Some tracks may have no singers (these are instrumental rather than vocal tracks, although this dichotomy is left implicit).

Table 5.13 shows an extract from another report from the same application. It lists the quantity in stock and recommended retail price (in US dollars) of each compact disc. This table is updated when required, on a daily basis. The stock quantity of a disc may drop to zero. For simplicity, let's assume that only the current stock and price figures are recorded (no history).

An extract from a third report required of the information system is shown in Table 5.14. For simplicity, let's assume that sales records are kept only for the current calendar year of operation (otherwise the year needs to be included). For each month that has passed, figures are kept of the quantity of copies sold and the net revenue (profit) accruing from sales of the compact discs in that month.

Table 5.13 Stock quantity and recommended retail price of compact discs.

CD#	CD name	Stock quantity	RRP
654321-2	Special Oldies	5	17.95
792542-2	The Other Side of the Mirror	100	25.00
836419-2	Money for Nothing	10	20.00
925838-2	Fleetwood Mac Greatest Hits	50	23.95
...	...	...	...

Table 5.14 Monthly sales figures (small sample only).

Month	CD#	CD name	Quantity sold	Net revenue
Jan	654321-2	Special Oldies	0	0.00
	836419-2	Money for Nothing	30	180.00
	925838-2	Fleetwood Mac Greatest Hits	50	400.00
			80	580.00
Feb	654321-2	Special Oldies	5	33.50
	792542-2	The Other Side of the Mirror	70	630.00
	836419-2	Money for Nothing	15	90.00
	925838-2	Fleetwood Mac Greatest Hits	50	350.00
			140	1103.50

For simplicity, these figures are restricted to the four compact discs met earlier. In reality this table would have thousands of rows and much larger totals. This table is updated on a monthly basis. Daily sales figures are kept manually but are not part of the application. For each month, if a disc was on the stock list and had no sales for that month, then a figure of zero is recorded for it. If a disc is a new stock item in the month, then it has no sales figures recorded for previous months (e.g., disc 792542-2 was not in stock in January).

This is the last report we need to model. Before reading on, try to verbalize this report, and then schematize the whole application. Include all uniqueness and mandatory role constraints and derivation rules.

How did you fare with the monthly sales report? The reference schemes here are obvious: Month (code), CompactDisc (cdNr), Quantity (nr)+, MoneyAmt (usd)+. The totals for quantity sold and net revenue are obviously derived. You may have schematized the stored fact types thus: CompactDisc has CDname; CompactDisc in Month sold in Quantity; CompactDisc in Month earned MoneyAmt. This is acceptable (although as we see later, an equality constraint then needs to be added).

However, it is better to nest the common part of the two ternaries, as shown in Figure 5.41. Here the name "Listing" is used for the objectified association that records which compact discs were listed for sale in what months. For each individual listing (of a given compact disc in a given month) the number sold (possibly zero) and profit earned (also possibly zero) are recorded. Apart from a more compact schema, the nested solution leads to a more efficient relational schema (as discussed later).

Other aspects of the schema are straightforward and are not discussed here. Two main points arising from this case study are that care is often required in choosing and identifying object types, and sample populations are not always significant.

5.6   Summary

For a given state of the database, the *population* of a role r, *pop(r)*, is the set of objects referenced as playing that role in that state. $A \cup B$, the *union* of sets A and B, is the set of all elements in A or B or both. The *null set* or empty set, { }, has no members. The population of an entity type A, *pop(A)*, is the union of the populations of its roles. Roles of a fact type are called *fact roles*. A relationship type used purely to identify or reference some object is a reference type; its roles are called *reference roles*. For a given state, the population of a fact type (stored or derived) is its set of fact instances.

Step 5 of the conceptual schema design procedure requires us to *add mandatory role constraints, and check for logical derivations*. A role r is *mandatory* (or *total*) for an object type A **iff** each member of pop(A) is known to play r (for each state of the knowledge base); otherwise the role is *optional*. A mandatory role is indicated by a large dot where the role connects to the object type: ⊙–. The dot may instead be placed at the role end.

By default, if a primitive entity type plays only one fact role in the global schema, this role is mandatory—in this case the dot may be omitted since it is implied. Schema constraints apply to the model, not necessarily to the real world. If a role is optional in the real world, it is optional in the model. But a role that is mandatory in the real world

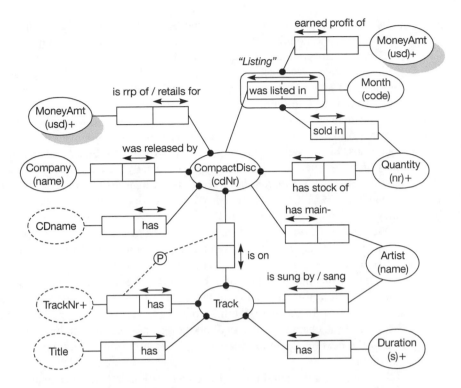

Figure 5.41 One way of schematizing the application.

may be optional in the model (e.g., the information may be unknown or omitted for privacy).

A *disjunction* of roles $r_1,..., r_n$ is *mandatory* for an object type *A* **iff** each member of pop(*A*) is known to play at least one of these roles (in each state). This *disjunctive mandatory,* or *inclusive-or,* constraint is shown by a circled dot ⊙ connected by a dotted line to the roles. Alternatively it may be shown as a large dot where the role arcs connect to the object type: ⚭.

By default, the disjunction of fact roles played by a primitive entity type in the global schema is mandatory—in this case the dot may be omitted since it is implied. However, a simple or disjunctive mandatory role constraint should be shown explicitly if it applies to an object type that has either an explicit identification scheme or a subtype.

To simplify the depiction of an object type with many roles, the object type may be *duplicated* on a schema page as well as over several pages. In this case the rule for implicit mandatory role disjunctions applies to the union of all the duplicates. An *external object type* is imported from another schema in which it is defined. Different CASE tools use different notations (e.g., arrow tip marker or shading for duplication in the same model, and double-ellipse notation or slash fill for external object types).

Derived fact types are normally omitted from the diagram—just the derivation rule is shown. If a derived fact type is included on the diagram, all its constraints should normally be shown. *By default, all constraints shown on a derived fact type are derivable* (from its derivation rule and other constraints).

Once mandatory role constraints are added, a *logical derivation check* should be performed to see if some fact types are derivable using logical rather than arithmetic operations. First check for missing fact types by asking: *Are there any other relationships of interest* between the object types, especially functional relationships? A binary relationship type is *functional* if at least one of its roles is functional (i.e., the role is a simple key: ○—▭). Each column entry for a functional role functionally determines the entry for the other role.

We now ask: *Can any fact type be derived* from the others? To help decide this, remember that constraints on a derived fact type should normally be derivable. If we have a chain of two or more functional fact types with uniqueness constraints on all the first roles, then a functional binary from the start to the end of this chain is derivable if it is defined by projecting on the join of these fact types—its uniqueness constraint is *transitively implied*. In this case, the first role of the derived fact type is mandatory iff the first role of the chain is mandatory and the second role of each binary subsets the first role of the next binary in the chain (e.g., if the first role of each binary in the chain is mandatory).

Derivation rules should normally be biconditionals (i.e., their main operator is **iff**). If their main operator is **if**, the fact type is only *partly derived*. Derived fact types do not need to have simple keys. Whether derived or not, a fact type should be excluded from the schema unless it is of interest for the application.

Each entity type must have one or more candidate reference schemes. One of these is picked as the *primary identification* scheme, and the others are treated as fact types. Primary reference schemes should be as simple and stable as possible. A *rigid identifier* identifies the same object throughout the application lifetime. The primary identification must provide a mandatory 1:1 map of each entity to a tuple of one or more values.

A *simple reference* scheme maps each entity to a single value (e.g., Subject to SubjectCode). A *compound reference* scheme maps each entity to two or more values (e.g., Person to Surname and Initials). Apart from nested cases, the identification aspect of compound reference is denoted by an external uniqueness constraint: ⓤ. With *disjunctive reference,* the number of values may vary for different entities of the same type (e.g., Person to Surname and Firstname and optionally Middlename).

Candidate identifiers for the same entity are called *synonyms*. When more than one candidate identification scheme exists, the primary reference scheme is indicated on the schema as follows: if simple, parenthesize it; if compound use ⓟ; if a 1:1 link to an entity type, mark it ⓟ.

If *different units* are used for the same quantity, the semantic connection between these units must be modeled. Different units may be modeled as reference modes or by use of a Unit object type. For any given quantity, one unit is often picked as the standard unit, and conversion rules are supplied to map the derived units to the standard unit.

Chapter Notes

Some versions of ORM use a universal quantifier (∀) instead of the mandatory role dot and place it along the role connector instead of at the start (e.g., DeTroyer et al. 1988). As discussed in Chapters 8 and 9, ER and UML support simple mandatory role constraints but not disjunctive mandatory role constraints. Some versions of ER use a solid line for mandatory and a broken one for optional (e.g., Barker 1990), some use double lines for mandatory (e.g., Elmasri and Navathe 1994), and some, including UML, use cardinality or multiplicity markers such as 0 for optional and 1 (or more) for mandatory (e.g., Batini et al. 1992). UML allows attributes to be declared mandatory or optional, but not all ER notations allow this.

The botanical example used in the discussion of disjunctive reference schemes came from Peter Ritson, who worked with me to develop a method for modeling such schemes. For a technical discussion of this topic see Halpin and Ritson (1992).

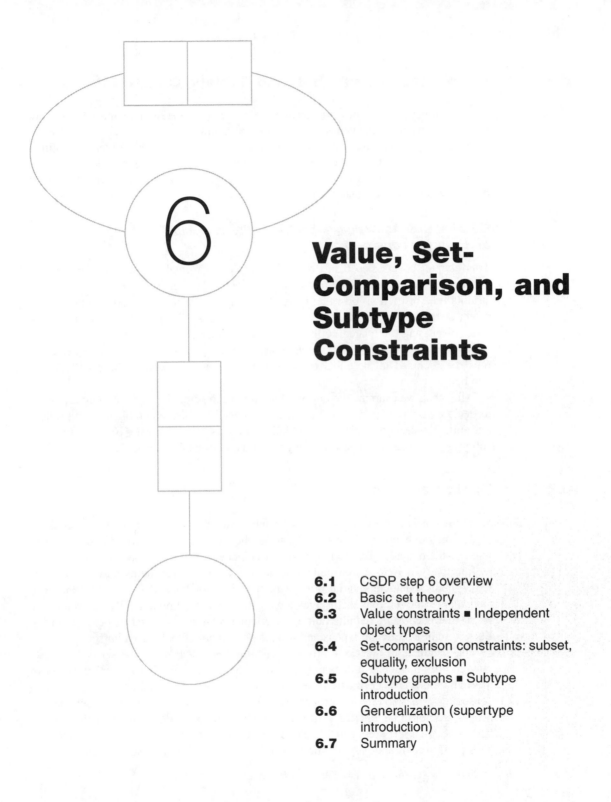

Value, Set-Comparison, and Subtype Constraints

6.1   CSDP Step 6: Value, Set, and Subtype Constraints

So far you have learned how to verbalize examples in terms of elementary facts, draw the fact types, mark uniqueness constraints and mandatory roles, specify rules for derived fact types, and use simple and complex reference schemes to identify entities. The next step of the conceptual schema design procedure covers three kinds of constraints: value, set comparison, and subtype. Set-comparison constraints are themselves of three kinds: subset, equality, and exclusion.

CSDP step 6: Add value, subset, equality, exclusion, and subtype constraints.

This chapter covers step 6 in detail. To clarify the formal concepts underlying the constraints, some basic set theory is first reviewed. Then we consider value constraints (i.e., restrictions on value types). For example, in modeling color monitors we might restrict the values of ColorCode to 'R', 'G', and 'B' (for Red, Green, and Blue). After discussing the related notion of independent objects, we examine the three set-comparison constraints—these declare whether the population of one role sequence must be included in, be equal to, or be mutually exclusive with the population of another.

After that, we examine the notion of subtyping in some depth. Subtyping allows us to declare how types are related (e.g., each manager is also an employee) and refines our ability to declare precisely what kinds of objects play what roles. Our treatment of subtyping proceeds from basics through to some reasonably advanced aspects.

6.2   Basic Set Theory

Since the constraints in step 6 make substantial use of sets and set operations, let's take some time out here to review some basic set theory. To provide a comprehensive summary of the required background, some ideas met earlier are included.

Intuitively, a *set* is a well-defined collection of items. The items may be concrete (e.g., people, computers) or abstract (e.g., numbers, points), and are called *elements* or *members* of the set. Sets themselves are abstract. They are numerically definite in the sense that each has a definite number of elements. A *type* is a set of possible items. Each item of a particular type is an instance or element of that particular set.

The members of a set collectively constitute the *extension* of the set. While a set may *contain* members, it does not *consist* of those members. For example, the set of Martian moons is an abstraction over and above its members (Phobos and Deimos) and consequently has no physical properties such as mass or volume. Although sets (unlike heaps) are not to be equated with their members, they are determined by their members, since two sets are *identical* or **equal** if and only if they have the same extension. Using "iff" for "if and only if", the *Law of Extensionality* may be stated thus:

Given any sets A and B, $A = B$ iff A and B have the same members.

Since sets are determined by their members, one simple way of *defining* a set is to *enumerate* or list the elements of the set. In so doing, braces are used as delimiters and commas as item separators (e.g., $A = \{3, 6\}$). Here A is defined as the set containing just the elements 3 and 6. One consequence of the Law of Extensionality is that a set is unchanged by *repeating* any of its members. For instance, if $A = \{3, 6\}$ and $B = \{3, 6, 6\}$, it follows that $A = B$, since both sets contain precisely the same members (3 and 6).

When enumerating sets, it is usual not to repeat the members. However, it is sometimes useful to permit this. For example, when stating general results about the set variable $\{x, y\}$, it may be handy to include the case $x = y$. Sometimes repetition of members occurs undetected. For instance, some people do not realize that the entity set {Morning Star, Evening Star} contains just one member (the planet Venus). Of course, the value set {'Morning Star', 'Evening Star'} contains two members.

If repetition is made significant, we have a *bag* or *multiset*. To help distinguish between bags and sets, it is advisable to use different delimiters. I use square brackets for bags and braces for sets. For instance the bag [3, 6, 6] has a count of 3 and is not equal to [3, 6], which has a count of 2. One use of bags is in collecting values for statistical work. For example, the set $\{3, 6, 6\}$ has an average of 4.5 but the bag [3, 6, 6] has an average of 5. Bags are frequently used with languages like SQL.

Another consequence of the Law of Extensionality is that the *order* in which elements are listed is irrelevant. For example, if $A = \{3, 6\}$ and $B = \{6, 3\}$, then $A = B$, since each set contains the same members. Bags are also insensitive to order, as in [3, 6] = [6, 3]. If order is made significant, we have an "ordered set".

Usually, when order is made significant, so is repetition. In this case we have a *sequence* or list or permutation or tuple. Thus a sequence is an ordered bag. Sequences are often delimited by parentheses or angle brackets, for example, (1, 2) or $\langle 1, 2 \rangle$. The sequence (6, 3, 6) has three members and differs from the sequence (3, 6, 6). In practice, several different delimiting notations are used. For example, "[", "]" are used as set delimiters in Pascal and list delimiters in Prolog.

If a set is enumerated in full, the ordering does not matter. However, a natural ordering often provides an obvious pattern; in such cases a partial enumeration can define the set. For example, the set of decimal digits may be shown as {0..9}, where the ".." indicates the missing digits. Here 0..9 is often called a *range*. Infinite sets may be represented with ".." at one or both ends. For example, the set of natural numbers may be shown as {1, 2, 3..}.

The preceding set definitions enumerate, wholly or partially, the extension of the set and are thus examples of an *extensional definition*. A set may also be defined by an *intensional definition*. Here the *intension* or meaning is declared using a property that applies to just the members of the set. That is, a description is given that constitutes both a necessary and sufficient condition (an "iff condition") for an item to belong to the set.

For example, the set A, defined extensionally as $\{1, 2, 3\}$, may be defined intensionally as $A =$ the set of natural numbers less than 4. This definition may be recast in set builder notation as $\{x: x$ is a natural number less than 4$\}$ or more briefly as $\{x: x \in \mathbb{N}\ \&\ x < 4\}$, where "$\in$" abbreviates "is a member of" and $\mathbb{N}$ is the set of natural numbers. In set builder notation, a stroke "|" may be used instead of a colon, for example, $\{x \mid x < 4\}$. The number of elements in a set is called the *cardinality* of the set (e.g., the set $\{2, 4, 6\}$ has a cardinality of 3).

Some set operations result in propositions, while others result in sets. Note the following *proposition-forming operators:* =, ≠, ⊆, ⊂, ⊇, and ⊃. These are read respectively as "equals", "is not equal to", "is a subset of", "is a proper subset of", "is a superset of", and "is a proper superset of".

Given any sets A and B, we say that A is a **subset** of B iff every member of A is also a member of B. For example, $\{1, 3\} \subseteq \{1, 2, 3\}$. An equivalent definition is the following: A is a subset of B iff A has no members that are not in B. This second definition makes it easy to see that the *null set* is a subset of every set. The null or empty set has no members and may be represented as $\{\ \}$ or $\varnothing$.

Every set is a subset of itself. For example, $\{1, 3\} \subseteq \{1, 3\}$. We say that A is a *proper subset* of B if and only if A is a subset of B but not equal to B. For instance, $\{1, 3\} \subset \{1, 2, 3\}$. We say that A is a **superset** of B iff B is a subset of A, and that A is a *proper superset* of B iff B is a proper subset of A. For example, $\{1, 2, 3\}$ is both a superset and a proper superset of $\{1, 3\}$.

Comparison relationships between two sets are often depicted by *Euler diagrams*. As developed by the Swiss mathematician Leonhard Euler, these were *spatial* and *existential*. Each set is pictured as a set of points inside an ellipse. This enables the relationship between the sets to be "seen" by the spatial arrangement of the ellipses. For example, placing ellipse A inside B shows that A is a proper subset of B (see Figure 6.1). Here we see that every element of A is also an element of B (so A is a subset of B). The existential viewpoint implies that each of the regions in the Euler diagram contains some elements. So B has some elements not in A. Hence A is a proper subset of B.

To show that A is a subset of B on standard Euler diagrams, we need to use a disjunction of two diagrams, as shown in Figure 6.2. The right-hand diagram caters to the possibility that $A = B$.

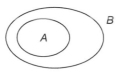

Figure 6.1   Standard Euler diagram for A is a proper subset of B.

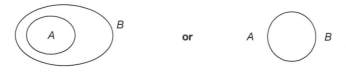

Figure 6.2   A disjunction of standard Euler diagrams denotes A is a subset of B.

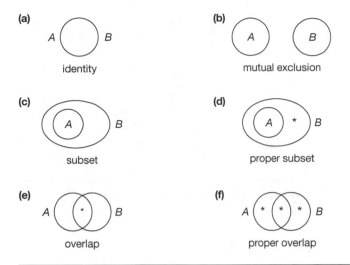

Figure 6.3 Hypothetical Euler diagrams for set comparisons.

The notion of subsethood is actually more useful than proper subsethood. Partly to depict such relationships on a single diagram, I use a notation that I call *Hypothetical Euler Diagrams* (HEDs). In a HED, an asterisk is placed in a region to show something exists there, while shading the region indicates that it is empty. If a region is unmarked, the question of whether any elements exist there is left open or hypothetical. Figure 6.3 shows the HEDs for the six most important comparisons between two sets.

Figure 6.3(a) shows *equality* or identity (e.g., $A = B = \{1, 2\}$). In Figure 6.3(b), A and B are *disjoint* or *mutually exclusive;* that is, they have no members in common (e.g., $A = \{1\}$, $B = \{2\}$). In Figure 6.3(c), A is a *subset* of B (equivalently, B is a superset of A). In Figure 6.3(d), A is a *proper subset* of B (equivalently, B is a proper superset of A). For example, both $A = \{1\}$, $B = \{1, 2\}$ and $A = \{1\}$, $B = \{1\}$ are instances of a subset, but only the former is an instance of a proper subset. Figure 6.3(e) shows *overlap:* the sets have some members in common. Figure 6.3(f) shows *proper overlap:* the sets have common as well as extra members. For example, both $A = \{1, 2\}$, $B = \{2, 3\}$ and $A = \{1\}$, $B = \{1, 2\}$ are instances of overlap, but only the former is a case of proper overlap.

Let's now consider *set-forming operations,* where the result is a set rather than a proposition. Given any sets A and B, we define $A \cup B$ (i.e., A union B) to be the set of all elements in A or B, reading "or" in the inclusive sense. $A \cap B$ (i.e., A intersect B) is the set of all elements common to both A and B. Each of these operations is commutative, so the order of the operands doesn't matter. That is, $A \cup B = B \cup A$, and $A \cap B = B \cap A$.

The *set difference* (or relative complement) operation is defined thus: $A - B$ (i.e., A minus B) is the set of all elements that are in A but not in B. This operation does not commute (i.e., cases may arise where $A - B \neq B - A$). If we let U = the *universal set* (i.e., the set of all elements under consideration), we define the *complement* of A as A'

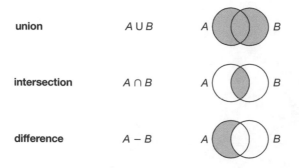

union $A \cup B$

intersection $A \cap B$

difference $A - B$

Figure 6.4 Venn diagrams for three set-forming operations.

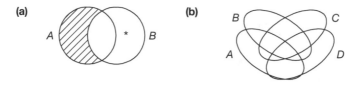

Figure 6.5 Venn diagrams for (a) A is a proper subset of B and (b) four sets.

$= U - A$. The symmetric difference between A and B is the set of elements in just one of A or B (i.e., the union minus the intersection).

The three most important set-forming operations are union, intersection, and difference. These are depicted in Figure 6.4 by means of *Venn diagrams,* using shading to indicate the result of the operation. Unlike Euler diagrams, the ellipses in Venn diagrams always overlap. Like HEDs, Venn diagrams adopt the hypothetical viewpoint. As examples of these operations, if $A = \{1, 2, 3\}$ and $B = \{2, 4\}$, then $A \cup B = \{1, 2, 3, 4\}$, $A \cap B = \{2\}$, $A - B = \{1, 3\}$, and $B - A = \{4\}$.

Venn diagrams are sometimes used to discuss comparisons between two sets. For example, Figure 6.5(a) indicates that $A \subset B$, using slash fill and "*" for empty and nonempty regions, respectively. However, Venn diagrams become extremely unwieldy as soon as the number of sets exceeds three—consider the Venn diagram for four sets in Figure 6.5(b). Euler diagrams have a similar scalability problem. Section 6.5 introduces a directed graph notation for diagramming subtype connections that enables many compatible object types to be related without incurring the jumble of line crossings that Euler and Venn diagrams would produce for such cases.

6.3   Value Constraints and Independent Objects

A **value constraint** indicates which values are allowed in a value type and is sometimes called a "domain constraint" or "object type constraint". A value constraint should be declared only if the value list is at least reasonably *stable;* otherwise we would need to continually change the constraint, and hence the schema, as the value list changed.

A value type may be defined by declaring its extension (set of possible values) as one or more enumerations or ranges enclosed in braces. On a schema diagram, a value constraint is declared by displaying the extension next to either the value type itself or the entity type that is referenced by the value type. Figure 6.6 shows several examples.

If the defining expression is short, it can be displayed in full on the diagram. If the value list is long, we can enter all the values in a CASE tool but choose to display just some leading values. A trailing ellipsis "..." then indicates that the display of later values has been suppressed. For example, for the object type WeekDay we might specify the value list {'Sunday', 'Monday', 'Tuesday', 'Wednesday', 'Thursday', 'Friday', 'Saturday'} but choose to display only the first two (see Figure 6.7). Although the list has been compacted on the diagram, it can be displayed in full textually when desired (e.g., by accessing a properties sheet for the object type).

Now consider Figure 6.8, which is a modified version of an Olympics example discussed earlier, together with a sample population from the final results of the 24th summer Olympics held in Seoul, Korea, in 1988 (ordered alphabetically by Country).

For this application, only three kinds of medals are allowed: gold, silver, and bronze, denoted by the codes "G", "S", and "B". This constraint is specified on the schema by listing the set of possible values {'G', 'S', 'B'} beside the entity type MedalKind.

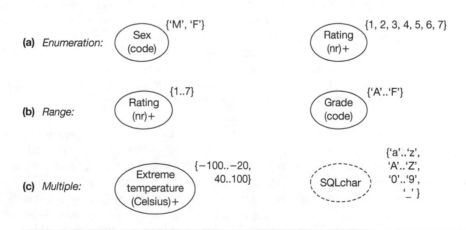

Figure 6.6 Value constraints may list the possible values of a value type.

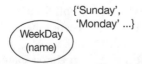

Figure 6.7 The display of later values is suppressed.

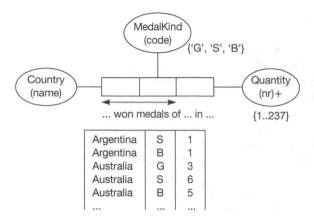

Figure 6.8 Value constraints are declared for MedalKind and Quantity.

In the 1988 Olympics there were 237 events, with one gold, silver, and bronze medal awarded for each event (assume there are no ties). It is logically possible (although highly unlikely) that the same country would win all medals of a given kind. So if Quantity is used only in this fact type, its largest value is 237. What is its smallest value?

If we want to store facts indicating that a country won no medals of a given kind, the lowest quantity is 0. However, if we want to minimize the size of the database, we would store only facts about actual wins—this approach is suggested by our sample population. In this case Quantity has a lower limit of 1. Taking the closed-world assumption, the fact that a country has won 0 gold medals could then be derived from the absence of a base fact about that country winning some gold medals. In principle, we could specify this restriction on Quantity by listing the numbers 1, 2, 3, and so on up to 237. However, this would be a lengthy listing!

Happily there are two aspects of this case that allow a convenient shorthand notation. First, because the values are integers, they have a clearly defined *order* (e.g., 1 is less than 2, which is less than 3, and so on). Second, we are talking about a *continuous* range of integers—we wish to include all the integers in the range from 1 to 237, without leaving any gaps that can be filled by other integers. So we may safely indicate the integers from 1 to 237 simply as {1..237}, where ".." abbreviates the integers in between. This is like a subrange definition in a language like Pascal. This value constraint is marked beside the relevant object type (see Figure 6.8).

Value constraints are declared for MedalKind and Quantity. What about Country? Here "Country" might denote the set of all nations on Earth, or perhaps just nations competing in the Olympics. In principle we could specify a full list of country names as a value constraint, but this would be impractical, mainly because the list is so long. For example, 161 nations competed in the 1988 summer Olympics. Also, the list of countries changes over the years (e.g., in 1991 the former Soviet Union fragmented into 15 nations). So if the schema is to be reused for different games, this value constraint would need to be continually updated.

Since the list of countries is both large and unstable, we will not specify a list of values for CountryName. However, we can declare a syntactic *data type*. For example, we might require each country name to be a string of at most 20 characters. Sometimes I use a shorthand notation for data types, to manually annotate various object types. For example, I use "a20" to denote a character string of at most 20 alpha characters (i.e., letters).

Many different shorthand conventions exist. In my personal system, "c" denotes a character, "a" a letter, and "d" a digit (i.e., 0..9). A number n before/after one of these indicates "exactly/at most n occurrences". Symbols may be concatenated. For example, the format of subject codes such as "CS114" might be specified as ⟨aaddd⟩ or ⟨2a3d⟩. The symbol "±" means a + or − sign, and "." is a decimal point. Optional components are placed in square brackets "[ ]". Here are some examples: c20 (a string of at most 20 characters); 20c (a string of exactly 20 characters); a15 (a string of at most 15 letters); d6.2d (at most 6 digits, followed by a decimal point and 2 digits); dddaaa (3 digits followed by three letters); 3d3a (same as previous); [±]d3 (optionally a + or − sign, followed by at most 3 digits). Some of these patterns map directly to an implementation data type, others are directly supported in some application languages, and others require separate checking code to be written.

Although such shorthand notations are useful for quickly jotting down requirements manually, they are not supported by CASE tools, which typically require you to specify data types by making choices from pull-down lists. For example, in Microsoft's ORM tool you can specify data types at a high level by choosing the portable data type option, then selecting your choice of category (e.g., Text, Numeric, Temporal), type (e.g., fixed length or variable length), size (single or double byte), and maximum length. For instance, to restrict country names to strings of at most 20 single-byte characters, you choose the settings Text, Fixed length, Single byte, 20. A portable data type is independent of the underlying DBMS. If you choose to show the physical data type, you see the type in the syntax of the chosen DBMS. For instance, the previous setting would appear as varchar(20) in IBM DB2 and Microsoft SQL Server, varchar2(20) in Oracle, and Text(20) in Microsoft Access.

Although choosing syntactic data types is not the most conceptual or exciting aspect of modeling, it's something you need to do before you implement the model. Otherwise you'll get whatever default data type the system provides, and this won't always be what you want.

Now suppose that the schema in Figure 6.8 is to be reused each time an Olympics is held, and that users want to know answers to the following questions. *Which countries competed? Which countries didn't compete?* The first question could be addressed by adding the unary predicate "competed" to Country; the competing countries would then all be entered in the single-column table for this unary fact type. Alternatively we could explicitly record zero for each competing country not winning a given kind of medal.

But what about the second question? This effectively asks: Which countries exist but didn't compete? This list is usually very small, but sometimes it may be large (e.g., because of a boycott). So somehow we need a way to record all the existing countries, whether or not they competed. As discussed earlier, putting this list of countries in a constraint is unwise because the list is large and unstable. Although schemas often do evolve, we usually try to design them to be as stable as possible. A classic strategy used is to model the feature so that the changes occur in the database population rather than the schema itself. How can we do this for the current example?

You might be tempted to add a unary predicate "exists" to Country. But such a predicate would apply to all object types in the schema. Moreover, there are formal problems with treating "exists" (an existential quantifier) as a predicate. In principle we could address the problem by adding another unary predicate "did not compete" for Country, and storing noncompetitors here. But such an approach is awkward—Country might play several roles (birthplace, location, etc.), and it may be arbitrary which role is negated to cater to the rest of the countries.

A cleaner approach is to allow all existing countries to be entered in a *reference table* for Country. A particular country may appear in this table without playing any fact roles in the schema. Such a country is said to be *independent,* since it exists in our model but doesn't need to do anything. We define an **independent object type** to be a *primitive object type whose fact roles are collectively optional* (assuming the object type plays at least one fact role). The term is not used for subtypes or for value types that play no fact roles. An independent object type plays one or more fact roles, but the disjunction of these roles is not mandatory (implicitly or explicitly). An independent type may have nonindependent instances. In the past, independent objects were sometimes called "lazy objects".

To signify that an object type is independent, an exclamation mark "!" is appended to its name. Figure 6.9 depicts Country as independent. Its reference table lists all existing nations. To save space, only the first six countries are shown in this figure—currently there are over 190 countries. The first row of this table may be verbalized as "The Country with name 'Afghanistan' exists"; this is classified as a reference, not a fact.

Figure 6.9 records wins of zero. So all competing nations play the first role of the ternary. This role is optional, since some nations don't compete (the data here is

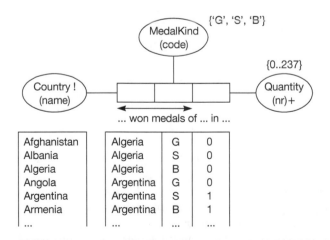

Figure 6.9 In this schema, Country is an independent object type.

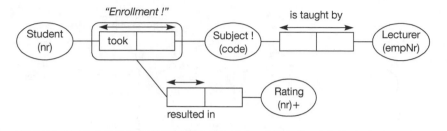

Figure 6.10 Objectified associations are often independent.

fictitious). If wins of zero were excluded (as in Figure 6.8) and the unary "competed" were added, the disjunction of this role and the wins role would be optional (and a subset constraint would run from the wins to the competed role—subset constraints are treated later). So the implied mandatory role rule does not apply to independent object types.

As with any entity type, the reference scheme of an independent entity type is mandatory. So no country may be recorded to compete or win unless it is recorded in the reference population of Country. To fully populate Country with a list of all nations is a tedious task, but once done it can be imported into various applications as required. In practice, most independent object types have fewer instances. As a minor point, the value constraint on Quantity may need to be updated or weakened to allow for more events.

If we did not want to know about noncompeting countries, then as an alternative to adding the unary "competed", we could restrict the meaning of Country to "Competing nation", mark it as independent, and record only nonzero wins.

Nested object types (objectified associations) are often independent, because we often wish to record an association before recording other facts about it. For example, the schema in Figure 6.10 allows us to record the fact that a student has enrolled in a subject (e.g., at the start of a semester) before knowing what result he or she achieves for that enrollment (e.g., at the end of the semester). In this example, the simple object type Subject is also independent. In this UoD, it is possible that all we know about a subject is its subject code. It is not necessary that all subjects be taught.

However, *simple object types are rarely independent.* In most academic applications we would need to know the title of any subject, not just its code. This more realistic situation is depicted in Figure 6.11, where Subject is no longer independent because there is a fact role that it must play. Similarly, in our Olympics example, if all countries had codes as well as names, and we chose code for primary reference, then Country has CountryName would become a mandatory fact type, and Country would no longer be independent.

Use of an independent object type or unary predicates instead of a value list constraint adds flexibility since the data can be changed without recompiling the schema (and relevant forms, etc.). Note however that the responsibility for this feature is now in the hands of the person entering the relevant data rather than the schema designer.

As a final note on independent object types, there is a Dutch version of ORM, known as Fully Communication Oriented Information Modeling (FCO-IM), that treats

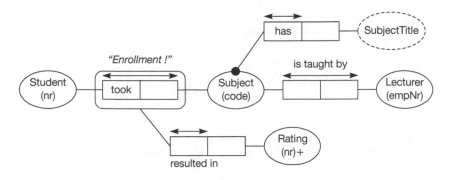

Figure 6.11 Simple object types are rarely independent.

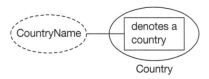

Figure 6.12 In FCO-IM, an entity type is an objectified predicate.

all entity types, independent or not, as objectified predicates. For example, in Figure 6.12 the entity type Country is depicted as the objectification of a role played by the value type CountryName. The notion of an entity type can then be treated as a derived, rather than a base, construct. This approach is not supported by Microsoft's ORM tool, which treats it as illegal to objectify a unary predicate.

Exercise 6.3

1. Schematize the following sample report about elementary particles. Include uniqueness, mandatory role, and value constraints. Set an upper limit of 2000 amu for mass.

Family	Particle	Charge	Mass (amu)
lepton	neutrino	0	0
	electron	−	1
	positron	+	1
meson	eta	0	1074
baryon	proton	+	1836
	neutron	0	1839

2. It is desired to record a list of all sports, and for each sport, which Olympic games (if any) included it. Some sports (e.g., running) have been included in each Olympics, some (e.g., judo) only in some, and others (e.g., surfing) never. Schematize this application. You may identify Olympics by its year or by an Olympiad number.

3. An Australian software retailer, SoftMart, maintains an information system to help with invoice and stock control. It has recently opened for business and has made only a few sales so far. The details of the software items it has in stock are shown. The software items are standardly identified by item codes, but also have unique titles. There are exactly three software categories, identified by codes (SS = spreadsheet, DB = database, WP = word processsor). The full names of these categories are not recorded. The list price of an item is the normal price at which the item is currently sold. However, SoftMart may sell an item at less than the current list price (e.g., SoftMart may give a discount for bulk orders or to favored clients, and the list price itself may change with time). There is no rule to enable the unit price (i.e., the actual price charged for a copy of an item) to be derived from the current list price.

Itemcode	Title	Category	Stock qty	Listprice
B123	Blossom 123	SS	8	799.50
DL	DataLight	DB	10	700.00
DB3	Database 3	DB	5	1999.99
Q	Quinquo	SS	6	400.00
SQL+	SQL plus	DB	4	1890.50
TS	TextStar	WP	5	500.00
WL	WordLight	WP	10	700.00

Customers are identified by a customer number, but the combination of their name and address is also unique. For simplicity, customer name is treated as a single character string, and so is address. Customers have at most one phone number recorded. The next table shows customer details.

Customer#	Name	Address	Phone
001	Starcorp	5 Sun St, St Lucia 4067	3765000
002	Eastpac	30 Beach Rd, Sandgate 4017	2691111
003	Dr I.N. Stein	7 Sesame St, St Lucia 4067	?

Customer details may be recorded before the customer places an order. Once an order is placed, the items are issued to the customer together with an invoice. At the time the database snapshot was taken for the output reports, only four invoices had been issued. When a customer pays for the items listed in an invoice, the date of payment is recorded. The following table lists the payments so far. Each invoice is identified by its invoice number. For this simple exercise, you may assume that an invoice is paid in full or not at all.

Invoice#	Date paid
0501	10/07/88
0502	20/07/88
0503	unpaid
0504	unpaid

The four actual invoices are shown. The invoice header giving the address of SoftMart is not stored. An invoice includes a table of one or more rows, called "invoice lines". Each invoice line lists details about the order of one or more units (copies) of a software item. For simplicity, assume that on a given invoice the same item can appear on only one invoice line. For each invoice line, the item code, title, quantity of units ordered, and unit price are listed.

The total charge for the invoice line is displayed as a subtotal. The total charge for the whole invoice is displayed as the amount due.

Schematize this UoD, including uniqueness, mandatory role, and value constraints. Identify a LineItem or invoice line by using the invoice number and the item code. If a fact type is derived, omit it from the diagram but include a derivation rule for it.

SoftMart, 46 Gallium Street, Brisbane 4001

invoice#: 0501   **date:** 07/03/88
customer#: 001   **customer name:** Starcorp
                         address: 5 Sun St, St Lucia 4067

Item code	Title	Qty ordered	Unit price	Subtotal
WL	WordLight	5	650.00	3250.00
Q	Quinquo	1	400.00	400.00
SQL+	SQL plus	5	1701.45	8507.25
B123	Blossom 123	1	799.50	799.50
		☞ **total amount due:**		$12956.75

SoftMart, 46 Gallium Street, Brisbane 4001

invoice#: 0502   **date:** 07/03/88
customer#: 002   **customer name:** Eastpac
                       address: 30 Beach Rd, Sandgate, 4017

Item code	Title	Qty ordered	Unit price	Subtotal
Q	Quinquo	4	400.00	1600.00
TS	TextStar	4	500.00	2000.00
		☞ **total amount due:**		$3600.00

SoftMart, 46 Gallium Street, Brisbane 4001

invoice#: 0503   **date:** 07/10/88
customer#: 001   **customer name:** Starcorp
                         address: 5 Sun St, St Lucia 4067

Item code	Title	Qty ordered	Unit price	Subtotal
Q	Quinquo	4	350.00	1400.00
		☞ **total amount due:**		$1400.00

SoftMart, 46 Gallium Street, Brisbane 4001

invoice#: 0504   **date:** 07/20/88
customer#: 003   **customer name:** Dr I.N. Stein
                       address: 7 Sesame St, St Lucia 4067

Item code	Title	Qty ordered	Unit price	Subtotal
B123	Blossom 123	1	799.50	799.50
DL	DataLight	1	700.00	700.00
		☞ **total amount due:**		$1499.50

4. Consider the previous question, but suppose that the same item may appear on more than one line of the same invoice. Devise an alternative identification scheme to deal with this situation. (*Hint:* Compare this with the compact disc example. Sometimes you need to identify things in terms of their position.)

5. Now suppose that a cumulative record of purchases from suppliers is also to be recorded, an extract of which is shown in the following table. Only a cumulative record is kept (individual deliveries from suppliers are not recorded in the information system). No supplier can be a customer.

Itemcode	Supplier	Quantity
B123	Macrosoft	7
	TechAtlantic	3
DL	Macrosoft	11
DB3	PacificTech	5
etc.		

(a) Draw a conceptual schema for this table.

(b) Assume this subschema is integrated with your solution to Question 3, and that your fact type for stock quantity is now declared to be derivable.

(i) Specify a derivation rule for this approach.

(ii) In a real business, how practical would it be to use such a rule to avoid storing stock quantity? Discuss.

6.4   Subset, Equality, and Exclusion Constraints

Set-comparison constraints restrict the way the population of one role, or role sequence, relates to the population of another. In Section 6.2, we considered six ways in which two sets might be related: subset, equality, exclusion, proper subset, overlap, and proper overlap. The last three of these require some objects to exist in at least one of the sets being compared. However, static constraints must apply to every state of the database, including the empty state. So the only set-comparison constraints of interest are subset, equality, and exclusion. These three kinds of constraints are examined in this section.

Suppose a local fitness club maintains an information system concerning its members, and that Table 6.1 is an extract of an output report from this system. Membership

Table 6.1 Details about members of a fitness club.

Member	Sex	Birth year	Sport	Booking	Reaction time (ms)	Heart rate (beats/min)
Anderson PE	M	1940	tennis	Mon 5 p.m.	250	80
Bloggs F	M	1940				
Fit IM	F	1975	squash		250	70
Hume D	F	1946	squash	Tue 9 a.m.		
Jones T	M	1965			300	93

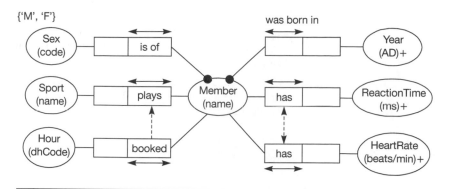

Figure 6.13 A conceptual schema for Table 6.1.

includes access to the club's normal fitness equipment (e.g., a weights gym). However, the club also has a few squash and tennis courts. To help ensure fair access to these courts, the club has a policy that members may play only one of these two racquet sports.

Members pay an extra fee for this right and optionally may book one regular weekly hour to use a court. For simplicity, the handling of casual bookings and court allocations is excluded from the UoD. As a service to its members, the club arranges a fitness test to measure the resting heart rate and reaction time of any member who requests it. For simplicity, let's assume only the latest results are kept for each member.

The determination of fact types, uniqueness constraints, mandatory roles, and value constraints for this example is straightforward (see Figure 6.13). For simplicity, let's agree that hours may be identified by a simple code (e.g., 'Mon. 5 p.m.'), without needing to separate out their day and time components.

However there are two more constraints that apply to this example. To begin with, only those members who have opted to play a sport may book a court. In terms of the schema diagram, each object in the population of the booking role must also appear in the population of the playing role. In other words, the set of members who book an hour must be a subset of the set of members who play a sport. As shown in Figure 6.13, we mark this **subset constraint** by a *dotted arrow* "--->" running from the subset role to the superset role.

Our sample data agrees with this constraint since {'Anderson PE', 'Hume D'} ⊆ {'Anderson PE', 'Fit IM', 'Hume D'}. If we tried to add a booking for Jones without also adding a sport for him, we would violate this constraint. In words, the subset constraint may be verbalized as **if** Member booked **some** Hour **then** Member plays **some** Sport. Using "**a**" and "**an**" as alternatives for "**some**", this may also be verbalized as **if** Member booked **an** Hour **then** Member plays **a** Sport.

The arrow notation for subset constraints derives from the arrow "→" often used for the logical connective "**if** ... **then** ...". Figure 6.14(a) summarizes the general case of a subset constraint from one role to another. For this comparison to make sense, both roles must be played by the same object type (or a supertype—see later). Figure 6.14(b)

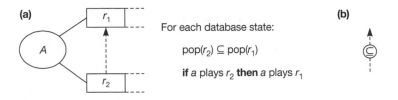

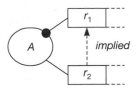

Figure 6.14 A subset constraint between two roles.

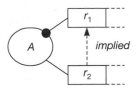

Figure 6.15 The implied subset constraint should not be shown.

shows an alternate, circled "⊆" notation using the mathematical symbol for subset-hood—since the circle can be moved independently of the line ends, it effectively provides a line elbow that may help to reduce line crossings in layout, as well as catering to rare cases where both roles are in the same predicate.

In Figure 6.14, a is any member of A. The reference to database states reminds us that the constraint applies to our application model (not necessarily to the real world). So "a plays r" means a plays r in our model. In terms of fact tables, the set of values in the column for r_2 is always a subset of the set of values in the column for r_1. It doesn't matter if any of these columns have duplicate values; we are comparing sets, not bags.

In Figure 6.14, it is assumed that A plays some other role and that both r_1 and r_2 are *optional*. If r_1 were mandatory, then a subset constraint to it would be *implied*, since the total population of A would then play r_1 (see Figure 6.15). In general, A has a mandatory role r only if there is a subset constraint to r from each of A's roles.

To reduce clutter, implied subset constraints should be omitted from conceptual schemas. Thus a subset constraint between two roles may be marked only if both of these roles are optional. This rule does not extend to composite subset constraints (see later).

Returning to our fitness club application, there is one more constraint to consider. Reaction time is recorded for a member if and only if his or her heart rate is too. Each member has both fitness measures taken or neither. This might be because the club wants to provide a balanced estimate of fitness, rather than risk reliance on a single figure. When the test data are entered, a compound transaction is used to enter both measures.

Such a constraint is called an **equality constraint,** since for any state of the database the set of people whose reaction time is recorded equals the set of people whose heart rate is recorded. This constraint is depicted by a *dotted arrow with two heads*

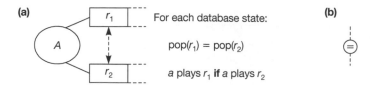

Figure 6.16 An equality constraint between two roles.

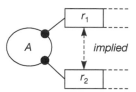

Figure 6.17 The implied equality constraint should not be shown.

("◄------►") connecting the relevant roles (look back at Figure 6.13). It asserts that the populations of these two roles must always be equal. As the notation suggests, an equality constraint is equivalent to two subset constraints, running in opposite directions.

One reason for using a double-headed arrow to mark an equality constraint is because a double arrow symbol "↔" is often used in logic for "if and only if". In words, the equality constraint in Figure 6.13 may be expressed as Member has a ReactionTime **iff** Member has a HeartRate.

Figure 6.16(a) summarizes the notion of an equality constraint between two optional roles. Figure 6.16(b) shows an alternate, circled "=" notation sometimes used to reduce line crossings in layout, or to cater to rare cases with both roles in the same predicate.

If both roles are mandatory, an equality constraint is implied since each of $pop(r_1)$ and $pop(r_2)$ equals $pop(A)$. Implied equality constraints should not be shown (see Figure 6.17). If one role is mandatory and the other is optional, then an equality constraint cannot exist between them since it is possible to have a state in which only some of A's population plays the optional role. If neither role is mandatory but their disjunction is, then there is no equality constraint; otherwise both the roles would be mandatory (why?).

In principle, all mandatory roles and equality constraints on a conceptual schema could be replaced by groups of subset constraints. In practice, however, this would lead to untidy schema diagrams, with subset constraint lines running all over them. Hence, the notions of mandatory role and equality constraint are very convenient.

Now consider the report extract shown in Table 6.2. In this UoD, employees may request a company parking space or a refund of their parking expenses, but not both. Employees may make neither request (e.g., they might not have a car, or they might simply want more time to decide).

Table 6.2 Employee details.

EmpNr	Employee name	Parking space	Parking claim ($)
001	Adams B	C01	−
002	Bloggs F	−	200
003	Collins T	B05	−
004	Dancer F	−	250
005	Eisai Z	?	?

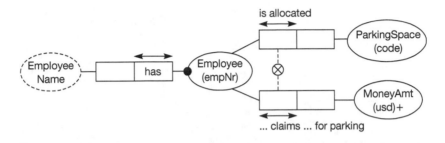

Figure 6.18 Conceptual schema for Table 6.2.

For this report, different kinds of null values are displayed differently. The "−" value indicates "not to be recorded" (because the other option is chosen). The "?" value simply indicates "not recorded"; an actual value might still be recorded for employee 005 later (e.g., after this employee buys a car). Once such a value is recorded, however, the system must disallow the other option.

Figure 6.18 shows a schema for this example. A circled X symbol "⊗" indicates an **exclusion constraint** between the roles it connects (X for eXclusion). This asserts that for each state of the database no employee can be recorded as playing both these roles. That is, the populations of these roles are *mutually exclusive*. A textual version of this constraint is **no** Employee is allocated **a** ParkingSpace **and also** claims **a** MoneyAmt for parking.

Figure 6.19 formalizes this notion of an exclusion constraint between two roles: their populations are exclusive just in case their intersection is the null set (i.e., they have no element in common). If two roles are played by different, primitive entity types, then an implied exclusion constraint exists between them (since the entity types are mutually exclusive); such implied exclusion constraints are always omitted.

An exclusion constraint may be asserted between two roles only if these roles are optional and are played by the same object type (or possibly a supertype—see later). If one of the roles were mandatory, any object playing the other role would also have to play the mandatory one, so an exclusion constraint could not apply. It is possible, however, that the disjunction of these two roles is mandatory.

Now consider Figure 6.20. In this simple application, married partners are identified by their first names, and their country of birth must be recorded. For the ring predicate "is husband of", the inverse predicate name "is wife of" is also shown. No partner can

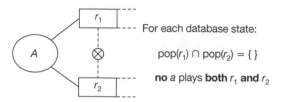

Figure 6.19 An exclusion constraint between two roles.

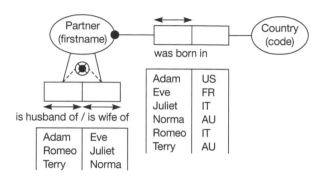

Figure 6.20 *Exclusive-or:* each partner is a husband or wife but not both.

be both a husband and a wife, so the husband and wife roles are mutually exclusive. Moreover, each partner is either a husband or a wife, so the same two roles are disjunctively mandatory.

Taken together, the exclusion and disjunctive mandatory role constraints assert that each partner is either a husband or a wife (of someone) but not both. These two constraints can be depicted together by superimposing the exclusion and mandatory symbols ($\otimes$ and $\odot$) to form the *life-buoy symbol* $\otimes$, connected by dotted lines to the relevant roles, as shown in Figure 6.20.

When disjunctive mandatory (inclusive-or) is combined with exclusion, we have an **exclusive-or constraint.** Each partner plays *exactly one* of the constrained roles. So each partner appears in one column of this fact table, but no partner can appear in both columns. Contrast this with the parenthood binary considered in an earlier chapter, where each person is a parent or child or both—a case of inclusive-or.

The life-buoy symbol is also called a *partition symbol,* since it effectively partitions an object type's population into separate role populations. We'll return to the notion of partitions when we discuss subtypes. Although the exclusive-or constraint may be depicted as a single symbol, it really denotes an orthogonal combination of two constraints and is normally verbalized as two separate constraints. In this case the verbalization is **each** Partner is husband of **a** Partner **or** is wife of **a** Partner; **no** Partner is husband of **a** Partner **and** is wife of **a** Partner. As an alternative to the life-buoy symbol, separate mandatory role and exclusion constraint symbols may be used, as shown in Figure 6.21.

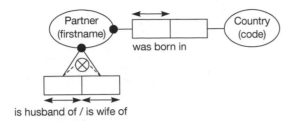

Figure 6.21 Alternative notation for exclusive-or.

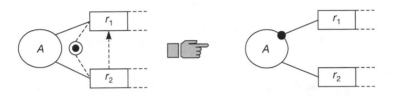

Figure 6.22 The left-hand schema should be redrawn as the right-hand schema.

Note that subset or equality constraints should not be displayed with disjunctive mandatory roles. For example, if the two constraints in the left-hand schema of Figure 6.22 apply, then it follows that role r_1 is mandatory (as an exercise, prove this). For clarity, the mandatory role should be shown explicitly; the subset constraint is now implied by this, and hence should be omitted (see right-hand schema of Figure 6.22).

Similarly, an equality constraint between disjunctive mandatory roles should be redrawn as two mandatory roles. Such redrawing rules are pragmatic. Formally the left-hand schema is equivalent to the right-hand one. However, the right-hand version is preferred because it is simpler for people to work with.

As another case of redrawing, an exclusion constraint among three or more roles may be depicted by a single "⊗" connecting the roles, in preference to exhaustively marking exclusion constraints between each pair of roles. A simple example of this is shown in Figure 6.23. In this UoD each person is limited to at most one of three vices.

In the left-hand diagram of Figure 6.23, three exclusion constraints are needed to cover all the ways in which the three roles may be paired. Four roles may be paired in six ways. In general, a single exclusion constraint across n roles replaces $n(n - 1)/2$ separate exclusion constraints between two roles. An equality constraint across n roles may also be specified using a single circled "=" instead of multiple binary equality constraints. No notation for a subset constraint over n roles is used, since direction is involved.

Although exclusion constraints between roles are not uncommon, in practice simple subset and equality constraints are seldom used on conceptual schemas (though they are often used on relational schemas). It is fairly common to encounter "qualified" set comparison constraints, but these are depicted by subtyping (see next section).

However, applications commonly involve *set comparison constraints between role sequences* (not just between single roles), which we cannot handle by subtyping. Let's

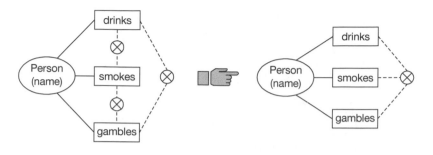

Figure 6.23 In this UoD, each person has at most one of three vices.

Table 6.3 Details about car owners and drivers.

Person	Sex	Cars owned	Cars driven
Fred	M	272NCP, 123BOM	272NCP, 123BOM
Sue	F	272NCP, 123BOM	272NCP
Tina	F	105ABC	
Tom	M		

consider some examples. Table 6.3 provides details about people and the cars they own or drive. For simplicity, assume that people are identified by their first name, and that each car is identified by a registration number stamped on its license plate. If we allowed a car to change its license plate, we would need to pick some other identifier (e.g., its vehicle identification number or compliance plate number).

Figure 6.24 shows the populated conceptual schema. The ownership association is many:many. A person may own many cars, and the same car may be owned by many people. For example, Fred and Sue are co-owners of two cars (e.g., they might be married). The drives association is also many:many.

Note that although Fred and Sue both own car 123BOM, only Fred drives it. For example, it might be Fred's "pride and joy" and he won't let Sue drive it; or perhaps it is a "bomb" of a car and Sue refuses to drive it! Tina owns a car but doesn't drive it (maybe she has a chauffeur). Tom neither owns nor drives a car.

For the population shown, people own every car that they drive. Although unusual, for discussion purposes let us assume the sample database is significant in this respect. In other words, in this UoD nobody may drive a car unless they own it.

This rule is indicated in Figure 6.24 by the *pair-subset constraint* running from the middle of the Drives predicate to the middle of the Owns predicate. This asserts that,

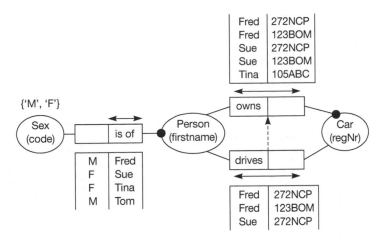

Figure 6.24 A populated conceptual schema for Table 6.3.

for each state of the database, the set of (Person, Car) pairs referenced in the Drives fact table is a subset of the set of pairs listed in the Owns table. We may think of each pair as a tuple of values from a row of a fact table.

For the database state shown, the Drives table has three pairs: (Fred, 272NCP), (Fred, 123BOM), and (Sue, 272NCP). The Owns table has five pairs. Each pair in the Drives table is also in the Owns table; the subset constraint indicates that this is true for each state of the database. This constraint may be expressed textually as **if a** Person drives **a** Car **then that** Person owns **that** Car. Here are some alternative verbalizations: Person drives Car **only if** Person owns Car; **if** Person *p* drives Car *c* **then** Person *p* owns Car *c*; Person *p* drives Car *c* **only if** Person *p* owns Car *c*.

As usual, the direction of the subset constraint is important. With our present example, if the arrow pointed instead to the Drives fact type this would signify that each person who owns a car also drives that car, which is quite a different constraint (false for this UoD, but as an exercise invent a population consistent with this new constraint).

To indicate that a subset constraint applies between role pairs rather than single roles, each end of the arrow is positioned at the junction of the two roles in the pair. This notation may be used whenever the roles in the pair are contiguous (see Figure 6.25).

In terms of the associated fact tables, the projection on columns r_3, r_4 of the lower table is a subset of the projection on columns r_1, r_2 of the upper table. If the roles in the pair are not contiguous, a connecting line is used between them. Role connectors are also used when the arguments to the constraint contain more than two roles (see Figure 6.26).

In general, a *tuple-subset constraint* may be specified between two compatible role tuples, where each tuple is a sequence of *n* roles ($n \geq 1$). However, *n* is rarely greater than two. In rare cases, roles may need to be reordered before being compared; in this case the constraint may be annotated by including the relevant permutation.

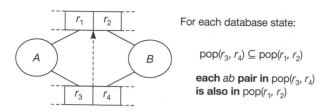

For each database state:

$$pop(r_3, r_4) \subseteq pop(r_1, r_2)$$

each *ab* pair in $pop(r_3, r_4)$
is also in $pop(r_1, r_2)$

Figure 6.25 A pair-subset constraint.

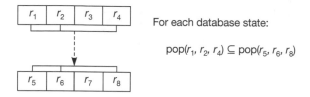

For each database state:

$$pop(r_1, r_2, r_4) \subseteq pop(r_5, r_6, r_8)$$

Figure 6.26 An example of a tuple-subset constraint between sequences of three roles.

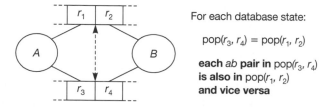

For each database state:

$$pop(r_3, r_4) = pop(r_1, r_2)$$

each *ab* pair in $pop(r_3, r_4)$
is also in $pop(r_1, r_2)$
and vice versa

Figure 6.27 A pair-equality constraint.

Now consider the case where people own a car if and only if they drive that car. Here we have subset constraints in both directions; this is a *pair-equality* constraint. In such cases where the role pairs form a whole predicate, we usually store only one fact type. For example, we might store Drives and derive Owns, or collapse both to IsOwnerDriverOf. However, if a role pair is embedded in a longer predicate, an equality constraint is not equivalent to a derivation rule (why not?). Figure 6.27 summarizes the case of pair equality for contiguous roles.

Exclusion constraints may be specified between two or more role sequences. As a simple example, suppose we want to record information about cars that people own and cars that they want to buy. Clearly, nobody would want to buy a car that they already own. We can indicate this by the *pair-exclusion constraint* shown in Figure 6.28.

This constraint is weaker than an exclusion constraint between just the first roles of these predicates (which would instead say that no car owner wants to buy any car, and hence would disallow Fred's appearance in both the fact tables shown). Although we must record each person's gender, both the owns and the wants-to-buy roles

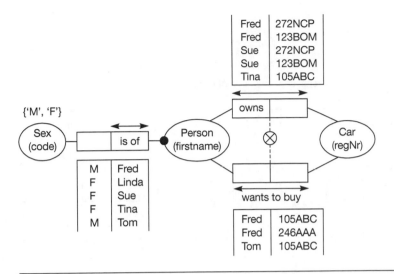

Figure 6.28 A pair-exclusion constraint: nobody wants to buy a car that they own.

are optional (even disjunctively). For example, Linda neither owns nor wants to buy a car.

In this section, set-comparison constraints have been considered between pairs of role sequences, where each role sequence comes from a single predicate. More generally, set-comparison constraints may be defined between compatible role paths formed by joining different predicates (join constraints are discussed in the next chapter).

To conclude this section, let's look at some general results, or theorems, about set-comparison constraints. Suppose we declare a tuple-subset constraint from role sequence rs_1 to role sequence rs_2, where each sequence has n roles ($n \geq 1$). Is it now possible for these role sequences to be exclusive?

If both role sequences are unpopulated, then both the subset and exclusion constraints are trivially satisfied. But for practical reasons, we need every conceptual schema to be *strongly satisfiable* (or *population consistent*). This means that each role sequence used as a predicate or as a constraint argument can be populated in some state. It is not necessary that these role sequences can be populated together in the same state.

Suppose we populate rs_1 with some sequence a. The subset constraint entails that a now populates rs_2 as well, thus violating the exclusion constraint. Swapping rs_1 with rs_2 in this reasoning shows a subset constraint in the other direction cannot hold either, if an exclusion constraint does.

This proves theorem NXS (No eXclusion with a Subset constraint), depicted in Figure 6.29. Here a long box depicts a sequence of one or more roles, and the constraints apply between the *whole* sequences (not different parts of them).

Recall that an equality constraint is equivalent to, and is used instead of, two subset constraints. Hence at most one set-comparison constraint may be declared between two (whole) role sequences. However, different set-comparison constraints may be declared

Figure 6.29   Theorem NXS: No eXclusion with a Subset constraint.

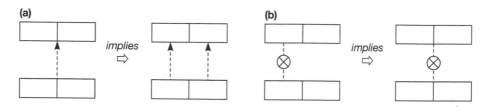

Figure 6.30   The implied constraints should not be shown.

between different parts of role sequences. For instance, we may have a subset constraint between the first roles and an exclusion constraint between the second roles. It is important to realize that subset or equality constraints between two role sequences imply similar constraints between the individual roles. In contrast, an exclusion constraint between single roles implies exclusion constraints between all sequences containing these roles.

These *constraint implication* results are depicted for role pairs in Figure 6.30, using "⇨" for "necessarily implies". In each case, the implication is in one direction only. Results for equality constraints are similar to the subset results. In the exclusion example, a similar result holds if a simple exclusion constraint is between the right-hand roles. Implied constraints should usually be omitted from a schema. As an exercise, you may wish to prove these results. If you have trouble here, try inventing some counterexamples to equivalence claims. For example, if $pop(r_1, r_2) = \{(a1, b1), (a2, b2)\}$ and $pop(r_3, r_4) = \{(a1, b2), (a2, b1)\}$, then $pop(r_1) = pop(r_3)$ and $pop(r_2) = pop(r_4)$ but $pop(r_1, r_2) \neq pop(r_3, r_4)$.

Other constraint implication theorems exist, some of which will be mentioned later in the book. One of the most important results deals with the case where the target of a pair-subset constraint includes a functional role. For example, consider the left pattern in Figure 6.30(a). Here we have a pair-subset constraint from the lower role pair to the top role pair. Suppose we add a simple uniqueness constraint over the left-hand role of the top role pair. What does this imply about the left-hand role of the lower role pair? If the lower predicate is just a binary, this role must also be unique! As an exercise, prove this. An important corollary of this result is that if the lower predicate is longer than a binary, then it must split in this case, since there will be an implied FD from the first role to the second role. This result is illustrated in Section 12.6 when we discuss normalization.

Exercise 6.4

1. A company allows some of its employees to use one or more of its company cars. The rest of its employees are given a travel allowance instead. The following report is an extract from the company's records in this regard. Schematize it.

EmpNr	Emp name	Cars used	Driver's license	Travel allowance ($)
001	Harding J	123ABC	A74000	–
002	Oh C	111KOR, 123ABC	A51120	–
003	Halpin T			200

2. The diagram below indicates the conceptual schema and current population for a particular UoD. Reference schemes are omitted for simplicity. Fact tables are shown below their fact types. Predicates are identified as **R..U**, and constraints as $C_1..C_9$.

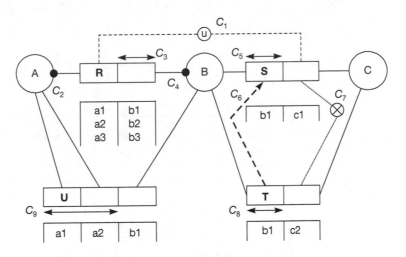

Each of the following requests applies to the **same** database population as shown above (i.e., treat each request as if it were the *first* to be made with this population). For each request, indicate the CIP's response. If the request is legal, write "accepted". Otherwise, indicate the constraint violated (e.g., "C_2 violated").

(a) add: a1 R b2   (b) add: b4 S c3   (c) add: b1 S c3   (d) delete: b1 S c1

(e) add: b2 S c2   (f) add: b3 T c3   (g) add: U a2 a1 b2   (h) add: U a1 a2 b2

(i) begin
    add: a1 R b4
    add: b4 S c1
  end

3. Draw the conceptual schema diagram for the UoD declared in Exercise 2.2, Question 2, adding constraint labels $C_1..C_5$ to the relevant constraints marked on the diagram.

4. The following table records details about various (fictitious) movies. Schematize this UoD. The population is not fully significant, so make some educated guesses.

Movie	Director	Stars	Supporting cast
Earth Song	Ima Beatle	Bing Crosby Elvis Presley Hugh Who	Neil Diamond Tina Turner
Me and My Echo Kangaroos	Hugh Who Doc U. Mentary		

5. A software company has a large number of shops located in the state of Queensland and requires detailed knowledge of their distribution. The table shows some of their locations. City shops are located in suburbs, but country shops are located in towns. City and town names are unique (other states are not of interest). Schematize this UoD, revealing the reference scheme of the entity type Location in full detail. Model street addresses as values but towns, suburbs, and cities as entities.

Shop#	Location			
	Suburb	City	Town	Street address
1	St Lucia	Brisbane		Suite 5, 77 Sylvan Rd
2			Strathpine	Unit 3, 1000 Gympie Rd
3	Sandgate	Brisbane		7 Sun St
4	Clontarf	Redcliffe		25 Beach Rd
5	Sandgate	Cairns		25 Beach Rd

6. The application described here is partly based on a real-life banking system, but simplifications and changes have been made. To help you appreciate the privacy implications of a universal identification scheme, all clients and staff of the bank are identified throughout the application by their tax file number (taxNr). Thus, all bank customers and personnel are taxpayers.

An information system is required to manage accounts and staff records for Oz Bank, which has branches at various locations. Each branch is standardly identified by its branch number but also has a unique name. The first table is an extract from staff records of Oz Bank. Each employee works at exactly one branch and has at most one phone listed. The mark "?" denotes a null value. The mark "..." indicates "etc." (other instances exist but are not shown here).

BranchNr	Branch name	Emp taxNr	Emp name	Emp phone
1	Uni. of Qld	200	Jones E	3770000
		390	Presley E	?
		...	...	...
2	Toowong Central	377	Jones E	?
		...	...	...
3	Strathpine	222	Wong M	2051111
		...	...	...

Within the one branch, each account has a unique serial number, but different accounts in different branches may have the same serial number. Account users are identified by their taxNr, but also have a name and possibly a phone number (see the second table).

Account		User		
BranchNr	SerialNr	TaxNr	Name	Phone
1	55	200	Jones E	3770000
		311	Jones T	3770000
1	66	199	Megasoft	3771234
2	55	199	Megasoft	3771234
2	77	377	Jones E	?
3	44	300	Wong S	2051111

Each account is a passbook account. Five sample passbook entries are shown. For each account, transactions are numbered sequentially 1, 2, 3, ... Dates are formatted day/month/year. For simplicity, assume each transaction is either a deposit (DEP) or withdrawal (WDL). In practice, other types of transactions are possible (e.g., interest and fees). The balance column shows the account balance after the transaction is executed.

OZ BANK

BranchNr	SerialNr
1	55

Branch name: Uni. of Qld
Users: Jones E; Jones T

TranNr	Date	Deposit	Withdrawal	Balance
1	3/1/90	1000		1000
2	5/1/90		200	800
3	5/1/90		100	700

OZ BANK

BranchNr	SerialNr
1	66

Branch name: Uni. of Qld
Users: Megasoft

TranNr	Date	Deposit	Withdrawal	Balance
1	10/2/90	2000		2000
2	10/2/90		500	1500

OZ BANK

BranchNr	SerialNr
2	55

Branch name: Toowong Central
Users: Megasoft

TranNr	Date	Deposit	Withdrawal	Balance
1	23/1/90	9000		9000
2	7/2/90	5000		14000
3	10/2/90		2000	12000
4	2/3/90		5000	7000

OZ BANK				
BranchNr	**SerialNr**	**Branch name:** Toowong Central		
		Users: Jones E		
2	77			

TranNr	**Date**	**Deposit**	**Withdrawal**	**Balance**
1	3/1/90	500		500

OZ BANK				
BranchNr	**SerialNr**	**Branch name:** Strathpine		
3	44	**Users:** Wong S		

TranNr	**Date**	**Deposit**	**Withdrawal**	**Balance**
1	5/1/90	100		100
2	12/1/90			700

Although the balance is derivable, for efficiency purposes *the balance is stored as soon as it is derived.* For example, this speeds up production of monthly statements for the bank's customers (Oz Bank has a few million customers who average several transactions each month). This *derive-on-update* (eager evaluation) decision contrasts with our normal *derive-on-query* (lazy evaluation) policy.

(a) Draw a conceptual schema diagram for this UoD. Make use of an entity type indicating the type of transaction: Trantype (code) { 'DEP', 'WDL' }. Include the account balance fact type on the diagram; mark it with "**" since it is derivable but it is required to be stored. Express the derivation rule as clearly as you can.

(b) Consider the fragment of your conceptual schema that captures the kind of information required for deposits and withdrawals (only two fact types are involved). Transform this subschema into an equivalent subschema that uses two different fact types, removing the entity type Trantype altogether.

(c) In a realistic banking application there are several kinds of transactions besides deposits and withdrawals. In such a situation is it better to include Trantype as an object type, or to extend the alternative approach you proposed in (b)?

6.5   Subtyping

If an object type is classified into one or more specific types, these specialized types are known as **subtypes.** Consider, for example, the object type Person, shown in Figure 6.31. For discussion purposes, this is populated with eight people. Each person's gender and birth country is recorded. The two instances of Gender are denoted by the biological symbols for male and female. Countries are denoted by their map shapes (only Australia, Italy, and Mexico are shown here).

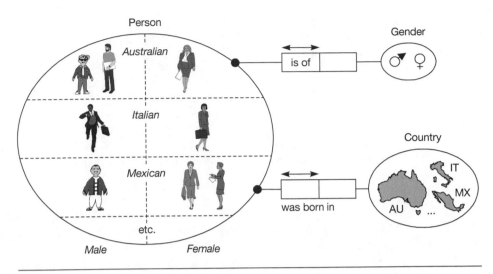

Figure 6.31 Person may be classified into subtypes according to gender or birthplace.

Based on gender, we could classify Person into the two subtypes MalePerson and FemalePerson. I've placed the males on the left and the females on the right in Figure 6.31, so you can visualize creating these subtypes by vertically dividing the Person type in two. We could also classify persons into different subtypes based on their country of birth. In Figure 6.31 this is depicted by the horizontal division of Person into Australian, Italian, Mexican, etc. For the small population shown, we have three Australians, two Italians, and three Mexicans, with other nationalities in various layers below (simply marked "etc." here to save space). For simplicity, let's ignore issues about naturalization, so the term "Australian" is used here in the sense of "Australian born", and so on.

The main reason for using a subtype in modeling is to *declare a constraint that a specific role is played only by that subtype*. For example, a medical database might record whether a patient was circumcised, but this would be recorded only for male patients.

A second reason for subtyping is to *encourage reuse of model components*. For example, if we already have an elaborate subschema describing the object type Employee and want to talk about managers, we can declare Manager as a subtype of Employee and simply add the extra details specific to managers. If Employee is defined in a reference model, it can be imported into many different models and specialized as appropriate for each case. If an object type has behavior defined for it, this can be reused as well as the data aspects. In programming applications, this can significantly reduce code duplication.

A third reason for subtyping is to reveal a *taxonomy* or classification scheme being used in the UoD. However, in ORM, we normally avoid introducing subtypes purely to expose a classification scheme. Why? First, taxonomies may be modeled in more economical ways. For example, to indicate there are two genders we may simply add a

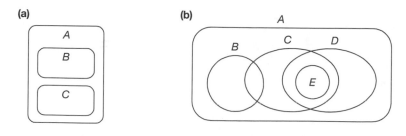

Figure 6.32 Euler diagrams are OK for simple subtyping (a) but not complex cases (b).

value constraint such as {'M', 'F'} on Gender (code). There is no need to introduce Male and Female subtypes unless we have some specific roles for them to play in our application domain.

Second, the number of subtypes can rapidly get out of hand if we use them purely for taxonomy. For example, suppose we are interested in classifying people based on country of birth. All we need is the fact type Person was born in Country. If instead we modeled this by introducing subtypes of Person, one for each country, this would lead to almost 200 subtypes in the schema! This is crazy. If one of these subtypes plays a specific role, then we should introduce it; but if it doesn't, we should not do so. For example, suppose we wanted to record whether Australians want their country to become a republic, but had nothing specific to record about the other nationalities. In that case, Australian is the only subtype we should introduce.

Earlier in the chapter, Euler diagrams were used to depict one set as a subset of another. In designing a conceptual schema we often need to introduce subtypes, and in so doing spell out clearly what is a subtype of what. Euler diagrams may be used to do this for simple cases, like Figure 6.32(a), where B and C are subtypes of A. Interpreting this as a hypothetical Euler diagram, the question is open as to whether A contains any elements not in B or C. If A does have more elements, this can be shown by adding an asterisk to the region outside B and C. As discussed in Section 8.2, the Barker notation for ER uses a special type called "Other" for this purpose instead of an asterisk.

The good thing about Euler diagrams is that they show containment intuitively, by placing one set or type spatially inside another. This works well for simple cases. In practice, however, an object type may have many subtypes, which might overlap, and a subtype may have many supertypes. For example, the subtype pattern in Figure 6.32(b) depicts the following information: B, C, and D are subtypes of A, and E is a subtype of both C and D. Moreover, B *overlaps* with C (i.e., they may have a common instance) and C overlaps with D, but B and D are *mutually exclusive* (cannot have a common instance). For example: A = Person; B = Asian; C = Consultant; D = American; E = TexanConsultant. For such cases, Euler diagrams become hopelessly complicated. Moreover, individual subtypes may have many specific details recorded for them, and there is simply no room to attach these details if the subtype nodes are crowded together inside their supertype nodes.

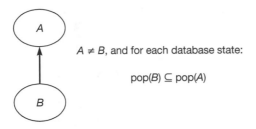

$A \neq B$, and for each database state:

$$pop(B) \subseteq pop(A)$$

Figure 6.33 *B* is a proper subtype of *A*.

For such reasons, Euler diagrams are eschewed for nontrivial subtyping. What we need is a simple notation that can be used to display subtypehood and subtype roles no matter how large or complex the situation is. This is achieved by displaying subtypes *outside* their supertype(s) and depicting the subtype-supertype connections by means of an *arrow*. To distinguish it from a subset constraint, the arrow line is thicker and unbroken. The basic idea is shown in Figure 6.33.

Here *A* and *B* are object types. Suppose *A* = Employee and *B* = Manager. The type Employee is the set of all employees about which facts might possibly be recorded. The subtype Manager is the set of all managers about which facts might be recorded. At any given database state, pop(Employee) and pop(Manager) are, respectively, the set of employees and the set of managers actually referenced in the database.

In general, *B* is a **proper subtype** of *A* if and only if pop*(B)* is always a subset of pop*(A)*, and *A* ≠ *B*. In this case, *A* is a *proper supertype* of *B*. If *A* = *B*, we do not specify any subtype connection. With this understanding, we usually omit "proper" when speaking about subtypes and supertypes. The adjective "proper" applies to the type relationship, but not necessarily to the *population* relationship. There may be a database state in which pop*(A)* = pop*(B)*. For example, if no facts about *A* have yet been entered, both pop*(A)* and pop*(B)* equal { }, and with our example, we may choose to enter information about managers before the other employees.

This notation is less intuitive than Euler diagrams because a subtype is shown "outside" its supertype even though every object instance within the subtype must also be contained inside the supertype. Moreover, information about subtype overlapping is lost unless we add some way to capture it. This is a consequence of depicting subtype connections by arrows rather than spatial containment. However, this disadvantage is more than offset by the ability to conveniently represent subtype patterns of arbitrary complexity, while still allowing plenty of space around each node for details to be attached.

Using this notation, the complex subtype pattern shown in the Euler diagram of Figure 6.32(b) may be modeled as shown in Figure 6.34. Here *A* is a *common supertype* of *B* and *C* and *D*, and *E* is a *common subtype* of *C* and *D*. In general, a common supertype is at least the union of its subtypes; if it is the union of its subtypes, then its subtypes are said to *exhaust* it. In our example, *B, C,* and *D* do not exhaust *A*. Note that Figure 6.34(a) depicts only the subtype connections. Figure 6.32(b) contained the

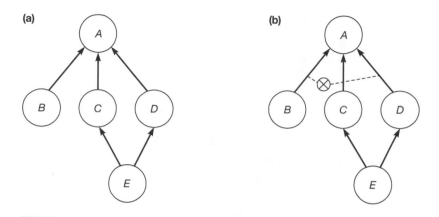

Figure 6.34 Another way to model the subtype connections in Figure 6.32(b).

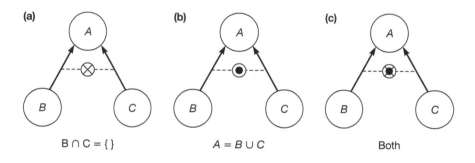

Figure 6.35 *B* and *C* are mutually exclusive (a), exhaustive (b), or both (c).

additional information that *B* overlaps with *C, C* overlaps with *D,* and *B* and *D* are mutually exclusive. Hence, if the subtype arrow notation is used, some other means must be used to convey whether or not subtypes are mutually exclusive.

One way of doing this in ORM is to attach an *exclusion* symbol "⊗" via dotted lines to the relevant subtype links. The absence of such a symbol indicates that the populations of the types may overlap. With this additional symbol, Figure 6.34(b) now conveys the exclusion/overlap information of the Euler diagram in Figure 6.32(b).

To indicate that two or more subtypes are *exhaustive* of their supertype (i.e., their union equals the supertype), a *mandatory* symbol "⊙" may be connected by dotted lines to the relevant subtype links. This constraint applies to the populations as well as the types. So each instance in the population of the supertype must appear in the population of at least one of the subtypes.

Implicitly, underlying each subtype arrow there is a 1:1 binary association named "is/is". The subtype exclusion and exhaustion constraints correspond to exclusion and disjunctive mandatory constraints on the roles played by the supertype in these associations. In combination they provide an exclusive-or constraint. Hence the choice of symbols for these constraints. In this light, the constraints in Figure 6.35 may be verbalized

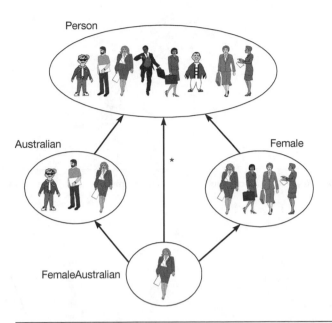

Figure 6.36 The indirect subtype connection is implied, so it should be omitted.

respectively as **no** A is **both** B **and** C; **each** A **is at least one of** B **or** C; **each** A **is exactly one of** B **or** C. Although these constraint symbols help clarify basic concepts, they are rarely used in practice because they are typically implied. This claim will be justified shortly.

Subtypes may overlap, especially if they are based on different classification schemes. For example, in Figure 6.36 the subtypes Australian and Female overlap. Since overlapping subtypes have elements in common, a common subtype may be formed from one or more elements in their intersection. For example, the subtype FemaleAustralian is a subtype of both Australian and Female.

In general, the relation of subtypehood is *transitive:* if A is a subtype of B, and B is a subtype of C, then A is a subtype of C. In this case, A is said to be an *indirect subtype* of C. In Figure 6.36, for example, FemaleAustralian is a direct subtype of Australian, which is a direct subtype of Person. Hence, FemaleAustralian is an indirect subtype of Person. For exposition purposes, this indirect link is marked on the diagram with an asterisk to show its derived nature. To avoid clutter, however, indirect subtype links should be omitted from diagrams since they are transitively implied.

If a subtype has two or more direct supertypes, this is called *multiple inheritance.* For example, in Figure 6.36 FemaleAustralian inherits from both Australian and Female. In general, a common subtype is at most the intersection of its supertypes. If a subtype has only one direct supertype, this is called *single inheritance.*

A supertype may have many direct subtypes, and a subtype may have many direct supertypes, so in general we have a *subtype graph* rather than a tree. The supertype and subtypes are referred to as the *nodes* of the graph. Since the arrowheads provide direction, we have a directed graph. Since no type can be a proper subtype of itself, it

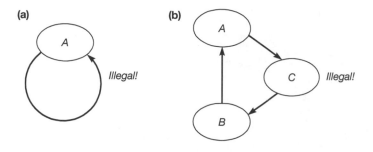

Figure 6.37 No cycles are permitted in a subtype graph.

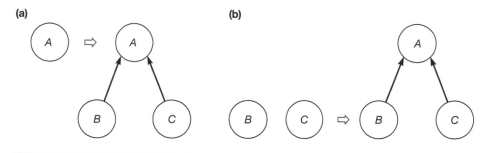

Figure 6.38 A subtype graph may arise by (a) specialization or (b) generalization.

follows that no cycles or loops are permitted, no matter what the length of the cycle (Figure 6.37 shows two illegal cycles). Thus any pattern of type-subtype relationships forms a *directed acyclic graph* (DAG).

An entity type that is not a proper subtype of any other entity type in the schema is said to be a *primitive entity type* for the schema. In Figure 6.31, for example, Person, Gender, and Country are primitive entity types. A single conceptual schema may have many subtype graphs (e.g., one based on Person and one based on Vehicle). Each subtype graph must stem from exactly one primitive entity type (possibly nested), which is the common supertype, or *root* node (or *top*) of that graph.

Subtype graphs have only one top, since primitive entity types are mutually exclusive. In contrast, subtypes in a graph necessarily overlap with their supertype(s) and may even overlap with one another (e.g., Australian and Female). Since root types are mutually exclusive, there is no overlap between subtypes that belong to different subtype graphs. To reinforce these general ideas about subtypes, you may wish to try Question 1 of the section exercises before continuing.

A subtype graph may arise in a top-down way, by *specializing* an object type into subtypes (subtype introduction), as in Figure 6.38(a). A subtype graph may also arise in a bottom-up way, by *generalizing* object types to a common supertype, and retaining the subtypes for specific details (supertype introduction), as in Figure 6.38(b). Sometimes a subtype graph arises from a combination of specialization and generalization.

Table 6.4 Details about hospital patients.

PatientNr	Name	Sex	Phone	Prostate status	Pregnancies
101	Adams A	M	2052061	OK	–
102	Blossom F	F	3652999	–	5
103	Jones E	F	?	–	0
104	King P	M	?	benign enlargement	–
105	Smith J	M	2057654	?	–

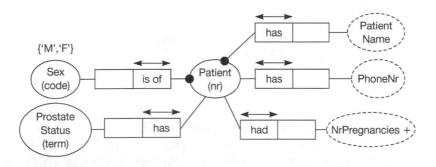

Figure 6.39 An incomplete conceptual schema for Table 6.4.

The rest of this section discusses the specialization process, and the following section deals with the generalization process.

Now consider a hospital application where all the patients are adults, and hence may be classified as men or women. An extract from the hospital records is shown in Table 6.4. Only males have a prostate gland. In later life this gland may suffer various medical problems. Only women can become pregnant.

In this table, a question mark "?" is an ordinary null value, indicating that an actual value is unknown. The minus sign "−" is a special null value, indicating that an actual value is *not to be recorded* in that spot. We met something like this when we considered subset and exclusion constraints. But there is a difference. Here the "−" means that an actual value is *inapplicable because of the specific value of some other entry* (or entries) for the entity involved.

On the first row, pregnancies must not be recorded for patient 101 because that patient is male (as shown by the "M" entry for sex). Similarly, prostate status must not be recorded for women. The number of pregnancies must be recorded for women, even if this number is zero. In contrast to "−", the "?" merely indicates that the information is missing. For example, patients 103 and 104 might have no phone, and patient 105 might not have had his prostate checked. Suppose we schematize this UoD as in Figure 6.39.

Notice the optional roles. Although correct as far as it goes, this schema fails to express the constraints that prostate status is recorded *only for* men and the number of

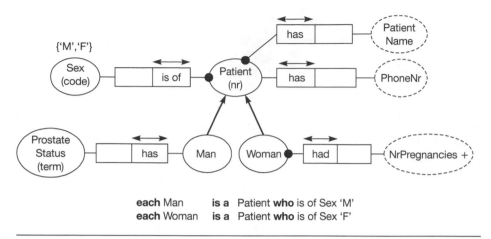

each Man   is a Patient who is of Sex 'M'
each Woman is a Patient who is of Sex 'F'

Figure 6.40 Subtyping completes the conceptual schema for Table 6.4.

pregnancies is recorded *just for* the women. The phrase "just for" means "for and only for" (i.e., "for all and only"). To capture these constraints, we introduce subtypes and attach their specific roles, as shown in Figure 6.40. The subtypes Man and Woman are formally defined beneath the diagram. By default, subtypes inherit the identification scheme of their supertype, so there is no need to repeat it.

Recall that a role is played only by the object type to which it is attached. Hence the subtyping reveals that prostate status is recorded **only if** the patient is male, and pregnancy count is recorded **only if** the patient is female. The role attached to Man is optional. Not all men need to have their prostate status recorded. However, the role attached to Woman is mandatory. So pregnancy count is recorded **if** the patient is female. The combination of the subtype constraint and mandatory role on Woman means that a pregnancy count is recorded **if and only if** the patient is female.

In this case, the Man subtype plays only one role, and this is optional. Unlike primitive entity types, there is no default assumption of mandatory if only one role is attached. *With subtypes, and objectified predicates, any mandatory role constraints must be explicitly shown* (including disjunctive cases).

Don't introduce a subtype unless there is at least one specific role recorded only for that subtype. As with primitive entity types, *each subtype must have an attached role.* Some other modeling methods allow inactive subtypes that play no specific roles. For example, Man and Woman subtypes might be introduced merely to display that patients can be classified in this way. As discussed earlier, it is better to display such a classification scheme as a binary fact type with a value constraint (e.g., Figure 6.40 uses Patient is of Sex {'M', 'F'}) or as unaries (e.g., isMan and isWoman may be attached to Patient as exclusive, disjunctively mandatory unaries). The binary form is much neater when the classification scheme involves several subtypes.

While specific fact types are attached to the relevant subtype, common fact types are attached to the supertype. In this example, name, sex, and phone may be recorded for any patient, so they are attached directly to Patient. In general, each subtype inherits all the roles of its supertype(s). Although drawn outside its supertype, the subtype is totally contained inside the supertype. In Figure 6.40 all instances of Man or Woman have their name, sex, and possibly phone recorded. Attaching a common fact type to the supertype avoids duplicating it on all the subtypes.

To determine membership of subtypes, *each subtype must be defined in terms of at least one role played by its supertype(s)*. With the present example, the sex fact type is used to determine membership in Man and Woman. The subtype definitions are shown below the diagram. These definitions are formal—they are not just comments. The operator **"is a"** or **"is an"** is used for "is defined as", and **"who"**, **"that"**, or **"which"** is used after the supertype name. For persons, "who" sounds more natural than "that". Optionally, **"each"** may be used before the name of the subtype being defined, as shown in Figure 6.40. Here each Man is a Patient, but since we require subtypes to be well defined, this "is a" connection must be *qualified* in some way. For example: **each** Man **is a** Patient **who** is of Sex 'M'. Subtyping provides a means of *qualifying an optional role, a simple subset constraint, or a simple exclusion constraint.*

Subtyping may also be used *instead of unqualified, simple set-comparison constraints, especially if the subtype plays many specific roles.* Consider a UoD where each employee drives cars or catches buses but not both. Cars or buses are recorded for all employees, bus allowance is recorded just for the bus catchers, and driver's license numbers are recorded only for the drivers. This can be modeled without subtypes, using exclusion, equality, and subset constraints. As an exercise draw the schema for this, and then try a subtyping solution.

Different subtyping approaches are possible. One solution is to specify the fact type Employee drives Car, then introduce the subtypes Driver (Employee **who** drives **some** Car) with the license predicate attached, and NonDriver (Employee **who** drives **no** Car) with both the bus and bus allowance predicates attached. The more subtype-specific information required (e.g., total distance traveled by bus, driving violations), the tidier the subtyping portrayal becomes in comparison to the nonsubtyping alternative. Note, however, that subtyping cannot replace composite set-comparison constraints (between sequences of two or more roles).

Be careful to avoid circular definitions—don't try to define a subtype in terms of itself. For example, suppose we defined BusCatcher as Employee **who** catches **some** Bus, and then attached the bus predicate to this subtype (i.e., BusCatcher catches Bus). This specifies that the role of catching a bus is played only by those who play the role of catching a bus. Such circular reasoning is not very informative! In very rare cases, a role used to define a subtype may be a reference role. For example, we might record some fact only for people whose surname begins with the letter Z.

The *specialization* (subtype introduction) procedure may be summarized as follows. Here "well-defined" means a precise subtype can be defined in terms of roles played by its supertype(s). A subtype definition is stronger than a set-comparison constraint if it adds a restriction to the defining predicate (e.g., Sex 'M', Rating > 3). The procedure is recursive: since a subtype may itself have optional roles, we apply the procedure to it to see if we need to form subtypes of it.

Specialization Procedure (SP):

Specify all mandatory roles

For each optional role:

(a)

Patient

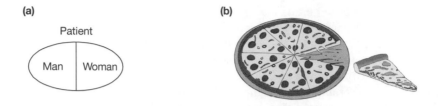

(b)

Figure 6.41 A partition of Patient (a) and a pizza (b).

> **if**   it's recorded only for a well-defined subtype of its attached object type
> **and**   (the subtype definition is not just a set-comparison constraint
>   **or** another role is recorded only for this subtype)
>
> **then**   introduce the subtype;
>   attach its specific roles;
>   add the subtype definition;
>   apply SP to the subtype

For the schema of Figure 6.40, the subtypes Man and Woman are mutually exclusive and collectively exhaustive. When these two conditions are met, the subtypes are said to form a partition of their supertype. We may display this situation on a hypothetical Euler diagram as shown in Figure 6.41(a). This is analogous to the process of partitioning or slicing a pie or pizza into pieces, as shown in Figure 6.41(b). The pieces don't overlap (mutual exclusion), and all the pieces together make up the whole pizza (collective exhaustion).

Our background understanding of the subtype names "Man" and "Woman" helps us to "see" a partition. But such names are only character strings to the computer system, so how is the partition formally captured in the model? Look back at Figure 6.40. The mutual exclusion between Man and Woman is implied by their definitions, together with the uniqueness constraint on the sex predicate (**each** Patient is of **at most one** Sex). The constraint that Man and Woman exhaust Patient is implied by the subtype definitions, the {'M','F'} constraint, and the mandatory role on the sex predicate (**each** Patient is of **at least one** Sex). Because ORM demands that subtypes be well defined and all relevant constraints on defining predicates be declared (graphically or textually), *any subtype exclusion or exhaustion constraints that do exist are always implied.*

As humans, we can use our background understanding of meaningful subtype names to immediately "see" whether subtypes are exclusive or exhaustive. This shortcut for us depends on a judicious choice of subtype names. For example, if it is not clear that the terms "Man" and "Woman" cover all patients (e.g., we might want to include children), then the exhaustion constraint is more clearly "seen" by using the subtype names "MalePatient" and "FemalePatient" instead of "Man" and "Woman".

In rare cases, we may wish to highlight subtype exclusion and exhaustion constraints by showing them explicitly on the schema diagram. As discussed earlier, mutual exclusion or exhaustion among subtypes may be shown by connecting "⊗" or "☉", respectively, by dotted lines to their subtype arrows. For a partition, these two symbols

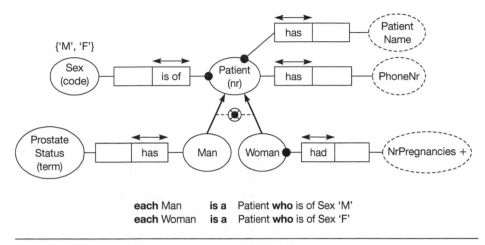

each Man   **is a** Patient **who** is of Sex 'M'
each Woman **is a** Patient **who** is of Sex 'F'

Figure 6.42 The implied subtype exclusion and exhaustion shown explicitly.

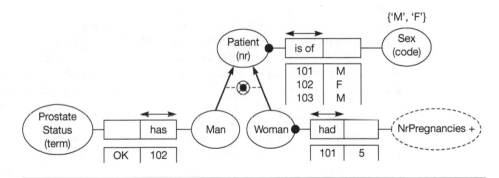

Figure 6.43 The constraints are satisfied, but can you spot a problem?

are overlaid (e.g., Figure 6.42). With complex subtype graphs, the explicit display of
such implied constraints makes the diagram appear cluttered. Ideally a CASE tool
should enable display of such constraints to be toggled on or off by the user.

Since Man and Woman are exclusive, and an object type must be populatable, no
object type can be a subtype of both, since such a type would always be empty (nobody
is simultaneously both a man and a woman). In general, *exclusive object types cannot
have a common subtype.*

In some other modeling methods a classification predicate or attribute (e.g., sex)
may be specified, then subtypes introduced but not formally defined, and relevant
exclusion and exhaustion constraints added. This alternative approach suffers two
problems. First, exclusion and exhaustion constraints are weaker than subtype definitions. For example, consider the populated schema in Figure 6.43. Here the partition
constraint is declared but the subtype definitions are removed. The sample population

satisfies all the constraints, but there is still something wrong. Can you spot the problem?

Prostate status is recorded for patient 102 (a female), and a pregnancy count is recorded for patient 101 (a male). This is nonsense. We need to record the sex of each patient regardless of their subtype roles, but if they do play a subtype role, we need to check that they are in the right subtype. The way to do this is to define the subtypes formally in terms of their sex, and then enforce the definition.

Omitting subtype definitions may also lead to inconsistency. For example, the exclusion constraint between Man and Woman might be missed or an exhaustion constraint applied wrongly (e.g., between SeniorLecturer and Professor when ordinary lecturers also exist). Hence if a classification predicate is used in addition to subtyping, these should be related by formal subtype definitions.

If subtyping is used without a classification predicate, the problems above can be avoided if the exclusion and exhaustion constraints themselves provide the classification constraints. However, sometimes a classification predicate is required. For example, we may need to record the salary of employees, then use this to subtype employees. Employees with a salary $\geq$ \$50,000 might be classified as HighPaidEmployee, for instance. Here exclusion and exhaustion constraints cannot convey the full semantics of the subtyping. For such reasons as well as uniformity, we should always declare formal subtype definitions based on predicates attached to the supertype(s).

If subtypes collectively exhaust their supertype, we have a "total union" or "completeness" constraint, since the union of the subtypes equals the total supertype. This holds for the type populations too, since a subtype population is determined by applying the subtype definition to the supertype population. However, unless each subtype has a specific mandatory role, the union of the populations of the subtype-specific roles need not equal the population of the supertype. For example, in Figure 6.42 the population of Man is the set of male patients, but some of these might not have their prostate status recorded.

Note that exclusion and exhaustion constraints among subtypes are to be interpreted in a *static* sense. For example, since the subtypes Man and Woman are exclusive, in any given database state their populations cannot overlap. However, this does not rule out an object migrating from one type to another between database states. This is unlikely for our present example! However, our next example includes the subtypes SeniorLecturer and Professor (see Figure 6.44). SeniorLecturer and Professor are exclusive, in the sense that no academic can be a member of both types simultaneously. However, a senior lecturer in one state can be promoted to professor in a later state.

In this application, academics have exactly one rank (lecturer, senior lecturer, or professor) and have been awarded one or more degrees. Each professor holds a unique "chair" (e.g., information systems), indicating the research area that he or she manages. Each student has at most one counselor, and this must be a senior lecturer. Nothing special is recorded for lecturers, so we don't bother introducing a subtype for them. The subtype definitions and the constraints on the rank predicate imply that the SenLec (Senior Lecturer) and Prof (Professor) subtypes are exclusive but not exhaustive. To avoid clutter, the implied exclusion constraint is omitted from the diagram.

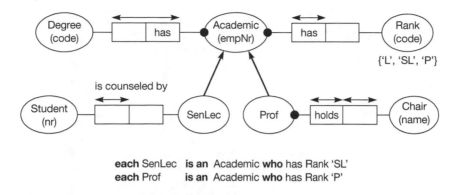

each SenLec is an Academic who has Rank 'SL'
each Prof   is an Academic who has Rank 'P'

Figure 6.44 The subtypes are exclusive but not exhaustive.

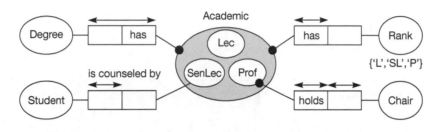

Figure 6.45 The subtyping of Figure 6.44 shown with a hypothetical Euler diagram.

Although subtypes are drawn outside their supertypes, every member of a subtype is also a member of its supertype(s). To clarify this point, Figure 6.45 depicts the subtyping of Figure 6.44 by means of a hypothetical Euler diagram; the shaded region is empty. For simplicity, reference schemes and subtype definitions are omitted. Although such diagrams may be used in simple cases for explanatory purposes, they are too awkward for complex cases and are no replacement for our subtyping notation.

Consider now a UoD peopled just by lecturers and students. Gender and PersonKind (L = Lecturer; S = Student) are recorded for all persons, salary is recorded just for lecturers, and course of study is recorded just for students (see Figure 6.46).

In this UoD a person may be both a lecturer and a student, as indicated by the many:many constraint. So the Student and Lecturer subtypes overlap. Although not exclusive, they are exhaustive, given the mandatory role and {'L','S'} constraint on the personkind fact type. Figure 6.47 displays the subtyping on a HED. Since these subtypes overlap, they may have a common subtype. For example, if some further information were required only for those lecturers studying a course, we could introduce a subtype StudentLecturer (both Student and Lecturer).

Suppose we expanded the UoD to include administrative staff, who may be students but not lecturers. This classification scheme may be depicted by three unaries (studies,

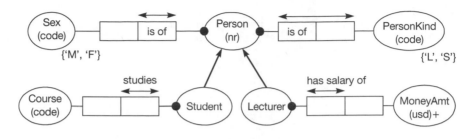

each Student **is a** Person **who** is of PersonKind 'S'
each Lecturer **is a** Person **who** is of PersonKind 'L'

Figure 6.46   In this UoD, a student may be a lecturer.

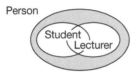

Figure 6.47   Overlapping and exhaustive subtypes of Figure 6.46 depicted by a HED.

Table 6.5   What determines whether we record a person's favorite group?

Person	Age	Favorite group
Bill	17	Abba
Fred	12	–
Mary	20	–
Sue	13	Dire Straits
Tom	19	Beatles

lectures, administrates) with an exclusion constraint between the last two. If specific details were required for administrators, we would introduce a third subtype for this. As an exercise, draw a schema diagram and a HED to depict this situation.

The rest of this section focuses on the problem of providing a correct definition for subtypes. Sometimes it is not obvious from an output report what criteria have been used to decide whether some fact is to be recorded. As a simple example, consider Table 6.5. What rule determines when to record a person's favorite group?

One pattern that fits the sample data is to record a person's choice of favorite group if and only if the person is aged between 13 and 19 inclusive (i.e., the person is a teenager). This is not the only pattern that fits, however. Maybe favorite group is recorded just for people with odd ages (13, 17, and 19 are odd numbers). While these might be argued to be the two most "obvious" patterns, there are very many patterns that are

Figure 6.48 What pattern matches the data?

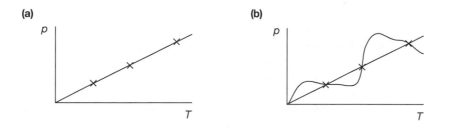

Figure 6.49 More than one pattern fits the data.

consistent with the data. Just based on age, we could specify any set of natural numbers minus the set $\{12, 20\}$ and within the age range of the UoD.

A database population is *significant with respect to a constraint type* if and only if it satisfies just one constraint from this type (excluding weaker constraints implied by this choice). In this case, the constraint may be deduced from the population. Obtaining a sample population that is significant with respect to uniqueness constraints can be tedious, but at least it can be done in a modest amount of time. Unfortunately, no decision procedure exists to automatically churn out the correct subtype definitions.

If we remove the restriction that a computer system has finite memory, then we open ourselves up to the problem that for any finite set of data there will always remain an infinite number of possible patterns that fit the data. This is the basis of the philosophical "problem of induction". As a scientific example, consider the graph shown in Figure 6.48. This shows three data points determined from an experiment in which the pressure *(p)* and absolute temperature *(T)* of a gas are measured at a fixed volume. What pattern, rule, or law does this suggest for the connection between pressure and temperature?

One pattern that fits the data is the linear relationship between pressure and temperature shown by the straight line in Figure 6.49(a). This indicates that when the volume of gas is fixed, its pressure is directly proportional to its absolute temperature. You may recall learning this law of physics in high school. However, the curved line in Figure 6.49(b) also fits the data. How do we know which (if any) is correct?

An obvious move is to pick a temperature where the two patterns differ in their pressure reading, and then measure what the actual reading is. The result is shown in Figure

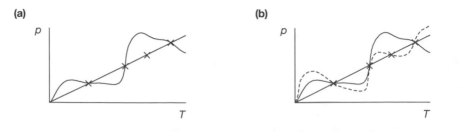

Figure 6.50 Extra data can eliminate a pattern, but other patterns may still fit.

6.50(a). Here the extra data point (the third "×") fits the straight line hypothesis, but not the curved line. This counterexample is enough to disprove that curved line. Does this prove that the straight line law is correct? No. We can always add another curved line to fit the expanded data, as shown by the dotted line in Figure 6.50(b). Indeed there are infinitely many curved lines that fit the data points. You can keep this process going as long as you like. Any finite set of data is consistent with infinitely many rules. Hence you never really prove any scientific law.

Returning to our subtype definition problem, it is clear that any subtype data sample is consistent with infinitely many subtype definitions. Rather than get bogged down in philosophical speculation at this point, you can use the following pragmatic approach to finalizing subtype definitions. Look carefully at the data, use "common sense" to spot the simplest pattern, then check with the domain expert whether this pattern is the one intended. Since the subtyping constraints reflect the decision of the domain expert on what should be recorded for what, the domain expert will always be able to resolve the matter. In a sense, it's like asking God what the rules are for the universe He/She created.

Although output reports cannot be significant with respect to subtype definitions, input forms such as tax returns or application forms often do provide a significant set of conditional instructions from which the subtyping definitions can be deduced. Typically such forms include a number of fields that are to be filled in only by certain kinds of people. To let users know which questions they must answer, instructions are included that reveal the conditions under which the specific details are to be recorded. From these instructions it is usually fairly easy to determine the subtyping. As a simple example, consider the media survey form shown in Figure 6.51.

Each copy of the form has a unique form number. Each form is filled out by a different person, and each person fills out only one form. The enforcement of this 1:1 correspondence between people and forms is the responsibility of the company conducting the survey rather than the information system itself. This correspondence is left implicit in the model, where people are identified directly by the form number.

The conditional instructions on this form are shown in italics. Everybody must answer Questions 1, 2, and 4. Anybody who answers 0 to Question 2 is told to skip Question 3. Hence favorite TV channel is recorded just for those who indicate they do watch some TV; let's call this subtype Viewer. People who answered 0 for Question 4 are told to skip all later questions. Hence favorite newspaper (Question 5) is recorded just for those who read newspapers; let's call this subtype Reader.

FormNr: 5001

1. Age (years): _____

2. Nr hours spent per week watching TV: _____
   If you answered 0, then go to Question 4.

3. What is your favorite TV channel? _____

4. Nr hours spent per week reading newspapers: _____
   If you answered 0, then Stop (no more answers are required).

5. What is your favorite newspaper? _____
   If you are younger than 18, or answered 0 to Question 2 or 4,
   then Stop (no more answers are required).

6. Which do you prefer as a news source?   ❏ Television
   (Check the box of your choice.)
                                                    ❏ Newspaper

Figure 6.51 A sample media survey form.

People who are younger than 18 or are not viewers or readers skip Question 6. Hence preferred news source is recorded just for adult viewers who are also readers; let's call this subtype MediaAdult. This analysis leads to the schema of Figure 6.52.

Alternatively, an output report from the application might be used to help with the modeling (see Table 6.6). The sample data have been carefully chosen to be significant with respect to the subtype graph. Given this, and recalling that the "−" sign means "not to be recorded", we may reason as follows. Age, viewing, and reading figures are recorded for everybody. The set of people for which favorite channel is recorded properly overlaps with the set of people for which favorite paper is recorded, so these correspond to overlapping subtypes. The set of people for which preferred news source is recorded is a proper subset of the previous two sets, so this corresponds to a common subtype.

This analysis yields the "diamond-shaped" subtype graph of Figure 6.52, as well as the information recorded for each node in the graph. However, we can only make educated guesses as to the actual subtype definitions—these should be checked with a domain expert if one is available.

In practice, reports often display different kinds of null values in the same way. For example, a blank space might be used for both our simply unknown "?" and inapplicable "−" marks. So you should clarify the meaning of any null values with the domain expert before deciding how to handle them.

To help you do the section exercises without a domain expert, the populations provided are significant with respect to the subtype graph. However, this is an artificial situation. In designing real-world applications, you would rarely be handed a

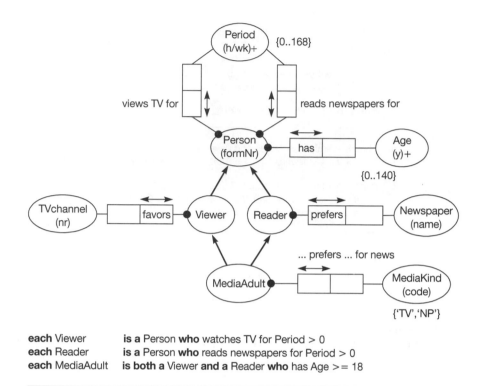

each Viewer   is a Person who watches TV for Period > 0
each Reader   is a Person who reads newspapers for Period > 0
each MediaAdult   is both a Viewer and a Reader who has Age >= 18

Figure 6.52 The conceptual schema for the media survey example.

Table 6.6 An output report from the media survey.

Person	Age (y)	Television (h/week)	Newspaper (h/week)	Favorite channel	Favorite paper	Preferred news
5001	41	0	10	–	The Times	–
5002	60	0	25	–	The Times	–
5003	16	20	2	9	The Times	–
5004	18	20	5	2	Daily Mail	TV
5005	13	35	0	7	–	–
5006	17	14	4	9	Daily Sun	–
5007	50	8	10	2	Daily Sun	NP
5008	33	0	0	–	–	–
5009	13	50	0	10	–	–

population guaranteed to be significant in this way. Only the domain expert could provide this guarantee, and to do this he or she must know the subtyping constraints anyway. It is better to get these constraints directly from the domain expert simply by asking.

Apart from the methods discussed, the online Appendix B discusses two matrix algorithms to deduce the configuration of a subtype graph from a population significant in this regard. Although it is unsafe to assume populations are significant, such procedures can be used to check whether a population is significant with respect to a known subtype graph.

Exercise 6.5

1. (a) For each of the following subtype graphs assume that type $A = \{1, 2, 3\}$. Provide examples for the subtypes to complete a satisfying model for each diagram.

   (b) Explain what is wrong with each of the following subtype graphs.

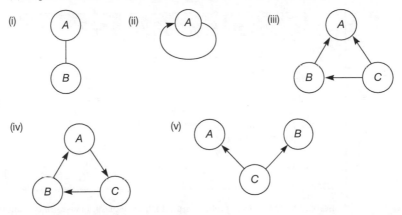

   Note: In the following questions, populations are significant with respect to the subtype graph, and "−" means "not to be recorded".

2. The following table is a sample weekly report about animals in a certain household. Provide a conceptual schema for this UoD, including uniqueness constraints, mandatory roles, value constraints, and subtype constraints. Include a definition for each subtype.

Animal	Animal kind	Sex	Nr cars chased	Nr mice caught
Fido	dog	M	12	−
Felix	cat	M	−	1
Fluffy	dog	F	0	−
Tweetie	bird	F	−	−

3. A simplified fragment of an income tax return form is shown.
    (a) Schematize this UoD, assuming that in section 5 the same employer can appear on only one line.
    (b) Modify your solution to part (a) to handle these changes. The same employer may appear on more than one line of section 5. For each of these lines, the taxpayer attaches a wage and tax statement from his or her employer that includes the employer's name as well as the employee's tax file number, gross salary, and tax installments deducted (i.e., tax paid). Wage and tax statements are identified by serial numbers.

---

1. Your tax file number: _____

2. Your full name: _____

3. Indicate the kind(s) of income you received from an employer by checking the relevant box(es).
   If you had no employer income, leave this blank and go to Question 7.

   ❏ salary   ❏ benefit (employment related)

4. Your main employment occupation: _____

5. If you earned a salary, complete the following income details:

Employer	Tax paid	Gross salary

6. If you earned employment-related benefits indicate total benefit: _____

7. etc.

---

4. Schematize the following table. Here a supervisor supervises one or more persons. You may find it helpful to draw a tree showing who supervises whom. The missing value "−" means "inapplicable because of some other information". The missing value "---" means "does not exist".

EmpNr	Emp name	Supervisor	Smoker?	Home phone	Health bonus ($)	Company car
101	Brown CA	102	N	–	300	–
102	Jones E	103	Y	2053771	–	–
103	White TA	---	N	2062050	500	597VTP
104	Mifune K	103	N	3651000	500	123KYO
105	Nelson HF	102	N	–	300	–
106	Adams PC	102	N	3719872	400	321ABC
107	Wong S	104	N	–	300	–
108	Collins T	104	Y	–	–	–
109	Smith JB	106	Y	–	–	–

5. A loan agency records information about clients. The following report is extracted from this information system. Clients are identified by clientNr. Marital codes are "D" (divorced), "M" (married), "S" (single), "W" (widowed). Residential codes are "B" (home buyer), "O" (home owner), "R" (home renter).

ClientNr	Marital status	Residential status	Number of dependents	Home value ($)	Spouse's income ($)	Spouse's share of home (%)
103	M	O	3	100,000	40,000	50
220	M	R	3	–	0	–
345	S	O	–	150,000	–	–
444	W	B	2	90,000	–	–
502	D	R	0	–	–	–
600	S	R	–	–	–	–
777	M	B	0	100,000	0	40
803	D	B	1	60,000	–	–
905	W	O	0	90,000	–	–

Each client has borrowed zero or more loans. For this agency, any given loan can be borrowed by only one client. The following report from the same information system provides details on some of the loans. Schematize this UoD.

ClientNr	Loans borrowed		
	LoanNr	Amount ($)	Term (years)
103	00508	25000	7
345	00651	25000	7
	00652	3000	1
etc.			

6. The following three reports come from an information system about the following bodies in our solar system: the Sun, the naked-eye planets, and their moons. Planets travel in roughly circular orbits about the Sun. A planet is in inferior conjunction if it is directly lined up between the Earth and the Sun. A planet is in opposition if the Earth is directly lined up between it and the Sun. The missing value "---" means "does not exist". The symbol "M_E" denotes one Earth mass. One astronomical unit (a.u.) equals 150,000,000 km. Schematize this UoD.

Sun:

Name	Mass (M_E)	Radius (km)
The Sun	34,000	696,000

Planets:

Name	Nr of moons	Mean distance from Sun (a.u.)	Mass (M_E)	Radius (km)	Orbital period (y d)	Next inf. conj.	Next oppos.	Atmosphere (main gases)
Mercury	0	0.39	0.06	2,440	0y 88d	Dec	–	---
Venus	0	0.72	0.81	6,050	0y 224d	Jan	–	CO_2
Earth	1	1.0	1.0	6,378	1y 0d	–	–	N_2, O_2
Mars	2	1.5	0.11	3,095	1y 322d	–	Feb	CO_2
Jupiter	16	5.2	318	71,400	11y 315d	–	Sep	H_2, He
Saturn	24	9.5	95	60,000	29y 167d	–	Sep	H_2, He

Moons:

Name	Planet orbited	Radius (km)	Orbital period (y d)	Mean apparent magnitude
Luna	Earth	1,737	0y 27.3d	−13.0
Phobos	Mars	6	0y 0.3d	11.5
Deimos	Mars	4	0y 30.0d	12.0
Io	Jupiter	1,867	0y 1.7d	5.5
etc.				

6.6   Generalization of Object Types

The previous section discussed a specialization procedure, in which subtypes of a more general object type are introduced to declare that specific roles are recorded only for these subtypes. Apart from this top-down procedure, a subtype graph may also arise in a bottom-up way, when we need to introduce a supertype of object types that already occur in the model. The process of introducing a supertype for object types that already exist is known as object type *generalization*. Hence, generalization is the reverse of specialization. A supertype is a more general form of its subtypes, and a subtype is a special form of its supertype(s).

Step 3 of the CSDP outlined the main reasons for generalizing existing object types (e.g., Doctor, Dentist, Pharmacist) into a more general type (e.g., Practitioner), but at that stage we ignored any need to retain any of the original object types as subtypes of the new general type. This need arises when the original object types have specific roles. As a simple example, consider Figure 6.53. Here sex is recorded for each kind of practitioner.

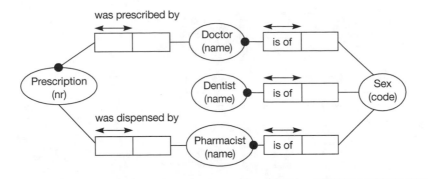

Figure 6.53 A schema before generalization has been applied.

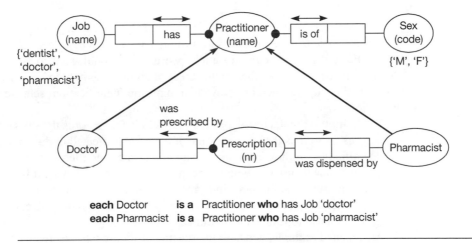

each Doctor　　**is a**　Practitioner **who** has Job 'doctor'
each Pharmacist　**is a**　Practitioner **who** has Job 'pharmacist'

Figure 6.54 The schema after generalization has been applied.

If we want to list all the practitioners together in some query, then we should introduce a practitioner supertype, attach the common role to it, and add a fact type to retain the classification scheme (see Figure 6.54). This assumes that all practitioners can be identified simply by their name, and that pharmacists, dentists, and doctors are mutually exclusive.

The original schema shows that prescriptions may be prescribed only by doctors and dispensed only by pharmacists. These constraints are retained in the new schema by using Doctor and Pharmacist subtypes for the prescription predicate. Here, no specific role is recorded only for dentists, so there is no need for a dentist subtype.

Pharmacist, Dentist, and Doctor were exclusive, but were generalized partly because of their common role (having a sex). In practice, further common information would normally be recorded (e.g., name, address, birth date), making this generalization more worthwhile. However, as pointed out in step 3, the sharing of a common

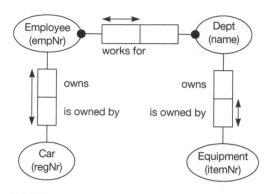

Figure 6.55 Should the object types be generalized?

role is not by itself sufficient to justify generalization. *If the object types are exclusive, we needn't generalize them unless we want to list common details for them in the same query.* For our medical clinic example, we usually would want to issue queries like "List the name, phone number, and address of all the practitioners". Generalization facilitates this, if we thereby provide a uniform identification scheme for all the practitioners.

To clarify this point, consider a veterinary clinic that records the sex and name of its employees, as well as the sex and name of the animals treated in the clinic. Employees are identified by employee numbers, but animals are identified by some other scheme (e.g., combining their name with the client number of their owner). It is highly unlikely that we would ever list the same information about the staff and the animals together in the same query. So Employee and Animal may be left as primitive object types, without generalizing them to EmployeeOrAnimal.

As a related example, consider the schema of Figure 6.55. Here an organization records the cars owned by its employees (e.g., to help the car park attendant to check whether a car is legally parked). It also records equipment (e.g., computers, photocopiers) owned by its departments. Cars are identified by their registration number and equipment items by an item number. Here the ownership predicate appears twice in the schema. Employee and Department are exclusive, but both play the role of owning. Car and Equipment are exclusive, but both play the role of being owned.

Suppose we generalize Employee and Department to Owner and Car and Equipment to Asset. As an exercise, you might like to draw the resulting schema for yourself before peeking at the solution.

The result of this generalization is shown in Figure 6.56. It's quite messy. The ownership predicate now appears just once, in the fact type Owner owns / is owned by Asset. But the rest of the schema is harder to conceptualize. New identifiers are required for the general types, and predicates to classify owners and assets by OwnerKind and AssetKind must be added to retain the original type information.

It would be wrong to model the working predicate as Owner works for Owner. Because of their specific roles (working, employing), Employee and Department are retained as

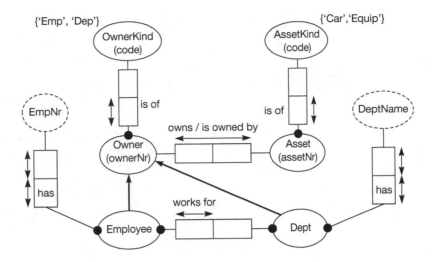

each Employee **is an** Owner **that** is of OwnerKind 'Emp'
each Dept **is an** Owner **that** is of OwnerKind 'Dep'

Other constraints: each Asset **that** is of AssetKind 'Equip' is owned by **at most one** Owner
each Owner **that** owns an Asset **that** is of AssetKind 'Equip' **is a** Dept
each Owner **that** owns an Asset **that** is of AssetKind 'Car' **is an** Employee

Figure 6.56   Don't generalize the types in Figure 6.55 like this unless you need to.

---

subtypes, so we still have the fact type Employee works for Department. Subtype definitions need to be added as shown.

Assuming the subtypes inherit the identifiers of their supertype, the employee number and department name predicates must now be explicitly depicted as fact types. Moreover, additional textual constraints must declare that each equipment item is owned by at most one Department (note the different constraints on the original ownership predicates), that only employees own cars, and that only departments own equipment.

Should we generalize exclusive object types in such a case? Not unless we want to ask a common question for all members of the general type (e.g., list all owners and their assets). If the objects are not to be listed together in the same column of an output report, then there is no need to generalize them. The more common properties there are, the more likely it is that such queries would be formulated. For example, in many applications such as banking or insurance, a customer might be a person or a company. Because common information needs to be accessed for them in the same query, it is worthwhile generalizing Person and Company to Customer (or Party, or whatever term is appropriate for the application). Of course we still retain Person and company as subtypes to record details specific to them.

If two fact types have the same predicate and object type names, they are treated as the same fact type. However, different predicates can have the same name. This often

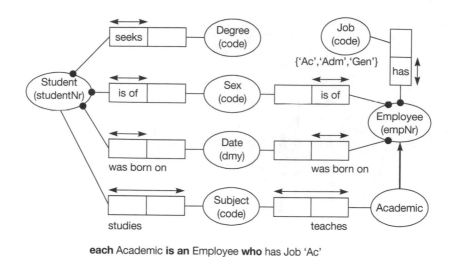

each Academic **is an** Employee **who** has Job 'Ac'

Figure 6.57 Students and employees have some details in common.

happens with trivial predicates such as "has' and "is of". It can also happen if we don't generalize object types that share common roles. For example, in Figure 6.55 there are two predicates called "owns". On a diagram, we can distinguish between these predicates by their containing fact types (e.g., Employee owns Car differs from Dept owns Equipment). In a CASE tool environment, two predicates with the same external name may be distinguished internally by surrogates or expanded names (e.g., P56, P57, or "owns1", "owns2"). Apart from such obvious cases as "has" and "is of", however, if we find ourselves duplicating a predicate name on a schema, we should ask ourselves whether we ought to generalize. CASE tools can assist here by prompting the designer appropriately.

The examples so far have considered exclusive types. What about *overlapping types?* Recall that primitive entity types on a conceptual schema are taken to be mutually exclusive. The only way to allow different entity types on a schema to overlap is to make them subtypes of something else. So generally speaking, if we find two primitive entity types that do overlap, then we should introduce a supertype for them. In rare cases, however, we might portray entity types that overlap in reality to be mutually exclusive in our model, because we are simply not interested in knowing about any overlap.

Consider the schema shown in Figure 6.57. This might be part of a model for a university system. Students are identified by their student number, and university employees are identified by an employee number. Employees are classified as academics, administrators, or general staff. Only academics can teach subjects, and only students can study subjects. Apart from their specific roles, students and employees both have their sex and birth date recorded. In the global schema, other specific information would be recorded for students (e.g., enrollment mode) and employees (e.g., department), and other common properties would be recorded (e.g., name, address, phone, marital status).

If you cut Figure 6.57 vertically down the middle, but duplicate Sex, Date, and Subject in both, the left-hand subschema deals with student records, and the right-hand subschema deals with employee records. In the past, it was common practiceto develop such subsystems independently of one another. Nowadays many organizations are integrating their subsystems into a general system to provide access to more information and to enforce constraints between the formally separate schemas.

Suppose Student and Employee are mutually exclusive. In spite of their common roles, it is unlikely that we want to list such information for both students and employees in the same query. In this case we may leave the schema as it is.

Now suppose that in the real world Student and Employee overlap (i.e., a student may be an employee at the same time). If we want to model this possibility, we must introduce a supertype (e.g., Person). Suppose, however, that we are not interested in knowing whether a student is an employee. If we are sure about this, and we have no common question for the two types, then we may leave the schema as is. However, our model now differs in this respect from the real world.

By presenting Student and Employee as primitive, our model declares that these types are exclusive, whereas in reality they overlap. To avoid misunderstanding, any such disagreement between the model and reality must be clearly documented in the technical and user manuals for the application, so that people are adequately warned of this decision.

Such decisions should not be taken lightly, as there will often be good reasons for wanting to know whether some instance is a member of both types. For example, suppose we want to enforce the constraint that no academic can be enrolled in a subject he or she is teaching. If we want the information system to enforce this constraint for us, we have to provide it with a way of detecting whether some student is an employee. To do this we must introduce a supertype (e.g., Person) preferably with a global identification scheme (e.g., personNr).

Moreover, we might want to record specific data for student employees (e.g., study leave). In this case, we also need to introduce StudentEmployee as a subtype of both Student and Employee. Figure 6.58 depicts the subtype graph for this situation. As an exercise, expand this graph to the full schema by adding fact types and subtype definitions. The sex and birth date fact types attach to Person. If included, the constraint about teachers should be specified textually.

Note that one or more predicates should be attached to Person to classify people into students and employees. We could use the unary predicates IsStudent and IsEmployee if we made their disjunction mandatory. The procedure for generalizing object types may now be summarized as follows. Here A and B are entity types that are initially depicted separately, with no common supertype.

Generalization Procedure (GP):

if A and B overlap, or can be compared (e.g., to compute ratios)
     and we wish to model this
  or

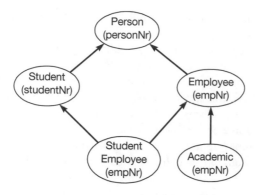

Figure 6.58 The subtype graph after generalization and further specialization.

A and B are mutually exclusive
and common information is recorded for both
and we wish to list A and B together for this information

then   introduce their supertype A ∪ B with its own identification scheme;
add predicate(s) to the supertype to classify members into A, B;
attach common roles to the supertype;
if A (or B) plays some specific roles
then define it as a subtype and attach these roles

Another feature of Figure 6.58 needs discussion. Up to now we have assumed that subtypes always inherit the identification scheme of the root supertype, and hence we have omitted reference display from the subtype nodes. In practice, however, we may sometimes meet a subtype with a primary identification scheme that differs from that of its supertype. In this case we have a *context-dependent reference scheme,* since the primary identifier of an object depends on the context in which it is being considered.

Suppose that within the context of student records, we want to identify students by studentNr, and in the context of employee records we want to identify employees by empNr. We can indicate this choice on the subtype graph by *specifying the primary reference scheme for each node in the subtype graph* (as in Figure 6.58). Note that StudentEmployee still inherits studentNr, but now as a fact type, not a reference type.

A composite reference scheme may be declared primary by using the following symbol for the external uniqueness constraint: "Ⓟ". To avoid ambiguity, the following rules apply to a subtype graph that uses context-dependent rather than uniform reference. Subtypes with the same reference scheme must have a common supertype with this reference scheme (e.g., consider Student_employee and Academic). Context-dependent reference should not be displayed by "shorthand" reference modes (e.g., name, code, nr). Although context-dependent reference is supported in Microsoft's ORM tool, some versions of ORM do not permit context-dependent reference at all.

It should be emphasized that the decision to generalize or specialize is a conceptual one. This does not commit us to a particular way of mapping the resulting subtype graph to a logical database schema. A number of mapping options exist (e.g., subtypes may be absorbed into the same table as their supertype, or mapped to separate tables). Chapter 10 discusses these mapping options in detail.

Exercise 6.6

1. A taxi company records these details about its employees: employeeNr, name, address, sex, phone, salary, and weight. It records these details about its cars: regNr, model, year manufactured, cost, and weight. It also records who drives what cars (optional *m:n*).
   (a) Schematize this with no subtyping. Use two predicates with the name "weighs".
   (b) Generalize Employee and Car, so that "weighs" appears only once.
   (c) Which of these solutions is preferable? Discuss.

2. A hospital maintains an information system about its employees and patients. The following report is an extract from its **employee records.** Employees are standardly identified by their employee number (empNr). Each employee has exactly one job: administrator (admin), doctor (doc), or pharmacist (pharm). A pager is a portable electronic device that beeps when its number is rung. Some employees are assigned unique initials, which may be used as a secondary identifier. The mark "−" means "inapplicable because of other data".

EmpNr	Name	Job	Office	PagerNr	Initials
e10	Adams A	admin	G17	−	−
e20	Watson M	doc	302	5333	MW1
e30	Jones E	pharm	−	−	EJ
e40	Kent C	admin	G17	−	−
e50	Kildare J	doc	315	5400	JK
e60	Brown C	pharm	−	−	CB
e70	Collins T	pharm	−	−	TC
e80	Watson M	doc	315	5511	MW2

In the following extract from the **patient records,** patients are standardly identified by their patient number (patNr), and are typed as inpatients (in) or outpatients (out), but not both. Some patients are placed in wards. Patients may be allergic to various drugs. Prescriptions are identified by their scriptNr. Each dispensed prescription has been prescribed by a doctor, dispensed by a pharmacist, and issued to a patient. Each prescription specifies exactly one drug. Since initials are easier for humans to remember, they are used in this report; however, the system uses empNr as the primary identifier for employees. Unlike "−", a blank simply means "not recorded".

The population is significant with respect to mandatory roles and the subtype graph. Note, however, that any patient may be dispensed a prescription, any doctor may prescribe one, and any pharmacist may dispense one.

PatNr	Type	Ward	Allergies	Prescriptions dispensed to patients			
				Script	Prescriber	Dispenser	Drug
p511	in	5B	aspirin doxepin	7001	MW1	EJ	warfarin
p632	out	–		7132 7250	JK MW1	CB EJ	aspirin paracetamol
p760	in	4C	warfarin	8055	JK	EJ	aspirin
p874	in	5B					

(a) In the real world, *no patient can be an employee.* Schematize this UoD.

(b) In reality, a patient may be an employee. However, we are not interested in knowing facts of this kind. What changes, if any, should you make to the model or the system documentation?

(c) In reality, a patient may be an employee. Moreover, the hospital has recently decided that facts of this kind should be known. For example, we may want to ensure that no doctor prescribes a drug for him- or herself. The hospital is willing to replace its old identification schemes for employees and patients by a new one. Modify your schema to deal with this situation.

(d) In reality, a patient may be an employee, and we want to know this. However, the hospital demands that empNr and patNr be retained as primary identifiers within their context. Modify your schema to deal with this situation.

6.7   Summary

A *set* is determined by its members, so order and repetition don't matter; for example, {3, 6} = {6, 3, 6}. A *bag* or *multiset* makes repetition significant; for example, [3, 6] = [6, 3], but [3, 6] ≠ [3, 6, 6]. A *sequence* is an ordered bag; for example, (3, 6) ≠ (6, 3). A set A is a *subset* of B (written $A \subseteq B$) iff each member of A belongs to B; in this case B is a *superset* of A. A is a *proper subset* of B iff $A \subseteq B$ and $A \neq B$. A and B are *mutually exclusive* or disjoint iff they have no common members; that is, their *intersection* $A \cap B = \{ \ \}$. If sets have common members they *overlap;* if each also has extra members, we have a case of *proper overlap.*

CSDP step 6 adds any value, set-comparison (subset, equality, exclusion), and subtype constraints. A *value constraint* specifies the members of a value type. It may provide a *full listing* or *enumeration* of all the values, for example, {'M', 'F'}; a *subrange definition,* for example, {1..7}, {'A'..'E'}; or a combination of lists and ranges. It may also indicate a syntactic *data type* (e.g., variable-length text of at most 20 single-byte characters). Various shorthand notations can be used to specify format patterns on a data type; for example, c20 allows any string of up to 20 characters, and aaddd requires two letters followed by three digits.

An *independent object type* is a primitive object type whose fact roles are collectively optional. Independent object types have "!" appended to their name. For example, we may populate a reference table for "Country!" with the names of all existing countries, even if some of these countries do not play in any facts. In principle, the values that reference members of an independent object type could instead be declared in a value constraint; however, this is awkward if the values may change or there are many values that cannot be specified as a range.

Set-comparison constraints restrict the way the population of a role, or role sequence, relates to the population of another. Let rs_1 and rs_2 be role sequences (of one or more roles) played by compatible object types. A *subset constraint* from rs_1 to rs_2 is denoted by a dotted arrow "□··►□", indicating pop(rs_1) ⊆ pop(rs_2). An alternative notation for subset constraints uses a circled "⊆". An *equality constraint* is equivalent to subset constraints in both directions; it is shown by a two-headed dotted arrow "□◄··►□", demanding that pop(rs_1) = pop(rs_2). An alternative notation for equality constraints uses a circled "=". An *exclusion constraint* among two or more role sequences is shown by connecting them to "⊗" with dotted lines; this means their populations must be disjoint.

If a set of roles is disjunctively mandatory and mutually exclusive, this may be shown by the life-buoy symbol ⊗. This *exclusive-or constraint* symbol is simply the inclusive-or constraint symbol ⊙ overlaid on the exclusion constraint ⊗.

If each role sequence contains two roles, we talk of pair-subset, pair-equality, and pair-exclusion constraints. A tuple-subset constraint implies simple subset constraints. A simple exclusion constraint implies tuple exclusion. Theorem NXS states that no exclusion constraint can have exactly the same arguments as a subset constraint.

An object type A is a (proper) subtype of B iff ($A \neq B$ and) for each database state, *pop(A)* ⊆ pop(B). We show this by a *solid arrow* from A to B: if A is a subtype of B, and B is a subtype of C, then it is transitively implied that A is a subtype of C; such indirect subtype links should not be displayed.

An object type may have many subtypes and many supertypes. Subtype connections among a family of compatible object types are displayed in a directed, acyclic *subtype graph*. This graph has exactly one root node (or top), which must be a primitive object type (or, in rare cases, a nested object type).

In ORM, subtypes are introduced to declare that one or more roles are played only by that subtype. The process of introducing subtypes is called *specialization*. Subtypes inherit all the roles of their supertype(s), as well as having at least one specific role. By default, a subtype inherits the primary reference scheme of the root supertype; in this case the reference scheme is not displayed on the subtype. With subtypes (and objectified associations), any mandatory roles must be explicitly shown.

Each subtype must be formally defined using one or more roles of its supertype(s). For example, **each** Woman **is a** Person **who** is of Sex 'F'. Subtypes must be well defined, and all relevant constraints on defining predicates must be declared; this ensures that any subtype exclusion "⊗" or totality "⊙" constraints that do exist are implied. Exclusive object types (e.g., Man, Woman) cannot have a common subtype.

Output reports often have missing values or null values. Subtyping is indicated if a missing value means "not to be recorded" (i.e., inapplicable because of other recorded data). This book uses a minus sign " − " for this purpose. If an output report is significant with respect to the subtype graph, we can determine the graph by examining the pattern of "−" marks. However, background knowledge is required to determine the subtype definitions and hence meaningful subtype names. Input forms often provide a set of conditional instructions that indicate the conditions under which particular entries on the form are needed. Such instructions can be used to deduce the subtyping constraints.

If we don't have a full set of output reports, we may wrongly declare object types to be primitive. There is then a need to introduce supertypes; this is called object type *generalization.* This process is the reverse of specialization. We introduce a supertype if object types overlap, and we want to know about this. A supertype is also introduced if the object types are exclusive, have common roles, and we want to list them together for this common information. If the original object types have specific roles as well, they must be retained as subtypes. In this way a subtype graph may be developed in a bottom-up fashion. The usual rules about subtype graphs still apply.

In some cases there is a need for subtypes to have a primary reference scheme different from that of their supertype. Such *context-dependent reference* is indicated by displaying the primary reference scheme for each node in the subtype graph.

Chapter Notes

Not all versions of ORM allow independent entity types. FCO-IM (Bakema et al. 1994) handles the problem by treating entity types as objectifications of unaries.

Most versions of ER do not allow subset, equality, or exclusion constraints between role sequences, or attributes, to be included on the schema diagram (see Chapter 8). UML includes graphic symbols for subset constraints only between whole associations and for exclusion constraints only in the context of an exclusive-or constraint between roles (see Chapter 9). Most recent versions of ER, as well as UML, offer basic support for subtyping, but ignore the need for formal subtype definitions or context-dependent reference (see Chapters 8 and 9).

Some versions of ORM allow subtypes with no specific roles, do not require formal subtype definitions, but do require subtype exclusion and exhaustion constraints to be shown explicitly (e.g., see De Troyer 1991). Context-dependent reference is not supported in some versions. The PSM variant adopts a different approach to generalization in which the supertype uses a disjunction of the identification schemes of its subtypes (e.g., see ter Hofstede et al. 1993). Although this raises additional implementation problems when a common query is executed on overlapping subtypes, this does provide another solution to the problem.

For further discussion of subtyping from an ORM perspective, an informal treatment can be found in Halpin (1995) and a formal treatment in Halpin and Proper (1995b).

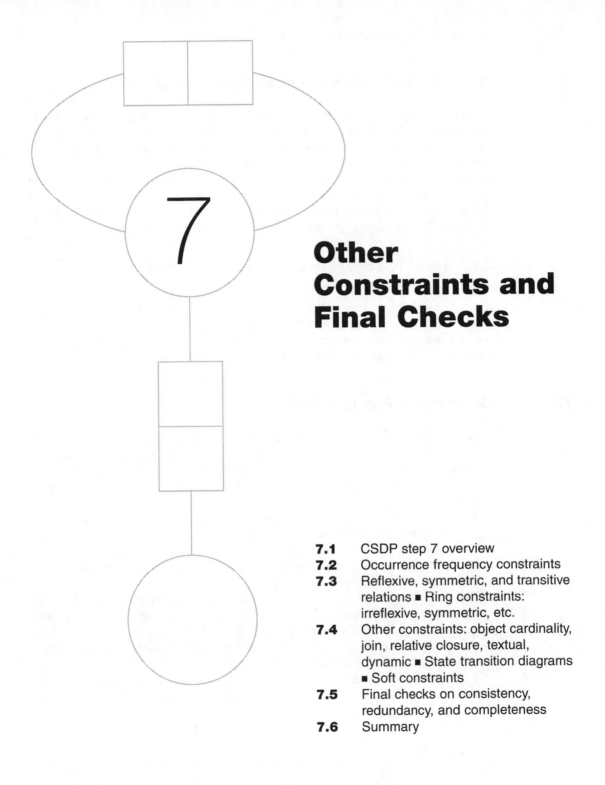

Other Constraints and Final Checks

7.1   CSDP Step 7: Other Constraints and Final Checks

In previous steps of the CSDP, we verbalized familiar examples in terms of elementary facts, sketched the fact types on a diagram, then added various constraints and derivation rules. Most applications include uniqueness, mandatory role, value, set-comparison, and subtyping constraints. Though less common, other kinds of constraints may also apply. Some of these have graphic notations. The rest are specified textually rather than on the diagram. Once all the constraints are specified, some final checks can be made to help ensure our information model is consistent and free of redundancy. This concludes the basic conceptual schema design procedure.

CSDP step 7: Add other constraints, and perform final checks.

This chapter deals with step 7 in detail. The next two sections discuss some important graphic constraints (occurrence frequencies and ring constraints). Then some other graphic constraints are briefly introduced (e.g., join constraints, relative closure). After that, we consider some constraints that must be declared textually. Finally we examine some ways of checking that the schema is consistent and redundancy free.

7.2   Occurrence Frequencies

Let n be some positive integer. To indicate that each entry in a fact column must occur there *exactly* n *times,* the number n is written beside the role (see Figure 7.1). This is an example of an **occurrence frequency constraint.** If $n = 1$, this is equivalent to a uniqueness constraint—in this case the usual arrow-tipped bar notation for uniqueness should be used instead of a "1" mark.

Like uniqueness constraints, frequency constraints are *local* constraints on the role(s), not global constraints on the object type. The constraint in Figure 7.1 means that *if* an instance of *A* plays role *r,* it must do so n times. It does *not* mean that each instance of *A* must play that role n times. If the role is optional, some instances of *A* might not play the role at all.

One use of occurrence frequencies is to ensure that if details are recorded, then they must be recorded for all instances of an enumerated type. For example, suppose a company stocks and sells three kinds of computer drives (F = floppy disk drive, H = hard disk drive, T = tape drive) and operates in just two cities (Los Angeles and Tokyo). Now consider the populated conceptual schema shown in Figure 7.2.

The frequency constraint of 3 on the first role requires each city that occurs in the first column to do so three times. The uniqueness constraint across the first two roles

Each member of pop(*r*) occurs there exactly *n* times

Figure 7.1   A simple occurrence frequency constraint on role *r.*

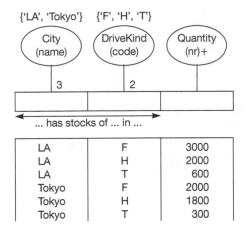

Figure 7.2 If stock figures are recorded, they are recorded for each city and drive kind.

ensures that each City-DriveKind pair appears on only one row. Hence if any stock figures are recorded for a city, then figures for all three kinds of drives must be recorded. Similarly, the frequency constraint of 2 on the second role ensures that each drive kind in the second column must appear there twice. Because of the uniqueness constraint, this means that if stock is recorded for a drive kind, then figures for both cities must be included.

The combination of occurrence frequency, uniqueness, and value constraints ensures that any recorded stock figures are *complete* with respect to both cities and drive kinds. A compound transaction is needed to initially populate this fact type, requiring at least six facts to be added.

Sometimes, an occurrence frequency constraint spans two or more roles of a fact type. In this case, we link the relevant roles by a line and write the number beside it. This is called a *compound occurrence frequency*. For example, in Figure 7.3 each Year-City pair in the fact table must occur there three times. Given the uniqueness constraint across the first three roles, sales must be recorded for all three drives for each Year-City pair in the table. Note that this does not require that yearly sales be recorded for both cities. The sample population includes only one city, yet it satisfies all the constraints.

Figure 7.4 strengthens the constraints by requiring yearly sales figures for both cities as well as the three kinds of drives. Given the uniqueness and value constraints, this is achieved by the simple occurrence frequency of 6 on the first role—as an easy exercise, prove this. The compound frequency of 3 across Year-City is omitted since it is implied. A compound frequency of 2 across Year-DriveKind is also implied, and hence omitted.

Just as internal uniqueness constraints can be generalized to internal frequency constraints, external uniqueness constraints can be generalized to external frequency constraints. However, such constraints are rarely encountered in practice.

Frequency ranges may also be specified. Use "≤ n" for "at most n", where $n ≥ 2$. Use "≥ n" for "at least n", where $n ≥ 1$. Use "$n .. m$" for "at least n and at most m",

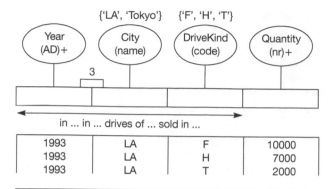

Figure 7.3 Yearly sales figures may omit a city but not a drive kind.

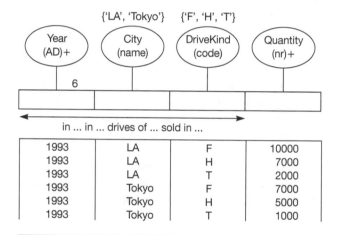

Figure 7.4 Yearly sales figures must cover all cities and drive kinds.

where $2 \leq n < m$. A lower frequency of 1 is the smallest frequency allowed and is assumed by default, since each entry in a column is already there once. Because the constraint applies to the population of the role(s), not the population of the object type(s), it doesn't make sense to declare an occurrence frequency of zero. An optional role indicates some members of the object type population might not play that role.

As an example, consider Figure 7.5. This is part of a schema for a conference application. Each expert is on at least one panel (as shown by the mandatory role) and referees at most five papers (possibly none, since the role is optional). Each panel with members has at least four and at most seven members. Since Panel is independent, we may record the existence of a panel before assigning members to it. Each refereed paper has at least two referees. It is possible that some papers have not been assigned referees yet. In principle, frequency constraints may combine values and ranges (e.g., "1, 5..7") but in practice this is extremely rare.

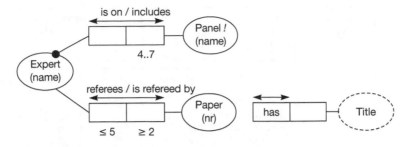

Figure 7.5 Examples of minimum and maximum frequency constraints.

Exercise 7.2

1. The following annual report provides information about two kinds of DBMSs (R = relational, NR = nonrelational) for each of the four seasons. Schematize this UoD, including uniqueness, mandatory role, value, and frequency constraints.

Database	Season	Nr sold
R	spring	50
NR	spring	70
R	summer	60
NR	summer	60
R	autumn	80
NR	autumn	40
R	winter	120
NR	winter	15

2. A software retailer maintains a database about various software products. Two sample output reports are shown below. There is a sales tax of 20 percent on all software. The *ex tax* price excludes this tax; the *with tax* price includes it. The functions of a software product are the tasks it can perform. A "✓" indicates the rating of the product for the criterion listed on that row (e.g., both products shown have a good performance). A "?" denotes missing information. Schematize this UoD, including uniqueness, mandatory role, value, and frequency constraints and any derivation rules. Don't nest or subtype. Model the information about product evaluation (ratings for performance, etc.) in terms of a single fact type.

Product: WordLight 4.0 **Functions:** word processor		**List price:** *ex tax* $500	*with tax* $600
	Poor	*OK*	*Good*	*Excellent*

	Poor	OK	Good	Excellent
Performance			✓	
Documentation				✓
Ease of learning			✓	
Ease of use			✓	
Error handling				✓
Support			✓	
Value				✓

Release date: 2001 Feb
Next upgrade: ?

Product:	PCjobs 1.0			**List price:** *ex tax*	*with tax*
Functions:	word processor			$1000	$1200
	spreadsheet				
	database				

	Poor	*OK*	*Good*	*Excellent*
Performance			✓	
Documentation	✓			
Ease of learning		✓		
Ease of use	✓			
Error handling		✓		
Support			✓	
Value		✓		

Release date: 2000 Oct
Next upgrade: 2002 Jun

3. Megasoft Corporation has a sales force. At the start of each year, each salesperson is assigned at most three different software products to sell during that year (not necessarily the same each year). At the end of each year, each salesperson reports how many of each product he or she sold in each month of that year. Historical information is kept on who is assigned what to sell in each year, and the monthly sales figures for that person (when the figures are available). No month may be omitted in these annual sales figures. The system retains information from previous years. Schematize this, including relevant value and frequency constraints. Make use of nesting.

4. (Acknowledgment: This question is based on an exercise devised by Dr. E. D. Falkenberg and is used by permission.)

   The following tables are sample reports from a system that maintains information about communities and roads. A "−" mark means "inapplicable because of other data" (see the asterisked notes). Mayors are identified by the combination of their first name and surname. A person can be mayor of only one city, and each city has exactly one mayor. Each road connects *exactly two* communities. Schematize this UoD, including uniqueness, mandatory role, value, subtype, and frequency constraints.

Community	*Population*	*Longitude* *	*Latitude* *	*Size* ** *(sq. km)*	*Mayor* ***	
					Firstname	*Surname*
Astraluna	900,000	−	−	145	Fred	Bloggs
Bradman	90,000	+120°50′	+48°45′	12	−	−
Cupidville	9,000	+120°50′	+48°40′	−	−	−

*   Recorded only for villages and towns (at most 100,000 inhabitants).
**   Recorded only for towns and cities (more than 10,000 inhabitants).
*** Recorded only for cities (more than 100,000 inhabitants).

Road Nr	Road kind*	Connection**		Length (km)	Avg. travel time***	Max. slope (%)****
		Community	Community			
11000	f	Astraluna	Bradman	25	0 h 20 m	–
11500	h	Astraluna	Bradman	22	0 h 25 m	2
11561	p	Bradman	Cupidville	17	0 h 20 m	2
11562	d	Bradman	Cupidville	15	–	15

*   f = freeway; h = highway; p = paved minor road; d = dirt road.
**   All connections are two-way (so the order of the connection is irrelevant).
***   Recorded only for freeways, highways, and paved minor roads.
**** Recorded only for dirt roads, paved minor roads, and highways.

7.3   Ring Constraints

When two roles in a predicate are played by the same object type, the path from the object type through the role pair and back to the object type forms a "ring". If the roles are played by subtypes with a common supertype, the path from and back to the supertype also forms a ring. The role pair may form a binary predicate or be part of a longer predicate (see the shaded role pairs in Figure 7.6). A *ring constraint* may apply only to a pair of roles like this.

Before discussing the various kinds of ring constraints, some standard definitions from the logic of relations are noted. Figure 7.7 is used as a template to discuss any ring binary (the predicate R might be obtained from a longer predicate by projecting on

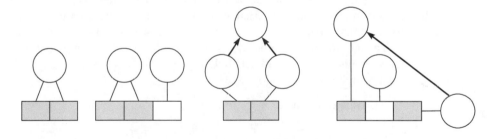

Figure 7.6 Ring constraints may apply to the shaded role pairs.

Figure 7.7 A ring binary (possibly embedded in a longer fact type).

roles r_1 and r_2, and A might be a supertype of the object types playing r_1 and r_2). For each state of the database, pop(r_1,r_2) is a set of ordered pairs, and hence a relation, of type R. Derived as well as base relations are allowed.

The infix notation "xRy" (read "x Rs y") is convenient for defining various properties of relations such as reflexivity, symmetry, and transitivity. Let's discuss such notions by way of example. Consider the populated fact type shown in Figure 7.8. The fact table or relation contains three facts. Note that, for this population, each person likes him- or herself. Suppose that in our UoD, this is true for all possible populations—each person who plays the role of liking or of being liked must like him- or herself. In this case, the Likes predicate is said to be *reflexive over its population*. For the general case shown in Figure 7.7, we have

R is **reflexive over its population** iff xRx for each x in pop(r_1) $\cup$ pop(r_2)

If we picture an object as a black dot and the Likes association as an arrow, we can picture this reflexion as a relationship line starting and ending at the same object, as shown in Figure 7.8. We can imagine less happy universes. For example, if we are allowed to delete just the third row from Figure 7.8, then Bill doesn't like himself, and the relation would then not be reflexive.

However, many important relations are reflexive (e.g., $=$, $\leq$, is parallel to, implies). A relation that is reflexive over the population of the whole universe is said to be "totally reflexive" (i.e., for all x, xRx). Of the four examples cited, only "$=$" is totally reflexive. For example, "implies" is defined for propositions but not for people (people do not imply people). When we say a relation is reflexive, we usually mean reflexive over its population (not necessarily over everything in the universe).

Now consider a UoD where anybody who likes a person is also liked by that person. One satisfying population comprises the three facts: Ann likes Bill; Bill likes Bill; Bill likes Ann (see Figure 7.9). Here given any persons x and y, not necessarily distinct, if x likes y, then y likes x. If this is always the case, we say that Likes is *symmetric*.

The dot-arrow figure conveys the idea that if the relationship holds in one direction, it also holds in the other direction. Using "$\rightarrow$" for "implies", we may define this notion for any predicate R as follows:

R is **symmetric** iff for all x, y $xRy \rightarrow yRx$

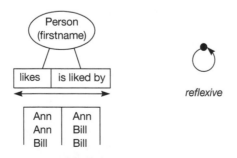

reflexive

Figure 7.8   In this world, the Likes relation is reflexive.

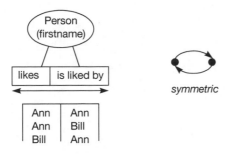

Figure 7.9 In this world, the Likes relation is symmetric.

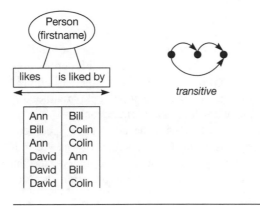

Figure 7.10 In this world, the Likes relation is transitive.

Now consider a UoD where, if one person likes a second, and the second person likes a third, then the first person must like the third. In this case we say that Likes is *transitive*. The definition includes the case where the persons are the same. The populated schema in Figure 7.10 illustrates this property.

The dot-arrow figure indicates that if a chain of relationships exists, the relationship also applies from the first to the last member of the chain. In general, transitivity may be defined as follows. Here we use "&" for "and", and give "&" precedence over "→" (so that the & operation is evaluated first). Note that x, y, and z need not be distinct.

R is **transitive** iff for all x, y, z xRy & yRz → xRz

I leave it as an exercise to prove that a relation that is both symmetric and transitive must also be reflexive over its population. A relation that is reflexive, symmetric, and transitive is called an "RST relation" or "equivalence relation". The classic example of this is the identity relation "=".

Relational properties such as reflexivity, symmetry, and transitivity might be thought of as constraints, since they limit the allowable relations. However, such properties are *positive* and are more often used to *derive* additional facts than constrain existing facts.

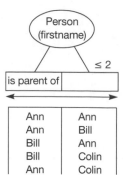

Figure 7.11 What is wrong here?

We now turn to a study of *negative* relational properties such as irreflexivity and asymmetry. Given the existence of some facts, such negative properties imply the nonexistence of certain other facts. Such properties are best handled as simple constraints. An example will help to clarify things. Look at the populated parenthood fact type in Figure 7.11, and see if you can spot anything that seems wrong.

The population shown is consistent with the constraints specified. Parenthood is many:many, and each person has at most two parents. But as you no doubt noticed, some of the facts in the table are inconsistent with the real-world concept of parenthood. We need to add more constraints so that the information system is able to reject such erroneous populations.

To begin with, the first fact (Ann is parent of Ann) has to be rejected since nobody can be their own parent. We say that the parenthood relation is *irreflexive,* and define this notion for any relation type *R* as follows. Here tilde "~" denotes the logical "**not**" (i.e., "it is not the case that").

R is **irreflexive** iff for all x ~xRx

To indicate that parenthood is irreflexive, we write ""$^\circ ir$" beside this predicate on the diagram. The inclusion of the ring-shaped ""$^\circ$"" symbol reminds us that this is a ring constraint. The textual version of this constraint is "**no** Person is parent of **itself**".

Figure 7.12 adds this constraint and reduces the population accordingly. A ring constraint may be written beside either role of the role pair, as in Figure 7.12(a). If the predicate contains more than two compatible roles, a role link is needed to mark out which roles are governed by the constraint. Some ORM tools use a role link in all cases, as in Figure 7.12(b). For explanatory purposes only, a dot-arrow icon for irreflexivity is also shown here. It is the same icon as for reflexivity, except a stroke is added to exclude the possibility of an object relating to itself in that way.

Note that "irreflexive" is stronger than "not reflexive". For example, if Likes is irreflexive, then nobody likes themselves. If some but not all people like themselves, then Likes is neither reflexive nor irreflexive. Irreflexivity is an intrarow constraint (i.e., violation of the constraint by a row can be determined by examining that row only). It specifies that no entry may occur in both cells of the same row. This makes the

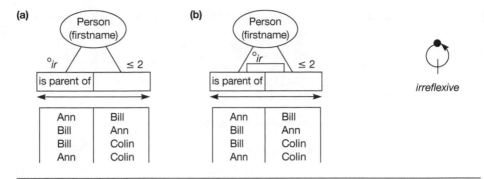

Figure 7.12 The relation is now irreflexive, but something is still wrong.

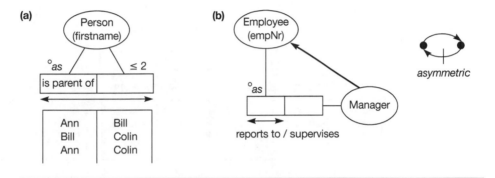

Figure 7.13 Examples of asymmetric constraints.

constraint easy and inexpensive to enforce. Note that the parenthood relation is irreflexive but not exclusive. For example, Bill may appear both as a parent of Colin and as a child of Ann.

There are still some problems with Figure 7.12. If we accept the first row, we should reject the second. If Ann is a parent of Bill, then it cannot be true that Bill is a parent of Ann. The parenthood relation is *asymmetric*. In general, for any relation type *R*:

R is **asymmetric** iff for all *x, y* $xRy \rightarrow \sim yRx$

That is, if the first object *R*s the second, then the second cannot *R* the first. Here, if one person is parent of another, then that other cannot be parent of the first. To say that a relation is asymmetric is stronger than saying the relation is not symmetric (you may wish to prove this as an exercise). Asymmetry is declared by writing "*°as*" beside the role pair (see Figure 7.13). With this constraint enforced, the parenthood population is reduced as shown. Figure 7.13(b) shows another example of the asymmetry constraint, where subtyping is involved. The dot-arrow icon captures the idea intuitively.

The irreflexive constraint is omitted from Figure 7.13. Is this a mistake? No. Any relation that is asymmetric must be irreflexive. The proof is left as an exercise. (*Hint: x and y* need not be distinct.) The converse does not hold. Some irreflexive relations are

Table 7.1 Extract from a poorly constructed table of synonyms.

Word	Synonyms
abandon	leave, forsake, relinquish
abate	diminish, lessen, reduce, decline
abbreviate	shorten, reduce, condense
:	:
condense	compress, consolidate, abridge
:	:
reduce	shorten, weaken, abate
:	:

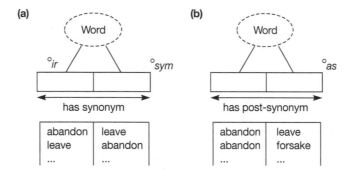

Figure 7.14 Examples of (a) symmetric and (b) asymmetric fact types.

not asymmetric (e.g., is sister of). To avoid implied constraints, omit "°ir" if "°as" applies.

If we remove the requirement for irreflexivity, we obtain the weaker property of antisymmetry. For example, ≤ and ⊆ are *antisymmetric* (°ans) but not asymmetric. It should be clear that °as is just the combination °ans and °ir.

> *R* is **antisymmetric** iff for all *x, y* $x \neq y$ & $xRy \rightarrow \sim yRx$

Before continuing with the parenthood example, let's look at some other examples to clarify the ideas discussed so far. Our first case deals with a system to record synonyms. A synonym for a word has roughly the same meaning as that word. A sample taken from a poorly designed book of synonyms is shown in Table 7.1.

Suppose we decide to store this information in the has-synonym binary shown in Figure 7.14(a). Is this reflexive? Although we might argue that each word is a synonym of itself, this is a trivial result that we are not usually interested in seeing. So, as far as this relation goes, let us agree that no word is its own synonym. This makes the relation irreflexive, as shown.

If one word is a synonym of another, then the other is a synonym for it. So has-synonym is symmetric. But Table 7.1 violates this condition. For example, the pair ("abbreviate", "reduce") appears in this order only. If we look up the word "reduce", we won't see "abbreviate" as one of its synonyms. This is a defect of the synonym book that we should avoid in a computerized synonym system. How can we avoid this problem?

One solution is to add the constraint that the has_synonym predicate is symmetric. This can be specified on the diagram using °*sym,* as in Figure 7.14(a). Suppose the symmetric constraint is declared, the table is currently empty, and the following update is attempted: **add:** Word 'abbreviate' has synonym Word 'shorten'.

A naive information processor would simply reject this for violating the symmetry constraint. A sophisticated processor might accept the fact and automatically add its converse: "shorten" has synonym "abbreviate". A consistent scheme would be adopted for the delete operation. Although this approach works, it doubles the size of the table, since each pair of synonyms is stored twice, once for each ordering.

To save space, we could store each pair in one order only. The post-synonym binary in Figure 7.14(b) has the second word alphabetically after the first. The pair ("abandon", "leave") is stored in this order only. The relation is then asymmetric, indicated by °*as.* The larger synonym relation can now be derived, using a derivation rule such as

Word$_1$ has synonym Word$_2$ **iff**   Word$_1$ has post_synonym Word$_2$
                             or
                             Word$_2$ has post_synonym Word$_1$

In SQL, the derived relation could be defined as a view on the base relation by using the **union** operator. For speed, both columns can be indexed. Users might perform updates on the base relation, but issue queries on the derived relation. Thus, we can sometimes choose whether to capture an aspect of the UoD in terms of a database constraint or as a derivation rule. Here we distinguished the base and derived fact types by name. It is also possible to have the same fact type partly stored and partly derived.

Now what about transitivity of synonymy? This issue is complex. You may be familiar with the "bald-hairy paradox" based on the following premise. In all cases, if we add one hair to the head of a bald man, he is still bald (where is the paradox?). A similar slippery-slope argument argues against synonym transitivity (sequences of approximations finally lead to nonapproximations). Moreover, the same word may have different meanings, leading to different groups of synonyms. If we still want to pursue with some transitivity, we might include a derivation rule for synonym transitivity but constrained by a maximum length of the transitivity chain and relativized to group meanings.

Now consider the marriage fact type in Figure 7.15. The husband and wife roles are mutually exclusive. In contrast to an irreflexive constraint, which requires inequality between entries on the same row, an exclusion constraint applies between columns and hence is much stronger. If no entry may occur in both columns, we cannot have two rows of the form (a, b) and (b, a). So *exclusion implies asymmetry.* Moreover, *asymmetry implies irreflexivity.* Since they are implied, neither the asymmetric nor the irreflexive constraint should be added to the schema.

Now let's return to the populated parenthood model in Figure 7.13. There is still a problem with it. Can you spot it? Let us agree that incest cannot occur in our UoD. If

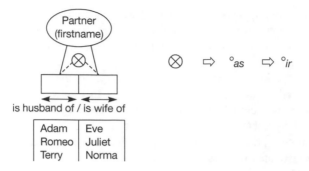

Figure 7.15 The exclusion constraint implies asymmetry and hence irreflexivity.

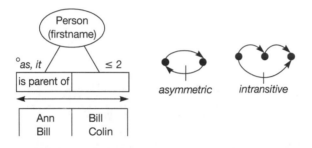

Figure 7.16 The relation is now asymmetric and intransitive.

Ann is parent of Bill and Bill is parent of Colin, then Ann cannot be parent of Colin. The parenthood relation is *intransitive*. In general, for any relation type *R*:

R is **intransitive** iff for all x, y, z xRy & $yRz \rightarrow \sim xRz$

Here, if one person is a parent of a second and the second person is parent of a third, then the first person cannot be parent of the third. To signify that parenthood is intransitive, we write "°*it*" beside the fact type. Since we already have an asymmetry constraint, we may list the two ring constraints together as shown in Figure 7.16. The population has been reduced to satisfy the constraints. The icon shown for intransitivity intuitively suggests that it is forbidden for a relationship to jump across a relationship chain.

As an exercise, prove that intransitivity implies irreflexivity. (*Hint: x, y,* and *z* need not be distinct.) The term "atransitive" is sometimes used instead of "intransitive". Saying a relation is intransitive is stronger than saying the relation is not transitive. Note that antisymmetry, asymmetry, and intransitivity are not intrarow constraints, since their enforcement requires comparing the row in question with other existing rows.

If an irreflexive relation includes a functional role (rather than being *m:n*), it must also be intransitive. Figure 7.17 illustrates the proof of this by *reductio ad absurdum*.

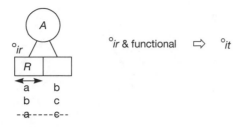

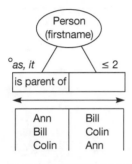

Figure 7.17 An irreflexive, functional relation must be intransitive.

Figure 7.18 What's wrong with this?

Let R be an irreflexive relation whose first role is functional (i.e., it has a simple uniqueness constraint). Now populate R with the first two rows shown. Since R is irreflexive, $a \neq b$ and $b \neq c$. Assume that R is not intransitive. This allows us to add the third row shown. Since $b \neq c$, rows 1 and 3 are distinct rows. This means that a plays the first role of R twice. But this contradicts the uniqueness constraint. So row 3 must be rejected (shown here by the dotted line through the third row). Hence the relation must be intransitive.

Are we finished with ring constraints? Not quite. Have a look at the parenthood population in Figure 7.18. All the specified constraints are satisfied, but something is still wrong. Can you spot the problem?

Here Ann is a parent of Bill, who is a parent of Colin who is a parent of Ann. This makes Ann a great-grandparent of herself. While reincarnation might make this possible, let's assume that we wish to exclude this possibility from our UoD. We can do this by declaring the relation to be **acyclic.** This means the relation has no cycles (i.e., there is no path via the relation from an object back to itself). Acyclicity is declared by placing $^\circ ac$ beside the relevant role pair, as shown in Figure 7.19(a).

A homogeneous binary relation can be displayed as a graph, using named circular nodes for the objects and arrows for the relationship instances, as in Figure 7.19(b). This makes it obvious whether a given population forms an acyclic relation. The icon

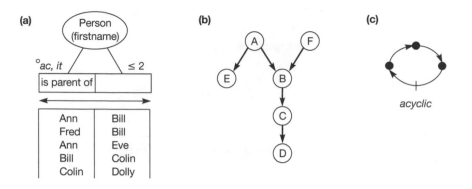

Figure 7.19 In an acyclic relation, no loops are allowed.

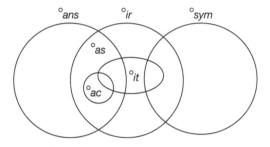

Figure 7.20 Relationships between ring constraints.

in Figure 7.19(c) conveys the idea of no cycles. However, cycles may be of any length. Asymmetry is just the special case of acyclicity with two links in the cycle. Since *acyclic implies asymmetric,* if a role pair is declared acyclic, then don't declare it asymmetric.

A recursive definition for *acyclicity* is provided in the section exercise. Recall that the graph of a subtype family is directed and acyclic. Because of their recursive nature, acyclic constraints may be expensive or even impossible to enforce in some database systems. To reduce system overhead, such recursive constraint checks might be run in batch mode overnight, or even left to the data entry operators to do manually. In any case, the constraints should be identified so a conscious decision can be made about their enforcement. Of all the ring constraints, irreflexivity is the least expensive to enforce.

The Euler diagram in Figure 7.20 shows the relationships between the ring constraints discussed so far. For example, the set of acyclic relations forms a proper subset of the set of asymmetric relations, so if a relation is acyclic, it must be asymmetric.

Some other results you can read off include the following: an intransitive relation must be irreflexive; an asymmetric relation is an irreflexive, antisymmetric relation.

In some applications, other properties of ring relations might apply (e.g., connectivity), but these are not discussed here. A classic example of an embedded ring relation is the "Bill of Materials" or "Parts Explosion" problem, which was included in Exercise 4.4. This involved the ternary Product contains Product in Quantity. You are invited to provide a more complete solution to this problem in the exercise that follows.

Exercise 7.3

1. For each predicate shown state which, if any, of the following properties hold: reflexive, irreflexive, symmetric, asymmetric, transitive, intransitive.
   (a) has the same age as   (b) is brother of
   (c) is sibling of   (d) is shorter than
   (e) is an ancestor of   (f) is at least as clever as
   (g) lives next to

2. Schematize the following report, which indicates composition of items (e.g., Item A contains 2 B parts and 3 C parts). Read "contains" as "directly contains" (e.g., A does not contain D). A more general reading for "contains" is taken in a later exercise. To help decide about ring constraints, draw a labeled graph for the containment relation, using an arrow for binary containment labeled with a number for the quantity.

Item	Part	Quantity
A	B	2
A	C	3
B	C	1
B	D	1
B	E	3
C	E	3
C	F	2

3. If you are familiar with predicate logic, prove the following theorems:
   (a) irreflex(R) & trans(R) → asym(R)
   (b) R is reflexive over its population iff $\forall xy(xRy \lor yRx \rightarrow xRx)$. Show this is implied by sym(R) & trans(R).

4. The diagram shows the conceptual schema and current population for a given UoD. Reference schemes are omitted for simplicity. Fact tables appear next to their fact types. Predicates are identified as **R..W**. Constraints are identified as $C_1..C_{15}$.

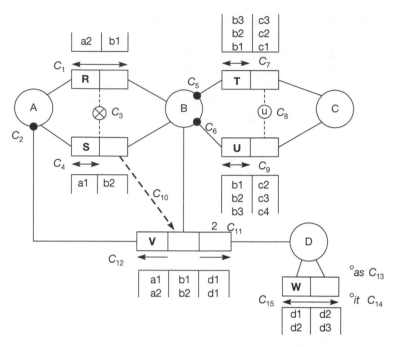

Each of the following requests applies to the **same** database population as shown (i.e., treat each request as if it were the *first* to be made on this population). For each request, indicate the CIP's response. If the request is legal, write "accepted". Otherwise, indicate a constraint violated (e.g., "C_2 violated").

(a) add: a1 S b1   (b) add: a3 R b3   (c) add: V a1 b1 d2   (d) add: a1 R b2

(e) add: a1 R b3   (f) add: a2 S b3   (g) delete: b3 T c3

(h) begin   (i) begin   (j) begin

    add: b4 T c1   add: b4 T c3   add: V a1 b2 d2

    add: b4 U c2   add: b4 U c2   add: V a1 b3 d2

  end   end   end

(k) add: d1 W d3   (l) add: d1 W d1

5. Schematize the following output report. Here "bordering" means sharing a land border. In this sense, countries like Australia have no bordering nations.

Nation	Bordering nations
Australia	
Belgium	France, Germany, Luxembourg, Netherlands
France	Belgium, Germany, Italy, Luxembourg, Spain, Switzerland
...	...

6. (a) Which, if any, of $°as$ and $°it$ are implied by $°ac?$

  (b) Convince yourself that the following recursive definition of acyclicity is correct. Model relationships of type R graphically; consider the fact xRy as a directed line from x to y. The quantifier "$\forall$" = "for all", and "$\exists$" = "there exists".

    x has path to y **iff** xRy **or** $\exists z(xRz$ & z has path to $y)$

    R is acyclic   **iff** $\forall x \sim(x$ has path to $x)$

7.4 Other Constraints

We now have covered most of the constraints that commonly occur in practical applications. This section considers other constraints that occur less frequently. Three of these may be specified on the schema diagram: object cardinality constraints, join constraints, and relative closure constraints. Other static constraints are specified in a textual language. Some dynamic constraints may be declared using state transition tables or graphs. These additional constraints are now discussed, in the order stated.

Figure 7.21 portrays a fragment of a conceptual schema used by a government department, the staff of which act as advisors in foreign countries. A strict ceiling has been placed on the size of the department: no more than 50 advisors may be employed at any one time. This *object cardinality constraint* is indicated by the notation "# ≤ 50" next to the object type Advisor. This is a constraint on populations of the type rather than the type itself. For any state of the database, the cardinality of (i.e., number of objects in) the population of advisors must be less than or equal to 50. Over a long period, the total number of advisors who were ever employed could be much higher. So the cardinality of the Advisor type, as opposed to its population, could be higher than 50.

Object cardinality constraints are rarely included on diagrams, since they are often implied by existing value constraints or occurrence frequency constraints. For example, an {'m','f'} constraint on Sex(code) implies "# ≤ 2" on Sex.

The pair-subset constraint in Figure 7.21 declares that if an advisor serves in a country, then he or she must speak at least one language used in that country. This may be verbalized as follows: **each** Advisor **who** serves in **a** Country **also** speaks **a** Language **that** is used by **that** Country. For example, an advisor serving in Belgium would need to speak Dutch or French since these are the official languages used there. This is an example of a *join constraint* since the Advisor-Country pair in the superset position of this constraint is formed by projecting on a conceptual join of the Speaks and Uses predicates. The join path is the compound fact type Advisor speaks Language **that** is used by Country. The role pair is obtained by projecting on the first and last roles of this path. For explanation purposes, Figure 7.21 shades these roles, but on a schema diagram they are simply connected by a line. This role pair is then targeted by the subset constraint. To understand this constraint, it helps to populate the fact types with a few lines of data. I'll leave this as an exercise.

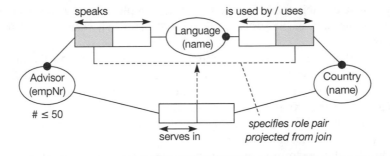

Figure 7.21 An object cardinality constraint and a join-subset constraint.

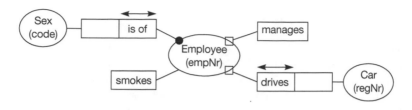

Figure 7.22 If a recorded employee manages or drives a car, these facts are known.

In general, if the population of a sequence of roles connected by a line is determined by joins or unnesting of the predicates involved, the role sequence may be used in the declaration of compatible set-comparison (subset, equality, or exclusion), external uniqueness, or frequency constraints. In those rare cases where an object type plays more than one role in the join, extra marks are needed to indicate which role(s) is/are used for the join in order to disambiguate the role path.

Now consider Figure 7.22. Suppose we populate this schema with just the single fact "Employee 501 is of Sex 'M'". In our model, this employee is not recorded as smoking. Does this mean the employee doesn't smoke in the real world? With a *closed-world* approach, the model contains complete information about the UoD; in this case we may deduce that employee 501 does not smoke. With an *open-world* approach, the model may have only incomplete information about the UoD; in this case, employee 501 might actually smoke, but we don't know it. This is the approach I take by default, but some people prefer to take the closed-world approach by default.

If we adopt an underlying open-world semantics, we can allow aspects of a schema to be closed by adding constraints. For example, mandatory role and frequency constraints ensure various kinds of completeness in our knowledge. We can also demand completeness of optional information by marking optional roles accordingly. In Figure 7.22 the "□" on the optional manages role indicates that if an employee recorded in the database is a manager, this information is known (to the system).

Intuitively, the "□" symbol "boxes in" or closes the relevant aspect: it applies only to that role and the population of that object type. As a relative form of the closed-world assumption, it's called a *relative closure* constraint. If a known employee is not recorded to manage, then the system may deduce that the employee is not a manager. The absence of this symbol on the smokes role implies that if a known employee is not recorded to smoke, the system must reply "unknown" when asked if that employee smokes.

The other relative closure constraint in Figure 7.22 indicates that if a known employee drives a car, this is known to the system. Relative closure is defined in such a way that the schema in Figure 7.22 is treated as an abbreviation of the schema in Figure 7.23. Notice the different value constraints in the binary version of the unaries. The schema is implicitly transformed into this unabbreviated version before being mapped to an actual database implementation.

While relative closure constraints provide a safe, convenient way of clarifying how complete our knowledge of optional information is, some modelers may prefer to

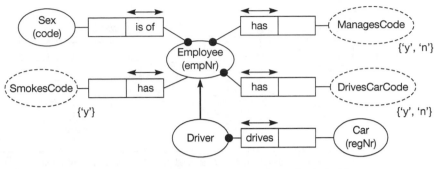

Figure 7.23 An equivalent version of the schema in Figure 7.22.

assume that users fully understand the semantics of optionality and null values that occur in the database implementation.

Like the mandatory role dot, the relative closure box marks a constraint on the population of the object type. Recall that a functional role has a simple uniqueness constraint. For mandatory functional roles, the closure constraint is implied and hence omitted. For disjunctive mandatory roles that are exclusive, we assume closure by default. For disjunctive mandatory roles that are not exclusive, the closure box is positioned at the relevant role end(s).

There are degrees of information completeness. A stronger form of completeness is closure relative to the actual population of the object type in the UoD (e.g., this also demands that all employees must be known). A weaker form is closure relative to the role population. If a role is nonfunctional, relative closure is not implied by a mandatory role constraint. For example, if each employee must drive a car but may drive several cars, we might want complete information about this. Such cases are ignored in this book.

At the time of writing, object cardinality and relative closure constraints are not yet supported in ORM tools. Join constraints may be declared, but are not yet mapped to code. So if you are using an ORM tool, you may need to look after these constraints yourself, at least in the short term.

You have now met essentially all the graphical notations used in ORM models. Although we could invent new graphic notations for further constraints, this could make the graphical language hard to learn and lead to cluttered diagrams. A conceptual schema diagram provides a human-oriented, unambiguous, but often incomplete specification of the UoD structure.

Static constraints that cannot be expressed using the predefined graphic symbols may be specified as *textual rules,* preferably in a high-level formal language. Elements affected by these constraints may be marked with a circled "R", preferably numbered, to remind us that extra rules apply. If the same rule applies to more than one element, it may be connected by a dotted line to each or replicated for each. The constraints themselves may be displayed in text boxes (along with any subtype definitions and

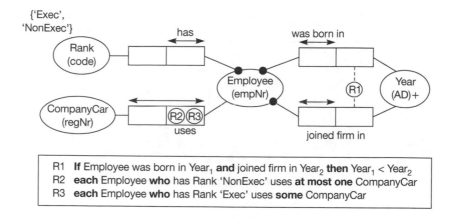

R1 **If** Employee was born in Year$_1$ **and** joined firm in Year$_2$ **then** Year$_1$ < Year$_2$
R2 **each** Employee **who** has Rank 'NonExec' uses **at most one** CompanyCar
R3 **each** Employee **who** has Rank 'Exec' uses **some** CompanyCar

Figure 7.24   Three examples of textual rules.

derivation rules). Ideally tools should allow the display of such extra rules to be toggled on or off by the user (e.g., by placing them on a layer of their own).

Figure 7.24 shows one way to display three textual rules. Rule R1 declares that employees joined the firm after their birth year. A pair-exclusion constraint also exists between the birth and appointment predicates, but is omitted since it is implied by R1.

Rule R2 says that nonexecutives use at most one company car. This is a *restricted uniqueness constraint,* since it strengthens the uniqueness constraint on Employee uses CompanyCar, but restricts this to a subtype of Employee.

Rule R3 says that each executive must have use of a company car. This is a *restricted mandatory role constraint,* since it makes a role mandatory for a subtype of Employee. Some other versions of ORM declare restricted constraints by repeating the predicate on the subtype, with the stronger constraint shown there. Restricted constraints could also be displayed in views that restrict the supertype to the subtype.

So far, our constraints have been *static*—they apply to database states, taken one at a time. *Dynamic constraints* restrict changes between database states. These often constrain *successive states* by specifying what transitions are allowed from one state to the next state. Sometimes they refer to *periods* (e.g., payment is due 30 days after shipping). Constraints over successive states may be declared textually using *formulas with state markers.* For example, using "old" for the current state and "new" for the next state, we might define a rule to prevent pay decreases thus: no_salary_drop :: new_salary >= old_salary.

Constraints on successive states are often visualized using *state transition diagrams.* For example, suppose that the possible ranks of an academic are associate lecturer (AL), lecturer (L), senior lecturer (SL), reader (R), and professor (P). Here the term "reader" denotes a high-ranking position with similar research expectations to "professor".

On a conceptual schema we include the object type Rank (code) {'AL', 'L', 'SL', 'R', 'P'}. Now suppose that no academic may be demoted, and promotions must comprise a single step to the next rank on the list, except that senior lecturers may be

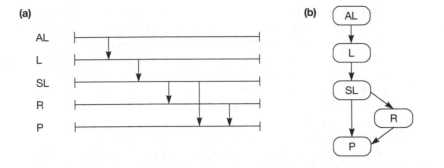

Figure 7.25 Two state transition diagram notations indicating possible rank changes.

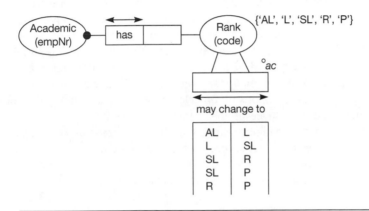

Figure 7.26 A transition constraint may be captured as data.

promoted to either reader or professor. Figure 7.25 lists the possible rank changes in a state transition diagram. Two commonly used notations are shown. In Figure 7.25(a) each state is shown as a named, horizontal bar and allowed transitions are depicted as vertical arrows. In Figure 7.25(b) each state is shown as a named, soft rectangle—this notation is used in UML *statecharts*. Transition constraints may also be declared in a transition matrix with from/to dimensions (recall the marital state example from Exercise 2.2).

We could store the allowed transitions in a fact table, as shown in Figure 7.26. This effectively demotes metadata (in this case a constraint) to object data. This simplifies schema evolution, since changes to the promotion rule are now data changes rather than schema changes. However, we still need some way of telling the system to use this table in checking updates on the relevant fact type (here: Academic has Rank).

Notice that the no_salary_drop rule considered earlier cannot be specified in this way, because its formula involves an operator, not just values. A *guarded transition diagram* allows a guard condition expressed as a formula to be applied to a transition.

An extreme version of a transition constraint is to make a fact *immutable* (unchangeable). In other words, once an elementary fact is entered it cannot be deleted. This might be used in an application such as banking, where auditing requires a complete historical record of any transactions. Suppose an error is made in a transaction (e.g., an actual deposit of $1,000 was incorrectly entered as $10,000). The record of this transaction is retained, but the error is compensated for by a following transaction (e.g., system withdrawal of $9,000). In general, however, you need to be wary of applying such constraints, because in most cases it is far more convenient to correct errors directly simply by replacing the erroneous fact with the correct one.

In practice many different diagrams and formalisms are used to specify various kinds of dynamic constraints. These include statecharts, activity diagrams, state nets, colored Petri nets, process-algebras structures, and ECA (Event-Condition-Action) declarations. ECA languages allow statements of the form **if** *event* **then on** *condition* **then** *action1* [**else** *action2*]. Among other things, this provides a general framework for *controlling the action to be taken on violation of a constraint.* An update is an example of an event, and a constraint is an example of a condition.

With a *hard constraint,* if the update violates the constraint, it is simply *rejected.* By default, this is the expected behavior of a conceptual information processor, as discussed in this book. At the relational level, other actions (e.g., on delete cascade) can be specified instead. For example, if you delete a department, you might want to automatically delete all the employees in the department as well.

In practice, we sometimes want to specify *soft constraints.* These are rules that should normally be obeyed, but for which exceptions are allowed. If a soft constraint is violated, the update may be allowed, but some action is taken to ensure that such violations are rare (e.g., send a message to a human to take appropriate action). For instance, the desired maximum size for classes might be 30 students, but if a 31st student applies to join a class, we can leave it to the instructor to decide whether to accept the student. In a monogamous society, if the 1:1 constraint on current_marriage is violated, we can record the violation and send a message to a law enforcement agency to investigate. Various categories of soft constraints exist (e.g., deontic). When specifying rules, you need to consider whether to allow any exceptions and what to do about them.

To conclude this section, let's consider an example that involves textual constraints and some other interesting issues. Suppose our information system is to maintain details about computer networks. In a bus network, one or more computer workstations (WS) are connected along a bus or transmission line to a file server (FS) at one end. Figure 7.27 provides a topological picture of one such network (i.e., it shows which computers are connected to which but not their distance apart or directional pattern).

To simplify our discussion, the computers are identified by a single letter. The main memory (MM) of each node and the hard disk (HD) capacity of the file server are recorded. This diagram packs in a lot of information. Our task is to design a schema to record this information, and similar details about other bus networks, so that users can extract as much information from this model as they could extract from the actual network diagrams. Try this yourself before reading on. There are many different, correct solutions.

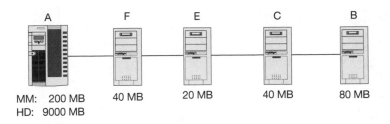

Figure 7.27 Topology of network 1.

Verbalizing the diagram in terms of elementary facts leads to several fact types, such as Node belongs to Network; Node is of NodeKind {'FS', 'WS'}; Node has main memory of Capacity; FileServer has disk of Capacity. The reference schemes are obvious. For a subtype definition, we may use **each** FileServer is **a** Node **that** is of NodeKind 'FS'. Now comes the hard part. How do we describe how the nodes are linked together?

Depending on our choice of primitive predicates, there are various options. If we find it hard initially to express the information in terms of elementary sentences, we can begin by just jotting down samples of whatever comes to mind. For example:

1. Node 'A' is directly connected to Node 'F'.
2. Node 'F' is directly connected to Node 'A'.
3. Node 'A' is indirectly connected to Node 'E'.
4. Node 'A' is an end node.
5. There is at most one link between each pair of nodes.
6. No link connects a node to itself.
7. Each node is directly connected to at most two nodes.

Let's stand back from the problem for a minute. There are two basic aspects about the topology that need to be captured. First, the nodes in a given network all lie along the same *continuous line segment* (in contrast to other shapes such as star networks, ring networks, fancy loop structures, separate segments, etc.). Second, the nodes are *positioned in some order* on this line.

If we consider the linearity of the structure to be a constraint, then how do we express the order of the nodes? Given that the nodes are positioned on a line, and that the file server is at one end of this line, let's first establish a *direction* for the line by saying the line starts at the file server. This avoids potential redundancy problems associated with an undirected, symmetric predicate (e.g., is directly connected to).

The ordering may be specified in terms of relative ordering or absolute ordering. With the first approach, we use a predicate for *directed linkage* (e.g., is just before). With the second approach, we assign each node an absolute position (e.g., 0, 1, 2, 3, 4, numbered from the file server end). The first approach leads to the ring fact type shown in Figure 7.28. This is populated with data from the sample network.

The disjunctive mandatory role constraint is displayed explicitly, since Node plays other roles in the complete schema. You are invited to add the relevant ring constraints, as well as the other fact types. If only complete networks are considered, the kind of

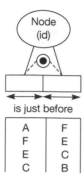

Figure 7.28 A fact type for direct, directed links (some constraints missing).

node can now be derived (e.g., a node is a file server if and only if it has no nodes before it).

By storing linkage information only for direct, directed links, we reduce the size of our database as well as avoiding the problems of symmetry and transitivity. If desired information about indirect links can be derived by using a recursive rule such as

$Node_1$ is before $Node_2$ **iff** $Node_1$ is just before $Node_2$ **or**
$Node_1$ is just before **a** $Node_3$ **that** is before $Node_2$

Other constraints exist. For example, each network has exactly one file server. If we are using the fact type Node belongs to Network, this must be specified textually. We can specify it graphically if we instead use separate fact types: Node is file server for Network; Node is workstation for Network. However, some constraints have to be specified textually no matter how we choose our fact types. For example: directly linked nodes belong to the same network. You are invited to express this constraint (and any others) formally.

As an exercise, try to model the linkage information using node position numbers instead, and notice the impact on constraints and derivation rules. Note that this absolute position approach makes it more awkward to add, delete, or swap nodes in the network since global changes to positional information would be required. For instance, if we add a node, say, D, between F and E, then not only will D be assigned the position 2, but nodes E, C, and B will all need to have their position numbers increased by 1. With our previous approach, only a local change would be needed. Swapping nodes is simple with both approaches. As an exercise, set out the compound transactions for some sample updates.

Exercise 7.4

1. An information system maintains details about politicians, the party they belong to, and the bills they vote for. A politician may vote for a bill only if his or her party supports it. Politicians have the option of not voting. A bill may be supported by many parties. There are positions in government for at most 200 politicians. Schematize this UoD.

2. Job applications are submitted by various people. These applications are recorded and later will receive a status of accepted or rejected. Model this UoD:
   (a) making use of relative closure
   (b) without using relative closure

3. A television survey on soap operas is conducted. Participants in this survey are identified by a number, but their sex is recorded as well as what soap operas they watch. Women may nominate all the soap operas they watch, if any, but to be included in the survey each man must specify exactly one soap opera. Model this UoD.

4. An information system keeps track of changes in the seasons over the years, as they cycle through spring, summer, autumn, and winter. Specify the dynamic constraint using
   (a) a state transition diagram
   (b) a transition matrix or table

5. A *star network* has a centrally located file server directly linked to zero or more work stations. A sample star network is shown.

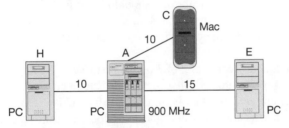

   For each node the generic kind of computer is recorded (PC or Mac). Only for the file server is the processor speed recorded. The maximum number of computers in any network is 20. The cable distance (in meters) of each node from the file server is shown beside each link. Schematize.

6. With reference to the Community-Roads UoD of Exercise 7.2, assume that roads are continuous, but may connect more than two communities. Discuss whether or not it is appropriate to use the ternary fact type "Road connects Community to Community".

7. With reference to the Bill of Materials question in Exercise 7.3, an output report is required to display parts contained at all levels (e.g., the fact that A contains part D is to be shown). Design a conceptual schema for this UoD.

8. A *ring network* has a central file server with workstations arranged in a ring. A sample network is shown. Details are as for Question 5, except no metric information is required. Specify the conceptual schema for this UoD.

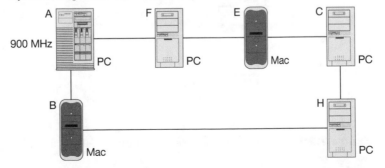

7.5   Final Checks

The conceptual schema design procedure facilitates early detection of errors by various checks, including communication with the user by way of examples. Four final checks may also be performed, to help pick up any errors that might have slipped through. These are designed to ensure internal consistency, external consistency, lack of redundancy, and completeness. We now consider these in order.

A conceptual schema is *internally consistent* if and only if each role sequence used as a predicate or constraint argument can be populated in some state. This topic was discussed in the previous chapter, where it was called "population consistency" or "strong satisfiability". Basically it means that the specified constraints do not contradict one another. For example, the schema in Figure 7.29 has three faults. Can you spot them?

First, the frequency constraint of 2 on predicate R clashes with the uniqueness constraint; moreover any frequency above 1 should be rejected if it spans the whole predicate. Second, the mandatory roles on A imply an equality constraint between these roles, so if A is populated, the exclusion constraint cannot be satisfied (recall theorem NXS).

Finally, the frequency constraint of 3 on the first role of S cannot be satisfied once A is populated. If it were satisfied, then C would include at least three instances (since each row of S is unique); but this is impossible since C is a proper subtype of B and hence has a maximum cardinality of 2 (the value constraint shows B has only three possible values).

With practice, it is usually easy to spot contradictory constraint patterns. CASE tools can be of assistance here. For example, Microsoft's ORM tool prevents most inconsistencies from even being entered, as well as performing a detailed consistency check before the conceptual schema is mapped to an implementation.

A conceptual schema is *externally consistent* if it agrees with the original examples and requirements used to develop the schema. If not done earlier, we populate the schema with some of the sample data and look to see if some constraints are violated by the population. If they are, then the constraints are *too strong* in this respect, since they reject legal examples. We should then modify the schema, typically by removing or softening some constraints, until the population is permitted.

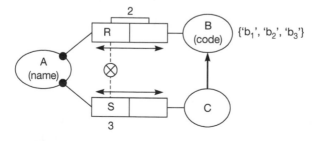

Figure 7.29 This schema is population inconsistent on three counts.

Table 7.2 Student details.

Person	Subject	Degree
Ann	CS112	BSc
Ann	CS100	BSc
Bob	?	BA
Sue	CS112	BA
Tom	CS213	BSc

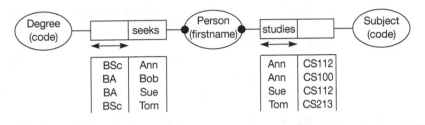

Figure 7.30 The constraints are inconsistent with the data.

As a simple illustration, consider Table 7.2. To simplify the discussion, assume that people may be identified by their first name. The null value indicates that Bob seeks a BA degree, but we do not know any of Bob's subjects.

Now suppose that we propose the schema in Figure 7.30. Assuming our fact types are correct, we might still get the constraints wrong. As well as asking the client directly about the constraints, we check by populating the fact tables with the sample data, as shown in the figure. Consider first the uniqueness constraint on studies. This asserts that each entry in this column is unique (i.e., each person studies at most one subject).

However, 'Ann' appears twice here. So this constraint is wrong. The sample population makes it clear that the uniqueness constraint should span both columns. Now consider the uniqueness constraint on Person seeks Degree. This asserts that each entry in the degree column is unique. But the entry 'BSc' appears twice there, and so does the entry 'BA'. The presence of either of these cases proves that this constraint is wrong. This does not imply that the correct uniqueness constraint should span both columns; although the population is consistent with this weaker constraint, it is also consistent with a uniqueness constraint over the Person column.

To decide between the two possibilities, we ask the domain expert an appropriate question (e.g., Can the same person seek more than one degree at the same time?). If the answer to this is "no", then we should replace the old uniqueness constraint with one across the Person column for this fact type.

Finally, note that the mandatory role constraint on studies is violated by the sample data, since Bob is referenced elsewhere in the database but does not play this role. So this role should be made optional. Figure 7.31 shows the fully corrected schema.

Figure 7.31   The corrected conceptual schema for Table 7.2.

While populating the schema with original examples may detect constraints that shouldn't be there, this will not automatically reveal missing constraints. In other words, while this check can pick up aspects of the constraint section that are too strong, we require significant examples or background knowledge to determine whether the constraint section is *too weak* in other respects.

We now check that the schema is free of *redundancy,* by ensuring that no elementary fact can appear twice. Stored redundancy was covered in step 4, in the context of arity checking. We now turn to the notion of *derived redundancy.* The most common case of this is when a recorded fact can be derived from other facts by means of specified derivation rules.

The task of identifying derived fact types was considered in earlier steps. For example, the markup of an article was derived by subtracting its wholesale price from its retail price. Here it would be redundant to store the markup values. If markup values are not stored, then they need to be computed upon request; this has the disadvantage of adding slightly to the response time for markup queries.

If markup values are stored, this takes up extra storage. Moreover, if the wholesale or retail price of an article is changed, then failure to update markup accordingly leads to an inconsistent database. If such an update anomaly can occur, the redundancy is *unsafe.*

You can arrange for *safe redundancy* or *controlled redundancy* in derived cases by having the derivation rule triggered by relevant updates. For example, the system can be configured to automatically "recalculate" the markup prices whenever wholesale or retail prices are updated (we assume markup prices may not be updated directly; this avoids the further overhead of a mutual recalculation between the three prices). This kind of approach is often used with spreadsheets.

Another derived case of safe redundancy occurs when the relevant facts are made nonupdatable. For example, a bank account balance may be computed at the end of each transaction, and then stored immediately. This is a case of "derive-on-update" rather than "derive-on-query". This "eager evaluation" of derived information can improve the performance of an application considerably. For example, if a bank with millions of customers produces monthly statements of account for each customer, accessing stored balances can save lots of recomputation. This is safe if the bank has a policy of never overwriting any balances. If an accounting error is found, it is left there but compensated for by a later correcting transaction. This practice can also facilitate the task of auditing.

We sometimes meet cases where a stored fact type is *partially derivable.* Recall the owner-driver example from the previous chapter (reproduced in Figure 7.32). In this

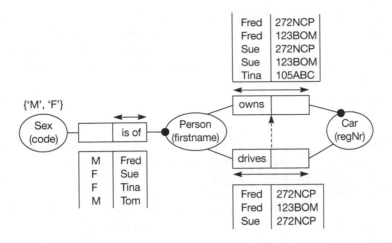

Figure 7.32 Some owner facts are both base and derived.

UoD if a person drives a car, then that person also owns that car. This feature is captured by the pair-subset constraint shown. From a logical point of view, the subset constraint may be specified instead as a derivation rule: Person owns Car **if** Person drives Car. Unlike most derivation rules, which have **iff** as their main operator, this is an **if** rule. Some people might own a car but not drive it. So the ownership fact type must be at least partly stored.

From an implementation viewpoint, it is usually better to store the whole of the ownership relation, under the control of the subset constraint. This may take up a bit more storage, but access to ownership facts is fast. Moreover, this approach is safe and easy to understand.

If storage space is a problem, you could reduce storage of owner facts about owner-drivers by using the derivation rule. In the extreme case, a pair-exclusion constraint could even be enforced between owner and driver facts. However, this exclusion constraint approach requires great care, especially for managing updates. For example, consider deleting a driver fact for a person who remains an owner. Unless memory is tight, the subset constraint approach has much to recommend it. From the *external* rather than the conceptual viewpoint, a user interface may be constructed to automatically add the required owner fact when a driver fact was added, and to delete the required driver fact when its owner fact was deleted. Such an interface could inform the user of its intended action and provide the option of canceling the transaction if this was not desired.

Apart from stored and derived redundancy, redundancy can occur within the set of derivation rules. For instance, it might be possible to derive a fact in more than one way, using different rules. Moreover, some rules might be derivable from more primitive rules. This situation is fairly common in formal inference systems (e.g., computer-aided reasoning systems).

In a wider context, redundancy can sometimes be very useful from the point of view of information retrieval, understanding (e.g., human communication), and coping with partial system failure (e.g., backup systems). This book itself exhibits a great deal of redundancy (e.g., by repeating important points). Although this makes the book longer, it hopefully makes it easier to follow.

The last check in the conceptual schema design procedure is to see if it is *complete* with respect to the original requirements specified for the application. This can be done systematically by going through each of the requirements, one at a time, and identifying which aspects of the conceptual design cater to it. If some requirements are found to be unfulfilled, the design should be extended to cater to them.

This completes the conceptual schema design procedure. In terms of the application development life cycle, there are still several things to be done (e.g., mapping the conceptual design to a database schema; implementing the internal and external schemas; testing; and maintenance). However, the most crucial and important stages of the cycle have now been considered.

Exercise 7.5

1. Discuss any problems with the following schema (reference schemes omitted for simplicity).

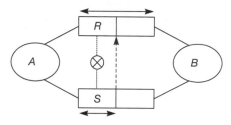

2. From the sample output report shown, a student draws the conceptual schema diagram shown. Check to see if the data in the original report can be a legal population of this schema. If not, modify the schema accordingly.

Particle	Family	Charge (e)
neutrino	lepton	0
electron	lepton	−1
muon	lepton	−1
pion	meson	1
kaon	meson	1
proton	baryon	1
neutron	baryon	0

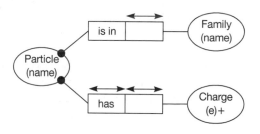

3. Is the following schema guilty of redundancy? If so, correct it.

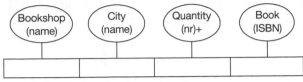

... located in ... has ordered ... copies of ...

Bookland	New York	100	300705
Websters	New York	100	300705
Bookland	New York	50	123555
OKBooks	London	200	123555

4. With respect to the previous question, suppose it is now possible that bookshops in different cities have the same name. For example, the following population is legal. Draw the correct conceptual schema diagram for this UoD.

Bookland	New York	100	300705
Websters	New York	100	300705
Bookland	New York	50	123555
Bookland	London	200	123555

5. In Prolog, relations are often partly stored and partly derived. For example, at one state the knowledge base might consist of the following facts and rules. Discuss this situation, making reference to the notion of derived redundancy.

    parent_of(ann,bob).
    parent_of(bob,chris).
    grandparent_of (david,chris).
    grandparent_of (X,Y) **if** parent_of(X,Z) **and** parent_of(Z,Y).

6. An information system is to deal with various colors that are classified as primary (P), secondary (S), or tertiary (T). There are three primary colors: blue, red, and yellow. A secondary color is comprised of a mixture of exactly two primary colors. A tertiary color comprises a mixture of exactly three primary colors.

    Each color has a unique, identifying trade name (e.g., "forest green"). The trade names of the primary colors are "blue", "red", and "yellow". Each color has a (perhaps zero) percentage of blue, red, and yellow. This percentage is expressed as a whole number in the range 0..100. For example, forest green is 70 percent blue and 30 percent yellow but has no red. The following extract from a sample output report indicates the sort of information that needs to be accessed.

Color	% blue	% red	% yellow	Class
forest green	70	0	30	S
mud brown	30	30	40	T
red	0	100	0	P

It is required to reduce the size of the database as much as possible by using derivation rules. For example, the percentage of a given color that is yellow should be derived from the percentages for blue and red. Schematize this UoD, clearly indicating all constraints. State each derivation rule—you may use obvious abbreviations (e.g., "%B", "%R", and "%Y"). So long as circularity is avoided, the rule for computing the percent yellow may be assumed in formulating other rules (i.e., other rules may use the term "%Y").

7.6   Summary

CSDP step 7 adds other constraints and performs final checks. An *occurrence frequency constraint* indicates that an entry in a column (or column combination) must occur there exactly *n* times (*n*), at most *n* times ($\leq n$), at least *n* times ($\geq n$), or at least *n* and at most *m* times (*n .. m*). A simple occurrence frequency appears next to the role. A compound occurrence frequency appears next to a line connecting the relevant roles.

A *ring constraint* may apply only to a pair of roles played by the same (or a compatible) object type. The role pair may form a binary predicate or be embedded in a longer predicate. Let *R* be the relation type comprising the role pair. *R* is *reflexive* (over its population) iff for all *x* playing either role, *xRx*. *R* is *symmetric* iff for all *x, y, xRy* → *yRx*. *R* is *transitive* iff for all *x, y, z, xRy* & *yRz* → *xRz*. These positive properties tend to be used for derivation rather than as constraints. However, symmetry is sometimes used, marked as °*sym*.

The following negative properties may be marked as ring constraints next to the role pair (or role connector). *R* is *irreflexive* (°*ir*) iff for all *x*, ~*xRx*. *R* is *asymmetric* (°*as*) iff for all *x, y, xRy* → ~*yRx*. *R* is *antisymmetric* (°*ans*) iff for all *x, y, x ≠ y* & *xRy* → ~*yRx*. *R* is *intransitive* (°*it*) iff for all *x, y, z, xRy* & *yRz* → ~*xRz*. Asymmetry and intransitivity each imply irreflexivity. Exclusion implies asymmetry (and irreflexivity). An irreflexive functional relation must be intransitive. A recursive ring constraint that may be difficult to enforce is *acyclicity* (°*ac*).

An *object cardinality constraint* limits the cardinality of each population of an object type. An upper limit of *n* is denoted by "# $\leq n$" next to the object type. If the population of a role sequence is determined by joins or unnesting of the predicates involved, the role sequence may be used in declaring compatible set-comparison, external uniqueness, or frequency constraints. These constraints are called *join constraints*.

A *relative closure constraint* marked as "□" on an optional functional role indicates that if an object in the population of the object type plays that role in the real world, it also plays that role in the model. These constraints are converted to equivalent open-world constructs before mapping.

Constraints for which no graphic symbol exists may be specified as *textual rules*. The relevant elements are marked with a circled "R*n*" to indicate an extra rule is involved. The rule itself may be displayed in a text box. A restricted uniqueness constraint declares stronger uniqueness for a given subtype. A restricted mandatory role constraint indicates an optional role is mandatory for a given subtype.

Dynamic constraints restrict changes between database states. Allowed transitions from one database state to the next may be specified in a *state transition diagram*, matrix, table, or formula.

All constraints discussed so far have been "hard constraints"; updates that violate a hard constraint are rejected. *Soft constraints* may also be needed; updates that violate a soft constraint typically generate a warning rather than being rejected.

When modeling connections between nodes, choose directed, immediate links for the stored relation. Indirect links may then be derived recursively.

At the end of the CSDP, final checks are made to ensure the conceptual schema is internally consistent (its constraint pattern can be populated without contradiction), is externally consistent (agrees with original data and conditions), is redundancy free (elementary facts can't be repeated), and is complete (covers all the requirements). Various cases of derived redundancy can be safely managed.

Chapter Notes

In contrast to our usage, occurrence frequencies are sometimes defined as the number of times members of an object type population must play a role—frequencies of 0 are then allowed and mean optional. Ring constraints are often discussed in logic books, within the context of the theory of dyadic relations, but are rarely discussed in modeling approaches other than ORM. Some extended versions of intransitivity were introduced by Peter Ritson, who also collaborated with me in developing the notion of relative closure. For some further discussion of this topic, see Halpin and Ritson (1992).

Join constraints were formalized in Halpin (1989b). The original "®" notation was introduced by Jim Harding for the InfoModeler tool. Basic state transition diagrams are ancient and are covered in most systems analysis books. For a discussion of statecharts and activity diagrams in UML, see Booch et al. (1999). State nets are used in OSM and are discussed in Embley et al. (1992) and Embley (1998). Some basic procedures for automatically checking the internal consistency of an ORM conceptual schema are covered in Halpin and McCormack (1992).

An extensional uniqueness constraint, denoted by a circled "eu", was introduced in the PSM (Predicator Set Model) variant of ORM to enable unnamed collections to be uniquely defined by their extension (membership). For further discussion of this constraint, see ter Hofstede and Weide (1994) and Halpin (2000b).

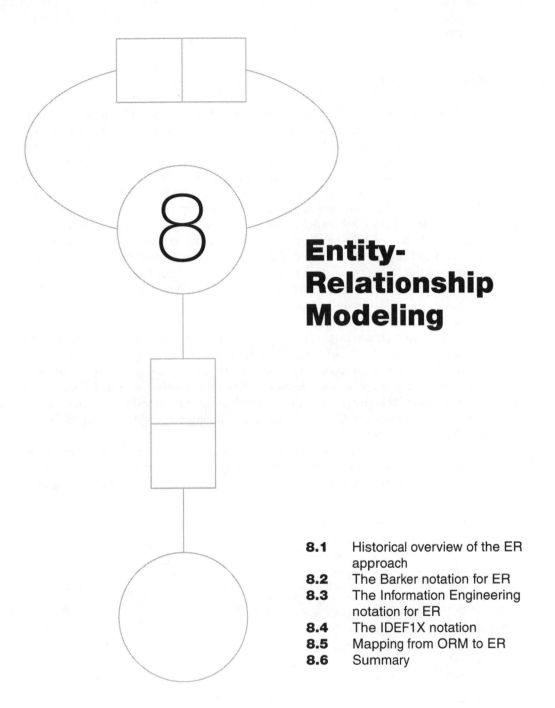

8 Entity-Relationship Modeling

8.1   Overview of ER

The *Entity-Relationship* (ER) modeling approach views an application domain in terms of entities that have attributes and participate in relationships. For example, the fact that an employee was born on a date is modeled by assigning a birth date attribute to the Employee entity type, whereas the fact that an employee works for a department is modeled as a relationship between them. This view of the world is quite intuitive, and in spite of the recent rise of UML for modeling object-oriented applications, ER is still the most popular data modeling approach for database applications.

In Chapter 1, I argued that ORM is better than ER for conceptual analysis. However, ER is widely used, and its diagrams are good for compact summaries, so you should become familiar with at least some of the mainstream ER notations. This is the main purpose of this chapter. A second purpose is to have a closer look at how ORM compares to ER. To save some explanation, I'm going to assume you have already studied the basics of ORM in earlier chapters, so that we can examine ER from an ORM perspective.

The ER approach was originally proposed by Dr. Peter Chen in the very first issue of an influential journal (Chen 1976). Figure 8.1 is based on examples from this journal paper. Chen's original notation uses rectangles for entity types and diamonds for relationships (binary or longer). Attributes may be defined, but are excluded from the ER diagram. As in ORM, roles are defined as parts played in relationships. Rolenames may optionally be shown at relationship ends (e.g., Employee plays the worker role in the Proj-Work relationship).

Chen formalized relationships in terms of ordered tuples of entities, allowing the order to be dropped if rolenames are used (as with attribute names in the relational model). Though not displayed on the ER diagram, relationships may have attributes,

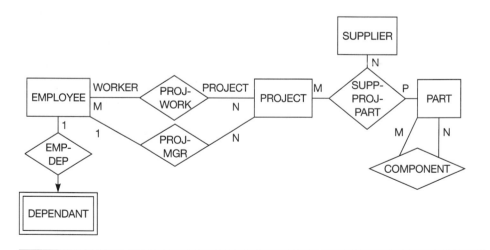

Figure 8.1 The original ER notation used by Chen.

but cannot play roles in other relationships. So objectified associations are not fully supported. Roles may be annotated to indicate a maximum cardinality of 1 or many. For example, read left to right, the Proj-Mgr relation is one to many (each employee manages zero or more projects, but each project is managed by at most one employee).

As shown in Figure 8.1, Chen used noun phrases for relationships, eliminating natural verbalization. Even if verb phrases are used, the direction in which relationship names are to be read is formally undecided, unless we add some additional marks (e.g., arrows) or rules (e.g., always read from left to right and from top to bottom). For example, does the employee manage the project, or does the project manage the employee? Although we can use our background knowledge to informally disambiguate this example, it is easy to find examples of relationships whose direction can only be guessed at by anybody other than the model's creator (e.g., Person killed Animal).

This problem is exacerbated if the verb phrase used to name the relationship is shortened to one word (e.g., "work", "love"), unfortunately still a fairly common practice. If we populate the Component relationship in Figure 8.1 with the pair (a, b), we don't know whether this means a is a component of b or vice versa. To disambiguate this, we need to add rolenames (e.g., "subpart", "superpart") or use a verb phrase (e.g., "is a component of") with a defined direction.

A rectangle with a double border denotes a *weak entity type*. This means that the entity type's identification scheme includes a relationship to another entity type. In Figure 8.1, for example, an entity of type Dependant might be identified by having the given name "Norma" and being related via the Emp-Dep relation to employee 007. In ORM this would be modeled by the coreferenced object type Dependant (has GivenName, is a dependant of Employee(empNr)). The arrow tip at the Dependant end of the relationship indicates that Dependant is existence dependent on Employee (its existence depends on the existence of the other). Given that Dependant is weak, this is basically redundant.

A far better approach is to introduce the concept of a mandatory role, as in ORM and many other ER versions (e.g., **each** Dependant is a dependant of **at least one** Employee). This ability to establish a minimum multiplicity of at least one for any given role was absent from Chen's original notation. Over time, many variant notations developed. Attributes were sometimes displayed as named ellipses, connected by an arrow from their entity type, with double ellipses for identifier attributes. Chen's current ER-Designer tool uses hexagons instead of diamonds. One problem with the ER approach is that there are so many versions of it, with no single standard. In industry, the most popular versions of pure ER are the Barker and Information Engineering (IE) notations. These are discussed in the next two sections. Another popular data modeling notation is IDEF1X, which is a hybrid of ER and relational notation, and so is not a true ER representative. Nevertheless, many people talk of IDEF1X as a version of ER, so I'll cover it in this chapter.

The best way to develop an ER or IDEF1X model is to derive it from an ORM model, and I'll briefly discuss mapping from ORM later in the chapter. The UML class diagram notation can be regarded as an extended version of ER, but because of the importance of UML, it is considered separately in the next chapter.

8.2   Barker Notation

I use the term "Barker notation" for the ER notation discussed in the classic treatment by Richard Barker (Barker 1990). Originating at CACI in the United Kingdom, the notation was later adopted by Oracle Corporation in its CASE design tools. Oracle now supports UML as an alternative to the traditional ER notation, though for database applications, many modelers still prefer the Barker notation over UML.

Dave Hay, an experienced modeler and fan of the Barker notation, argues that "UML is ... not suitable for analyzing business requirements in cooperation with business people" (Hay 1999b). While I agree with him that UML class diagrams are less than ideal for data modeling, his preferred ER notation shares some of UML's weaknesses in being attribute based. As discussed in Chapter 1, using attributes in a base conceptual model adds complexity and instability, and makes it harder to validate models with domain experts using verbalization and sample populations. Attributes are great for logical design, since they allow compact diagrams that directly represent the implementation data structures (e.g., tables or classes). However, for conceptual analysis, I just want to know what the *facts* and *rules* are about the business, and communicate this information in *sentences,* so that the model can be understood by the domain experts. I sure don't want to bother about how facts are grouped into multifact structures. Whether some fact ends up in the design as an attribute should not be a conceptual issue.

As Ron Ross (1998, p. 15) says, "Sponsors of business rule projects must sign off on the sentences—not on graphical data models. Most methodologies and CASE tools have this more or less backwards". ORM allows the domain expert to inspect ORM models fully verbalized into sentences with examples, making validation much easier and safer.

Now that I've stated my bias up front, let's examine the Barker notation itself. The basic conventions are illustrated in Figure 8.2. *Entity types* are shown as soft rectangles (rounded corners) with their name in capitals. *Attributes* are written below the entity type name. Some constraint information may appear before an attribute name. A "#" indicates that the attribute is, or is a component of, the primary identifier of the entity type.

An asterisk (*) or heavy dot (•) indicates the attribute is mandatory (i.e., each instance in the database population of the entity type must have a non-null value recorded for this attribute). A "°" indicates the attribute is optional. Some modelers also use a period "." to indicate the attribute is not part of the identifier.

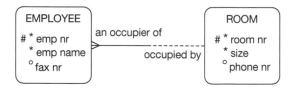

Figure 8.2 A simple ER model in the Barker notation.

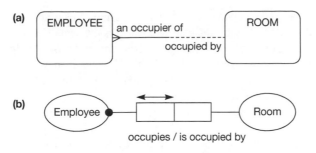

Figure 8.3 The ER diagram (a) is equivalent to the ORM diagram (b).

Relationships are restricted to binaries (no unaries, ternaries, or longer relationships) and are shown as lines with a relationship name at the end from which that relationship name is to be read. This name placement overcomes the ambiguous direction problem mentioned earlier. Both forward and inverse readings may be displayed for a binary relationship, one on either side of the line. This makes the Barker notation superior to UML for verbalizing relationships.

From an ORM perspective, each end (or half) of a relationship line corresponds to a role. Like ORM, Barker treats role optionality and cardinality as distinct, orthogonal concepts, instead of lumping them together into a single concept (e.g., multiplicity in UML). A *solid half-line* denotes a *mandatory* role, and a *dotted half-line* indicates an *optional* role. For cardinality, a *crow's foot* intuitively indicates *many,* by its many "toes". The absence of a crow's foot intuitively indicates "one". The crow's foot notation was invented by Dr. Gordon Everest, who originally used the term "inverted arrow" (Everest 1976) but now calls it a "fork". Figure 8.3 shows the basic correspondence with the ORM notation for simple mandatory and uniqueness constraints

To enable the optionality and cardinality settings to be verbalized, Barker (1998, p. 3-5) recommends the following *naming discipline for relationships.* Let *A R B* denote an infix relationship *R* from entity type *A* to entity type *B*. Name *R* in such a way that each of the following four patterns results in an English sentence:

each *A* (must | may) be *R* (one and only one *B* | one or more *B-plural-form*)

Use "must" or "may" when the first role is mandatory or optional, respectively. Use "one and only one" or "one or more" when the cardinality on the second role is one or many, respectively. For example, the optionality/cardinality settings in Figure 8.3(a) verbalize as **each** Employee **must be** an occupier of **one and only one** Room; **each** Room **may be** occupied by **one or more** Employees.

The constraints on the left-hand role in the equivalent ORM model shown in Figure 8.3(b) verbalize as **each** Employee occupies **some** Room; **each** Employee occupies **at most one** Room. If desired, these constraints may be combined to verbalize as **each** Employee occupies **exactly one** Room. Since the right-hand role has no constraints, this is not normally verbalized in ORM (unlike Barker ER). However, the lack of any uniqueness constraint could be verbalized explicitly as **it is possible that the same** Room is occupied by **more than one** Employee. If no inverse reading is available, it can be verbalized as **it is possible that more than one** Employee occupies **the same** Room.

Regarding the lack of an explicit mandatory role constraint on the right-hand role, I am less inclined to want that verbalized explicitly because it may well be unstable. If Room plays no other fact roles, the role is mandatory by implication (Room has not been declared independent), so verbalization may well confuse here. If Room does play another fact role, and we decide that some rooms may be unoccupied, we could declare this explicitly as **it is possible that some** Room is occupied by **no** Employee. Or equivalently, **it is not necessary that each** Room is occupied by **some** Employee. If no inverse reading is available, it could be verbalized thus: **it is possible that no** Employee occupies **some** Room.

To its credit, the Barker verbalization convention is good for basic mandatory and uniqueness constraints on infix binaries. However, it is far less general than ORM's

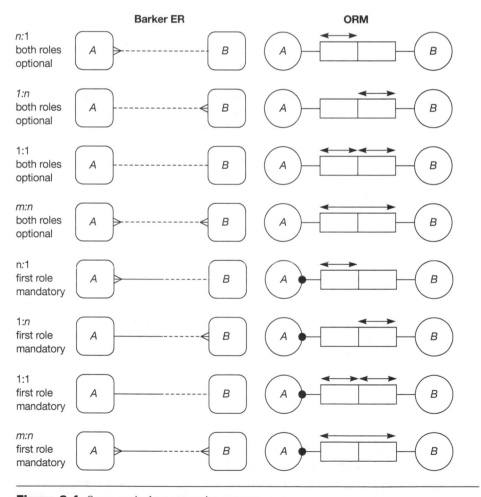

Figure 8.4 Some equivalent constraint patterns.

approach, which applies to instances as well as types, for predicates of any arity, infix or mixfix, and covers many more kinds of constraints, with no need for pluralization. As a trivial example, the fact instance "Employee '101' an occupier of Room 23" is not proper English, but "Employee '101' occupies Room 23" is good English.

If each of the two roles in a binary association may be assigned one of optional/ mandatory and one of many/one, there are 16 patterns. The equivalent Barker ER and ORM diagrams for the first eight of these cases are shown in Figure 8.4.

The other eight cases are shown in Figure 8.5. Although all eight are legal in ORM, the last case where both roles of a many:many relationship are mandatory is considered illegal by Barker.

Ring associations that are considered illegal by Barker are shown in Figure 8.6(a). Although rare, they sometimes occur in reality, so they should be allowed at the

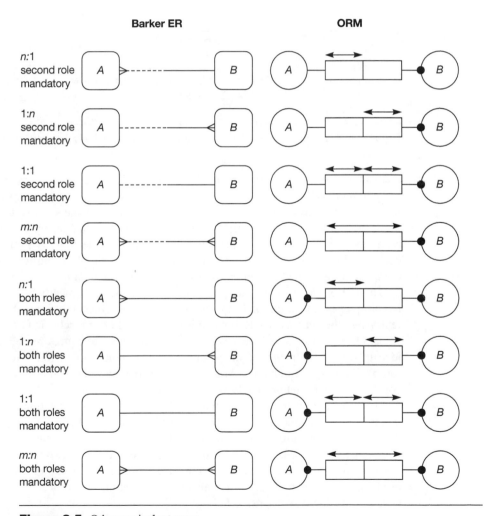

Figure 8.5 Other equivalent cases.

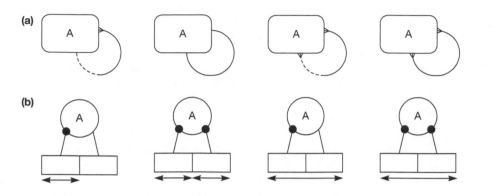

Figure 8.6 Illegal ring associations in Barker ER (a) that are allowed in ORM (b).

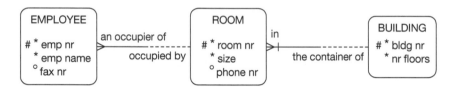

Figure 8.7 Room is identified by combining its room nr and its relationship to Building.

conceptual level, as permitted in ORM. As an exercise, you may wish to invent satisfying populations for the ORM associations in Figure 8.6(b). Although considered illegal by Barker, at least some of these patterns are allowed in Oracle's CASE tools.

In the Barker notation, a bar "|" across one end of a relationship indicates that the relationship is a component of the primary identifier for the entity type at that end. For example, in Figure 8.7, Employee and Building have simple identifiers, but Room is compositely identified by combining its room number and building.

The use of identification bars provides some of the functionality afforded by external uniqueness constraints in ORM. For example, the schemas in Figure 8.8 are equivalent. Any other attributes of Room and Building would be modeled in ORM as relationships. ORM's external uniqueness notation seems to me to convey more intuitively the idea that each RoomNr, Building combination is unique (i.e., refers to at most one room). But maybe I'm biased. At any rate, this constraint (as well as any other graphic constraint) can be automatically verbalized in natural language.

Some people misread the bar notation for composite identification as a "1", since this is what the symbol means in many other ER notations. But the main problem with the bar and "#" notations is that they cannot be used to declare certain kinds of uniqueness constraints (see later). A second problem is that they are two very different notations for the same fundamental concept (uniqueness). ORM allows constraints to be used wherever they make sense and always uses relationships instead of attributes, so it doesn't have these problems.

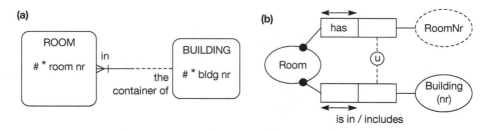

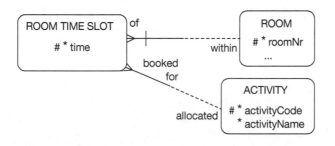

Figure 8.8 Composite identification in Barker ER (a) and ORM (b).

Figure 8.9 A room schedule model in Barker notation.

Section 1.2 used a room scheduling example to illustrate several fundamental differences between ORM and modeling approaches such as ER and UML. You may recall that the schema shown in Figure 8.9 was used to model the application in the Barker notation. If you skipped Section 1.2, you may wish to read it now, since it discussed this example in a lot of detail. The use of attributes and the binary-only relationship restriction in this model make it hard to verbalize and populate the schema for validation purposes. Moreover, there is at least one constraint missing.

A populated ORM schema for this example is reproduced in Figure 8.10 (minus the counterexample rows discussed in Section 1.2). Here the facts are naturally verbalized as a ternary and a binary, and the constraints are easily checked using verbalization and sample data. With the ER model there is no way of specifying the right-hand uniqueness constraints on either fact type, since the Barker notation doesn't capture uniqueness constraints on attributes or relationships unless they are used for primary identification.

In case it looks like I'm just bashing attribute-based approaches like ER, let me say again that I find attribute-based models useful for compact overviews and for getting closer to the implementation model. However, I generate these by mapping from ORM, which I use exclusively for conceptual analysis. This makes it easier to get the model right in the first place, and to modify it as the underlying domain evolves.

Unlike ER (and UML for that matter), ORM was built from a linguistic basis, and its graphic notation was carefully chosen to exploit the potential of sample populations. To

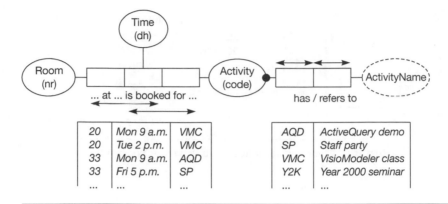

Figure 8.10 A populated ORM model for room scheduling.

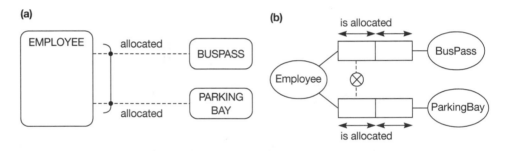

Figure 8.11 A simple exclusion constraint in (a) Barker notation and (b) ORM.

reap the benefits of verbalization and population for communication with and validation by domain experts, it's better to use a language that was designed with this in mind. An added benefit of ORM is that its graphic notation can capture many more business rules than popular ER notations. Although not as rich as ORM, the Barker notation is more expressive than many ER notations. The rest of this section discusses its support for advanced constraints and subtyping.

In Barker notation, an exclusion constraint over two or more roles is shown as an *exclusive arc* connected to the roles with a small dot or circle. For example, Figure 8.11(a) includes the constraint that no employee may be allocated both a bus pass and a parking bay. In ORM this constraint is depicted by connecting "⊗" to the relevant roles by a dotted line, as shown in Figure 8.11(b).

To declare that two or more roles are mutually exclusive and disjunctively mandatory, the Barker notation uses the exclusive arc, but each role is shown as mandatory (solid line). For example, in Figure 8.12(a) each account is owned by a person or a company, but not both.

This notation is liable to mislead, since it violates the orthogonality principle in language design. Viewed by itself, the first role of the association Account owned by Person

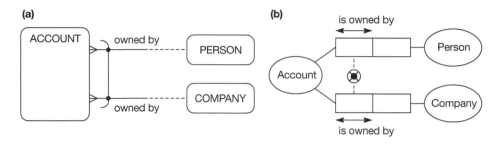

Figure 8.12 An exclusive-or constraint in (a) Barker notation and (b) ORM.

would appear to be mandatory, since a solid line is used. But the role is actually optional, since superimposing the exclusive arc changes the semantics of the solid line to mean the role belongs to a set of roles that are disjunctively mandatory.

Contrast this with the equivalent ORM model shown in Figure 8.12(b). Here an exclusion constraint ⊗ is orthogonally combined with a disjunctive mandatory (inclusive-or) constraint ⊙ to produce an exclusive-or constraint, shown here by the "life-buoy" symbol formed by overlaying one constraint symbol on the other.

The ORM notation makes it clear that each role is individually optional, and that the exclusive-or constraint is a combination of inclusive-or and exclusion constraints. Suppose we modified our business so that the same account could be owned by both a person and a company. Removing just the exclusion constraint from the model leaves us with the inclusive-or constraint ⊙ that each account is owned by a person or company. Like UML, the Barker ER notation doesn't even have a symbol for an inclusive-or constraint, so it is unable to diagram this or the many other cases of this nature that occur in practice.

In the Barker notation, a role may occur in at most one exclusive arc. ORM has no such restriction. For example, in Figure 8.13(a) no student can be both ethnic and aboriginal, and no student can be both an aboriginal and a migrant (these rules come from a student record system in Australia). Even if the Barker notation supported unaries (it doesn't), this situation could not be handled by exclusive arcs. Like UML, Barker ER does not provide a graphic notation for exclusion constraints over role sequences. For instance, it cannot capture the ORM pair-exclusion constraint in Figure 8.13(b), which declares that no person who wrote a book may review the same book. Such rules are very common. Moreover, the Barker notation cannot express any ORM subset or equality constraints at all, even over simple roles.

The Barker notation for ER allows simple *frequency constraints* to be specified. For any positive integer n, a constraint of the form $= n$, $< n$, $\leq n$, $> n$, $\geq n$ may be written beside a single role to indicate the number of instances that may be associated with an instance playing the other role. For example, the frequency constraint "≤ 2" in Figure 8.14 indicates that each person is a child of at most two parents.

In the Barker notation, this constraint is placed on the parent role, making it easy to read the constraint as a sentence starting at the other role. In ORM the constraint is placed on the child role, making it easy to see the impact of the constraint on the

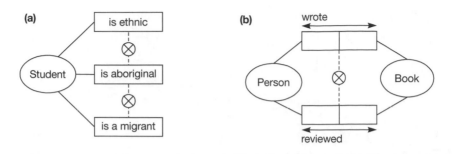

Figure 8.13 Some ORM exclusion constraints not handled by Barker's exclusive arcs.

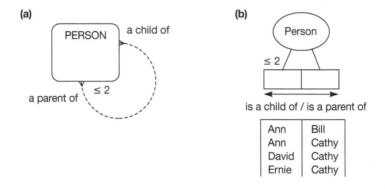

Figure 8.14 A simple frequency constraint in (a) Barker notation and (b) ORM.

population (each person appears at most twice in the child role population). Unlike the Barker notation, ORM allows frequency constraints to include ranges (e.g., 2..5) and to apply to role sequences.

In Barker notation, *subtyping* is depicted with a version of Euler diagrams. In effect, only partitions (exclusive and exhaustive) can be displayed. For example, Figure 8.15(a) indicates that each patient is a male patient or a female patient, but not both. As discussed in Section 6.5, ORM displays subtyping using directed acyclic graphs (DAGs). Subtype exclusion and exhaustion constraints are normally omitted in ORM, as in Figure 8.15(b), since they are implied by the subtype definition and other constraints (e.g., mandatory, uniqueness, and value constraints on Patient is of Gender). However, they can be explicitly displayed as in Figure 8.15(c).

Euler diagrams are good for simple cases, since they intuitively show the subtype inside its supertype. However, unlike DAGs, they are hopeless for complex cases (e.g., many overlapping subtypes), and they make it inconvenient to attach details to the subtypes. For the latter reason, attributes are often omitted from subtypes when the Barker notation is used.

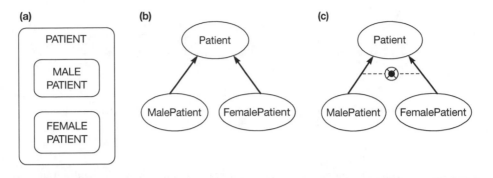

Figure 8.15 A subtype partition in (a) Barker, (b) implicit ORM, and (c) explicit ORM.

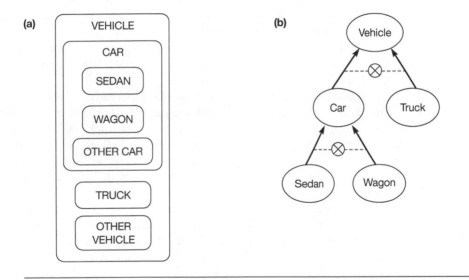

Figure 8.16 Nonexhaustive, exclusive subtypes in (a) Barker ER and (b) ORM.

In the Barker notation, if the original subtype list is not exhaustive, an "Other" sub-type is added to make it so, even if it plays no specific role. For example, in Figure 8.16 a vehicle is a car or truck or possibly something else, and a car is a sedan or wagon or possibly something else. In ORM, there is no need to introduce subtypes for OtherCar or OtherVehicle unless they play specific roles.

A major problem with the Barker notation for subtyping is that it does not depict overlapping subtypes (e.g., Manager and FemaleEmployee as subtypes of Employee) or multiple inheritance (e.g., FemaleManager as a subtype of FemaleEmployee and Manager). While it is possible to implement multiple inheritance in single-inheritance systems (e.g., Java) by using some low-level tricks, for conceptual modeling purposes

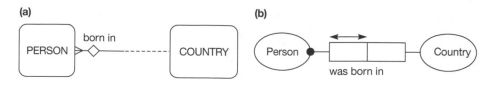

Figure 8.17 Nontransferable nature of a relationship declared in Barker (a), but not ORM (b).

multiple inheritance should be simply modeled as multiple inheritance. As a final comparison point about subtyping, Barker ER lacks ORM's capability for formal subtype definitions and context-dependent identification schemes.

In addition to its static constraints, Barker ER includes a dynamic "changeability constraint" for marking *nontransferable relationships*. This constraint declares that once an instance of an entity type plays a role with an object, it cannot ever play this role with another object. This is indicated by an open diamond on the constrained role. For example, Figure 8.17(a) declares that the birth country of a person is nontransferable.

As indicated in Figure 8.17(b), ORM does not currently include a notation for this constraint. It would be possible to add a notation for this, but it is at least debatable whether this is advisable. If we were to add such a notation, we would need to ensure that the implemented model is still open to error corrections by duly authorized users. For example, if my birth country was mistakenly entered as Austria, it should be possible to change this to Australia. I'll discuss this issue further in Chapter 9 when examining changeability properties in UML.

Well, that pretty well covers the Barker notation for ER. As we've seen, it does a good job of expressing simple mandatory, uniqueness, exclusion, and frequency constraints; simple subtyping; and also nontransferable relationships. However, if a feature is modeled as an attribute instead of as a relationship, very few of these constraints can be specified for it.

Unlike ORM, the Barker notation does not support unary, *n*-ary, or objectified associations (nesting). Moreover it lacks support for most of the advanced ORM constraints (e.g., subset, multirole exclusion, ring constraints, and join constraints). It does not include a formal textual language such as ConQuer for specifying queries, other constraints, and derivation rules at the conceptual level. Nevertheless, it is better than many other ER notations and is still widely used. If you ever need to specify a model in Barker ER notation, I suggest you first do the model in ORM, then map it to the Barker notation and make a note of any rules that can't be expressed there diagrammatically.

Rather than giving you some exercises on the Barker notation at this point, I'll wait till the end of the chapter, when we've covered the main ER notations in use as well as some techniques for mapping from ORM to ER. You can then decide which notation(s) you would like to have some practice with.

8.3   Information Engineering Notation

The *Information Engineering* (IE) approach began with the work of Clive Finkelstein in Australia, and CACI in the UK, and was later adapted by James Martin. Different versions of IE exist, with no single standard. In one form or other, IE is supported by many data modeling tools and is one of the most popular notations for database design.

In the IE approach, *entity types* are shown as named rectangles, as in Figure 8.18(a). *Attributes* are often displayed in a compartment below the entity type name, as in Figure 8.18(b), but are sometimes displayed separately (e.g., bubble charts). Some versions support basic constraints on attributes (e.g., Ma/Op/Unique).

Relationships are typically restricted to binary associations only, which are shown as named lines connecting the entity types. Relationship names are read left to right and top to bottom. As with the Barker notation, a half-line or line end corresponds to a role in ORM. Optionality and cardinality settings are indicated by annotating the line ends. To indicate that a role is *optional,* a circle "○" is placed at the other end of the line, signifying a minimum participation frequency of 0. To indicate that a role is *mandatory,* a stroke "|" is placed at the other end of the line, signifying a minimum participation frequency of 1. After experimenting with different notations for a cardinality of *many,* Finkelstein settled on the intuitive crow's foot symbol suggested by Dr. Gordon Everest.

In conjunction with a minimum frequency of 0 or 1, a stroke "|" is often used to indicate a maximum frequency of 1. With this arrangement, the combination "○|" indicates *at most one,* and the combination "||" indicates *exactly one.* This is the convention used in this section. However, different IE conventions exist. For example, some assume a maximum cardinality of 1 if no crow's foot is used, and hence use just a single "|" for "exactly one". Clive Finkelstein uses the combination "○|" to mean "optional but will become mandatory", which is really a dynamic rather than static constraint—this can be combined with a crow's foot. Some conventions allow a crow's foot to mean the minimum (and hence maximum) frequency is many. So if you are using a version of IE, you should check which of these conventions applies.

Figure 8.19 shows a simple IE diagram and its equivalent ORM diagram. With IE, as you read an association from left to right, you verbalize the constraint symbols at the right-hand end. Here, each employee occupies exactly one (at least one and at most one) room. Although inverse predicates are not always supported in IE, you can supply these yourself to obtain a verbalization in the other direction. For example: "Each room

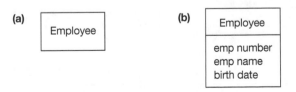

Figure 8.18 Typical IE notation for (a) entity type and (b) entity type with attributes.

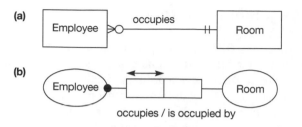

Figure 8.19 The IE diagram (a) is equivalent to the ORM diagram (b).

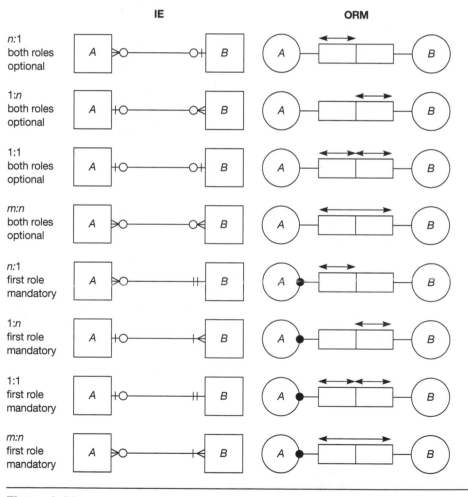

Figure 8.20 Some equivalent constraint patterns.

is occupied by zero or more employees". As with the Barker notation, a plural form of the entity type name is introduced to deal with the many case.

The IE notation is similar to the Barker notation in showing the maximum frequency of a role by marking the role at the other end. But unlike the Barker notation, the IE notation shows the optionality/mandatory setting at the other end as well. In this sense, IE is like UML (even though different symbols are used). As discussed earlier, there are 16 possible constraint patterns for optionality and cardinality on binary associations. Figure 8.20 shows eight cases in IE notation together with the equivalent cases in ORM. The other eight cases are shown in Figure 8.21.

An example using the different notation for IE used by Finkelstein is shown in Figure 8.22. Here the single bar on the left end of the association indicates that each computer is located in exactly one office. The circle, bar, and crow's foot on the right end of

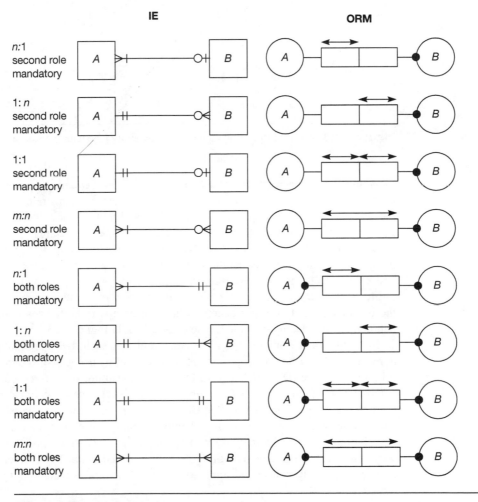

Figure 8.21 Other equivalent cases.

Figure 8.22 In Finkelstein's notation, circle-bar means "optional becoming mandatory".

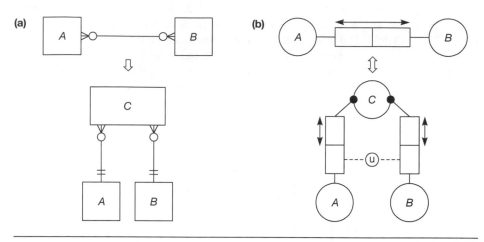

Figure 8.23 An *m:n* association remodeled as an entity type with *n:*1 associations.

the association collectively indicate that each office must eventually house one or more computers. Although this "optional becoming mandatory" constraint has no counterpart in ORM and is unsupported by most IE modeling tools, it could be used to refine decisions on how to group fact types into implementation structures.

Some modeling tools support the IE notation for *n:*1, 1:*n,* and 1:1 associations but not *m:n* (many-to-many) associations. For such tools, 4 of the 16 cases in Figures 8.20 and 8.21 can't be directly represented. In this situation, you can model the *m:n* cases indirectly by introducing an *intersection entity type* with mandatory *n:*1 associations to the original entity types. For example, the *m:n* case with both roles optional may be handled by introducing the object type *C* as shown in Figure 8.23.

In IE this transformation loses the constraint that each *A-B* combination relates to at most one *C* (unless we drop to the relational level by using two foreign keys for *C*'s primary key—see IDEF1X later). In ORM, the constraint is captured conceptually as external uniqueness, making *C* a *coreferenced* object type—the transformation is a flatten/coreference equivalence (see Chapter 12). As an example, the *m:n* association Person plays Sport can be transformed into the uniquely constrained, mandatory *n:*1 associations Play is by Person; Play is of Sport. However, such a transformation is often very unnatural, especially if nothing else is recorded about the coreferenced object type. So any truly conceptual approach must allow *m:n* associations to be modeled directly.

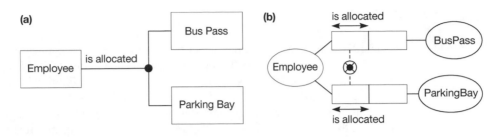

Figure 8.24 An exclusive-or constraint in (a) IE and (b) ORM.

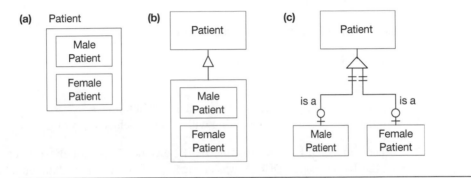

Figure 8.25 Some different IE notations for subtyping.

Some versions of IE support an *exclusive-or constraint,* shown as a black dot connected to the alternatives. Figure 8.24(a) depicts the situation where each employee is allocated a bus pass or parking bay, but not both. The equivalent ORM schema is shown in Figure 8.24(b). Unlike ORM, IE does not support an inclusive-or constraint. Nor does it support exclusion constraints over multirole sequences.

Subtyping schemes for IE vary. Sometimes Euler diagrams are used, adding a blank compartment if needed for "Other". Sometimes directed acyclic graphs are used, possibly including subtype relationship names and optionality/cardinality constraints. Figure 8.25 show three different subtyping notations for partitioning Patient into MalePatient and FemalePatient. There is no formal support for subtype definitions or context-dependent reference. Multiple inheritance may or may not be supported, depending on the version.

Although far less expressive than ORM, IE does a good job of covering basic constraints. Its founder Clive Finkelstein is an amiable Aussie who is still actively engaged in the Information Engineering discipline. He developed a set of modeling procedures to go with the notation, extended IE to Enterprise Engineering (EE), and recently began applying data modeling to work in XML (Extensible Markup Language). For details on Clive's recent work, see Finkelstein and Aiken (2000).

8.4   **IDEF1X**

In the 1970s, the U.S. Air Force began work on a program for Integrated Computer Aided Manufacturing (ICAM). This was the genesis of a family of *IDEF modeling languages.* The acronym "IDEF" originally denoted "ICAM DEFinition", but now stands for "Integration DEFinition", reflecting its possible use for exchanging information between different modeling languages. Rather than specifying one universal modeling language, the ICAM project defined the following languages for different tasks:

- IDEF0: activity modeling
- IDEF1: conceptual data modeling
- IDEF2: simulation modeling

Later, other languages were added, including

- IDEF1X: logical data modeling
- IDEF3: process modeling
- IDEF4: object-oriented software design
- IDEF5: knowledge engineering of enterprise ontologies
- IDEF1X$_{97}$: logical data modeling with object-oriented extensions

The name "IDEF1X" stands for "IDEF1 eXtended". Although based on the conceptual IDEF1 language, IDEF1X was changed to focus on logical data modeling. Though regretted by some, the introduction of IDEF1X effectively spelled the end of IDEF1. Over time, IDEF3 subsumed much of IDEF2 and more recently IDEF5. Nowadays, IDEF0 and IDEF1X are the most popular IDEF languages. Both are supported in a variety of CASE tools and are widely used in U.S. government sectors, especially defense. The IDEF3 language is also used, though to a lesser extent.

IDEF1X is a hybrid language, combining some conceptual notions (e.g., entity, relationship) with relational database constructs (e.g., foreign keys). It was accepted as a standard by the National Institute of Standards and Technology (NIST) in 1993 (NIST 1993). A proposed successor called IDEF1X$_{97}$ was approved in June 1998 by the IEEE-SA Standards Board (IEEE 1999). Also known as IDEF$_{object}$, this extended IDEF1X with object-oriented features to make it suitable for implementation in object-oriented databases and programming languages, while maintaining compatibility with IDEF1X for implementation in relational databases. This backward compatibility gives IDEF1X$_{97}$ one advantage over UML for adoption in U.S. government sectors.

Nevertheless, the future of IDEF1X$_{97}$ is uncertain, since its object-oriented extensions are less encompassing than those in UML. Although UML is yet to be widely used for database design, it is by far the most widely used language for designing object-oriented code, is supported by many CASE tools, and is being considered for standardization by the International Standards Organization (ISO). At the time of writing, few practitioners or tool vendors have expressed interest in adopting IDEF1X$_{97}$. In contrast, the original (1993) version of the IDEF1X language continues to be very widely used for database design and is supported by many modeling tools. For these reasons, I'll restrict my attention to the original IDEF1X in the rest of this section.

To model facts, IDEF1X uses the three main constructs of ER: entities, attributes, and relationships. Unfortunately, the IDEF1X standard uses the term "entity" to mean "entity type", not "entity instance". Even more unfortunately, this misusage has been adopted by some practitioners. So you may have to use the word "instance" more than you want to, simply to ensure you are not misunderstood. Each entity type has one or more attributes that are based on domains. A domain is a named set of data values of the same data type. Relationships are restricted to binary associations between entity types.

IDEF1X allows models to be developed in phases using at least *three views:* ER view, key-based view, and fully attributed view. The essential differences between these views are summarized in Table 8.1.

The *ER view* may be used early in the analysis but is very inexpressive compared with true ER. No identification schemes are specified for entity types, and no attributes need be declared. If attributes are specified, no constraints (e.g., mandatory) are declared for them. An ER view in IDEF1X is basically an incomplete sketch of an ER model. In principle, it could be refined into a true ER model. Unfortunately, instead of carrying out the refinement at the conceptual level, IDEF1X drops down to the logical level to add the extra detail. Any ER view must be resolved into a key-based view and ultimately a fully attributed view to complete the model. Key-based views and fully attributed views are similar to a relational model in many respects. Some CASE tools that support IDEF1X do not support its ER view, and I'll ignore the ER view from this point on.

In key-based and fully attributed views, IDEF1X entity types are basically relational tables, and the "relationships" are foreign key to primary key references. Recall that a foreign key is a set of one or more attributes whose values (possibly composite) must occur as a value of some primary key. The source or referencing entity (type) is called the *child,* and the target or referenced entity (type) is called the *parent.* The relationships may be assigned forward and inverse readings as if they were conceptual associations or subtype links. However, they ultimately represent subset constraints. The actual facts are all stored in attributes, as in the relational model.

An entity type is classified as identifier-independent or identifier-dependent. An entity type is *identifier-independent* if and only if its identifier does not depend on other entity types. In other words, its identification scheme does not include a conceptual

Table 8.1 Three different views in IDEF1X.

ER view	Entity types: No identification scheme or keys defined No need to specify any attributes No attribute constraints (e.g., mandatory) Relationships: Many:many relationships are allowed Identifying/nonidentifying distinction is not made
Key-based view	Include at least all the key-based attributes Classify connection relationships as identifying or nonidentifying
Fully attributed view	Include all attributes

relationship to another entity type. In terms of keys, this means that *an entity type is identifier-independent if and only if its primary key has no component that is a (complete) foreign key*—its primary key may, however, contain an attribute that is just part of a foreign key. Otherwise the entity type is *identifier-dependent.* The terms "identifier-independent" and "identifier-dependent" are often shortened to "independent" and "dependent". This notion of "independent" has nothing to do with the notion of independent object types in ORM.

In IDEF1X, an independent entity (type) is depicted as a hard rectangle (square corners), with its name written above, as shown in Figure 8.26(a). A dependent entity type is depicted as a soft rectangle (rounded corners), as shown in Figure 8.26(b).

Attributes of an entity type are listed inside its rectangle. *Primary key* attributes appear in the top compartment. These provide the entity type's primary identification scheme. *Alternate keys* are marked by appending "(AKn)", where $n > 0$. These provide an alternate identification scheme. If an alternate key is composite, each of its components has the same value for n. Different alternate keys must have different values for n. *Foreign keys* are indicated by appending "(FK)". Attributes are *mandatory by default.* To show that an attribute is *optional,* "(O)" is appended. All attributes are single-valued.

In Figure 8.27, empNr is the primary key of Employee, and the bldgNr, roomNr pair provides the composite primary key for Room. The social security number attribute (ssn) is an alternate key for Employee. In Employee, the pair bldgNr, roomNr is a foreign key (referencing the primary key of Room). In Room, bldgNr is a foreign key (referencing the primary key of a Building entity type not shown here). All attributes are mandatory except for fax and phoneNr, which are marked optional.

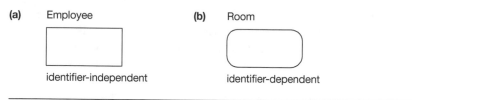

(a)   Employee   **(b)**   Room

identifier-independent   identifier-dependent

Figure 8.26 An independent entity type (a) and a dependent entity type (b).

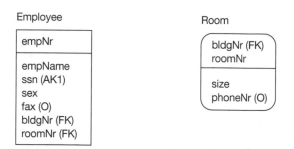

Employee

empNr

empName
ssn (AK1)
sex
fax (O)
bldgNr (FK)
roomNr (FK)

Room

bldgNr (FK)
roomNr

size
phoneNr (O)

Figure 8.27 Attributes with key (primary, alternate, and foreign) and optional indicators.

Figure 8.28 An identifying connection "relationship".

In all views, *relationships* are binary only. In the ER view, relationships are conceptual associations and may be "nonspecific" (many-to-many). In key-based and fully attributed views, each "relationship" is either a *connection* (*foreign key to primary key reference*) or a *categorization* (*subtype link*). Connections are *specific* (many-to-one) binary associations between a child entity type and parent entity type, where each child has at most one parent.

Connection relationships are either identifying or nonidentifying. In principle, an *identifying relationship* is an association that is conceptually used in the identification scheme of the child. In actuality, it is simply a *reference from a foreign key in the child's primary key to the parent's primary key.* In a *nonidentifying* relationship, the child *nonkey* attributes include a foreign key attribute.

All connection relationships are denoted as a named line with a *dot* "●" *at the child end.* An *identifying* relationship is shown as a named, *solid line,* as shown in Figure 8.28. Here *a* and *b* are attributes (possibly compound). With an identifying connection, each child entity is associated with *exactly one* parent instance. This is because each child instance has a non-null value for the foreign key (in the child's primary key) that references the parent. By definition, the child must be identifier-dependent, as shown by the soft rectangle. The parent is identifier-independent (as shown here) unless it is made dependent by some other relationship.

IDEF1X allows both forward and inverse predicate readings for relationships. These may be written together, as shown in Figure 8.29(a), or on different sides of the relationship line, as shown in Figure 8.30(a).

The forward reading of a specific connection relationship is always toward the child, and hence *toward the dot* "●". This forward or "parent-perspective" reading must be supplied. The inverse or "child-perspective" reading, if supplied, is toward the parent (away from the dot). If both readings are supplied, a slash "/" is appended to the forward reading. In Figure 8.29(a) the forward reading is Building contains Room, and the inverse reading is Room is in Building. Because the child in this case is on the left, the forward reading is right to left. For nonspecific (*m:n*) relationships, however, the forward reading is always read from left to right (or top to bottom if the relationship line is vertical). Recall, however, that *m:n* relationships exist only at the ER view level.

The equivalent ORM diagram in Figure 8.29(b) makes it clear that the association Room is in Building is part of the composite reference scheme for Room. In the IDEF1X diagram, this association is actually depicted by including bldgNr as part of the key for Room, and the connection "relationship" shows the foreign key reference. We can partially lift the IDEF1X discussion to a conceptual level by talking of the parent's primary key *migrating* to the child (see Figure 8.30).

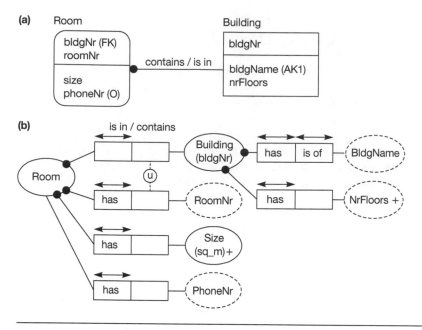

Figure 8.29 The IDEF1X schema (a) is equivalent to the ORM schema (b).

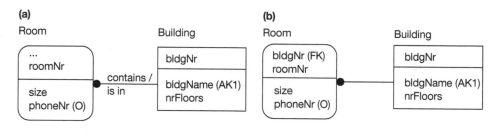

Figure 8.30 The primary key of Building "migrates" to become a foreign key in Room.

Although not a legal IDEF1X diagram, Figure 8.30(a) helps to portray Room as being partly identified by its room number and partly by its relationship to Building. Compare this with the Barker notation depiction in Figure 8.7. At this level, the association Room is in Building is conceptual.

Now imagine a copy of Building's primary key migrating to complete the primary key of Room, as shown in Figure 8.30(b). At this stage, we have dropped to the logical level. The conceptual relationship between Room and Building is now depicted by Room's bldgNr attribute. We still need to indicate that any value for this attribute must also occur as a primary key value of Building, and this foreign key reference is what the connection line now represents. I've removed the "relationship" name to stress this point. You can now think of the connection line as a foreign key arrow.

For identifying relationships, each child (instance) is associated with exactly one parent (instance), as shown by a solid line with no adornments. By default, a parent is associated with zero or more children, as shown by an unadorned dot "•" at the line end. If you are familiar with UML, you can think of this as equivalent to "*". You can override this default child cardinality by adorning the dot with a *cardinality constraint* mark. The main cases are shown in Figure 8.31 along with their ORM counterpart. Here "P" indicates a positive number (at least one), and "Z" indicates zero or one (at most one). A single number (e.g., 3) indicates exactly that number.

You can also indicate ranges. For example, "2–5" indicates at least 2 and at most 5. To make sense of these cardinality constraints, think of them as applying to the conceptual relationship that existed before the key was migrated to the child (cardinality constraints on a foreign key reference are rather pointless). The "Z" mark is unintuitive for "at most one", and in IDEF1X$_{97}$ an alternative notation for this constraint is to use a hollow dot "°".

A *nonidentifying relationship* is shown as a named, *dashed line.* Child and parent are independent unless made dependent by some other relationship. If the dashed line is unadorned, each child (instance) is associated with *exactly one parent* (instance), as in Figure 8.32(a). If a *diamond* is added at the parent end, each child is associated with *at most one parent,* as in Figure 8.32(b). The corresponding ORM diagrams are also shown.

In a nonidentifying relationship, the child *nonkey* attributes (those not in the primary key) include a foreign key that references the parent's primary key. If the foreign key is mandatory (each component is non-null), then each child instance is associated with

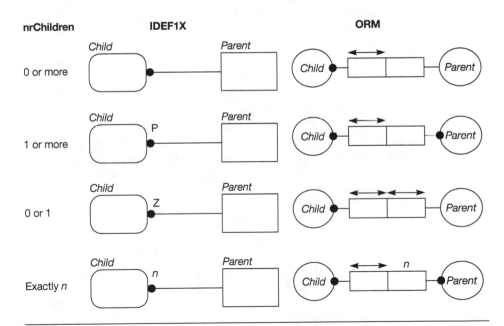

Figure 8.31 The main child cardinality cases for identifying relationships.

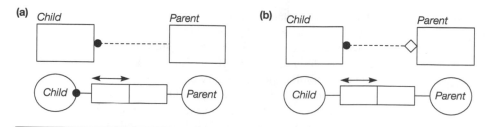

Figure 8.32 Nonidentifying connection "relationships".

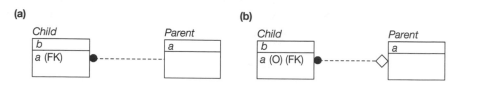

Figure 8.33 "Mandatory" (a) and "optional" (b) nonidentifying connection "relationships".

exactly one parent instance. This is referred to as a *mandatory* relationship, but actually means that the child role of the conceptual relationship that (before migration) gave rise to the foreign key reference is mandatory. Figure 8.33(a) depicts this situation in more detail. Here *a* and *b* are simple or composite attributes. If the foreign key is optional (its components may all be null), then each child instance is associated with at most one parent instance. Figure 8.33(b) depicts this situation. In IDEF1X this is referred to as an *optional* relationship.

In both the mandatory and optional cases, each instance of the child's foreign key that has no null components must occur as an instance of the parent's primary key. This is the default meaning of a foreign key constraint in SQL. For the mandatory case, of course, there can be no null components.

An example of a mandatory, nonidentifying connection relationship is shown in Figure 8.34(a). Here each employee is identified by an employee number, must have a name, and must work for a department. Each department is identified by its code and must have a unique name. The fact (conceptual relationship) that a given employee works for a given department is stored by instantiating the empNr and deptCode attributes of Employee (e.g., empNr = 101, deptCode = 'HR'). The connection "relationship" is simply a foreign key reference indicating that each department code of an employee must be a department code of a department.

The same example is shown in IE notation in Figure 8.34(b) and in ORM notation in Figure 8.34(d). Here the association Employee works for Department is depicted conceptually, rather than by including deptCode as an attribute of Employee. This would also be the case for the Barker notation. Figure 8.34(c) depicts the situation in a relational notation. Here facts about who works for what department are stored in the Employee table, which includes a deptCode attribute referencing the Department table. If

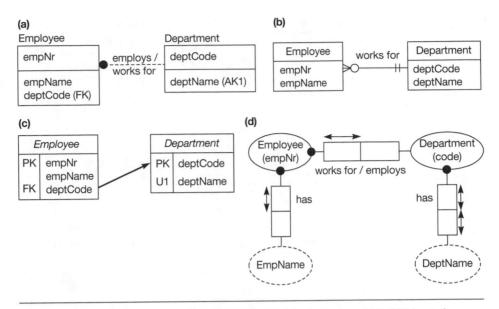

Figure 8.34   Same example in (a) IDEF1X, (b) IE, (c) relational, and (d) ORM notation.

you compare this with the IDEF1X notation in Figure 8.34(a), it should be clear that they are just two notational variations of the same structure. In key-based and fully attributed views, the IDEF1X notation is essentially a logical notation rather than a conceptual one.

As another example of nonidentifying relationships, the room-scheduling example considered in Sections 1.2 and 8.2 is modeled in IDEF1X in Figure 8.35(a). The ORM model for this situation is reproduced in Figure 8.35(b), without the fact populations.

The primary key and alternate key constraints in the IDEF1X model correspond to the uniqueness constraints in the ORM model. Although the IDEF1X schema does capture all of the constraints, it is a logical rather than a conceptual representation, and unlike ORM it does not facilitate validation by verbalization and population.

In an ER view or "entity-level diagram", all entity types are depicted by hard rectangles, and nonspecific (*m:n*) relationships are permitted. Each nonspecific relationship line must end in a dot, possibly adorned by a cardinality mark. If unadorned, a cardinality of exactly one is assumed. In moving to a key-based or fully attributed view, each *m:n relationship* must be resolved into an *intersection entity type* with two *n:*1 relationships. Figure 8.36 shows an example, in both IDEF1X and ORM.

An intersection entity type is sometimes called an *associative entity type.* Although conceptually this corresponds to a coreferenced object type in ORM, in IDEF1X the identifying attributes must be "migrated" to become foreign keys inside the primary key of the intersection entity type, which therefore must be identifier-dependent, appearing as a soft rectangle. This foreign key depiction effectively lowers the representation to the relational level. Although this resolution is often unnatural, it does allow attributes to be added to what was once a relationship. For example, we might wish to

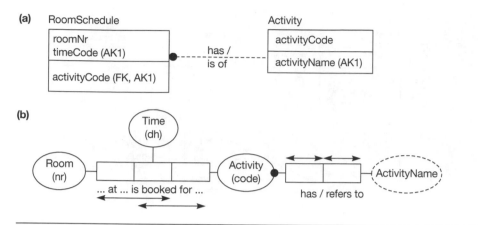

Figure 8.35 The room schedule example in (a) IDEF1X and (b) ORM.

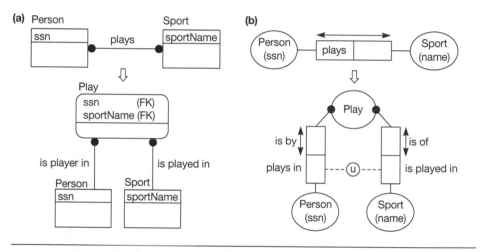

Figure 8.36 (a) In IDEF1X, *m:n* relationships must be resolved into *n:*1 relationships. (b) The same example in ORM.

record a skill level for Play. In ORM and UML, this objective can also be achieved by simply permitting a relationship to be objectified (as an objectified association or association class), but this conceptual alternative is not allowed in IDEF1X.

If the *m:n* relationship is a ring association, rolenames may be prepended to the names of the migrated foreign keys to distinguish them. For example, in Figure 8.37(a) the rolenames "subPartNr" and "superPartNr" are prepended to "partNr" to disambiguate the primary key attributes of Containment. Although the IDEF1X standard uses a dot after the rolename, this dot notation is not supported in some CASE tools. However, the distinction can be easily achieved without the dot by using just a rolename (e.g., "subPartNr" can be used instead of "subPartNr.partNr"). In either case, the

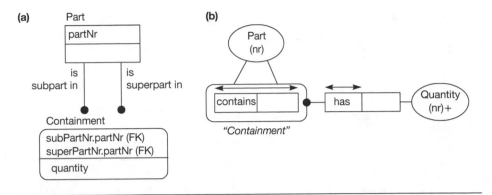

Figure 8.37 (a) In IDEF1X, rolenames may be used if needed to distinguish attributes. (b) The same example in ORM.

rolename should be shown as a noun phrase that identifies the attribute even without appending the name of the referenced primary key. In ORM, a more natural way to model this situation is to objectify the containment association, as shown in Figure 8.37(b).

In IDEF1X, an entity type may be classified into one or more clusters of mutually exclusive *categories* (subtypes). The supertype is called the *generic* entity (type). Each subtype inherits the primary key of its supertype, and hence is identifier-dependent. The subtype linkage is called a *categorization relationship*. This version of subtyping is very restricted compared with ORM subtyping, which allows overlapping types within a "cluster" as well as context-dependent reference. In effect, the subtyping approach of IDEF1X treats entity types as tables, and the "categorization relationships" are simply foreign key references. In sharp contrast, ORM subtyping is purely conceptual, and different mapping strategies may be chosen at implementation time (see Chapter 10).

However, there are two aspects of the subtyping approach in IDEF1X that express more than simple foreign key references. These are the completeness and discriminator declarations. A subtype link is shown as a line with an underlined circle at the supertype end. A *single underline* means the cluster is *incomplete* (i.e., the supertype is more than the union of its subtypes). This means that the population of the supertype may contain instances not present in any of its subtypes. For example, in Figure 8.38(a), the subtypes TallPerson and ShortPerson are mutually exclusive, but not collectively exhaustive. A person may be of medium height without being classified as either tall or short. In contrast to IDEF1X, ORM requires that subtypes must be defined in terms of roles played by their supertype(s). Figure 8.38(b) shows one way of modeling this situation in ORM.

Here a person's height is used to determine whether he or she is a member of TallPerson or ShortPerson. The subtype definitions and the lack of a value constraint on Height indicate that these subtypes are exclusive but not exhaustive. This can also be depicted explicitly by an implied exclusion constraint as shown. As an alternative to using height, you could attach the optional and exclusive unaries "is tall" and "is short" to Person and supply the obvious definitions.

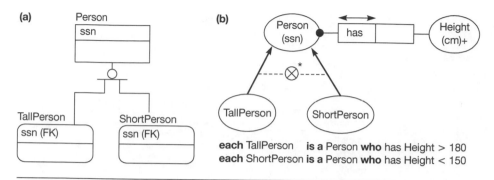

Figure 8.38 An incomplete and exclusive subtype cluster in (a) IDEF1X and (b) ORM.

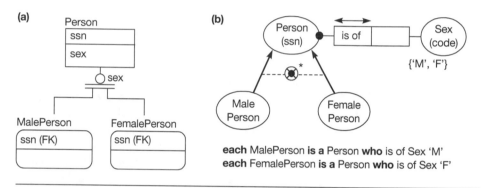

Figure 8.39 A complete, exclusive subtype cluster in (a) IDEF1X and (b) ORM.

In IDEF1X, a *double underline* at the supertype end means the cluster is *complete*. This means the supertype is the union of its subtypes. Since members of an IDEF1X cluster are also exclusive, this means we have a partition. In Figure 8.39(a), for example, Person is partitioned into MalePerson and FemalePerson.

A mandatory attribute of a supertype may be used as a *discriminator* and written beside the circle to indicate the basis for the subtyping. In Figure 8.39(a), for example, sex is used as a discriminator to classify Person into MalePerson and FemalePerson. The corresponding ORM schema is shown in Figure 8.39(b). The partition constraint shown explicitly here is implied by the subtype definitions and other constraints.

Well, that pretty much covers the IDEF1X notation. Although it is a widely used standard, especially in the defense industry, I find it less suitable than the Barker or IE notations for conceptual modeling. To capture any detail or even basic constraints in IDEF1X, you have to resolve the model into what is essentially a relational model. Moreover, the IDEF1X set of concepts and its notation are unnecessarily complex and forgettable. For conceptual analysis and validation, it also suffers from the weaknesses of an attribute-based approach. In spite of such drawbacks, IDEF1X can be used effectively by experienced modelers, who often associate connection relationships with the conceptual relationships from which they are migrated. Even for such experienced modelers, however, the best way to model in IDEF1X is to first do an ORM model, then map it to IDEF1X, expressing any additional ORM constraints as supplementary text or implementation code. An ORM modeling tool can perform this mapping automatically.

8.5   Mapping from ORM to ER

In mapping from ORM to ER or IDEF1X, first replace any objectified associations by coreferenced object types. For example, if the fact type Company sold Product is objectified as Sale, replace this by Sale was made by Company and Sale is of Product. Now binarize any nonbinary predicates. For example, replace the unaries "is male" and "is female" by "is of Sex", and replace the ternary "Room at Time is booked for Activity" by forming an entity type for a composite of Room and Time (or perhaps Time and Activity).

Now decide which $n{:}1$ and 1:1 ORM associations to remodel as attributes. If you have specified rolenames, these can usually be used as attribute names, with the object type name becoming the attribute's domain name. Any $m{:}n$ associations should remain that way, unless the target notation doesn't support them (e.g., IDEF1X). In that case, you can replace the association by an intersection entity type as discussed earlier.

The simplest constraints in ORM usually map in an obvious way to mandatory or cardinality constraints, as illustrated earlier. The more complex ORM constraints have no counterpart in ER, so you need to record these separately in textual form.

With these few hints, and the examples discussed earlier in this chapter, you should now have enough background to do the mapping manually for yourself. The mapping procedure is fairly boring and is best done automatically with a CASE tool. In Chapter 10 we discuss in detail how to map from an ORM schema to a relational database schema. For mapping to IDEF1X, the relational mapping procedure discussed there may be used essentially as is, treating the relationships as foreign key references and making the relevant notational variations.

Exercise 8.5

1. Model the following application in your preferred version of ER or IDEF1X. I suggest you do an ORM model first, but that's up to you.

   A video store has a library of videotapes that may be lent to customers. Six extracts are shown from the information system used by the store. Several aspects have been simplified or removed to reduce the size of this problem. For example, addresses are shown as a single entry, and financial aspects are ignored. Data about a movie may be recorded before the store obtains a videotape of it. Each videotape contains a copy of exactly one movie and is either purchased or leased from another supplier. The status or condition (Good, OK, Poor, X) of each tape is noted on a regular basis. A status of "X" indicates the tape is excluded from the list of tapes that may be borrowed.

Movie	Title	Category	Copy Nr	Purchase date	Lease expiry	Status
AP2K	Apocalypse 2000	R	1	01/10/00		Good
BMF	Batman Forever	M				
CJ	City of Joy	MA	1	07/01/00		OK
			2		01/01/01	X
DS	Donovan Sings	G	1	01/03/99		Good
			2	01/03/99		OK
GHST	Ghost	M	1	06/06/91		X
			2	07/10/91		Poor
			3	07/10/91		X
GQ	Galaxy Quest	PG	1	01/10/00		OK
			2		07/01/01	Good
MTX	The Matrix	R	1	11/11/99		Good
			2	11/11/99		Good
MTX2	The Matrix 2	R				

For excluded videotapes, a record is kept to indicate the reason for their exclusion and whether they are written off for taxation purposes. Here is a sample extract.

Movie	CopyNr	Comment	Written off?
CJ	2	faulty	Y
GHST	1	faulty	N
GHST	3	stolen	Y

The following table records details about the categories in which movies are classified.

Category	Description
G	For General exhibition
PG	Parental Guidance recommended for persons under 15
M	Recommended for Mature audiences 15 years and over
MA	For Mature Adults: restrictions apply to persons under the age of 15 years
R	Restricted to adults 18 years and over

For the current calendar year, a record is kept of which movies are the best sellers.

Month	Rank	Movie	Title
1	1	MTX	The Matrix
	2	AP2K	Apocalypse 2000
	3	DS	Donovan Sings
	...	...	...
2	1	MTX	The Matrix
	2	GQ	Galaxy Quest
	2	DS	Donovan Sings
	4	AP2K	Apocalypse 2000
	...	...	...

Loans are charged to customers, who are identified by the number on their video store card presented at the time of borrowing. The combination of name and address is unique for a customer. Customers who indicate a phone number must also indicate what periods of the day they may be contacted on that phone (D = day only; N = night only; D&N = day and night). Customer details may be recorded before they take out any loan.

Customer	Name	Address	Phone	Call period
1	Frog F	5 Ribbit Rd, Bellevue	425 555 7000	N
2	Jones E	3 Sun Ave, Spokane		
3	Smith J	520 Pike St, Seattle	206 555 6789	D
4	Jones E	520 Pike St, Seattle	206 555 6701	D
5	Frog K	5 Ribbit Rd, Bellevue	425 555 7000	D&N

Each loan is identified by a loan number and may involve more than one tape. Customers may borrow tapes as often as they like and may even borrow the same tape more than once on the same day (after returning it). The rental of a videotape within a loan is called a LoanItem. Although return data for loan items may be derived from videotape returns and other data, to simplify the problem you can ignore this.

Loan date	Loan Nr	Customer		Videotape		Date returned
		Nr	Name	Movie	Copy	
10/01/00	9001	2	Jones E	GQ	1	?
				MTX	1	10/02/00
	9002	3	Smith J	GQ	2	10/01/00
10/02/00	9003	3	Smith J	MTX	1	10/03/00
				DS	2	10/03/00
				GQ	2	10/03/00
	9004	4	Jones E	GHST	2	?
10/03/00	9005	1	Frog F	AP2K	1	10/03/00
				MTX	1	?

2. The following ORM schema models information about university academics. As a challenge exercise, map this to your preferred ER or IDEF1X notation, including some comments to cater to advanced constraints and multiple inheritance. You may wish to delay this till you have studied the relational mapping procedure in Chapter 10.

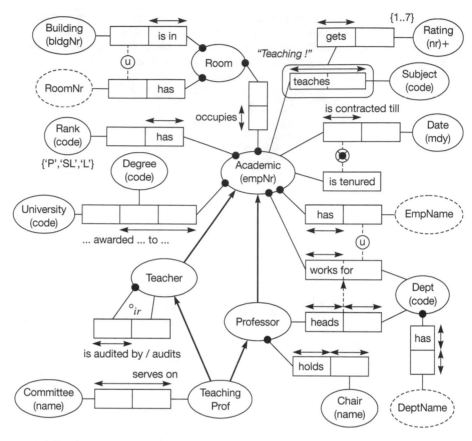

each Teacher   **is an** Academic **who** teaches **some** Subject
each Professor   **is an** Academic **who** has Rank 'P'
each TeachingProf   **is both a** Teacher **and a** Professor

8.6   **Summary**

The *Entity-Relationship* (ER) modeling approach was originated by Peter Chen in the 1970s and allows facts to be expressed via relationships (e.g., Person was born in Country) or attributes (e.g., birth date). Of the dozens of different ER versions in existence, the most widely used are the Barker notation and Information Engineering (IE). The popular IDEF1X approach is often referred to as a version of ER, but is actually a mixture of ER and relational approaches, with the emphasis on relational.

The *Barker notation* represents entity types as named, soft rectangles with a list of one or more attributes. A "*" or "●" indicates an attribute is mandatory, and a "°" indicates the attribute is optional. All relationships are binary and are shown as named lines. A solid half-line denotes a mandatory role, and a dotted half-line denotes an optional role. A crow's foot at the end of the line indicates the cardinality "many", and its absence indicates "one". A hash "#" in front of an attribute indicates it is the primary identifier, or is a part of the primary identifier. A bar "|" across one end of a relationship indicates that the relationship is a component of the primary identifier for the entity type at that end. An exclusive arc across roles indicates the roles are mutually exclusive; if the role lines are solid, we have an exclusive-or constraint. Subtype partitions are denoted by Euler diagrams, placing the subtypes inside the supertype.

In the *Information Engineering* approach, entity types are displayed as named rectangles, with a list of attributes. Relationships are binary and are denoted by named lines. A crow's foot at the end indicates "many", a stroke "|" indicates "one", and a circle "O" indicates "optional". Two strokes "||" indicate "exactly one". Some IE versions depict an exclusive-or constraint as a black dot joining relationship lines. Different subtype notations exist for IE, some using Euler diagrams and some "is a" relationship lines.

IDEF1X models may be viewed at three levels. In a high-level ER view, $m:n$ relationships may be shown directly, but these must be resolved into an intersection entity type with two $n:1$ relationships as the model is refined into key-based or fully attributed views. An entity type is identifier-dependent if its primary key includes a foreign key, and it is shown as a named, soft rectangle. Otherwise it is identifier-independent and is shown as a named, hard rectangle. Attributes are listed inside the rectangle, with the primary key in the top compartment. Alternate keys are denoted by appending "(AKn)" and foreign keys by appending "(FK)". An attribute is mandatory unless followed by "(O)".

Connection relationships are foreign key references from the child to the parent and are shown as a named line with a dot "●" at the child end. For a specific connection relationship, its forward name is always read toward the dot. If an inverse name is added, a slash "/" is appended to the forward reading. For nonspecific relationships, the forward reading is left to right (or top to bottom if the line is vertical).

A line end has a cardinality of 1 unless it is annotated. A dot indicates "0 or more" but can be strengthened by adding "P" (1 or more), "Z" (0 or 1), or "n" (exactly n). A foreign key reference starting from a primary key is an identifying relationship and is shown as a solid line. A foreign key reference starting from a nonkey is a nonidentifying relationship and is shown as a dashed line; in this case, a diamond at the parent end indicates each child is associated with at most one parent.

An entity type may be classified into one or more clusters of mutually exclusive categories. Subtype links are depicted as categorization relationships with a circle at the supertype end. The cluster is incomplete or complete according to whether the circle has a single underline or double underline, respectively.

ER or IDEF1X models are best developed by mapping them from ORM models and noting any additional ORM constraints as comments.

Chapter Notes

This chapter is largely based on some of my articles for the *Journal of Conceptual Modeling* (*www.inconcept.com*). There are dozens of ER notations in existence, and minor variations exist in CASE tool implementations of the main notations discussed in this chapter. Dr. Peter Chen is still active in the field and is on the steering committee for the international Entity-Relationship conferences, which have been held yearly since 1981 and have been broadened in scope to include all forms of conceptual modeling. The proceedings of the ER conferences are published by Springer-Verlag.

Clive Finkelstein, the "father of Information Engineering", is also still active in the field. Finkelstein (1989) discusses the basic concepts and history of IE. Finkelstein (1992) provides practical advice on using IE, as well as a treatment of entity dependency. For a short, authoritative overview of the IE method, see Finkelstein (1998). A detailed treatment of his latest work, including the application of data modeling to XML for building corporate portals, can be found in Finkelstein and Aiken (2000). You can access his Web site at *www.ies.aust.com/~ieinfo/*. For a look at the IE approach used by James Martin, see Martin (1993). Martin's more recent books tend to use the UML notation instead. In practice, however, IE is still used far more extensively for database design than UML, which is mostly used for object-oriented code design.

An overview of the IDEF family of languages is presented in Menzel and Mayer (1998). For further details on IDEF1X, see Bruce (1992) and NIST (1993). The IDEF1X$_{97}$ standard is described in IEEE (1999).

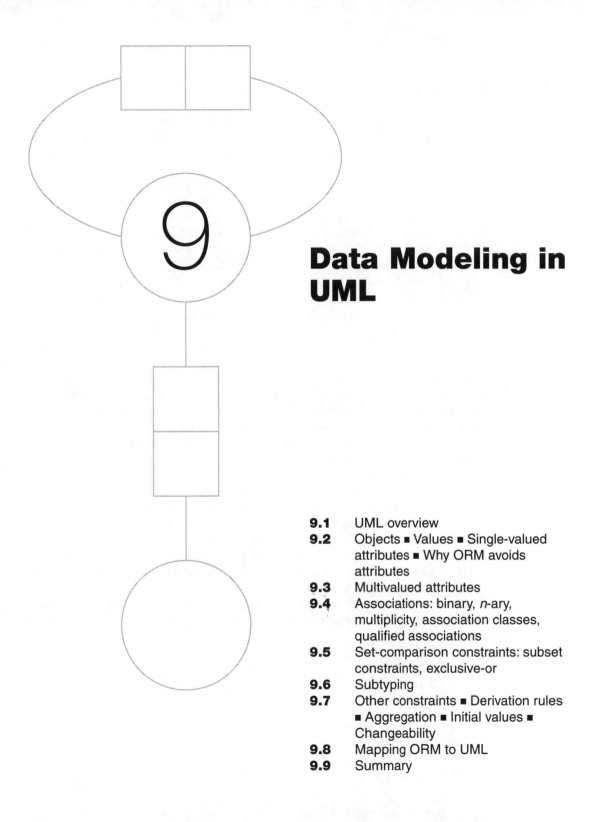

Data Modeling in UML

9.1   Introduction

Although semantic approaches to information modeling appeared in the early 1970s, no single approach has yet achieved universal adoption. By and large, the history of information systems modeling has been characterized by a plethora of techniques and notations, with occasional religious wars between proponents of different approaches. Each year, dozens of new approaches would be proposed, leading to groans from the academic community who were charged with teaching the state of the art. This is referred to as the "yama" (Yet Another Modeling Approach!) or "nama" (Not Another Modeling Approach!) syndrome. Figure 9.1 pictures this as a mountain of modeling methods, piled on top of one another, which nicely ties in with the Japanese meaning of "yama" (mountain), depicted as a kanji that is high in the middle and low on the ends.

While diversity is often useful, clearly the modeling industry would benefit if practitioners agreed to use just a few standard modeling approaches, individually suited for their modeling scope, and collectively covering the tasks needed to model a wide variety of practical applications. This would improve communication between modelers and reduce training costs, especially in an industry with high turnaround of employees.

Recently, the rapid rise of UML (Unified Modeling Language) has been accompanied by claims that UML by itself is an adequate approach for modeling any software application. Some UML proponents have even been so bold as to claim that "the modeling wars are over—UML has won". This claim has been strongly rejected by several experienced data modelers, including Dave Hay, who argues that "there is no such thing as 'object-oriented analysis'" (Hay 1999a), only object-oriented design, and that "UML is ... not suitable for analyzing business requirements in cooperation with business people" (Hay 1999b).

To date, UML is mainly used in industry for designing object-oriented program code. Although it can be used for designing databases, UML has so far had little success in displacing other approaches such as ER for this purpose. Given UML's object-oriented focus, and the dominance of relational DBMSs, this is perhaps not surprising. Nevertheless, UML is a very important language that could well become popular for database design in the future. Indeed, whole books are now devoted to the use of UML to design databases (e.g., Muller 1999).

Initially based on a combination of the Booch, OMT (Object Modeling Technique), and OOSE (Object-Oriented Software Engineering) methods, UML was refined and

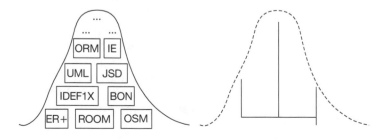

Figure 9.1 "Yama" (Yet Another Modeling Approach), or Japanese for "mountain".

extended by a consortium of several companies working within the Object Management Group (OMG). Version 1.1 of UML was adopted in November 1997 by OMG as a language for object-oriented analysis and design. Late in 1999, version 1.3 was approved (OMG 1999), and work began on version 1.4, with a major revision (2.0) planned for some years later. Though not yet a standard, UML has been proposed for standardization by the International Standards Organization (ISO), and approval may come as early as 2001 (Kobryn 1999).

The UML notation includes a vast number of symbols, from which various diagrams may be constructed to model different perspectives of an application. The nine main diagram types are

- Use case: use case diagram
- Static structure: class diagram and object diagram
- Behavior: statechart and activity diagram
- Interaction: sequence diagram and collaboration diagram
- Implementation: component diagram and deployment diagram

Some of these diagrams (e.g., collaboration diagrams) are useful only for designing object-oriented program code, some (e.g., activity diagrams and use case diagrams) can be useful in requirements analysis, and some (e.g., class diagrams) have limited use for conceptual analysis and are best used for logical design. Although all the UML diagram types are worth studying, the focus of this book is on information modeling for databases. This chapter focuses on data modeling in UML, so it considers only the static structure (class and object) diagrams. Class diagrams are used for the data model, and object diagrams provide a limited means to discuss data populations. Some of the other UML diagram types are briefly discussed in Chapter 13.

UML facilitates object-oriented code design because it covers both data and behavioral modeling, and it lets you drill down into physical design details relevant to OO code. Using a class diagram, for example, you can declare whether an attribute is private, public, or protected; what operations are encapsulated in an object; and whether an association can be navigated in one direction only. By omitting such implementation details, class diagrams can be used for analysis. When used in this way, class diagrams essentially provide an extended ER notation. Like ER, UML uses attributes. As discussed in earlier chapters, attributes are great for logical models, but are best modeled as relationships when performing conceptual analysis, since this facilitates validation and minimizes the impact of change. For reasons discussed in Section 1.2, I believe the best way to develop UML data models is to first do an ORM model and then map it to UML.

For specifying the logical design of a database, UML class diagrams offer no major benefits over traditional database design notations. Currently, UML has no standard notation for candidate keys or foreign key relationships, but you can add your own notations for these until some standard notation eventuates.

This chapter discusses the main data modeling constructs in UML and how they relate to ORM. Along the way, some comparative advantages of ORM are noted. If you're a UML advocate, please don't take offense when I note these advantages. This is not to disparage UML, which does have its strengths, but to suggest ways to overcome some of its weaknesses. No language is perfect, ORM included. Overall, UML provides a useful suite of notations for both data and process modeling, and its class diagram notation has some advantages over popular ER notations.

9.2   Object Reference and Single-Valued Attributes

If you haven't already read Section 1.2, you might like to do that now to get a quick idea of why I believe the fact-oriented approach of ORM provides an ideal precursor to the object-oriented approach of UML. Since ORM will be used to clarify the data modeling concepts in UML, I'll summarize the relevant ORM concepts along the way. This will also help make this chapter reasonably self-contained.

ORM classifies objects into entities (nonlexical objects) and values (lexical objects) and requires each entity to be identified by a well-defined reference scheme used by humans to communicate about the entity. For example, employees might be identified by social security numbers and countries by ISO country codes. ORM uses "object", "entity", and "value" to mean "object instance", "entity instance", and "value instance", appending "type" for the relevant set of all possible instances. For example, you are an instance of the entity type Person. Entities might be referenced in different ways and typically change their state over time. Glossing over some subtle points, values are constants (e.g., character strings and numbers) that basically denote themselves, so they do not require a reference scheme to be declared.

Figure 9.2(a) depicts explicitly a simple reference scheme in ORM. Object types are shown as named ellipses, using solid lines for entity types (e.g., Employee) and dashed lines for value types (e.g., EmpNr). Relationship types are depicted as a named sequence of one or more roles, where each role appears as a box connected to its object type. In ORM, relationships may be of any arity (1 = unary, 2 = binary, 3 = ternary, etc.). In base ORM, each relationship must be elementary (i.e., it cannot be split into smaller relationships covering the same object types without information loss).

Read from left to right, the binary relationship in Figure 9.2(a) is Employee has EmpNr. Read backwards, we have EmpNr is of Employee. The verb phrases "has" and "is of" are predicate names. To enable navigation in any direction around an ORM schema, each *n*-ary relationship (*n* > 0) may be given *n* predicate names (one starting at each role).

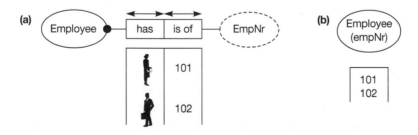

Figure 9.2 A simple reference scheme in ORM, shown (a) explicitly and (b) implicitly.

If an entity type has more than one candidate reference scheme, one may be declared primary to assist verbalization of instances (or to reflect actual business practice). Relationship types used for primary reference are called reference types. All other relationship types are called fact types. A primary reference scheme for an entity type maps each instance of it onto a unique, identifying value (or a combination of values). In Figure 9.2(a), the reference type has a sample population shown in a reference table (one column for each role). Here icons are used to denote the real-world employee entities.

To conserve space, simple reference schemes may be abbreviated by enclosing the reference mode in parentheses below the entity type name, as in Figure 9.2(b), and an object type's reference table includes values but no icons. References verbalize as existential sentences, for example, "There is an Employee who has the EmpNr 101". The constraints in the reference scheme enable entity instances to be referenced elsewhere by definite descriptions, for example, "The Employee who has the EmpNr 101".

Reference modes indicate how values refer to entities. Contrast Mass(kg) with Mass(lb). The black dot is a mandatory role constraint: **each** Employee has **at least one** EmpNr. The arrow-tipped bar over the left role is a uniqueness constraint: each instance in its associated column appears there only once (i.e., **each** Employee has **at most one** EmpNr). The uniqueness constraint on the right role indicates that each employee number refers to at most one employee. Hence the reference type provides an injection (mandatory, 1:1-into mapping) from Employee to EmpNr. The sample population clarifies the 1:1 property.

In a relational implementation, we might use the primary reference scheme to provide value-based identity, or instead use row ids (system-generated tuple identifiers). In an object-oriented implementation we might use oids (hidden, system-generated object identifiers). Such choices can be added later as annotations to the model. For analysis and validation purposes, however, we need to ensure that humans have a way to identify objects in their normal communication. It is the responsibility of humans (not the system) to enforce constraints on primary reference types. Assuming humans do enforce the reference type constraints, the system may be used to enforce fact type constraints.

UML classifies instances into objects and data values. UML *objects* basically correspond to ORM entities, but are assumed to be identified by oids. UML *data values* basically correspond to ORM values: they are constants (e.g., character strings or numbers) and hence require no oids to establish their identity. Entity types in UML are called *classes,* and value types are called *data types.* Note that "object" means "object instance", not "object type". A relationship instance in UML is called a *link,* and a relationship type is called an *association.*

Because of its reliance on oids, UML does not require entities to have a value-based reference scheme. This ignores the real-world database application requirement that humans have a verbal way of identifying objects. It is important therefore to include value-based reference in any UML class diagram intended to capture all the conceptual semantics about a class. To do this, we often need to introduce nonstandard extensions to the UML notation, as seen in the following example.

Like other ER notations, UML allows relationships to be modeled as attributes. For instance, in Figure 9.3(b) the Employee class has eight attributes. Classes in UML are depicted as a named rectangle, optionally including other compartments for attributes and operations. The corresponding ORM diagram is shown in Figure 9.3(a). ORM models the world in terms of just objects and roles, and hence has only one data structure—the relationship type. This is a fundamental difference between ORM and UML (and ER for that matter). Wherever an attribute is used in UML, ORM uses a relationship instead. In consequence, ORM diagrams are often larger than corresponding UML or ER diagrams, as Figure 9.3 illustrates. But this is a small price to pay for the resulting benefits. Before discussing these advantages, let's see how to translate between the relevant notations.

The ORM model indicates that employees are identified by their employee numbers. The top three mandatory role constraints indicate that every employee in the database must have a name, title, and sex. The circled black dot connecting two roles is a disjunctive mandatory role (or inclusive-or) constraint, indicating that these roles are collectively mandatory (each employee has a social security number or passport number or both).

In UML, *attributes are mandatory by default.* In the ORM model, the unary predicate "smokes" is optional (not everybody has to smoke). UML does not support unary relationships, so it models this instead as the Boolean attribute "isSmoker". In UML the domain of any attribute may optionally be displayed after it (preceded by a colon). In this example, the domain is displayed only for the isSmoker attribute. By default, ORM tools usually take a closed-world approach to unaries, which agrees with the

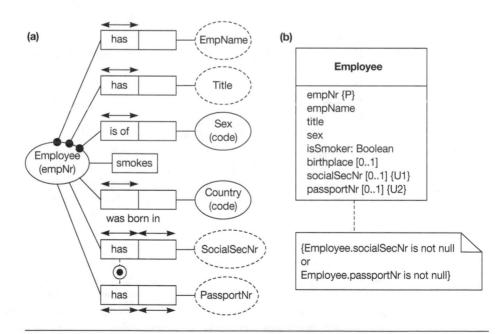

Figure 9.3 ORM relationship types (a) depicted as attributes in UML (b).

isSmoker attribute being mandatory. The ORM model also indicates that Sex and Country are identified by codes (rather than names, say). We could convey some of this detail in the UML diagram by appending domain names. For example, "Sexcode" and "Countrycode" could be appended after "sex:" and "birthplace:" to provide syntactic domains.

In the ORM model it is *optional* whether we record birthplace, social security number, or passport number. This is captured in UML by appending [0..1] after the attribute name (each employee has 0 or 1 birthplace and 0 or 1 social security number). This is an example of an *attribute multiplicity constraint*. UML does not have a graphic notation for disjunctive mandatory roles, so this kind of constraint needs to be expressed textually in an attached note, as in Figure 9.3(b). Such *textual constraints* may be expressed informally or in some formal language interpretable by a tool. In the latter case, the constraint is placed in *braces*. Although UML provides the Object Constraint Language (OCL) for this purpose, it does not mandate its use, allowing users to pick their own language (even programming code). This of course weakens the portability of the model. Moreover, the readability of the constraint is typically poor compared with the ORM verbalization (**each** Employee has **a** SocialSecNr **or** has **a** PassportNr).

The uniqueness constraints over the left-hand roles in the ORM model (including the EmpNr reference scheme shown explicitly earlier) indicate that each employee has at most one employee number, employee name, title, sex, country of birth, social security number, and passport number. Unary predicates have an implicit uniqueness constraint, so each employee instantiates the smokes role at most once (for any given state of the database). All these uniqueness constraints are implicitly captured in the UML model, where *attributes are single valued by default* (multivalued attributes are discussed later).

The uniqueness constraints on the right-hand roles (including the EmpNr reference scheme) indicate that each employee number, social security number, and passport number refers to at most one employee. UML does not have a standard graphic notation for these *attribute uniqueness constraints*. It suggests that boldface could be used for this (or other purposes) as a tool extension, but clearly this is not portable. I've chosen my own notation for this, appending textual constraints in braces after the attribute names (P = primary identifier, U = unique, with numbers appended if needed to disambiguate cases where the same U constraint might apply to a combination of attributes). The use of "P" here does not imply the model must be implemented in a relational database using value-based primary keys; it merely indicates a primary identification scheme that may be used in human communication.

Because UML does not provide standard graphic notations for such constraints, and it leaves it up to the modeler whether such constraints are specified, it is perhaps not surprising that many UML models in practice simply leave such constraints out.

Now that we've seen how single-valued attributes are modeled in UML, let's briefly see why ORM refuses to use them in its base modeling. The main reasons may be summarized thus:

- Attribute-free models are more stable.
- Attribute-free queries are more stable.
- Attribute-free models are easy to populate with multiple instances.

- Attribute-free models facilitate verbalization in sentences.
- Attribute-free models highlight connectedness through semantic domains.
- Attribute-free models are simpler and more uniform.
- Attribute-free models make it easier to specify constraints.
- Attribute-free models avoid arbitrary modeling decisions.
- Attribute-free models may be used to derive attribute views when desired.

Let's begin with semantic stability. ORM models and queries are inherently more stable because they are free of changes caused by attributes evolving into entities or relationships, or vice versa. Consider the ORM fact type Employee was born in Country. In ER and OO approaches, we might model this using a birthplace attribute. If we later decide to record the population of a country, then we need to introduce Country as an entity type. In UML, the connection between birthplace and Country is now unclear. Partly to clarify this connection, we would probably reformulate our birthplace attribute as an association between Employee and Country. This is a significant change to our model. Moreover, any object-based queries or code that referenced the birthplace attribute would also need to be reformulated.

Another reason for introducing a Country class is to enable a listing of countries to be stored, identified by their country codes, without requiring all of these countries to participate in a fact. To do this in ORM, we simply declare the Country type to be independent. The object type Country may be populated by a reference table that contains those country codes of interest (e.g., 'AU' denotes Australia).

A typical counterargument is this: "Good ER or OO modelers would declare country as an object type in the first place, anticipating the need to later record something about it, or to maintain a reference list; on the other hand, features such as the title and sex of a person clearly are things that will never have other properties, and hence are best modeled as attributes". This attempted rebuttal is flawed. In general, you can't be sure about what kinds of information you might want to record later, or about how important some feature of your model will become. Even in the title and sex case, a complete model should include a relationship type to indicate which titles are restricted to which sex (e.g., "Mrs.", "Miss", "Ms.", and "Lady" apply only to the female sex). In ORM this kind of constraint can be captured graphically as a join-subset constraint between the relevant fact types, or textually as a constraint in a formal ORM language (e.g., **if** Person$_1$ has **a** Title **that** is restricted to Sex$_1$ **then** Person$_1$ is of Sex$_1$). In contrast, attribute usage hinders expression of the relevant restriction association (try expressing and populating this rule in UML).

An ORM model is essentially a connected network of object types and relationship types. The object types are the semantic domains that glue things together and are always visible. This *connectedness* reveals relevant detail and enables ORM models to be queried directly, using traversal through object types to perform conceptual joins. For example, to list the employees born in a country with a population below 10 million, we simply say: **list each** Employee **who** was born in **a** Country **that** has **a** Population < 10000000.

Avoiding attributes also leads to greater simplicity and uniformity. For example, we don't need notations to reformulate constraints on relationships into constraints on attributes or between attributes and relationships. Another reason is to minimize arbitrary modeling choices (even experienced modelers sometimes disagree about whether to model some feature as an attribute or relationship).

ORM sentence types (and constraints) may be specified either textually or graphically. Both are formal and can be automatically transformed into the other. In an ORM diagram, since a predicate appears as a named, linear sequence of one or more role boxes, fact types may be conveniently populated with fact tables holding multiple fact instances, one column for each role. This allows all fact types and constraints to be validated by verbalization as well as sample populations. Communication between modeler and domain expert can thus take place in a familiar language, backed up by population checks. The practical value of these validation checks is considerable, especially since many clients find it much easier to work with instances rather than types. As discussed later, attributes and UML-style associations make it harder to populate models with multiple instances and often lead to unnatural verbalization.

For summary purposes, ORM includes algorithms for dynamically generating ER-style diagrams as attribute views. These algorithms assign different levels of importance to object types depending on their current roles and constraints, redisplaying minor fact types as attributes of the major object types. Modeling and maintenance are iterative processes. The importance of a feature can change with time as we discover more of the global model, and the application being modeled itself changes. To promote semantic stability, ORM makes no commitment to relative importance in its base models, instead supporting this dynamically through views. Elementary facts are the fundamental conceptual units of information and are uniformly represented as relationships. How they are grouped into structures is not a conceptual issue.

In short, you can have your cake and eat it too, by using ORM for analysis, and if you want to work with UML class diagrams, you can use your ORM models to derive them.

9.3   Multivalued Attributes

Suppose that we are interested in the names of employees, as well as the sports they play (if any). In ORM, we might model this as shown in Figure 9.4(a). The mandatory role dot indicates that each employee has a name. The absence of a mandatory role dot on the first role of the Plays fact type indicates that this role is optional (it is possible that some employee plays no sport). Since an employee may play many sports, and a sport may be played by many employees, Plays is a *many-to-many* (*m:n*) relationship type. This is shown in ORM by the uniqueness constraint spanning both roles. Visually, this indicates that each employee-sport pair can occur on at most one row of the associated fact table. Read from left to right, the EmpName relationship type is *many-to-one* (*n:1*), since employees have at most one name, but the same name may refer to many employees.

One way of modeling the same situation in UML is shown in Figure 9.4(b). Here the information about who plays what sport is modeled as the *multivalued attribute* "sports". The "[0..*]" appended to this attribute is a *multiplicity constraint* indicating

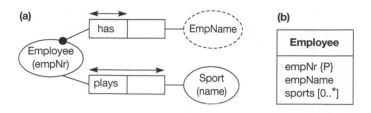

Figure 9.4 Plays depicted as (a) ORM *m:n* fact type and (b) UML multivalued attribute.

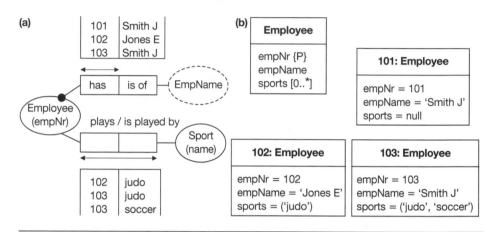

Figure 9.5 Populated models in (a) ORM and (b) UML.

how many sports may be entered here for each employee. The "0" indicates that it is possible that no sports might be entered for some employee. Unfortunately, the UML standard uses a *null value* for this case, just like the relational model. The presence of nulls in the base UML model exposes users to implementation rather than conceptual issues, and adds considerable complexity to the semantics of queries. By restricting its base structures to elementary fact types, ORM avoids the notion of null values, enabling users to understand models and queries in terms of simple two-valued logic. The "*" in "[0..*]" indicates there is *no upper bound* on the number of sports of a single employee. In other words, an employee may play many sports, and we don't care how many. If "*" is used without a lower bound, this is taken as an abbreviation for "0..*".

As mentioned earlier, an attribute with no explicit multiplicity constraint is assumed to be mandatory and single valued (exactly one). This can be depicted explicitly by appending "[1]" to the relevant attribute. For example, to indicate explicitly that each employee has exactly one name, we would use "empName [1]".

ORM constraints are easily clarified by populating the fact types with sample populations. For example, see Figure 9.5(a). The inclusion of all the employees in the EmpName fact table, and the absence of employee 101 in the Plays fact table, clearly show that playing sports is optional. Notice also how the uniqueness constraints mark out which column or column-combination values can occur on at most one row. In the EmpName fact table, the first column values are unique, but the second column includes duplicates. In the Plays table, each column contains duplicates; only the whole rows are unique. Such populations are very useful for checking constraints with the subject matter experts. This validation-via-example feature of ORM holds for all its constraints, not just mandatory roles and uniqueness, since all its constraints are role based, and each role corresponds to a fact table column.

Instead of using fact tables for the purposes of instantiation, UML provides *object diagrams*. These are essentially class diagrams in which each object is shown as a separate class instance, with data values supplied for its attributes. As a simple example, the population of Figure 9.5(a) may be displayed in a UML object diagram as shown in Figure 9.5(b). For simple cases like this, object diagrams are useful. However, they rapidly become unwieldy if we wish to display multiple instances for more complex cases. In contrast, fact tables scale easily to handle large and complex cases.

Let's look at a couple more examples involving multivalued attributes. At my former university, employees could apply for a permit to park on campus. The parking permit form required you to enter the license plate numbers of those cars (up to three) that you might want to park. A portable sticker was issued that could be transferred from one car to another. Over time, an employee may be issued different permits, and we want to maintain a historical record of this. Suppose that it is also a rule that an employee can be issued at most one parking permit on the same day. One way to model this situation in ORM is set out in Figure 9.6.

Here the circled "u" depicts the external uniqueness constraint that any given employee on any given date may be issued at most one parking permit. Notice also the "<= 3" next to the first role of the fact type ParkPermit-is-for-Car. This frequency constraint indicates that each permit in the fact column for that role appears there at most three times. In other words, each parking permit allows at most three cars to be parked on campus. In ORM, both uniqueness and frequency constraints may be applied to one or more roles, possibly from different predicates.

One way to model the same application in UML is shown in Figure 9.7. In addition to the ParkPermit class, Employee and Car classes are included. The "..." shown here

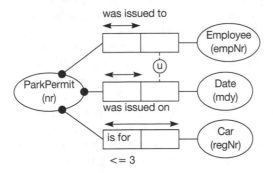

Figure 9.6 ORM diagram with external uniqueness and frequency constraints.

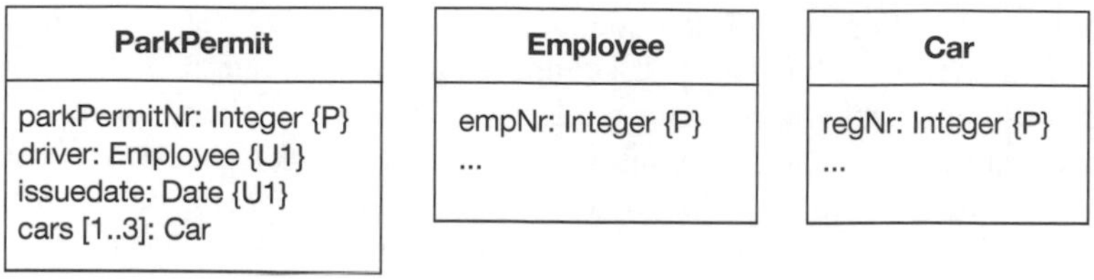

ParkPermit
parkPermitNr: Integer {P} driver: Employee {U1} issuedate: Date {U1} cars [1..3]: Car

Employee
empNr: Integer {P} ...

Car
regNr: Integer {P} ...

Figure 9.7 A UML alternative to the ORM model in Figure 9.6.

simply indicates that other attributes of these classes exist in the global schema (this use of "..." is not part of the UML notation). For discussion purposes, the attribute domains are displayed. In UML these domains are called "type expressions". Instead of defining a standard syntax for type expressions, UML allows them to be written in any implementation language, assuming the latter provides the relevant parser. For example, one type expression might be a C++ function pointer. To keep our analysis model at least semiconceptual, I've restricted type expressions to simple data types and classes. Data types are sets of pure values (no oids) and include primitive types (e.g., Integer, String) as well as enumeration types (including Boolean and user defined). In our example, the attribute domains include the data types Integer and Date, as well as the classes Employee and Car. By using classes as domains in this way, we can understand when an attribute corresponds to an association between entities, even if it is not displayed as such.

Constraints not included in the standard notation may be added in braces in some implementation language. In Figure 9.7 I've used "{P}" for "primary identifier" and "{U1}" on both driver and issuedate to indicate that this combination is unique. Taken together, the two "{U1}" annotations correspond to the ORM external uniqueness constraint in Figure 9.6. The "[1..3]" constraint on the cars attribute indicates that each parking permit is associated with at least one and at most three cars. The "at least one" part of this corresponds to an ORM mandatory role constraint, and the "at most three" corresponds to the "<= 3" ORM frequency constraint. Mandatory role constraints are separated out in ORM, mainly because they have *global* impact (each population instance of that type must play all the roles of that object type in the global schema). In contrast, other ORM constraints (e.g., frequency and uniqueness) are local, applying only to the population of the associated role(s).

As a final example of multivalued attributes, suppose that we wish to record the nicknames and colors of country flags. Let us agree to record at most two nicknames for any given flag, and that nicknames apply to only one flag. For example, "Old Glory" and perhaps "The Star-Spangled Banner" might be used as nicknames for the U.S. flag. Flags have at least one color. Figure 9.8(a) shows one way to model this in ORM. For verbalization we identify each flag by its country. Since country is an entity type, the reference scheme is shown explicitly (reference modes may abbreviate reference schemes only when the referencing type is a value type). The "<= 2" frequency constraint indicates that each flag has at most two nicknames, and the uniqueness constraint on the role of NickName indicates that each nickname refers to at most one flag.

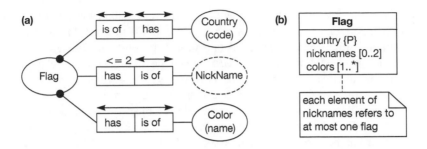

Figure 9.8 A flag model in (a) ORM and (b) UML.

Figure 9.8(b) shows one way of modeling this in UML. The "[0..2]" indicates that each flag has at most two (from zero to two) nicknames. The ["1..*] declares that a flag has one or more colors. An additional constraint is needed to ensure that each nickname refers to at most one flag. A simple attribute uniqueness constraint (e.g., {U1}) is not enough, since nicknames is set valued. Not only must each nicknames set be unique for each flag, but each element in each set must be unique (the second condition implies the former). This more complex constraint is specified formally in an attached note.

Here the attribute domains are hidden. Nickname elements would typically have a data type domain (e.g., String). If we don't store other information about countries or colors, we might choose String as the domain for country and color as well (although this is subconceptual because real countries and colors are not character strings). However, since we might want to add information about these later, it's better to use classes for their domains (e.g., Country and Color). If we do this, we need to define the classes as well, as in our previous example.

UML gives us the choice of modeling a feature as an attribute or an association. For conceptual analysis and querying, explicit associations usually have many advantages over attributes, especially multivalued attributes. This choice helps us verbalize, visualize, and populate the associations. It also enables us to express various constraints involving the "role played by the attribute" in standard notation, rather than resorting to some nonstandard extension (e.g., our braced comments). This applies not only to simple uniqueness constraints (as discussed earlier) but also to other kinds of constraints (frequency, subset, exclusion, etc.) over one or more roles that include the role played by the attribute's domain (in the implicit association corresponding to the attribute).

For example, if the association Flag is of Country is explicitly depicted in UML, the constraint that each country has at most one flag can be captured by adding a multiplicity constraint of "0..1" on the left role of this association. Although country and color are naturally conceived as classes, nickname would normally be construed as a data type (e.g., a subtype of String). Although associations in UML may include data types (not just classes), this is somewhat awkward, so in UML, nicknames might best be left as a multivalued attribute. Of course, we could model it cleanly in ORM first.

Another reason for favoring associations over attributes is stability. If ever we want to talk about a relationship, it is possible in both ORM and UML to make an object out of it and simply attach the new details to it. If instead we modeled the feature as an attribute, we would not be able to add the new details without first changing our original schema; in effect, we would need to first replace the attribute by an association. For example, consider the association Employee plays Sport in Figure 9.4(a). If we need to record a skill level for this play, we can simply objectify this association as Play and attach the fact type Play has SkillLevel. A similar move can be made in UML if the play feature has been modeled as an association. In Figure 9.4(b), however, this feature is modeled as the sports attribute, so this attribute needs to be removed and replaced by the equivalent association before we can add the new details about skill level. The notion of objectified relationship types or association classes is covered in the next section.

Another problem with multivalued attributes is that queries on them need some way to extract the components, and hence complicate the query process for users. As a trivial example, compare queries Q1 and Q2 expressed in ConQuer (an ORM query language) with their counterparts in OQL (the object query language proposed by the ODMG):

(Q1)   **List each** Color **that** is of Flag 'USA'.
(Q2)   **List each** Flag **that** has Color 'red'.

(Q1a)   **select** x.colors **from** x **in** Flag **where** x.country = "USA"
(Q2a)   **select** x.country **from** x **in** Flag **where** "red" **in** x.colors

Although this example is trivial, the use of multivalued attributes in more complex structures can make it harder for users to express their requirements.

For such reasons, multivalued attributes should normally be avoided in analysis models, especially if the attributes are based on classes rather than data types. If we avoid multivalued attributes in our conceptual model, we can still use them in the actual implementation. Both ORM and UML allow schemas to be annotated with instructions to override the default actions of whatever mapper is used to transform the schema to an actual implementation. For example, the ORM schema in Figure 9.8 (a) can be prepared for mapping by annotating the roles played by NickName and Color to map as sets inside the mapped Flag structure. Such annotations are not a conceptual issue and can be postponed till mapping.

9.4   Associations

UML uses Boolean attributes instead of unary relationships, but allows relationships of all other arities. Each association may be given at most one name, and this is optional. Association names are normally shown in italics, starting with a capital letter. Binary associations are depicted as *lines* between classes. Association lines may include elbows to assist with layout or when needed (e.g., for ring relationships). Association roles appear simply as line ends instead of boxes, but may optionally be given rolenames. Once added, rolenames may not be suppressed. Verbalization into sentences is possible only for infix binaries, and then only by naming the association with a predicate name (e.g., "Employs") and using an optional marker "▶" to denote the direction.

Figure 9.9 depicts two binary associations in both UML and ORM. On the UML diagram, the association names, their directional markers, and all the role names are displayed. All of these could have been omitted. To avoid ambiguity, however, either the directed association name or the rolenames should be shown. In the ORM diagram, both forward and inverse predicate names are shown; at most one of these may be omitted. Rolenames are not normally displayed on the ORM diagram but may be added elsewhere (e.g., on a predicate property sheet).

Ternary and higher arity associations in UML are depicted as a *diamond* connected by lines to the classes, as shown in Figure 9.10(a). Because many lines are used to denote the association, directional verbalization is ruled out, so the diagram can't be used to communicate in terms of sentences. This nonlinear layout also often makes it impractical to conveniently populate associations with multiple instances, unless we use rolenames for column names. Add to this the impracticality of displaying multiple populations of attributes, and it is clear that class diagrams are of little use for population checks.

As discussed earlier, UML does provide *object diagrams* for instantiation, but these are convenient only for populating associations with a *single* instance. Adding multiple instances leads to a mess (e.g., Blaha and Premerlani 1998, p. 31). Hence, as noted in the UML Notation Guide, "the use of object diagrams is fairly limited".

The previous section discussed how UML depicts *multiplicity constraints* on attributes. A similar notation is used for associations, where the relevant multiplicities are written beside the relevant roles. Figure 9.11(a) adds the relevant multiplicity constraints to Figure 9.9(a). A "*" abbreviates "0..*", meaning "zero or more", "1" abbreviates "1..1", meaning "exactly one", and "0..1" means "at most one". UML places

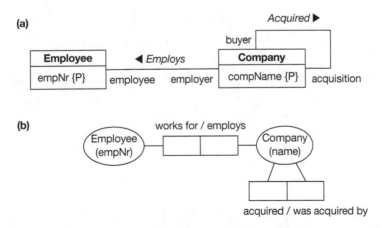

Figure 9.9 Binary associations in (a) UML and (b) ORM.

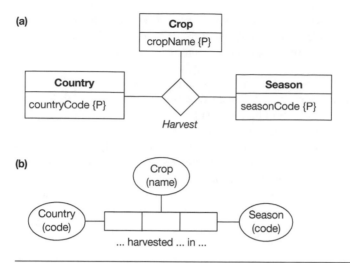

Figure 9.10 A ternary association in (a) UML and (b) ORM.

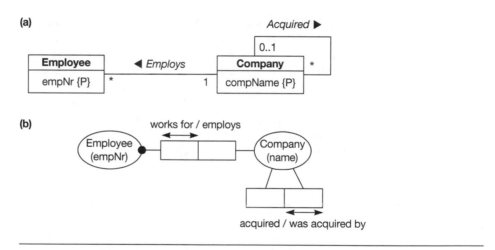

Figure 9.11 UML multiplicity constraints (a) and equivalent ORM constraints (b).

each multiplicity constraint on the "far role", in the direction in which the association is read. Hence the constraints in this example mean "each company employs zero or more employees"; "each employee is employed by exactly one company"; "each company acquired zero or more companies"; and "each company was acquired by at most one company".

The corresponding ORM constraints are depicted in Figure 9.11(b). Recall that multiplicity covers both cardinality (frequency) and optionality. Here the mandatory role constraint indicates that each employee works for at least one company, and the uniqueness constraints indicate that each employee works for at most one company, and each company was acquired by at most one company. As usual, the ORM notation facilitates verbalization and population. Microsoft's ORM tool allows these constraints to be entered graphically, by answering multiplicity questions, or by induction from sample populations, and it can automatically verbalize the constraints.

For binary associations, there are four possible uniqueness constraint patterns (n:1, 1:n, 1:1, m:n) and four possible mandatory role patterns (only the left role mandatory, only the right role mandatory, both roles mandatory, both roles optional). Hence if we restrict ourselves to a maximum frequency of one, there are 16 possible multiplicity combinations for binary associations. The first eight of these are shown in Figure 9.12, covering the cases where the second role is optional. The other eight cases, shown in Figure 9.13, cover the situation where the second role is mandatory.

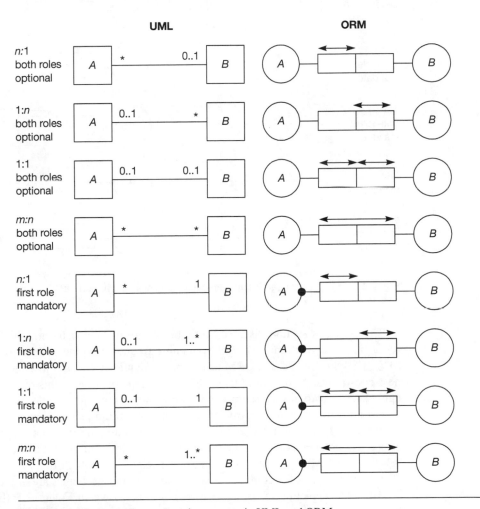

Figure 9.12 Equivalent constraint patterns in UML and ORM.

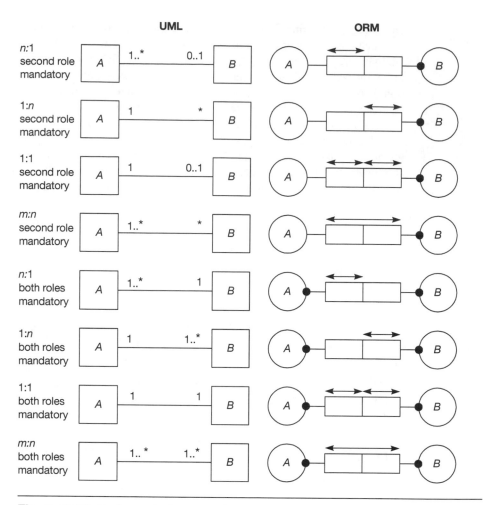

Figure 9.13 Further equivalent constraint patterns in UML and ORM.

The previous section discussed attribute multiplicity constraints involving occur-rence frequency lists and/or ranges containing frequencies other than zero or one (e.g., "1..7, 10"). For such cases, ORM uses general frequency constraints instead of unique-ness constraints. As discussed later, ORM is more expressive in this regard since it can apply such constraints to arbitrary collections of roles, not just single roles.

For an elementary n-ary association, each internal uniqueness constraint must span at least $n - 1$ roles. In UML, a multiplicity constraint on a role of an n-ary association effectively constrains the population of the other roles combined. For example, Figure 9.14(a) is a UML diagram for a ternary association in which both Room-Time and Time-Activity pairs are unique. For simplicity, reference schemes are omitted.

An ORM depiction of the same association is shown in Figure 9.14(b). The left-hand uniqueness constraint indicates that Room-Time is unique (i.e., for any given

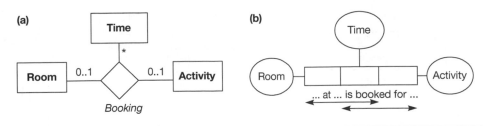

Figure 9.14 Constraints on a ternary in (a) UML and (b) ORM.

room and time, at most one activity is booked). The right-hand uniqueness constraint indicates that Time-Activity is unique (i.e., for any given time and activity, at most one room is booked). An extended version of this example was discussed in Section 1.2, where the ORM diagram better facilitated constraint checking by verbalization and population.

Because it covers some *n*-ary cases like this, UML's multiplicity constraint notation is richer than the optionality/cardinality notation of typical ER. However, there are many cases with *n*-ary associations where UML's multiplicity notation is incapable of capturing even a simple mandatory role constraint, or a minimum occurrence frequency constraint above one (Halpin 2000c). In contrast, ORM's mandatory, uniqueness, and frequency constraint notation can capture any possible constraint of this nature, on roles or role sequences, on predicates of any arity. So ORM is far richer in this regard.

Unlike many ER versions, both UML and ORM allow associations to be objectified as first class object types, *called association classes* in UML and *objectified associations* or *nested object types* in ORM. UML requires the same name to be used for the original association and the association class, impeding natural verbalization of at least one of these constructs. In contrast, ORM nesting is based on linguistic *nominalization* (a verb phrase is objectified by a noun phrase), thus allowing both to be verbalized naturally, with different names for each.

Although UML identifies an association class with its underlying association, it displays them separately, connected by a dashed line (see Figure 9.15). Each person may write many papers, and each paper is written by at least one person. Since authorship is *m:n*, the association class Writing has a primary reference scheme based on the combination of person and paper (e.g., the writing by person 'Norma Jones' of paper 33). The optional period attribute stores how long that person took to write that paper. Instead of distancing the objectified association from its underlying association, ORM intuitively envelops the association with an object type frame. Writing is marked independent (by the "!") to indicate that a writing object may exist, independently of whether we record its period. ORM displays Period as an object type, not an attribute, and includes its unit.

Objectified relationships in standard ORM must have at least two roles and must either have a single, spanning uniqueness constraint or be a 1:1 binary. A Dutch variant of ORM known as Fully Communication Oriented Information Modeling (FCO-IM) allows unaries to be objectified, but this adds no extra expressibility. UML allows any

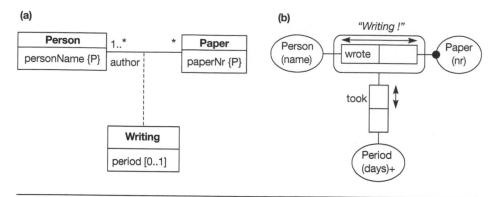

Figure 9.15 Writing is depicted as an objectified association in (a) UML and (b) ORM.

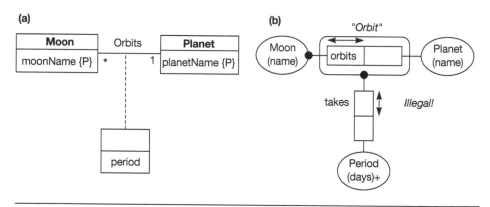

Figure 9.16 Objectification of *n:*1 associations is allowed in UML (a) but not ORM (b).

association (binary and above) to be objectified into a class, regardless of its multiplicity constraints. In particular, UML allows objectification of *n:*1 associations, unlike ORM (see Figure 9.16).

ORM currently forbids such cases, mainly to encourage modelers to conceptualize facts in elementary rather than compound form. For example, since each moon orbits only one planet, we can specify its orbital period without having to mention its planet. Hence ORM requires this case to be modeled using two separate fact types, as shown in Figure 9.17. This also facilitates removal/addition of mandatory role constraints on the fact types independently (e.g., the nested version has to be completely remodeled if we now decide to keep period facts mandatory but make planet facts optional).

However, if an experienced modeler aware of the implications still finds it easier to think about a situation as a nested *n:*1 association, there may be some argument for relaxing ORM's restriction, just as we relaxed it for 1:1 cases such as current marriage to avoid arbitrary decisions about relative importance. If enough people feel this way,

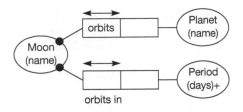

Figure 9.17 ORM models *n:*1 association classes as separate, elementary fact types.

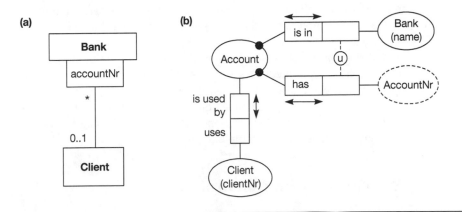

Figure 9.18 (a) Qualified association in UML and (b) coreferenced object type in ORM.

ORM could be relaxed to downgrade this error to a warning, and mapping algorithms would add a preprocessing step to reattach roles and adjust constraints internally.

Earlier we saw that UML has no graphic notation to capture ORM external uniqueness constraints across roles that are modeled as attributes in UML. Hence I introduced a {U*n*} notation to append textual constraints to the constrained attributes. Simple cases where ORM uses an external uniqueness constraint for *coreferencing* can also be modeled in UML using *qualified associations.* Here, instead of depicting the relevant ORM roles or object types as attributes, UML uses a class, adjacent to a *qualifier,* through which connection is made to the relevant association role. A qualifier in UML is a set of one or more attributes, whose values can be used to partition the class, and is depicted as a rectangular box enclosing its attributes. Figure 9.18 is based on an example from the official UML specification, along with the ORM counterpart.

Here each bank account is used by at most one client, and each client may use many accounts. In the UML model, the attribute accountNr is a qualifier on the association, effectively partitioning each bank into different accounts. In the ORM model, an Account object type is explicitly introduced and referenced by combining its bank with its (local) account number. The circled "u" may be replaced by a "P" for primary reference.

The UML notation is not only less clear, but less adaptable. For example, if we now want to record something about the account (e.g., its balance), we need to introduce an Account class, and the connection to accountNr is unclear. For a similar example, see Fowler (1997, p. 92, Figure 5.10), where product is used with Order to qualify an order line association; again, this is unfortunate, since we would normally introduce a Product class to record data about products, and relevant connections are then lost.

As a complicated example of this deficiency, see Blaha and Premerlani (1998, p. 51, Figure 3.14), where the semantic connection between Node and nodeName is lost. The problem can be solved in UML by using an association class instead, although this is not always natural. The use of qualified associations in UML is hard to motivate, but may be partly explained by their ability to capture some external uniqueness constraints in the standard notation, rather than rely on nonstandard textual notations (such as our {Un} notation).

ORM's concept of an external uniqueness constraint that may be applied to a set of roles in one or more predicates provides a simple, uniform way to capture all of UML's qualified associations and unique attribute combinations, as well as other cases not expressible in UML graphical notation (e.g., cases with $m{:}n$ predicates or long join paths). As always, the ORM notation has the further advantage of facilitating validation through verbalization and multiple instantiation.

9.5   Set-Comparison Constraints

Set-comparison constraints declare a subset, equality, or exclusion relationship between the populations of role sequences. This section compares support for these constraints in ORM and UML. A detailed discussion of these constraints in ORM can be found in Section 6.4.

ORM allows a *subset constraint* to be graphically specified between any pair of compatible role sequences by connecting them with a dashed arrow. This declares that the population of the source role sequence must always be a subset of the target role sequence (the one hit by the arrowhead). Each sequence may comprise one or more roles. These constraints have corresponding verbalizations. For example, in Figure 9.19 the subset constraint between single roles indicates that students have second names only if they have first names. The other subset constraint is between Student-Course role pairs and declares that students may pass tests in a course only if they enrolled in that course. Since the role of having a surname is mandatory for Student, subset constraints to it from all the other student roles are implied (and hence not shown).

As an extension mechanism, UML allows subset constraints to be specified between *whole associations* by attaching the constraint label "{subset}" next to a dashed arrow between the associations. For example, the subset constraint in Figure 9.20 indicates that any person who chairs a committee must be a member of that committee.

However, UML does not provide a graphic notation for subset constraints between single roles or between parts of associations. Hence, if a UML diagram depicted the relationship types in Figure 9.19 as associations, it would not be able to capture the subset constraints graphically.

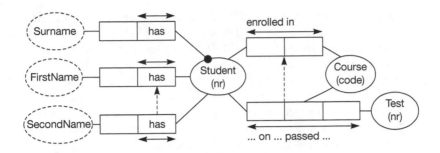

Figure 9.19 Subset constraints in ORM.

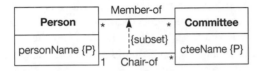

Figure 9.20 A subset constraint in UML.

However, other options are available in UML. For instance, if we model surname, firstName, and secondName as attributes of Person, we can express the single-role subset constraint by attaching a comment including the following textual constraint (see Figure 9.21):

Student.firstName **is not null or** Student.secondName **is null**

Although this does capture the subset constraint, it is at a lower level than ORM's graphic or verbalized form, and is basically the same as the check clause generated by an ORM tool when mapping the constraint down to a relational implementation.

One way in UML to capture the pair-subset constraint from Figure 9.19 is to transform the ternary into a binary association with a subset constraint to the enrollment association, and with a binary association to Test. A better solution is to use ORM's overlap algorithm (see Section 12.3) to objectify the enrollment association and associate this with Test. As discussed earlier, the equivalent UML action is to make a class out of enrollment (see Figure 9.21). Although in this situation an association class provides a good way to cater to a compound subset constraint, sometimes this nesting transformation leads to a very unnatural view of the world. Ideally the modeler should be able to view the world naturally, while having optimization transformations that reduce the clarity of the conceptual schema performed under the covers.

ORM has a mature formalization, including a rigorous theory of such topics as schema consistency, equivalence, and implication. UML has only recently been specified and is still undergoing revisions. Since formal guidelines for working with UML are somewhat immature, extra care is needed to avoid logical problems. As a simple example, look back at Figure 9.20, which comes directly from the UML specification, with reference schemes added. Do you spot anything confusing about the constraints?

You probably noticed the problem. The multiplicity constraint of 1 on the chair association indicates that each committee must have at least one chair. The subset constraint tells us that a chair of a committee must also be a member of that committee. Taken together, these constraints imply that each committee must have a member. Hence we would expect to see a multiplicity constraint of "1..*" (one or more) on the Person end of the membership association. However, we see a constraint of "*" (zero or more) instead, which at best is very misleading.

An ORM schema equivalent to Figure 9.20 is shown in Figure 9.22(a). The implied mandatory role constraint (each Committee includes at least one Person) is added explicitly in Figure 9.22(b). Which do you prefer?

Although display options for implied constraints may sometimes be a matter of taste, practical experience has shown that in cases like this it is better to show implied constraints explicitly rather than expect modelers or domain experts participating in the modeling process to figure them out for themselves. If you enter the schema of Figure 9.22(a) in Microsoft's ORM tool and attempt to build a database schema, the tool will

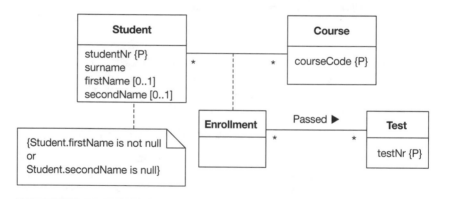

Figure 9.21 A UML version of the ORM schema in Figure 9.19.

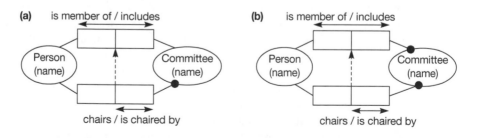

Figure 9.22 (a) Model with an implied mandatory role constraint; (b) model with mandatory role constraint shown explicitly.

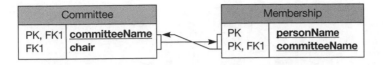

Figure 9.23 The relational schema mapped from the schema of Figure 9.22(b).

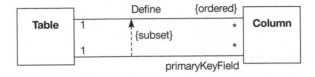

Figure 9.24 Spot anything wrong?

detect the misleading nature of the constraint pattern and ask you to resolve the problem. Human interaction is the best policy here, since there is more than one possible mistake (e.g., is the subset constraint correct or is the optional role correct?).

If the schema of Figure 9.22(b) is mapped to a relational database, it generates a referential cycle, since the mandatory fact types for Committee map to different tables (so each committee must appear in both tables). Referential cycles can be awkward to work with. Microsoft's ORM tool issues a warning in such a case, but still generates the code to cope with it. The relational schema is shown in Figure 9.23 (the arrows show the foreign key references, one simple and one composite, that correspond to the subset constraints). Relational mapping is covered in detail in the next chapter.

As another constraint example in UML, consider Figure 9.24, which is the UML version of an OMT diagram used in Blaha and Premerlani (1998, p. 68) to illustrate a subset constraint between associations. Can you spot any problems with the constraints?

There are some fairly obvious problems with the multiplicity constraints. For example, the "1" on the primary key association should be "0..1" (not all columns belong to primary keys), and the "*" on the define association should presumably be "1..*" (unless we allow tables to have no columns). Assuming that tables and columns are identified by oids or artificial identifiers, the subset constraint makes sense, but the model is arguably suboptimal since the primary key association and subset constraint could be replaced by a Boolean isaPKfield attribute on Column.

From an ORM perspective, heuristics lead us to initially model the situation using natural reference schemes as shown in Figure 9.25. Here ColName denotes the local name of the column in the table. I've simplified reality by assuming tables may be identified just by their name. The external uniqueness constraints suggest two natural reference schemes for Column: name plus table or position plus table. We can choose one of these as primary, or instead introduce an artificial identifier. The unary predicate indicates whether a column is, or is part of, a primary key. If desired, we could derive the

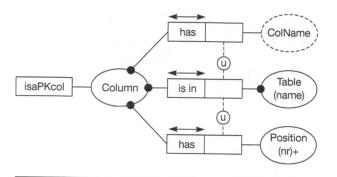

Figure 9.25   An ORM model for relational columns.

association Column is a primary key field of Table from the path Column is in Table **and** Column isaPKcol (the subset constraint from the previous model is then implied).

What is interesting about this example is not that the authors of the earlier model may have made some trivial errors with constraints (I've made slips of the pen like that myself), but rather the difference in modeling approaches. Most OMT and UML modelers seem to assume that oids will be used as identifiers in their initial modeling, whereas ORM modelers like to expose natural reference schemes right from the start, and populate their fact types accordingly. These different approaches often lead to different solutions. The main thing is to first come up with a solution that is natural and understandable to the domain expert because here is where the most critical phase of model validation should take place. Once a correct model has been determined, optimization guidelines can be used to enhance it.

One other feature of the example is worth mentioning. The UML solution in Figure 9.24 uses the annotation "{ordered}" to indicate that a table is comprised of an *ordered set* (i.e., a sequence with no duplicates) of columns. In the ORM community, a debate has been going on for several years on the best way to deal with constructors for collection types (e.g., set, bag, sequence, unique sequence) at the conceptual level. My view (and that of several other ORM researchers) is that such constructors should not appear in the base conceptual model; hence the use of Position in Figure 9.25 to convey column order (the uniqueness of the order is conveyed by the uniqueness constraint on Column has Position). Keeping fact types elementary has so many advantages (e.g., validation, constraint expression, flexibility, and simplicity) that it seems best to relegate constructors to derived views. I'll have more to say about collection types later.

In ORM, an *equality constraint* between two compatible role sequences is shorthand for two subset constraints (one in either direction) and is shown as a double-headed arrow. Such a constraint indicates that the populations of the role sequences must always be equal. If two roles played by an object type are mandatory, then an equality constraint between them is implied (and hence not shown).

As a simple example of an equality constraint, consider Figure 9.26. Here the equality constraint indicates that if a patient's systolic blood pressure is measured, so is his

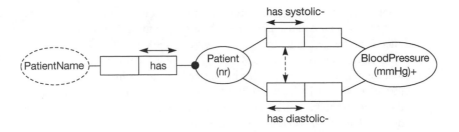

Figure 9.26 A simple equality constraint.

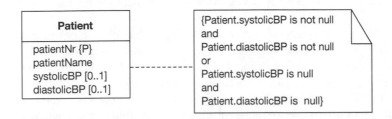

Figure 9.27 A simple equality constraint in UML.

or her diastolic blood pressure (and vice versa). In other words, either both measurements are taken or neither. This kind of constraint is fairly common. Less common are equality constraints between sequences of two or more roles.

UML has no graphic notation for equality constraints. For whole associations we could use two separate subset constraints, but this would be very messy. We could add a new notation, using "{equality}" beside a dashed arrow between the associations, but this notation would be unintuitive, since the direction of the arrow would have no significance (unlike the subset case).

In general, equality constraints in UML would normally be specified as textual constraints (in braced comments). For our current example, the two blood pressure readings may be modeled as attributes of Patient, and hence a textual constraint is attached to the Patient class as shown in Figure 9.27. This seems awkward, compared to the corresponding ORM constraint (graphic or verbalized).

Subset and equality constraints enable various classes of schema transformations to be stated in their most general form, and ORM's more general support for these constraints allows more transformations to be easily visualized (e.g., see the equivalence theorem PSG2 in Section 12.2).

Although UML does not include a graphic notation for a pure exclusion constraint, it does include an *exclusive-or constraint* to indicate that each instance of a class plays *exactly one* association role from a specified set of alternatives. To indicate the constraint, "{xor}" is placed beside a dashed line connecting the relevant associations.

Figure 9.28(a), which is based on an example from the UML specification, indicates that each account is used by a person or corporation, but not both. For simplicity, reference schemes and other constraints are omitted.

Prior to version 1.3 of UML, "{or}" was used for this constraint, which was misleading since "or" is typically interpreted in the inclusive sense. The equivalent ORM model is shown in Figure 9.28(b), where the exclusive-or constraint is simply an orthogonal combination of a disjunctive mandatory role (inclusive-or) constraint (black dot) and an exclusion constraint (circled "X").

Although the current wording of the UML specification describes the xor constraint as applying to a set of associations, we need to apply the constraint to a set of roles or association ends to avoid ambiguity in cases with multiple common classes. Visually this could be shown by attaching the dashed line near the relevant ends of the associations, as shown in Figure 9.29(a).

UML has no symbols for exclusion or disjunctive mandatory role constraints. If ever UML symbols for these constraints are considered, then "{x}" and "{or}", respectively, seem appropriate—this choice also exposes the composite nature of "{xor}". Even if such a proposal were accepted as a UML extension, this would capture only a fragment of ORM's expressive power in this area, since ORM's exclusion constraint applies not just to a set of roles, but a set of compatible role sequences, and hence is far more general than the kind of case considered here.

UML xor constraints apply between single roles. The current wording of the UML specification seems to imply that these roles must belong to different associations. If

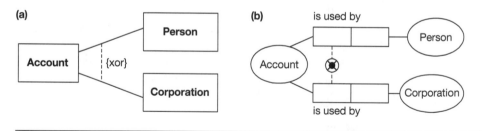

Figure 9.28 Exclusive-or: each account is used by a person or corporation, but not both.

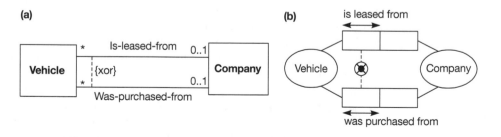

Figure 9.29 The exclusive-or constraint should apply between association roles.

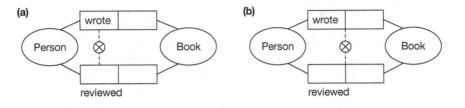

Figure 9.30 (a) Nobody wrote and reviewed a book; (b) nobody wrote and reviewed *the same* book.

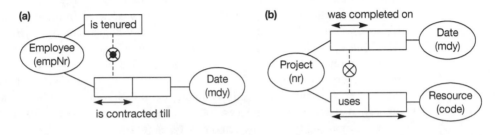

Figure 9.31 Some ORM examples that are awkward to capture in UML.

so, UML cannot use an xor constraint between roles of a ring fact type (e.g., between the husband and wife roles of a marriage association). ORM exclusion constraints cover this case, as well as many other cases not expressible in UML graphic notation. As a trivial example, consider the difference between the following two constraints: no person both wrote and reviewed a book; no person wrote and reviewed the same book. ORM clearly distinguishes these by noting the precise arguments of the constraint (see Figure 9.30).

The pair-exclusion constraint in Figure 9.30(b) can be expressed in UML by adding a comment box that includes a textual constraint written in some language (e.g., OCL), and connecting this by dotted lines to the two associations. However, this notation is both cluttered and nonstandard (since UML allows users to pick their own language to write textual constraints). One way to reduce the clutter would be to allow the display of textual constraints to be toggled on/off, so they are displayed only when desired.

UML has no graphic notation for exclusion between attributes or between attributes and associations. In Figure 9.31(a), the unary predicate may be modeled in UML as a Boolean attribute, and the contract predicate would normally be modeled as a contractDate attribute. In Figure 9.31(b), the completion predicate would be modeled in UML as a completionDate attribute of the Project class, while resource usage would normally be modeled as an association between Project and Resource classes. If we made these modeling choices in UML, we must resort to nonstandard notations or textual constraints to add exclusion constraints between attributes or between an attribute and an association. There are other ways to model these cases in UML (e.g., using subtypes) that offer more chance to capture the constraints graphically.

9.6   **Subtyping**

Both UML and ORM support *subtyping,* using substitutability ("is-a") semantics, where each instance of a subtype is also an instance of its supertype(s). For example, declaring Woman to be a subtype of Person entails that each woman is a person, and hence Woman inherits all the properties of Person. Given two object types, *A* and *B,* we say that *A* is a *subtype* of *B* if, for each state of the database, the population of *A* is included in the population of *B.* For data modeling, the only subtypes of interest are *proper* subtypes. We say that *A* is a proper subtype of *B* if and only if *A* is a subtype of *B,* and there is a possible state where the population of *B* includes an instance that is not in *A.* From now on, I'll use "subtype" as short for "proper subtype".

In both UML and ORM, *specialization* is the process of introducing subtypes, and *generalization* is the inverse procedure of introducing a supertype. Both UML and ORM allow single *inheritance* as well as multiple inheritance (where a subtype has more than one direct supertype). For example, AsianWoman may be a subtype of both AsianPerson and Woman. In UML, "subclass" and "superclass" are synonyms of "subtype" and "supertype", respectively, and generalization may also be applied to things other than classes (e.g., interfaces, use case actors, and packages). This section restricts its attention to subtyping between object types (classes).

In ORM, a subtype inherits all the roles of its supertypes. In UML, a subclass inherits all the attributes, associations, and operations/methods of its supertype(s). An operation implements a service and has a signature (name and formal parameters) and visibility, but may be realized in different ways. A method is an implementation of an operation, and hence includes both a signature and a body detailing an executable algorithm to perform the operation. In an inheritance graph, there may be many methods for the same operation (*polymorphism*), and scoping rules are used to determine which method is actually used for a given class. If a subclass has a method with the same signature as a method of one of its supertypes, this is used instead for that subclass (*overriding*). For example, if Rectangle and Triangle are subclasses of Shape, all three classes may have different methods for display(). This section focuses on data modeling, not behavior modeling, covering inheritance of static properties (attributes and associations), but ignoring inheritance of operations or methods.

Subtypes are used in data modeling to assert typing constraints, encourage reuse of model components, and show a classification scheme (taxonomy). In this context, typing constraints ensure that subtype-specific roles are played only by the relevant subtype. Both approaches use subtyping for reuse. Since a subtype inherits the properties of its supertype(s), only its specific roles need to be declared when it is introduced. Apart from reducing code duplication, the more generic supertypes are likely to find reuse in other applications. At the coding level, inheritance of operations/methods augments the reuse gained by inheritance of roles/attributes/associations. Using subtypes to show taxonomy is of little use, since taxonomy is often more efficiently captured by predicates. For example, the fact type Person is of Sex {male, female} implicitly provides the taxonomy for the subtypes MalePerson and FemalePerson.

Both UML and ORM display subtyping using *directed acyclic graphs* (DAGs). A directed graph is a graph of nodes with directed connections, and "acyclic" means there are no cycles (a consequence of proper subtyping). Figure 9.32 shows a subtype pattern in UML and ORM. An arrow from one node to another shows that the first is a subtype of the second. UML uses a thin arrow shaft with an open arrowhead, while ORM uses a solid shaft and arrowhead. As an alternative notation, UML also allows separate shafts to merge into one, with one arrowhead acting for all (e.g., *E* and *F* are subtypes of *C*).

Since subtypehood is transitive, indirect connections are omitted (e.g., since *E* is a subtype of *C* and *C* is a subtype of *A,* it follows that *E* is a subtype of *A,* so there is no need to display this implied connection).

UML includes four predefined constraints to indicate whether subtypes are exclusive or exhaustive. If subtype connections are shown with separate arrowheads, the constraints are placed in braces beside a dotted line connecting the subtype links, as in the top part of Figure 9.32(a). I assume this line may include elbows, as shown for the disjoint constraint—without elbows or a similar device, some cases can't be specified. If the subtype connections are shared, the constraints are placed near the shared arrowhead, as in the lower part of Figure 9.32(a). The key word "overlapping" indicates the subtypes overlap. The key word "disjoint" indicates the subtypes are mutually exclusive. Originally the key word "complete" simply meant that all subtypes had been declared, but this was redefined to mean total or exhaustive (i.e., the supertype equals the union of its subtypes). The key word "incomplete" means the supertype is more than the union of its subtypes. Other key words may be added by users.

By default, ORM subtypes may overlap, and subtypes need not collectively exhaust their supertype. ORM allows graphic constraints to indicate that subtypes are mutually exclusive (a circled "X" connected to the relevant subtype links), collectively exhaustive (a circled dot), or both (a circled, crossed dot), as shown in Figure 9.32(b). ORM's approach is that exclusion and totality constraints are enforced on populations, not types. For example, an overlapping "constraint" does not mean that the populations must overlap, just that they may overlap. Hence, from an ORM viewpoint, this is not really a constraint at all, so there is no need to depict it. Neither is explicit depiction of

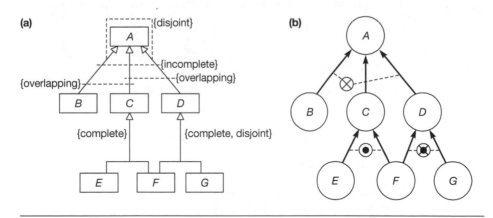

Figure 9.32 Subtyping displayed by directed acyclic graphs in (a) UML and (b) ORM.

exclusion and totality constraints needed in ORM, since these constraints are implied by other constraints in conjunction with formal subtype definitions.

For any subtype graph, the top supertype is called the *root,* and the bottom subtypes (those with no descendants) are called *leaves.* In UML this can be made explicit by adding "{root}" or "{leaf}" below the class name. If we know the whole subtype graph is shown, there is little point in doing this; but if we were to display only part of a subtype graph, this notation makes it clear whether or not the local top and bottom nodes are also like that in the global schema. For example, from Figure 9.33, we know that globally Customer has no supertype, and MalePerson and FemalePerson have no subtypes. Since Organization is not marked as a leaf node, it may have other subtypes not shown here.

UML also allows an ellipsis "..." in place of a subclass to indicate that at least one subclass of the parent exists in the global schema, but its display is suppressed on the diagram. Currently ORM does not include a root/leaf notation or an ellipsis notation for subtypes. Although a text box could be added to convey this information, this would merely be informal, so it may be worthwhile adding similar formal notations to ORM.

UML also distinguishes between *abstract* and *concrete* classes. An abstract class cannot have any direct instances and is shown by writing its name in italics or by adding "{abstract}" below the class name. Abstract classes are realized only through their descendants. Concrete classes may be directly instantiated. This distinction seems to have little relevance at the conceptual level and is not depicted explicitly in ORM. For code design, however, the distinction is important (e.g., abstract classes provide one way of declaring interfaces, and in C++ abstract operations correspond to pure virtual operations, while leaf operations map to nonvirtual operations). For further discussion of this topic, see Fowler (1997, pp. 85–88) and Booch et al. (1999, pp. 125–26).

Like other ER notations, UML provides only weak support for defining subtypes. A *discriminator* label may be placed near a subtype arrow to indicate the basis for the classification. For example, Figure 9.34 includes a "sex" discriminator to specialize Person into MalePerson and FemalePerson. The UML specification says that the discriminator names "a partition of the subtypes of the superclass". In formal work, the term "partition" usually implies the division is both exclusive and exhaustive. In UML,

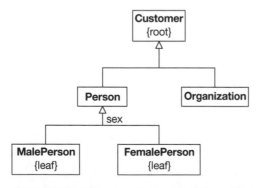

Figure 9.33 Organization may have other subtypes not shown here.

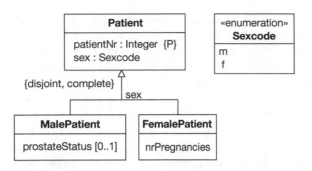

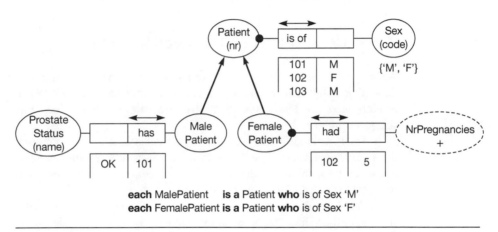

Figure 9.34 Sex is used as a discriminator to partition Patient.

each MalePatient   **is a** Patient **who** is of Sex 'M'
each FemalePatient **is a** Patient **who** is of Sex 'F'

Figure 9.35 With formal subtype definitions, subtype constraints are implied.

the use of a discriminator does not imply that the subtypes are exhaustive or complete, but at least some authors argue that they must be exclusive (Fowler 1997, p. 78). If that is the case, there does not appear to be any way in UML of declaring a discriminator for a set of overlapping subtypes. The same discriminator name may be repeated for multiple subclass arrows to show that each subclass belongs to the same classification scheme. This repetition can be avoided by merging the arrow shafts to end in a single arrowhead, as in Figure 9.34.

In Figure 9.34, the sex attribute of Patient is used as a discriminator. This attribute is based on the enumerated type Sexcode, which is defined using the stereotype «enumeration», and listing its values as attributes. By itself, this model fails to ensure that instances populating these subtypes have the correct sex. For example, there is nothing to stop us populating MalePatient with patients that have the value 'f' for their sexcode.

This error is allowed because the model hasn't formally related the subtypes back to their precise sex. ORM overcomes this problem by requiring that *formal subtype definitions* be declared for all subtypes. These definitions must refer to roles played by the supertype(s). The correct schema is shown in Figure 9.35, together with a satisfying population. Note that the ORM partition (exclusion and totality) constraint has been removed from the diagram since it is now implied by the combination of the subtype definitions and the three constraints on the fact type Patient is of Sex.

While the subtype definitions in Figure 9.35 are trivial, in practice more complicated subtype definitions are sometimes required. As a basic example, consider a schema with the fact types City is in Country, City has Population, and now define LargeUScity as follows: **each** LargeUScity **is a** City **that** is in Country 'US' **and** has Population > 1000000. There does not seem to be any convenient way of doing this in UML, at least not with discriminators. We could perhaps add a derived Boolean isLarge attribute, with an associated derivation rule in OCL, and then add a final subtype definition in OCL, but this would be less readable than the ORM definition above. For a more detailed discussion of subtyping in ORM, including the notion of context-dependent reference, see Section 6.5. Mapping of subtypes is discussed in the next chapter.

9.7   Other Constraints and Derivation Rules

A *value constraint* restricts the population of a value type to a finite set of values specified either in full (*enumeration*), by start and end values (*range*), or some combination of both (*mixture*). The values themselves are primitive data values, typically character strings or numbers.

In UML, enumeration types may be modeled as classes, stereotyped as enumerations, with their values listed (somewhat unintuitively) as attributes. Ranges and mixtures may be specified by declaring a textual constraint in braces, using any formal or informal language. For example, see Figure 9.36(a).

In ORM, a value constraint is shown by declaring the possible values in braces beside either the value type or an entity type with a reference mode. In the latter case, the constraint is understood to apply to the implicit value type. For example, in Figure 9.36 the constraints apply to Sexcode and RatingNr. Value constraints other than enumeration, range, and mixture may be declared in UML or ORM as textual constraints, for example, {committeeSize must be an odd number}. For further UML examples, see Rumbaugh et al. (1999, pp. 236, 268).

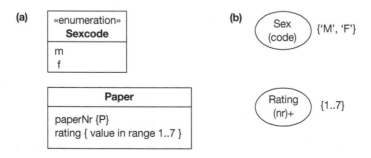

Figure 9.36 Data value restrictions declared as enumerations or textual constraints.

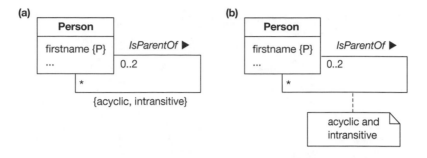

Figure 9.37 Ring constraints expressed as (a) textual constraints or (b) comments.

A ring fact type has at least two roles played by the same object type (either directly, or indirectly via a supertype). A *ring constraint* applies a logical restriction on the role pair. For example, the association Person is parent of Person might be declared acyclic and intransitive.

UML does not provide ring constraints built in, so the modeler needs to specify these as a textual constraint in some chosen language. In UML, if a textual constraint applies to just one model element (e.g., an association path), it may be added in braces beside that element, as in Figure 9.37(a).

It is the responsibility of the modeling tool to ensure the constraint is linked internally to the relevant model element and to interpret any textual constraint expressions. If the tool cannot interpret the constraint, it should be placed inside a note (dog-eared rectangle), without braces, showing that it is merely a comment, and explicitly linked to the relevant model element(s), as shown in Figure 9.37(b). ORM provides six built-in ring constraints: antisymmetric (^{o}ans), asymmetric (^{o}as), acyclic (^{o}ac), irreflexive (^{o}ir), intransitive (^{o}it), and symmetric (^{o}sym), which can be formally declared by writing them beside the relevant role pair (Section 7.3 has examples).

A *join constraint* applies to one or more role sequences, at least one of which is projected from a path from one predicate through an object type to another predicate. The act of passing from one role through an object type to another role invokes a conceptual join, since the same object instance is asserted to play both the roles. Although join constraints arise frequently in real applications, UML has no graphic symbol for them. To declare them on a UML diagram, write a constraint or comment in a note attached to the model elements involved. For example, Figure 9.38 links a comment to three associations. This example is based on a room-scheduling application at a university with built-in facilities in various lecture and tutorial rooms. Example facility codes are PA = personal address system, DP = data projection facility, INT = Internet access.

ORM provides deep support for join constraints. An external uniqueness constraint is one simple example. Role sequences featuring as arguments in set-comparison constraints may also arise from projections over a join path. For example, in Figure 9.39, the subset constraint runs from the Room-Facility role pair projected from the path Room at **a** Time is booked for **an** Activity **that** requires **a** Facility. This path includes a

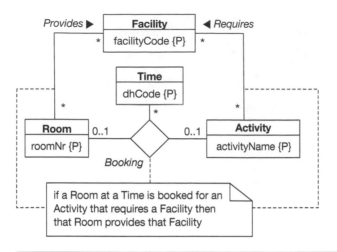

Figure 9.38 Join constraint specified as a comment in UML.

conceptual join on Activity. The constraint may be formally verbalized as **if a** Room at **a** Time is booked for **an** Activity **that** requires **a** Facility **then that** Room provides **that** Facility. Figure 9.39 includes a satisfying population for the three fact types. This again illustrates how ORM facilitates validation constraints via sample populations. The UML associations in Figure 9.38 are not so easily populated on the diagram.

As another example, consider the Employee class shown in Figure 9.40(a). This is nice and compact, but it makes it hard to express the business rule that some titles determine sex (e.g., "Lady" applies only to females). In ORM this can be captured by a populated join-subset constraint as shown in Figure 9.40(b). In ConQuer, this constraint verbalizes as **if** $Person_1$ has **a** Title **that** determines Sex_1 **then** $Person_1$ is of Sex_1.

As an example of a join-exclusion constraint, consider the following rule from a conference paper review application: **no** Person **who** works at **an** Institute **that** employs **a** Person **who** wrote **a** Paper reviews **that** Paper. As discussed later, subset and equality constraints also provide one way of specifying derivation rules.

In UML, the term *aggregation* is used to describe a *whole/part relationship.* For example, a team of people is an aggregate of its members, so this membership may be modeled as an aggregation association between Team and Person. Several different forms of aggregation might be distinguished in real-world cases. For example, Jim Odell and Conrad Bock discuss the following six varieties of aggregation: component-integral, material-object, portion-object, place-area, member-bunch, and member-partnership (Martin and Odell 1998, Chapter 18; Odell 1998, pp. 137–65).

Currently, UML associations are classified into one of three kinds: ordinary association (no aggregation), shared (or simple) aggregation, and composite (or strong) aggregation. Hence UML recognizes only two varieties of aggregation: shared and composite. Although early planning for UML 2.0 foreshadows further kinds of aggregation being introduced, I'll consider only shared and composite aggregation here. Some

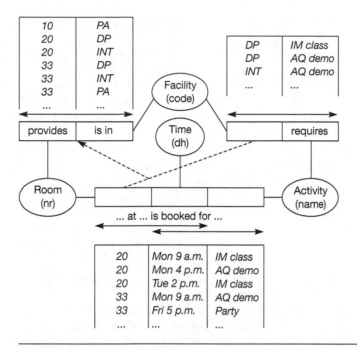

Figure 9.39 A join-subset constraint in ORM.

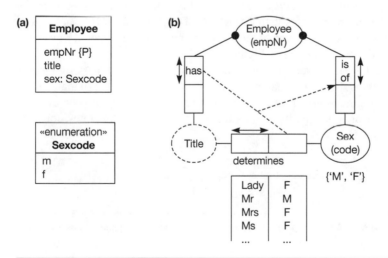

Figure 9.40 ORM makes it easy to capture the constraint between title and sex.

versions of ER include an aggregation symbol (typically only one kind). ORM, as well as many versions of ER, includes no special symbols for aggregation.

These different stances with respect to aggregation are somewhat reminiscent of the different modeling positions with respect to null values. Although over 20 kinds of null have been distinguished in the literature, the relational model recognizes only one kind of null, Codd's version 2 of the relational model proposes two kinds of null, and ORM argues that nulls have no place in base conceptual models (because all its base facts are elementary). But let's return to the topic at hand.

Shared aggregation is denoted in UML as a binary association, with a *hollow diamond* at the "whole" or "aggregate" end of the association. *Composition* (*composite aggregation*) is depicted with a *filled diamond*. For example, Figure 9.41 depicts a composition association from Club to Team and a shared aggregation association from Team to Person.

In ORM, which has no special notation for aggregation, this situation would be modeled as shown in Figure 9.42. Does Figure 9.41 convey any extra semantics, not captured in Figure 9.42? At the conceptual level, it is doubtful whether there is any additional useful semantics. At the implementation level, however, there is additional semantics. Let's discuss this in more detail.

The UML specification declares that "both kinds of aggregation define a transitive ... relationship". The use of "transitive" here is somewhat misleading, since it refers to indirect aggregation associations rather than base aggregation associations. For example, if Club is an aggregate of Team, and Team is an aggregate of Person, it follows that Club is an aggregate of Person. However, if we wanted to discuss this result, it should be exposed as a *derived association*. In UML, derived associations are indicated by prefixing their names with a *slash* "/". The *derivation rule* can be expressed as a constraint, either connected to the association by a dependency arrow or simply placed beside the association as in Figure 9.43.

In ORM, derived fact types may be diagrammed by marking them with an asterisk, and derivation rules may be specified in an ORM textual language such as ConQuer (see Figure 9.44). In many cases, derivation rules may also be diagrammed as a join-subset or join-equality constraint. As this example illustrates, the derived transitivity

Figure 9.41 Composition (composite aggregation) and shared aggregation in UML.

Figure 9.42 The Figure 9.41 example modeled in ORM.

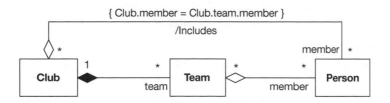

Figure 9.43 A derived aggregation in UML.

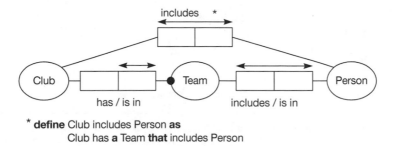

Figure 9.44 The derived aggregation of Figure 9.43 modeled in ORM.

of aggregations can be captured in ORM without needing a special notation for aggregation.

The UML specification declares that "both kinds of aggregation define a transitive, antisymmetric relationship (i.e., the instances from a directed, noncyclic graph)". Recall that a relation R is antisymmetric if and only if, for all x and y, if x is not equal to y, then xRy implies that yRx. It would have been better to simply state that paths of aggregations must be acyclic.

At any rate, this rule is designed to stop errors such as that shown in Figure 9.45. If a person is part of a team, and a team is part of a club, it doesn't make sense to say that a club is part of a person.

Since ORM does not specify whether an association is an aggregation, illegal diagrams like this can't occur in ORM. Of course, it is possible for an ORM modeler to make a silly mistake by adding an association such as Club is part of Person, where "is part of" is informally understood in the aggregation sense, and this would not be formally detectable. But avoidance of such a bizarre occurrence doesn't seem to be a compelling reason to add aggregation to ORM's formal notation. There are plenty of associations between Club and Person that do make sense and plenty that don't. In some cases, however, it is important to assert constraints such as acyclicity, and this is handled in ORM by ring constraints.

Composition does add some important semantics to shared aggregation. To begin with, it requires that each part belongs to at most one whole at a time. In ORM, this is captured by adding a uniqueness constraint to the role played by the part (e.g., see the

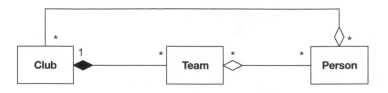

Figure 9.45 Illegal UML model. Aggregations should not form a cycle.

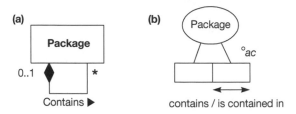

Figure 9.46 Direct containment modeled in (a) UML and (b) ORM.

role played by Team in Figure 9.42). In UML, the multiplicity at the whole end of the association must be 1 or 0..1. If the multiplicity is 1 (as in Figure 9.41), the role played by the part is both unique and mandatory (as in Figure 9.42).

As an example where the multiplicity is 0..1 (i.e., where a part optionally belongs to a whole), consider the ring fact type of Figure 9.46: Package contains Package. Here "contains" is used in the sense of "directly contains". The UML specification notes that "composition instances form a strict tree (or rather a forest)". This strengthening from directed acyclic graph to tree is an immediate consequence of the functional nature of the association (each part belongs to at most one whole), and hence ORM requires no additional notation for this. In this example, the ORM model explicitly includes an acyclic constraint. This direct containment association is intransitive by implication (acyclicity implies irreflexivity, and any functional, irreflexive association is intransitive).

UML allows some alternative notations for aggregation. If a class is an aggregate of more than one class, the association lines may be shown joined to a single diamond, as in Figure 9.47(a). For composition, the part classes may be shown nested inside the whole by using rolenames, and multiplicities of components may be shown in the top right-hand corners, as in Figure 9.47(b).

Some authors list kinds of association that are easily confused with aggregation but should not be modeled as such—for example, topological inclusion, classification inclusion, attribution, attachment, and ownership (Martin and Odell 1998; Odell 1998). For example, Finger belongs to Hand is an aggregation, but Ring belongs to Finger is not. There is some disagreement among authors about what should be included on this list. For example, attribution is treated by some as a special case of aggregation,

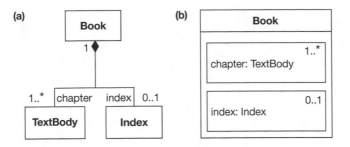

Figure 9.47 Alternative UML notations for aggregation.

namely, a composition between a class and the classes of its attributes (Rumbaugh et al. 1999).

My viewpoint is that for conceptual modeling purposes, agonizing over such distinctions doesn't seem to be worth the trouble, and there seems little justification for introducing the notion of aggregation at all as a separate concept at the conceptual level. Obviously there are different stances you could take about how, if at all, aggregation should be included in the conceptual modeling phase. You can decide what's best for you. The chapter notes provide some further discussion on this issue.

Let's now look at the notion of *initial values*. The syntax of an attribute specification in UML includes six components as shown below. Square and curly brackets are used literally here as delimiters (not as BNF symbols to indicate optional components).

visibility name [multiplicity] : type-expression = initial-value {property string}

If an attribute is displayed at all, its name is the only thing that must be shown. The visibility marker (+, #, − denote public, protected, and private, respectively) is an implementation concern and will be ignored in our discussion. Multiplicity has been discussed earlier and is specified for attributes in square brackets, for example, [1..*]. For attributes, the default multiplicity is 1, that is, [1..1]. The type expression indicates the domain on which the attribute is based (e.g., String, Date). Initial value and property string declarations may optionally be declared. Property strings may be used to specify changeability (see later).

An attribute may be assigned an initial value by including the value in the attribute's declaration after an equals sign (e.g., diskSize = 9; country = USA; priority = normal). The language in which the value is written is an implementation concern. In Figure 9.48, the nrColors attribute is based on a simple domain (e.g., PositiveInteger) and has been given an initial value of 1. The resolution attribute is based on a composite domain (e.g., PixelArea) and has been assigned an initial value of (640, 480).

Unless overridden by another initialization procedure (e.g., a constructor), declared initial values are assigned when an object of that class is created. This is at least similar to the database notion of *default values*, where during the insertion of a tuple an attribute may be assigned a predeclared default value if a value is not supplied by the user.

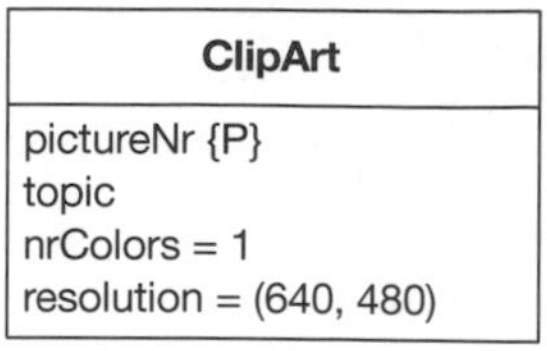

ClipArt
pictureNr {P}
topic
nrColors = 1
resolution = (640, 480)

Figure 9.48 Attributes may be assigned initial values in UML.

However, UML uses the term "default value" in other contexts only (e.g., template and operation parameters), and some authors claim that default values are not part of UML models (Rumbaugh et al. 1999, p. 249).

The SQL standard treats **null** as a special instance of a default value, and this is supported in UML, since the specification notes that "a multiplicity of 0..1 provides for the possibility of null values: the absence of a value" (OMG 1999). So an optional attribute in UML can be used to model a feature that will appear as a column with the default value of null, when mapped to a relational database. Presumably a multiplicity of [0..*] or [0..n] for any $n > 1$ also allows nulls for multivalued attributes, even though an empty set could be used instead.

Currently, ORM has no explicit support for initial/default values. However, UML initial values and relational default values could be supported by allowing default values to be specified for ORM roles. At the metalevel, we add the fact type Role has default- Value. At the external level, instances of this could be specified on a predicate properties sheet, or even entered on the schema diagram (e.g., by attaching an annotation such as d: *value* to the role, and preferably allowing this display to be toggled on/off). For example, the role played by NrColors in Figure 9.49 is allocated a default value of 1. When mapped to SQL, this should add the declaration "default 1" to the column definition for ClipArt.nrColors.

To support the composite initial values allowed in UML, composite default values could be specified for ORM roles played by compositely identified object types (coreferenced or nested). When coreferencing involves at least two roles played by the same or compatible object types, an order is needed to disambiguate the meaning of the composite value. For example, in Figure 9.49 the role played by Resolution is assigned a default composite value of (640, 480). To ensure that the 640 applies to the horizontal pixelcount and the 480 applies to the vertical pixelcount (rather than the other way around), this ordering needs to be applied to the defining roles of the external uniqueness constraint. In Microsoft's ORM tool, this ordering is determined by the order in which the roles are selected when entering this constraint.

If all or most roles played by an object type have the same default, it may be useful to allow a default value to be specified for the object type itself. This could be supported in ORM by adding the meta–fact type ObjectType has default- Value, and proving some notation for instantiating it (e.g., by an entry in the Object Type Properties sheet or by annotating the object type ellipse with d: *value*). This corresponds to the default clause permitted in a create-domain statement in SQL-92. Note that an object type

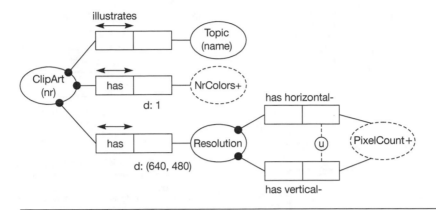

Figure 9.49 A possible extension to ORM to capture default values.

default can always be expressed instead by role-based defaults, but not conversely (since the default may vary with the role).

Specification of default values does not cover all the cases that can arise with regard to default information in general. A detailed proposal for providing greater support for default information in ORM is discussed in Halpin and Vermeir (1997), but this goes beyond the built-in support for defaults in either UML or SQL. Default information can be modeled informally by using a predicate name to convey this intention to a human. For example, we might specify default medium (e.g., 'CD', 'DVD', 'T') preferences for delivery of soft products (e.g., music, video, software) using the 1:n fact type Medium is default preference for SoftProduct.

In cases like this where default values overlap with actual values, we may also wish to classify instances of relevant fact types as actual or default (e.g., Shipment used Medium). For the typical case where the uniqueness constraint on the fact type spans $n - 1$ roles, this can be achieved by including fact types to indicate the default status (e.g., Shipment was based on Choice {actual, default}), resulting in extra columns in the database to record the status. While this approach is generic, it requires the modeler and user to take full responsibility for distinguishing between actual and default values.

Now let's examine the notion of *derived data*. In UML, derived elements (e.g., attributes, associations, or association roles) are indicated by prefixing their names with "/". Optionally, a *derivation rule* may be specified as well. The derivation rule can be expressed as a constraint or note, connected to the derived element by a dashed line. This line is actually shorthand for a dependency arrow, optionally annotated with the stereotype name «derive». Since a constraint or note is involved, the arrow tip may be omitted (the constraint or note is assumed to be the source). For example, Figure 9.50(a) includes area as a derived attribute. Figure 9.50(b) shows the ORM schema.

The UML dependency line may also be omitted entirely, with the constraint shown in braces beside the derived element (in this case, it is the modeling tool's responsibility to maintain the graphical linkage implicitly). A club-membership example of this was included earlier. As another example, Figure 9.51(a) expresses uncle information

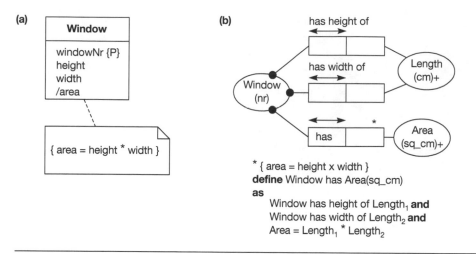

Figure 9.50 Derivation of area in (a) UML and (b) ORM.

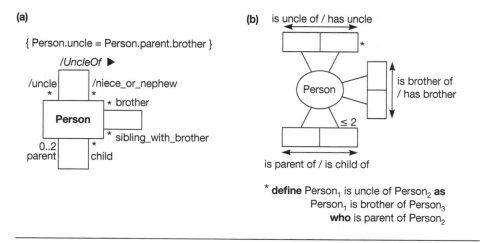

Figure 9.51 Derived uncle association (and roles) in (a) UML, with derivation rule, and (b) ORM.

as a derived association. For illustration purposes, rolenames are included for all association ends. The corresponding ORM schema is shown in Figure 9.51(b).

Although precise rolenames are not always elegant, the use of rolenames in derivation rules involving a path projection can facilitate concise expression of rules, as shown here in the UML model. More complex derivation rules can be stated informally in English or formally in a language such as OCL.

Some but not all derivations can be modeled graphically in ORM using equality constraints. In other cases, a fact type may be partly base and partly derived. These are sometimes called *hybrid* fact types. Some hybrid fact types may be handled in ORM using a subset constraint (see Section 7.5). As an example of a hybrid fact type, suppose that we know somebody's uncles but not his or her parents, and we wish to record this information about uncles. In this case, some uncle facts may be derived (as discussed earlier) while others must be entered directly. One way of dealing with this is to store the entered facts in a base uncle fact type, separate from the derived fact type discussed earlier, which might be renamed, and specify the disjunction of these two fact types as another derived fact type.

UML and ORM both provide support for derived information. As the examples illustrate, the use of attributes and association rolenames in UML often enables derivation rules to be expressed concisely using attribute notation. In contrast, the predicate-based derivation rules of ORM may appear verbose, especially for derivations of a mathematical rather than logical nature. While many ORM derivation rules appear neater than the corresponding UML rules, the attribute style of UML is definitely more convenient in many cases. To address this reality, ORM now allows rolenames as well as predicate names, and ConQuer has been enhanced to support this alternative notation. The main advantage of ORM's predicate-based notation is that it is more stable than an attribute-based notation, since it is not impacted by schema changes such as attributes being remodeled as associations. So the choice of an attribute or relational style for derivation rules can involve a trade-off between convenience and stability.

In UML, restrictions may be placed on the *changeability* of attributes, as well as the roles (ends) of binary associations. It is unclear whether changeability may be applied to the ends of *n*-ary associations, but this is probably forbidden. The following three values for changeability are recognized, only one of which can apply at a given time:

- changeable
- frozen
- addOnly

The value "changeable" was previously called "none". Although the new term "changeable" was approved for UML 1.3, some instances of "none" still occur in the specification; this oversight should be remedied in a later version. The default changeability is "changeable" (any change is permitted). Although the UML specification and Rumbaugh et al. (1999, p. 166) indicate that "changeable" is a value, the specification also says that "there is no symbol for whether an attribute is changeable", so it appears that this default cannot be explicitly declared. However, it makes sense to allow explicit declaration of this default, and it would not be surprising to see the specification revised to permit it. The other settings (frozen and addOnly) may be explicitly declared in braces. For an attribute, the braces are placed at the end of the attribute declaration. For an association, the braces are placed at the opposite end of the association from the object instance to which the constraint applies.

Recall that in UML a "link" is an instance of an association. The term *frozen* means that once an attribute value or link has been inserted, it cannot be updated or deleted, and no additional values/links may be added to the attribute/association (for the constrained object instance). The term *addOnly* means that although the original value/link cannot be deleted or updated, other values/links may be added to the attribute/

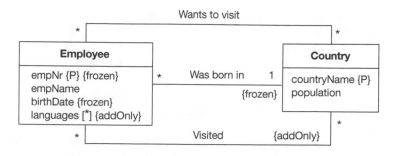

Figure 9.52 Changeability of attributes and association roles may be specified in UML.

association (for the constrained object instance). Clearly, addOnly is only meaningful if the maximum multiplicity of the attribute/association role exceeds its minimum multiplicity.

As a simple if unrealistic example, see Figure 9.52. Here empNr, birthDate, and country of birth are frozen for Employee, so they cannot be changed from their original value. For instance, if we assign an employee the empNr 007, and enter his or her birth date as 02/15/1946 and birth country as 'Australia', then we can never make any changes or additions to that.

Notice also that for a given employee, the set of languages and the set of countries visited are addOnly. Suppose that when facts about employee 007 are initially entered, we set his or her languages to {Latin, Japanese} and countries visited to {Japan}. So long as employee 007 is referenced in the database, these facts may never be deleted. However, we may add to these (e.g., later we might add the facts that employee 007 speaks German and visited India).

By default, the other properties are changeable. For example, employee 007 might legally change his name from 'Terry Hagar' to 'Hari Seldon', and the set of countries he wants to visit might change, after some traveling, from {Ireland, Italy, USA} to {Greece, Ireland}.

Some traditional data modeling approaches also note some restrictions on changeability. As discussed in the previous chapter, the Barker ER notation includes a diamond to mark a relationship as nontransferable (once an instance of an entity type plays a role with an object, it cannot ever play this role with another object). Although changeability restrictions may at first appear very useful, in practice their application in database settings is limited.

One reason for this is that we almost always want to allow facts entered into a database to be changed. With snapshot data, this is the norm, but even with historical data changes can occur. The most common occurrence of this is to allow for corrections of mistakes, which might be because we were told the wrong information originally or because we carelessly made a misspelling or typo when entering the data.

In exceptional cases, we might require that mistakes of a certain kind be retained in the database (e.g., for auditing purposes) but be corrected by entering later facts to

Transaction
tranNr {P} {frozen}
accountNr {P} {frozen}
tranDate {frozen}
tranType {frozen}
tranAmount {frozen}
/balance {frozen}

Figure 9.53 All attributes of Transaction are frozen.

compensate for the error. This kind of approach makes sense for bank transactions (see Figure 9.53). For example, if a deposit transaction for $100 was mistakenly entered as $1,000, the record of this error is kept, but once the error is detected it can be compensated for by a bank withdrawal of $900. As a minor point, the balance is both derived and stored, and its frozen status is typically implied by the frozen settings on the base attributes, together with a rule for deriving balance.

Although not stated in UML 1.3, some authors allow changeability to be specified for a class, as an abbreviation for declaring this for all its attributes and opposite association ends (Booch et al. 1999, p. 184). For instance, all the {frozen} constraints in Figure 9.53 might be replaced by a single {frozen} constraint below the name "Transaction". While this notation is neater, it would be rarely used. Even in this example, we would probably want to allow for the possibility of adding nonfrozen information later (e.g., a transaction might be audited by zero or more auditors).

Changeability settings may have more use in the design of program code than in conceptual modeling (e.g., {frozen} corresponds to const in C++). Although changeability settings are not supported in ORM, which focuses on static constraints, they could be added as role properties if desired. In the wider picture, being able to completely model security issues (e.g., who has the authority to change what) would provide greater value.

UML includes an *{ordered} constraint* to indicate mapping to an *ordered set* (i.e., a sequence with no duplicates). For example, Figure 9.54(a) shows one way of modeling authorship of papers in UML. Each paper has a list or sequence of authors, each of whom may appear at most once on the list.

This may be modeled in flat ORM by introducing a Position object type to store the sequential position of any author on the list, as shown in Figure 9.54(b). The uniqueness constraint on the first two roles declares that for each paper an author occupies at most one position; the constraint covering the first and third roles indicates that for any paper, each position is occupied by at most one author. The textual constraint indicates that the list positions are numbered sequentially from 1.

Though not shown here, the ternary solution can also be modeled in UML. Although this ternary representation may appear awkward, it is easy to populate and it facilitates any discussion involving position (e.g., who is the second author for

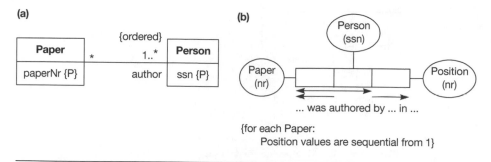

Figure 9.54 An ordered set constraint in UML (a) may be modeled in ORM using Position (b).

paper 21?). From an implementation perspective, a sequence structure could still be chosen.

An ordered set is an example of a collection type. As discussed in Chapter 13, some versions of ORM allow collections to be specified as mapping annotations in a similar way to UML, and some ORM versions allow collections to be modeled directly as first class objects.

9.8   Mapping from ORM to UML

Object types and value types map to object classes and data types, including attribute domains when associations are replaced by attributes. Unary associations (e.g., smokes) may be mapped to Boolean attributes (e.g., isSmoker) or to subtypes (e.g., Smoker), or may be transformed into binary associations (e.g., has SmokerStatus { 'S', 'NS'}) before mapping.

Now decide which $n{:}1$ and 1:1 associations in ORM you would like to remodel as attributes. If you have specified rolenames, these can usually be used as attribute names, with the object type name becoming the attribute's domain name. Any $m{:}n$ associations should remain that way. Binary associations between entity types are normally best mapped into binary associations between classes. Functional ($n{:}1$ or 1:1) associations to a value type may be mapped into attributes. Nonfunctional and longer associations may be mapped directly to associations.

Objectified associations map to association classes. Some cases of coreference could be mapped into qualified associations, but mapping to separate attributes or associations supplemented by a textual composite uniqueness constraint offers a more general solution.

Internal uniqueness constraints map to a maximum multiplicity of 1. External uniqueness maps to a textual constraint or qualified association. A simple mandatory role constraint maps to a minimum multiplicity of 1. A disjunctive mandatory role constraint maps to a textual constraint. Simple frequency constraints map to multiplicity constraints; more complex cases map to textual constraints. Value constraints map to enumeration or textual constraints. Subset constraints between full associations map to subset constraints; other subset constraints map to textual constraints. And similarly for exclusion constraints. Equality constraints are preprocessed into two subset constraints before mapping. Subtyping maps fairly directly, with trivial notation changes. Formal subtype definitions, ring constraints, and join constraints map to textual constraints. Object cardinality maps to class multiplicity.

With these hints, and the examples discussed earlier, you should now have enough background to do the mapping manually for yourself. The following short exercise will give you some practice at this. If you are keen on using UML for data modeling, you may wish to use UML to model some of the many modeling exercises in other chapters.

Exercise 9.8

1. Model the following application in UML. I suggest you do an ORM model first, but that's up to you. The universe of discourse is based on a simplified fragment of a database application used by an electrical utility to help manage delivery of electricity to consumers in Australia. A line link is a section of an electrical feeder or main power line that connects two adjacent nodes (e.g., power poles, pillar boxes).

The figure shown illustrates a tiny part of the electrical power network. Here three power poles (also called telephone poles) carry power lines to supply electricity. The house is one of many receiving electricity from the power company.

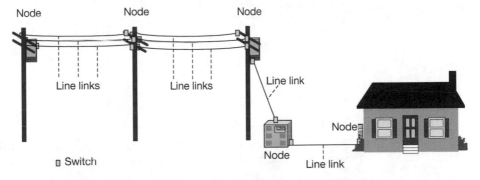

The following output report provides an extract of sample data about line links. The link types listed are not exhaustive.

Line link	Link type	Linktype description	Voltage (V)	Current (A)	Power (kW)	Length (m)
33	OW	open wire	11,000	400	4,400	200
40	UGC	underground cable	11,000	400	4,400	150
55	ABC	aerial bundled conductor	415	300	124.5	170
56	ABC	aerial bundled conductor	240	200	72	180

The following report shows details about line links to help with fault detection and correction. Each power line link has a switch at both ends. The switches can be remotely toggled open (to break the circuit) or closed. Line status has only two values, as shown.

Line link	From node	To node	Status	Start switch	End switch
33	B	D	OK	Closed	Closed
40	D	E	OK	Closed	Open
55	F	G	Faulty	Open	Open
56	F	G	OK	Closed	Closed

The following report extract lists details about nodes and any consumers serviced with electricity by those nodes. Only nodes with a transformer (i.e., nodes for which we record a transformer type) can service a consumer. A consumer may be serviced by many nodes, and has exactly one, two, or three phases supplied (regardless of which node supplies the power). The transformer types shown here (PT = pole transformer, PMT = pad-mounted transformer, GT = ground transformer) are not meant to be exhaustive. Codes of transformer types are stored, but descriptions are not.

Note: In reality a consumer has only one node for normal service and possibly other nodes for backup in the case of a fault—however, we ignore this refinement since its modeling requires subtypes, which we avoid in this simple exercise. Data models of electrical applications usually include many subtypes.

Node	Nr fuses	Transformer type	Consumer serviced	Nr phases supplied
B	3	PT	?	?
D	0	?	?	?
E	1	PMT	3001	2
			3005	3
...	...	...		
F	2	GT	5678	2
			5700	1
...	...	...	...	...
G	2	GT	5678	2
...	...	...	...	...

The following report extract lists details about electrical faults suffered by consumers. Timestamps may be treated as a single value (including both date and time of day).

Consumer	Fault type	Reported	Fixed	Fault cause
3005	Dim lights	1996–04–29 09:30	1996–04–30 10:45	?
	Dim lights	1997–07–12 17:25	?	Wires down
5678	Blackout	1996–04–30 11:20	1996–05–01 6:30	Lightning strike
	Cold water	1996–04–30 11:20	?	?

The following report extract indicates electrical energy consumption (in kilowatt hours) by consumers on a quarterly basis. Some consumers (e.g., recent ones) might not yet appear in the report. Although consumption can be derived from other data not shown here, for this exercise assume that it is simply stored.

Consumer	Quarter		Consumption (kW.h)
	Year	QtrNr	
3001	1996	4	1622
	1997	1	1500
	1997	2	2001
	...	...	...
5678	1997	2	2001
...	...	...	...

(a) Specify a UML schema for this UoD, including constraints and derivation rules.

(b) Suppose that in the model, Fault is an association class to objectify the association Consumer reported FaultType at Instant. Suggest a new identification scheme for Fault to improve the usability of the model.

2. Model the academic schema in Exercise 8.5, Question 2, in UML.

9.9   Summary

The Unified Modeling Language (UML) has been adopted by the OMG as a method for object-oriented analysis and design. Though mainly focused on design of object-oriented programming code, it can be used for modeling database applications by supplementing its predefined notations with user-defined constraints.

UML includes the following nine main diagram types: use case diagram, class diagram, object diagram, statechart, activity diagram, sequence diagram, collaboration diagram, component diagram, and deployment diagram. When stripped of implementation details, class diagrams are essentially an extended form of ER diagrams.

The basic correspondence between data structures and instances in UML and ORM is summarized in Table 9.1. Classes are basically entity types and are depicted as named rectangles, with compartments for attributes, operations, and so on. In UML, facts are stored either in attributes of classes or in associations among two or more classes. Binary associations are depicted as lines. Ternary and longer associations include a diamond. Rolenames may be placed at association ends, and an association may be given a name. An association may be objectified as an association class, corresponding to nesting in ORM. Associations may be qualified to provide a weak form of coreference.

Table 9.2 summarizes the main correspondences between constraints in UML and ORM. Attributes and association ends may be annotated with multiplicity constraints, which indicate both optionality and cardinality (e.g., 0..1 = at most one, 1 = exactly one, * = zero or more). Attributes have a default multiplicity of 1.

Subset constraints are allowed only between whole associations and are denoted by "{subset}" next to a dashed arrow. An exclusive-or constraint is depicted by "{xor}" beside a dashed line connecting the relevant associations. Subtypes are connected to their supertypes by a line with an open arrowhead at the supertype end. Subtyping may

Table 9.1 Correspondence between ORM and UML data instances and structures.

ORM	UML
Entity	Object
Value	Data value
Object	Object or Data value
Entity type	Class
Value type	Data type
Object type	Class or Data type
—{ use relationship type }	Attribute
Unary relationship type	—{ use Boolean attribute }
2^+-ary relationship type	Association
2^+-ary relationship instance	Link
Nested object type	Association class
Coreference	Qualified association §

§ = incomplete coverage of corresponding concept

be annotated using the key words "{complete}", "{incomplete}", "{disjoint}", "{overlapping}", "{root}", and "{leaf}". A discriminator (e.g., sex) may be used to indicate the basis for a subtype graph.

Whole/part associations may be displayed as aggregations using a small diamond at the whole end. A hollow diamond denotes shared aggregation (a part may belong to more than one whole), and a filled diamond indicates composition or composite aggregation (a part may belong to at most one whole at a time).

Attributes may be assigned initial values. Derived attributes and associations are indicated by prepending "/" to their name. Attributes and binary association roles may be assigned a changeability setting: changeable, frozen, or addOnly. Frozen means that once an attribute value or link has been inserted, it cannot be updated or deleted, and no additional values/links may be added to the attribute/association (for the constrained object instance). AddOnly means that although the original value/link cannot be deleted or updated, other values/links may be added to the attribute/association (for the constrained object instance).

An association end may be adorned with "{ordered}" to indicate implementation as an ordered set. One way of modeling this in ORM is to explicitly introduce a Position type to indicate the order.

UML models are best developed by mapping them from ORM models and noting any additional ORM constraints as comments.

Table 9.2 Correspondence between ORM and UML data model constraints.

ORM	UML
Internal uniqueness	Multiplicity of ..1 §
External uniqueness	—{ use qualified association § }
Simple mandatory role	Multiplicity of 1.. §
Disjunctive mandatory role	—
Frequency: internal; external	Multiplicity §;—
Value	Enumeration and textual
Subset and equality	Subset §
Exclusion	xor constraint §
Subtype link and definition	Subclass discriminator, etc. §
Ring constraints	—
Join constraints	—
Object cardinality	Class multiplicity
—{ use unique and mandatory §}	Aggregation/composition
—	Defaults/changeability
Textual constraints	Textual constraints

§ = incomplete coverage of corresponding concept

Chapter Notes

Much of the material in this chapter is based on my series of articles on data modeling in UML from an ORM perspective that appeared in the *Journal of Conceptual Modeling (www.inconcept. com)*. For related publications on UML from an ORM perspective, see Halpin and Bloesch (1999) and Halpin (1999b, 2000a, 2000c). The last of these references (Halpin 2000c) discusses several weaknesses in UML, including the failure of its multiplicity notation to generalize properly for *n*-ary associations, and investigates which concepts from ORM might be used to address some of these deficiencies. For details on the Dutch version of ORM that allows unaries to be objectified, see Bakema et al. (1994).

The UML specification is accessible online at *www.omg.org/uml/*. A simple introduction to UML is contained in Fowler (1997). For a detailed discussion of UML by "the three amigos" (Booch, Rumbaugh, and Jacobson), see Booch et al. (1999) and Rumbaugh et al. (1999). Their suggested modeling process for using the language is discussed in Jacobson et al. (1999). Martin and Odell (1998) provide a general coverage of object-oriented modeling using the UML notation. Muller (1999) provides a detailed treatment of UML for the purposes of database modeling. A thorough discussion of OMT for database applications is given in Blaha and Premerlani

(1998), although its notation for multiplicity constraints differs from the UML standard. The Object constraint language is covered in detail in Warmer and Kleppe (1999).

On the topic of aggregation, Rumbaugh et al. (1999, p. 148) argue:

> Aggregation conveys the thought that the aggregate is inherently the sum of its parts. In fact, the only real semantics that it adds to association is the constraint that chains of aggregate links may not form cycles ... Some authors have distinguished several kinds of aggregation, but the distinctions are fairly subtle and probably unnecessary for general modeling.

There are plenty of other distinctions (apart from aggregation) we could make about associations, but don't feel compelled to do so. For a very detailed discussion arguing for an even more thorough treatment of aggregation in UML, see Barbier et al. (2000).

The view that security issues have priority over changeability settings is nicely captured by the following comment of John Harris, in a thread on the inconcept Web site:

> Rather than talk of "immutable" data I think it is better to talk of a privilege requirement. For instance, *you* can't change your recorded salary but your boss can, whether it's because you've had a pay rise or because there's been a typing error. Privileges can be as complicated or as simple as they need to be, whereas "immutable" can only be on or off. Also, privileges can be applied to the insertion of new data and removal of old data, not just to updates.

A recent collection of readings critiquing UML is contained in Siau and Halpin (2000). The precise UML group, comprised largely of European academics, has published several papers mainly aimed at providing a more rigorous semantic basis for UML. A useful collection of their papers is accessible from their Web site, *www.puml.org*.

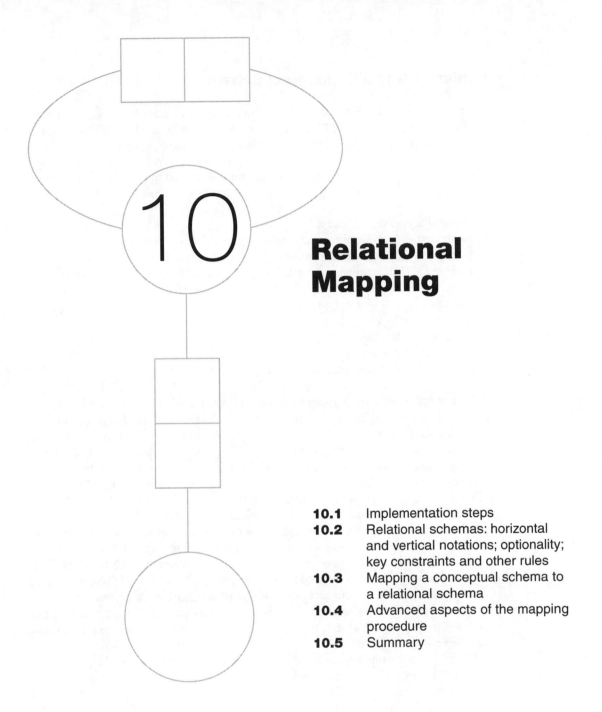

Relational
Mapping

10.1   Implementing a Conceptual Schema

Most database modeling tools allow you to enter a data model in one or more high-level notations (e.g., ER, IDEF1X, ORM, or UML) as well as a logical-level notation (e.g., relational). Typically a high-level (conceptual or semiconceptual) schema must be mapped down to a logical and then physical schema in order for the database to be populated and queried. Assuming you do the right thing and model first at the conceptual level, the main steps in implementing your data model are as follows:

- Design the conceptual schema.
- Annotate the conceptual schema with mapping choices as needed.
- Map the design to a logical schema (e.g., relational or object-relational).
- Finesse the logical schema as needed (e.g., rename or reorder some columns).
- Generate the internal schema (e.g., in Microsoft Access or SQL Server).
- Create external schema(s): (e.g., forms, reports).
- Enforce security levels as needed.
- Populate the database.
- Issue queries and updates.
- Update the schemas as needed.

Earlier chapters discussed how to design the conceptual schema. The focus of this chapter is on mapping from conceptual to logical. Because of the dominance of relational database systems, the relational model is used for the logical schema. Basic ideas about relational databases were introduced in Chapters 1 and 2. Section 10.2 summarizes these points, and expands briefly on them. Section 10.3 discusses the basic procedure for mapping an ORM conceptual schema onto a relational schema. This can be easily adapted to cover mapping from other notations such as ER or UML. Mapping from IDEF1X to relational is trivial, as discussed in Chapter 8.

Section 10.4 discusses advanced aspects of relational mapping, including the use of conceptual annotations to override default mapping choices (e.g., to control how subtypes or 1:1 associations are mapped). After automated mapping, some finessing of table and column names may be needed to meet naming standards, and columns may be reordered to improve performance. Once the logical schema is determined, if not before, the target DBMS is selected. The internal schema can then be generated for this specific platform. Some aspects of tuning the physical model to improve performance are covered later in Chapter 12 (e.g., index selection and denormalization).

Updates and queries tend to be carried out either in a logical query language (e.g., SQL or QBE) or via an external forms and reporting interface defined on top of the logical schema. Some aspects of external schema design are covered in Section 13.5. With multiuser applications, access rights to the tables, forms, and reports for different user groups should be enforced by the database administrator. The next chapter indicates how table updates, queries, and access rights can be declared in SQL.

All the major relational DBMSs either support SQL directly, or provide translation facilities to/from SQL. Recently some higher-level query languages have appeared that allow users to formulate queries directly in terms of dimensions (for data warehousing) or even conceptual schema constructs. Some of these are discussed in Chapter 13.

The next section summarizes the fundamental constructs in relational database schemas using a generic notation. The following two sections then discuss basic and advanced mapping of conceptual to relational schemas. The final section provides the chapter summary.

10.2 Relational Schemas

A *relational schema* (or relational database schema) is a set of relational table definitions, constraints, and perhaps derivation rules. You may wish to review Sections 1.3 and 2.3, where the basic ideas were discussed. The structure of a single relational table is called a *table scheme.* This is basically a named set of *attributes* (columns) that draw their values from *domains.* Each table scheme may be populated by a set of unnamed *tuples* (rows) of data, but the population is not part of the table scheme itself.

Many *notations* exist for table schemes. To save space, and to facilitate discussion of populations, this book normally uses a *horizontal layout,* where the table name precedes a parenthesized list of column names, separated by commas. If desired, domain names may be displayed after the column names, using a colon separator.

For example, ignoring constraints, the ORM conceptual schema in Figure 10.1 maps to the table scheme

Employee (empNr: EmpNr, salary: Money, tax: Money)

Here the table name is "Employee", the attribute empNr is based on the domain EmpNr, and the attributes salary and tax are both based on the domain Money. I adopt the convention of starting table and domain names with a capital letter and attribute names with a lowercase letter. This case convention is similar to that of UML and is fairly popular. However, many other case preferences are also used in practice. Whichever convention you choose, using it consistently will help make your schemas more readable.

When using horizontal layout, I usually write the table name in italics. I also prefer to concatenate name components, with later components capitalized (e.g., empNr) rather than using a separator such as an underscore or space (e.g., emp_nr or "emp nr").

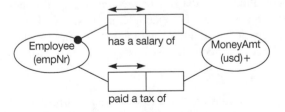

Figure 10.1 A simple ORM model for employees.

As discussed in the next chapter, the SQL standard requires double quotes around a name that includes a space character. Modeling tools usually give you control over how such names are generated. You can pick your own style and stick with it. For compactness, it is usual to omit the domain names in setting out table schemes. For example:

Employee (empNr, salary, tax)

In theory, the relational model supports semantic domains that basically correspond to ORM conceptual object types. Prior to 1992, the SQL standard required that each attribute be defined directly over a numeric or character string data type. For example:

Person (surname: **char**(20), city: **char**(20), height: **smallint,** weight: **smallint**)

This can lead to semantic nonsense, such as comparing people and cities or height and weight. SQL-92 allows attributes to be defined over user-defined syntactic domains that specify an underlying data type and optionally a value list and/or default value. The underlying data types in standard SQL support date, time, and bit strings but not Money, which is instead defined in terms of a numeric data type, for example, **decimal**(9,2). SQL:1999 introduced user-defined types, which can be used as semantic domains (see Chapter 11). However, many commercial SQLs still provide no support for user-defined domains or types, so I'll typically ignore domain details from this point on.

Let's now consider the main notations used for specifying *constraints* in a relational schema. Later sections discuss how to group fact types into table schemes and how to map constraints and rules in more detail.

Using horizontal layout, **uniqueness constraints** on relational columns are shown by underlining. Each unique column, or unique column combination, provides a *candidate key* for identifying rows in the table. A key is a *minimal* set of uniquely constrained attributes. In other words, if an attribute is removed from a compound key, the remaining attributes are not spanned by a uniqueness constraint. If there is only one candidate key, this is automatically the *primary key*. For example, we may indicate that empNr is the primary key of the Employee table thus:

Employee (empNr, salary, tax)

If more than one candidate key exists, one of these must be selected as the primary key. The others are then called *alternate keys* or *secondary keys*. Primary keys are doubly underlined if alternate keys exist. For example, suppose we also record the name and department of each employee, and the combination of employee name and department is unique. The primary and secondary keys may be shown thus:

Employee (empNr, empName, deptCode, salary, tax)

The order in which the columns are listed is semantically irrelevant, since each column has a name unique to its table. If columns in a composite key are not listed consecutively, arrowheads must be added to the underlines to show that a single, composite

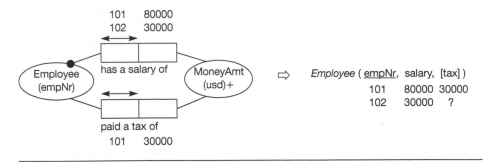

Figure 10.2 The populated ORM model maps to the populated table scheme shown.

uniqueness constraint applies rather than multiple simple constraints. For example, the previous Employee table scheme may also be displayed thus:

Employee (empNr, empName, salary, deptCode, tax)

A column that does not allow null values is said to be **mandatory** *(for its table)*. A column that does allow null values is said to be *optional*. For horizontal layout, this book adopts the following conventions: optional columns are enclosed in *square brackets;* a column is mandatory in its table unless it is marked optional. This practice is consistent with the well-known BNF (Backus-Naur Form) notation. For example, since paying tax is optional, the previous ORM schema maps to the following table scheme, with the tax column optional (null values allowed):

Employee (empNr, salary, [tax])

This mapping is illustrated with a sample population in Figure 10.2. The conceptual population includes three elementary facts: employee 101 has a salary of $80,000 (US); employee 102 has a salary of $30,000; and employee 101 paid a tax of $30,000. No tax payment is yet recorded for employee 102.

Recall that each row of a relational table expresses one or more elementary facts. Since both fact types have been grouped into the same table, each row expresses one or two facts. The first row records the salary and tax facts about employee 101. The second row records the salary fact about employee 102. The second row also contains a null value (shown here as "?"), indicating the absence of a tax fact for employee 102. The order in which the rows are displayed is not semantically relevant.

If all roles played by an object type map to the same table, its mandatory roles can be specified simply as mandatory columns. However, the relational model often requires different facts about the same object to be stored in different tables. In general, *mandatory role constraints are captured by making their columns mandatory in their table, and running a subset constraint from other tables (if any) that contain facts about that object type.* Consider Figure 10.3, which adds two fact types to Figure 10.1. Each employee's sex is now recorded, as well as any cars driven by the employee.

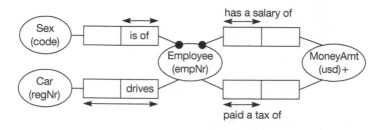

Figure 10.3 The drives fact type will map to a separate table.

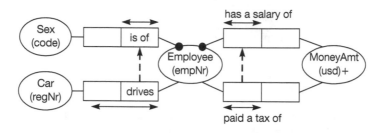

Figure 10.4 Some implied subset constraints from optional roles.

As discussed in the next section, the *m:n* nature of the drives fact type requires it to be mapped to a different relational table from the other three fact types, so information about Employee is spread over two relational tables as shown below. Here, the mandatory role constraints have only been partly captured—there is nothing to stop us entering employee numbers in the Drives table that do not occur in the Employee table.

Employee   (<u>empNr</u>, sex, salary, [tax])
Drives   (<u>empNr, carRegNr</u>)

How then do we map the conceptual mandatory role constraints? A role *r* is mandatory for an object type *O* if and only if the population of each other role played by *O* must be a subset of the population of *r*. Hence each optional role of an object type has an implied subset constraint to each mandatory role of that object type. Figure 10.4 shows one implied subset constraint from each optional role in the current example. Each optional role has another subset constraint targeting the other mandatory role. Equality constraints are implied between the mandatory roles, but are irrelevant to our discussion.

The three *n:*1 fact types for salary, sex, and tax are all grouped into the Employee table. The mandatory salary and sex predicates map to mandatory columns, and the subset constraint on the tax role is captured by having tax as the only optional column in the Employee table. The drives fact type maps to a separate table. So to capture the subset constraint from the drives role, we add to the relational schema a subset constraint from the empNr column of the Drives table to the empNr column of the Employee table.

In horizontal layout, this subset constraint is depicted as a dotted arrow, as shown below. This ensures that any employee listed as driving a car is also referenced in the Employee table, where sex and salary are mandatorily recorded.

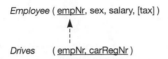

In relational jargon, this subset constraint is said to be a *referential integrity constraint,* and the empNr attribute of the Drives table is a *foreign key* that *references* the empNr attribute of the Employee table. In the relational model, foreign keys can reference only primary keys, but SQL allows foreign keys to also target alternate keys.

The relational model has two basic integrity rules. The *entity integrity rule* demands that primary keys contain no null values (i.e., each column in a primary key is a mandatory column for its table). The *referential integrity rule* basically says that each non-null value of a foreign key must match the value of some primary key. The relational model also allows for user-defined constraints and derivation rules.

To get a feel for how a relational schema might be implemented in practice, let's extend our example a little and map it to SQL. Figure 10.5 adds fact types to record the department and name of each employee. It also adds three constraints other than internal uniqueness and simple mandatory constraints. Employee names are unique within a given department, the possible sex codes are 'M' and 'F', and each employee drives at most three cars.

The external uniqueness constraint on employee name and department maps to a composite uniqueness constraint spanning two attributes. In the horizontal layout, this is denoted by underlining the relevant columns as discussed before. The value constraint on sex codes and the frequency constraint that each employee drives at most three cars are specified in the horizontal layout by annotating the table schemes with a conceptual-like notation, as shown in Figure 10.6(a).

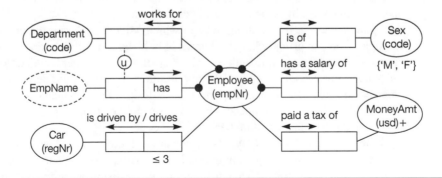

Figure 10.5 A more detailed ORM model for employees.

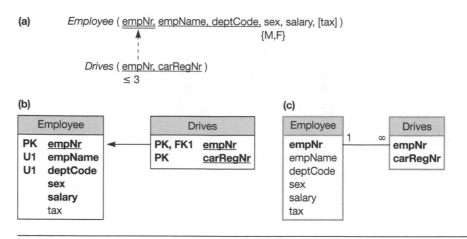

Figure 10.6 A relational schema in (a) horizontal, (b) one vertical (Visio), and (c) another vertical (Microsoft Access) layout.

Most ORM conceptual constraint notations may be used in a similar way in setting out relational schemas. Sometimes we adapt these notations or introduce new ones (see later sections). While our semigraphical notation is compact and fairly intuitive, commercial tools usually depict relational schemas diagrammatically using a *vertical layout,* supplemented by textual rules stored in property sheets or code. Though it takes up more space, vertical layout is convenient when a table contains many columns.

Figure 10.6(b) shows one of the ways in which Visio diagrams the same example. Here the table name is listed in the top compartment with the column names listed vertically below. Mandatory columns are shown in bold, so tax is the only optional column. Primary key columns are underlined and annotated with "PK". If desired, primary keys can also be displayed in a separate compartment. Foreign keys are annotated with "FKn" ($n > 0$), and an arrow depicts the subset constraint from the foreign key to the target table. Nonprimary uniqueness constraints are denoted by "Un". The value constraint on sexcode and the frequency constraint on CarRegNr are not displayed on the diagram but can be inspected in the associated code.

Figure 10.6(c) is based on the way in which Microsoft Access diagrams the same example. Here the primary keys are shown in bold, and the foreign key constraint is depicted as a relationship line with a cardinality of 1 at the target end and "∞" (infinity, for "many") at the source end. Although no other constraints are depicted here, some other constraints can be inspected in a table design view: mandatory is specified as "Required = Yes" and uniqueness by "Indexed = Yes (No Duplicates)". Other constraints need to be inspected in the associated code.

As these sample vertical layouts demonstrate, there is no industry standard that is uniformly adopted for diagramming relational schemas. This is another reason for this book's use of a generic horizontal notation. When using a particular CASE tool or DBMS, you need to familiarize yourself with its specific relational notation.

The same relational schema may be specified in SQL-92 as set out below. Reserved words are shown in bold, but this is not required. To save some writing, domains on which more than one column are based are declared initially (EmpNr and Money), and constraint names are omitted. In SQL:1999, types may be declared instead of domains. The **create table** statements declare the schemes for the Employee and Drives tables. A **not null** clause indicates a column is mandatory for its table. Primary keys are declared with **primary key** clauses. A **unique** clause specifies the alternate compound key. The intertable subset constraint is declared with a **references** clause. **Check** clauses are used to declare the value and frequency constraints. Further explanation of SQL syntax is given in the next chapter.

```
create domain EmpNr smallint;
create domain Money decimal(9,2);

create table Employee (
   empNr      EmpNr        not null    primary key,
   empName    varchar(20)  not null,
   deptCode   varchar(5)   not null,
   sex        char         not null    check( sex in ('M','F') ),
   salary     Money        not null,
   tax        Money,
      unique ( deptCode, empName ) );

create table Drives (
   empNr      EmpNr        not null    references Employee,
   carRegNr   char(6)      not null,
      primary key ( empNr, carRegNr ),
      check( not exists
               (select empNr from Drives
               group by empNr
               having count(*) > 3) );
```

Although the above SQL syntax is legal as far back as SQL-92, some commercial versions of SQL do not yet support all of this syntax. For data definition, some versions have barely progressed beyond the old SQL-89 standard (which had no domain clauses, and restricted check clauses to conditions on a single row). In practice, some features of a relational schema may need to be specified as procedural code rather than declaratively.

A conceptual schema comprises three sections: fact types, constraints, and *derivation rules*. Conceptual derivation rules may be specified in an appropriate language, using either relational or attribute style notation. For example, an employee's net pay might be derived using the rule **for each** Employee, **if** tax > 0 **then** netpay = salary − tax **else** netpay = salary. This rule may be simplified to a simple subtraction if we make tax mandatory with a default of 0, or assume that nulls are treated as zero for subtraction. The next chapter discusses in detail how SQL handles nulls. Various options exist for mapping derivation rules to the relational level. For example, a rule may be declared within a view (virtual table), or a derived column can be included in the relevant base table with triggers specified to compute and store the derived value on update.

Exercise 10.2

1. The following table contains details about members of a martial arts club. A null value "?" indicates that a member has no phone or is unranked in any martial art. Black belt ranks are known as dan grades and lower ranks are kyu grades.

Member	Sex	Phone	Arts and ranks
Adams B	M	2052777	judo 3-dan; karatedo 2-kyu
Adams S	F	2052777	judo 2-kyu
Brown C	F	3579001	?
Collins T	M	?	aikido 2-dan; judo 2-dan
Dancer A	F	?	?

(a) Specify a conceptual schema for this UoD, assuming that rank (e.g., 3-dan) may be stored as a single value. Many other martial arts are possible.

(b) Explain why the table shown is not a relational table.

(c) Given that any fact type with a composite uniqueness constraint must be stored as a separate table, map your conceptual schema to a relational schema. Underline keys, mark optional fields in square brackets, and show any intertable subset constraint as a dotted arrow.

(d) In a "nested relational database", the data may be stored in a single table. For example, an entry in the Arts_and_Ranks column may itself be viewed as a relation with attributes sport and rank (or as a set of ordered pairs). Discuss any advantages or disadvantages you feel might result from this approach.

10.3   Relational Mapping Procedure

The previous section introduced a generic notation for setting out a relational schema, and discussed an example of mapping from a conceptual to a relational schema. We now discuss the main steps of a general procedure for performing such a mapping. The following section deals with advanced aspects of this procedure.

For a given conceptual schema, several different relational designs might be chosen. Ideally the relational schema chosen should be *correct, efficient, and clear.* Correctness requires the relational schema to be equivalent to the conceptual schema (within the completeness allowed by relational structures). Efficiency means good response times to updates and queries, with reasonable demands on storage space. Clarity entails the schema should be relatively easy to understand and work with.

Since correctness of data is usually more important than fast response times, and correctness requires adequate constraint enforcement, a high priority is normally placed on simplifying the enforcement of constraints at update time. The main way to simplify the management of updates is to avoid redundancy. This strategy can lead to more tables in the design, which can slow down queries and updates if extra table joins are now required. For efficiency, we should try to keep the number of tables down to an acceptable limit.

With these criteria in mind, the **Rmap** (relational mapping) procedure guarantees a redundancy-free relational design and includes strategies to restrict the number of tables. Rmap extends and refines an older mapping procedure known as the ONF ("Optimal Normal Form") algorithm. The full version of Rmap includes details for completely mapping all graphical conceptual constraints and is beyond the scope of this text. However, the central steps of this procedure are covered in this section and the next. As discussed in Chapter 12, more efficient relational designs with fewer tables may possibly result if the conceptual schema is transformed by an optimization algorithm before Rmap is applied, and sometimes lower-level optimization using controlled redundancy may be needed to meet critical performance requirements.

Even without such further optimization, the Rmap procedure is extremely valuable since it guarantees a safe, reasonably efficient, normalized design. Happily, the basic steps of the procedure are simple. Recall that redundancy is repetition of an elementary fact. Having gone to the trouble of ensuring that our conceptual fact types are elementary, we can easily avoid redundancy in our relational tables.

Typically each relational table stores one or more elementary fact types. Otherwise the table stores a single reference type, corresponding to an independent, unnested object type with no functional fact roles, which may be thought of as an existential fact type (e.g., a lookup table of country codes). Hence we can automatically *avoid redundancy* in tables by ensuring that *each fact type maps to only one table, in such a way that its instances appear only once.* To achieve this, there are two basic rules, as follows. As an exercise, convince yourself that grouping fact types like this makes it impossible for any fact to be duplicated.

1. Fact types with compound uniqueness constraints ☐⋯☐ map to separate tables.
2. Fact types with functional roles attached to the same object type ○━☐ are grouped into the same table, keyed on the object type's identifier.

These two rules show how to group fact types into table schemes. The first rule is illustrated in Figure 10.7. Any nonobjectified predicate with a uniqueness constraint spanning two or more of its roles must map to a table all by itself. Hence *m:n* binaries, and all *n*-aries ($n \geq 3$) on the conceptual schema, map to a separate table (unless they are objectified associations, as discussed later). Each object type maps to one or more attributes depending on the number of components in its reference scheme. If the predicate has only one uniqueness constraint, the table's primary key is the attribute(s) spanned by this constraint. Otherwise one of the uniqueness constraints spans the

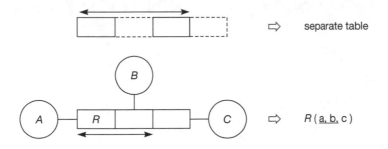

Figure 10.7 Each fact type with a compound, internal UC maps to a table by itself.

primary key, and the others span alternate keys. Microsoft's ORM tool allows you to specify which constraint you prefer for the primary key before mapping.

When mapping conceptual schemas, care should be taken to *choose meaningful table and column names*. In the case of Figure 10.7, the table is used to store instances of the conceptual relationship type, so it is often given a name similar to the conceptual predicate name. If the object types involved are different, their names or the names of their value types, or a concatenation of the object and value type names, are often used as column names. For instance: *Drives*(empNr, CarRegNr).

When information about the same object is spread over more than one table, it is usually better to consistently use the same column name for this object (e.g., empNr was also used in the Employee table to refer to employees). Apart from helping the designer to see the connection, this practice can simplify the formulation of natural joins in the SQL standard. However, if different roles of the same predicate are played by the same object type, different column names must be chosen to reflect the different roles involved. For example: *Contains*(superpart, subpart, quantity).

A typical example of the second grouping rule is illustrated in Figure 10.8. Here two functional roles are attached to the object type *A*. However, the rule also applies when there is just one functional role, or more than two. The handling of mandatory and optional roles was considered earlier (optional column in square brackets).

The identification schemes of *A, B,* and *C* are not shown here, but may be simple or composite. The fact types are grouped together into a single table, with the identifier of *A* as the primary key (shown here as *a*). The name of *A* is often chosen as the table name. To avoid confusion, it is best never to use the same name for both a table and a column, so the name of *A*'s value type is often chosen for *a*. The names of *B* and *C* (or their value types or rolenames) are often chosen as the other column names (here *b* and *c*). For example: *Employee* (empNr, sex, [phone], salary, [tax]).

Once table groupings have been determined, keys underlined, optional columns marked in square brackets, and other constraints (e.g., subset, value list) mapped down, any derivation rules are also mapped, as discussed in the previous section.

To help understand the Rmap procedure, it will help to consider several examples. In our initial examples, all entity types have simple identifiers, and no subtypes or objectified associations occur.

Consider the conceptual schema in Figure 10.9. The many:many fact type maps to a separate table (using rule 1), while the functional fact types map to a table keyed on the identifier of Employee (using rule 2). The primary keys are underlined and the

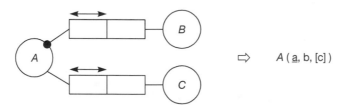

Figure 10.8 Functional fact types of the same object type are grouped together.

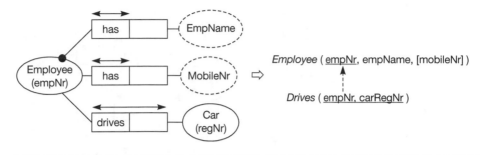

Figure 10.9 A simple relational mapping.

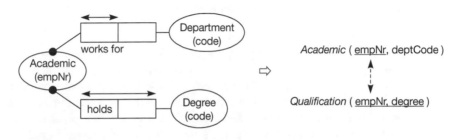

Figure 10.10 The equality constraint entails a referential cycle.

optionality of mobileNr is shown by the square brackets. The dotted arrow depicts the *subset constraint* that each employee referenced in the Drives table is also referenced in the primary key of the Employee table (referential integrity).

Now consider the conceptual schema in Figure 10.10. Notice the *equality constraint,* shown as an arrow-tipped dotted line between the empNr fields of both tables. This is needed since both roles played by Academic are mandatory, and each maps to a different table. An equality constraint is equivalent to two subset constraints, going in opposite directions. This causes a *referential cycle,* since each table refers to the other.

The subset constraint from Qualification.empNr to Academic.empNr is a simple foreign key constraint, since it references a primary key. But the subset constraint from Academic.empNr to Qualification.empNr is not a foreign key constraint, since it targets only part of a primary key. This latter subset constraint may be enforced in various ways (e.g., by assertions, triggers, or stored procedures). Referential cycles typically result from a role that has a mandatory constraint but no simple uniqueness constraint. Since referential cycles require special care to implement, this conceptual constraint pattern should be avoided if possible. In our example, however, the business rule that each academic holds at least one degree does seem reasonable, so in this case we leave it as is.

Before leaving this example, a few more comments about naming are worth making. The table name "Qualification" is one of many possible choices to convey the notion of

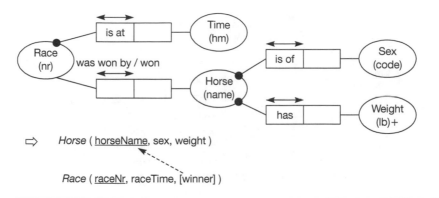

Figure 10.11 An ORM model for horse races.

academics being qualified by their degrees. Two other choices are to use the association name ("Holds") or to concatenate the object type names ("AcademicDegree"). The department column is named "deptCode" because I expect other departmental facts (not shown here) to be recorded in a department table, and I want to avoid using "department" to name both a column and a table. The degree column is named "degree" since I don't expect to record any other facts about degrees. However, if I did expect to record such facts (e.g., degree titles), I would have named this column "degreeCode". In general, if the object type underlying a column will also underlie the primary key of another table, it is advisable to include the reference scheme in the column name.

Now consider Figure 10.11. Here each horse has its sex and weight recorded. Each race has at most one winner (we do not allow ties). There are no composite keys for rule 1 to work on. The sex and weight fact types have functional roles attached to Horse. By rule 2, these two associations must be grouped into the same table keyed on the identifier for Horse. Similarly the time and win fact types are functions of race and are grouped into the Race table. I chose the column name "raceTime" instead of "time" mainly because "time" is a reserved word in SQL. It's best to avoid using reserved words for names, since they require double quotes. Section 11.4 includes a list of SQL reserved words. The column name "winner" is used instead of "horseName" to convey the semantics better.

Mapping 1:1 Associations

Let's now consider some examples involving *1:1 fact types*. In the conceptual schema of Figure 10.12, both Bankcard and Client share a 1:1 association. If we are certain that no other functional roles will be recorded about Bankcard, it is usually best to group the 1:1 fact type together with the other functional fact types into the same table, as shown.

The bankcard column is optional, but the disadvantage of null values here is usually outweighed by the advantage of having all the information in one table. The underlining of bankcard indicates a uniqueness constraint for its non-null values. Because it

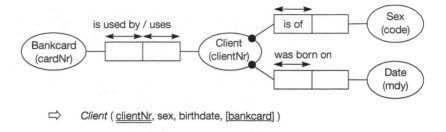

$\Rightarrow$ *Client* (<u>clientNr</u>, sex, birthdate, [<u>bankcard</u>])

Figure 10.12 Mapping choice if Bankcard plays no other functional roles.

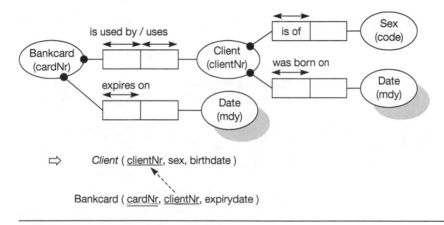

$\Rightarrow$ *Client* (<u>clientNr</u>, sex, birthdate)

Bankcard (<u>cardNr</u>, <u>clientNr</u>, expirydate)

Figure 10.13 Mapping choice if Bankcard plays another functional role.

may contain more than one null, the bankcard column cannot be used to identify rows, and hence cannot be the primary key. With two uniqueness constraints, we doubly underline clientNr to highlight it as the primary key.

If Bankcard does play other functional roles, however, the bankcard usage association should be grouped into a Bankcard table, as shown in Figure 10.13. Notice that the usage role played by Bankcard is now explicitly mandatory; in the previous example it was only implicitly mandatory (because it was the only role played by Bankcard). Notice that *only one role of this 1:1 association is mandatory*. In asymmetric cases like this, it is usually better to *group on the mandatory role side* as shown here.

To illustrate this idea further, consider the conceptual schema in Figure 10.14. Here each employee is primarily identified by his or her employee number, but also has a unique name. Each department has one head, who heads only one department. Since not all employees are department heads, the role of heading is optional. So the 1:1 association between Employee and Department is optional for Employee but mandatory for Department. Since it is usually better to group on the mandatory role side, here this means including the headEmpNr column in the Department table, as shown.

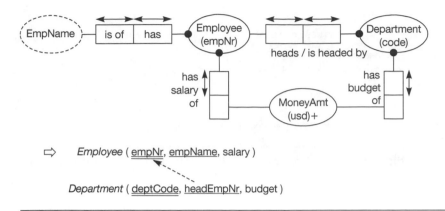

⇨   *Employee* (<u>empNr</u>, <u>empName</u>, salary)

Department (<u>deptCode</u>, <u>headEmpNr</u>, budget)

Figure 10.14 The heads fact type is grouped on the mandatory role side.

Suppose we grouped on the optional side instead, by adding a deptHeaded column to the Employee table. This leads to the following relational schema:

Employee (<u>emplNr</u>, [deptHeaded], <u>empName</u>, salary)

Department (<u>deptCode</u>, budget)

This alternative has two disadvantages. First, the optional deptHeaded column permits null values (unlike the mandatory headEmpNr column). All other things being equal, null values should be avoided if possible. Besides consuming storage, they are often awkward for people to work with. The second disadvantage is that we now have an equality constraint between the tables, rather than just a subset constraint.

In principle, we might group into one table all the functional predicates of both object types involved in a 1:1 association. With our example this gives the scheme *EmployeeDept*(<u>empNr</u>, <u>empName</u>, salary, [deptHeaded, deptBudget]). Here enclosing the last two columns in the same square brackets declares that one is null if and only if the other is.

However, apart from requiring two optional columns and a special constraint that requires them to be null together, this grouping is unnatural. For example, the primary key suggests the whole table deals with employees rather than their departments. For such reasons, this single-table approach should normally be avoided.

Now consider Figure 10.15(a). Here each employee has the use of exactly one company car, and each company car is allocated to exactly one employee. Employees are identified by their employee number and cars by their registration number. The names of employees and the car models (e.g., Mazda MPV) are also recorded, but these need not be unique. Here both roles of the 1:1 association are mandatory, and each is attached to an entity type with another functional role. Should the 1:1 fact type be grouped into an Employee table or into a Car table?

Unlike the previous example, we now have a symmetrical situation with respect to mandatory roles. An arbitrary decision could be made here. We could group to the left,

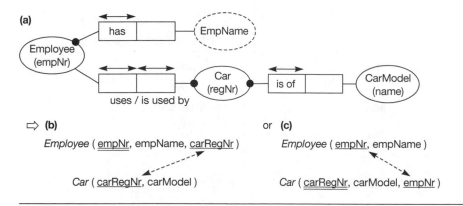

Figure 10.15 The conceptual schema (a) may map to schema (b) or to schema (c).

as in Figure 10.15(b), or to the right, as in Figure 10.15(c). Either of these approaches is reasonable.

We might also try a single table: *EmployeeCar*(empNr, empName, carRegNr, carModel). Although this could be used, it is unnatural, requiring an arbitrary choice of primary key. This becomes more awkward if other facts about employees (e.g., sex, birth date) and cars (e.g., color, purchase date) are recorded in the table. Also, consider the additional update overhead to change the car used by an employee, compared with the two-table approach.

Now what about the case of a 1:1 fact type with both roles optional? For example, consider a UoD identical to that just discussed except that only some employees are given company cars and only some company cars are used by employees (e.g., some may be reserved for important visitors). The two-table approach is recommended. Because of the symmetry with respect to mandatory roles, we could map the 1:1 association into the Employee table to give the schema *Employee*(empNr, empName, carRegNr); *Car*(carRegNr, carModel); Employee.carRegNr references Car. Alternatively we could map it to the Car table yielding the schema *Employee*(empNr, empName); *Car*(carRegNr, carModel, empNr); Car.empNr references Employee. The *percentage of null values* is likely to differ in these two designs. In this case, the design with fewer null values is usually preferable.

Yet another option is a three-table approach, in which the 1:1 association is placed in a table by itself. This option becomes more attractive if the two-table approach yields high percentages of nulls. For example, if only 1 percent of employees and 1 percent of cars are likely to be involved in Employee uses Car, we might map this fact type into a table all by itself, giving three tables overall. A fourth option for 1:1 cases is to use two tables, but include the 1:1 association in both, with a special equality constraint to control the redundancy. More detailed discussions of mapping 1:1 fact types are referenced in the chapter notes. Our simple, default procedure is summarized in Figure 10.16; here "functional role" means a functional role in a fact type (not a reference type).

Each 1:1 fact type maps to only one table:

if   only one object type in the 1:1 predicate has another functional role
              then group on its side   { case (a) }
else if   both object types have other functional roles
              and only one role in the 1:1 is explicitly mandatory
              then group on its side   { case (b) }
else if   no object type has another functional role
              then map the 1:1 to a separate table
else   the grouping choice is up to you

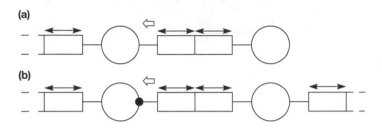

Figure 10.16 Default procedure for mapping 1:1 fact types.

In Figure 10.16, the arrow "⇐" indicates that the 1:1 fact type should be grouped into the functional table of the left-hand object type. In case (a), the right-hand object type may play nonfunctional roles not shown here, and any role in the 1:1 fact type may be optional or mandatory. The third case (no other functional roles) is rare and requires a choice of primary key in the separate table. The final line in the procedure refers to the symmetric cases where the roles of the 1:1 predicate are both mandatory or both optional, and both object types play another functional role—here we have a grouping choice.

To understand some further cases, it will help to recall the fundamental bridge between conceptual and logical levels. This is summarized in Figure 10.17.

In the populated conceptual schema in Figure 10.17(a), the mandatory role pattern anticipates other roles being added later to Employee but not Sex. Figure 10.17(a) abbreviates the primary reference schemes shown explicitly in Figure 10.17(b). The shaded, derived association abbreviates the conceptual path from EmpNr through Employee and Sex to SexCode. This unpacks the semantics underlying the relational schema in Figure 10.17(c).

Recall that uniqueness constraints on reference predicates are the responsibility of humans to enforce. The information system can't stop us from giving the same employee number to two different employees, or giving the same employee two employee numbers. Hence, *uniqueness constraints on primary reference schemes are not mapped.* Instead, we must enforce them in the real world.

Assuming we have enforced the primary reference constraints, however, the system can enforce constraints on the fact types. For example, it enforces the uniqueness constraint in *Employee*(empNr, sex) by ensuring each employee number occurs only once in that column and hence is paired with at most one sex code. Assuming the reference

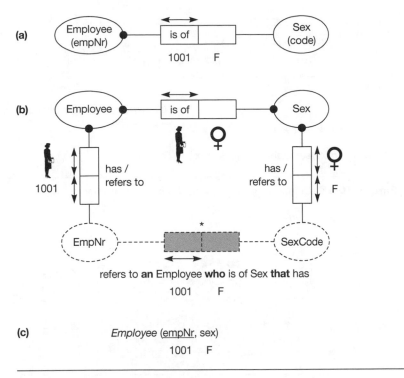

Figure 10.17   The conceptual/logical bridge.

types really are 1:1, this uniqueness constraint on empNr corresponds to the uniqueness constraint on the conceptual fact type (i.e., **each** Employee is of **at most one** Sex). It does not capture any uniqueness constraint from the reference types.

Mapping External Uniqueness Constraints

Let's now consider cases involving *external uniqueness constraints.* In the conceptual schema of Figure 10.18, employees are identified by combining their surname and initials. Since the external uniqueness constraint relates to the primary reference scheme, it is not mapped. In the resulting table scheme *Employee*(surname, initials, sex), the uniqueness constraint corresponds to the uniqueness constraint on the conceptual fact type Employee is of Sex.

A good way to visualize the mapping is as follows:

- Mentally erase the identification scheme of each object type.
- Group facts into tables, using simple surrogates for the real-world objects.
- Replace each surrogate by the attribute(s) used to identify it in the table.

For example, the conceptual schemas of Figures 10.17 and 10.18 each map initially to *Employee*(*e, s*) with the meaning Employee *e* is of Sex *s*. In both cases, *s* is then replaced by "sex". With Figure 10.17, *e* is replaced by empNr; but with Figure 10.18, *e* is

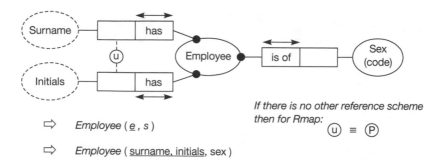

$\Rightarrow$ *Employee (e , s)*

$\Rightarrow$ *Employee (surname, initials, sex)*

Figure 10.18 Composite primary identifier and functional fact type.

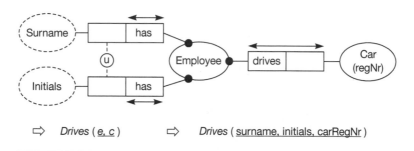

$\Rightarrow$ *Drives (e, c)* $\Rightarrow$ *Drives (surname, initials, carRegNr)*

Figure 10.19 Composite primary identifier and nonfunctional fact type.

unpacked into surname, initials since the identification scheme is composite. Since the uniqueness constraint spans *e*, it must also span the attribute combination that replaces it.

Now consider the conceptual schema of Figure 10.19. The structural difference here is that the fact type has a composite uniqueness constraint. We may initially think of it as mapping to the table *Drives*(*e, c*), where *e* and *c* are surrogates for the employee and car. Replacing the surrogates by the real identifiers results in the table scheme *Drives* (surname, initials, carRegNr). Since *e* was just part of a longer key, so is the composite identifier for employee that replaces it.

Now consider the conceptual schema of Figure 10.20. This is like that of Figure 10.18 except that Employee now has empNr as its primary identifier. The external uniqueness constraint now applies to two fact types rather than reference types, and hence can be mapped and enforced by the information system. As shown, this maps to a uniqueness constraint spanning surname and initials in the relational table (ensuring each surname, initials combination is paired with only one employee number). The uniqueness constraint on the table's primary key, empNr, captures the three simple uniqueness constraints on the three conceptual fact types (since each empNr is unique, it is paired with only one surname, only one sequence of initials, and only one sex).

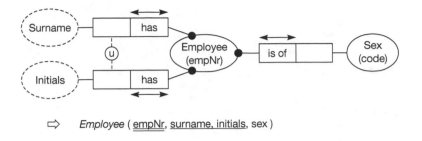

⇨   *Employee* (<u>empNr</u>, <u>surname, initials</u>, sex)

Figure 10.20 Composite secondary identifier and functional fact type.

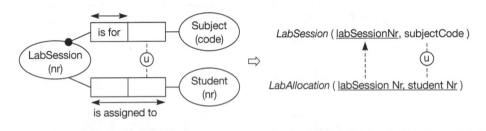

Figure 10.21 External uniqueness constraint involving a nonfunctional fact type.

Now consider the conceptual schema of Figure 10.21. Here each laboratory session is primarily identified by a session number and is used for a particular subject. Once these subject bookings have been made, sessions are assigned for use by students. The external uniqueness constraint says that each student is assigned at most one session for each subject (e.g., laboratory resources might be scarce). Since this constraint involves fact types rather than reference types, it can be mapped.

An unusual feature of this example is the association of the external uniqueness constraint with an *m:n* fact type (LabSession is assigned to Student). Because the *m:n* fact type must map to a table by itself, the external uniqueness constraint ends up spanning two tables in the relational schema. This is equivalent to an internal uniqueness constraint spanning subject and studentNr in the natural join of the two tables.

Let's now discuss some cases involving *nesting*. Recall that by default, a uniqueness constraint is assumed to span any objectified predicate. In Figure 10.22 the associa-tion "worked on" is objectified as Work. This nested object type plays one mandatory and one optional role, both of which are functional. As with other object types, we *ini-tially treat the nested object type as a "black box", mentally erasing its identification scheme.*

From this viewpoint, the conceptual schema appears to have just two fact types, both having functional roles attached to the object type "Work". *Fact types are now grouped in the usual way.* So these two fact types are grouped into the same table. Visual-izing the nested object type "Work" as a black box, "■", results in the table *Work*

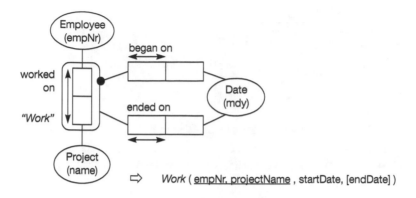

Figure 10.22 An active, objectified association with functional roles.

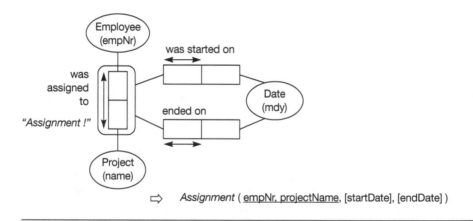

Figure 10.23 An independent, objectified association with functional roles.

(■, startDate, [endDate]). Finally we *unpack* ■ *into its component attributes* (empNr and projectName), giving *Work*(empNr, projectName, startDate, [endDate]).

Mapping Independent Object Types

Now consider the conceptual schema of Figure 10.23. Here employees might be assigned to projects before their actual starting date is known. So some instances of the objectified Assignment association might be recorded that (in some database state) do not play either of the attached roles.

Recall that the disjunction of roles attached to an objectified predicate is not assumed to be mandatory. In this example, since even the disjunction of the attached roles is optional, the nested object type is *independent*—this is noted by the exclamation mark in "Assignment !". Contrast this with the previous example, where the nested object type Work was active. Independent object types, whether nested or not, require special treatment in mapping, as follows:

- Map each independent object type and its functional fact types (if any) to a separate table, with the object type identifier as the primary key and all other attributes optional.

For example, in Figure 10.23 both the start date and end date attributes are optional. If we wish to record just the fact that an employee is assigned to a particular project, we enter values just for empNr and projectName. Details about start and end dates for work on the project can be added later when they are known.

Figure 10.24 shows another way to model this UoD. Here the independent object type has no functional roles attached. In this case, it maps to a table all by itself. The *m:n* fact type maps to another table. A subset constraint captures its optionality. If instead we tried to map everything to one table, this would violate entity integrity (why?).

You may have noticed that some constraints are missing in Figures 10.23 and 10.24. To begin with, the date on which a worker ends work on a project must be after or on the starting date. This should be specified as a textual constraint. Moreover, in the real world an employee can end work on a project only if he or she started the project. The schemas shown allow us to record an end date without a start date.

In practical applications, we sometimes allow things like this because our information may be incomplete. For example, we might want to record the date somebody ended a project, but not *know* when that person started. For the same reason, conceptual schemas sometimes have fewer mandatory roles than the ideal world suggests, and in consequence relational schemas may have more optional columns than complete knowledge would allow.

Suppose, however, that if we know an end date, then we *do* know the starting date. To enforce this constraint in Figure 10.23, add a subset constraint on the conceptual schema from the first role of the "ended on" predicate to the first role of the "was

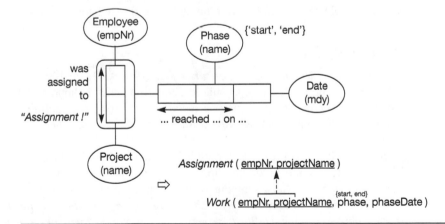

Figure 10.24 An independent, objectified association with no functional roles.

started on" predicate. This constraint may be declared in the relational schema by using *nested option brackets*. Here we enclose the option brackets for endDate *inside* the option brackets for startDate, giving *Assignment*(empNr, projectName, [startDate, [endDate]]). This indicates a (non-null) value is recorded for endDate only if a value is recorded for startDate.

To add this constraint to Figure 10.24 is not as easy. A textual constraint is required at both conceptual and relational levels to declare that for each employee-project pair, phase "end" is recorded only if phase "start" is. Apart from complicating the enforcement of this constraint, should it be required, the approach of Figure 10.24 spreads the information over more tables and demands an intertable constraint. This is usually undesirable, since it typically slows down the execution of queries and updates. For such reasons, the approach of Figure 10.23 is normally preferred to that of Figure 10.24.

Chapter 12 examines in detail the notion of "equivalent" conceptual schemas and provides guidelines for transforming a conceptual schema to improve the efficiency of the relational schema obtained from Rmap.

If the date on which an employee begins work on a project is recorded, a derivation rule can be specified to compute the period for the employee to complete work on the project (by subtracting the start date from the end date, if known). Since each computer system has an internal clock, conceptually there is a unary fact type of the form Date is today. So for someone still working on a project we could also derive the time spent so far on the project, by subtracting the start date from the current value for "today".

By default, derived facts are not stored. So *by default, derived columns are excluded from the base tables* (i.e., stored tables) of the relational schema. However, the derivation rules should be mapped. These may be set out using view definitions, triggers, and so on (recall the earlier net pay example).

In some cases, efficiency considerations may lead us to derive on update rather than at query time, and store the derived information. In such cases the derived fact type is marked "**" on the conceptual schema diagram. During the relational mapping, the fact type is mapped to a base table, and the derivation rule is mapped to a rule that is triggered by updates to the base table. As well as derivation rules, *all* conceptual constraints should be mapped (not just uniqueness and mandatory constraints).

Mapping Subtypes

Let's now consider the *mapping of subtype constraints*. Table 10.1 was met earlier in Chapter 6. Although we have no rule to determine when a phone number is recorded, we know that prostate status may be recorded only for men, and pregnancies are recorded for all women and only for women. The conceptual schema is reproduced in Figure 10.25.

Some limited support for subtyping is included in the SQL standard, but current relational systems typically do not directly support this concept. Nevertheless, there are three main ways in which subtyping can be implemented on current systems: absorption, separation, and partition. With *absorption,* we *absorb the subtypes back into the (top) supertype* (giving *qualified optional roles*), *group the fact types as usual,* and then *add the subtyping constraints as textual qualifications,* as shown in Figure 10.25.

Table 10.1 Details about hospital patients.

PatientNr	Name	Sex	Phone	Prostate status	Pregnancies
101	Adams A	M	2052061	OK	—
102	Blossom F	F	3652999	—	5
103	Jones E	F	?	—	0
104	King P	M	?	benign enlargement	—
105	Smith J	M	2057654	?	—

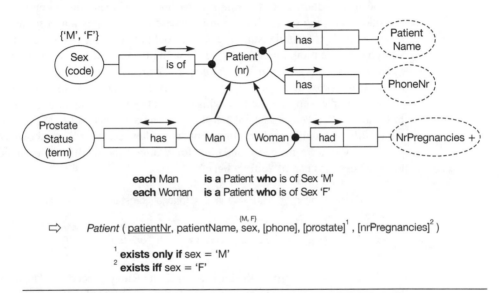

each Man **is a** Patient **who** is of Sex 'M'
each Woman **is a** Patient **who** is of Sex 'F'

⇨   *Patient* (<u>patientNr</u>, patientName, sex$^{\{M, F\}}$, [phone], [prostate]^1 , [nrPregnancies]^2)

    ^{1} **exists only if** sex = 'M'
    ^{2} **exists iff** sex = 'F'

Figure 10.25 Subtype constraints on functional roles map to qualified optionals.

To best understand this example, visualize the subtypes on the conceptual schema being absorbed back into the supertype Patient, with the subtype roles now attached as qualified optional roles to Patient. All the roles attached to Patient are functional, so the fact types all map to the same table as shown. The phone, prostate, and nrPregnancies attributes are all optional, but the latter two are qualified.

In the qualifications, "**exists**" means the value is not null. Qualification 1 is a pure subtype constraint, indicating that a non-null value for prostate is recorded on a row **only if** the value of sex on that row is 'M'. Some men might have a null value recorded here. Qualification 2 expresses both a subtype constraint (number of pregnancies is recorded **only if** sex is 'F') and a mandatory role constraint (nrPregnancies is recorded **if** sex is 'F'). Recall that "**iff**" is short for "if and only if".

Since only functional fact types are involved in this example, the absorption approach leads to a table that basically matches that of the original output report (except that most relational systems support only one kind of null value). The main advantage of this approach is that it maps all the functional predicates of a subtype family into a single table. This usually makes related queries and updates more efficient. Its main disadvantage is that it generates null values.

The second main approach, *separation,* creates separate tables for the subtype-specific facts. With this approach, the conceptual schema of Figure 10.25 maps to three tables: one for the common facts, one for the man-specific facts, and one for the woman-specific facts. The third main approach, *partition,* may be used when the subtypes form a partition of their supertype. Since Man and Woman are exclusive and exhaustive, this approach may be used here, resulting in two tables, one containing all the facts about the male patients and the other all the facts about female patients.

The next section discusses the relative merits of these three approaches and also considers mapping of a subtype family where the subtypes may use an identification scheme different from the supertype's. Our default approach, however, is to absorb the subtypes before grouping. Note that even with this approach, *any fact types with a non-functional role played by a subtype map to separate tables, with their subtype definitions expressed by qualified subset constraints* targeting the main supertype table.

For example, suppose the following *m:n* fact type is attached optionally to Woman in Figure 10.25: Woman attended prenatal clinic on Date. This fact type maps to a separate table with the qualified subset constraint "**only where** sex = 'F'", as shown below. If the new fact type were instead mandatory for Woman, the qualification would read "**exactly where**" instead of "**only where**".

$$Patient \; (\; \underline{patientNr}, \; patientName, \; sex, \; [phone], \; [prostate]^1 \; , \; [nrPregnancies]^2 \;)$$
$$\{M, F\}$$

▲
$$\vdots \; 3$$
$$PreNatalVisit \; (\; \underline{patientNr, \; attendanceDate} \;)$$

^{1} **exists only if** sex = 'M'
^{2} **exists iff** sex = 'F'
^{3} **only where** sex = 'F'

We have now covered all the basic steps in the Rmap procedure. These may be summarized as shown below. Even if you are using a CASE tool to do the mapping for you, it's nice to understand how the mapping works.

Step 0 may be thought of as a preparatory mental exercise. Erasing all explicit primary reference schemes (i.e., those other than parenthesized reference modes) ensures that all the remaining predicates on display (as box sequences) belong to fact types (rather than reference types). Recall that a *compositely identified object type* is either a nested object type (objectified association) or a coreferenced object type (primarily identified with an external uniqueness constraint).

Basic Rmap procedure:

0   Absorb subtypes into their top supertype.
    Mentally erase all explicit primary identification schemes;
    treat compositely identified object types as "black boxes".

1   Map each fact type with a compound UC ⬓⬓ to a separate table.

2   Fact types with functional roles attached to the same object type ○—▭
    are grouped into the same table, keyed on the object type's identifier.
    Map 1:1 cases to a single table, generally favoring fewer nulls.

3 Map each independent object type with no functional roles to a separate table.

4 Unpack each "black box column" into its component attributes.

5 Map all other constraints and derivation rules.
Subtype constraints on functional roles map to qualified optional columns, and on nonfunctional roles to qualified subset constraints.

There are plenty of questions in the section exercise to give you practice at performing the mapping manually. As preparation for this exercise, some larger examples are now considered.

Figure 10.26 shows the conceptual schema for the compact disc case study discussed in Chapter 5. If you feel confident, you might like to try mapping this to a relational schema yourself before reading on.

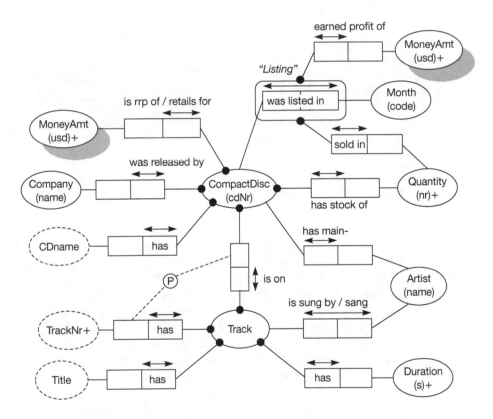

* totalQtySold(*Month*) ::= **sum**(Quantity) **from** (Listing(CompactDisc,*Month*) sold in Quantity)
* totalProfit(*Month*) ::= **sum**(MoneyAmt)
             from (Listing(CompactDisc,*Month*) earned profit of MoneyAmt)

Figure 10.26 The conceptual schema from the compact disc case study.

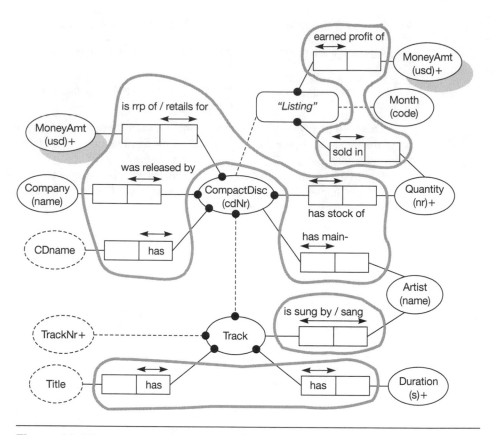

Figure 10.27 Reference types are erased, and fact types are lassoed into groups.

As there are no subtypes in this example, step 0 amounts to mentally erasing any primary reference schemes that are shown explicitly. There are only two, each involving a compositely identified object type: Track and Listing. Figure 10.27 depicts this erasure by removing the predicate boxes and showing their connections to object types as dashed lines. For steps 1–3 we treat these two compositely identified object types just like any other object type.

We now proceed to group fact types into tables. To help visualize this we *place a lasso around each group of predicates that map to the same table* (see Figure 10.27). We lasso only the predicates, not the object types. Since each fact type should map to exactly one table, *all predicates must be lassoed,* and *no lassos may overlap.*

In step 1 we look around for a predicate with a compound uniqueness constraint. Since the objectified association is now hidden, we see only one such predicate: is sung by. So we lasso this predicate, indicating it goes to a table all by itself.

In step 2 we group functional fact types of the same object type together. For example, CompactDisc has five functional roles attached to it, so these five fact types are grouped into a table keyed on the identifier for CompactDisc. Similarly the two

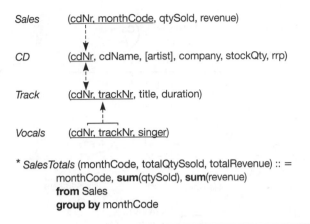

Sales (<u>cdNr, monthCode</u>, qtySold, revenue)

CD (<u>cdNr</u>, cdName, [artist], company, stockQty, rrp)

Track (<u>cdNr, trackNr</u>, title, duration)

Vocals (<u>cdNr, trackNr, singer</u>)

* *SalesTotals* (monthCode, totalQtySsold, totalRevenue) :: =
   monthCode, **sum**(qtySold), **sum**(revenue)
   from Sales
   group by monthCode

Figure 10.28 Relational schema mapped from the conceptual schema of Figure 10.26.

functional fact types for Track are lassoed together, as are the two functional fact types of the nested object type. This example has no 1:1 cases and no independent object types. We have now roped all the predicates, and there are four lassos, so the conceptual schema maps to four tables.

The final relational schema is shown in Figure 10.28. Since five functional fact types map to the CD (CompactDisc) table, and all the objects involved have simple identifiers, this table has six columns (one for the key and one for each fact attribute). The other three tables involve a compositely identified object type, which is unpacked into its component attributes (step 4).

The keys of the tables are already determined, but the mandatory role constraints are enforced by mandatory columns and intertable subset/equality constraints. Note the composite subset constraint from the pair cdNr, trackNr in Vocals to the primary key of Track. Finally the two derivation rules are mapped (step 5).

If you lasso fact types into groups before writing down the table schemes, you may mentally erase all primary identification schemes (including reference modes) in step 0 (thus treating all object types as black boxes), then in step 4 replace each column by its identifying attribute(s). This alternative formulation of the Rmap procedure is logically cleaner. If performing Rmap manually, you might find it convenient to photocopy the conceptual schema and use colored pencils to cross out the reference types and lasso the fact types. As a complicated example, consider the conceptual schema in Figure 10.29.

This concerns television channels. Notice that Time is modeled as a coreferenced entity type (a time point is identified as a given hour on a given day). For variety, the object types Office and Dept are modeled as objectified associations. A television channel may have different offices in different suburbs. For this application, a channel may have only one office in any given suburb. A given office may have many departments. For example, one department might be the advertising department for the channel 9 office located in the suburb Toowong. Alternatively (and arguably more naturally) the

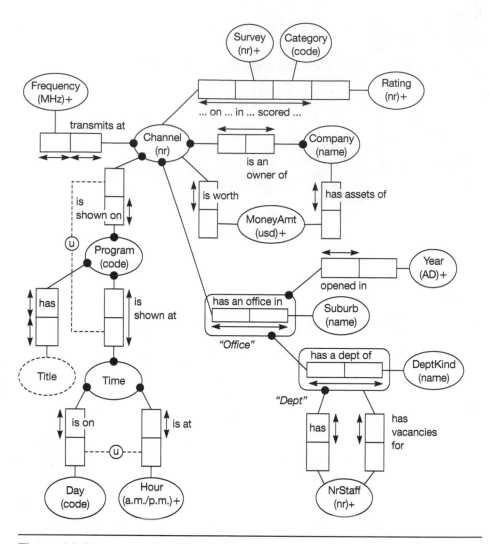

Figure 10.29 An ORM model for TV channels.

object types Office and Dept could have been modeled as coreferenced object types. However, this would not change the mapping.

The external uniqueness constraint on Program indicates that a channel can screen only one program at a given time. As an exercise, try to map this yourself before reading on. Start by mentally erasing the reference types, and lassoing the fact types that should be grouped together, before you write down the relational schema.

Figure 10.30 hides the identifying predicates for Time, Office, and Dept, and lassos the fact types into groups. The 1:1 associations must be grouped with Channel and Program since these have other functional roles, but Frequency and Title do not.

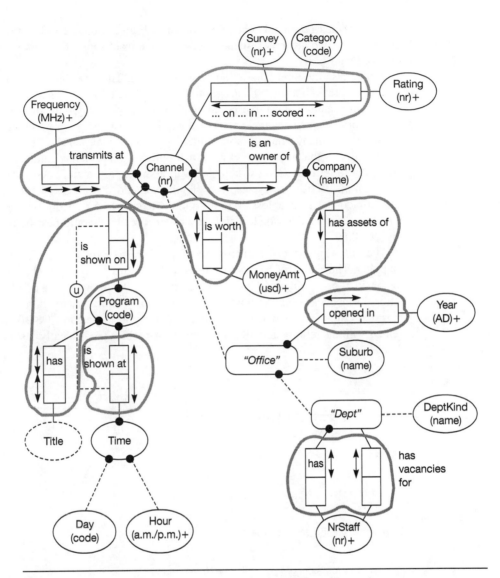

Figure 10.30 Reference types are erased, and fact types are grouped.

The detailed relational schema is shown in Figure 10.31. The identifier for Office unpacks into two attributes, while the Dept key unpacks into three (two for Office and one for DeptKind).

Notice also the intertable uniqueness constraint. This indicates that when a natural join is performed between the Program and ProgTime tables, there will be a uniqueness constraint spanning the three columns channelNr, progDay, and progHour. In other words, for any given channel and time, there is at most one program being shown.

Notice the many equality constraints in the relational schema. These lead to referential cycles that may be awkward to implement. The many mandatory roles also entail that a lot of data must be entered in a single transaction. As discussed earlier, to minimize referential cycles, you should not add a mandatory role constraint to a nonfunctional role unless it is absolutely required. As an optional exercise, you may wish to consider which mandatory role constraints would best be removed from Figure 10.29.

The following exercise contains lots of questions to give you practice with relational mapping. The choice of names for tables and columns is up to you, but you may wish to consider the naming guidelines discussed earlier. Mapping from a conceptual to a relational schema is a bit like doing CSDP step 1 in reverse. Try to choose names for tables and columns that would make it easier for you to perform CSDP step 1 if presented with the relational tables. Remember that tables are basically just collections of facts.

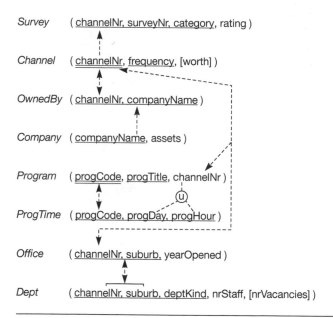

Figure 10.31 Relational schema mapped from the model in Figure 10.29.

Exercise 10.3

1. Map the following conceptual schema onto a relational schema, using the Rmap procedure. Use descriptive table and column names. Underline the keys, and enclose any optional columns in square brackets. Indicate any subset or equality constraints.

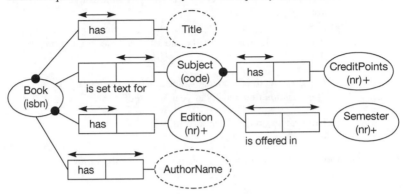

2. Rmap the following conceptual schema.

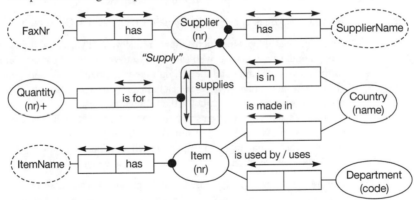

3. (a) The conceptual schema for a given UoD is shown below. A novice designer maps the likes and costs fact types into a single table: *Likes* (<u>woman, dress</u>, cost). Explain with the aid of a small sample population why this table is badly designed. Use surrogates w1, w2, ... for women and d1, d2, ... for dresses.

   (b) Rmap the conceptual schema.

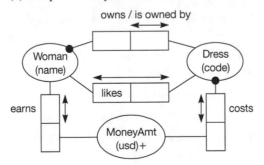

4. In a given UoD, each lecturer has at least one degree and optionally has taught at one or more institutions. Each lecturer has exactly one identifying name and at most one nickname. Each degree is standardly identified by its code, but also has a unique title. Some degrees might not be held by any current lecturer. Each institution is identified by its name. The sex and birth year of the lecturers is recorded, as well as the years in which their degrees were awarded.

   (a) A novice designer develops a relational schema for this UoD that includes the following two tables. Explain, with the aid of a sample population, why these tables are badly designed.

   Lecturer (lecturerName, sex, degreeCode, degreeTitle)
   Qualification (degreeCode, yearAwarded)

   (b) Draw a conceptual schema for this UoD.
   (c) Rmap your answer to (b).

5. Add constraints to your conceptual schema for the following, then perform Rmap.
   (a) Exercise 3.5, Question 2.
   (b) Exercise 3.5, Question 3.

6. Rmap the Invoice conceptual schema for Exercise 6.3, Question 3.

7. Rmap the Oz Bank conceptual schema for Exercise 6.4, Question 6.

8. Consider a naval UoD in which sailors are identified by a sailorNr and ships by a shipNr, although both have names as well (not necessarily unique). We must record the sex, rank, and birth date of each sailor and the weight in tonnes (metric tons) and construction date of each ship. Each ship may have only one captain and vice versa. Specify a conceptual schema and relational schema for this UoD for the following cases.
   (a) Each captain commands a ship, but some ships might not have captains.
   (b) Each ship has a captain, but some captains might not command a ship.
   (c) Each captain commands a ship, and each ship has a captain.
   (d) Some captains might not command a ship, and some ships might not have captains.

9. Consider a UoD in which students enroll in subjects and later obtain scores on one or more tests for each subject. Schematize this conceptually using nesting, then Rmap it.
   (a) Assume that scores are available for all enrollments.
   (b) Assume that enrollments are recorded before any scores become known.

10. Rmap the conceptual schema in Figure 6.44 (absorb the subtypes before mapping).

11. Refer to the MediaSurvey conceptual schema in Figure 6.52.
    (a) Rmap this schema (absorb subtypes).
    (b) Set out an alternative relational schema with separate tables for each node in the subtype graph. Which schema is preferable?

12. (a) Rmap the Taxpayer conceptual schema for Exercise 6.5, Question 3(a).
    (b) Rmap the Taxpayer conceptual schema for Exercise 6.5, Question 3(b).

13. Rmap the SolarSystem conceptual schema for Exercise 6.5, Question 6.

14. Rmap the conceptual schema in Figure 7.5 (note that Panel is an independent object type).

15. Rmap the CountryBorders conceptual schema for Exercise 7.3, Question 5.

16. Rmap the following conceptual schema.

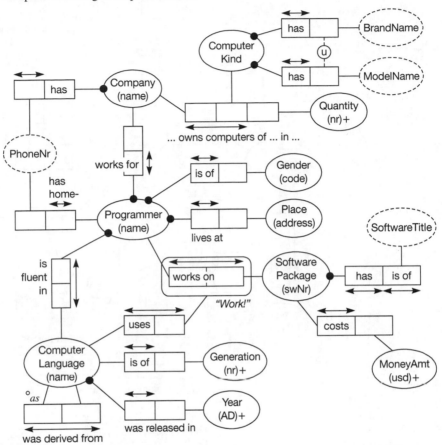

17. Rmap the following conceptual schema. Note that Degree is compositely identified (e.g., a Ph.D. from UCLA and a Ph.D. from MIT are treated as different degrees). Student is also compositely identified (by the time you finish the mapping you will appreciate how much better it would be to use a studentNr instead!). The codes 'y', 'n', 'PT', 'FT', 'int', and 'ext' abbreviate "yes", "no", "part time", "full time", "internal", and "external".

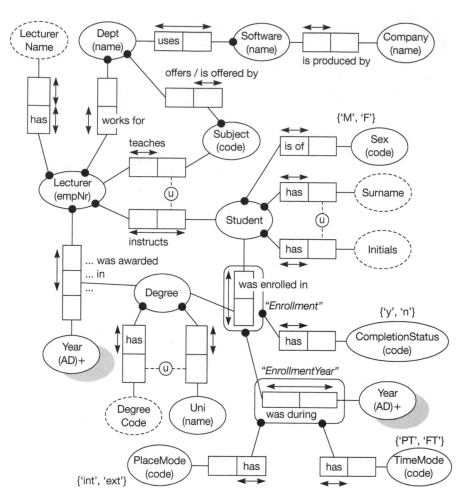

18. Rmap the following conceptual schema. Ignore the implicit semantic connection between Year and Date.

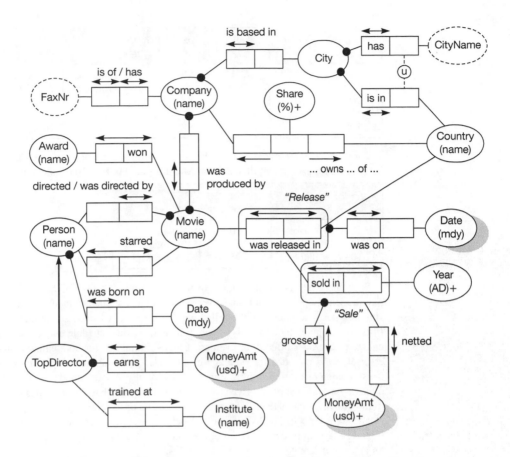

each TopDirector **is a** Person **who** directed a Movie **that** won **an** Award

19. A life insurance company maintains an information system about its clients. The following information samples are extracted from a fragment of this system. For simplicity, several data items (e.g., client's name and address) are omitted and may be ignored for this question. Each client is identified by his or her client number (clientNr).

    The following table uses these abbreviations: Emp. = employment (EA = employed by another; SE = self-employed; NE = not employed); Acct = accounting; NS = nonsmoker; S = smoker. Some clients are referred by other clients (referrers) to take out a policy (this entitles referrers to special benefits outside our UoD). The value "?" is an ordinary null value meaning "not recorded" (e.g., nonexistent or unknown). The value "−" means "inapplicable" (because of some other data).

ClientNr	Referrer	Birth date	Smoking status	Emp. status	Job	Work phone	Acct. firm
101	?	15/2/46	NS	EA	lecturer	3650001	–
102	?	15/2/46	S	SE	builder	9821234	Acme
103	101	1/1/70	NS	NE	–	–	–
104	103	3/4/65	S	EA	painter	?	–
105	?	1/1/70	NS	SE	painter	2692900	?

For each client a record of major illnesses (if any) is kept; one recovery figure and hospital is noted for each client illness. The extract for clients 101–105 is shown:

ClientNr	Illness	Degree (%) of recovery	Hospital treated
102	stroke	90	Wandin Valley
	diabetes	80	Burrigan
103	diabetes	95	Wandin Valley

Each client selects one insurance coverage (currently $25,000, $50,000, or $100,000) and pays a monthly premium for this coverage. Premiums are determined by coverage, age, and smoking status, as shown in the following schedule. This schedule is stored in the database (it is not computed by a formula). From time to time, this schedule may change in premiums charged, coverages offered, or even age groups. Premiums for both smokers and nonsmokers are always included for each age group/coverage combination. For simplicity, only the latest version of the schedule is stored (a history of previous schedules is not kept). Moreover, payments must be for 1 year at a time, and are calculated as 12 times the relevant premium current at the date of payment (using the age of the client at that date).

The computer system has an internal clock, which may be conceptually viewed as providing an always up-to-date instance of the fact type "Date is today". You may use **"today"** as an initialized date variable in derivation rules.

Age (y)	Nonsmoker premiums ($)			Smoker premiums ($)		
	25,000 coverage	50,000 coverage	100,000 coverage	25,000 coverage	50,000 coverage	100,000 coverage
21–39	5.00	7.50	12.50	6.50	10.50	18.50
40–49	6.50	10.50	18.50	10.00	17.50	32.50
50–59	13.00	23.50	34.00	24.00	45.50	88.50
60–69	36.50	70.50	138.50	57.50	112.50	222.50

Though not shown in the schedule, age groups are primarily identified by an age group number (currently in the range 1..4).

Assume all clients have paid their 12-month fee by completing a form like that shown below (details such as name and address are omitted for this exercise). The first four fields are completed by the insurance agency and the rest by the client. Records of any previous payments are outside the UoD.

```
┌─────────────────────────────────────────────────────────────┐
│  ClientNr: _____                                         │
│                                                              │
│  Insurance coverage: $ _____                        │
│                                                              │
│  Date: _____                                      │
│                                                              │
│  Payment for next 12 months' insurance: $ _____ │
│                                                              │
│                                                              │
│  Method of payment (Please check one): ❏ cash  ❏ check  ❏ credit card │
│                                                              │
│  If paying by credit card, complete the following:           │
│                                                              │
│  ❏ Visa         ❏ Mastercard        ❏ Bankcard              │
│                                                              │
│  Card Number: ❏❏❏❏ ❏❏❏❏ ❏❏❏❏ ❏❏❏❏                          │
│                                                              │
│  Card expiration date: ❏❏❏❏                                 │
└─────────────────────────────────────────────────────────────┘
```

Choose suitable codes to abbreviate payment methods and card types. Each credit card is used by at most two clients (e.g., husband and wife). In practice the card type could be derived from the starting digits of the card number, but ignore this possibility for this question.

(a) Specify a conceptual schema for this UoD. Include **all** graphic constraints and any noteworthy textual constraints. Include subtype definitions and derivation rules. If a derived fact type should be stored, include it on the diagram with an "**" mark.

(b) Should the payment by a client be derived only, stored only, or both? Discuss the practical issues involved in making this decision.

(c) Map your conceptual schema to a relational schema, absorbing subtypes while maintaining subtype constraints. Underline keys and mark optional columns with square brackets. Include **all** constraints. As an optional exercise, map any derivation rules.

10.4   Advanced Mapping Aspects

The previous section discussed the main steps in the default relational mapping procedure (Rmap). Step 0 of this procedure may be refined as shown below. This section discusses these refinements in order and clarifies some fine points. If desired, this section may be safely skipped on a first reading.

Rmap Step 0:

0.1 Mentally binarize any unaries, and cater to any relative closure.
0.2 Mentally erase all reference (primary identification) predicates.
    Treat compositely identified object types as "black boxes".
0.3 Indicate any absorption overrides for subtypes.
0.4 Identify any derived fact types that must be stored.
0.5 Indicate mapping choices for symmetric 1:1 cases.
0.6 Consider replacing any disjunctive reference schemes, by using an artificial or concatenated identifier or mandatory defaults.
0.7 Indicate mapping choice where required for any objectified associations that have no spanning uniqueness constraint.

As background to step 0.1, please review the discussion of relative closure in Section 7.4. Now consider a UoD about applications (e.g., for jobs or loans). Suppose that Figure 10.32 is used to model part of this UoD.

The relative closure boxes (□) on the unaries indicate that if an application succeeded or failed this must be known. Since the disjunction of these unaries is optional, it is possible that the fate of some applications is undecided. As explained in detail in Chapter 12, a schema transformation may be performed to replace these exclusive unaries by the binary shown in Figure 10.33.

Here the status of the application is identified by a code (S = succeeded, F = failed, U = undecided). This transformation is understood to be performed automatically as a preprocessing stage to the rest of Rmap. For analysis purposes, you may still work with the original conceptual schema unless you prefer the transformed version. The final result of the mapping is shown at the bottom of Figure 10.33. For another example of step 0.1, see the model used to illustrate relative closure in Section 7.4 (the final mapping is left as an exercise).

Step 0.2 involves mentally erasing any reference predicates and treating objectified associations as simple object types. The previous section discussed typical cases. Figure 10.34 depicts a special case. Here each Olympic games is identified by the year in which it is held. There are three fact types (Athlete competes in Games; Athlete was born in Year; City hosts Games) and one reference type (Games is held in Year).

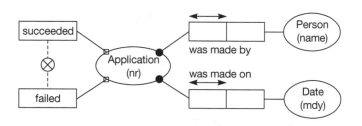

Figure 10.32 How do the unaries map?

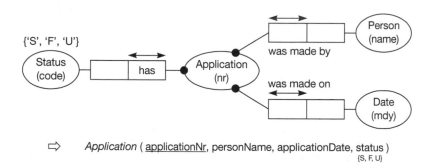

Figure 10.33 The result of binarizing the unaries in Figure 10.32.

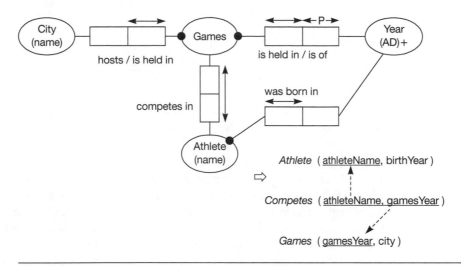

Figure 10.34 Games is identified by a single, explicit reference type.

The reference type must be shown explicitly, since Year is an entity type, not a value type. Using this reference type and the birth fact type we may derive, if desired, the approximate ages of athletes at various games. One instance of the hosts fact type is: The City with name 'Sydney' hosts the Games that is held in the Year 2000 AD.

It is rare to have an object type identified by means of a single, explicit reference type. To map this case, first mentally erase the reference type, leaving the three fact types to be grouped into tables. As an exercise, try the mapping yourself and then check your answer with the solution shown in Figure 10.34.

By default, subtypes are absorbed into their root supertype for mapping purposes. Although the subtype constraints are still mapped (as qualifications on optional columns or intertable subset constraints), absorption generally causes any functional roles of subtypes to be grouped together with the functional roles of the root supertype. In step 0.3 we may wish to override this default. Let's consider some examples, starting with the usual case where the subtypes inherit the primary reference scheme of their top supertype.

Figure 10.35 depicts a simple subtype graph with functional roles. Reference schemes and subtype definitions are omitted for simplicity. As discussed in the previous section, there are three basic ways in which the functional fact types associated with the nodes may be grouped into tables: *absorption, separation,* and *partition.*

The first option *absorbs* the subtypes back into the supertype before grouping. For example, assume all the roles played by *A, B,* and *C* are functional (i.e., they have a simple uniqueness constraint). In this case we generate just one table (with subtype constraints expressed as qualifications on the optional subtype attributes). This absorption default has two main advantages: better performance is achieved for queries that require attributes from more than one node (no joins required), and subtype constraints are usually easy to specify and cheap to enforce (no joins).

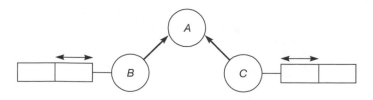

Figure 10.35 How do we map functional fact types played by subtypes?

The main disadvantages of subtype absorption are the following: nulls are required for objects that belong to only one of the subtypes; the functional table of the supertype is larger (more columns); queries about only one subtype require a restriction; and viewing just a subtype is less convenient (projection and restriction needed). Usually the advantages outweigh the disadvantages. Note that any nonfunctional roles of the subtypes map to separate tables anyway, so these are not affected by our subtype mapping choice.

The second option, *separation,* groups the functional roles attached directly to each object type node into separate tables, one for each node. Here the functional predicates of *A* map to one table (the common properties), the attributes specific to *B* map to another table, and the attributes specific to *C* map to a third table. The main advantages of separation are that it minimizes nulls, and queries about each subtype are fast. Its main weaknesses are the following: queries requiring attributes from more than one node are slower (joins needed), and insertions to subtype tables are slower (subtype constraints are now specified as qualified subset constraints, so access to a supertable is required to enforce them).

The third option is to horizontally *partition* the instances of *A*. This should normally be considered only if *B* and *C* form a partition of *A* (i.e., they are exclusive and exhaustive: $B \cap C = \{ \}$; $B \cup C = A$). In this case one table holds all the functional predicates of *B* (including those attached to *A*), and another holds all the functional predicates of *C*. However, if *B* and *C* do not exhaust *A*, a separate table is needed for $A - (B \cup C)$.

If *B* and *C* overlap, redundancy results for the facts about $B \cap C$, and this must be controlled. This partition option departs from the usual practice of grouping each fact type into only one table and tends to be useful only in distributed or federated database settings.

The main advantages of partitioning the supertype are the following: it minimizes nulls; queries about all the properties of *B* (or *C*) are fast; and subtype constraints typically need not be coded (because implied) or are trivial to code (e.g., Man and Woman tables without/with sex field). Its main disadvantages are the following: it results in slow queries about all of *A*, or *B* and *C* (joins needed); it is very awkward unless *B* and *C* form a partition of *A*; and if *B* and *C* are exclusive, enforcement of this constraint normally requires intertable access.

The criteria discussed can help us decide whether to override the default absorption option. Override decisions may be indicated by annotating the schema in an

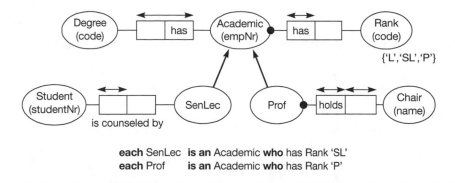

each SenLec   **is an** Academic **who** has Rank 'SL'
each Prof   **is an** Academic **who** has Rank 'P'

Figure 10.36 Senior lecturers and professors play specific roles.

appropriate way, or perhaps by selecting from an option list in a CASE tool. For larger subtype graphs, the mapping choices increase rapidly, as mixtures of the three options might be used.

To clarify some of the previous discussion, let's look at a couple of examples. Consider the conceptual schema in Figure 10.36. Here academics have one of three ranks (L = lecturer, SL = senior lecturer, P = professor). Students may be counseled only by senior lecturers, and academic chairs are held only by professors. Since the subtypes do not form a partition of Academic, we would normally choose either absorption or separation to map them. As an exercise try both these options yourself before reading on.

In the counseling predicate, the role attached to SenLec is not functional. So this predicate maps to a separate table regardless of whether we choose absorption or separation. Also, being *m:n*, the degrees fact type maps to a separate table regardless. So the only choice we have in the subtype mapping is whether or not to group the rank and chair fact types together. With absorption, we do so (see Figure 10.37(a)). With separation we do not (see Figure 10.37(b)). Note the different ways of specifying the subtype and mandatory role constraints for the Professor subtype.

In the subset constraint qualifications, the **"only where"** captures the subtype constraint, while **"exactly where"** covers both subtyping and mandatory role constraints. Let's now restrict our attention to the mapping of functional predicates of the nodes in the subtype graph, since the mapping of other predicates to separate tables with qualified subset constraints is straightforward.

As an example with multiple inheritance, consider Figure 10.38. This figure also shows one way of displaying an ER view of an ORM diagram. Here all attributes are single valued; underlining an attribute indicates the 1:1 nature. The absence of a mandatory role dot on nrKids (number of children) indicates that recording of this attribute is optional for female academics.

Suppose we decide on separate tables for each subtype. This yields the relational schema in Figure 10.39. Note that qualified subset constraints from FemaleProf.empNr to Professor.empNr and FemaleAc.empNr are implied. For efficiency reasons we adopt the default policy of specifying qualified subset constraints with respect to the root

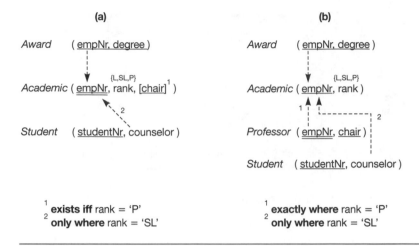

Figure 10.37 Mapping Figure 10.36, using subtype absorption (a) or separation (b).

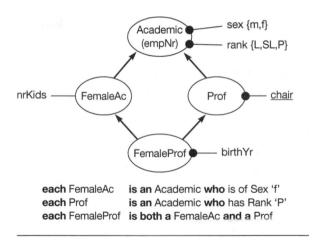

each FemaleAc   **is an** Academic **who** is of Sex 'f'
each Prof   **is an** Academic **who** has Rank 'P'
each FemaleProf   **is both a** FemaleAc **and a** Prof

Figure 10.38 An ER view with multiple inheritance.

supertable where possible. The order of table creation then does not matter so long as the root table is created first, and the schema is easier to change.

Mixed approaches may be adopted. For example, if we absorb FemaleProf and Prof into Academic, but map roles specific to FemaleAc to a separate table, we obtain the relational schema in Figure 10.40. Notice that qualification 2 captures two subtype constraints. Other mixtures are possible, but this gives the idea.

In Section 6.6, we discussed the awkward situation of *context-dependent reference schemes,* where a subtype may have a different primary identification scheme from its supertype(s). Let's briefly discuss how such cases may be mapped.

Recall that a *direct* supertype of a subtype is connected directly to the subtype (i.e., with no intermediate subtypes on the connecting path). On a conceptual schema

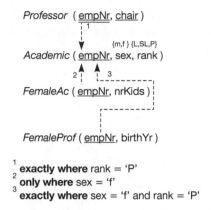

$Professor$ (<u>empNr</u>, <u>chair</u>)

$Academic$ (<u>empNr</u>, sex, rank) {m,f} {L,SL,P}

$FemaleAc$ (<u>empNr</u>, nrKids)

$FemaleProf$ (<u>empNr</u>, birthYr)

[1] **exactly where** rank = 'P'
[2] **only where** sex = 'f'
[3] **exactly where** sex = 'f' and rank = 'P'

Figure 10.39 Relational map of Figure 10.38, choosing subtype separation.

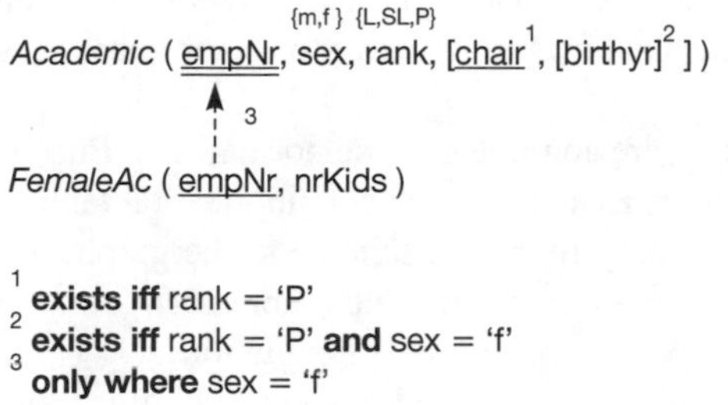

$Academic$ (<u>empNr</u>, sex, rank, [chair][1], [birthyr][2]) {m,f} {L,SL,P}

$FemaleAc$ (<u>empNr</u>, nrKids)

[1] **exists iff** rank = 'P'
[2] **exists iff** rank = 'P' **and** sex = 'f'
[3] **only where** sex = 'f'

Figure 10.40 Relational map of Figure 10.38, separating FemaleAc only.

diagram, a subtype's primary reference scheme is shown if and only if the subtype has at least one direct supertype with a different primary reference scheme.

In mapping, all specific roles attached to an entity type require the object type to be identified by its primary reference scheme. Adopting this requirement avoids some extremely complex reference constraints that could otherwise arise in practice.

If two overlapping subtypes have the same primary reference scheme, and one is not a subtype of the other, they must have a common supertype with this primary reference scheme (if not, create one). This is needed to avoid redundancy later.

For example, consider FemaleStudent (sNr) and PostGradStudent (sNr) as direct subtypes of Person (pNr). Mapping pNr down into tables for both subtypes creates redundancy of the facts that associate pNr and sNr for the intersection of the subtypes, so insert the intermediate supertype Student (sNr) as a target for mapping pNr.

We confine our discussion here to the subtype separation option (separate tables are created for functional roles specific to each subtype) and assume all reference schemes are simple (not composite). For each subtype with a primary reference mode different from the root's, we define its *total table* (if any) as set out in the total table procedure below. The basic idea is that the total table of an object type contains its total population (i.e., it includes all instances in the population of the object type). If an object type does have a total table, this procedure will find it.

Total table procedure:

if the object type has a mandatory disjunction of one or more functional roles
then the table to which its functional roles map is its total table
else if it has a mandatory nonfunctional role
    then select one of these roles arbitrarily;
        the table to which this role maps is its total table
    else { all roles are optional }
        if the object type is independent
        then its table is the total table
        else if the object type plays only functional roles or only one role
            then the table for this is its total table
            else the object type has no total table.

In what follows, where total tables exist we basically ignore other tables of the object type (the other tables are linked by foreign keys to the primary ones in the normal way).

The root supertype table(s) is/are computed in the normal way. Push the primary reference of the root supertype down as an extra attribute in the total table of each subtype that "introduces" a different primary reference scheme to the graph; if the introducing subtype has no total table, create an extra reference table for it (to store just the fact connecting the two identifiers for the object type's population).

In specifying, at the relational level, subtype links between object types with different primary reference schemes use the root reference scheme; if the object types have the same reference scheme, use this common reference scheme.

These guidelines are best understood by way of example. Consider the schema in Figure 10.41. Here "StudEmp" is short for "Student Employee". Better students are often employed to do some tutoring. If known, the number of hours tutoring undertaken by such a student is recorded. In practice many other fact types might be stored about each node. Within the student records subschema, students are identified by their student number (studentNr). Within the staff record subsystem, all employees are identified by the employee number (empNr). A student may be an employee, and we want to know when this occurs. If it did not already exist, we introduce a person number (personNr) to enable people to be identified across the global schema. For student employees, we have three possible identifiers: personNr, studentNr, or empNr.

In this example, we have chosen empNr as the primary identifier for student employees in the context of roles played by StudEmp. This choice is shown by including empNr in parentheses on StudEmp. Although StudEmp inherits its identification scheme from Employee, it also has Student as a direct supertype. In this case, Employee is said to be the *primary supertype* for StudEmp, and the subtype link to the secondary supertype (Student) is shown as a dotted arrow.

Each of the three supertypes has a total table that is identical to its functional table. The functional fact types of the nodes in the subtype graph map to the four tables

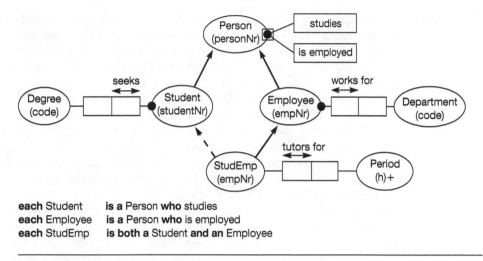

each Student   **is a** Person **who** studies
each Employee   **is a** Person **who** is employed
each StudEmp   **is both a** Student **and an** Employee

Figure 10.41 A subtype graph with differing reference schemes.

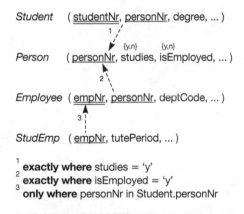

Figure 10.42 The relational map of Figure 10.41, choosing subtype separation.

shown in Figure 10.42. Here an ellipsis "..." denotes any other (functional) attributes omitted in Figure 10.41.

If there are some other mandatory columns in StudEmp, then tutePeriod becomes optional. Because of the relative closure on the disjunctively mandatory unaries on Person in Figure 10.41, both the studies and employed columns of Person are mandatory, with yes/no values.

Notice that personNr is not included in the StudEmp table; this avoids duplicating any instances of the fact type "Person (with personNr) has StudentNr". This is not the only possible way to handle the mapping. For example, we might absorb StudEmp into Employee.

To get a deeper understanding of this mapping example, you need to be aware that subtype links are equivalent to *is associations* as depicted in the underlying explanatory schema of Figure 10.43. The primary inheritance link from StudEmp to Employee is actually a reference type: StudEmp is Employee. The subtype links from Student and Employee to Person are actually fact types, since they introduce a different reference scheme, allowing us to express facts such as "The employee with empNr 23 is the person with personNr 507". Finally the subtype link from StudEmp to Student is actually a derived association, equivalent to the longer path from StudEmp through Person to Student, as shown in the derivation rule included in Figure 10.43.

By default, derived fact types are not stored. Instead, their derivation rules are used to compute the derived values on request. Apart from saving storage space, this "derive-on-query" (lazy evaluation) approach ensures that every time the derived information is requested it will be based on the latest values of the stored data. Sometimes, however, the same derivations are required many times with large volumes of stable data. In such cases, it can be much more efficient to store the derived information, so that it can be accessed immediately at later times without having to be recomputed. Typically in such cases a "derive-on-update" (eager evaluation) approach is used, so that as soon as the base data is updated, the derived information is computed and stored. Recall the bank balance example from Exercise 6.4.

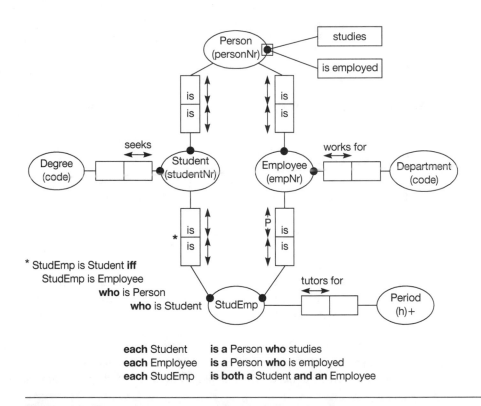

Figure 10.43 Subtype links to new reference schemes are treated as base fact types.

In step 0.4 of the mapping procedure, any derived fact types to be stored should be included on the schema diagram and marked "**", with the derivation rule also declared. The fact type should then be grouped into a table in the normal way, and the derivation rule mapped as well. For example, the Window schema in Figure 10.44(a) uses the default mapping so no column for area is included in its base table. However, the area fact type in Figure 10.44(b) is marked "**" for storage, so it maps to a base table column. The rule for computing area may be included in insert and update triggers (or in a view or stored procedure). Care is required with storing derived data. For example, unless the derivation rule is fired every time the relevant base data is updated, the derived values can become outdated.

For symmetric 1:1 binaries (roles are both optional or both mandatory, and both object types have other functional roles), we have a choice as to how the 1:1 binary should be mapped. This mapping choice should be noted in step 0.5 (e.g., by annotation or option selection) and adhered to when the fact type is mapped in step 2.

In rare cases a conceptual schema may include a disjunctive primary reference scheme (identification by a mandatory disjunction of two or more roles, at least one of which is optional). In Figure 10.45, PlantKind is identified in this way (this botanical naming convention was discussed in Chapter 5). When mapped to a relational schema, such schemes can prove awkward to handle.

For example, the conceptual schema in Figure 10.45 maps to the following relational schema. This violates the relational entity integrity rule, since the primary keys may contain null values. We enclose both infraRank and infraName in the same pair of

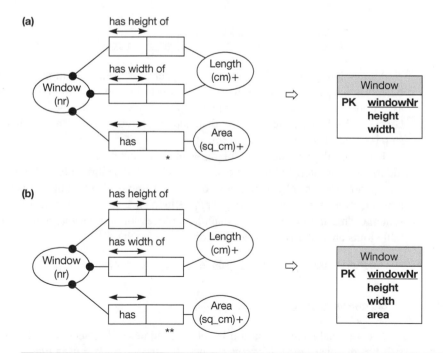

Figure 10.44 Derived fact types may be evaluated lazily (a) or eagerly (b).

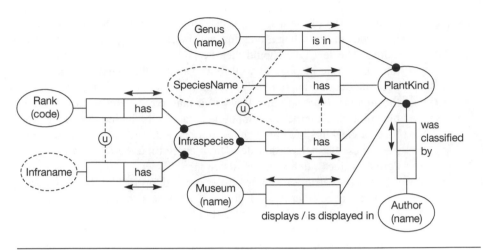

Figure 10.45 PlantKind has a disjunctive reference scheme.

square brackets to indicate that the qualification applies to *both,* and that if one is null so is the other. Enclosing both of these inside the option brackets for species indicates that they can only be given a non-null value when species is non-null.

PlantKind   (genus, [species, [infraRank, infraName]], author)

DisplayedIn (genus, [species, [infraRank, infraName]], museum)

Although forbidden by the relational model, this is allowed in most relational data-base systems, and the relevant uniqueness constraint can be enforced by a procedure or assertion. However, a simpler implementation can often be obtained by altering the conceptual schema to replace the disjunctive reference with a nondisjunctive one. In step 0.6, we consider such replacements.

There are three basic ways of replacing a disjunctive reference scheme: artificial identifiers, concatenated identifiers, or use of special default values. Let's look at these three alternatives briefly, using this botanical example. The first option is to introduce a new identifier for PlantKind (e.g., plantKindNr), leading to the following relational schema. This approach has two main advantages: the primary keys have no nulls, and table joins are faster (now based just on plantKindNr).

PlantKind   (plantKindNr, genus, [species, [infraRank, infraName]], author)

DisplayedIn (plantKindNr, museum)

The artificial identifier option is not all good news. The secondary key in PlantKind still has optional fields. Moreover, since this secondary key uses the natural reference scheme, this is what users will normally want to see (not the artificial plantKindNr).

For example, to find what kinds of plant are on display in a museum, we now need to join the tables since we want to see the natural plant names.

A simpler solution is just to concatenate the formerly separate parts of the identifier into a single name. This leads to the very simple relational schema

PlantKind   (<u>plantKindName, author</u>)

DisplayedIn (<u>plantKindName, museum</u>)

This simple schema is the best solution, so long as we are not interested in listing or grouping the formerly separate parts of the identifier. However, if we wanted to issue a query such as "Which species has the most plant kinds?" there is now no simple way of formulating this query.

The third option is to keep the original components of the reference scheme separate but make each of them mandatory by using special default values when no actual value exists. For example, the plant kind *Acacia interior* could be stored as the tuple ('Acacia', 'interior', 'nil', 'nil') using "nil" as a special default value (different from null) to indicate that plant kind has no actual value for infraRank and infraName. The conceptual schema in Figure 10.45 is modified by making the species and infraspecies predicates mandatory for PlantKind, deleting the subset constraint, and adding "nil" to any value list for Rank, for example, {'ssp', 'var', 'forma', 'n-ssp', 'n-var', 'n-forma', 'nil'}. The following relational schema is obtained (value list omitted):

PlantKind   (<u>genus, [species, [infraRank, infraName]]</u>, author)

DisplayedIn (<u>genus, [species, [infraRank, infraName]], museum</u>)

In this case the default value "nil" is unlikely to ever be confused with an actual value. However, in some cases such confusion might arise (e.g., a default score of 0) and the user may then be burdened with the responsibility of distinguishing default from actual values.

The final refinement to step 0 of the mapping procedure (step 0.7) deals with cases where an objectified predicate is not spanned by a uniqueness constraint. Many versions of ORM forbid this from happening anyway, since it violates elementarity. However, if the version you are using does allow it, then some preprocessing is needed before executing the grouping part of the procedure.

In nested 1:1 cases, a decision should be made to favor one of the roles in grouping. For example, suppose the schema in Figure 10.46 is used to model current marriages in a monogamous society. This schema violates elementarity. It can be split into two fact types: one about the marriage and one about the marriage year. If no other functional roles are played by Person, we might map this to either of the table schemes shown in Figure 10.46. For such 1:1 cases a choice must be made (e.g., by choosing one of the uniqueness constraints as primary).

If only one role in the objectified predicate is functional, it is automatically chosen for the primary key. For example, in a polyandrous society where a man may be married to at most one woman but not vice versa, the husband column would be chosen as

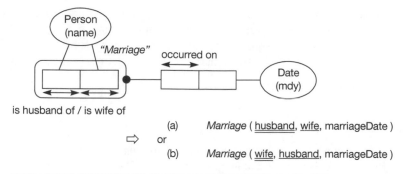

Figure 10.46 Two possible mappings for an objectified 1:1 association.

the primary key (and wife would no longer be a key). In spite of the provisions of step 0.7, objectified *n:*1 associations should normally be avoided.

Once the columns and constraints are determined in a relational mapping, you may wish to consider changing the *order of columns* within a table. Although the relational model treats column order as irrelevant, in practice column order can have an impact on both readability and performance. A CASE tool will choose an ordering for you, but you can override this. Usually it is best to include primary key columns first, and to group columns together if they are components of a compositely identified object type or have a strong semantic affinity. In such cases, a top-down order is usually preferable (e.g., buildingNr, roomNr instead of roomNr, buildingNr). For such composite cases, placing the attributes with fewer values first can help speed up joins in some cases. A similar comment applies to composite indexes. Some systems also perform better if optional columns are placed last.

Exercise 10.4

1. (a) Rmap the conceptual schema in Figure 7.22.
   (b) Add the optional unary "is a nonsmoker" to Figure 7.22, with an exclusion constraint. The unaries are not closed. How does this affect the mapping?
   (c) If the unaries are closed, is their disjunction mandatory? Why?
   (d) If the unaries are disjunctively mandatory, how does this affect the mapping?

2. Suppose heads of government are identified by the country that they head, and have their salary and country of birth recorded. Schematize this and Rmap it.

3. Refer to the hospital UoD of Exercise 6.6, Question 2. Rmap the conceptual schema for part (a), then discuss any changes in the mapping for parts (b), (c), and (d).

4. Consider a UoD in which people are identified by the combination of their surname, first given name, and (if it exists) second given name. Each person's weight is recorded, as well as the sports they play (if any).
   (a) Schematize this UoD.
   (b) Rmap this, using the given identification scheme for persons.
   (c) Introduce personNr as the primary identifier. Rmap the new conceptual schema.
   (d) Instead, concatenate surname and given names to a single name. Rmap this.

(e) Instead, introduce "nil" as a default for no second given name. Rmap this.

(f) Which do you prefer?

5. Consider the functional fact type "Moon (name) orbits Planet (name)". Suppose that facts about the orbital period of moons are modeled by objectifying the previous predicate, giving this the alias of "Orbit", and attaching the fact type "Orbit takes Period (day)".

(a) Draw the conceptual schema.

(b) Does this violate elementarity?

(c) Unnest the schema.

(d) Rmap it.

10.5   Summary

Conceptual schemas are normally implemented by mapping them to a logical schema (e.g., relational), finessing this, then generating internal and external schemas (including security controls). Updates and queries may then be performed on the databases and schema(s).

A *relational (database) schema* is a set of table definitions (stored base tables or derived views) and constraints. A *table scheme* is a named set of *attributes* (columns) that draw their values from *domains*. Each column, or column set, spanned by a uniqueness constraint is a *candidate key*. Keys are underlined. Each table row is identified by its *primary key* (doubly underlined if another key exists). The *entity integrity* rule demands that primary keys have no null values. Optional columns allow null values and are enclosed in square brackets. For example: *Employee*(empNr, empName, address, sex, [phone]).

Mandatory roles are mapped to nonoptional columns, with subset constraints running from any other tables that contain facts about that object type. A *referential integrity constraint* is a subset constraint from a foreign key to some primary key. Subset constraints between tables appear as dotted arrows. Other constraint notations are used.

The relational mapping procedure (Rmap) groups each fact type into a single table, using two basic ideas: each fact type with a compound UC ⊏⊐ is mapped to a separate table; fact types with functional roles attached to the same object type ○—⊏ are grouped into the same table, keyed on the object type's identifier.

The *basic Rmap procedure* may be summarized as follows. Absorb subtypes into their top supertype. Mentally erase all explicit primary identification schemes, treating compositely identified object types as "black boxes". Map each fact type with a compound UC to a separate table. Group fact types with functional roles attached to the same object type into the same table, keyed on the object type's identifier. Map 1:1 cases to a single table, generally favoring fewer nulls. Map each independent object type with no functional roles to a separate table. Unpack each "black box column" into its component attributes. Map all other constraints and derivation rules. Subtype constraints on functional roles map to qualified optional columns, and on nonfunctional roles to qualified subset constraints.

If the total population of an object type is included in one table, this is called a *total table* for the object type. See the *total table procedure* on page 449 for more details. Advanced mapping aspects in the *Rmap step 0 procedure* may be summarized as follows. Mentally binarize any unaries, and cater to any relative closure. Mentally erase all reference (primary identification) predicates. Treat compositely identified object types as "black boxes". Indicate any absorption overrides for subtypes. Identify any derived fact types that must be stored. Indicate mapping choices for symmetric 1:1 cases. Consider replacing any disjunctive reference schemes by using an artificial or concatenated identifier or mandatory defaults. Indicate mapping choice where required for any objectified associations with no spanning uniqueness constraint.

Chapter Notes

Many modern database textbooks discuss mapping ER schemas to relational schemas (e.g., Batini et al. 1992). For mapping UML class diagrams to relational schemas, see Blaha and Premerlani (1998) and Muller (1999). The mapping extensions to the old ONF algorithm to develop Rmap were developed jointly by Dr. Peter Ritson and myself. For more details on mapping 1:1 predicates, see Ritson and Halpin (1993a). For further details on Rmap and its SQL version, see Ritson and Halpin (1993b).

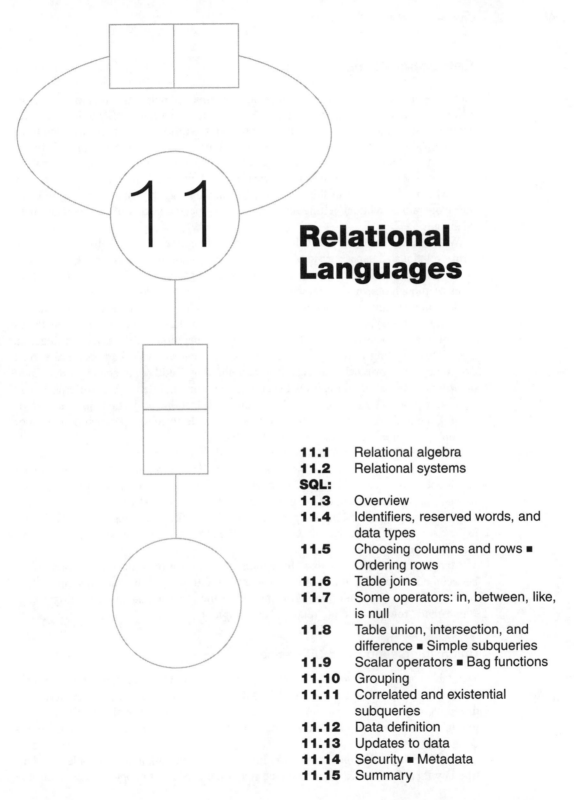

Relational Languages

11.1   Relational Algebra

So far we've seen how to design a conceptual schema and map it to a relational schema. The relational schema may now be implemented in a relational DBMS and its tables populated with data. To retrieve information from the resulting database, we need to issue queries. In practice the most popular query languages are *SQL* (popularly, if incorrectly, called "Structured Query Language") and *QBE* (Query By Example). Both of these are based, at least partly, on a formal query language known as *relational algebra,* which is discussed in this section. Studying this algebra first clarifies the basic query operations without getting distracted by the specific syntax of commercial query languages.

With the algebra under our belt, we will be able define what is really meant by the term "relational database system". The following sections then cover SQL in some depth, starting with the basics and moving on through intermediate to advanced concepts. Although our focus is on the SQL standard(s), some additional detail will be included about commercial dialects of SQL. Now let's begin with relational algebra.

In the relational model of data, all facts are stored in tables (or relations). New tables may be formed from existing tables by applying operations in the relational algebra. The tables resulting from these operations may be named and stored, using relational assignment. The original relational algebra defined by Codd contained eight *relational operators:* four based on traditional set operations (union, intersection, difference, and Cartesian product) and four special operations (selection, projection, join, and division). Each of these eight relational operators is a table-forming operator on tables. For example, the union of two tables is itself a table.

Relational algebra includes six *comparison operators* ($=, <>, <, >, <=, >=$). These are proposition-forming operators on terms. For example, $x <> 0$ asserts that x is not equal to zero. It also includes three *logical operators* **(and, or, not).** These are proposition-forming operators on propositions (e.g., $x > 0$ **and** $x < 8$). Since the algebra does not include arithmetic operators (e.g., $+$) or functions (e.g., count), it is less expressive than SQL. Proposed extensions to the algebra to include these and other operators are ignored here.

Many different notations exist for expressing the relational algebra. A comparison between our notation and a common academic notation is given later. To simplify discussion, I'll often use informal terms instead of the strict relational terminology (e.g., "table" and "row" instead of "relation" and "tuple").

Union, Intersection, and Difference

Two tables are *union-compatible* if and only if they have the same number of columns, and their corresponding columns are based on the same domain (the columns may have different names). Treating a table as a set of rows, the traditional set operations of union, intersection, and difference may be defined between tables that are union-compatible.

Consider the conceptual schema in Figure 11.1. In this small UoD, people are identified by their first name. We record facts about the foods that people eat and about the

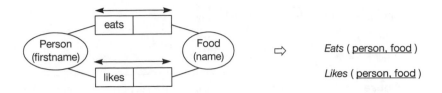

Figure 11.1 The conceptual schema maps to two tables.

Eats:

person	food
Ann	pizza
Ann	spinach
Bill	pizza

Likes:

person	food
Ann	chocolate
Ann	pizza
Bill	pizza
Bill	steak

Eats ∪ Likes ⇨

person	food
Ann	pizza
Ann	spinach
Bill	pizza
Ann	chocolate
Bill	steak

Figure 11.2 The union of two tables is the set of rows that occur in either table (or both).

foods that they like. The relational schema comprises two tables as shown. The populations of the tables may properly overlap or even be disjoint. Hence there are no intertable constraints in the relational schema—this situation is fairly unusual.

Figure 11.2 includes sample data. The **union** of tables A and B is the set of all rows belonging to A or B (or both). We write this as "$A \cup B$" or "A **union** B". Suppose we want to pair each person up with foods that they either eat or like. This may be specified simply as the union of the tables, Eats ∪ Likes. Figure 11.2 includes this query expression, and the resulting (unnamed) table, which includes all the rows in the Eats table as well as all the rows in the Likes table. As with any table, duplicate rows are excluded. So rows that appear in both the Eats and Likes tables appear only once in the result.

Note that "Eats ∪ Likes" is an expression describing how the result may be derived in terms of tables stored in the database (i.e., base tables); it is not a table name. We may refer to a query result as a result table, answer table, or derived table. The order of the rows in this result (or the base tables) has no significance, since we are dealing with sets. Actual query languages like SQL provide ways to display the rows in any preferred order.

The **intersection** of tables A and B is the set of rows common to A and B. We write this as "$A \cap B$" or "A **intersect** B". For instance, to list facts about foods that people

Eats ∩ Likes ⇨

person	food
Ann	pizza
Bill	pizza

Figure 11.3 The intersection of two tables is the set of rows common to both.

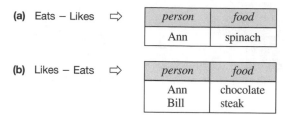

(a) Eats − Likes ⇨

person	food
Ann	spinach

(b) Likes − Eats ⇨

person	food
Ann	chocolate
Bill	steak

Figure 11.4 (a) $A - B$ is the set of rows in A that are not in B; (b) $B - A$.

both eat and like, we may specify this as the intersection of our two base tables, Eats ∩ Likes (see Figure 11.3).

We define the **difference** operation between tables thus. $A - B$ is the set of rows belonging to A but not B. We may also write this as A **minus** B, or A **except** B. For example, the expression Eats − Likes returns details about people who eat foods they don't like (see Figure 11.4(a)).

As in ordinary set theory, the union operation is *commutative* (i.e., the order of the operands is not significant). So, given any tables A and B it is true that $A \cup B = B \cup A$. Likewise, the intersection operation is commutative, that is, $A \cap B = B \cap A$. The difference operation, however, is not commutative, so it is possible that $A - B$ does not equal $B - A$. For example, Likes − Eats returns facts about who likes a food but doesn't eat it (see Figure 11.4(b)). Compare this with the previous result.

Cartesian Product (Unrestricted Join)

In mathematics, the **Cartesian product** of sets A and B is defined as the set of all ordered pairs (x, y) such that x belongs to A and y belongs to B. For example, if $A = \{1, 2\}$ and $B = \{3, 4, 5\}$ then $A \times B = \{(1, 3), (1, 4), (1, 5), (2, 3), (2, 4), (2, 5)\}$. We write this product as $A \times B$ (read "A cross B"). This definition applies also to tables, although the ordered pairs of rows (x, y) are considered to be single rows of the product table, which inherits the corresponding column names. Thus if A and B are tables, $A \times B$ is formed by *pairing each row of A with each row of B*. Here "pairing" means "prepending". The expression "$A \times B$" may also be written as "A **times** B". The Cartesian product is also called the "cross join" or "unrestricted join".

Since $A \times B$ pairs each row of A with all rows of B, if A has n rows and B has m rows, then the table $A \times B$ has $n \times m$ rows. So *the number of rows in $A \times B$ is the* *product of the number of rows in A and B.* Since the paired rows are concatenated into single rows, *the number of columns in A × B is the sum of the number of columns in A and B.*

Let's look at a simple example. In Figure 11.5, A is a 3 × 2 table (i.e., 3 rows × 2 columns) and B is a 2 × 1 table. So A × B has six (3 × 2) rows of three (2 + 1) columns. The header rows that contain the column names *a1, a2, b1* are not counted in this calculation. In this example, dotted lines have been ruled between rows to aid readability. Note that the Cartesian product A × B exists for any tables A and B; it is not necessary that A and B be union-compatible.

If we define Cartesian products in terms of tuples treated as ordered sequences of values, the × operator is not commutative (i.e., A × B need not equal B × A). This is the usual treatment in mathematics. With relational databases, however, each column has a name, so a tuple may instead be treated as an (unordered) set of attribute-value pairs (each value in a row is associated with its column name). In this sense, columns are said to be "ordered by name". With this view of tuples, the × operator is commutative.

To clarify this, compute B × A for the example in Figure 11.5. Although the resulting table has its columns displayed in the order *b1, a1, a2,* and the values are ordered accordingly, the information is the same as for A × B, since each value can be linked to its column name. For example, the first row of B × A may be represented as {(b1, 7), (a1, 1), (a2, 2)}, which equals {(a1, 1), (a2, 2), (b1, 7)}, which represents the first row of A × B. Once columns are named, their physical order has no semantic significance.

As in standard set theory, the operations of union, intersection, and Cartesian product are *associative.* For instance, A ∪ (B ∪ C) = (A ∪ B) ∪ C. Since no ambiguity results, parentheses may be dropped in such cases. For example, the expression "A ∪ B ∪ C" is permitted. Of the four table operations considered so far, difference is the only one that is not associative; that is, it is possible that A − (B − C) is not equal to (A − B) − C. As an exercise, use Venn diagrams to check these claims.

Recall that column names of a table must be unique. If A and B have no column names in common, then A × B uses the simple column names of A and B. If A and B are different but have some common column names, the corresponding columns in

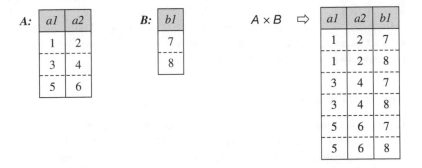

Figure 11.5 *A* × *B* pairs each row of *A* with each row of *B*.

Person:	firstname	sex
	Fred	M
	Sue	F

Person × Person ⇨

firstname	sex	firstname	sex
Fred	M	Fred	M
Fred	M	Sue	F
Sue	F	Fred	M
Sue	F	Sue	F

Figure 11.6 What is wrong with this Cartesian product?

define alias Person2 **for** Person

Person × Person2 ⇨

Person.firstname	Person.sex	Person2.firstname	Person2.sex
Fred	M	Fred	M
Fred	M	Sue	F
Sue	F	Fred	M
Sue	F	Sue	F

Figure 11.7 Table aliases are needed to multiply a table by itself.

$A \times B$ are uniquely referenced by using *qualified names* (with the prefix "*A.*" or "*B.*"). However, what if A and B are the same (i.e., we wish to form the Cartesian product of a table with itself)?

Consider the Person × Person table in Figure 11.6. This breaks the rule that column names in a table must be unique. In this case, simply using the qualified column names will not solve the problem either because we would have two columns named "Person.firstname" and two columns named "Person.sex".

This problem is overcome by introducing **aliases** for tables. For example, we could use "Person2" as an alternative name for the table, and form the product as shown in Figure 11.7. If desired, we could have introduced two aliases, "Person1" and "Person2", say, to specify the product Person1 × Person2. The need to multiply a table by itself may arise if we have to compare values on different rows. Aliases can also be used simply to save writing (by introducing shorter names).

Relational Selection

Let us now consider the four table operations introduced by Codd. The first of these is known as **selection** (or *restriction*). Don't confuse this with SQL's select command. In relational algebra, the selection operation chooses just those rows that satisfy a specified condition. Visually we can picture the operation as returning a *horizontal subset,* or row subset, since it returns zero or more rows from the original table (see Figure 11.8).

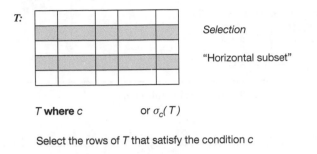

T **where** *c*   or $\sigma_c(T)$

Select the rows of *T* that satisfy the condition *c*

Figure 11.8 The selection operation in relational algebra.

Player:

name	sex	height
David	M	172
Norma	F	170
Selena	F	165
Terry	M	178

Player **where** sex = 'M' ⇨

name	sex	height
David	M	172
Terry	M	178

Figure 11.9 The selection operation picks those rows that satisfy the condition.

The selection operation may be specified using an expression of the form *T* **where** *c*. Here *T* denotes a *table expression* (i.e., an expression whose value is a table) and *c* denotes a *condition*. The selection operation returns just those rows where the condition evaluates to True, filtering out rows where the condition evaluates to False or Unknown. The "**where** *c*" part is called a *where* clause. This notation encourages top-down thinking (find the relevant tables before worrying about the rows) and agrees with SQL syntax. The alternative notation $\sigma_c(T)$ is often used in academic journals. The "σ" is sigma, the Greek *s* (which is the first letter of "selection").

In Figure 11.9, the Player table stores details about tennis players. To list details about just the male tennis players, we could formulate this selection as indicated, giving the result shown. Here the selection condition is just the equality sex = 'M'. The use of single quotes with 'M' indicates that this value is literally the character 'M'. Single quotes are also used when referencing character string values such as 'David'. Numeric values should not be quoted. Although the table resulting from the selection is unnamed, its columns have the same names as the original.

The condition *c* may contain any of six *comparison operators:* = (equals), <> (is not equal to), < (is less than), > (is greater than), <= (is less than or equal to), and >= (is greater than or equal to). Sometimes the result of a table operation is an empty

Player **where** (sex = 'F') **and** (height < 170)

⇨

name	sex	height
Selena	F	165

Figure 11.10   Are the parentheses needed in this query?

table (cf. the null set). For instance, no rows satisfy the condition in Player **where** height > 180.

If conditions do not involve comparisons with null values, they are Boolean expressions—they evaluate to True or False. If conditions do include comparisons with nulls, a three-valued logic is used instead, so that the condition may evaluate to True, False, or Unknown. This is also what happens in SQL. In either case, the selection operation returns just those rows where the condition is true. Any row where the condition evaluates to false or unknown is filtered out.

Besides comparison operators, conditions may include three *logical operators:* **and, or, not.** As usual, **or** is inclusive. As an exercise, formulate a query to list details of those females who are shorter than 170 cm. Also refer to the Player table and see if you can state the result. Then check your answer with Figure 11.10. To aid readability, reserved words are in bold.

The query in Figure 11.10 used parentheses to clarify the order in which operations are to be carried out. With complicated expressions, however, large numbers of parentheses can make things look very messy (cf. LISP). Unlike several programming languages (e.g., Pascal), most query languages (e.g., SQL) give *comparison operators higher priority than logical operators.*

So the operators $=$, $<>$, $<$, $>$, $<=$, and $>=$ are given precedence over **not, and,** and **or** for evaluation purposes. We make the same choice in relational algebra since this reduces the number of parentheses needed for complex expressions. With this understood, the query in Figure 11.10 may be rewritten more concisely as

Player **where** sex = 'F' **and** height < 170

To further reduce the need for parentheses, the algebra adopts the logical operator priority convention commonly used in computing languages such as Pascal and SQL. First evaluate **not,** then **and,** then **or.** Table 11.1 shows the evaluation order for both comparison and logical operators. This operator precedence may be overridden by the use of parentheses.

For example, suppose we want details about males who are taller than 175 cm or shorter than 170 cm. The query in Figure 11.11(a) looks like it should work for this, but the wrong result is obtained. Why?

Because the **and** operator is evaluated before the **or,** this query is interpreted as Player **where** (sex = 'M' **and** height > 175) **or** height < 170. Notice that line breaks have no significance to the meaning of the query. So the result includes details about anybody shorter than 170 cm (including females). The query in Figure 17.11(b) corrects this by

Table 11.1 Priority convention for the operators (1 = first).

Priority	Operators
1	=, <>, <, >, <=, >=
2	**not**
3	**and**
4	**or**

(a)   Player **where** sex = 'M'
       and height > 175 or height < 170   ⇨

name	sex	height
Selena	F	165
Terry	M	178

(b)   Player **where** sex = 'M'
       and (height > 175 or height < 170)   ⇨

name	sex	height
Terry	M	178

Figure 11.11 Unless parentheses are used, **and** is evaluated before **or.**

(a)   Player **where** sex = 'M' **and** height > 175
      or sex = 'F' **and** height >=170   ⇨

name	sex	height
Terry	M	178
Norma	F	170

(b)   Player **where** (sex = 'M' **and** height > 175)   ⇨
      or (sex = 'F' **and** height >=170)

Figure 11.12 Two equivalent queries; if in doubt, include parentheses.

including parentheses around the height disjunction to evaluate the **or** operator before the **and** operator.

To obtain details about players who are either males over 175 cm or females at least 170 cm tall, either of the queries shown in Figure 11.12 may be used. In the query in Figure 11.12(b), the parentheses are redundant, since the **and** operators are evaluated before the **or** operator anyway. If ever in doubt about whether parentheses are needed, put them in.

Figure 11.13 shows three equivalent queries for listing information on players who are neither taller than 172 cm nor shorter than 168 cm. Operator precedence ensures that the query in Figure 11.13(a) means Player **where** (**not** (height > 172)) **and** (**not** (height < 168)). Note that the six comparison operators may be grouped into three pairs

(a)   Player **where not** height >172 **and not** height <168   ⇨

(b)   Player **where** height <=172 **and** height >=168   ⇨

(c)   Player **where not** (height >172 **or** height <168)   ⇨

name	sex	height
David	M	172
Norma	F	170

Figure 11.13 Three equivalent queries.

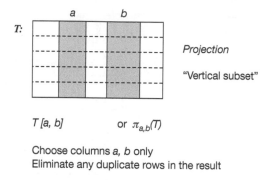

T:

a   b

Projection

"Vertical subset"

T [a, b]   or $\pi_{a,b}(T)$

Choose columns *a, b* only
Eliminate any duplicate rows in the result

Figure 11.14 The projection operation in relational algebra.

of opposites: =, <>; <, >=; and >, <=. So the query in Figure 11.13(a) may be replaced by the shorter query in Figure 11.13(b).

De Morgan's laws, named after the famous logician Augustus De Morgan, are the following:

not (p **and** q) ≡   **not** p **or not** q
not (p **or** q) ≡   **not** p **and not** q

Here *p* and *q* denote any proposition or logical condition. These laws hold in both two-valued and three-valued logic, so they are safe to use with null values. Using the second of these laws, it is easy to see that the query in Figure 11.13(c) is equivalent to the query in Figure 11.13(a).

Relational Projection

The next table operation, known as **projection,** was introduced in Chapter 4. This operation involves *choosing one or more columns* from a table, and *then eliminating any duplicate rows* that might result. It is said to produce a *vertical subset* or *column subset*. Figure 11.14 illustrates a projection on two columns.

We may represent the projection operation as *T [a,b,...]* where *T* is a table expression and *a, b,...* are the names of the required columns (this column list is called the *projection list*). To delimit the projection list, we use square brackets rather than parentheses, since the latter have other uses in queries (e.g., to change the evaluation order of operations). Italicizing the square brackets "*[ ]*" helps to distinguish them from the use of "[ ]" to delimit optional items, or bags, and to indicate an extra task (duplicate elimination) once the columns are chosen.

The alternative notation $\pi_{a,b..}(T)$ is common in academic journals. The "π" symbol is pi, the Greek p (the first letter of "projection"). Like SQL, this notation lists the required columns before the tables. Our preferred notation instead encourages top-down thinking by identifying the relevant tables before listing the columns.

Figure 11.15 gives two examples, based on the table *Player*(name, sex, height). When projecting on a single base table, if the chosen columns include a candidate key, then no duplicate rows can result. If not, duplicates may arise. For example, choosing just the sex column gives the bag ['M', 'F', 'F', 'M']. To complete the projection, the duplicate values are eliminated, giving the set {'M', 'F'}. If we project on all columns, we end up with the same table. For instance, Player *[name, sex, height]* is the same table as Player.

The same column must not be mentioned twice in a projection. For example, Player *[name, name]* is illegal (why?). If desired, projection may be used to display columns in a different order. For example, Player *[height, sex, name]* reverses the order. Since column names are listed in the result, this doesn't change the meaning.

If the relational schema is fully normalized, it is fairly unusual to have base tables that are union-compatible (the Eats and Likes tables considered earlier being an exception). So the ∪, ∩, and − operations tend to be used almost exclusively with result tables that have become union-compatible because of projections.

Let's look now at some examples that are a little harder. To facilitate a discussion of a step-by-step approach to such cases, I'll use the **relational assignment** operation. Because their contents may vary, tables may be regarded as *variables*. In fact, tables are the only kind of variable allowed in relational algebra. The notion of relational assignment, which is strictly separate from the algebra itself, is similar to that in

Player:

name	sex	height
David	M	172
Norma	F	170
Selena	F	165
Terry	M	178

Player *[name,sex]* ⇨

name	sex
David	M
Norma	F
Selena	F
Terry	M

Player *[sex]* ⇨

sex
M
F

Figure 11.15 Projection involves picking the columns and removing any duplicates.

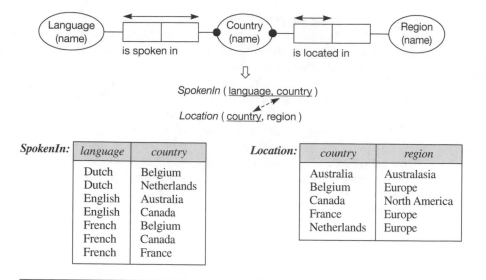

Figure 11.16 Conceptual and relational schemas, with sample population.

programming languages. Using the symbol ":=" for "becomes" or "is assigned the value of", we may write assignment statements of the form

table variable := table expression

This is an instruction to first evaluate the expression on the right, and then place its value in the variable named on the left. If this variable had a previous value, the old value would simply be replaced by the new value. For example, if *X, A,* and *B* are tables, then the statement "$X := A - B$" means *X* is assigned the value of $A - B$.

Once named in a relational assignment, result tables may be used just like base tables in later expressions. For example, to store details about male tall players in a table called "MaleTallPlayer", we could make the following three assignments. To list these details, our query is simply the table name MaleTallPlayer.

```
MalePlayer      :=   Player where sex = 'M'
TallPlayer      :=   Player where height > 175
MaleTallPlayer  :=   MalePlayer ∩ TallPlayer
```

As a harder example, consider the UoD of Figure 11.16. How may we formulate this query in relational algebra: Which non-European countries speak French? Try this yourself before reading on.

We could formulate the query in steps, using intermediate tables on the way to obtaining our final result table. For example:

```
NonEuroCountry := (Location where region <> 'Europe') [country]
FrenchSpkCountry := (SpokenIn where language = 'French') [country]
FrenchSpkNonEuroCountry := NonEuroCountry ∩ FrenchSpkCountry
```

Here our first step was to find the non-European countries: {Australia, Canada}. Then we found the French-speaking countries: {Belgium, Canada, France}. Finally we took the intersection of these, giving the result: {Canada}.

Setting queries out this way is known as *stepwise formulation*. Doing things in stages can sometimes make it easier to formulate difficult queries. However, it saves writing to express a query by means of a single expression. For instance, the three assignment statements just considered can be replaced by

(Location **where** region <> 'Europe')*[country]*
∩
(SpokenIn **where** language = 'French')*[country]*

This lengthy expression is said to be a *nested formulation* because it nests one or more queries inside another. For complex queries we might perform the stepwise formulation in our heads, or scribbled down somewhere, and then convert this into the nested formulation. In general, any information capable of being extracted by a series of relational algebra queries can be specified in a single relational algebra query.

Note that projection does not distribute over intersection. In other words, given tables A and B, and a projection list p, it is possible that $(A \cap B)[p] \neq A[p] \cap B[p]$. For instance, the following query is *not* equivalent to the previous one (why not?).

((Location **where** region <> 'Europe') ∩ (SpokenIn **where** language = 'French'))*[country]*

This query is illegal, since the table operands of ∩ are not compatible. Even if A and B are compatible, projection need not distribute over ∩ or over −. If A and B are compatible, projection does distribute over ∪, that is, $(A \cup B)[p] = A[p] \cup B[p]$. As an exercise, you may wish to prove these results.

Relational Joins

Object joins at the conceptual level were introduced in Section 4.4 to help clarify the meaning of external uniqueness constraints. We now consider the relational **join** operation between two tables (or two occurrences of the same table), which compares attribute values from the tables, using the comparison operators (=, <, >, <>, <=, >=). There are several kinds of join operations, and we discuss only some of these here. Columns being compared in any join operation must be defined on the same domain; they do not need to have the same name. Where it is necessary to distinguish between join columns with the same local name, we use their fully qualified names.

Let Θ (theta) denote any comparison operator (=, <, etc.). Then the Θ-**join** of tables A and B on attributes a of A and b of B equals the Cartesian product $A \times B$, restricted to those rows where $A.a \Theta B.b$. We write this as shown below. An alternative, academic notation is shown in braces.

$A \times B$ **where** c { or $A \bowtie_c B$ }

The condition c used to express this comparison of attributes between tables is called the *join condition*. The join condition may be composite (e.g., a1 < b1 **and** a2 < b2). Because of the Cartesian product, the resulting table has a number of columns equal to the sum of the number of columns in A and $B;$ but because of the selection operation, it typically has far fewer rows than the product of the numbers of rows of the joined tables.

With most joins, the comparison operator used is $=$. The Θ-join is then called an **equijoin.** Thus the equijoin of A and B equating values in column a of A with column b of B is $A \times B$ restricted to the rows where $A.a = B.b$. If the join column names occur in only one of the tables, there is no need to qualify them with the table names. We write this as shown below. In general, the join condition may contain many equalities.

$A \times B$ **where** $A.a = B.b$

or

$A \times B$ **where** $a = b$ { if a, b occur in only one of A, B }

Let's consider an example. Figure 11.17 includes a simple conceptual schema and its corresponding relational schema. A sample population is given in Figure 11.18.

Before formulating queries you should *familiarize yourself with the structure and contents of the database.* From the schema, we see that employees are identified by their employee number, and their name and sex must also be recorded. An employee may drive many cars, and the same car may be driven by many employees. The population is not significant, since it does not include instances where the same name applies to more than one employee. However, it does illustrate that driving cars is optional

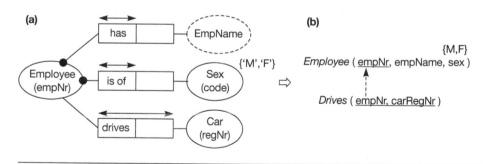

Figure 11.17 The ORM schema (a) maps to the relational schema (b).

Employee:	empNr	empName	sex
	001	Hagar, T	M
	002	Wong, S	F
	003	Jones, E	F
	004	Mifune, K	M

Drives:	empNr	carRegNr
	001	ABC123
	003	ABC123
	003	TAH007

Figure 11.18 A sample population for the schema in Figure 11.17.

Employee:	empNr	empName	sex
	001	Hagar, T	M
	002	Wong, S	F
	003	Jones, E	F
	004	Mifune, K	M

Drives:	empNr	carRegNr
	001	ABC123
	003	ABC123
	003	TAH007

(Employee × Drives)
where Employee.empNr = Drives.empNr

	Employee.empNr	empName	sex	Drives.empNr	carRegNr
⇨	001	Hagar, T	M	001	ABC123
	003	Jones, E	F	003	ABC123
	003	Jones, E	F	003	TAH007

Figure 11.19 An equijoin.

(employees 002 and 004) and that an employee may drive more than one car (employee 003). Now consider the following query: "List the employee number, name, and cars for each employee who drives a car."

We could specify this by the equijoin in Figure 11.19, which joins the tables by equating their empNr attributes. To help explain this, I've added dotted lines between the base tables to indicate which rows match on their empNr value. Only the first and third rows from the Employee table are able to find a match. The third row (003) finds two matches. Check the result for yourself.

Here the join columns have the same local name, "empNr". So qualified names are used to distinguish these columns in the query and the join result. The join columns don't have to have the same (unqualified) name—so long as they belong to the same domain, the join can be made. For example, if the employee number column in the Drives table were named "empId", the join condition could be specified as "empNr = empId".

As this example illustrates, an equijoin contains two matching columns resulting from each join attribute (note the two empNr columns). If these columns actually refer to the same thing in the UoD (and they typically do), then one of these columns is re-dundant. In this case, we lose no information if we *delete one of these matching columns* (by performing a projection on all but the column to be deleted). This is done in Figure 11.20.

If the *columns used for joining have the same name in both tables,* then the unquali-fied name is used in the join result. The resulting table is then said to be the **natural in-ner join** of the original tables. Joins may be inner or outer. Since "inner" is assumed by default, the natural inner join may be expressed simply as "natural join". This is by far the most common join operation in practice. The natural join of tables A and B may be written as A ⋈ B, or in words as "A **natural join** B". This may be summarized as follows:

To compute $A \bowtie B$:   Form $A \times B$
For each column name c that occurs in both A and B
   Apply the restriction $A.c = B.c$
   Remove $B.c$
   Rename $A.c$ to c

There is no need to name the join columns because these are the ones with the same names in both tables (and of course these must be based on the same domain). To help remember the bow-tie "$\bowtie$" notation, note that "$\bowtie$" looks like a cross "$\times$" with two vertical lines added, suggesting that a natural join is a Cartesian product plus two other operations (selection of rows with equal values for the common columns, followed by projection to delete redundant columns). Figure 11.21 shows the natural join for our driving example. Note that the empNr column appears just once and is unqualified.

If the tables have no column names in common, then the natural join is simply the Cartesian product. Like Cartesian product, natural join is associative: $(A \bowtie B) \bowtie C = A \bowtie (B \bowtie C)$. So expressions of the form $A \bowtie B \bowtie C$ are unambiguous.

Tables being joined may have zero, one, or more common columns. In any case, the natural join is restricted to those rows where all the common attributes have the same value in both tables. The number of columns in $A \bowtie B$ equals the sum of the number of columns in A and B, minus the number of columns common to both.

To illustrate a natural join on many attributes, consider the UoD in Figure 11.22. First examine the conceptual schema. Within a bank branch, an account may be identified by its accountNr (local account number). But different accounts in different branches may have the same local account number. So globally, the bank identifies its

(Employee × Drives)
where Employee.empNr = Drives.empNr
[Employee.empNr, empName, sex, carRegNr]

$\Rightarrow$

Employee.empNr	empName	sex	carRegNr
001	Hagar, T	M	ABC123
003	Jones, E	F	ABC123
003	Jones, E	F	TAH007

Figure 11.20 The duplicate column is removed by projection on the equijoin.

Employee $\bowtie$ Drives $\Rightarrow$

empNr	empName	sex	carRegNr
001	Hagar, T	M	ABC123
003	Jones, E	F	ABC123
003	Jones, E	F	TAH007

Figure 11.21 A natural join.

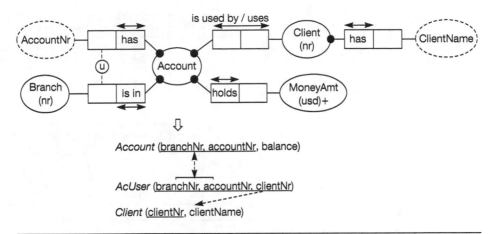

Figure 11.22 Account has a composite identification scheme.

Account:

branchNr	accountNr	balance
10	54	3000.00
10	77	500.55
23	54	1000.00

Client:

clientNr	clientName
1001	Jones, ME
1002	Jones, TA
2013	Jones, ME
7654	Seldon, H
8005	Shankara,TA

AcUser:

branchNr	accountNr	clientNr
10	54	1001
10	54	1002
10	77	2013
23	54	7654

Figure 11.23 Sample population for the bank schema.

accounts by a combination of branch and account number. Clients are identified by a global client number and have a name (not necessarily unique). Not all clients need an account.

The relational schema is included in the figure. Notice the subset and equality constraints between the tables. Joins are usually, though not always, made across such constraint links. Simple joins may be performed on clientNr, and composite joins on branchNr-accountNr pairs (which identify accounts). Figure 11.23 shows sample data.

The two queries in Figure 11.24 use natural joins to display users and balances of accounts. The first query matches accounts by joining on both branchNr and accountNr. To add the client names, the second query also matches clients by joining on clientNr.

(a) Account ⋈ AcUser ⇨

branchNr	accountNr	balance	clientNr
10	54	3000.00	1001
10	54	3000.00	1002
10	77	500.55	2013
23	54	1000.00	7654

(b) Account ⋈ AcUser ⋈ Client

⇨

BranchNr	AccountNr	balance	clientNr	clientName
10	54	3000.00	1001	Jones, ME
10	54	3000.00	1002	Jones, TA
10	77	500.55	2013	Jones, ME
23	54	1000.00	7654	Seldon, H

Figure 11.24 Two queries using natural joins.

Drinker:

patient	liver
Bloggs, F	OK
Smith, S	poor
Stoned, IM	bad

Smoker:

patient	lungs
Bloggs, F	bad
Stoned, IM	bad

(Drinker × Smoker)
where Drinker.patient <> Smoker.patient
[Drinker.patient, Smoker.patient]

⇨

Drinker.patient	Smoker.patient
Bloggs, F	Stoned, IM
Smith, S	Bloggs, F
Smith, S	Stoned, IM
Stoned, IM	Bloggs, F

Figure 11.25 Example of a <>-join.

In rare cases, comparison operators other than equality are used in joins. As a simple example, consider the Drinker and Smoker tables in Figure 11.25. These might result from a decision to map subtypes of Patient to separate tables.

Suppose we wanted a list of drinker-smoker pairs, where the drinker and smoker are distinct persons. This can be formulated by a <>-*join* as shown. Here the comparison operator is "<>". Notice that because drinkers and smokers overlap, some patient doubles may appear twice (in different order). Similarly, <-joins, >-joins, <=-joins, and >=-joins may be defined.

Other kinds of joins can be defined. For example, left, right, and full *outer joins* are used to include various cases with null values. An outer join is basically an inner join, with extra rows padded with nulls when the join condition is not satisfied. For example, Client **left outer join** AcUser includes a row to indicate that client 8005 has the name

Figure 11.26 A simple example to explain relational division.

Figure 11.27 A practical example of relational division.

"Shankara, TA" but uses no account (branchNr and accountNr are assigned null values on this row). The left outer join includes all the clients from the left-hand table (i.e., the table on the left of the join operator), whether or not they are listed in the right-hand table. Outer joins are discussed in detail later for SQL.

Relational Division

The final relational operation we consider is relational **division.** A table A is divisible by another table B only if A has more columns. Let B have n columns. The operation $A \div B$ is defined if and only if the domains of the last n columns of A match the domains of the columns of B (in order). In this case, $A \div B$ is formed by deleting the last n columns from A, then restricting the result to those rows that, in the original A, are paired with (at least) *all* the rows of B. The expression $A \div B$ may also be written as A **divide-by** B. Figure 11.26 shows a trivial example, where the attribute domains are denoted by D1..D3.

Although not used very often, the division operation can be useful in listing rows that are associated with at least *all* rows of another table expression (e.g., who can supply all the items on our stock list?). As a practical example, suppose the table *Speaks* (country, language) stores facts about which countries speak (i.e., use) which languages. A sample population is shown in the large table within Figure 11.27. Now

Table 11.2 Operator priority (1 = highest).

Priority	Operator type	Operator(s)
1	Comparison	= <> < > <= >=
2		**not**
3	Logical	**and**
4		**or**
5	Relational	selection (... **where** ...), projection ...[*a, b*]
6		∪ ∩ − × ⋈ ÷

consider the query "Which countries speak *all* the languages spoken in Canada?" To answer this, we first find all the languages spoken in Canada, using the expression Speaks **where** country = 'Canada' [language]. This returns the table {English, French}. We then divide the Speaks table by this result, as shown, to obtain the final answer {Canada, Dominica}. That completes all the main operators in relational algebra.

Table 11.2 indicates the operator precedence adopted in this book. The comparison operators have top (and equal) priority, so they are evaluated first. Next the logical operators are evaluated (first **not,** then **and,** then **or**). Then relational selection and projection are evaluated (equal priority). Finally the other six relational operators (union, intersection, difference, Cartesian product, natural join, and division) are evaluated (equal priority). Operators with equal priority are evaluated left to right. Expressions in parentheses are evaluated first. Some systems adopt a different priority convention for the relational operators.

To help formulate queries in relational algebra, the following *query strategies* are useful:

- Phrase the query in natural language, and understand what it means.
- Which tables hold the information?
- If you have table data, answer the query yourself, then retrace your mental steps.
- Divide the query up into steps or subproblems.
- If the columns to be listed are in different tables, declare joins between the tables.
- If you need to relate two rows of the same table, use an alias to perform a self-join.

Our first move is to formulate the query in natural language, ensuring that we understand what the query means. Next determine what tables hold the information needed to answer our query. The information might be in a single table or spread over two or more tables. If the columns to be listed come from different tables (or different copies of the same table), then we must normally specify joins between these tables. These joins might be natural joins, theta-joins, or cross joins (Cartesian products).

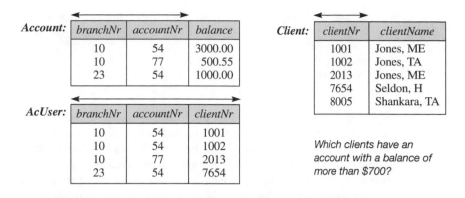

Figure 11.28 How can this query be formulated in relational algebra?

Apart from some cases involving ∪, ∩, or −, relational algebra requires joins whenever different tables must be accessed to determine the result, even if the result columns come from the same table. In contrast, SQL allows use of subqueries instead of joins when the result columns come from the same table.

Let's look at an example using our bank account database. To reduce page turning, the database is reproduced in Figure 11.28. Now consider the query: Which clients have an account with a balance of more than $700? Before formulating this in relational algebra, we should ensure that we understand what the natural-language query means. In some cases we may need to clarify the meaning by asking the person who originally posed the query. For example, do we want just the client number for the relevant clients, or do we want their name as well? Let's assume we want the client name as well. Looking at the tables, we can now see that all three tables are needed. The Account table holds the balances, the Client table holds the client names, and the AcUser table indicates who uses what account.

Since we have sample data, we can first try to answer the English query, then examine what we did, and finally try to express this in the formal language of relational algebra. If we were answering the request ourselves, we might go to the Account table and select just the rows where the balance exceeded $700. This yields the account (10, 54) and the account (23, 54). We might then look at the AcUser table to see who uses these accounts. This yields the clients numbered 1001, 1002, and 7654. Now we look to the Client table to find out their names ('Jones, ME', 'Jones, TA', 'Seldon, H'). So our answer is {(1001, 'Jones, ME'), (1002, 'Jones, TA'), (7654, 'Seldon, H')}.

Retracing and generalizing our steps, we see that we joined the Account and AcUser tables by matching the account (branchNr and accountNr), and we linked with the Client table by joining on clientNr. Since these attributes have the same names over the tables, we can use natural joins. We may set this out in relational algebra as

(Account **where** balance > 700) *[branchNr, accountNr]*
⋈ AcUser
⋈ Client *[clientNr, clientName]*

This isn't the only way we could express the query. For instance, using a top-down approach, both joins could have been done before selecting or projecting, thus:

```
(Account ⋈ AcUser ⋈ Client)
where balance > 700
[clientNr, clientName]
```

Notice how queries may be spread over many lines to make them more readable. A useful syntax check is to ensure that you have the same number of opening and closing brackets. Although these two queries are logically equivalent, if executed in the evaluation order shown, the second query is less efficient because it involves a larger join. Relational algebra can be used to specify transformation rules between equivalent queries to obtain an optimally efficient, or at least a more efficient, formulation. SQL database systems include a *query optimizer* to translate queries into an optimized form before executing them. So in practice we often formulate queries in ways that are easy for us to think about them, rather than worrying about efficiency considerations.

Since relational algebra systems are not used in practice, you can ignore efficiency considerations when doing exercises in the algebra. However, for complex queries in SQL, practical optimizers are not perfect, and you may need to tune your queries to achieve the desired performance. In some cases, hand-tuning a complex query can dramatically reduce its execution time (e.g., from hours to minutes).

As our next example, let's return to the Speaks table mentioned earlier. Consider the query: list each pair of countries that share a common language. For example, one pair is Australia and Canada since they both have English as an official language. Before looking at the solution provided, you might like to try solving this yourself. As a hint, *if you need to relate different rows of the same table, then a self-join is needed.* Also, recall that table aliases are required to join a table to itself.

The solution is shown in Figure 11.29. First, we define two aliases, "Speaks1" and "Speaks2", for the Speaks table. You can think of this as two different copies of the table, as shown. By using the original table name we could have got by with only one alias. Check to make sure that you understand the solution. Notice that we should *not* use the natural join for this query (why?).

The query of Figure 11.29 could have used ">" or "<>" instead of "<". However, "<" nicely arranges for the first name of each pair to be alphabetically prior to the second name. Moreover, "<>" is inadvisable since it would result in each pair being listed twice, once for each order (recall our earlier example about drinkers and smokers).

For a couple of harder examples, we return to the compact disc retailer UoD discussed earlier in the book. The relational schema for the base tables is set out in Figure 11.30. As an exercise, try to formulate the following English queries in relational algebra before checking the solutions provided. These queries are much harder than our earlier examples. Recall that the month codes for January and February are 'Jan' and 'Feb'.

(a) List the cd number and name of each compact disc that *either* had sales of more than 20 copies in each of the months January and February *or* has no track with a duration longer than 300 seconds.

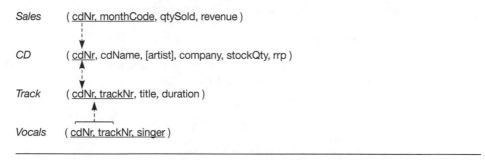

Speaks1:

country	language
Australia	English
Belgium	Dutch
Belgium	French
Canada	English
Canada	French
Cuba	Spanish
Dominica	English
Dominica	French

Speaks2:

country	language
Australia	English
Belgium	Dutch
Belgium	French
Canada	English
Canada	French
Cuba	Spanish
Dominica	English
Dominica	French

define alias Speaks1 **for** Speaks
define alias Speaks2 **for** Speaks

(Speaks1 × Speaks2)
where Speaks1.language = Speaks2.language
    and Speaks1.country < Speaks2.country
[Speaks1.country, Speaks2.country]

⇨

Speaks1.country	*Speaks2.country*
Australia	Canada
Australia	Dominica
Belgium	Canada
Belgium	Dominica
Canada	Dominica

Figure 11.29 A self-join is needed to list pairs of countries with a common language.

Sales   (cdNr, monthCode, qtySold, revenue)

CD   (cdNr, cdName, [artist], company, stockQty, rrp)

Track   (cdNr, trackNr, title, duration)

Vocals   (cdNr, trackNr, singer)

Figure 11.30 Base table schema for compact disc retailer UoD.

(b) Who sings a track lasting at least 250 seconds, *and* sings on *each* compact disc that sold more copies in February than its current stock quantity?

The relational algebra query for (a) is shown in QA. Intersection is required since the quantity sold must be greater than 20 in *each* month (i.e., January *and* February). As an exercise, explain why this can't be done using **"and"** or **"or"**. Union is used for the *or* since the disjuncts are not available on the same row. Subtraction is used to enforce the condition about *no* track. The join provides the cdName.

(QA) (Sales **where** monthCode = 'Jan' **and** qtySold > 20 *[cdNr]*
       ∩
       Sales **where** monthCode = 'Feb' **and** qtySold > 20 *[cdNr]*
       ∪
       (Track *[cdNr]* − Track **where** duration > 300 *[cdNr]*)
       ⋈
       CD) *[cdNr, cdName]*

Query QB formulates the query for (b). Intersection handles the *and* operation, while relational division is used to enforce the *each* requirement.

(QB)   (Vocals ⋈ Track) **where** duration >= 250 *[singer]*
    ∩
    (Vocals *[singer, cdNr]*
    ÷
    (Sales ⋈ CD) **where** monthCode = 'Feb' **and** qtySold > stockQty *[cdNr]*)

Such queries are best formulated by noting the overall structure (e.g., a union), then working on each part. These queries are unusual in requiring frequent use of ∪, ∩, and −. Remember in using these operators to ensure that the operands are compatible—this usually means a projection has to be done first.

Sometimes a query requires several tables to be joined. In this case, if you are joining n tables, remember to specify $n − 1$ joins. For example, the query for Figure 11.28 joined three tables and hence required two joins.

Of the eight table operations covered, only five are primitive (i.e., cannot be defined in terms of the other operations). While some choice exists as to which to consider primitive, the following list is usual: ∪, −, ×, selection, and projection. The other three (∩, ⋈, and ÷) may be defined in terms of these five operations (the proof is left as an exercise). Talking about exercises, you must be bursting to try out your relational algebra skill on some questions. So here they are.

Exercise 11.1

1. The conceptual schema for a particular UoD is shown below. Here "computer" is used as an abbreviation for "kind of computer".

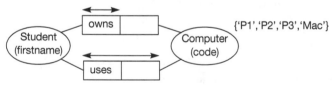

(a) Map this onto a relational schema. Then populate the tables with these data:

    Ann uses a P2.
    Fred uses a P2 and a Mac, and owns a P2.
    Sue uses a P3 and owns a P1.
    Tom owns a Mac.

Given this schema and database, formulate the following queries in relational algebra and state the result. Make use of ∪, ∩, −, and *[ ]*.
(b) List the students who own or use a computer.
(c) List the students who use a computer without owning one of that kind.
(d) List the students who use a computer but own no computer.
(e) List the students who own a computer but do not use a computer.
(f) List the students who own a computer without using one of that kind.
(g) List the students who use a computer and own a computer of that kind.
(h) List the students who use a computer and own a computer.
(i) List the computers used (by some student) but owned by no student.
(j) List the computers owned (by some student) but used by no student.

2. (a) If A is a 200 × 10 table and B is a 300 × 10 table, under what conditions (if any) are the following defined?

 (i) $A \cup B$ (ii) $A \cap B$ (iii) $A - B$ (iv) $A \times B$

 (b) If A is 200 × 10 and B is 100 × 5, what is the size of $A \times B$?

3. The relational schema and a sample population for a student database are shown below. Students are identified by their student number. It is possible for two students to have the same name. All students have their name, degree, gender, and birth year recorded, and optionally subjects (e.g., a student might enroll in a degree before picking which subjects to study). Subjects are identified by their codes. Two subjects may have the same title. For each subject, we record the title and credits. Some subjects might not be studied (e.g., PY205 might be a newly approved subject to be introduced in the next year). This schema applies to a one-semester period only, so we can ignore the possibility of a student repeating a subject. Subject enrollments are entered early in the semester, and ratings are assigned at the end of the semester (so rating is optional). Formulate each of the following queries as a single relational algebra query.

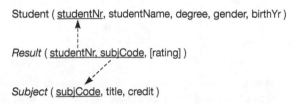

Student (<u>studentNr</u>, studentName, degree, gender, birthYr)

Result (<u>studentNr, subjCode</u>, [rating])

Subject (<u>subjCode</u>, title, credit)

Student:

studentNr	studentName	degree	gender	birthYr
861	Smith J	BSc	M	1967
862	Jones E	BA	F	1965
863	Brown T	BSc	M	1950

Subject:

subjCode	title	credit
CS113	Databases	8
PD102	Logic	10
PY205	Xenoglossy	5

Result:

studentNr	subjCode	rating
861	CS113	7
861	PD102	5
862	PD102	7
863	CS113	4
863	PD102	5

 (a) List the code, title, and credits for the subject CS113.

 (b) List the student number, name, and degree of male students born after 1960.

 (c) List the codes of the subjects studied by the student(s) named "Brown T".

 (d) List the studentNr and name of those students who obtain a 7 rating in at least one subject.

 (e) List the studentNr and name of all students who obtain a 5 in a subject called Logic.

 (f) List the studentNr and degree of those students who study all the subjects listed in the database.

(g) List the studentNr, name, and gender of those students who either are enrolled in a BSc or have obtained a rating of 7 for PD102.

(h) List the studentNr, name, and birth year for male students born before 1970 who obtained at least a 5 in a subject titled "Databases".

4. The following table contains details on students who are to debate various religious topics. For this UoD, students are identified by their first name. Each debating team is to comprise exactly two members of the same religion but opposite sex.

Debater:

firstname	gender	religion
Anne	F	Buddhist
Betty	F	Christian
Cathy	F	Hindu
David	M	Christian
Ernie	M	Buddhist
Fred	M	Hindu
Gina	F	Christian
Harry	M	Buddhist
Ian	M	Christian
Jane	F	Christian
Kim	F	Hindu

Phrase each of the following as a single relational algebra query:

(a) List the name and religion of all females who are not Buddhists.

(b) List the name and sex of those who are either male Hindus or female Christians.

(c) List all possible debating teams, mentioning females before males. For example, one team comprises Anne and Ernie.

5. (a) Map the following conceptual schema to a relational schema.

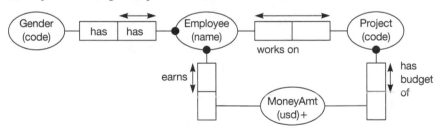

Use your schema to formulate each of the following in relational algebra.

(b) Find names and salaries of all female employees who earn more than $25,000 or work on project "5GIS".

(c) List the name and gender of those employees who work on all projects with a budget of at least $100,000.

6. The Employee table stores the employee number and name of each employee, the department they work for, and the year they joined the firm. The Department table indicates the manager and budget for each department. Each employee manages at most one department (which must be the department for which he or she works).

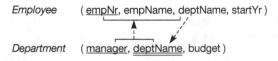

Employee   (empNr, empName, deptName, startYr)

Department   (manager, deptName, budget)

(a) Draw a conceptual schema diagram for this UoD.

Phrase each of the following requests as a single relational algebra query:
(b) Who works for the Accounting department and started with the firm before 1970?
(c) What is the budget of the department in which employee 133 works?
(d) List the departmental managers and the year they joined the firm.
(e) Which employees are not departmental managers?
(f) Give the empNr, name, and year started for those managers of departments with a budget in excess of $50,000.
(g) Which employees worked for the firm longer than their departmental managers?

7. (a) Define A ∩ B in terms of −.
   (b) Let relation A have attributes x, y and relation B have attributes y, z, where both y attributes are defined over the same domain. Define the natural inner join operation $A \bowtie B$ in terms of ×, selection, and projection.
   (c) Let A have attributes x, y and B have the attribute y, where both y attributes are defined over the same domain. Define $A \div B$ in terms of ×, −, and projection.

8. In the following schema, a person is identified by combining the surname and forename. Formulate each of the following as single queries in relational algebra.

Person (<u>surname, forename</u>, sex, weight)

Plays (<u>surname, forename, sport</u>)

(a) Which females play judo?
(b) Which males in the weight range 70..80 kg play either judo or karatedo?
(c) Which females over 50 kg play judo but not karatedo?
(d) Who plays both judo and aikido? (Do *not* use a join.)
(e) Who plays both judo and aikido? (*Do* use a join.)

9. The following relational schema relates to the software retailer UoD from Exercise 6.3. The category codes are DB = database, SS = spreadsheet, WP = word processor.

Customer (<u>customerNr</u>, <u>customerName, address</u>, [phoneNr])

Invoice (<u>invoiceNr</u>, customerNr, issueDate, [paidDate])

LineItem (<u>invoiceNr, itemCode</u>, qty, unitPrice)

Item (<u>itemCode</u>, <u>title</u>, category, stock, listPrice) {DB,SS,WP}

Formulate the following as single queries in relational algebra.
(a) List the customerNr of each customer who has been charged less than the list price for at least one software item, but has been sold no word processor.
(b) List the name of each customer who was sold at least one copy of *all* the spreadsheets on the stock list.
(c) List the customerNr of each customer who has purchased a copy of *all* the word processors that are in stock but who has never purchased a database.
(d) List the customerNr of those customers who purchased both a spreadsheet and a word processor *on the same invoice.*

11.2   Relational Database Systems

We may now define a **relational DBMS** as a DBMS that has the relational table as its only essential data structure, and supports the selection, projection, and join operations without needing specification of physical access paths. A relational system that supports all eight table operations of the relational algebra is said to be *relationally complete*. This doesn't entail eight distinct operators for these tasks; rather, the eight operations must be expressible in terms of the table operations provided by the system.

The two main relational languages are SQL and QBE, with SQL being the most important. Most SQL systems are relationally complete. A system that supports all aspects of the relational model, including domains and the two basic integrity rules (entity integrity and referential integrity), is sometimes said to be "fully relational". The relational model of data itself is evolving.

For version 1 of the relational model, Codd proposed 12 basic rules to be satisfied by a relational DBMS. These may be summarized as follows:

1. All information is represented in relational tables.
2. All data is accessible using the table name, primary key value, and column name.
3. Systematic support for missing information (null values, independent of data type) must be provided.
4. The relational schema itself is represented in tables and is accessible in the same way as the database.
5. A relational query language must be provided that supports data definition, view definition, data manipulation, integrity constraints, authorization, and transaction boundaries (begin, commit, and rollback).
6. Basic support for view updatability is provided.
7. Table-at-a-time retrieval and update operations are provided.
8. Application programs are logically unaffected by changes to internal storage or access methods.
9. Application programs are logically unaffected by information-preserving changes to the base tables.
10. Integrity constraints must be definable in the query language and storable in the system tables.
11. The DBMS has distribution independence.
12. If record-at-a-time processing is supported, this cannot be used to bypass the constraints declared in the set-oriented query language.

Version 2 of the relational model as proposed by Codd (1990) includes 333 rules, including support for two kinds of missing information. While some of the proposed revisions have merit, others are debatable, and it is doubtful whether any commercial DBMS will ever try to satisfy all these rules. In practice, the SQL language itself has become more influential than the relational model in standardization efforts for relational DBMSs. Some SQL systems are fully relational with respect to Codd's original 12 rules, but most provide only weak support for domains. For example, many require heights and weights to be defined as numeric data types, allowing comparisons such as "height = weight".

In SQL-89 the union operation is allowed only between select statements, not between table expressions, and separate operators for ∩, −, and ⋈ (natural join) are not explicitly provided (though expressible in terms of other SQL primitives). In 1992 the SQL standard was substantially improved, and all the table operators are explicitly included in SQL-92 (for example, ∩, −, and ⋈ are called "**intersect**", "**except**", and "**natural join**"). The ability to declare constraints was also substantially improved.

The latest SQL standard, SQL:1999, was approved in 1999, but it will be years before commercial systems provide strong support for it. New features in SQL:1999 include triggers, user-defined data types, object identifiers, array-valued fields, recursive union, and procedural control structures.

Relational DBMSs provided higher-level query facilities than prerelational DBMSs but were originally slower. So they were first used for decision support and low-volume online applications. Nowadays their performance has improved greatly, and they are dominant even for large-scale OLTP (On-Line Transaction Processing) applications.

SQL products (e.g., DB2, Microsoft SQL Server, Oracle) dominate on larger relational systems. Initially, many smaller relational systems (e.g., Access, Paradox, FoxPro) used a version of QBE or Xbase as their main query language. Nowadays, most relational systems, small or large, provide good support for SQL, with basic QBE support offered as an alternative for simpler queries.

In addition to relational algebra operations, relational DBMSs provide further capabilities such as sorting, arithmetic, grouping, and formatting. Most systems also provide powerful tools for creating external interfaces (e.g., screen forms), report writing, and security. In spite of such productivity benefits, the success of any database application still depends critically on the database design.

11.3   SQL: Historical and Structural Overview

The rest of the chapter focuses on SQL. A full coverage of SQL would require a large book itself, so many advanced features of the language are omitted. The treatment assumes familiarity with relational schemas and the main operations of relational algebra, as discussed earlier. This section provides a brief history and structural overview of SQL.

After the publication of Dr. Codd's classic paper on the relational model of data (Codd 1970), some early prototypes were developed to provide a relational DBMS, including a language for querying and updating relational databases. In 1974, Don Chamberlin and Raymond Boyce published a paper on a language called "SEQUEL" (Structured English Query Language) being implemented by a team at the IBM San Jose Research Laboratory as an interface to its System R relational prototype, within a project also called System R. By 1977, a revised version of this language (SEQUEL/2) had been defined and largely implemented by IBM. In the late 1970s it was discovered that "Sequel" was an existing trademark, so the language was renamed "SQL". Although "SQL" is often pronounced "Sequel", officially it is pronounced simply "ess-cue-ell".

The System R project ran from 1971 through 1979, and later evolved into a distributed database project (System R*). Using the experience gained from its System R project, IBM built its first commercial relational DBMS, known as SQL/DS, which it released in 1981. Its second and highly influential SQL product, known as DB2, was released in 1983. As the SQL language had been widely publicized in the 1970s in research papers, other firms began developing their own systems. Relational Software Inc. (later renamed Oracle Corporation) actually beat IBM to the market by releasing its commercial SQL product in 1979. In 1982, the American National Standards Institute (ANSI) began standardization work on the language. The first SQL standard was completed in 1986 and is known as SQL-86.

In 1987, the ANSI SQL-86 standard was adopted by the International Organization for Standardization (ISO). In 1989 a more comprehensive standard, SQL-89, was adopted by both ANSI and ISO. This defined a basic Level 1 version, a richer Level 2 version, and included an addendum on integrity enhancements (including declarative entity integrity and referential integrity).

In 1992 the next standard, known as SQL-92, was approved by both ANSI and ISO. Because of its size (over 600 pages), it was defined at three levels: entry, intermediate, and full. The latest standard, SQL:1999, was approved on December 8, 1999. SQL:1999 represents a significant departure from earlier versions in its inclusion of object-oriented features (e.g., object identifiers and references, array-valued fields, and procedural control structures). SQL is now object-relational rather than purely relational.

Because of its enormous size, the SQL:1999 standard (ANSI 1999) was divided into five separate parts: Framework, Foundation, Call Level Interface, Persistent Stored Modules, and Host Language Bindings. The Foundation part itself comprises 1,151 pages. Other parts are currently under development, and work on a subsequent standard, code-named "SQL:200n" (previously known as "SQL4") is under way.

Currently, most commercial DBMSs have implemented significant portions of SQL-92 and some of the new features in SQL:1999 (e.g., triggers, row types, and large objects), and are working on other aspects of SQL:1999 as well as SQL4. However, it is highly unlikely that any commercial system will ever implement all of SQL-92, much less the later standards. Commercial dialects use their own, nonstandard syntax for some features that they do implement from the standard, and also have their own extensions that are not included in the standard. This overlap is portrayed in Figure 11.31, where dialects A and B denote commercial versions of SQL (e.g., DB2 and Microsoft SQL Server).

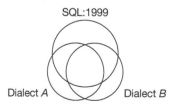

Figure 11.31 Proper overlap between standard SQL and commercial dialects.

Commercial SQL systems are slowly replacing much of their nonstandard syntax with standard syntax, while retaining most of their alternative syntax for backward compatibility. When a feature is supported in both standard and nonstandard syntax, you should use the standard syntax. This makes your SQL code more portable and more understandable to users of other SQLs. This chapter focuses on the SQL-89, SQL-92, and SQL:1999 standards, but also includes some details about commercial implementations.

The SQL language is vast. To help come to terms with it, SQL is sometimes informally classified into the following sublanguages: *DDL* (data definition language), *DML* (data manipulation language), *DCL* (data control language), and *DPL* (data procedural language). The DDL includes statements for creating, altering, and dropping various kinds of database objects, such as tables and views (e.g., **create table, alter table, drop table, create view, drop view**). The DML includes statements for querying and updating the database (e.g., **select, insert, update**, and **delete** statements). The DCL is used for security, controlling who has what kind of access to database objects (e.g., **grant** and **revoke** statements). The three previous sublanguages are essentially declarative, in that statements are used to declare what is to be done rather than how it is to be done. The DPL is a procedural language that supports branching, looping, and other programming constructs (e.g., **if** and **while** statements). This classification is only approximate (e.g., a **create view** statement includes a **select** query, and a **create trigger** statement may include procedural code). Our main focus is on the DML and DDL.

11.4   SQL: Identifiers and Data Types

For a given schema, some database objects such as base tables, views, domains, and constraints are identified by name. A column is identified by appending its (local) name to the name of its table, using a "dot notation". This distinguishes columns with the same local name in different tables. For example, the second columns of the tables *Subject*(subjectCode, title, credit) and *Book*(isbn, title) are identified as "Subject.title" and "Book.title", respectively. In SQL, all names (including local names) are called *identifiers,* even though local names provide identification only within a limited context.

In SQL-89, identifiers were restricted to at most 18 characters, and all letters had to be in upper case. In SQL-92 and SQL:1999, an identifier is either regular or delimited. A *regular identifier* is a string of at most 128 characters, the first of which must be a letter ("a".."z","A".."Z"). Each later character must be a letter, digit ("0".."9"), or underscore ("_"). Moreover, *no reserved word may be used as a regular identifier.* You may, however, use a reserved word as part of an identifier. For example, "note" is fine as an identifier even though it includes the reserved word "**not**".

Commercial SQLs may require shorter identifiers or allow some other characters. In Oracle, the length of identifiers is restricted to 30 characters. Microsoft SQL Server allows identifiers of up to 128 characters, but also allows the first character to be "_", "#", or "@", and later characters to be "#", "@", or "$". It uses "#" to start names of temporary objects and "@" to start variable names.

Table 11.3 Which names may be used as regular identifiers?

Allowed as (regular) identifiers?	SQL-89	SQL-92	SQL:1999
A, R2D2, CUSTOMER_NR	Yes	Yes	Yes
a, This_is_a_long_identifier, CustomerNr	No	Yes	Yes
2B, CUSTOMER NR, SPEED(MPH)	No	No	No
date, first, level	Yes	No	No
before, row, trigger	Yes	Yes	No

Some examples are shown in Table 11.3. The names in the third row cannot be used as regular identifiers since they start with a digit or include an illegal character (e.g., a space or parenthesis). The names in the fourth and fifth rows were first introduced as reserved words in SQL-92 and SQL:1999, respectively.

Since the list of reserved words grows with each new standard, identifiers in existing applications might become illegal at a later stage. For example, Tables 11.4 and 11.5 show that many words became reserved for the first time in SQL-92 and SQL:1999. Different SQL dialects may omit some of these words from their reserved word lists, while adding others, which makes portability between dialects even harder. Partly to avoid such problems, the SQL-92 standard introduced delimited identifiers.

A *delimited identifie*r is a string of at most 128 characters, delimited by (i.e., enclosed in) double quotes. Any character at all may be used, as well as reserved words, within the double quotes. For example, the following are legal delimited identifiers: "customer nr", "speed (km/h)", "&^%!!", "date", "group". Unlike regular identifiers, delimited identifiers are case sensitive (i.e., uppercase letters are not equated to lowercase letters). For example, the delimited identifiers "invoiceNr", "InvoiceNr", and "INVOICENR" are unequal, but the regular identifiers InvoiceNr and INVOICENR are equal.

In SQL, a string constant is delimited by single quotes. For example, 'USA' might be a value in a countryCode column. Some commercial SQLs allow string constants to be delimited by double quotes instead of single quotes, for example, "USA". This practice should be discouraged, since it conflicts with the now standard use of double quotes for delimited identifiers. In Microsoft SQL Server, the command "**set quoted_identifer on**" ensures that double quotes are used only for delimited identifiers, forbidding their use to delimit string constants.

Words that were reserved may cease to be so in later versions. As shown in Table 11.5, the names of several functions and operators were downgraded from reserved words to nonreserved key words in SQL:1999 (e.g., **avg, between, exists, sum**). *Key words* are words that have predefined meanings. Reserved words are key words that cannot be used as regular identifiers.

As mentioned, a reserved word may be embedded within an identifier. Suppose a column is to store the names of tutorial groups. Since **group** is a reserved word, we cannot use this (unquoted) for the column name. However, we may add quotes to make it a delimited identifier or include "group" in a longer regular identifier (e.g., "group", TuteGroup, GroupName).

Table 11.4 Reserved words in SQL-89 and SQL-92.

Reserved words in SQL-89 (and SQL-92)	Extra reserved words in SQL-92
all and any as asc authorization avg	absolute action add allocate alter are assertion at
begin between by	bit bit_length both
char character check close commit continue count create current cursor	cascade cascaded case cast catalog char_length character_length coalesce collate collation column connect connection constraint constraints convert corresponding cross current current_date current_time current_timestamp current_user
dec decimal declare default delete desc distinct double	date day deallocate deferrable deferred describe descriptor diagnostics disconnect domain drop
end escape exec exists	else end-exec except exception execute external extract
fetch float for foreign found from	false first full
go goto grant group	get global
having	hour
in indicator insert int integer into is	identity immediate initially inner input insensitive intersect interval isolation
	join
key	
language like	last leading left level local lower
max min module	match minute month
not null numeric	names national natural nchar next no nullif
of on open option or order	octet_length only outer output overlaps
precision primary privileges procedure public	partial position prepare preserve prior
real references rollback	read relative restrict revoke right rows
schema section select set smallint some sql sqlcode sqlerror sum	scroll second session session_user size sqlstate substring system_user
table to	temporary then time timestamp timezone_hour timezone_minute trailing transaction translate translation trim true
union unique update user	unknown upper usage using
values view	value varchar varying
whenever where with work	when write
	year
	zone

Table 11.5 Key words in SQL:1999.

Reserved words	Some nonreserved words
absolute action add admin after aggregate alias all allocate alter and any are array as asc assertion at authorization	abs ada avg
before begin binary bit blob boolean both breadth by	between bit_length
call cascade cascaded case cast catalog char character check class clob close collate collation column commit completion condition connect connection constraint constraints constructor continue corresponding create cross cube current current_date current_path current_role current_time current_timestamp current_user cursor cycle	c cobol contains convert count
data date day deallocate dec decimal declare default deferrable deferred delete depth deref desc describe descriptor destroy destructor deterministic dictionary diagnostics disconnect distinct do domain double drop dynamic	
each else elseif end end-exec equals escape every except exception exec execute exit external	exists extract
false fetch first float for foreign found from free full function	
general get global go goto grant group grouping	
handler having host hour	
identity if ignore immediate in indicator initialize initially inner inout input insert int integer intersect interval into is isolation iterate	instance
join	
key	
language large last lateral leading leave left less level like limit local localtime localtimestamp locator loop	length lower
map match minute modifies modify module month	max method min mod
names national natural nchar nclob new next no none not null numeric	name nullable number
object of off old on only open operation option or order ordinality out outer output	overlaps
pad parameter parameters partial path postfix precision prefix preorder prepare preserve primary prior privileges procedure public	position
read reads real recursive redo ref references referencing relative repeat resignal restrict result return returns revoke right role rollback rollup routine row rows	row_count
savepoint schema scroll scope search second section select sequence session session_user set sets signal size smallint some space specific specifictype sql sqlexception sqlstate sqlwarning start state statement static structure system_user	self substring sum system
table temporary terminate than then time timestamp timezone_hour timezone_minute to trailing transaction translation treat trigger true	transform translate trim type

Table 11.5 (*continued*)

Reserved words	Some nonreserved words
under undo union unique unknown unnest until update usage user using	unnamed upper
value values varchar variable varying view	{ there are many more }
when whenever where while with without work write	
year	
zone	

A first impression of how a given SQL dialect compares with the standards may be gained by inspecting its list of key words, and especially its reserved words. For the rest of this chapter, key words are usually distinguished by displaying them in bold.

Values entered in a table column belong to the *data type* declared for that column. Table 11.6 lists the standard data types in SQL-89 and SQL-92. Here, square brackets indicate optional components. All SQL dialects support at least character string and numeric types. In the standard, "**char**(n)" means the value is stored as a fixed-length string of n characters. If the value has fewer than n characters, blanks are appended to fill out the length. If no size (n) is specified, this is treated as a string with only one character. A value of type **varchar**(n) is stored as a string of at most n characters. If the value is shorter, it is stored as it is, without padding it with extra blanks. SQL-92 allows various national character sets to be declared. The use of "**nchar**" indicates that characters are selected from the designated national character set.

With the **numeric** data type, the precision p is the maximum number of digits included in the number, and the scale s is the number of digits after the decimal point. For example, columns declared **numeric**(6, 2) allow values in the range $-9,999.99..+9,999.99$. The **decimal** type is like the numeric type except that an implementation may sometimes provide a precision greater than p. Many systems implement numeric and decimal as the same type. The **integer** and **smallint** data types allow integers only (no fractions). The three approximate numeric data types allow very large or very small numbers to be stored to a specified precision as a mantissa times an exponent of 10. The abbreviations **char, dec, int,** and **nchar** may be expanded to **character, decimal, integer,** and **national character**.

As set out in Table 11.6, SQL-92 provides direct support for bit strings as well as time points and time intervals. Times are local unless the **with time zone** option is specified. This option includes the offset from UTC (Universal Time, Coordinated, formerly called Greenwich Mean Time (GMT)). Various temporal operators are provided (e.g., to allow computation of intervals by subtracting one time point from another).

In SQL:1999, all of the previous data types are called *predefined types.* As Table 11.7 indicates, SQL:1999 adds four more predefined types: character large object, national character large object, binary large object, and boolean (true or false). In addition SQL:1999 allows *row types, user-defined types, reference types,* and *collection types.* A

Table 11.6 Standard data types in SQL-89 and SQL-92.

SQL-89 (and SQL-92)	Extra in SQL-92

character string:
    char(*n*)
    char
 	
exact numeric:
    numeric (*p* [, *s*])
    dec (*p* [, *s*])
    int
    smallint
 	
approximate numeric:
    float [*p*]
    real
    double precision
 	
{ *p* = precision
  s = scale }
	character string:
	    varchar(*n*)
	
	national character string:
	    nchar(*n*)
	    nchar varying(*n*)
	
	bit string:
	    bit(*n*)
	    bit varying(*n*)
	
	datetime:
	    date { year, month, day }
	    time { hour, minute, second }
	    timestamp {date and time }
	    time with time zone
	    timestamp with time zone
	
	interval:
	    year-month periods
	    day-time periods

Table 11.7 Extra data types in SQL:1999.

Predefined type	As for SQL-92 plus:
	    character string: **clob**(*n*) { character large object }
	    national character string: **nclob**(*n*) { national character large object }
	    binary large object string: **blob**(*n*)
	    boolean type: **boolean**

Row type	**row**(*field-defn* [, ...])
User-defined type	*UDT name*
Reference type	**ref**(*UDT*)
Collection type	*data-type* **array**(*n*)

row type is basically a sequence of fields and can be used as the basis for defining a table. A user-defined type (UDT) is identified by its name and may include a list of method specifications. If based on a single, predefined type, it is called a *distinct type.* If specified as a list of attribute definitions, it is called a *structured type.* The only collection type constructor allowed in SQL:1999 is array. It is anticipated that further constructors will be added in SQL:200n (e.g., set and multiset).

Currently, most commercial SQLs support all the SQL-89 data types, almost all the additional SQL-92 data types, a few of the extra SQL:1999 data types, and some additional nonstandard data types (e.g., **money**). Many differences exist. For example, Oracle treats **varchar** as **char,** and uses **varchar2** to denote the standard **varchar.** Informix implemented sets, multisets, and lists years ago. SQL Server includes many extra types such as **tinyint, real, money, smallmoney, text, image**, and **uniqueidentifier.** The range of most standard types is usually implementation defined rather than standardized. For example, the range for **smallint** is often, but not always, $-32,768..32,767$.

Exercise 11.4

1. Which of the following are legal identifiers in which of SQL-89, SQL-92, or SQL:1999?

(a) Payroll#	(b) PayrollNr	(c) "Payroll#"	(d) 1994Tax
(e) Tax in 1994	(f) "Tax in 1994"	(g) Tax_in_1994	(h) Deposit_in_$
(i) Mass_(kg)	(j) Order	(k) WorldWideWebIdentifier	(l) count

11.5   SQL: Choosing Columns, Rows, and Order

Recall that relational algebra includes the following eight table operations: union, intersection, difference, Cartesian product, selection, projection, join, and division. All of these operations (as well as others) can be expressed using SQL's powerful select statement. This section discusses how SQL is used to perform relational projection and selection, as well as bag projection and row ordering.

First let's see how to *choose columns*. Consider a small UoD where people are identified by their first name. Table 11.8 provides sample data for the table scheme: *Person* (firstname, sex, starsign, birthyr). The whole table may be retrieved by projecting on all its columns. In relational algebra this may be formulated as Person, or as Person *[firstname, sex, starsign, birthyr]*. In SQL, this is expressed as follows:

select * from Person

Here the asterisk "*" means "all columns" and may be read as "everything" or "all". The table named after "from" indicates the table from which the data is to be retrieved. When this command is executed, the result is an *unnamed* table with the same column names and contents as the original Person table.

If only some of the columns are required, then instead of "*" the relevant columns should be listed (separated by commas). If the columns include a key, no duplicate rows can occur in the result, so the result corresponds to a relational projection on those columns (e.g., see Figure 11.32). To improve readability, an SQL query is usually spread over many lines (e.g., a new line is used to start the **from** clause). Except for quoted string constants, the case (upper or lower) in which letters are written has no significance. I prefer to use lower case most of the time, but start table names with a capital letter. Many organizations have their own detailed standards on use of upper or lower case.

Table 11.8 A relational table storing personal details.

Person:

firstname	sex	starsign	birthyr
Bob	M	Gemini	1967
Eve	F	Aquarius	1967
Fred	M	Gemini	1970
Norma	F	Aries	1950
Selena	F	Taurus	1974
Terry	M	Aquarius	1946

select firstname, starsign
from Person   ⇨

firstname	starsign
Bob	Gemini
Eve	Aquarius
Fred	Gemini
Norma	Aries
Selena	Taurus
Terry	Aquarius

Figure 11.32 Projecting on columns that include a key.

If the chosen columns do not include a key, then duplicate rows may occur in the result. For example, the query in Figure 11.33(a) returns a bag (multiset) rather than a set, since ('M', 'Gemini') appears twice. This operation may be called a *bag projection*. It is sometimes useful to include duplicates (e.g., listing all the scores awarded by judges for a gymnastics event). You can explicitly request inclusion of duplicate rows, by using the qualifier **all** before the select-list, but this is what happens by default in SQL anyway. So a query of the form **select all** *a, b,...* **from** *T* is equivalent to **select** *a, b,...* **from** *T*.

To eliminate duplicates, include the qualifier **distinct** before the select-list. This ensures that rows displayed will be distinct, thus providing a relational projection. Hence the **distinct** qualifier converts a bag of rows to a set of rows. For example, the query in Figure 11.33(b) eliminates the duplicate ('M', 'Gemini') row.

Columns are displayed in the order in which they are specified in the select-list. If "*" is used, all the columns are displayed in the same order as the original table. So the command **select** * **from** Person is merely shorthand for **select** firstname, sex, starsign, birthyr **from** Person.

In general, the relational projection *T[a, b,...]* of relational algebra may be expressed by an SQL statement of the form

select distinct *a, b,...* **from** *T*

We may summarize that portion of the select statement covered so far in the following EBNF (Extended Backus Naur Form) notation. The symbol "::=" may be read "is defined as". Here items in square brackets are optional. The expression "[,...]" means

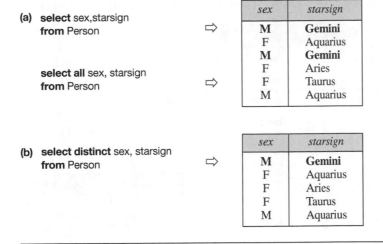

(a) **select** sex,starsign
   from Person ⇨

sex	starsign
M	**Gemini**
F	Aquarius
M	**Gemini**
F	Aries
F	Taurus
M	Aquarius

   select all sex, starsign
   from Person ⇨

(b) **select distinct** sex, starsign
   from Person ⇨

sex	starsign
M	**Gemini**
F	Aquarius
F	Aries
F	Taurus
M	Aquarius

Figure 11.33 The **distinct** qualifier may be used to remove duplicate rows.

the previous construct may be repeated any number of times, with its occurrences separated by commas. A stroke "|" is used to separate alternatives. By default, "|" has minimum scope (i.e., it applies just to the terms immediately beside it). Key words are shown in bold. The final line of the select-query shown here is called the **from** clause. From a logical point of view, it would be better to specify the **from** clause before the select-list, but the syntax of the language does not allow this.

select-list   ::=   *columnname* [,...]

select-query   ::=   **select** [**all** | **distinct**] *select-list* | *
                 from *tablename*

Now let's see how to *choose rows* in SQL. A relational *selection* (or restriction) is the operation of selecting those rows that satisfy a specified condition. In SQL, the syntax for this operation is essentially the same as we adopted for relational algebra. A **where** clause is added to the **select** statement just after the **from** clause, and the specified condition is known as the *search condition*. Do not confuse the relational operation of selection with the **select** statement itself, which is used to perform other operations as well. The formulations in relational algebra and SQL listed in Table 11.9 are equivalent. For example, the query in Figure 11.34 may be used to list details about the Aquarians mentioned in our earlier Person table.

Notice that the character string 'Aquarius' contains a mixture of upper- and lower-case characters. Suppose this is the way it is stored in the table, but the query has the starsign typed in upper case, that is,

select * **from** Person
where starsign = 'AQUARIUS'

Table 11.9 Equivalent formulations in relational algebra and SQL.

Relational algebra	SQL
T **where** *c*	**select * from** *T* **where** *c*
T **where** *c* *[a, b,...]*	**select distinct** *a, b, ...* **from** *T* **where** *c*

select *
from Person
where starsign = 'Aquarius' ⇨

firstname	sex	starsign	birthyr
Eve	F	Aquarius	1967
Terry	M	Aquarius	1946

Figure 11.34 A **where** clause is used to select just the Aquarians.

Unless the system has been configured to convert character strings into the same case before comparing them, no match would be made since the string 'AQUARIUS' is different from 'Aquarius'. To make string comparisons case insensitive in SQL-92 or SQL:1999, either declare a collation set to act this way, or use string functions to convert the case. For example, given a string expression *s,* the fold functions *upper(s)* and *lower(s)* return the uppercase and lowercase versions of *s.* Hence the following query will retrieve the Aquarians regardless of the case used for the letters in 'Aquarius' in the column entries:

select * from Person
where upper(starsign) = 'AQUARIUS'

Although many commercial dialects of SQL, such as SQL Server, support the standard upper and lower string functions, some dialects provide other ways of controlling case sensitivity of string constants.

The next example, shown in Figure 11.35, illustrates three new features. The sample data for the table scheme *Actor*(surname, firstname, sex) includes the surname "D'Abot", which includes a single quote as one of its characters. As discussed earlier, string constants are delimited by single quotes. To embed a single quote within a string like this, we need to inform the SQL system that the quote is part of the string rather than ending it. To do this, we *use two adjacent single quotes to denote an embedded single quote.*

The following **insert** statement may be used to add the second row of data to the table: **insert into** Actor **values** ('D''Abot', 'Maryam', 'F'). Notice that this uses two single quotes in 'D''Abot'. Although this may display simply as "D'Abot" when queried, we must use the two single quotes when using the value in an SQL statement. For example, note the search condition surname = 'D''Abot'.

Actor:

surname	firstname	sex
Bardot	Brigitte	F
D'Abot	Maryam	F
D'Abot	Tony	M

select *, 'This isn''t hard' **as** comment
from   Actor
where surname = 'D''Abot'   ⇨

surname	firstname	sex	comment
D'Abot	Maryam	F	This isn't hard
D'Abot	Tony	M	This isn't hard

Figure 11.35 Two single quotes embed a single quote, and **as** introduces an alias.

The second thing to note about the query is that *we may include a constant as select-item.* Here the select-list includes the string constant 'This isn''t hard'. Note again the use of two single quotes to embed a single quote. Any constant included as an item in the select-list will be included in each row returned by the query. In our example, two rows were returned.

The third aspect illustrated by the example is that the key word **as** *may be used to introduce an alias for a select-item.* This alias will appear as the name of the column for that item in the result table. This example introduced the alias "comment" for the string constant that was added to the select-list. In practice, aliases for select-items are used mainly to provide a simple name for more complex expressions, as discussed later.

Search conditions may include terms, *comparison operators* (=, <>, <, >, <=, >=) and *logical operators* (**not, and, or**). Some SQL dialects allow symbols other than "<>" for "is not equal to" (e.g., "^=", "!="). SQL Server also includes "!<" for "is not less than" and "!>" for "is not greater than", which are equivalent to ">=" and "<=", respectively. For portability, you should avoid such nonstandard symbols. The same priority convention as for relational algebra is adopted. So unless parentheses determine otherwise, *comparison operators are evaluated before logical operators,* which are evaluated in the order **not,** then **and,** then **or.**

Consider the query in Figure 11.36. This lists the name and starsign of people born after 1950 who are either Aquarians or Geminis. If the parentheses were omitted, the condition would be interpreted as starsign = 'Aquarius' **or** (starsign = 'Gemini' and birthyr > 1950). This is different, since it would result in the older Aquarians (in this case Terry) being listed as well.

The selection operation becomes a bit trickier if null values may be present. Consider the relation scheme *Employee*(empNr, empName, dept, [carType]). Here the carType column is optional. Some employees might not drive a car, and even if they do, perhaps it is not recorded. Figure 11.37 provides a sample population for this table, as well as two queries and their results. Suppose we want to know who drives a Ford and who doesn't. We might formulate these questions as the queries in Figure 11.37. Although each employee in real life either does or does not drive a Ford, employee 1002 is absent from both the query results. Can you make sense of this?

Where null values are concerned, SQL operates on a *three-valued logic.* A condition may evaluate to true, false, or unknown. More correctly, a condition is known-to-be-

select firstname, starsign
from   Person
where   (starsign = 'Aquarius' **or** starsign = 'Gemini')
    and birthyr > 1950   ⇨

firstname	starsign
Bob	Gemini
Eve	Aquarius
Fred	Gemini

Figure 11.36 Parentheses are needed to evaluate **or** before **and**.

Employee:

empNr	empName	dept	carType
1001	Thompson, E.	Sales	Ford
1002	Jones, E.	Sales	?
1003	Smith, F.	R&D	Toyota
1004	Adams, A.	Sales	Ford
1005	Dennis, A.	Admin	?

(a) **select** empNr, empName
    from   Employee
    where   cartype = 'Ford'   ⇨

empNr	empName
1001	Thompson, E.
1004	Adams, A.

(b) **select** empNr, empName
    from   Employee
    where   cartype <> 'Ford'   ⇨

empNr	empName
1003	Smith, F.

Figure 11.37 Rows are selected when the condition is true (not false and not unknown).

true, known-to-be-false, or unknown. *A comparison between terms, one of which is null, always evaluates to unknown.* This holds for any comparison operator (=, <>, <, etc.). Consider the row for employee 1002, where a null value (displayed here as "?") is recorded for the carType. For the query in Figure 11.37(a), the condition is "null = Ford", and for the query in Figure 11.37(b), the condition is "null <> Ford". In both cases, the condition evaluates to unknown.

The selection operation performed by the ***where*** *clause returns just those rows that evaluate to true* (i.e., known-to-be-true). Rows that evaluate to false or unknown are filtered out. Hence the rows for employees 1002 and 1005 (Jones and Dennis) are filtered out in both queries. Filtering out the unknown helps us to avoid making unwarranted assumptions. As discussed later, SQL provides a special function for detecting null values.

Now let's discuss how to control the *ordering* of columns and rows in a result table. Columns are displayed in the order in which they appear in the select-list, so if you want a different column order, simply reorder the select-list. However, the order in which *rows* are displayed may be controlled by means of an **order by** clause. If used, the

order by clause must come at the end of the **select** statement. One or more columns in the select-list (identified by name or by position in the select-list) may be used as ordering criteria.

Ordering for a criterion is ascending by default. You can also explicitly specify ascending order by appending **asc** to the column identifier. To specify descending order, you must append **desc.** For numeric values, "ascending" means smaller numbers are listed first. For example, 1 < 3 < 7, so 1, 3, and 7 are in ascending order. For character string values, "ascending" means strings that come earlier in the collating sequence are listed first. As a rough guide, words that come earlier in alphabetical order usually come first.

As a simple example, each of the queries in Figure 11.38 may be used to list the employees in alphabetical order. Although highly undesirable, "2" may be used here instead of "empName" in the **order by** clause, since empName is the second item in the select-list (it doesn't have to be the second column of the base table). This use of position numbers creates problems if you later modify the select-list, makes the query harder to understand, and is a deprecated feature of the SQL standard (i.e., it may be removed in a later version). Because **as** can be used if needed to introduce a result column name, there is never any need to resort to position numbers for ordering. So don't use them.

Character strings are ordered according to the character collating sequence. For example, if ASCII is used, then space (" ") precedes digits (0..9), which precede uppercase letters (A..Z), which precede lowercase letters (a..z). For instance, in ASCII, 'M2' < 'MY' < 'Ma' < 'Ma Kettle' < 'MacTavish' < 'Zen' < 'apple'. However, other collating sequences may differ from this. For example, in EBCDIC, lowercase letters precede uppercase letters, which precede digits.

The **order by** clause may be thought of as a way of converting a *bag* of rows to a *sequence* of rows. For ordering purposes, null values are treated as equal, and depending on the implementation are either less than all non-null values (as in SQL Server) or greater than all non-null values. Consider the following query:

```
select carType from Employee
order by carType
```

This returns the sequence 'Ford', 'Ford', 'Toyota', either preceded or followed by the two null values, depending on the implementation.

		empNr	empName
select empNr, empName **from** Employee **order by** empName	⇨	1004	Adams, A.
or		1005	Dennis, A.
select empNr, empName **from** Employee **order by** empName **asc**	⇨	1002	Jones, E.
		1003	Smith, F.
		1001	Thompson, E.

Figure 11.38 Listing employees in ascending order of employee names.

select firstname, sex
from Person
order by sex, firstname **desc**   ⇨

firstname	*sex*
Selena	F
Norma	F
Eve	F
Terry	M
Fred	M
Bob	M

Figure 11.39 Ordering on two criteria.

select starsign, firstname, sex, birthyr
from Person
where starsign <> 'Taurus'
   and starsign <> 'Aries'
order by starsign, sex **desc,** birthyr   ⇨

starsign	*firstname*	*sex*	*birthyr*
Aquarius	Terry	M	1946
Aquarius	Eve	F	1967
Gemini	Bob	M	1967
Gemini	Fred	M	1970

Figure 11.40 If no order is specified after an **order by** item, **asc** is assumed.

If the column chosen for ordering does not have a uniqueness constraint, then further ordering can be obtained within its duplicate values by specifying more columns in the **order by** clause. Criteria listed first in the **order by** clause are ordered first. For any particular column, the ascending or descending option may be applied. For instance, a query of the form

   select * **from** T **order by** a, b **desc**

first sorts the rows in ascending order of a, and then each set of rows with the same a value is sorted in descending order of b. For example, see Figure 11.39. Here the females are listed first, since 'F' < 'M', and within each sex the names are shown in reverse alphabetical order.

Notice in Figure 11.39 that **desc** has *minimum back scope,* applying just to firstname, not to sex. If descending order of both were required, we would use sex **desc,** firstname **desc.** If an item in an **order by** list is not qualified by either an **asc** or **desc** option, then **asc** is always assumed by default. Hence, to list in ascending order of sex, then name, we may use just sex, firstname, since this is taken to abbreviate sex **asc,** firstname **asc.** To test your understanding, see if you can predict the result of the query in Figure 11.40 and then check your answer with the table shown.

Did you get it right? The rows are first sorted on starsign in ascending order, since **asc** is assumed after starsign (see column 1). Then males of the same starsign as females are listed before those females as a second criterion (see rows 1, 2) since this is descending order of sex. Finally, for those of the same starsign and sex, the younger appear first using the third criterion of ascending order by birth year (see rows 3, 4). The **order by** clause may be specified explicitly by including the implied ordering options:

> **order by** starsign **asc**, sex **desc**, birthyr **asc**

Let us use the term *colname* to indicate a column name and *col* to indicate a column specification (either by name or number). The syntax of that portion of the select statement so far covered may be summarized in EBNF as follows. Although a column-alias can be introduced immediately after a select-item without using **as**, it is better to include **as** in such cases since it aids readability.

> **select** * | [**all** | **distinct**] *colname* | *constant* [[**as**] *column-alias*] [,...]
> **from** *tablename*
> **where** *condition*
> **order by** *col* [**asc** | **desc**] [,...]

Exercise 11.5

1. The following table concerns statements provided in Modula 2. In the column Extra, the values 'Y' and 'N' indicate respectively whether the statement is extra to or already included in Pascal. Formulate each of the following requests as a single SQL query.

Statement:	*kind*	*composition*	*extra*
	assignment	simple	N
	procedure call	simple	N
	if	structured	N
	case	structured	N
	for	structured	N
	while	structured	N
	repeat	structured	N
	loop	structured	Y
	with	structured	N
	exit	simple	Y
	return	simple	Y
	empty	simple	N

(a) List the kind of each statement.

(b) List all information in the table.

(c) List the kind and composition of all statements.

(d) List the kind of each statement and whether it is extra.

(e) List the possible composition values of the statements. (Avoid duplicates.)

(f) Which statements are structured?

(g) Which simple statements are extra to Pascal?

(h) List the kind and composition of those statements that are extra to Pascal.

(i) List, in alphabetical order, the kinds of those statements already found in Pascal.

(j) List the kind and composition of all the statements, starting with the simple statements.

(k) List the kind and composition of all the statements, starting with the structured state-ments and listing statements of the same composition in alphabetical order.

(l) List the kind, composition, and extra status of all the statements, giving precedence to statements extra to Pascal. Statements with the same extra status should be listed starting with those of simple composition, with those of similar composition being shown in re-verse alphabetical order.

(m)List alphabetically the kinds of those statements that are neither structured nor extra to Pascal.

(n) List in reverse alphabetical order the kinds of those statements that are either structured and extra to Pascal or simple.

(o) As for (n) but exclude the exit statement from consideration and include the composition of each. Show all the structured statements first, in reverse alphabetical order, followed by the simple statements, in reverse alphabetical order.

11.6   SQL: Joins

We have seen how to choose, and order, columns and rows from a single table. But sup-pose the information we need from a single query is spread over many tables. SQL pro-vides two main methods to access such information. The first of these uses relational **joins,** and is discussed in this section. The second involves subqueries, and is treated in a later section. The following discussion assumes a basic familiarity with the concept of joins from the relational algebra section.

A *cross join* (Cartesian product) of tables pairs all the rows of one with all the rows of the other. In SQL-89, a cross join of tables is specified by listing the tables in the **from** clause, using a comma to denote the Cartesian product operator (depicted by "×" in relational algebra). A *conditional join* (Θ-join) selects only those rows from the Car-tesian product that satisfy a specified condition. In SQL-89, the condition is specified in a **where** clause, just as we did in relational algebra. So the query expressions in Table 11.10 are equivalent.

Although the SQL-89 syntax has the advantage of being supported by every com-mercial dialect of SQL, it has drawbacks. First, it fails to distinguish join conditions (intertable comparisons) from nonjoin conditions (intratable comparisons on the same base row), instead lumping them together in a single **where** clause. This makes the query harder to understand. Second, it uses a comma for the cross join operation. This is unintuitive and also overloads the comma with different meanings (e.g., it is also

Table 11.10 SQL-89 syntax for joins.

Join type	Relational algebra	SQL-89
Cross join	$A \times B$	**select** * **from** A, B
Conditional join	$A \times B$ **where** $A.a \ominus B.b$	**select** * **from** A, B **where** $A.a \ominus B.b$

used in SQL simply to separate items in lists). Third, it does not provide any direct support for operations such as outer joins, which often occur in practical queries.

For such reasons, SQL-92 (and SQL:1999) uses special syntax for various kinds of joins. In addition to supporting the SQL-89 syntax, these newer standards include special notations for the following types of joins (any text after two hyphens "--" is a comment):

```
cross join
qualified join:    conditional join      -- on clause
                   column-list join      -- using clause
natural join
union join
```

Qualified and natural joins may be further classified into the following types:

```
inner              -- this is the default
outer:   left
         right
         full
```

The new and old syntax for these is summarized in Table 11.11. In this summary, if tables A and B have any common columns (with the same local name), these columns are collectively referred to as "c". For the column-list join, "c_1, ..." denotes one or more of these common columns. Some entries for SQL-89 syntax include unions and subqueries, and are explained in later sections. Many dialects of SQL now support the new syntax for cross joins and qualified joins (including outer joins), but few yet support the new syntax for natural joins. Let's now consider each of the new join notations.

For *cross join,* the more descriptive **cross join** may be used instead of a comma. This syntax is best reserved for unrestricted joins (full Cartesian products). As an example, the Male and Female tables in Figure 11.41 store details about tennis players, and the query lists all possible male-female pairs for mixed-doubles teams.

Cross joins are fairly rare in practice. Much more common are *conditional joins.* The new syntax includes the **join** operator in the **from** clause and the join condition in an **on** clause. Figure 11.42 shows a relational schema, sample population, and a conditional join query to retrieve the name of each female employee and their department. To aid readability, it's a good idea to indent the **on** clause, as shown. Each column mentioned in the query occurs in just one of the tables, so there is no need to qualify the column names with the table names. In this case, the join takes place along the foreign key reference shown in the figure. Although joins often involve foreign key references, they don't have to. All we need is that the columns being joined are based on the same domain.

The same query may be formulated in SQL-89 as follows:

```
select empName, deptName
from   Employee, Department
where dept = deptCode and sex = 'F'
```

Table 11.11 Joins in SQL-92/SQL:1999 and SQL-89.

Join type	New syntax in SQL-92, SQL:1999	SQL-89 syntax
cross	**select** * **from** A **cross join** B	**select** * **from** A, B
conditional	**select** * **from** A **join** B **on** *condition*	**select** * **from** A, B **where** *condition*
column-list	**select** * **from** A **join** B **using** (c_1, ...) -- c_1, ... are unqualified	**select** A.c_1, ... , ... -- omit B.c_1, ... **from** A, B **where** A.c_1 = B.c_1 **and** ... -- join columns are qualified
natural inner	**select** * **from** A **natural [inner] join** B -- join column in result is c	**select** A.c,... -- omit B.c **from** A, B **where** A.c = B.c -- join column in result is A.c

left outer	**select** *
	from A **natural left [outer] join** B
	-- join cols are unqualified;
	-- nulls generated for nonmatches
	
	-- to join on fewer cols use:
	A **left [outer] join** B **using** (c_1, ...)
	
	-- to join cols with different names:
	A **left [outer] join** B
	        on *condition* }
		select A.c,... { omit B.c }
		from A, B
		where A.c = B.c
		union all
		select c, ..., ' ? ', ...
		from A
		where c **not in**
		        (**select** c **from** B)
		-- for composite c, use **exists** with a
		-- correlated subquery.
		-- fewer or different cols cases
		-- are not shown here

right outer	**select** * **from** A **natural right [outer] join** B -- other cases: cf. left join	**select** B.c, ... -- omit A.c ... -- rest as for left join, -- but swap A and B
full outer	**select** * **from** A **natural full [outer] join** B -- other cases: cf. left join; -- rarely used	union of left and right outer joins
union	**select** * **from** A **union join** B -- rarely used	**select** A.*cols*, ' ', ... --' ' $\forall$ B col **from** A **union all** **select** ' ', ..., B.*cols* --' ' $\forall$ A col **from** B

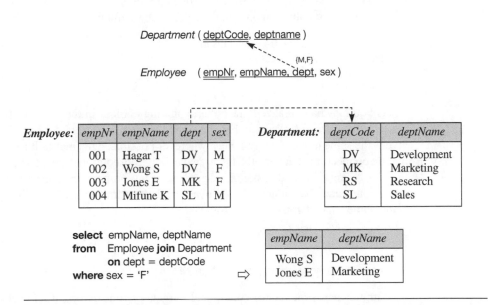

Figure 11.41 Listing all possible male-female pairs.

Figure 11.42 A conditional join specifies the join condition in an **on** clause.

However, the formulation in Figure 11.42 is better, since it separates out the join condition (in the **on** clause) from the intratable condition (in the **where** clause). Although declaring the join conditions up front is logically cleaner, in practice SQL optimizers typically evaluate the intratable conditions before the join conditions, since this reduces the size of intermediate tables created to compute the result (why?).

Column-list joins match values on the specified columns with the local same name in both tables. The new syntax uses the word **join** in the **from** clause, with the relevant columns listed in a **using** clause. As an example, consider the following schema. This is semantically equivalent to the previous schema, but different choices are made for some column names. The department code is denoted by "deptCode" in both tables, and the local identifier "name" is used for the department name as well as the employee name.

Department (<u>deptCode</u>, <u>name</u>)

Employee   (<u>empNr</u>, <u>name, deptCode</u>, sex ^{M,F})

Now consider the previous query: list the name of each female as well as their department name. How do we formulate this query for this new schema? The tables have two local column names in common: "deptCode" and "name". Here we want to perform an equijoin between only some of the columns with common names (just "deptcode", not "name"). The common column names used for the join are listed in a **using** clause, as shown below. Here only one column is used for the join. To disambiguate the query, the column names in the select-list are qualified by their table name.

```
select Employee.name, Department.name
from   Employee join Department
       using (deptCode)
where sex = 'F'
```

As you may have realized, the column naming choices in the previous two schemas are less than ideal. If a column has the same meaning in different tables, it is better to give it the same name in those tables, wherever possible. This makes it easier to see semantic connections between the tables, especially those without foreign key references. For the schema under discussion, "deptCode" may be uniformly used for the department code, and the names of employees and departments may be distinguished as "empName" and "deptName", as follows:

Department (<u>deptCode</u>, deptname)

Employee   (<u>empNr</u>, empname, deptCode, sex ^{M,F})

With this new schema, the conditional join query considered earlier needs to qualify the column names used in the join, since their unqualified names occur in both tables. This gives

```
select empName, deptName
from   Employee join Department
       on Employee.deptCode = Department.deptCode
where sex = 'F'
```

For the new schema, the column-list query does not require any qualifications to the column names, as shown below:

```
select empName, deptName
from   Employee join Department
       using (deptCode)
where sex = 'F'
```

As you might have noticed, the underlying join operation in the previous two queries is now a *natural join,* since we are equijoining on *all* the columns with the same name (in this case there is only one such column: deptCode).

As discussed in relational algebra, *natural inner joins* perform an equijoin to match all columns with the same local names, then remove the extra copies of these columns. In SQL-89, natural inner joins are specified by first forming the Cartesian product (of the tables listed in the **from** clause), then specifying any join conditions in a **where** clause, using the select-list to filter out unwanted duplicate columns. In SQL-92 and SQL:1999, natural inner joins may be declared simply by inserting **natural** or **natural inner** before **join** in the **from** clause (qualified and natural joins are inner by default).

The new notation has three main advantages: it is more descriptive; the **natural join** operator gives direct support for the natural inner join operator of relational algebra (⋈); and it is often more concise. For example, the query just considered can be reformulated more concisely as

```
select empName, deptName
from   Employee natural join Department
where sex = 'F'
```

There is no need to explicitly declare the join condition Employee.deptCode = Department.deptCode, since this is implied by the use of **natural** and the fact that "deptCode" is the only common column name for the tables listed in the **from** clause. The compactness of this new notation is more obvious as the number of natural joins in a query grows. For example, consider the following relational schema:

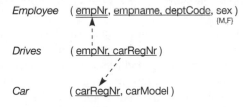

Suppose we want to list the employee number and name of each employee who drives, as well as the model of their cars. Looking at the schema, the information is spread over three tables. As indicated in Figure 11.43, we can join the Employee and Drives tables by matching empNr, and join with the Car table by matching carRegNr (join values are shown in bold). Using the special syntax for natural joins, this can be formulated simply as shown.

Currently, most SQL dialects (including SQL Server) do not support the natural join syntax. Instead, the conditional join syntax is often used to handle natural joins. For example, the query in Figure 11.43 may be reformulated thus:

```
select Employee.empNr, empName, carModel
from   Employee join Drives
          on Employee.empNr = Drives.empNr
       join Car
          on Drives.carRegNr = Car.carRegNr
```

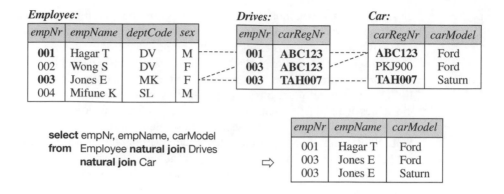

Employee:

empNr	empName	deptCode	sex
001	Hagar T	DV	M
002	Wong S	DV	F
003	Jones E	MK	F
004	Mifune K	SL	M

Drives:

empNr	carRegNr
001	**ABC123**
003	**ABC123**
003	**TAH007**

Car:

carRegNr	carModel
ABC123	Ford
PKJ900	Ford
TAH007	Saturn

select empNr, empName, carModel
from   Employee **natural join** Drives
       natural join Car

⇨

empNr	empName	carModel
001	Hagar T	Ford
003	Jones E	Ford
003	Jones E	Saturn

Figure 11.43 A projection on the natural join of three tables.

Alternatively, SQL-89 syntax can be used as follows:

select Employee.empNr, empName, carModel
from   Employee, Drives, Car
where Employee.empNr = Drives.empNr
      and Drives.carRegNr = Car.carRegNr

When the natural join operator is used, any join columns in the select-list must be denoted by their local (unqualified) names. If a natural join is specified using other syntax (e.g., conditional join or SQL-89 syntax), the join columns must be qualified.

Although most joins in practice are natural inner joins, sometimes natural joins should be avoided. The natural join operation cannot be used to join columns with different names. For example, it can't join dept and deptCode in the query of Figure 11.42. Moreover, the natural join operation must not be used if different tables in the **from** clause include columns with the same name that should not be equated. For example, consider the table schemes for our column-list join example: *Department* (deptCode, name); *Employee* (empNr, name, deptCode, sex). A natural join between Department and Employee would equate not just deptCode but name as well. Any row in the result would equate the employee's name with the department's name, which is nonsense.

Sometimes we do wish to naturally join two tables on more than one column. For example, recall the following schema discussed in the relational algebra section.

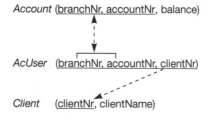

To list the balance and client details for all the accounts requires a composite join on account (compound identifier) and a simple join on client. This may be specified with the natural join syntax as

select * **from** Account **natural join** AcUser **natural join** Client

or as a conditional join:

select   Account.branchNr, Account.accountNr, balance,
            Client.clientNr, clientName
from   Account **join** AcUser
           on Account.branchNr = AcUser.branchNr
             and Account.accountNr = AcUser.accountNr
        join Client
           on AcUser.clientNr = Client.clientNr

For conditional, column-list, and natural joins, **join** is assumed to mean inner join unless an outer join is explicitly specified (see later). In these cases, **inner** may be explicitly declared (e.g., **inner join** or **natural inner join**). If **natural** is declared, an **on** clause or a **using** clause must not be. If three or more tables are included in a join expression, the joins are normally evaluated in a left-to-right order. The join order can also be controlled by inserting parentheses. Since natural inner joins are associative, the order doesn't affect the actual result.

As a more complex example, consider the relational schema in Figure 11.44. As an exercise, you might like to draw the conceptual schema. In the first table "mgrEmpNr" denotes the employee number of the department manager (where there is a manager). The pair-subset constraint indicates that an employee manages a department only if he or she works in it. The (2, 1) item-list marker on this constraint indicates the reordering to (mgrEmpNr, deptCode) before comparing with (empNr, deptCode).

Now consider the following query: for each department with a manager, list its code and name and the employee number and name of its manager. We must match employee numbers between the Department and Employee tables. The department codes must also match, but do we need to specify this? No, because if the manager referenced in the department table is the same as the employee referenced in the Employee table,

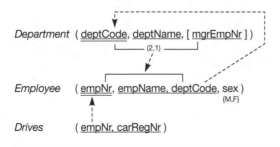

Figure 11.44 A relational schema about employees.

the matching of department codes is implied by the constraints in the schema (why?). So the query may be formulated with the following conditional join:

```
select Department.deptCode, deptName, mgrEmpNr, empName
from   Department join Employee
       on mgrEmpNr = empNr
```

Can we do this with a natural join? No, since the join columns have different names ("mgrEmpNr" and "empNr").

So far we have discussed four of the eight joins listed in Table 11.11. There are also three outer joins, as well as a union join. The union join is rarely used and will not be discussed further. *Outer joins* may be *left, right,* or *full.* Left and right outer joins are often encountered in commercial applications. Given two tables *A* and *B,* their left/right/full outer join is formed by first computing their inner join, then adding the rows from the left/right/both table(s) that don't have a match in the inner join and padding them with null values to fill the extra columns in the result table.

Figure 11.45 provides a simple example of a natural left outer join. The query lists the employee number, name, and car registration numbers (if any) of all the employees (including those who don't drive cars). Each of the two formulations shown is legal in SQL-92 and SQL:1999. The first uses the natural join syntax, but this is not yet supported by most SQL dialects. The second formulation uses the conditional outer join syntax, which is typically supported.

The natural inner join results in the three rows shown for the two drivers (employees 001 and 003). Employees 002 and 004 have no match in the Drives table. The left outer join adds their rows padded with a null value for car registration number. In this book, a null value is displayed as "?". Some systems display it instead as a blank or as "NULL". Many systems allow you to choose how you would like null values to display.

Employee:

empNr	empName	deptCode	sex
001	Hagar T	DV	M
002	Wong S	DV	F
003	Jones E	MK	F
004	Mifune K	SL	M

Drives:

empNr	carRegNr
001	ABC123
003	ABC123
003	TAH007

```
select empNr, empName, carRegNr
from   Employee natural left outer join Drives      ⇨
```

```
select Employee.empNr, empName, carRegNr
from   Employee left outer join Drives
       on Employee.empNr = Drives. empNr             ⇨
```

empNr	empName	carRegNr
001	Hagar T	ABC123
002	Wong S	?
003	Jones E	ABC123
003	Jones E	TAH007
004	Mifune K	?

Figure 11.45 Two equivalent formulations of a natural left outer join.

Although the conditional join syntax requires qualified column names for join columns, when the result table is displayed, some systems (e.g., SQL Server) are clever enough to omit the table qualification from the column header (as in Figure 11.45). Some systems support an alternative outer join syntax that was introduced before outer joins became part of the SQL-92 standard. This alternative syntax often has different semantics and should never be used unless the standard syntax is unsupported.

SQL-92 and SQL:1999 are *orthogonal*. So anywhere a value is legal, so is any expression that returns that value. This makes the language much easier to use, and increases the expressive power of single queries. However, many commercial systems are not fully orthogonal. In particular, they often place restrictions on outer join queries. For example, at most one outer join might be allowed, or no other joins might be allowed after an outer join. With such systems, it is sometimes necessary to formulate a single standard query as a series of queries using intermediate tables to store results on the way.

Right outer join is analogous to left. Full join is the union of left and right. The word **outer** is assumed for left/right/full joins, so it may be omitted (e.g., **natural left join** or **left join**). Outer joins are not associative, so be careful with the join order when outer-joining three or more tables. As discussed later, outer joins can be emulated in the old SQL-89 syntax by means of **union** and subqueries.

When different rows of the same table must be compared, we need to join the table to itself. Such *self-joins* were discussed in Section 11.1. Recall that this requires introducing an alias for the table. In SQL, a *temporary alias* may be declared as a *tuple variable* in the **from** clause after the table it aliases. This variable may be assigned any row from the table and is sometimes called a "correlation variable", "range variable", or "table label". For clarity, **as** may be used to introduce the alias.

Figure 11.46 provides a simple example. The base table Scientist stores the name and sex of various scientists, and the query lists pairs of scientists of opposite sex. Here the aliases S1 and S2 are declared in the **from** clause. To understand the self-join, it helps to think of S1 and S2 as copies of the original base table, as shown. The conditional join performs a $<>$-join on sex (to ensure opposite sex) and a $<$-join on PersonName (to ensure each pair appears only once, rather than in both orders).

Some versions of SQL also provide a "create synonym" command for declaring a permanent alias definition. However, this is not part of the standard. In simplified form, the **from** clause syntax of SQL queries may be summarized in BNF as follows (for alternatives in braces, exactly one is required):

```
from table [[as] alias]
    [, | cross join table [[as] alias]
       | natural [inner | [outer] {left | right | full}] join table [[as] alias]
       | [inner | [outer] {left | right | full}] join table [[as] alias]
                                          { on condition | using (col-list) }
       | union join table [[as] alias]
       [,...]]
```

In formulating an SQL query, the guidelines discussed in relational algebra usually apply. First state the query clearly in English. Then try to solve the query yourself,

Scientist:

personName	*sex*
Curie, Marie	F
Curie, Pierre	M
Edison, Thomas	M
Lovelace, Ada	F

S1:

personName	*sex*
Curie, Marie	F
Curie, Pierre	M
Edison, Thomas	M
Lovelace, Ada	F

S2:

personName	*sex*
Curie, Marie	F
Curie, Pierre	M
Edison, Thomas	M
Lovelace, Ada	F

← ---- "copies" ---- →

```
select S1.personName, S2.personName
from   Scientist as S1 join Scientist as S2
       on S1.sex <> S2.sex
          and S1.personName < S2.personName
```

⇒

personName	*personName*
Curie, Marie	Curie, Pierre
Curie, Marie	Edison, Thomas
Curie, Pierre	Lovelace, Ada
Edison, Thomas	Lovelace, Ada

Figure 11.46 A self-join is used to list pairs of scientists of opposite sex.

watching how you do this. Then formalize your steps in SQL. This usually entails the following moves. What tables hold the required information? Name these in the **from** clause. What columns do you want, and in what order? Name these (qualified if needed) in the select-list. If the select-list doesn't include a key, and you wish to avoid duplicate rows, use the **distinct** option. If you need n tables, specify the $n - 1$ join conditions. What rows do you want? Specify the search condition in a **where** clause. What order do you want for the rows? Use an **order by** clause for this.

The new join syntax introduced in SQL-92 is convenient, but adds little in the way of functionality. The most useful notations are those for conditional and natural joins (both inner and outer). If you are using a version of SQL that does not support the new syntax, you should take extra care to specify the join conditions in detail and to qualify column names when required.

Any SQL statement may include *comments*. These might be used for explanation, documentation, or to simply comment out some code for debugging (comments are ignored at execution time). In SQL-92, a comment begins with two contiguous hyphens "--" and terminates at the end of the line. In addition to these single-line comments, SQL:1999 supports multiline comments, starting with "/*" and ending with "*/". SQL Server supports both of these comment styles. Here's an example:

```
-- This query retrieves details about the employees who drive a car
select *                          -- select all the columns
from   Employee natural join Drives
/* If the above natural join syntax is not supported,
   then omit "natural", and specify the join condition in an on clause */
```

Exercise 11.6

1. This question refers to the student database discussed in Exercise 11.1. Its relational schema is shown. Formulate the following queries in SQL.

Student (<u>studentNr</u>, studentName, degree, gender, birthYr)

Result (<u>studentNr, subjCode</u>, [rating])

Subject (<u>subjCode</u>, title, credit)

(a) List studentNr, name, degree, and birthYr of the students in ascending order of degree. For students enrolled in the same degree, show older students first.
(b) For each student named 'Smith J', list the studentNr and the codes of subjects (being) studied.
(c) List the studentNr, name, and gender of all students studying CS113.
(d) List the titles of the subjects studied by the student with studentNr 863.
(e) List the studentNr, name, and degree of those male students who obtain a rating of 5 in a subject titled 'Logic'. Display these in alphabetical order of name.
(f) List the code and credit points of all subjects for which at least one male student enrolled in a BSc scores a rating of 7. Display the subjects with higher credit points first, with subjects of equal credit points listed in alphabetical order of code. Ensure that no duplicate rows occur in the result.
(g) List the code and title of all the subjects, together with the ratings obtained for the subject (if any).

2. The relational schema shown is a fragment of an application dealing with club members and teams. Formulate the following queries in SQL.

Team (<u>teamName</u>, [captain], [coach])

Member (<u>memberNr</u>, memberName, sex) {M,F}

(a) List the teams as well as the member numbers and names of their captains.
(b) Who (member number) is captain and coach of the same team?
(c) Who (member number) captains some team and coaches some team?

To record who plays in what team, the following table scheme is used:

PlaysIn (<u>memberNr, teamName</u>)

(d) What intertable constraints apply between this table and the other two tables?

Formulate the following queries in SQL:
(e) List details of all the members as well as the teams (if any) in which they play.
(f) List details of all the members as well as the teams (if any) that they coach.
(g) Who (memberNr) plays in the judo team but is not the captain of that team?
(h) Who (memberNr and name) plays in a team with a female coach?

11.7   SQL: in, between, like, and is null Operators

This section examines four special operators (other than the comparators =, <, etc.) that SQL provides for use within search conditions: *in;* ...*between*...*and*...; *like*; and *is null*. These are sometimes called "functions", and the conditions they are used to express are called "predicates" in the SQL standard.

A function is something that takes zero or more values as arguments and returns a single value as its result. You are probably familiar with functions from mathematics or programming, such as $\cos(x)$ or $\text{sqrt}(x)$. As these examples illustrate, syntactically a function is usually represented as a function identifier preceding its arguments, which are typically included in parentheses.

When the action performed by a function is represented without bracketing all the arguments, we usually describe the notation as involving operators and operands rather than functions and arguments. Operators may be represented in infix, prefix, postfix, and mixfix notation according to whether the operator appears between, before, after, or mixed among the operands. For instance, in mathematics the sum of 2 and 3 might be set out as

```
sum(2, 3)        -- function
2 + 3            -- infix operator
+ 2 3            -- prefix operator
2 3 +            -- fix operator
sum of 2 and 3   -- mixfix operator
```

The four operators we are about to discuss are used to express search conditions. The first three return the value True, False, or Unknown, while the **is null** operator returns True or False. Our initial treatment focuses on the SQL-89 version of these operators. Extensions for SQL-92 and SQL:1999 are mentioned later. Most of our examples are based on the Person table, reproduced here as Table 11.12.

Suppose we want the names and birth years of the people born in 1950, 1967, or 1974. One way of requesting this information is shown in the following SQL query. As an exercise, check that this results in four rows.

```
select firstname, birthyr from Person
where birthyr = 1950 or birthyr = 1967 or birthyr = 1974
```

Table 11.12 A relational table storing personal details.

Person:	*firstname*	*sex*	*starsign*	*birthyr*
	Bob	M	Gemini	1967
	Eve	F	Aquarius	1967
	Fred	M	Gemini	1970
	Norma	F	Aries	1950
	Selena	F	Taurus	1974
	Terry	M	Aquarius	1946

Imagine how tedious this way of phrasing the request would be if there were a dozen or more years involved. Partly to make life easier in such situations, SQL includes an *in* operator to handle *bag membership* and hence *set membership*. Using this infix operator, the above request may be formulated more briefly as

select firstname, birthyr **from** Person
where birthyr **in** (1950,1967,1974)

Here the search condition is that the birthyr value is a member of the bag containing the values 1950, 1967, and 1974. The order in which these values are written does not matter, nor would it matter if any are duplicated. In general, if x is some expression (e.g., a column name) and a, b, and so on are data values (e.g., numeric or string constants), then the SQL condition shown below on the left is equivalent to the mathematical expression shown on the right:

x **in** $(a, b, ...)$ means $x \in [a, b, ...]$

We use **in** instead of "$\in$", and parentheses "( )" instead of square brackets "[ ]" for *bag delimiters*. Since a set may be thought of as a bag with no duplicates, the **in** operator may also be used for set membership. Unlike many programming languages, SQL allows bags or sets to contain character strings (not just numbers). For example, the following query lists the Aquarians and Taureans (Eve, Selena, and Terry):

select firstname **from** Person
where starsign **in** ('Aquarius','Taurus')

To indicate that the value of an expression does *not* belong to a bag or set, the logical **not** operator may be used with the **in** operator. As with the ordinary comparison operators, SQL gives the **in** operator higher priority than the logical operators (unlike most programming languages). So in SQL the condition "not (x in S)" may be rendered more briefly as not x in S. Even better, SQL also allows **not in** for "$\notin$". So this may set out more naturally as x not in S.

x **not in** $(a, b, ...)$ means $x \notin [a, b, ...]$

For example, to obtain the names and birth years of those not born in any of the years 1950, 1967, or 1974, the following query may be used (yielding Fred and Terry):

select firstname, birthyr **from** Person
where birthyr **not in** (1950,1967,1974)

Sometimes we wish to determine whether an expression has a value occurring in a *range* of values. In mathematics, to say that some variable x has a value in the range from a to b we usually express this as $a \leq x \leq b$. This notation is illegal in SQL. Instead we could say: $a <= x$ **and** $x <= b$. For the sample population, the following query returns the name and birth year of all but Terry:

select firstname, birthyr **from** Person
where 1950 <= birthyr **and** birthyr <= 1974

As another way to specify range membership, SQL provides the ternary mixfix operator "... **between** ...**and**...", which may be defined as shown, where x, a, and b may be scalar expressions:

x **between** a **and** b means $a <= x$ **and** $x <= b$

For example, the previous query may be reformulated as

select firstname, birthyr **from** Person
where birthyr **between** 1950 **and** 1974

Note carefully that, in contrast to ordinary English, **between** in SQL is read in an *inclusive sense*. For instance, both 1950 and 1974 are included in the above range.

Notice also that here **and** is just part of the mixfix operator; it is not a logical operator. As already noted, the $<=$ operator may be used to order strings as well as numbers, so strings may be used as operands. For example, the following query returns the bag ('Bob', 'Eve', 'Fred').

select firstname **from** Person
where firstname **between** 'Bob' **and** 'Fred'

Nonmembership in a range may be expressed with the help of the **not** operator, which has lower priority than **between**, and may be placed just before the word **between**. Thus each of the following conditions is equivalent to $x < a$ **or** $x > b$.

x **not between** a **and** b **not** (x **between** a **and** b)   **not** x **between** a **and** b

The **not between** formulation is easier to read. For example, the following query returns just the tuple ('Terry', 1946):

select firstname, birthyr **from** Person
where birthyr **not between** 1950 **and** 1974

In the pure relational model, column values are atomic. However, SQL provides a number of ways of accessing substrings within character string values. In particular, the *like* operator may be used for *pattern matching* with character strings. The general form of the condition in SQL-89 may be set out in BNF thus:

char-col [**not**] **like** *quoted-string* [**escape** *quoted-char*]

Here char-col is the name of a column based on a character string data type. The quoted string is a character string, surrounded by single quotes, which may contain wildcard characters. You may be familiar with the use of wildcards for matching filenames at the operating system level (e.g., "*" and "?" in MS-DOS). In the absence of an escape clause, SQL gives the percentage character "%" and the underscore character "_" the following special meanings if included in a quoted string operated on by **like:**

% = 0 or more characters
_ = any single character

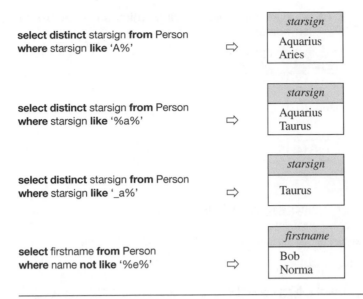

| **select distinct** starsign **from** Person
where starsign **like** 'A%' | ⇨ | *starsign*
Aquarius
Aries |

| **select distinct** starsign **from** Person
where starsign **like** '%a%' | ⇨ | *starsign*
Aquarius
Taurus |

| **select distinct** starsign **from** Person
where starsign **like** '_a%' | ⇨ | *starsign*
Taurus |

| **select** firstname **from** Person
where name **not like** '%e%' | ⇨ | *firstname*
Bob
Norma |

Figure 11.47 "%" and "_" wildcards for pattern matching with the **like** operator.

The "%" is generally more useful, but "_" is needed if the character's position in the string is important. Figure 11.47 provides a few examples based on Table 11.12. The **like** operator has priority over logical operators, so "*x* **not like** *s*" means "not (*x* like *s*)".

Note that the "%" and "_" are interpreted as wildcard characters only in the context of a **like** condition. For example, the following query returns the null set. There are no rows that satisfy the condition, since if "=" is used instead of **like**, the expression 'A%' is taken literally.

> **select** starsign **from** Person
> **where** starsign = 'A%'

As discussed earlier, to include a single quote in a string, we use two single quotes. For example, for the table scheme *Actor* (surname, firstname, sex) considered earlier, the following query returns each actor whose surname begins with "D'": **select** surname **from** Actor **where** surname **like** 'D''%'.

To see a few examples where the like operator is quite useful, consider Table 11.13, which indicates which subjects are offered in which semester at a given university. The sample population is small to save space. At this university, subject codes have the following meaning: the first two characters indicate the discipline area (e.g., "CS" denotes Computer Science and "PD" denotes Philosophy), and the third character denotes the year level (e.g., "1" for first-year level).

Try to formulate the following queries yourself before peeking at the answers:

Table 11.13 A relational table showing which subjects are offered in which semesters.

Offering:

subject	semester
CS112	1
CS112	2
PD102	1
PD102	2
CS225	2
CS314	1

List the computer science subjects.
List the first-year-level subjects.
List subjects higher than first level that are offered in semester 2.

The queries in order are

select distinct subject **from** Offering **where** subject **like** 'CS%'

select distinct subject **from** Offering **where** subject **like** '__1%'

select distinct subject **from** Offering
where distinct subject **not like** '__1%' **and** semester = 2

Another common example of a string that is often interpreted as having structure is a person name. Usually a person's surname as well as either a first name or initials are recorded (e.g., "Smith, James" or "Smith JB"). Suppose we wish to distinguish between these two parts of a person's name. One way to implement this is to include two columns, one for the surname and another for the first name (or initials). The structure is then known to the system, and each of these two parts of the name can be accessed individually (this is especially handy for SQL's **group by** facility). Alternatively, we might use just one column to store the whole name and then use the **like** operator to distinguish the two parts—the name structure then becomes derived rather than stored.

For example, consider Table 11.14, which provides details of players in a mixed-doubles tennis match. Try the following queries and then check your answers.

List details of people with surname "Smith".
List details of people with first name "James".

In order, the queries are

select * **from** Player **where** personName **like** 'Smith, %'
select * **from** Player **where** personName **like** '%, James'

Conditions using the **like** operator may optionally include an *escape character.* If chosen, it may be used as a lead-in character to have "%" and "_" interpreted literally rather than as wildcards. For example, the query in Figure 11.48 lists the starships with an underscore character in their name. Here "\" is used as the lead-in character; any

Table 11.14 A relational table concerning tennis players.

Player:

personName	sex	height
Smith, James	M	180
Smith, Sue	F	?
Smithers, James	M	175
James, Susan	F	170

Starship:

shipName	maxSpeed
Alpha_1	warp 5
Enterprise	warp 8
Epsilon_33	warp 7
Galactica	warp 5

select shipName **from** Starship
where shipName **like** '%_%' **escape** '\'   ⇨

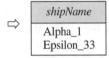

shipName
Alpha_1
Epsilon_33

Figure 11.48 Here "\" is used as an escape character to detect an underscore.

character that doesn't occur in the string being investigated could be used. Some SQL dialects extend the capability of the **like** operator with additional wildcards. For example, SQL Server uses [] to include a range of characters and [^] to exclude characters.

Although null values may be displayed (e.g., as "?"), they cannot be used with the usual comparison operators. Instead, a special postfix Boolean ...**is null** operator is used. This operator is placed after the name of the column on which it operates. It returns True if the column value is null and False otherwise. For example, the following query on the Player table returns 'Smith, Sue', since her height is unknown:

select personName **from** Player
where height **is null**

Neither of the expressions "height = null" or "height = '?'" is allowed. To specify that a value is not null, use the logical **not** operator before the column name or the word **null**. For instance, either query below returns the names of the three other players.

select personName **from** Player **where not** height **is null**
select personName **from** Player **where** height **is not null**

Using "col" to denote a column, the BNF syntax for null comparisons in SQL-89 is

col **is** [**not**] **null**

While the **is null** operator always returns true or false, other comparison operators return unknown when one of the arguments is the null value. Suppose we want the names of the players who are between 170 cm and 175 cm tall (inclusive). The following query returns just two names: 'Smithers, James', 'James, Susan'.

select personName **from** Player
where height **between** 170 **and** 175

Although in the real world Sue Smith's height might be in this range, she is excluded from this result. The system does not know her height, so it will not evaluate the condition to True in her case. Suppose now we want the names of those players whose height is not in the range 170..175. The following query returns just one name: 'Smith, James'.

select personName **from** Player
where height **not between** 170 **and** 175

Notice that Sue Smith is excluded from this result as well. As far as the system is concerned, in her case the truth value of the condition "height between 170 and 175" is neither true nor false; rather it is unknown.

A row is included in a result only if it satisfies the search condition—that is, the condition is (known by the system to be) true for that row. If the condition is either false or unknown, the row is excluded from the result. As an extreme example, the following query returns all the players except Sue Smith.

select personName **from** Player
where height = 170 **or** height < > 170

For Sue Smith's row, each comparison in this condition evaluates to unknown, and applying the **or** operator to unknowns also gives an unknown. The truth value of any condition is evaluated according to a *three-valued logic,* as set out in Figure 11.49. Here "1", "0", and "?" denote the values "true", "false", and "unknown", respectively.

Although SQL-89 and SQL-92 allow only one kind of null value, Codd (1990) proposed a four-valued logic in version 2 of the relational model, to allow for two kinds of unknowns (applicable and inapplicable), but this has not had popular approval.

p	$not\ p$
1	0
0	1
?	?

p	q	$p\ and\ q$
1	1	1
1	0	0
1	?	?
0	1	0
0	0	0
0	?	0
?	1	?
?	0	0
?	?	?

p	q	$p\ or\ q$
1	1	1
1	0	1
1	?	1
0	1	1
0	0	0
0	?	?
?	1	1
?	0	?
?	?	?

Figure 11.49 Truth tables for three-valued logic (1 = true, 0 = false, ? = unknown).

A summary of the SQL-89 syntax of the four operators introduced in this section is shown below. Here *"expn"* denotes an expression such as a column name or constant (or a combination of these connected by arithmetic operators +, −, *, /, ...; see later).

expn [**not**] **in** (*constant-list*)
expn [**not**] **between** *expn* **and** *expn*
char-col [**not**] **like** *quoted-string* [**escape** *quoted-char*]
col **is** [**not**] null

In addition to the above, SQL-89 allows the **in** operator to be used with subqueries and the use of quantified comparisons and the **exists** quantifier in search conditions (see later). SQL-92 and SQL:1999 significantly extended the kinds of expressions and operators allowed in search conditions.

For example, SQL-92 allows a *row value expression* (e.g., a tuple of values) as the left argument of any comparator (e.g., =, **in**) and includes **unique, match**, and **overlaps** predicates. **Unique** is used to check whether each null-free row returned by a subquery is unique, **match** is used to check whether a row matches a row returned by a subquery, and **overlaps** is used to test whether two datetime periods overlap.

SQL:1999 goes further, adding **similar, distinct**, and **type** predicates for use in search conditions. **Similar** allows character strings to be compared by means of a regular expression, **distinct** tests whether two row values are distinct, and **type** tests whether a user-defined type value expression conforms to a user-defined type specification. Dialects of SQL differ in their support for these standard predicates. However, all SQL dialects now support the SQL-89 syntax discussed in this section.

Exercise 11.7

1. The table contains data about computer languages. Phrase the following queries in SQL.

CompLanguage:	title	releaseYr
	FORTRAN	1957
	ALGOL	1958
	COBOL	1959
	Logo	?
	Pascal	1971
	Prolog	1972
	SQL	?
	Modula	1975
	Modula 2	1979
	Goodo Pascal 1.0	1983
	Goodo Pascal 2.0	1984
	Goodo Pascal 3.0	1985
	Goodo Prolog	1986

(a) Which languages were released in the years 1959, 1975, or 1979?
(b) Which languages were released in the period 1959–1979?
(c) Which languages do not have their release year recorded?
(d) List the name and release year of any Goodo language.
(e) List the name of any language ending with 'OL'.

    (f) List the name and release year of any Pascal language.

    (g) List language names that are five characters long.

    (h) List language names with 'o' as the second character.

    (i) List the name of any language containing the letter 'O' or 'o'.

    (j) List the name and release year of languages not starting with 'P' that were released after 1959 and before 1979.

    (k) List language names that either are six characters long and have 'a' as the last or second-to-last character, or are five characters long and end with 'OL'.

2. Suppose that in later years computer languages with the following titles were released: Modula_3, Oberon_2, Ada%93, COBOL%93. Write an SQL query to list all languages whose title includes an underscore or a percentage sign.

11.8   SQL: Union and Simple Subqueries

This section discusses two ways in which select-queries may be used as components within a larger select-query. First we examine how to specify the operations of union, intersection, and difference in SQL. Next we look at basic subqueries in SQL. Let's begin with the **union** operation. The basic syntax is shown below. The reserved word **union** is allowed only between select-queries, not between table names.

> *select-query*
> **union** [**all**]
> *select-query*
> ...

The select-queries must be union-compatible (i.e., same number of columns, and corresponding columns are based on compatible data types). By default, a set is returned that is the union of the tables returned from the individual select-queries, with any duplicate rows eliminated. To return a bag, specify **all** to include duplicate rows. Note that this is the opposite of the SQL select-list syntax, which returns a bag by default and uses **distinct** to remove duplicates. SQL:1999 allows the **distinct** option to be explicitly declared after **union;** if omitted, it is assumed by default. The explicit use of **union distinct** is not supported by SQL Server.

    As an example, the query in Figure 11.50 lists each person who is an American or drives a Ford. The first **select** finds the Americans ('JimO', 'Lance'), the second **select** finds the Ford drivers ('Colleen', 'Lance'), and the **union** includes any person in either or both of these intermediate results. Although Lance appears in both of the tables to be unioned, he appears just once in the final union since duplicates are removed by default.

    If *duplicates* are desired, the **all** option must be specified after **union,** yielding a bag. For example, **union all** in the previous query would cause Lance to appear twice in the result. In general, if a row appears m times in one result table and n times in another, then it appears $m + n$ times in the bag union of those results.

    In our example, the corresponding columns (shortName and driver) are compatible but have different names. Since column headings in the final result are chosen from the

Person:	shortName	nationality
	Colleen	Irish
	JimO	American
	Lance	American
	Norma	Aussie
	Terry	Aussie
	Walter	American

Drives:	driver	carModel
	Colleen	Ford
	JimO	Honda
	Lance	Ford
	Lance	Honda
	Terry	Saturn

Who is an American or drives a Ford?

select shortName **from** Person
where nationality = 'American'
union
select driver **from** Drives
where carModel = 'Ford'   ⇨

shortName
Colleen
Lance
Walter
JimO

Figure 11.50 By default, **union** eliminates duplicates.

first query in the union, the heading "shortName" appears here. Although this query may be formulated in other ways (see subqueries later), the union operation provides the most natural method of merging results from compatible result tables.

Since base tables are rarely union-compatible, the **union** operator is mostly used on derived tables that have been made union-compatible by projection, as in this example. The **union** operation may be applied several times in a query. If an **order by** clause is used, it must come after the last query in the union. For example, appending the clause **order by** shortName sorts the result into 'Colleen', 'JimO', 'Lance', 'Walter'.

In SQL-92 (and SQL:1999), a **corresponding** option may be added to specify the common columns used for the union. For example, if the driver column in Figure 11.50 were instead named "shortName", the query could be declared as **select** * **from** Person **union corresponding** Drives, or as **select** * **from** Person **union corresponding by** (shortName) Drives. This option is not yet supported by most SQLs, including SQL Server.

Now consider the query "Who drives a Ford or Holden or Honda (i.e., who drives at least one of these car models)?" Although we could formulate this using two unions, the query can be answered with one scan of the rows from the Drives table. So it is simpler (and more efficient) to use the **or** operator thus:

select driver **from** Drives
where carModel = 'Ford' **or** carModel = 'Holden' **or** carModel = 'Honda'

When the operands of a **union** operator are disjoint (i.e., mutually exclusive), the **union** operator is sometimes used to add descriptions to the output even when only one base table is involved. As an example, consider the Expert and Novice tables in Figure 11.51. Suppose we want to list the names of the judo players, as well as a label to indicate who are the experts and who are the novices. To obtain the names, we can union a select-query for the judo experts with another select-query for the judo novices. We could then identify the expert and novice judoka, by including the strings 'expert judoka' and 'novice judoka' in the relevant select-lists. We can improve on this by

Expert:

person	sport
Ann	aikido
Ann	judo
Bill	judo
John	bojutsu

Novice:

person	sport
Ann	karatedo
Bill	karatedo
Cathy	aikido
Cathy	judo
David	kendo

```
select  person, 'expert' as "judo level"
from    Expert
where   sport = 'judo'
union
select  person, 'novice' as "judo level"
from    Expert
where   sport = 'judo'
order by "judo level", person
```

⇨

person	judo level
Ann	expert
Bill	expert
Cathy	novice

Figure 11.51 Constants may be used with **union** to indicate the source of the rows.

introducing "judo level" as an alias for the labels. This provides a meaningful column header for the labels, and allows us to shorten the labels to just "expert" and "novice", as shown. Notice the use of double quotes in "judo level" to allow an embedded space.

Although this technique of adding descriptive strings in unions is handy when the operands are disjoint, it is not of much use if they overlap. Any originally overlapping rows become disjoint when the string values are added into the rows (since they will differ in that string value). Hence, such rows would appear more than once in the union.

In SQL-92 (but not SQL-89), the **intersect** operator is provided for *set intersection,* and the **except** operator handles *set difference.* These work analogously to the **union** operator. They are allowed only between select-queries that return union-compatible tables, and duplicates are removed from the result unless the **all** option is specified.

Refer back to the tables *Person*(shortName, nationality) and *Drives*(driver, carModel) in Figure 11.50. Now consider the query "Which Americans drive a Ford?" This can be reworded: "Who is an American *and* drives a Ford?" Since the nationality facts and carModel facts are in separate tables, this logical "and" operator can naturally be implemented by a table intersection operator as follows, yielding the result {'Lance'}.

```
select shortName from Person
where nationality = 'American'
intersect
select driver from Drives
where carModel = 'Ford'
```

Similarly the query "Which Americans do not drive a Ford?" can be formulated as a set difference as follows, yielding the result {'JimO', 'Walter'}.

```
select shortName from Person
where nationality = 'American'
except
```

```
select driver from Drives
where carModel = 'Ford'
```

Unlike union and intersection, the difference operator is not commutative. For example, reversing the order of the operands in the previous query results in {'Colleen'}, since the reversed query has the different meaning "Which Ford drivers are not American?"

If the **all** option is used after **intersect** or **except,** it returns a bag intersection or bag difference, respectively. In general, if a row appears m times in one result table and n times in another, where $m \geq n$, then it appears $\min(m, n)$ times in the bag intersection and $\max(m - n, 0)$ times in the bag difference.

Although all the main commercial SQL dialects support the **union** operator, several (including SQL Server) do not yet support the **intersect** and **except** operators. As we now discuss, these two operators can be emulated using **subqueries,** so their absence does not entail a loss of functionality.

SQL subqueries are like component queries within nested formulations in relational algebra. Although SQL subqueries are queries in their own right, they must be enclosed in parentheses (unlike select-queries that are unioned), and they have some limitations on their use. Ideally, a language ought to be orthogonal—wherever a value or result is legal, an expression that returns that value or result should be legal. In SQL-89, however, subqueries are allowed only in a few places where their result is legal. Although SQL-92 removed these restrictions, few commercial SQLs are fully orthogonal.

A subquery is a parenthesized select-query embedded in a search condition. Let θ denote one of the comparison operators $(=, <>, <, >, <=, >=)$. In SQL-89, a subquery is legal only in the following three contexts:

```
expression [not] in (subquery)              -- membership subquery
expression θ [all | some | any] (subquery)  -- [quantified] comparison subquery
exists (subquery)                           -- existential subquery
```

A *membership subquery* follows an **in** operator. In SQL-89, a membership subquery must be a *singleton query* (i.e., it must return a single column). This is consistent with our earlier use of the **in** operator with a bag of values (a column is just a bag of values, displayed vertically). In SQL-92, the **in** operator may be preceded by a row value expression, in which case the subquery may return a multicolumn table.

A *comparison subquery* follows a comparator (e.g., =). If the comparator is modified by one of the quantifiers **all**, **some**, or **any**, this is a *quantified comparison.* In SQL-89, a comparison subquery must return a single column; if the comparison is not quantified, the subquery must return a single value. This is consistent with the normal use of comparison operators. In SQL-92, a comparator may be preceded by a row value expression, in which case the subquery may return a multicolumn table, or if unquantified, a row value. An *existential subquery* appears after the **exists** quantifier and may return any table.

In SQL-92, subqueries may be used in many other places (e.g., **from** clauses and **check** clauses), so long as their result table makes sense there (orthogonality). **From** clause subqueries require an alias for the derived table even if not needed. The syntax is

```
... from (subquery) [as] alias
```

SQL Server supports subqueries in a **from** clause, but not in a **check** clause. Some SQL dialects limit their subquery support to the three SQL-89 cases, each of which embeds the subquery in a **where** clause of an outer query, thus:

```
select ...          -- outer query
from ...
where ...
        ( select ...     -- subquery
        from ... )
```

If the subquery is self-contained (i.e., it makes no reference to the outer query), it is said to be *uncorrelated*. In this case, it is evaluated first and replaced by its result (e.g., a bag of values) before the outer query is processed. In contrast, *correlated subqueries* refer to their outer query. This section considers only simple, uncorrelated membership and comparison subqueries. Existential and correlated subqueries are covered later.

Let's now consider **membership subqueries.** The condition *expression* **in** (*subquery*) returns true if and only if the value of the expression is included in the subquery result. If the subquery returns the null set, the condition evaluates to unknown. The outer query result includes only the rows where the condition evaluates to true.

To discuss some examples, consider the tables shown in Figure 11.52. Assume there is a subset constraint from Mountain.countryName to Country.countryName. The opposite constraint does not apply (e.g., the Netherlands has no mountains). To save space, only some mountains are shown for the countries.

Consider the query: Which mountains are located in a country with more than 100 million people? This may be set out in SQL as follows:

```
select mtName from Mountain
where countryName in
        (select countryName from Country
        where population > 100000000)
```

The subquery is evaluated first, resulting in the bag ('India', 'USA'). After the subquery has been replaced by this intermediate result, the outer query is evaluated, finally resulting in a list of three mountains: Mana, McKinley, and Rainier. Of course, this query could have been phrased instead using a join. As an exercise, you may wish to do this.

Subqueries may be nested (i.e., their search conditions may include subqueries). To improve readability, subqueries should always be indented. The deeper the level of nesting, the greater the indentation should be.

Country:

countryName	population
Australia	19,000,000
India	1,000,000,000
Netherlands	16,000,000
USA	281,000,000

Mountain:

mtName	countryName
Kosciusko	Australia
Mana	India
McKinley	USA
Rainier	USA

Figure 11.52 Some countries and some of their mountains (if any).

Often, queries using subqueries may be replaced by join queries and vice versa. Some joins cannot be reformulated in terms of subqueries. In particular, *if the select-list includes columns from more than one table, a join must be used* (self-joins must be used if the select columns are from different copies of the same table). For example, the following query cannot be reformulated as a subquery:

select * **from** Country **natural join** Mountain

Now consider the relational schema for our software retailer UoD, which was discussed in Exercise 6.3 and is reproduced in Figure 11.53. Suppose we wish to issue the query "List the customer number, customer name, and invoice number of each invoice that records a shipment of the product titled 'Quinquo'". You might like to try this yourself in SQL before reading on.

The customer name, customer number, and invoice number are to be selected, but do not all occur in the same table. Hence we must include a join in the query to bring these together on the same row of the result table. Looking at the schema, the minimum join we require is to join the Customer and Invoice tables together on customerNr. The rest of the navigation between tables can be done with subqueries because we don't need to include any other columns from those tables in the select-list of the final result. This approach leads to a formulation with one join and nested subqueries as follows:

```
select customerNr, customerName, invoiceNr
from   Customer natural join Invoice
where invoiceNr in
     (select invoiceNr from Lineitem
   where itemCode in
     (select itemCode from Item
   where title = 'Quinquo')
```

Alternatively, we could replace any of the subqueries by a join. For example, the following formulation uses three joins and no subqueries:

```
select customerNr, customerName, invoiceNr
from   Customer natural join Invoice
       natural join Lineitem
       natural join Item
```

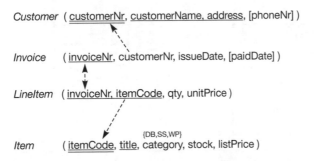

Customer (<u>customerNr</u>, <u>customerName, address</u>, [phoneNr])

Invoice   (<u>invoiceNr</u>, customerNr, issueDate, [paidDate])

LineItem (<u>invoiceNr, itemCode</u>, qty, unitPrice)

Item   (<u>itemCode</u>, <u>title</u>, category, stock, listPrice)   {DB,SS,WP}

Figure 11.53 The relational schema for an invoice application.

If your SQL dialect doesn't support the natural join syntax, use either the conditional join syntax or the old SQL-89 join syntax instead.

As a negated example of subqueries, the following query lists the countries with no mountains. For the given population, this results in just one country: Netherlands.

```
select countryName from Country
where countryName not in
        (select countryName from Mountain)
```

Can you replace a negated subquery with an inner join? No! However, you can replace it with an outer join. For example, the above query may be reformulated as

```
select countryName
from   Country natural left outer join Mountain
where mtName is null
```

The query may also be formulated using a *set difference* operation, thus:

```
select countryName from Country
except
select countryName from Mountain
```

To list those countries that *do* have mountains, the following query could be used:

```
select countryName from Country
where countryName in
        (select countryName from Mountain)
```

This performs a *set intersection* and is equivalent to

```
select countryName from Country
intersect
select countryName from Mountain
```

So, when just single columns are required, *the use of* in *and* not in *with subqueries enables set intersection and set difference operations to be formulated* even in SQL-89. To discuss this further, recall the *Person*(shortName, nationality) and *Drives*(driver, carModel) tables from the previous section. For convenience the sample population for these tables is repeated in Figure 11.54.

Person:	shortName	nationality
	Colleen	Irish
	JimO	American
	Lance	American
	Norma	Aussie
	Terry	Aussie
	Walter	American

Drives:	driver	carModel
	Colleen	Ford
	JimO	Honda
	Lance	Ford
	Lance	Honda
	Terry	Saturn

Figure 11.54 Two relational tables.

Recall that the following queries were used to list the Americans who drive a Ford or do not drive a Ford, respectively:

```
select shortName from Person        select shortName from Person
where nationality = 'American'       where nationality = 'American'
intersect                            except
select driver from Drives            select driver from Drives
where carModel = 'Ford'              where carModel = 'Ford'
```

For a dialect that does not support the intersect or except operators, these queries may reformulated using membership subqueries, thus:

```
select shortName from Person        select shortName from Person
where nationality = 'American'       where nationality = 'American'
and shortName in                     and shortName not in
  (select driver from Drives           (select driver from Drives
   where carModel = 'Ford')             where carModel = 'Ford')
```

This technique will not work in SQL-89 if we want to obtain the intersection or difference of tables with more than one column. However, the **exists** quantifier may be used with subqueries to handle such cases, as discussed later. In SQL-92, the multiple-column case can be handled with membership subqueries because the **in** operator works with row value expressions.

Now suppose we tried to list the Americans who did not drive a Ford by using the following query. Is this correct? Work out the result table for yourself before reading on.

```
select shortName
from Person join Drives
    on shortName = driver
where nationality = 'American' and carModel <> 'Ford'
```

The result from this query lists both JimO and Lance. The query is incorrect for two reasons. As formulated, the query actually asks for the Americans who drive a car other than a Ford. This is very different from the intended query. Lance is wrongly included since he drives a Honda (even though he does drive a Ford). Walter is wrongly eliminated because he drives no car. The condition of never matching a specified value (on any row) is quite different from the condition of matching a different value on some row.

Subqueries may be used with the **union** operator to emulate *outer joins*. For example, consider the query "List the empNr and name of each employee, as well as their car models (if any)". In SQL-92 syntax this may be set out as

```
select Employee.empNr, empName, carModel
from   Employee left outer join Drives
       on Employee.empNr = Drives.empNr
```

In SQL-89 syntax, this may be rephrased as follows. Here a string constant ' ? ' (padded with blanks if needed) is used to emulate a null value, since the standard forbids **null** as a select-item. However, many dialects, including SQL Server, do allow us to say **select null** ..., and this can be handy at times.

```
select Employee.empNr, empName, carModel
from   Employee, Drives
where Employee.empNr = Drives.empNr
union
select Employee.empNr, empName, ' ? '
from   Employee
where empNr not in
                (select empNr from Drives)
```

The remainder of this section discusses **quantified comparison subqueries.** Recall that comparison subqueries may be used to formulate conditions of the form

expression θ [**all** | **some** | **any**] (*subquery*)

where θ is a comparision operator (e.g., =, >), and **all**, **some**, or **any** are quantifiers. In the absence of a quantifier, the subquery must return a single value, which can be guaranteed by using a function (see next section). If such a quantifier is used, we have a quantified comparison subquery. The quantifiers have the following meanings:

some   means   *at least one*
any   means   *at least one*
all   means   *each* (taken one at a time)

In consequence, the following equivalences hold:

in   ≡   **= some** ≡   **= any**
not in   ≡   **<> all**

To avoid confusion, **in** and **not in** should be used instead of their equivalent quantified comparisons, and **some** should always be used instead of **any**. In SQL, **some** and **any** are treated as synonyms. However, this is not always the case in English. For example, "<> any" means "not in" in English, but not in SQL! To appreciate this point, compute the result of the following query for yourself:

```
select countryName from Country
where population <> any (select population from Country)
```

After evaluating the subquery, we may express the condition as "population <> any (190000000, 1000000000, 16000000, 281000000)". In English, "<> any" means "= none". Since each population equals itself, we would expect no rows to be returned. But the query returns all the populations, since each is not equal to some (i.e., at least one) of the populations, and SQL treats "<> any" to mean "<> some".

As a proper use of a quantified comparison, consider the query "Which country has the largest population?" This may be formulated as follows:

```
select countryName
from   Country
where population >= all (select population from Country)
```

Remember that **all** is interpreted distributively as "each, taken individually" rather than collectively. The query result correctly lists India. As discussed in the next section, a **max** function could alternatively be used to reformulate the search condition as population = (**select max**(population) **from** Country). As discussed later, however, quantified comparisons can also handle some cases not amenable to functions (e.g., group extrema).

Exercise 11.8

1. A database is used to store information on diets. The relational schema and a sample population are provided. Weight (or more correctly, mass) is measured in kg.

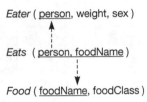

Eater (person, weight, sex)

Eats (person, foodName)

Food (foodName, foodClass)

Eater:

person	weight	sex
Ann	70	F
Bill	70	M
Humphrey	150	M
Sue	60	F

Food:

foodName	foodClass
apple	fruit
beef	meat
chicken	meat
orange	fruit
peas	vegetable
potato	vegetable

Eats:

person	foodName
Ann	apple
Ann	beef
Ann	potato
Bill	apple
Bill	potato
Humphrey	apple
Humphrey	beef
Humphrey	chickcn
Humphrey	orange
Humphrey	peas
Humphrey	potato
Sue	apple
Sue	chicken
Sue	orange
Sue	peas

For this database, formulate each of the following queries in SQL:

(a) Who is either a male or a person weighing over 60 kg?

(b) Who is either a male or a person who eats peas?

(c) Who is female and weighs over 60 kg?

(d) Who is female and eats potatoes?

(e) Who weighs over 60 kg but does not eat beef?

(f) List all pairs of people who are of the same weight but opposite sex.

(g) Who eats vegetables?

(h) List the name and weight of those males who eat at least one kind of meat.

(i) Who eats some food other than meat?

(j) Who are vegetarians (i.e., who does not eat meat)?

(k) List the name, weight, and sex of all eaters, identifying each as either a vegetarian or meat-eater, and listing vegetarians first, then ordering by sex (females first), then by weight, and finally by name.

2. Consider the following relational schema and sample population (for simplicity, assume academics are identified by their surname):

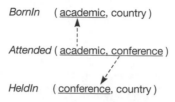

BornIn   (<u>academic</u>, country)

Attended (<u>academic, conference</u>)

HeldIn   (<u>conference</u>, country)

BornIn:

academic	country
Everest	America
Smith	America
Meersman	Belgium

Attended:

academic	conference
Everest	ER-99
Everest	ORM-1
Meersman	ORM-1
Meersman	CAiSE-00

HeldIn:

conference	country
CAiSE-00	Sweden
DAMA-00	America
ER-99	France
ER-00	America
ORM-1	Australia

Formulate queries (a)–(f) in SQL-89:

(a) For conference attendees, list their name, birth country, and conferences attended.

(b) As for (a), but include all academics.

(c) For those academics who attended conferences, list their surname and the name and place of their conferences.

(d) As for (c), but include the conferences not attended by the listed academics.

(e) List the name and birth country of academics born in a country that held a conference, as well as the conferences held there.

(f) As for (e), but include all countries (each additional country will have birth or conference details but not both).

(g)–(l) Formulate queries (a)–(f) in SQL:1999, making use of its extra join operators.

11.9   SQL: Scalar Operators and Bag Functions

A *scalar* is a data value (e.g., a number, string, or date). This section provides a brief discussion of the scalar operators and bag functions that are available in SQL-89, as well as some of the further operators and functions included in SQL-92 and SQL:1999.

In SQL-89, the scalar operators are the four *arithmetic operators* +, −, *, and /. As unary operators, + and − provide the sign of the number (e.g., +3 or −3). If omitted, + is assumed (e.g., 3 = +3). As binary operators, + and − perform *addition* and *subtraction.* The binary operators * and / perform *multiplication* and *division;* they have no unary version. Each is a number-forming operator on numbers. Their operands may appear as column names, constants, function calls, or expressions formed from these by use of arithmetic operators and perhaps parentheses. Scalar expressions may be used as items in a select-list or a search condition.

Let's begin by seeing how these operators may be used to provide a simple calculator facility in SQL to compute the value of an arithmetic expression. We simply include in our database a dummy table with just one row, and then include the expression as the sole item in a select-list for this table. Some DBMSs have dummy tables built in, but let's create our own by issuing the command **create table** C (c **char**) and then populating this table with the dummy value 'c' thus: **insert into** C **values** ('c'). We can now use this table to do simple calculations. As a trivial example, to compute the sum obtained by adding 2 to the product of 3 and 4, we can issue the following query:

select 2 + 3 * 4 **from** C   →   14

For such calculations, the contents of C are not accessed, and hence are irrelevant (except that by confining C to one row, the desired value is displayed just once). In SQL Server, the **from** clause is optional, so you can simply use "**select** 2 + 3 * 4" without having to create a dummy table. The arithmetic operators obey the usual priority convention. Multiplication and division have top priority, with addition and subtraction second. Operators on the same level are left associative (i.e., are evaluated left to right in the order in which they appear). Parentheses may be used to override this evaluation order (parenthesized expressions are evaluated before being operated on from outside). For example: 2 + 8 / 2 * 4 = 18.

For the division operation on exact numeric data, the SQL standard leaves it implementation defined as to the scale (number of digits after the decimal point) of the result. In many SQL dialects (including SQL Server), this scale is 0, so that the division operator performs integer division if its operands are integers. For example:

select 14/3 **from** C   →   4

In this case, real division can be obtained by making one of the operands real. For example:

select 14.0/3 **from** C   →   4.666666

In some dialects, this displays as 4.666666E+000. Here "E" is read "times 10 to the power", so the above value is read "4.666666 times 10 to the power 0". Since $10^0 = 1$, this result boils down to just 4.666666.

SQL-92 introduced the **cast** function to enable data to be recast or converted into data of another type (with some restrictions). This can be used to control the scale of a division result. For example, in SQL Server the following query results in 4.67. Whether results are rounded (as here) or truncated is implementation dependent.

select cast(14.0/3 **as numeric**(9,2)) **from** C   →   4.67

When arithmetic operands are of different type, the result is typically coerced into the "greater" type. For example, the result of the above division was coerced into real by including a real operand. When column names rather than constants are involved, coercion to real can be achieved by multiplying by 1.0 (e.g., **select** 1.0 * quantity/2).

The result of an arithmetic operation between two numbers of the same type (e.g., smallint) may be coerced into a larger type (e.g., integer) to avoid possible overflow problems. As not all SQL dialects behave in the same way, you should check the numeric computation rules for your own dialect.

As a practical example using scalar operators, consider the table scheme *LineItem*(invoiceNr, itemCode, qty, unitPrice). The items and line totals in Australian dollars for invoice 502 where the unit price is above 100 AUD may be requested as follows, assuming unit prices are stored in USD and a conversion rate of 1 AUD = 0.61 USD:

```
select itemCode, qty * unitPrice/0.61 as lineTotalAUD
from   LineItem
where invoiceNr = 502
   and unitPrice/0.61 > 100          -- unitPrice > 100 AUD
```

SQL-92 introduced just one more scalar operator, "||", for *concatenating strings* (character strings or bit strings). For example, suppose the table scheme *Pupil*(pupilNr, surname, firstname, sex, [iq]) is used to store information about school students. Figure 11.55 shows a sample population, as well as a query to list the full name of each student in the way it is normally stated in English, as well as how much above average their IQ is. Some dialects, including SQL Server, use "+" instead of "||" for the concatenate operator.

In the result, each fullname appears as the concatenation of the firstname, a single-space character, and the surname. This assumes the firstname and surname columns are defined using a **varchar** data type. If instead these columns used a fixed-length **char** type, extra spaces would appear between the fullname components, aligning the surnames.

Note that the IQ delta for Don Collins is unknown ("?" denotes the null value). This is because his IQ is unknown, and *a scalar operation returns unknown if any of its operands is null.*

SQL-92 extended the use of the +, −, *, and / operators to datetimes and intervals (e.g., subtracting one date from another yields an interval). SQL:1999 extended the use of the || operator to work with large object strings (clobs, nclobs, and blobs) and

Pupil:

pupilNr	surname	firstname	sex	iq
103	Adams	Ann	F	120
101	Brown	Tom	M	120
106	Brown	Chris	F	100
102	Collins	Don	M	?
104	Dancer	Ernie	M	95
105	Evans	Ann	F	115

```
select firstname || ' ' || surname as fullname,
       iq − 100 as iqDelta
from   Pupil
order by fullname
```

⇨

fullname	iqDelta
Ann Adams	20
Ann Evans	15
Chris Brown	0
Don Collins	?
Ernie Dancer	−5
Tom Brown	20

Figure 11.55 String concatenation using the "||" operator (sometimes rendered as "+").

Table 11.15 Operator priority (1 = highest).

Priority	Operator type	Operator(s)
1	Arithmetic/temporal	* /
2		+ −
	String/array	||
3	Comparison	= <> < > <= >= in between like null
4		not
5	Logical	and
6		or
7	Relational	union intersect except

Table 11.16 The five bag functions in SQL-89.

Bag function	Result
count (*) **count** (**distinct** *colname*)	number of rows in bag number of distinct values in column
sum (*numeric-expn*) **sum** (**distinct** *colname*)	sum of *expn* values in bag sum of distinct values in column
avg (*numeric-expn*) **avg** (**distinct** *colname*)	average of *expn* values in bag average of distinct values in column
max (*expn*)	maximum of *expn* values in bag
min (*expn*)	minimum of *expn* values in bag

arrays. No further scalar operators have yet been introduced in standard SQL. The precedence order for the main SQL operators is summarized in Table 11.15.

SQL-89 provides the following *five bag functions:* **count, sum, avg, max,** and **min.** Each operates on a bag of rows and returns a single, scalar value. In SQL-89, the return value must be a number in the case of **count, sum,** and **avg,** and is either a number or a character string in the case of **max** and **min.** Recall that a bag or multiset is a set in which repetition (though not order) is significant. Each function takes a bag as its argument. For **count** this may be a table (bag of rows) or a column (bag of data values); for the others it must be a column.

Table 11.16 summarizes the cases. The **distinct** option may also be applied with the **max** and **min** functions, but obviously would have no effect. SQL-92 and SQL:1999 introduced no new bag functions. Commercial dialects often support futher bag functions (e.g., SQL Server includes **stdev** and **stdevp** functions to compute standard deviations).

A function is called simply by naming it and placing its argument in parentheses after its name. In SQL-89 the argument must be an expression of the following kind: a column name; a constant; or an arithmetic expression formed from column names and constants with the use of arithmetic operators and perhaps parentheses. Any duplicate values are included in the computation unless the keyword **distinct** is placed inside the parentheses just before the expression.

Function calls may be included in a select-list. In this case, every other item in the select-list must also include a function call, unless the item is a constant or grouping is being performed (see later).

The **sum** and **avg** functions require numeric expressions, whereas **max** and **min** accept number or string expressions. **Count**(*) treats nulls like actual values. All other function calls remove the nulls before computing the result. If the argument bag is empty, **count** returns 0 and the other functions return **null.**

The **count** function may be used in only two ways. **Count**(*) returns the number of rows in the specified table, while **count(distinct** colname) returns the number of distinct values in the named column. If **distinct** is specified, any duplicates are excluded. If duplicates are wanted, the key word **all** may be used; however, since this is the default, it is often omitted.

A few examples based on the Pupil table in Figure 11.55 are shown in the following queries. With the third example, a **where** clause is used to filter out unwanted rows before the function is called.

```
select count(*) from Pupil          →   6
select count(distinct sex) from Pupil   →   2
select count(*) from Pupil
where iq > 100                      →   3
```

The **sum** function returns the sum of the values in the column, and **avg** returns the average of these values. For example:

```
select sum(iq) from Pupil           →   550
select sum(distinct iq) from Pupil  →   430
select avg(iq) from Pupil           →   110
```

Note the exclusion of null values here. Since Don Collins's IQ is unknown, there are only five IQ values to be considered. Since these total 550, their average is 110.

If the argument of the **avg** function is exact numeric, the SQL standard leaves the scale of the result implementation defined. For example, the following query returns different results depending on the SQL dialect used.

```
select avg(distinct iq) from Pupil   →   107.50   -- in some SQLs
                                     →   107      -- in SQL Server
```

In SQL Server the scale here is 0, so any fraction in the average result is lost. To include the fraction, you can multiply the argument by 1.0 to coerce it to real. For example:

```
select avg(distinct 1.0 *iq) from Pupil →   107.500000
```

The functions **max** and **min** return, respectively, the maximum and minimum values. If the data type is character string rather than numeric, these values are computed according to ordinal positions in the character collating. For example:

select max(iq) **from** Pupil	→	120
select min(iq) **from** Pupil	→	95
select max(surname) **from** Pupil	→	Evans

In SQL-89, the bag functions may be called only in a select-list (or in a **having** clause—see later). For example, consider the request: Who has an IQ above the average pupil IQ? The following formulation is illegal:

select firstname, surname **from** Pupil
where iq > **avg**(iq)   →   *Error!*

Instead, we need to embed the function call within a subquery as follows. This query correctly lists Ann Adams, Tom Brown, and Ann Evans in its result.

select firstname, surname **from** Pupil
where iq >
    (**select avg**(iq) **from** Pupil)

A few more examples are given in the following SQL queries. The first query computes the difference between the highest and lowest IQ. The second query determines the ratio of highest to lowest IQ (note the multiplication by 1.0 to ensure the decimal fraction is included). Similarly, in the third example, to compute the mean of the highest and lowest IQ, the divisor is 2.0 rather than 2. The fourth example lists those pupils where 80% of their IQ is greater than 90% of the minimum IQ. As an exercise, explain why it would be wrong in SQL-89 to express the search condition as 0.8 * IQ > 0.9 * (**select min**(IQ) **from** Pupil).

select max(iq) − **min**(iq) **from** Pupil   →   25

select 1.0 * **max**(iq) / **min**(iq)
from Pupil   →   1.263157

select (**max**(iq) + **min**(iq))/2.0
from Pupil   →   107.500000

select firstname, surname **from** Pupil
where 0.8 * iq >
    (**select** 0.9 * **min**(iq) **from** Pupil)   →   Ann   Adams
                                                          Tom   Brown
                                                          Ann   Evans

The above example illustrates the fact that in SQL-89, unlike a function call, an arithmetic expression may be used as a term to be compared in a search condition.

Our next example additionally illustrates the fact that built-in functions may take an arithmetic expression as an argument. Consider the relation scheme: *Window* (windowNr, height, width). The following query may be used to list details about those windows whose height exceeds their width by the greatest amount:

```
select * from Window
where height − width =
              (select max(height − width) from Window)
```

SQL-92 and SQL:1999 extended the range of expressions that may feature as arguments of bag functions. For example, **sum** and **avg** may apply to interval types, and **max** and **min** may be applied to user-defined types. Although SQL-92 and SQL:1999 did not add further bag functions, they did add many scalar functions. For example, SQL-92 introduced the following scalar functions, each of which takes zero or more arguments and returns a scalar: **bit_length, char_length, octet_length, case, cast, collate, convert, translate, current_date, current_time, current_timestamp, current_user, session_user, system_user, user, extract, lower, upper, position, substring**, and **trim.** Most dialects support some of these, as well as other scalar functions of their own.

The **lower** and **upper** functions return uppercase and lowercase versions of the argument, while the **cast** function converts the argument to another data type. Examples of these were given earlier. The **substring** function returns a part of a string, using the syntax **substring** (*string-expn* **from** *start-posn* [**for** *length*]). For example:

```
select substring(surname from 2 for 3)
from   Pupil
where surname = 'Adams'         →         dam
```

Some dialects use a nonstandard syntax for this function. For example, SQL Server uses commas instead of the **from** and **for** key words, for example, **substring**(surname, 2, 3).

The **case** function is quite useful for arranging different output for different cases. Conditions are placed after **when**, with their return option after **then**, and an **else** clause is used to specify the return option if all conditions fail. For example:

```
select firstname, surname,
    case
        when iq > 100 then 'above average IQ'
        when iq = 100 then 'average IQ'
        when iq < 100 then 'below average IQ'
        else 'IQ is unknown'
    end
from Pupil2   →   Ann    Adams    above average IQ
                  Tom    Brown    above average IQ
                  Chris  Brown    average IQ
                  Don    Collins  IQ is unknown
                  Ernie  Dancer   below average IQ
                  Ann    Evans    above average IQ
```

That covers the most important scalar operators and functions in SQL. A discussion of other scalar functions can be found in the references cited in the chapter notes.

Exercise 11.9

1. This question refers to the Diet database used in Exercise 11.8. The table schemes are *Eater* (person, weight, sex); *Eats*(person, foodName); *Food*(foodName, foodClass). Formulate SQL queries for the following.

(a) How many males are there above 100 kg in weight?
(b) How many different weights are there?
(c) What is the sum of the weights of the males?
(d) What is the average weight of the females?
(e) What is the heaviest weight of those who eat beef?

For each of the next two questions, give two equivalent solutions, one of which uses a function while the other uses an **all** or **some** quantifier.
(f) Which females are lighter than every male?
(g) State the name and weight of those females who are as heavy as at least one male.

2. *Log* (code, diameter, len, mass, cost_price, retail_price)

Log:

code	diameter	len	mass	cost_price	retail_price
2A	15	2	10	4.00	7.00
3B	20	3	20	6.00	9.50
5C	20	5	30	9.00	13.00
5D	20	5	25	8.00	12.00

The Log table shown is used by a hardware store to record details about wooden logs on sale. The diameter, length (here called "len"), mass, and price of the logs are measured in cm, m, kg, and $, respectively. Sample data are shown. Formulate the following in SQL.
(a) List the absolute markup (i.e., retail price − cost price) for all the logs.
(b) List the volume of each log in cubic meters, with the column heading "Volume (cubic m)". Use the formula $V = \pi D^2 L/4$ for the volume of a cylinder, approximating π as 3.14. Express each volume as a fixed-point number, truncated to three decimal places.
(c) List the density (i.e., mass/volume), in kg/m^3, of those logs that are 5 m long. Use an appropriate heading and show each density as a fixed-point number truncated to two decimal places.
(d) Which log has the highest relative markup (use ratio R.P./C.P.)?
(e) Which log has a less-than-average ratio of length to diameter? Include this ratio (dimensionless, two decimal places) in the output.

3. The following database is used by a library to record details of books. Authors are identified by name and books by their ISBN (International Standard Book Number). A sample population is shown. Formulate the following queries in SQL.
(a) Who are the Australian male authors?
(b) List the titles of books published in the period 1984..1986, ordered by title. (Explain the position of "dBaseIII" in the result.)
(c) List all details of books with "SQL" as part of the title, showing the most recently published ones first.
(d) Who wrote a book titled "Databases" published in 1980?
(e) List the ISBN and title of all books with at least one Australian author.
(f) List the name and nationality of author(s) of any book(s) titled "Informatics" published by Hall in 1986.
(g) List, with suitable descriptors, the name of the Australian male authors and the American female authors, with the former shown first.

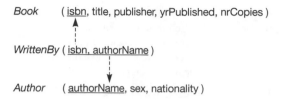

Book   (<u>isbn</u>, title, publisher, yrPublished, nrCopies)

WrittenBy (<u>isbn, authorName</u>)

Author   (<u>authorName</u>, sex, nationality)

Book:

isbn	title	publisher	yrPublished	nrCopies
101	Databases	Possum	1985	4
202	SQL Primer	Hall	1984	4
246	Databases	West	1980	1
345	dBase III	West	1986	1
400	Modula 2	Possum	1986	4
444	Advanced SQL	Hall	1986	2
500	Informatics	Hall	1986	2

WrittenBy:

isbn	authorName
101	Brown J
101	Collins T
202	Adams A
246	Smith JB
345	Jones S
400	Smith JA
444	Adams A
500	Brown J
500	Smith JA

Author:

authorName	sex	nationality
Adams A	F	Aussie
Brown J	M	Aussie
Collins T	M	Kiwi
Jones S	F	American
Smith JA	M	Aussie
Smith JB	M	American

4. Specify the following SQL queries for the Pupil table discussed in this section.
   (a) List the names of the female pupils in a single column, with surname first, followed by a comma, space, and firstname, for example, "Adams, Ann".
   (b) List the number of pupils as well as the number of pupils whose IQ is known.
   (c) List the pupilNr, surname, firstname, and sex of each pupil whose IQ is known, specifying sex as a name ("Female" or "Male") instead of a code ("F" or "M").

11.10   SQL: Grouping

Sometimes we wish to partition the rows of a table into a number of *groups* and display properties that apply to each group as a whole. SQL provides a **group by** clause that may be included in the **select** statement to retrieve such grouped data. *Each group is a bag of rows with the same value(s) for the grouping criteria* listed in the **group by** clause. *The final query result has at most one row for each group.* Figure 11.56 pictures grouping by column *a*. Here there are three groups, one for each of the *a* values. The result may include some group property or function of *a*, depicted here as *f(a)*.

Since the final result includes just one row for each group, the select-list may include group properties only. In other words, for each group, each select-item has only one value. To ensure this, each group property must be either a grouping criterion (a

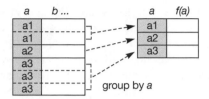

Figure 11.56 Partitioning rows into groups with the same value for column *a*.

Table 11.17 Some atomic particles.

Particle:	particleName	family	charge	mass
	neutrino	lepton	0	0
	mu neutrino	lepton	0	0
	electron	lepton	−1	1
	mu −	lepton	−1	207
	pi 0	meson	0	264
	pi +	meson	1	273
	pi −	meson	−1	273
	K +	meson	1	966
	K −	meson	−1	966
	K 0	meson	0	974
	eta	meson	0	1074
	proton	baryon	1	1836
	neutron	baryon	0	1839
	lambda	baryon	0	2183
	sigma +	baryon	1	2328
	sigma 0	baryon	0	2334
	sigma −	baryon	−1	2343
	xi −	baryon	−1	2585
	xi 0	baryon	0	2573

column name used for grouping), a function call (e.g., **count**(*)), a constant, or an expression formed from these terms (e.g., 2 * groupcol). The basic syntax is as follows:

```
select group-property1, ...
from ...
[where ...]
group by group-criterion1, ...
```

Table 11.17 will be used to help explain most of these ideas. The relation scheme is *Particle*(particleName, family, charge, mass). To help you visualize the grouping into families, I've sorted the rows by family, and added a blank line between the groups. The table lists the main atomic particles belonging to the lepton (light), meson (middle), and baryon (heavy) families. The charge of each particle is given in elementary charges (1 elementary charge = charge of proton = 1.6×10^{-19} Coulomb). The mass of each particle is expressed as a multiple of the electron mass (9.1×10^{-31} kg).

Consider the following query: List the families and the number of particles in each. This may be formulated in SQL as shown. For this section, the result tables are listed with the column headers underlined by hyphens (this is typical of most SQLs).

```
select family, count(*)  →    family  count(*)    -- function header
from   Particle               ——————————         -- may be omitted
group by family               baryon   8          -- in some SQLs
                              lepton   4
                              meson    7
```

Here the **group by** clause indicates that the particles are to be *grouped* into families (i.e., particles with the same family name are placed in the same group). The *items in the select-list are then applied to each group as a whole.*

If **count**(*) is used, it returns the number of rows in the group. In this case we have eight baryons, four leptons, and seven mesons. If an expression other than a column name is used in the select-list, some SQLs use the expression as a column header in the result (as shown here), while others, including SQL Server, omit the column header. It's normally best to use an **as** clause after the expression, to provide your own header.

In many versions of SQL, the use of **group by** causes a default ordering equivalent to a matching **order by** clause (e.g., order by family in this case). However, this is not part of the SQL standard. The syntax of the **group by** clause is

group by *col-name* [, ...]

Members of the same group must have matching values for all of the columns named in the **group by** clause. The next example places particles into groups having both the same family name and the same charge.

```
select family, charge, count(*) as tally    →    family   charge   tally
from   Particle                                   ————————————————————
group by family, charge                           baryon    −1      2
order by family, charge                           baryon     0      4
                                                  baryon     1      2
                                                  lepton    −1      2
                                                  lepton     0      2
                                                  meson     −1      2
                                                  meson      0      3
                                                  meson      1      2
```

If more than one column is used for grouping, the order in which these columns are specified is irrelevant to the content of the result. This is because the same set of groups must be formed. For example, if we group by attributes *a, b* or *b, a*, then the group with values $a = a1$, $b = b1$ is the same as the group with values $b = b1$, $a = a1$, and so on. However, if the row order is based on the group order, the order of rows in the result may be different. For example, the following query returns the same rows as the previous query, in a different order. You can adjust the **order by** clause to change the order:

```
select family, charge, count(*) as tally        →    family   charge   tally
from   Particle                                      ─────────────────────────
group by charge, family                              baryon    −1       2
order by charge, family                              lepton    −1       2
                                                     meson     −1       2
                                                     baryon     0       4
                                                     lepton     0       2
                                                     meson      0       3
                                                     baryon     1       2
                                                     meson      1       2
```

If a function call in the select-list is used as an ordering criterion, you should introduce an alias for it so you can reference it by name in the **order by** clause. For example, the following query lists each family and the mass of its lightest particle, ordering by that minimum mass. As an undesirable alternative, you can reference it by its position in the select-list (e.g., **order by** 2).

```
select family, min(mass) as minMass           →    family   minMass
from   Particle                                    ──────────────────
group by family                                    lepton       0
order by minMass                                   meson      264
                                                   baryon    1836
```

Use of a **group by** clause implies that items in the select-list are to be applied to each group as a whole, returning just one value for each group. So any columns mentioned in the select-list must either be grouped columns or must appear there as an argument to a built-in function (e.g., family and mass in the above query). So when grouping is being performed it makes no sense, and is in fact illegal, to include a nongrouped column as a whole item in the select-list. For example:

```
select family, mass from Particle             →    Error!
group by family
```

Since the same family may include several particles of different mass, this request is plain silly (which mass would we choose?). We can, however, obtain a single grouped value related to mass by using a built-in function, such as **min**(mass) or **avg**(mass), as we did with the previous query.

Although the select-list must not include any nongrouped columns, it is legal to group by columns that are not mentioned in the select-list. For example, the following query lists the minimum mass, but not the name, of each family.

```
select min(mass) as minMass                   →    minMass
from   Particle                                    ───────
group by family                                       0
                                                    264
                                                   1836
```

Within the **select** statement, *a* **where** *clause may be included to filter out unwanted rows before the groups are formed and functions are applied.* Sensibly, the **where** clause must be placed *before* the **group by** clause. For example, the following query lists each family and the average mass of its uncharged particles. To cater to dialects like SQL Server that truncate averages, the mass has been coerced to real by multiplying by 1.0, and the **cast** function is used to display just two digits after the decimal point. Note that it's OK to apply a scalar function to a bag function, for example, **cast**(**avg**(...)). It is, however, illegal to apply a bag function to a bag function, for example, **min**(**avg**(...)).

		family	avgUnchargedMass
select family, **cast**(**avg**(1.0*mass) as **decimal**(6,2)) **as** avgUnchargedMass			
from Particle			
where charge = 0	→	baryon	2232.25
group by family		lepton	0.00
		meson	770.65

Sometimes we wish to restrict our attention to only those groups that satisfy a certain condition. Just as a **where** clause may be used to impose a search condition on individual rows, a **having** clause may be used to impose a *search condition on individual groups*. In this case, the **having** clause must be placed straight after the **group by** clause to which it is logically connected. The syntax is

group by *col-name* [, ...]
having *group-condition*

The usual rules for search conditions apply. Logical and comparison operators may be included in the condition. Each comparison compares some property of the group, such as **min**(mass), with a constant or another group property. Although rare, it is possible to include a **having** clause without an associated **group by** clause; in this case, the entire table is treated as one group. As a simple example, the following query lists the families with more than four particles and the number of particles for each. Although it makes sense to allow aliases (e.g., tally) in the **having** clause, this is not allowed in many SQLs (e.g., SQL Server).

		family	tally
select family, **count**(*) **as** tally	→		
from Particle			
group by family		baryon	8
having count(*) > 4		meson	7

The next example is harder. To help clarify how it works, I've added numbers 1..6 to indicate the order in which the query lines are processed. These numbers are not part of the query. Trace through these six steps yourself to make sure you follow this order. With respect to the **having** clause, note that the charged leptons are included (the uncharged leptons with zero mass have been filtered out earlier by the **where** clause), and the charged baryons are excluded (their maximum mass exceeds 2,000).

Considering only the charged particles, form groups with the same family name, where the group's lightest particle has a mass above 0 and the group's heaviest particle has a mass below 2,000. List the family name, number of particles, and largest mass for each group, showing groups with more members first.

```
5   select family, count(*) as chargedTally, max(mass) as maxChargedMass
1   from Particle
2   where charge <> 0
```

```
3   group by family
4   having min(mass) > 0 and max(mass) < 2000
6   order by chargedTally desc
```

→

family	chargedTally	maxChargedMass
meson	4	966
lepton	2	207

One trivial use of grouping is simply to avoid duplicates. For example, the following query may be used as an alternative to **select distinct** family **from** Particle:

```
select family from Particle
group by family
```

→

family
baryon
lepton
meson

Now suppose we issue the following query. What will be the result?

```
select family from Particle
group by family
having count(*) = 4
```

By comparing this with the previous query, you may feel that the count of each family will be 1 and hence that no rows will be returned (i.e., that the result is the null set). This is wrong! When the **group by** clause does its work, each group still has all its members (which of course all have the same group value). The **having** clause is now applied to filter out those groups that do not satisfy its search condition. Finally the select-list determines which group properties are listed. With this query, the groups are first sorted into three families, then two of these families are eliminated (the baryons and mesons), and finally just the family name "lepton" of the remaining group (the four leptons) is listed.

As a further application of grouping, let's consider how simple cases of *relational division* can be handled. Figure 11.57 shows an SQL query for an example handled earlier in Figure 11.27 by relational division. Here the column name "language" is double-quoted because it is a reserved word.

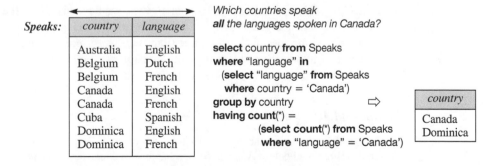

Figure 11.57 Grouping can be used to perform relational division.

Although SQL provides no operator for relational division, we can achieve the same effect by grouping as shown. The first subquery yields ('English', 'French'), so the **where** clause filters out the Dutch and Spanish rows before the groups are formed. Because of the uniqueness constraint on Speaks, the number of Canadian languages spoken by a country is now the number of rows in the group for that country. So the left **count**(*) of the **having** condition returns the values 1, 1, 2, 2 for Australia, Belgium, Canada, and Dominica, respectively. The second subquery evaluates to 2, so the overall query returns Canada and Dominica.

This approach can be adapted to handle cases when the relevant column association is not unique by using the **distinct** option. For example, consider the relation schemes *Localization*(productCode, "language") and *LanguageUse*("language", country, nrSpeakers). The query "Which products are localized into all languages spoken by a country where at least 10 million speak that language?" requires "**count**(**distinct**("language"))" instead of "**count**(*)" in the subquery of the **having** clause. As discussed later, this grouping approach can be extended to cater to queries that involve set comparisons other than those covered by relational division.

We have now covered most of the basic working of SQL's **select** statement. The BNF syntax covered so far may be summarized as shown below. Unlike the syntax shown here, the SQL standard actually allows a **having** clause without a **group by** clause (effectively meaning "group by no columns"), but the semantics are problematic so I'm ignoring this option.

```
select * | [all | distinct] expression [[as] column-alias ] [,...]
from table [[as] alias]
     [, | cross join table [[as] alias]
         | natural [inner | [outer] {left | right | full}] join table [[as] alias]
         | [inner | [outer] {left | right | full}] join table [[as] alias]
                                              { on condition | using (col-list) }
         | union join table [[as] alias]
         [,...]]
[where col-condition]
[group by colname [,...]
   [having group-condition]]
[union | intersect |except ...]
[order by col [asc | desc] [,...] ]
```

Of the eight table operations of relational algebra, we have discussed the equivalent SQL formulation for the general case of five (projection, selection, Cartesian product, θ-join, union) and for special cases of three (intersection, difference, and division). The general cases of intersection, difference, and division can be handled using correlated and existential subqueries, as discussed in the next section.

Exercise 11.10

1. This question refers to the library database discussed in Exercise 11.9. The relational schema is repeated below. Assume ISBN is based on a character data type. Formulate SQL queries for the following requests.

Book   (<u>isbn</u>, title, publisher, yrPublished, nrCopies)

WrittenBy (<u>isbn, authorName</u>)

Author   (<u>authorName</u>, sex, nationality)

(a) How many authors of each sex are there?

(b) Place authors into groups of the same sex and nationality, indicating how many there are in each group, with the larger groups shown first.

(c) Considering only the books published after 1980, list the publishers and the total number of copies of their books in the library.

(d) For each publisher having an average number of library copies per book above two, show the earliest publication year.

(e) List the ISBN and the number of authors for each book published before 1986 that has more than one author.

(f) Restricting attention to male authors of a book published by Hall or Possum, list the number of such authors for each nationality that has at least as many authors of this kind as there are copies in the library of the book with ISBN "444".

3. The relational schema for a dietary database is shown (for a sample population, see Exercise 11.8). Formulate the following queries in SQL.

Eater (<u>person</u>, weight, sex)

Eats (<u>person, foodName</u>)

Food (<u>foodName</u>, foodClass)

(a) Who eats all the foods?

(b) Which foods are eaten by all eaters?

11.11   SQL: Correlated and Existential Subqueries

This section extends the subquery work in Section 11.8 by considering correlated and existential subqueries. The subqueries discussed earlier were simple, uncorrelated subqueries. An uncorrelated subquery is computed once, then replaced by its result, and the outer query is run. In contrast, a **correlated subquery** relates its search condition to *each* row of a table named in the outer query and is effectively recomputed for each outer row (see Figure 11.58).

Because of repeated computation, correlated subqueries can sometimes be slow to run. However, they significantly extend the range of queries that can be expressed as a single SQL query and are well worth mastering. Let us refer to the condition inside the correlated subquery as the *correlation condition*. This condition typically takes the form

$a \; \Theta \; b$

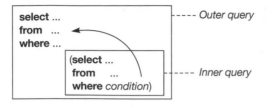

Figure 11.58 A correlated subquery relates its condition to each row of the outer query.

Table 11.18 Declaring a correlation between an inner column *a* and an outer column *b*.

Case	Situation	Declaration
1	*a* is the name of a column in inner table only. *b* is the name of a column in outer table only.	$a \ominus b$
2	*a*, *b* are the same column name but in different tables. *T* is the base name of the outer table.	$a \ominus T.b$
3	The inner and outer tables have the same base name. *X* is an alias introduced for the outer table.	$a \ominus X.b$

where *a* is an *inner column* (listed in the **from** clause of the subquery), *b* is an *outer column* (listed in the **from** clause of the outer query), and $\ominus$ is a comparator (e.g., $=$, $>$).

To avoid ambiguity, the column names for *a* or *b* may need to be qualified by a table name. The three basic cases are summarized in Table 11.18. Since local scope is assumed by default, we may normally leave *a* unqualified (unless it occurs in two inner tables). However, if *a* and *b* have the same unqualified name, we need to distinguish *b* by qualifying it with its outer table name. If the outer table has the same name as the inner table, we must introduce an alias for it to distinguish it from the inner table.

For example, consider the table scheme *Human*(firstname, sex, height). For simplicity, we assume that people in this UoD can be identified by their firstname. A sample population is provided in Figure 11.59, along with a correlated subquery to retrieve the name and height (in cm) of those who are above average height for *their* sex. In English, correlations are often made with a *pronoun,* such as "their", "his or her", "its", or "that". Pronouns effectively function as object variables.

Here the same table name "Human" appears in the **from** clause of both the inner and outer queries. So to distinguish the sex column in the inner table from the sex column in the outer table, the alias *X* is introduced for the outer table. This allows us to specify the correlation condition as "sex = *X*.sex", rather than "sex = sex" (which would always be true). Here *X* is said to be a *correlation variable.* You can think of *X* as an extra copy of the Human table.

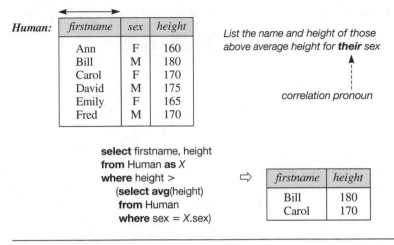

Figure 11.59 Correlation between inner and outer tables with the same base name.

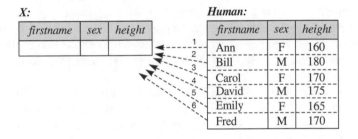

Figure 11.60 In the outer query, X is successively assigned one of the six rows.

Alternatively, you can think of it as a tuple variable that ranges over the rows of the Human table, as depicted in Figure 11.60. In spite of its set-oriented syntax, SQL queries are processed one row at a time. Here X is successively assigned each row of the Human table, passing through six states, in each of which it holds one row. For each of these states, the inner query is evaluated, computing the average height for the sex currently assigned to X. If you're familiar with programming languages, this should remind you of a nested **for** loop.

Let's walk through the execution of the query. At the outer level, we start at the top row, so X is assigned the tuple ('Ann', 'F', 160). Hence in the outer level, sex = 'F' and height = 160. In other words, X.sex = 'F' and X.height = 160. In the subquery, the correlation condition "sex = X.sex" now becomes "sex = 'F'". So the subquery returns the average height of the females, which is 165. The condition in the outer query now becomes "160 > 165", which is false. Since the top row does not satisfy the condition, it is filtered out, so Ann is excluded from the result.

Table 11.19 Who earns at least 80% of his or her boss's pay?

Employee:

empNr	empName	pay	bossNr
1	Davis, J	1000	?
2	Jones, E	900	1
3	Smith, J	700	1
4	Brown, T	780	2

At the outer level we now move on to the second row, so X is assigned the tuple ('Bill', 'M', 180). Hence X.sex = 'M' and height = 180. In the subquery, the condition "sex = X.sex" becomes "sex = 'M'". So the subquery returns the average height of the males, which is 175. The condition in the outer query now becomes "180 > 175", which is true. So Bill's firstname and height ('Bill', 180) is included in the result.

Similarly we move through rows 3, 4, 5, and 6 at the outer level, recomputing the subquery each time. Carol is accepted (170 > 165 is true), but the others are rejected (the conditions 175 > 175, 165 > 165, and 170 > 175 are all false). So the final result lists the firstname and height of just Bill and Carol as shown in Figure 11.59.

Now consider the table scheme *Employee*(empNr, empName, pay, [bossNr]), where pay stores the weekly pay, and bossNr is the employee number of the boss of the employee on that row. The foreign key constraint bossNr references empNr also applies. A sample population is shown in Table 11.19. Now consider the query "Who earns at least 80% of *his or her* boss's pay?"

Let's try answering the question first, using the sample data. Employee 1 is eliminated because he or she has no boss. Employee 2 earns 900/1000 or 90% of his or her boss's pay, employee 3 earns 70% of his or her boss's pay, and employee 4 earns 780/900 or 86.67% of his or her boss's pay. So the result should list employees 2 and 4. How can we formulate the query in SQL to work with any set of data? You might like to try it yourself before reading on.

The inclusion of the pronoun "his or her" in the question is a clue that the query can be formulated with a correlated subquery, as set out below. I've used E to denote the employee at the outer level. Though not needed, I've used a second alias B to help indicate that the inner employee is a boss.

```
select empNr
from Employee as E
where pay >=
    (select 0.8 * pay
     from Employee as B
     where B.empNr = E.bossNr)
```

As an alternative, you can formulate the query using a self-join as follows:

```
select E.empNr
from Employee as E join Employee as B
    on E.bossNr = B.empNr
    and E.pay >= 0.8 * B.pay
```

To help you understand the join approach, I've listed below the rows formed from the join before the final projection is made on *E*.empNr.

E empNr	empName	pay	bossNr	B empNr	empName	pay	bossNr
2	Jones, E	900	1	1	Davis, J	1000	?
4	Brown, T	780	2	2	Jones, E	900	1

As this example suggests, computing a correlated subquery is basically equivalent to computing a join, so some care is needed in the formulation of correlated subqueries to avoid unacceptable performance.

Now let's consider **existential subqueries.** In predicate logic, the proposition "There is a frog" may be formulated as "$\exists x\ Fx$". Here "$\exists$" is the existential quantifier, with the meaning "there exists at least one", "*x*" is an individual variable standing for some object, and "*F* ..." abbreviates the predicate "... is a frog". An existential subquery in SQL is somewhat similar. It appears in an *existential condition* of the form

exists (*subquery*)

Here **exists** is used instead of "$\exists$" for the existential quantifier, and *subquery* is effectively a tuple variable ranging over rows returned by the subquery. The **exists** quantifier may be thought of as a Boolean function, *returning true if the subquery returns a row and false otherwise*. The **exists** quantifier may be preceded by the logical **not** operator. The possible cases are shown below. Here the term "a row" means "at least one row". Since the system always knows whether or not a row is returned, a simple two-valued logic applies—existential conditions evaluate to true or false, never unknown.

exists (*subquery*)	→ True	-- a row is returned (by the subquery)
	→ False	-- no row is returned
not exists (*subquery*)	→ True	-- no row is returned
	→ False	-- a row is returned

Existential subqueries may be used within search conditions in a **where** clause, leading to overall queries of the following form:

```
select ...
from ...
where [not] exists
    (select * ...)
```

Since the mere existence of a row is all that counts in the subquery result, it is normal to simply use "*" instead of a column list in the select-list for the existential subquery. Prior to SQL-92, existential subqueries were the only subqueries that could return multiple columns, since in SQL-89 both membership and comparison subqueries had to return a single column. Some SQL dialects still have this restriction.

Let's look at some examples using the populated schema in Figure 11.61. The Member table stores details about members of a martial arts club. The Ranked table

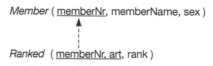

Member:	memberNr	memberName	sex
	1	Adams, Ann	F
	2	Brown, Ann	F
	3	Halpin, John	M
	4	Halpin, Terry	M

Ranked:	memberNr	art	rank
	2	kendo	3 kyu
	3	judo	2 dan
	3	karatedo	6 dan
	4	judo	1 dan
	4	karatedo	3 kyu

Figure 11.61 Martial arts club members and their ranks (if any).

indicates what rank (if any) members have achieved in what martial arts. Below black belt level, *kyu* grades are used, whereas *dan* grades are used for black belt ranks.

Consider the query "Who (member number and name) is a black belt in at least one art?" We can formulate this in SQL with an existential subquery as shown below. This is also a correlated subquery since the subquery condition refers back to the outer table (Member). Because the outer table has a different name from the inner table (Ranked), there is no need to introduce an alias for it. The existential condition checks to see if the member has a row in the Ranked table with a dan rank.

```
select memberNr, memberName
from Member                          →    memberNr    memberName
where exists                              ─────────────────────────
    (select * from Ranked                    3         Halpin, John
    where memberNr = Member.memberNr         4         Halpin, Terry
        and rank like '% dan')
```

The same query could have been formulated using a membership query instead, for example:

```
select memberNr, memberName
from Member
where memberNr in
    (select memberNr from Ranked
    where rank like '% dan')
```

To list the members who do *not* have a black belt, we simply substitute **not exists** for **exists** and **not in** for **in** in the previous queries. Would the following query also work for this?

```
select memberNr, memberName
from Member natural join Ranked
where rank not like '% dan'
```

As you no doubt realized, this fails because it also returns members with both a dan rank and a nondan rank (in this case, me!). By the way, my brother John really does have those ranks, and luckily for me he also has a gentle nature.

Member (surname, firstname, sex)

Ranked (surname, firstname, art, rank)

Member:

surname	firstname	sex
Adams	Ann	F
Brown	Ann	F
Halpin	John	M
Halpin	Terry	M

Ranked:

surname	firstname	art	rank
Brown	Ann	kendo	3 kyu
Halpin	John	judo	2 dan
Halpin	John	karatedo	6 dan
Halpin	Terry	judo	1 dan
Halpin	Terry	karatedo	3 kyu

Figure 11.62 Members have a composite reference scheme.

As a more complex example, suppose that club members are identified instead by combining their surname and firstname. The populated schema for this is shown in Figure 11.62.

Now consider the query: Who is not ranked in judo? The existential subquery solution is straightforward, matching on both surname and firstname:

```
select surname, firstname from Member
where not exists
    (select * from Ranked
    where surname = Member.surname
        and firstname = Member.firstname
        and art = 'judo')
```

→

surname	firstname
Adams	Ann
Brown	Ann

Although we can do this with a membership subquery, the logic is more complex because we cannot use a column-name pair (here surname, firstname) as an argument for the **in** operator. In the following query, the surname column is compared using the **in** operator, and the firstname is matched using a correlation:

```
select surname, firstname from Member
where surname not in
    (select surname from Ranked
    where firstname = Member.firstname
        and art = 'judo')
```

For such cases, the existential solution is easier to understand.

Yet another solution to this query is to use the concatenate operator to combine the name parts into a single string (recall that some dialects use "+" instead of "||"):

```
select surname, firstname from Member
where surname || firstname not in
    (select surname || firstname from Ranked
    where art = 'judo')
```

Further examples of correlated and existential subqueries are discussed in the context of set-comparison queries in the online SQL supplement (Appendix C).

Exercise 11.11

1. A population for the table scheme *Pupil* (<u>pupilNr</u>, <u>surname, firstname</u>, sex, [iq]) was provided in Figure 11.55. Formulate the following queries in SQL:
   (a) Which person has the highest IQ?
   (b) Who has the highest IQ for his or her sex?
   (c) List each male-female pair where both sexes have the same IQ.

2. For the Member and Ranked tables discussed in Figure 11.62, formulate the following in SQL:
   (a) Who holds a kyu rank?
   (b) Which sexes hold a kyu rank?
   (c) Who is not ranked?
   (d) Who does not hold a kyu rank?

3. The following schema refers to part of the student database considered in Exercise 11.1. Specify the following queries in SQL.

   Student (<u>studentNr</u>, studentName, degree, gender, birthYr)

   Result   (<u>studentNr, subjCode</u>, [rating])

   (a) List the student number and name of each student who did not score any 7s. (Use a subquery.)
   (b) Same question, but use a join instead of a subquery (*Hint:* 7 is the highest rating.)

11.12   SQL: Data Definition

The set of SQL statements for defining a database schema is traditionally known as the *data definition language* (DDL). In this section we'll focus on the main DDL statements used for creating, altering, and dropping base tables and creating and dropping views.

The population of a *base table* resides in the database (unlike result tables and views). Base tables must be created before they are populated. In SQL-92 and SQL:1999, base tables (and all other aspects of the database) are defined within the scope of a *database schema* that is created using a **create schema** statement. The schema may be deleted using a **drop schema** statement. Commercial SQLs often provide a different syntax for this (e.g., **create database**).

In the SQL standard, tables are created using a **create table** statement. In addition to this, most DBMSs provide a grid interface for users to create tables by entering text and choosing options. The SQL-89 syntax of the **create table** statement may be summarized as shown below. Here *literal* denotes a numeric or string constant, *col-list* denotes a list of one or more column names separated by commas, and *unique-col-list* denotes a column list that has collectively been declared to be the primary key or to be unique. If a constraint applies to a single column it may be declared at the end of the column definition. Multicolumn constraints must be declared at the end of the table definition. **Check** clauses are restricted to conditions that involve only one row of the table.

```
create table tablename (
    colname          data-type      [not null]
                                     [default literal | null | user]
                                     [primary key | unique]
                                     [references tablename]
                                     [check (col-condition-on-same-row)]
    [,...]
    [, primary key (col-list)]
    [, unique (col-list)]
    [, foreign key (col-list) references tablename[(unique-col-list)] [,...]]
    [, check (table-condition-on-same-row) [,...]] )
```

SQL-92 extended this syntax in many ways. Constraints may be named by inserting **constraint** *constraint-name* at the start of their definition. This facilitates meaningful error messages and dropping of constraints. **Check** clause conditions may range over many rows or tables, and general constraints may be declared using **create assertion** (mainly for intertable constraints). Foreign key constraints may include full/partial match conditions and referential actions. Constraints may be declared immediate or deferred. Macros for constrained data types may be declared with a **create domain** statement. SQL:1999 went much further. For example, an **of** clause may be used to declare a table to be of a user-defined type, previously declared as a row type with a **create type** statement. Subtables may be defined using an **under** clause to reference the supertable.

Commercial SQL dialects typically support all the SQL-89 functionality, possibly with some different syntax. They tend to support only some of the new syntax from SQL-92 and SQL:1999. For example, constraint names and referential actions are widely supported, but assertions and unrestricted **check** clauses are rarely supported. Most vendors also provide extra features and syntax of their own.

As an example, let's see how to declare the relational schema for our software retailer database. The graphical version of this schema is reproduced in Figure 11.63, along with the schema declaration in SQL-92 syntax. You can adapt this where needed to your SQL dialect of choice, and add constraint names as you see fit.

Notice the four intertable subset constraints (the equality constraint shows two of these). Unless we add these intertable constraints later, using an **alter table** or **create assertion** statement, the *order* in which we create the tables is important. If you wish to minimize the need for these later additions, you should wherever possible create the referenced table before the referring table. With our example, this entails creating the Customer table before the Invoice table and the Item table before the LineItem table.

Columns are optional by default, but may be declared mandatory using **not null**. SQL requires **primary key** columns to be declared not null. A **unique** constraint is assumed for primary keys, but may be explicitly declared for other columns or column lists, with the meaning that non-null values are unique. For example, if the optional phoneNr column had instead been declared **unique,** an actual phone number may appear at most once in that column, but there may be many null values in that column.

Foreign keys are declared with a **references** clause, indicating the referenced table, optionally followed by the referenced column list, which must already be declared to be the primary key or unique. If no referenced column list is given, the primary key is assumed to be the target. A **check** clause specifies a condition to be satisfied. A **check**

Customer (<u>customerNr</u>, <u>customerName, address</u>, [phoneNr])

Invoice　　(<u>invoiceNr</u>, customerNr, issueDate, [paidDate])

LineItem　(<u>invoiceNr, itemCode</u>, qty, unitPrice)

{DB,SS,WP}

Item　　　(<u>itemCode</u>, <u>title</u>, category, stock, listPrice)

create schema SoftwareRetailer;

create table Customer (
customerNr	**smallint**	**not null**	**primary key,**
customerName	**varchar**(20)	**not null,**	
address	**varchar**(40)	**not null,**	
phonenr	**varchar**(10),		

　　　　unique (customerName, address));

create table Item (
itemCode	**char**(4)	**not null**	**primary key,**
title	**varchar**(20)	**not null**	**unique,**
category	**char**(2)	**not null**	
		check (category **in** ('DB','SS','WP')),	
stock	**smallint**	**not null**	**default** 0,
listPrice	**decimal**(6,2)	**not null**);	

create table Invoice (
invoiceNr	**smallint**	**not null**	**primary key,**
customerNr	**smallint**	**not null**	**references** Customer,
issueDate	**date**	**not null,**	
paidDatepaid	**date**);		

create table LineItem (
invoiceNr	**smallint**	**not null**	**references** Invoice,
itemCode	**char**(4)	**not null**	**references** Item,
qty	**smallint**	**not null,**	
unitPrice	**decimal**(6,2)	**not null,**	

　　　primary key (invoiceNr, itemCode));

create assertion each_invoice_has_a_line_item
　check (**not exists**
　　　　　(**select * from** Invoice
　　　　　where invoiceNr **not in**
　　　　　　(**select** invoiceNr **from** LineItem)));

Figure 11.63　The relational schema for the software retailer database.

constraint is violated if and only if its condition evaluates to false (not true and not unknown).

Default options may be declared with a **default** clause. If a user inserts a row without specifying a value for a column, then the system automatically inserts the default value defined for that column. In SQL-89, the only allowed defaults were a literal value, **user**, or **null**. In the absence of a **default** clause for an optional column, **null** is assumed to be the default. SQL-92 expanded the possible defaults to include the nullary functions: **current_user, session_user, system_user, current_date, current_time, current_timestamp.** SQL:1999 added **current_role, current_path**, and any implicitly typed value specification (e.g., to deal with collection types).

The equality constraint in the graphical version of the software retailer schema is equivalent to two subset constraints in either direction between LineItem.invoiceNr and Invoice.invoiceNr—a referential cycle. The subset constraint from LineItem.invoiceNr to Invoice.invoiceNr is a foreign key constraint, since the target is a primary key. So this may be declared using a **references** clause as shown. However, the subset constraint from Invoice.invoiceNr to LineItem.invoiceNr is *not* a foreign key constraint, since its target is just one part of a composite primary key. In SQL-92 this constraint may be declared using an **assertion,** as shown. In SQL dialects that do not support assertions (e.g., SQL Server), assertions can be coded instead using triggers or stored procedures.

Here is a suggested procedure for deciding where to declare constraints in SQL that you may find useful if you want to minimize keystrokes:

> **If** a constraint applies to only one table
>   **or** is a foreign key constraint
> **then if** it applies to only one column
>   **then** declare it with the column
>   **else** declare it at the end of the table definition
> **else** declare it with an assertion (or trigger etc.)

Let's now discuss the notion of *referential integrity* in more detail. Recall that referential integrity is a special case of a subset constraint. The relational schema outline below shows a typical case, where $S.a$ is a foreign key referencing $R.a$. Basically the subset constraint is satisfied if each value in $S.a$ either occurs as a value of $R.a$ or is null.

$R\,(\underline{a},\,b,\,...\,)$
   ▲
   ¦
$S\,(\underline{a,\,c},\,d,\,...\,)$

The subset constraint may be violated in any of the following four ways:

1. Insert a row into S with a value for $S.a$ that is not a value in $R.a$
2. Update a row of S to replace the value for $S.a$ with a value that is not in $R.a$
3. Delete a row from R where the value of $R.a$ is also a value in $S.a$
4. Update a row of R to replace a value of $R.a$ that is also a value in $S.a$

Hence, instead of declaring the subset constraint as "$S.a$ **references** $R.a$", we could enforce the constraint by writing trigger code to handle each of these four cases. A *trigger* is basically a chunk of procedural code that is defined for a single table to carry out some action whenever a specified kind of event (insert, delete, or update) occurs for that table. SQL:1999 includes a full procedural trigger language with the power of a typical third-generation programming language.

Although triggers can be very useful for enforcing rules (such as constraints or derivation rules), if a declarative version of the rule is supported by the system, then the declarative approach is normally preferred. First, the declarative version of the rule is more easily understood, and hence easier to validate with domain experts. Second, the declarative version is shorter and easier to formulate than the procedural version. For example, the declaration "*S.a* **references** *R.a*" is trivial compared to the code for the corresponding triggers. Finally, the system can often do a better job of optimizing declarative code than procedural code. Having said that, there are still many cases where triggers or stored procedures provide the only way of getting the system to carry out some action. Until recently, referential actions fit into this category.

A *referential action* is an action to be taken in response to a violation of a referential integrity constraint. In SQL-89, if an attempted update (insert/delete/update) violates a foreign key constraint, the update is simply rejected—in other words, no action is taken. In SQL-92, this "no action" default may be replaced for update and delete operations by other options, by declaring the appropriate referential action(s) at the end of the **references** clause. SQL-92 also allows a **match** clause, with **full** or **partial** options for finer control over null value matching. SQL:1999 added the **simple** option to allow the default option for matching to be explicitly declared, but otherwise uses the same syntax for the **references** clause, the full syntax of which is

references *table* [(*col-list*)]
[**match** { **full** | **partial** | **simple** }]
[*delete-action* [*update-action*] | *update-action* [*delete-action*]]

where *delete-action* has the syntax

on delete   { **no action** | **cascade** | **set null** | **set default** }

and *update-action* has the syntax

on update { **no action** | **cascade** | **set null** | **set default** }

If an attempt is made to change the database with an insert, delete, or update operation that would violate the referential constraint, the default **no action** option rejects the change. The other three referential action options accept the change, but also take some compensating action to keep the database consistent. The **cascade** option propagates the change to all referencing foreign key values; **set null** sets the relevant foreign key values to null; and **set default** sets the relevant foreign key values to the column default. For example, consider the following relational schema:

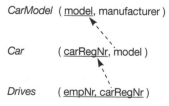

CarModel (<u>model</u>, manufacturer)

Car   (<u>carRegNr</u>, model)

Drives   (<u>empNr</u>, <u>carRegNr</u>)

Here we have a chain of two subset constraints. Suppose "**on delete cascade**" is declared for both constraints. If we attempt to delete the model "Ford T" from the CarModel table, the delete is accepted. But if there are any rows in the Car table with the model "Ford T", they will be deleted also, which in turn causes any rows in the Drives table with matching registration number to be deleted also.

SQL-92 introduced the **match** operator as a Boolean operator to test whether a tuple belongs to a set of tuples; that is, does $(a_1, ..., a_n) \in \{(b_1, ..., b_n), ...\}$? Except for its Boolean nature, it is a generalization of the **in** operator and may be used in search conditions of the form $(a_1, ..., a_n)$ **match** [**unique**] [**full** | **partial** | **simple**] (*subquery*). The **unique** option requires the tuple to match exactly one row. By default, or if **simple** is declared, the match operation returns true if all values $a_1..a_n$ match or *some* are null; otherwise it returns false. If full is specified, the match operation returns true if all values $a_1..a_n$ match or *all* are null; otherwise it returns false. If partial is specified, the match operation returns true if all *non-null* values match; otherwise it returns false. The match operator may also be used in a **references** clause in a similar way.

Although the **references** clause syntax for SQL-89 is now widely supported, most SQL dialects currently have little support for the further referential syntax in SQL-92 or SQL:1999. For example, SQL Server 2000 supports the **cascade** and **no action** options for delete and update, but does not support the **set null** or **set default** options, nor the **match** operator.

An *index* is typically an ordered binary tree of key values, with pointers to the disk addresses of the full records used to store the data. Because indexes are relevant only for physical modeling, not logical modeling, the SQL standard will never mention them. However, most commercial systems allow users to explicitly create and drop indexes, using syntax such as **create** [**unique**] **index** *indexname* **on** *tablename* (*index-column* [**asc** | **desc**] [,...]) and **drop index** *indexname*. Optimizers use indexes to improve performance and may create and drop indexes themselves. If supported, the **unique index** option provides one way of enforcing uniqueness constraints. However, most uniqueness constraints are better declared using primary key or unique declarations, although uniqueness constraints on optional columns usually require triggers. Indexes are often created automatically for primary and foreign keys.

Especially for large tables, indexes can dramatically improve query performance since indexes often allow random access in main memory rather than sequential disk access. Indexes may slow down updates since the relevant indexes must also be updated, not just the base tables. However, indexes may speed up constraint enforcement (e.g., a constraint may involve a query), so it all depends on the situation. Depending on the DBMS, there may be many different kinds of indexes, and strategies for choice of indexes may also vary. Since this book is primarily concerned with conceptual and logical modeling, index strategies will be ignored.

After a base table has been created and even populated, we may wish to change its definition. This was not possible in SQL-89. However, SQL-92 allows a table scheme to be changed using an **alter table** statement. SQL:1999 extended this slightly to cater to column scoping. Each change requires a separate statement. The basic syntax is as follows:

```
alter table tablename
  add [column] col-defn
  | alter [column] colname set default-defn | drop default
  | drop [column] colname restrict | cascade
  | add table-constraint-defn
  | drop constraint constraint-name restrict | cascade
```

Dropping a column is not allowed if **restrict** is specified and the column is referenced in constraint or view definitions. The **cascade** option causes the other definitions to be dropped too. Commercial SQLs typically do not support **restrict** or **cascade** options for dropping columns or constraints.

Although the standard forbids the data type of a column to be altered, some dialects allow a column's data type to be changed to a "larger type", for example, change char(2) to char(4) for a roomNr column. Some alter actions are not supported by many vendors, for example, **drop column.** To simplify automated table creation, some vendors prefer to add most table constraints in **alter table** statements. The following examples are self-explanatory:

```
alter table Person
        add column email_address varchar(20)
alter table Person
        add foreign key starsign references StarsignPeriod
```

SQL-92 allows a table (including its population) to be deleted from the database using a **drop table** statement. Although this is not allowed in SQL-89, all vendors support this. The syntax is

```
drop table tablename cascade | restrict
```

Dropping a table is not allowed if **restrict** is specified and the table is referenced in constraint or view definitions. The **cascade** option causes the other definitions to be dropped too. Most commercial SQLs do not require cascade/restrict here.

As a first step on the way to user-defined types, SQL-92 introduced statements for creating, altering, and dropping syntactic *domains*. Once a domain has been defined, it can be used in column definitions. For example:

```
create domain Money as decimal(9,2)
create domain Sexcode as char constraint ValidSexcode check( value in ('F','M'))
create domain Centimeters as smallint check( value > 0 )
create domain Kilograms as smallint check( value > 0 )
```

```
create table Employee (
    empNr    smallint  not null   primary key,
    sex      Sexcode   not null,
    salary   Money     not null,
    tax      Money,
    height   Centimeters,
    weight   Kilograms )
```

These domains are merely macros or abbreviations for their definitions. So nonsense queries such as "**select** * **from** Employee **where** height = weight" are still legal. However, SQL:1999 does support true user-defined types, with strong type checking. For example, if we replace the previous domain definitions for Centimeters and Kilograms by the following type definitions, the condition "height = weight" generates an error. If ever you do want to compare just the numbers rather than the height and weight entities, you can use the **cast** function to convert to compatible data types. The declaration of **final** means the type cannot have proper subtypes.

create type Centimeters **as smallint final**
create type Kilograms   **as smallint final**

Centimeters and Kilograms are defined in terms of a predefined scalar type, but are treated as distinct from their base type and are said to be *distinct types*. SQL:1999 also allows user-defined *structured types* involving many attributes. In SQL:1999, *array types* and *row types* may be introduced within a table definition. The type definition features in SQL:1999 are vast, but not yet widely supported. There is no space here to discuss them in detail, but here is an example:

```
create table Voter (
    voterId        smallint          primary key,
    preferences    smallint array[3],
    address        row( streetAddress varchar(20),
                        cityname        varchar(20),
                        zip             row( main char(5), ext char(4)))
```

Besides defining base tables, SQL also allows us to define **views,** or "virtual tables", which are basically *named, derived tables.* Their definition is stored, but their contents are not. By means of the view definitions, queries and updates on views are automatically translated into equivalent queries/updates on basc tables. Hence, unlike working tables that you might create to temporarily store results, views are always up-to-date.

Views have many uses. They may be used for security reasons by allowing a user group access to views but not their underlying base tables. They can also be used to hide unwanted details, simplify queries or updates, implement derivation rules, and allow base table reconstruction with minimum impact. Their main limitations are that some views cannot be updated, and queries on views sometimes lower performance.

A view is created using the **create view** statement. The SQL-89 syntax is as follows:

create view *viewname* [*(col-list)*] **as**
    select-query
    [**with check option**]

SQL-92 allows the check option to be qualified as local or cascaded, and SQL:1999 allows views to be recursive and to be based on user-defined types. Although SQL-89 does not allow views to be dropped, SQL-92 does, using the syntax

drop view *viewname* { **restrict** | **cascade** }

If the **restrict** option is specified, the view is not dropped if it is referenced in another view or a constraint. If the **cascaded** option is specified, the view is dropped as well as any views or constraints that reference it. Many dialects, including SQL Server, do not yet support these two options. Although the standard does not provide an **alter view** statement, some dialects, including SQL Server, do.

Table 11.20 A base table about academics.

Academic:	empNr	empName	dept	sex	grade
	101	Aldave, L	CS	F	Lec
	102	Jones, E	MA	?	Lec
	103	Codd, E	CS	M	Prof
	104	Rolland, C	CS	F	Prof

Table 11.21 A view.

FemaleCompScientist:	empNr	name	rank
	101	Aldave, L	Lec
	104	Rolland, C	Prof

Some restrictions apply to the select-query used to define a view, although details depend on the SQL dialect. Typically no **order by** clause or any of the union, intersect, or except operators are allowed. An *updatable view* can be used to insert, delete, or modify rows. Many more restrictions apply to updatable views (see later).

Consider the table scheme *Academic*(empNr, empName, dept, [sex], grade), used to store details about academic employees. Sample data are shown in Table 11.20. The dept column stores the code for the academic's department (e.g., CS = Computer Science, MA = Mathematics). Grade is the academic's rank (e.g., Lec = lecturer, Prof = professor).

The following statement may be used to create a view about just the female computer scientists. With this definition stored, we may now act as if a table corresponding to the view really exists, as shown in Table 11.21.

```
create view FemaleCompScientist (empNr, name, rank) as
    select empNr, empName, grade
    from Academic
    where dept = 'CS' and sex = 'F'
```

For example, to retrieve the female professors of computer science, we request

```
select empNr, name
from FemaleCompScientist
where rank = 'Prof'              → Rolland, C
```

When this query is processed, the view definition is accessed and used to automatically translate the query into the following equivalent query on the underlying base table. The base table query is then processed to produce the result:

```
select empNr, empName
from Academic
where dept = 'CS' and sex = 'F'
    and grade = 'Prof'          → Rolland, C
```

That view was based on just a projection and selection from a single table. Let's look at a harder case based on a join. Consider the table scheme *ParentOf*(parent, child). A sample population is shown in Figure 11.64. For simplicity, assume people are identified by their first name.

Now consider the query "Who are the grandparents of Fred?" To make it easy to answer the question, I've included a graph in Figure 11.64 where a dotted arrow from one node to another means the first is the parent of the second. Starting at Fred, you can easily find Chris as Fred's only recorded parent, and then move up to Chris's parents. So the answer is the set {Ann, Bill}. You can also follow this procedure using the table. The query is easy to formulate in SQL using a membership subquery, thus:

```
select parent from ParentOf
where child in
    (select parent from ParentOf
    where child = 'Fred')
```

But now suppose we often wanted to list the grandparents of different people on different occasions. We could save ourselves some work by defining a view for the *GrandparentOf*(grandparent, grandchild) relation thus:

```
create view GrandparentOf (grandparent, grandchild ) as
    select A.parent, B.child
    from ParentOf as A join ParentOf as B
    on A.child = B.parent
```

This view definition involves a projection on a self-join, where we match the child of the grandparent to the parent of the grandchild. Table 11.22 shows the virtual population, which could be listed using the command **select** * **from** GrandParentOf.

The grandparents of Fred can be listed using **select** * **from** GrandParentOf **where** grandchild = 'Fred'. The grandparents of any other person can be requested by using their name in place of 'Fred'. Although the view is obviously useful for queries, can it also be used for updates?

As discussed in the next section, rows can be inserted into base tables using an insert command. Suppose we try to insert a row into the view thus:

```
insert into GrandparentOf
    values ('Bernie', 'Selena')
```

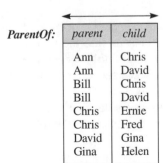
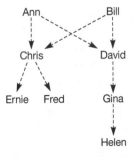

Figure 11.64 Who are the grandparents of Fred?

Table 11.22 A view based on a join.

GrandparentOf:	grandparent	grandchild
	Ann	Ernie
	Bill	Ernie
	Ann	Fred
	Bill	Fred
	Ann	Gina
	Bill	Gina
	David	Helen

An update on a view must be translated into an equivalent update on the base table(s). But since we don't know the intermediate parents (i.e., Selena's parents), the best we could hope for in this case is to add the following two rows into the ParentOf table:

ParentOf: parent child
─────────────
              Bernie   ?
              ?   Selena

But this is unacceptable because it doesn't really tell us that Bernie is a grandparent of Selena. In fact, the two rows would not satisfy the view definition anyway, since they fail the join condition A.child $= B$.parent. Since both values are null here, the condition evaluates to unknown, and the row ('Bernie', 'Selena') is excluded from the view. So the GrandparentOf view is *nonupdatable*.

SQL-92 places many restrictions (more than logically required) on what kinds of views are updatable. In particular, an updatable view must contain no joins, no union (or intersect or except), no **distinct** option, and no **group by** clause. SQL Server gets around many such restrictions by use of **instead of** triggers on views.

Even with no joins, similar problems with nulls arise if the view excludes a column used in its search condition. For example, suppose we try the following insertion on our FemaleCompScientist view:

insert into FemaleCompScientist
    values (105, 'Bird, L', 'Lec')

If we allow this update, is 'Bird, L' included in the result? Given our earlier view definition, if the update were accepted, it would translate into the following row being inserted into the Academic table: (105, 'Bird, L', **null, null,** 'Lec'). The new row fails the view definition since the condition (dept $=$ 'CS' **and** sex $=$ 'F') evaluates to unknown. So if the update is accepted, it is not part of the view!

It is better to reject any update that fails to satisfy the view definition. To do this, append "**with check option**" to the view definition. For example, the following view may be used for computer science professors:

create view CSProfessor (empNr, name, dept, rank) **as**
    select empNr, empName, dept, grade

    from Academic
    where grade = 'Prof' **and** dept = 'CS'
      with check option

The following attempts to update this view would now have the results shown.

insert into CSProfessor
 values (106,'Wirth N','CS','Prof') →   accepted

insert into CSProfessor
 values (107,'Russell B','MA','Prof') →   rejected

update CSProfessor
 set rank = 'Lec'
 where empNr = 103   →   rejected

These update attempts make use of data manipulation statements in SQL. The next section considers these in more detail.

Exercise 11.12

1. Specify SQL DDL statements to create the following relational schema:

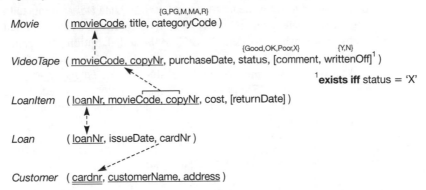

2. A conceptual subschema, its relational tables, and a sample population are shown.

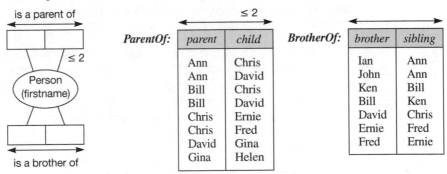

(a) Complete the following derivation rule: *Person₁* is an uncle of *Person₂* **if** ...

(b) Specify this rule as a view *UncleOf* (uncle, child) in SQL.

(c) Formulate the query "Who is an uncle of whom?" in SQL, using the view.

(d) Formulate (c) in SQL without using the view.

(e) Formulate in SQL: Who is recorded as having a parent but not an uncle?

11.13   SQL: Updating Table Populations

Generically, an "update" of the population of the database tables may involve any of three relational operations: insert a row into a table; delete a row from a table; modify one or more values on a row. In SQL, the modify operation is called "update", so the term is sometimes used in this restricted sense.

Let's first consider how to **insert rows** into a table. For this, SQL provides an **insert** statement in two basic forms. The first adds a *single row* of data to a table. Its SQL-89 syntax is

> **insert into** *tablename* [(*col-list*)]
> **values** (*constant-list*)

If no columns are listed, values for all columns must be given. Character strings must be delimited by single quotes. A null value may be entered as **null.** SQL-92 introduced the following form of the **insert** statement: **insert into** *tablename* **default values.** This adds a single row where each column is given its default value (possibly **null**). An error results if any column has no default. SQL:1999 added options for using constructors and overrides.

As a simple example, consider the table scheme *Employee*(empNr, surname, firstname, sex, [phone], [email]). Suppose a new female employee named "Eve Jones" is assigned the employee number 715. To add these details of the new employee to the table, we could use either

> **insert into** Employee
> **values** (715, 'Jones', 'Eve', 'F', **null, null**)

or

> **insert into** Employee (empNr, surname, firstname, sex)
> **values** (715, 'Jones', 'Eve', 'F')

Commercial systems also provide commands for fast bulk load of data from files (e.g., in delimited ASCII format). Data entry from users is typically via screen forms rather than directly to tables. Because of constraints on forms or between tables, a single row insert might require other data to be inserted in the same transaction. A *transaction* is a series of SQL statements, terminated by a **commit** statement:

> **commit [work]**

If not committed, a transaction may be canceled thus:

> **rollback [work]**

SQL:1999 allows inclusion of one or more *savepoints* within a transaction. Work can then be rolled back to a specific savepoint rather than rolling back the whole transaction. Releasing a savepoint acts like a tentative commit of the part of the transaction preceding the savepoint. Many SQL vendors do not yet support savepoints.

The most powerful form of the **insert** statement allows us to insert *multiple rows* into a table in one go. Its basic syntax is

```
insert into tablename [ (col-list) ]
    select-query
```

This inserts the set of rows returned from the subquery. This has many uses, such as making copies of tables, or temporarily storing join results to speed up later queries. For example, consider the software retailer database schematized earlier in Figure 11.63. Now suppose we want to run lots of queries about sales of the database products. To facilitate this, we could create an appropriate table called "DBsales", then populate it thus:

```
insert into DBsales
    select *
    from Invoice natural join LineItem natural join Item
    where category = 'DB'
```

For analysis purposes for a given period (e.g., 1 week), it may be OK to ignore updates to the underlying base tables. Queries can now be formulated on DBsales without the performance overhead of the original joins. This approach is used in data warehousing.

Now let's consider how to **delete rows.** In SQL, the **delete** statement is used to delete some or all rows from a table. After the deletion, the table structure still exists (until the relevant **drop table** command). The basic syntax of the **delete** statement is

```
delete from tablename
[ where condition ]
```

Here are two examples, based on our retailer database:

```
delete from Item              -- deletes all rows from the Item table

delete from Item
where category = 'DB'         -- deletes all the database item rows from Item
```

Now let's consider how to **update rows** (i.e., change one or more values in existing rows). In SQL, the **update** statement is used to modify rows. Its basic syntax is shown below. In SQL-89, expression must be a scalar expression, or **null** or **default.** A scalar expression may include column names, constants, and scalar operators.

```
update tablename
    set colname = expression [, ...]
    [where condition]
```

As an example, consider the table scheme *Employee*(<u>empNr</u>, ..., job, salary). The following statement gives all modelers earning less than $50,000 a 5 percent increase in salary:

```
update Employee
  set salary = salary * 1.05
  where job = 'Modeler'
    and salary < 50000
```

Because of the bulk updating power of insert, delete, and update commands, it is critical to have facilities for undo (rollback) and security (e.g., granting relevant access rights).

Triggers provide yet another way to change table populations. Although not included in the standard until SQL:1999, triggers have been used by commercial dialects for many years. As well as enforcing constraints, triggers may be used to perform other actions, including computation of derived columns, maintaining audit or summary data in other tables, and initiating external actions such as sending email. In SQL:1999, the statements for creating and dropping triggers have the following syntax:

```
create trigger triggername
        { before | after } { insert | delete | update [ of col-list ] } on tablename
        [ referencing   { old | new } [row] [as] correlation-name |
                        { old | new } table [as] table-alias        [, ...] ]
        [ for each { row | statement } ]
            [ when ( condition ) ]
            triggered-SQL-statement

drop trigger triggername
```

Although most SQL dialects support triggers, most of them (including SQL Server) do not yet conform to the standard syntax shown above for creating triggers. There is no space to discuss this topic any further.

11.14   SQL: Security and Metadata

This section looks briefly at two topics that any database administrator needs to be familiar with: security and metadata in SQL. Let's begin with security. A database is *secure* if and only if operations on it can be performed only by users authorized to do so. Each system user is assigned a user identifier (AuthID). The user who "owns" or creates a database has all access privileges on it, and can grant and revoke access privileges on it to other users. SQL provides a **grant** statement for granting various kinds of privileges to users. The SQL-92 syntax is

```
grant all privileges |
      select | insert [(col)] | update [(col)] | delete | usage | references [(col)] [,...]
on object
to user-list [ with grant option ]
```

where *object* is one of [**table**] *tablename*, **domain** *domainname*, and so on. The user list may include **public**, meaning all users. SQL:1999 extended the statement to cater to "roles" (user groups). If the **with grant option** is included, the user list has the power to grant the same privilege to others. For example, the following statement grants all users read access to the Stock table: **grant select on** Stock **to public.** The following grants the user with authorization id "Mgr" read access to the Stock table as well as the right to update values in the price column: **grant select, update**(price) **on** Stock **to** Mgr. Privileges may be removed with the **revoke** statement:

> **revoke** [**grant option for**] *privilege-list*
> **on** *object*
> **from** *user-list* [**restrict** | **cascade**]

For example, to revoke the update right granted earlier, use **revoke update**(price) **on** Stock **from** Mgr. The table name in **grant** or **revoke** statements may be the name of a base table or view. Granting access to views but not the base tables is one convenient way of enforcing security. The **restrict** and **cascade** options are not yet widely supported.

Now let's move on to *metadata* (data about data). SQL systems automatically maintain a set of *system tables* holding information about the database schema itself (e.g., base tables, views, domains, constraints, and privileges). In commercial DBMSs, such tables are collectively referred to under various names, for example, "system catalog". SQL-92 uses the term "catalog" in a different sense (for a collection of schemas within an environment). System tables of commercial systems also include physical information (e.g., about indexes) that is used by the optimizer. Users with access to the system tables may query them in SQL (just like the application tables).

Commercial system tables use their own specific names (e.g., SysTables, SysCatalog, Tab) and structures for the metadata. SQL-92 introduced an idealized set of system tables as well as a set of views (Domains, Tables, Columns, Assertions, etc.) comprising "the information schema", for standard access to metadata. SQL:1999 extended this further (e.g., to store metadata about types and triggers). To conform to the standard, a DBMS should support these views, and many popular DBMSs are at least in the process of doing so. As a simple example, the following query uses the standard Columns view to request the number of columns in the Customer table:

> **select count**(*)
> **from** Columns
> **where** table_name = 'CUSTOMER'

Well, that completes our basic coverage of SQL. Some aspects of SQL are considered later in the book in the context of the topic under consideration. More advanced SQL aspects are included in the online Appendix C, and the chapter notes provide further detail. While knowledge of the relevant SQL standards provides an excellent basis, the easiest way to learn the language is by using it, which entails discovering how your chosen SQL dialect differs from the standard. Fortunately, most commercial DBMSs provide extensive online resources to assist you in this regard.

11.15   **Summary**

The data manipulation aspect of the relational model includes *relational algebra* and *relational assignment* (:=). Apart from the use of logical and comparison operators in expressing conditions, the algebra includes eight basic table operations. Comparison operators have precedence over logical operators, which have precedence over table operators. Table 11.2 listed the six priority levels of the operators: $=, <>, <, >, <=,$ $>=$; **not**; **and**; **or**; selection (**where** ...) and projection (*[ ]*); and finally union ($\cup$), intersection ($\cap$), difference ($-$), Cartesian product ($\times$), natural join ($\bowtie$), and division ($\div$). Parentheses may be used to override this order. Operators on the same precedence level are left-associative (evaluated in left-to-right order as they appear in an expression). Our priority convention is designed to minimize use of parentheses and is stronger than some other conventions in use. If in doubt, or purely for the sake of clarity, feel free to add extra parentheses.

The table operators are summarized visually in Figure 11.65. Many different notations exist for selection, projection, and joins. A notation common in academic journals is shown on the left, with our notation on the right.

$$\sigma_c(T) \quad\equiv\quad T \textbf{ where } c$$
$$\pi_{a,b,...}(T) \quad\equiv\quad T \, [a,b,...]$$
$$A \bowtie_c B \equiv \quad A \times B \textbf{ where } c$$

The laws for the comparison and logical operators are well known. Table 11.23 sets out most of the main laws for the table operators. Some of these have not been discussed; their proof is left as an easy exercise. Here *A, B,* and *C* are tables; *c* is a condition; and *p* is a projection list of attributes. Various other distributive laws could be stated; recall, however, that *[ ]* does not distribute over $\cap$ or $-$.

A *relational DBMS* has the relational table as its only essential data structure and supports relational selection, projection, and join without needing to specify access paths. *SQL* is the dominant language used in relational DBMSs, and various versions have been standardized over the years, the most recent being SQL:1999. Most commercial SQL dialects support all of SQL-89, some of the extra features in SQL-92 and SQL:1999, and some of their own special features.

Database objects such as tables and columns may be named using standard identifiers or delimited identifiers (allowing any characters inside double quotes). Database fields may be defined in terms of predefined data types (e.g., varchar(20)). SQL:1999 added user-defined types, row types, reference types, and arrays. The SQL **select** statement is used for queries and has the following basic syntax.

```
select * | [all | distinct] expression [[as] column-alias ] [,...]
from table [[as] alias]
    [, | cross join table [[as] alias]
       | natural [inner | [outer] {left | right | full}] join table [[as] alias]
       | [inner | [outer] {left | right | full}] join table [[as] alias]
                                        { on condition | using (col-list) }
       | union join table [[as] alias]
       [,...]]
[where col-condition]
```

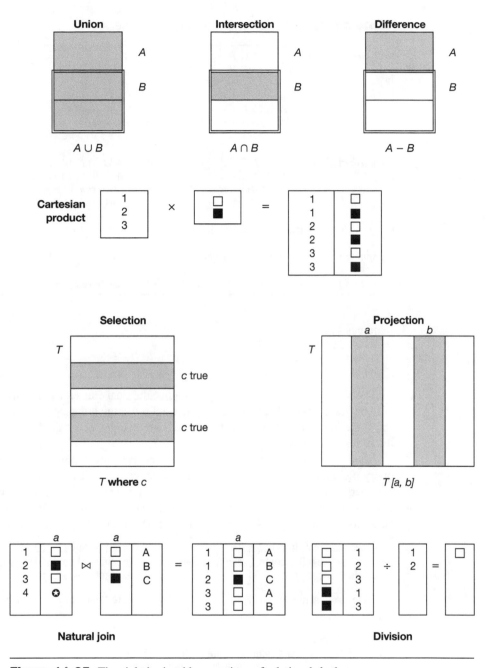

Figure 11.65 The eight basic table operations of relational algebra.

Table 11.23 Main laws for the relational operators.

Commutative laws:	$A \cup B$	$=$	$B \cup A$
	$A \cap B$	$=$	$B \cap A$
Associative laws:	$A \cup (B \cup C)$	$=$	$(A \cup B) \cup C$
	$A \cap (B \cap C)$	$=$	$(A \cap B) \cap C$
	$A \times (B \times C)$	$=$	$(A \times B) \times C$
	$A \bowtie (B \bowtie C)$	$=$	$(A \bowtie B) \bowtie C$
Distributive laws:	$A \cup (B \cap C)$	$=$	$(A \cup B) \cap (A \cup C)$
	$A \cap (B \cup C)$	$=$	$(A \cap B) \cup (A \cap C)$
	$(A \cup B)$ **where** c	$=$	A **where** $c \cup B$ **where** c
	$(A \cap B)$ **where** c	$=$	A **where** $c \cap B$ **where** c
If A, B are compatible:	$(A \cup B)$ *[p]*	$=$	$A[p] \cup B[p]$ -- false for $\cap$
Exportation:	A **where** $c1$ **where** $c2$	$=$	A **where** $c1$ **and** $c2$
Delayed projection:	$A[p]$ **where** c	$=$	$(A$ **where** $c)$ *[p]*

```
[group by colname [,...]
[having group-condition]]
[union | intersect |except ...]
[order by col [asc | desc] [,...] ]
```

The *select-list* chooses the result columns, the **from** clause declares the source tables and joins, the **where** clause is used to filter out rows, the **group by** clause forms groups of rows, the **having** clause is used to filter out groups, and the **order by** clause determines the order of rows.

A *subquery* is a parenthesized select-query used inside an outer query. If the subquery includes a condition that refers to the outer query, it is a *correlated* subquery. A subquery after an **exists** quantifier is an existential subquery. An **exists** condition is true if the subquery returns a row and false otherwise. The three most common forms of conditions with an embedded subquery are as shown, where θ is a comparison operator.

```
expression [not] in (subquery)           -- membership subquery
expression θ [all | some | any] (subquery)   -- [quantified] comparison subquery
exists (subquery)                         -- existential subquery
```

Base table schemes may be defined using a **create table** statement, whose main syntax is

```
create table tablename (
   colname        data-type       [not null]
                                   [default literal | null | user]
                                   [primary key | unique]
                                   [references tablename]
                                   [check (col-condition-on-same-row)]
   [,...]
   [, primary key (col-list)]
```

```
    [, unique (col-list)]
    [, foreign key (col-list) references tablename[(unique-col-list)] [,...]]
    [, check (table-condition-on-same-row) [,...]] )
```

Views may be created using a **create view** statement, with the syntax

```
create view viewname [ (col-list) ] as
    select-query
    [ with check option ]
```

View definitions are used to translate queries over views into equivalent queries on base tables. Some views are nonupdatable (e.g., views involving joins).

Table populations may be changed using **insert, update**, and **delete** statements, with the following basic syntax. Many other SQL statements exist for tasks such as altering and dropping tables, creating and dropping triggers, and granting and revoking privileges.

```
insert into tablename [ (col-list) ]
        values (constant-list) | select-query

update tablename
    set colname = expression [, ...]
    [where condition]

delete from tablename
[ where condition ]
```

Chapter Notes

Relational algebra is covered in most database texts (e.g., Elmasri and Navathe 1994; Date 2000). Arithmetic operators, set functions, semijoin, and other operators have been proposed to extend the relational algebra (e.g., Date 2000, Section 6.7). As an alternative to the relational algebra, the relational calculus may be used (e.g., Date 2000, Chapter 7). Codd (1990) proposed version 2 of the relational model, with 333 rules, but this has not achieved any significant adoption.

The SQL standards may be purchased online from *www.ncits.org,* including the SQL:1999 standard (ANSI 1999). For clear, thorough accounts of the SQL-92 standard, see Melton and Simon (1993) and Date and Darwen (1997).

The original SEQUEL language, described in Chamberlin and Boyce (1974), was itself based on an earlier relational language called "SQUARE". Chamberlin (1998) provides a very readable coverage of DB2, with Section 1.3 sketching an authoritative history of SQL, including an explanation for why SQL permits duplicate rows in base tables. For a comprehensive coverage of the latest version of Oracle, see Loney and Koch (2000). At the time of writing, books on the 2000 release of Microsoft SQL Server were yet to appear. For details on the latest books on SQL Server see any Web bookstore (e.g., *www.fatbrain.com*). *SQL Server Magazine* is a good source of technical articles on this product (*www.sqlmag.com*).

For a readable and practical discussion of many kinds of advanced queries in SQL, see Celko (2000). An in-depth critique of SQL and an alternative theoretical foundation for object-relational databases are provided by Date and Darwen (1998).

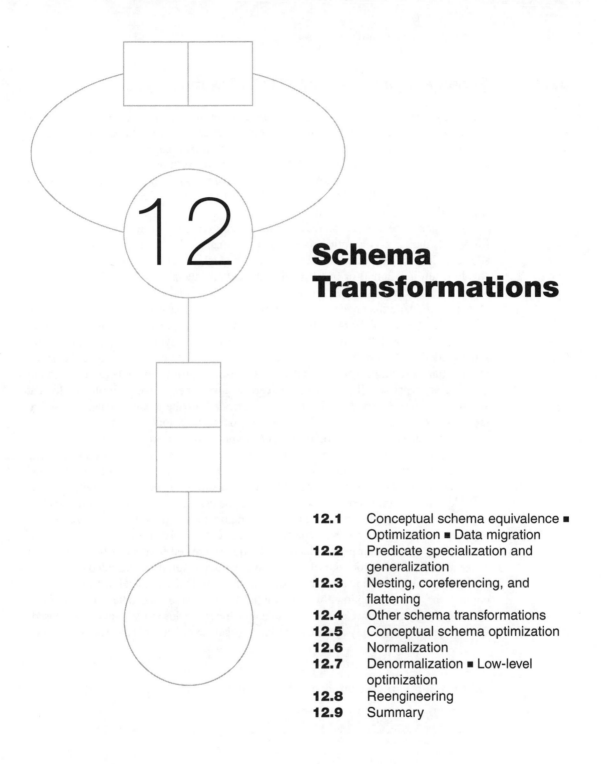

Schema
Transformations

12.1   Schema Equivalence and Optimization

Previous chapters discussed how to model the structure of an application in terms of a conceptual schema, and then map it to a logical schema for implementation in a relational database system. Although much of the design and mapping can be automated, humans are required to perform CSDP step 1, since verbalizing the relevant facts about the real world involves human understanding. Given the informal nature of this initial step in modeling the UoD, it is not surprising that people often come up with different ways of describing the same reality.

Hence the same application may be modeled by more than one conceptual schema. Moreover, the same conceptual schema may be mapped in different ways to a logical schema, either by choosing a different type of logical model (e.g., object-relational instead of pure relational) or by overriding the default mapping choices (e.g., choosing separate subtype tables or denormalizing). Finally the same logical schema may be implemented in more than one way in the physical schema (e.g., different index choices).

To help you choose from such a variety of different models, this chapter examines various ways in which schemas may be transformed to provide alternatives, then presents guidelines for optimizing your choice. On the way, we'll cover some theory on schema transformations and normalization, to ensure a proper understanding of the underlying concepts. We'll start at the conceptual level, then move down to the logical and physical levels. An example will then illustrate how the ideas can also be used to reengineer existing applications that have proved unsatisfactory.

The remainder of this section provides a simple introduction to schema transformation and optimization, using an example. Earlier chapters already introduced some modeling choices. For example, we might express a ternary fact type in either flattened or nested form. Basically, two conceptual schemas are **equivalent** if and only if whatever UoD state or transition can be modeled in one can also be modeled in the other.

As a simple example, consider the medical report shown in Table 12.1. Here a check mark in the appropriate column indicates that a patient smokes or drinks. Since both of these "vices" can impair health, doctors are often interested in this information. Try to schematize Table 12.1 for yourself before looking at the solutions provided.

Figure 12.1 shows one conceptual schema for this UoD, together with the sample population. Here two optional unaries are used for the smoker-drinker facts. In Table 12.1 the absence of a check mark might mean the patient doesn't smoke/drink (closed-world approach) or simply that we don't know (open-world approach). You would need

Table 12.1 A report on vices of medical patients.

PatientNr	Patient name	Smokes?	Drinks?
1001	Adams, A		✓
1002	Bloggs, F	✓	✓
1003	Collins, T		

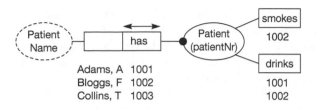

Figure 12.1 One way of modeling Table 12.1.

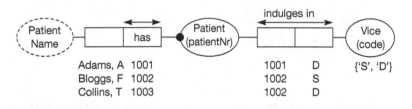

Figure 12.2 Another way of modeling Table 12.1.

to check with the domain expert as to what is intended here. If no check mark means "no" you could add a relative closure symbol to the unaries to make this clear.

Instead of using unaries, we may model the smoker-drinker facts using two functional binaries: Patient has SmokerStatus; Patient has DrinkerStatus. With the closed-world approach, both of these fact types are mandatory, with two values for each status type (e.g., {"yes", "no"}). A third way to model this is to generalize the smoking and drinking predicates into a single binary, introducing the object type Vice {S = smoking, D = drinking) to maintain the distinction (see Figure 12.2).

Intuitively, most people would consider the schemas of Figures 12.1 and 12.2 to be equivalent. Formally, this intuition can be backed up by introducing Vice as an "implicit object type" to the schema of Figure 12.1, and by specifying how the predicates of each can be translated into the predicates of the other. For example, facts expressed in the first model may be expressed in terms of the second model using the translations

Patient smokes   **iff** Patient indulges in Vice 'S'
Patient drinks   **iff** Patient indulges in Vice 'D'

and facts in the second model may be expressed in the first using the translation

Patient indulges in Vice **iff**   Patient smokes **and** Vice has ViceCode 'S'
                              or
                              Patient drinks **and** Vice has ViceCode 'D'

Like the schemas themselves, these FORML translations can be mapped into formulae of predicate logic. Formal logic may then be used to prove schema equivalence.

The equivalence just considered is an example of *contextual equivalence* since it adds definitional context to the original schemas. It also requires formal recognition of "implicit object types" (e.g., Vice exists implicitly in the first schema). This notion is called *object relativity,* since it effectively allows that "objects lie in the eye of the beholder". This permits classical logic proof techniques to be applied to such cases.

The next few sections discuss some theorems that can help us decide whether or not two schemas are equivalent. These theorems can also help us to transform one schema into an alternative schema that is either equivalent, or at least acceptably close to being equivalent (sometimes we may wish to strengthen or weaken our schema a little by adding or deleting information). The act of reshaping a schema like this is said to be a **conceptual schema transformation.**

Although the conceptual transformations are specified in ORM, they can be translated into other modeling notations. For example, the previous equivalence (minus definitional context) may be set out in UML as shown in Figure 12.3, using "⟺" for "is equivalent to". Using ORM enables many more complex transformations to be captured graphically, without needing to supplement the diagram with textual constraints. But if you want to work in a non-ORM notation, you should be able to translate the transformation theorems into your preferred notation without much trouble.

Knowledge of schema transformations helps us to see what different design choices are possible. Moreover, if two independently developed schemas are to be either fully or partly integrated, we often need to resolve the differences in the ways that each schema models common UoD features. To do this, we need to know whether one representation can be transformed into the other, and if so, how.

Another use of conceptual schema transformations is to reshape the original conceptual schema into one that maps directly to a more efficient implementation. This process is known as **conceptual schema optimization.** For example, the conceptual schema in Figure 12.1 maps to a single table. Taking a closed-world interpretation, we may use the table scheme shown in Figure 12.4. For discussion purposes, the population for the sample data is included. However, because the indulges fact type is *m:n,* the schema in Figure 12.2 maps to two tables, as shown in Figure 12.5. Again, the sample population is included.

For many applications, the single-table solution is more efficient. It enables us to list all the information about the patients without requiring a table join. It also avoids any intertable accesses required to enforce the subset constraint (e.g., when adding a vice

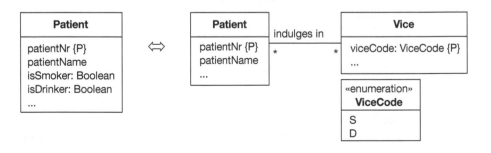

Figure 12.3 The schema equivalence example in UML.

$$\{Y, N\} \quad\quad \{Y, N\}$$

Patient (patientNr, patientName, isSmoker, isDrinker)

1001	Adams, A	N	Y
1002	Bloggs, F	Y	Y
1003	Collins, T	N	N

Figure 12.4 A relational model based on the conceptual model in Figure 12.1.

$$\{S, D\}$$

Patient (patientNr, patientName)   *Indulges* (patientNr, vice)

1001	Adams, A		1001	D
1002	Bloggs, F		1002	S
1003	Collins, T		1002	D

Figure 12.5 A relational model based on the conceptual model in Figure 12.2.

fact or deleting a patient). So the original schema of Figure 12.2 might be optimized by transforming it to that of Figure 12.1 before passing it to the normal Rmap procedure.

On the other hand, if the set of vices we wish to record often changes, the two-table solution may be preferable since it caters to such changes without requiring the schema itself to change. Guidelines for performing such optimizations are given later in the chapter. If the optimized conceptual schema still fails to give an efficient map, some denormalization may then be required, as discussed in Section 12.7.

In reengineering, optimization is applied to an existing database. So after the schema itself has been transformed, we have the additional task of *data migration,* to populate the new schema with the information stored in the original database. This task is not challenging, but can be lengthy and tedious without automated assistance.

Here is one basic way of transforming the populated two-table model in Figure 12.5 into the single-table model in Figure 12.4, assuming an SQL database is used. First add an optional isSmoker column to the Patient table, using the following statement:

```
alter table Patient
    add column isSmoker char check (isSmoker in ('Y','N'))
```

At this stage, the isSmoker column is populated with null values. The check constraint is not violated because it evaluates to unknown (not false). Now add the appropriate 'Y' or 'N' values to indicate who smokes:

```
update Patient
    set isSmoker = case
                    when patientNr in
                        (select patientNr from Indulges where vice = 'S')
                    then 'Y'
                    else 'N'
                end
```

Now make the isSmoker column mandatory:

alter table Patient
    add constraint isSmokerNonNull **check** (isSmoker **is not null**)

Similarly, add the isDrinker column to the Patient table, update its population, and finally drop the Indulges table. In practice, the most efficient way to migrate data may depend on the DBMS(s) being used.

That completes our high-level introduction to the basic concepts of schema equivalence and optimization. The following sections develop these concepts further, as well as providing a concise account of normalization theory.

12.2   Predicate Specialization and Generalization

The previous section illustrated how the same UoD structure may be described by different, but equivalent, schemas and discussed the use of transformations to reshape one schema into another. This section considers a class of schema transformations known as **predicate specialization,** as well as its inverse, **predicate generalization.**

If two or more predicates may be thought of as special cases of a more general predicate, then we may replace them by the more general predicate, so long as the original distinction can be preserved in some way. For example, if we transform the schema of Figure 12.1 into that of Figure 12.2, we *generalize* smoking and drinking into indulging in a vice, where vice has two specific cases. If we transform in the opposite direction, we *specialize* indulging in a vice into two predicates, one for each case.

Predicate specialization and generalization are similar notions to object type specialization and generalization, except that it is rare to specify any subtype connections between predicates (the predicates must be objectified for this to be legal).

A predicate may be specialized if a *value constraint or a frequency constraint* indicates that it has a finite number of cases. Examples with value constraints are more common, so we examine these first. The drinker-smoker example provides one illustration, where Vice has the value constraint {'S','D'}. As another example, recall the Olympic Games schema, reproduced in Figure 12.6(a).

Because there are exactly three kinds of medals, the ternary may be specialized into three binaries, one for each medal kind, as shown in Figure 12.6(b). You may visualize

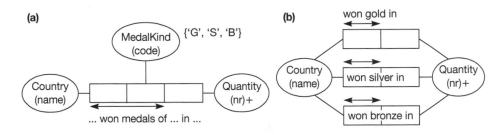

Figure 12.6 The ternary is specialized into three binaries by absorbing MedalKind.

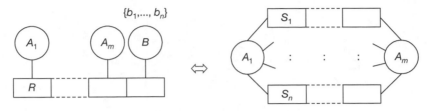

where $m \geq 1$, and each S_i corresponds to R where $B = b_i$

Figure 12.7 PSG1: R may be specialized into $S_1..S_n$ by absorbing B.

the transformation from the schema in Figure 12.6(a) into the schema in Figure 12.6(b) thus: when the object type MedalKind is *absorbed* into the ternary predicate, it divides it (or specializes it) into the three binaries. Hence this transformation is also known as *object type absorption*. The reverse transformation from Figure 12.6(b) to Figure 12.6(a) generalizes the three binaries into the ternary by extracting the object type MedalKind—this may be called *object type extraction*.

Notice that in the vices example, a binary is specialized into unaries. With the games example, a ternary is specialized into binaries. In general, when an n-valued object type is absorbed into a predicate, the n specialized predicates that result each have one less role than the original (since the object type has been absorbed). This general result is set out in Figure 12.7. Although the equivalence is set out diagrammatically to aid understanding, there is a formal mapping of the diagrams to predicate logic where the actual equivalence proofs were made (Halpin 1989b). In this sense, the results may be called theorems.

The schema equivalence in Figure 12.7 is called *Predicate Specialization/Generalization theorem 1* (PSG1). The predicates R and S, respectively, have $m + 1$ roles and m roles, where $m \geq 1$. The object types $A_1,.., A_m$ and B are not necessarily distinct. The value type for B has n values $b_1,.., b_n$. If $m = 1$, we have conversion between a binary and n unaries; if $m = 2$, the conversion is between a ternary and n binaries; and so on. Transforming from left to right specializes the predicate R into n predicates $S_1,.., S_n$ by absorbing the object type B. The reverse transformation from right to left generalizes the shorter predicates into the longer one by extracting B. As an exercise, draw the diagrams for the cases $m = 1, 2$, and 3.

The theorem PSG1 holds regardless of whatever additional constraints are added. However, *any constraint added to one of the schemas must be translated into an equivalent, additional constraint on the other schema.* For example, the uniqueness constraint in Figure 12.6(a) translates into the three shorter uniqueness constraints in Figure 12.6(b). This is an instance of the following corollary to PSG1 (using "UC" for "uniqueness constraint" and reading "spans" as "exactly spans").

If a UC in R spans a combination of B's role and other roles, a UC spans the specialization of these other roles in $S_1,..,S_n$, and conversely.

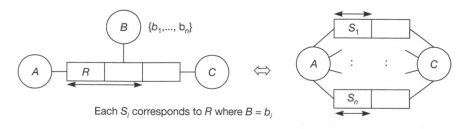

Each S_i corresponds to R where $B = b_i$

Figure 12.8 The UC on the left is equivalent to the UCs on the right.

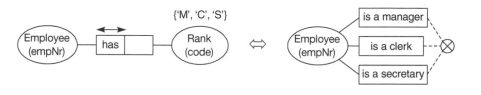

Figure 12.9 The UC on the left is equivalent to the exclusion constraint on the right.

Figure 12.8 illustrates the most common case, where R is a ternary with a UC spanning B's role and one other. However, the result applies for longer predicates too.

The games example of Figure 12.6 is an instance of the equivalence in Figure 12.8 where B = MedalKind, $n = 3$, and B's role is included in a compound uniqueness constraint. What happens, however, if B's role in the general predicate R is not included in a uniqueness constraint? Since R is elementary, its other roles must be spanned by a uniqueness constraint, and this constraint is transformed into a mutual *exclusion* constraint over the specialized predicates.

Exclusive unaries provide the simplest case of this. For example, suppose that workers in a company may hold at most one position (manager, clerk, or secretary). This may be rephrased in terms of exclusive unaries as shown in Figure 12.9, assuming appropriate translations between the predicates. For implementation purposes, the binary version is usually preferred (e.g., its relational schema simplifies both updates to a worker's position and schema updates to the list of allowable positions). The larger the number of unaries, the worse the unary solution becomes (why?).

Another example, this time with exclusive binaries, is shown in Figure 12.10. For simplicity, reference schemes are omitted. Here the task codes 'A' and 'R' denote authoring and reviewing. Note the two alternative ways of saying that a person cannot act both as an author and a reviewer of the *same* book.

These two examples illustrate unary ($m = 1$) and binary ($m = 2$) cases of the following, second corollary to theorem PSG1. This result applies to longer predicates as well (see Figure 12.11). Here the exclusion constraint means that no row of values may appear in more than one of the S_i fact tables.

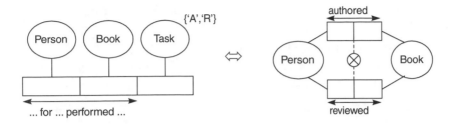

Figure 12.10 The UC on the left is equivalent to the exclusion constraint on the right.

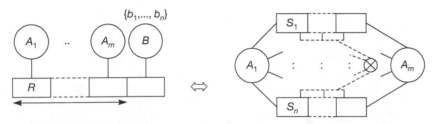

where $m \geq 1$, and each S_i corresponds to R where $B = b_i$

Figure 12.11 The UC on the left is equivalent to the exclusion constraint on the right.

If a UC spans all roles of R except for B's role, then $S_1 .. S_n$ are mutually exclusive, and conversely.

In rare cases, when a schema transformation is performed, a graphical constraint in one schema may have no corresponding graphical constraint in the other. In this case, the constraint should be expressed as a *textual constraint* in the other version. For example, consider the two schemas in Figure 12.12. The codes 'A' and 'S' indicate "assistant" and "supervisor", respectively. Reference schemes are omitted for simplicity. A person might supervise one project and assist on another. Assuming appropriate translations between the predicates, the schemas are still not equivalent. One schema has a constraint that is not captured in the other. Try to spot this for yourself before reading on.

Did you find it? The uniqueness constraint in Figure 12.12(a) translates to the exclusion constraint in Figure 12.12(b), and the top uniqueness constraint in Figure 12.12(b) is implied. However, the lower uniqueness constraint in Figure 12.12(b) declares that each project has at most one supervisor. This is missing from the ternary and cannot be expressed as a graphic constraint there since it is a *restricted uniqueness constraint* (this kind of constraint was discussed in Section 7.4). To ensure equivalence, this may be added to the left-hand schema as a textual constraint in FORML as follows:

each Project uses **at most one** Employee in Position 'S'

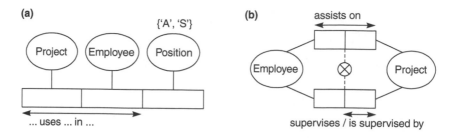

Figure 12.12 One schema has an additional constraint. Can you find it?

If Project plays other functional roles, the binary approach of the right-hand schema would normally be preferred since its relational version simplifies the enforcement of this supervision constraint. If Project has no other functional roles, the ternary approach might be preferred since it maps to a single table.

Since schema transformation theorems are typically applied to subschemas within some global schema, care must be taken to preserve any *mandatory role constraints* (implicit or explicit). For example, in Figure 12.6, if Country plays no other role, then its role in Figure 12.6(a) and the disjunction of its roles in Figure 12.6(b) are implicitly mandatory. If Country does play another role in the global schema, and at least one medal result must be recorded for it, then these simple and disjunctive mandatory role constraints must be explicitly shown. This illustrates our third corollary to theorem PSG1:

If A's role (or role disjunction) in R is mandatory, then the disjunction of its specialized roles is mandatory, and conversely ($1 \leq i \leq m$).

The inclusion of "(or role disjunction)" covers the rare case when the A_i plays more than one role in R (recall that $A_1 .. A_m$ are not necessarily distinct). Note also how our convention for implicit mandatory role constraints enables theorems such as PSG1 to be specified without any assumption about other roles played in the global schema.

Suppose in Figure 12.6(a) that Country's role is optional (this implies Country plays some other role in the global schema), but it has a *frequency constraint* of 3. So if any medal results are recorded for a country, all three medal results (gold, silver, and bronze) are required. To express this in Figure 12.6(b) we need to add an *equality constraint* between the roles played by Country. Since equality is transitive, we need only add two simple equality constraints, one between the top and middle roles of Country and one between the middle and bottom roles. This is an instance of the following, fourth corollary to theorem PSG1 (it may help to refer to Figure 12.8):

If R is a ternary with a UC spanning just B's role and one other role, then adding a frequency constraint of n to this other role is equivalent to adding an equality constraint over the specialized versions of that role.

Now consider Figure 12.13. The unfinished vertical lines indicate that Country plays another role in the global schema. Contrast this with Figure 12.6. In Figure 12.13(a) the

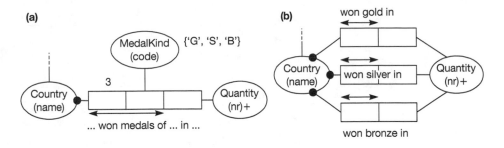

Figure 12.13 The impact of adding mandatory role and frequency constraints.

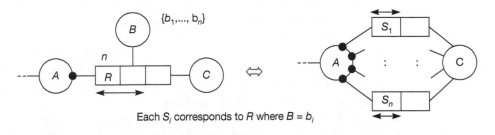

Figure 12.14 Fifth corollary to theorem PSG1.

medal role played by Country is mandatory and also has a frequency constraint of 3. The mandatory role, frequency, uniqueness, and value constraints together ensure that each country must have its medal tally recorded for each kind of medal. Hence Figure 12.13(b) has three mandatory roles.

This example is an instance of the following, fifth corollary to theorem PSG1:

> If R is a ternary with a UC spanning just B's role and one other role, then adding a mandatory role constraint and frequency constraint of n (the number of possible values for B) to this other role is equivalent to making each specialized version of that role mandatory.

This corollary is illustrated in Figure 12.14. It is implied by the previous two corollaries, since an equality constraint across a set of disjunctively mandatory roles implies that each of these roles is mandatory.

Other Kinds of Predicate Specialization/Generalization

As an introduction to a second equivalence theorem, consider Figure 12.15. The two schemas provide alternative models for a fragment of a car rally application. Each car in the rally has two drivers (a main driver and a backup driver), and each person drives exactly one car. The schema in Figure 12.15(a) is transformed into the schema in Figure 12.15(b) by absorbing the object type Status into the drives predicate, specializing this into the main driver and backup driver predicates. The reverse transformation

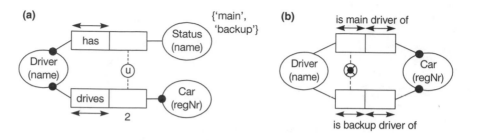

Figure 12.15 The drives predicate is specialized by absorbing Status.

generalizes the specific driver predicates into the general one by extracting the object type Status. Since this object type appears in a different fact type, this equivalence does not fit the pattern of PSG1.

Note how the constraints are transformed. The external uniqueness constraint in Figure 12.15(a) says that each car has at most one main driver and at most one backup driver. This is captured in Figure 12.15(b) by the uniqueness constraints on the roles of Car. The uniqueness constraint on the drives predicate in Figure 12.15(a) corresponds in Figure 12.15(b) to the uniqueness constraints on the roles of Driver. The uniqueness constraint on the status predicate in Figure 12.15(a) is captured by the exclusion constraint in Figure 12.15(b). The mandatory and frequency constraints on Car's role in Figure 12.15(a) require the two mandatory role constraints on Car in Figure 12.15(b). Finally, the mandatory role constraints on Driver in Figure 12.15(a) are catered to in Figure 12.15(b) by the disjunctive mandatory role constraint (shown explicitly here).

This example illustrates our *second predicate specialization/generalization theorem* (PSG2) as well as four of its corollaries (see Figure 12.16). The terms "LHS" and "RHS" abbreviate "left-hand schema" and "right-hand schema". In our example, *A, B,* and *C* correspond to Driver, Status, and Car, and the equality constraint is implied by the two mandatory role constraints on Driver. Theorem PSG2 can be derived from earlier results. For example, adding an exclusion constraint across *A*'s roles in the RHS of Figure 12.8 makes *A*'s role unique in the LHS, causing this compound fact type to split into two binaries to agree with the LHS of Figure 12.16. In Section 12.4 we consider two more general versions of this theorem.

Sometimes we may wish to transform a schema into another that is not quite equivalent. For example, suppose that in our car rally application we limit each car to at most two drivers, but do not classify the drivers in any meaningful way (e.g., as main or backup drivers). Let us also remove the constraint that drivers may drive only one car. This situation is schematized in Figure 12.17.

Although no Status object type is present, the frequency constraint in Figure 12.17 says that each car has at most two drivers. This enables us to introduce an artificial distinction to specialize the predicate into two cases, as shown in Figure 12.18. Since this distinction is not present in the original schema, the alternatives shown in Figure 12.18

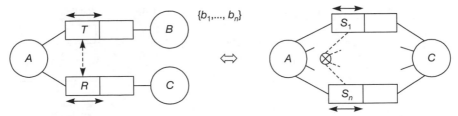

Each S_i corresponds to R where T is restricted to $B = b_i$

Corollary 1:	If A's roles are mandatory in the LHS, the disjunction of A's roles in the RHS is mandatory, and conversely.
Corollary 2:	If an external UC spans the roles of B and C in the LHS, then a UC applies to each of C's roles in the RHS, and conversely.
Corollary 3:	If C's role in the LHS is mandatory, then each of C's roles in the RHS is mandatory, and conversely.
Corollary 4:	An equality constraint over C's roles in the RHS is equivalent to a frequency constraint of $\geq n$ on C's role in the LHS; this constraint is strengthened to n if a UC exists on each of C's roles in the RHS.

Figure 12.16   PSG2: R may be specialized into $S_1..S_n$ by absorbing B.

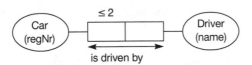

Figure 12.17   Can the predicate be specialized?

are *not equivalent* to the original. They are in fact *stronger*—each implies the original schema, but is not implied by it.

Notice the use of *hyphens* in the predicates of Figure 12.18 to bind adjectival phrases to their object terms. This improves verbalization of the fact types and constraints. The four predicates are Car has Driver-A; Car has Driver-B; Car has first-Driver; and Car has second-Driver. When Microsoft's ORM tool generates constraint verbalization, it binds the adjective to the object noun. For example, the upper uniqueness constraint in Figure 12.18(b) is verbalized as "**each** Car has **at most one** first Driver". Without the hyphen, the verbalization defaults to the awkward "**each** Car has first **at most one** Driver".

The schema in Figure 12.18(b) is actually stronger than the schema in Figure 12.18(a). If the Car role in Figure 12.17 is mandatory, then the Car roles in Figure

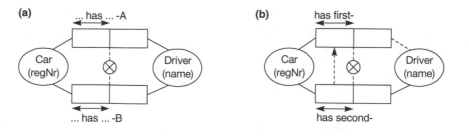

Figure 12.18 Two ways of strengthening the schema in Figure 12.17.

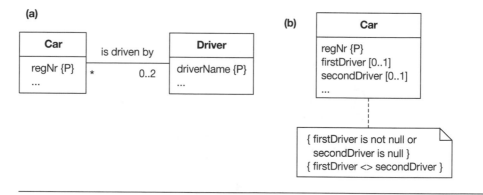

Figure 12.19 UML versions of the schemas in Figure 12.17 and Figure 12.18(b).

12.18(a) are disjunctively mandatory, and the top Car role in Figure 12.18(b) is mandatory (which then implies the subset constraint).

In an application where other facts are stored about cars but not about drivers, one of these alternatives may well be chosen to avoid a separate table being generated for car-driver facts when the schema is mapped (the specialized predicates are functional rather than *m:n*). In practice, the schema in Figure 12.18(b) would normally be chosen. The UML version of this choice is shown in Figure 12.19(b), using a note to declare the subset and exclusion constraints. Figure 12.19(a) shows the UML version of Figure 12.17.

Transforming from the original schema in Figure 12.17 to one of those in Figure 12.18 *strengthens* the schema by adding information. Transforming in the opposite direction *weakens* the schema by losing information. Any such transformations that add or lose information should be the result of conscious decisions that are acceptable to the client (for which the application is being modeled).

This example illustrates our *third specialization/generalization theorem* (PSG3), as shown in Figure 12.20. Note the use of "⇨" for "implies", since this result is a schema implication rather than an equivalence. In practice, the transformation is

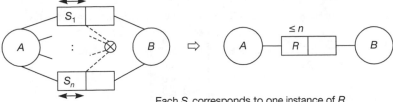

Each S_i corresponds to one instance of R

Corollary 1: If an equality constraint applies over A's roles in the LHS, then the frequency constraint in the RHS is strengthened to n, and conversely.

Corollary 2: Adding a UC to B's role in the RHS is equivalent in the LHS to adding UCs to B's roles (making the S_i 1:1) and strengthening the exclusion constraint to an exclusion constraint over B's roles.

Figure 12.20 PSG3: The left-hand schema implies the right-hand schema.

usually performed from right to left (strengthening the schema), with a subset constraint added from the first role of S_2 to that of S_1 if $n = 2$. Some corollaries for this result are also specified.

Well, that covers the most important results to do with predicate specialization and generalization. Note that the theorems require that the appropriate translations hold between the general and the special predicates. Humans are needed to provide natural names for the new predicate(s) and to confirm that the translation holds. This is not something that can be decided automatically by the system.

Exercise 12.2

1. Schematize the following table using (a) unaries and (b) a binary.

Male staff	Female staff
Creasy, PN	Orlowska, ME
Halpin, TA	Purchase, HC

2. A company committee has to decide whether to increase its budget on staff training. The following table indicates the current views of the committee members on this issue. Schematize this using (a) unaries and (b) a binary.

For	Against	Undecided
Alan	Betty	Chris
David	Eve	Fred
Gearty		

3. The following table is an extract from an output report indicating quarterly sales figures for software products marketed by a particular company.

(a) Schematize this using a ternary.

(b) Transform your solution into an equivalent one using binaries.

Software	Quarter	Sales ($)
DataModeler	1	200,000
	2	500,000
	3	500,000
	4	700,000
WordLight	1	90,000
	2	150,000
	3	155,000
	4	200,000

4. An embassy maintains details about how well its staff speak foreign languages. The following table is an extract from this system.

Language	Expert	Novice
Arabic		Smith, J
Dutch	Bruza, P Proper, HA	
French	Rolland, C	Bruza, P

(a) Schematize this using binaries.

(b) Transform this into a ternary.

5. University debating teams are to be selected, with four students in each team, with one student from each year level (1..4). No student may be in more than one team. Students are identified by their student number, but their name is also recorded. Debating teams are identified by codes.

(a) Schematize this UoD using YearLevel as an object type.

(b) Transform your schema by absorbing this object type

6. Employee records are kept that show the employee number, name, and up to two phone numbers for each employee.

(a) Schematize this in the natural way.

(b) Map this to a relational schema.

(c) It is now required to map all the information into a single relational table. Transform the conceptual schema to enable this to happen.

(d) Rmap your revised conceptual schema.

Each phone is now to be classified as a work phone or a home phone. At most one work phone and at most one home phone may be recorded for an employee.

(e) Modify your solution to (a) accordingly.

(f) Rmap this.

(g) Modify your solution to (c) accordingly.

(h) Rmap this.

7. The following conceptual schemas are meant to describe the same UoD, but each fails to capture some constraint in the other. Add a textual constraint to schema (1), and a graphical

constraint to schema (2), to obtain equivalence. The codes 'chr', 'sec', and 'ord' abbreviate "chairperson", "secretary", and "ordinary member".

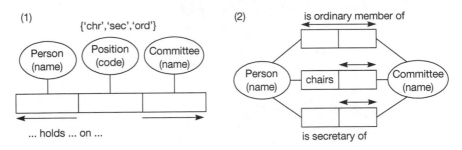

8. Consider the following academic UoD. Each subject is identified by its code but also has a unique title. Each subject has at most three assignments (possibly none), numbered 1, 2, and 3. Each subject has a second assignment only if it has a first assignment, and it has a third assignment only if it has a first and second assignment. Each assignment has exactly one due date. Although assignments for different subjects may be due on the same date, no subject has more than one assignment due on the same date.

Though unlikely, it is possible that within a subject the chronological order of due dates differs from the numerical order of the assignments (e.g., because of software problems the due date for CS400 assignment 1 might be postponed till after the due date for CS400 assignment 2).

(a) Model this by adding constraints (graphic, and textual if needed) to the schema:

Reference schemes:	Subject (code)
	Assignt (has AssigntNr, is for Subject)
Fact types:	Subject has Title
	Assignt is due on Date

(b) Map this to a relational schema, including all constraints.
(c) Specialize the is-due-on predicate in (a) by absorbing Assignt# into it.
(d) Map this to a relational schema including all constraints.
(e) Suppose that within each subject the chronological order of assignment due dates must match their numeric order. How does this affect the answers to (c) and (d)?

12.3   Nesting, Coreferencing, and Flattening

As humans, we have the freedom to think of the universe in different ways. One choice in modeling is whether to represent some feature in terms of an object type, and if so, how. The previous section discussed how to absorb or extract object types by predicate specialization and generalization. An object type with a composite identification scheme may be portrayed explicitly either as a nested object type or as a coreferenced object type. If we don't want to think of this feature in terms of an object type, we can model it with predicates using a flattened approach. In this section we consider transformations between nested, coreferenced, and flattened approaches.

Table 12.2 A relational table of student results.

Result:	studentNr	subject	rating
	1001	CS100	4
	1002	CS100	4
	1002	CS114	5

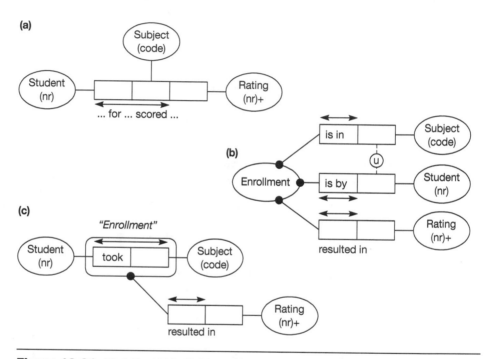

Figure 12.21 Modeling Table 12.2 by (a) flattening, (b) coreferencing, and (c) nesting.

Let's start with a familiar example. The report in Table 12.2 may be modeled in three ways, as shown in Figure 12.21. The schema in Figure 12.21(a) takes the flattened approach, using a ternary fact type. In the schema in Figure 12.21(b), Enrollment is a coreferenced object type, where its primary identification scheme combines two reference types. In the schema in Figure 12.21(c), Enrollment is modeled as a nested object type or objectified association. As discussed in Chapter 9, UML uses association classes for nesting and has a limited form of coreference.

In this example, the nested or coreferenced object type plays just one fact role, and this role is mandatory. In such a situation, the relational mapping is the same whether we nest, coreference, or flatten. In this case, each maps to the table scheme *Result* (studentNr, subjcode, rating). So we may choose whichever of the three approaches appeals most to us. Although this choice is partly subjective, there are a few guidelines that may be helpful.

Table 12.3 Length of departmental annual reports.

Year	Department	Report length (pp.)
1993	Research	40
1993	Sales	25
1993	Support	40
1994	Research	67
...	...	...

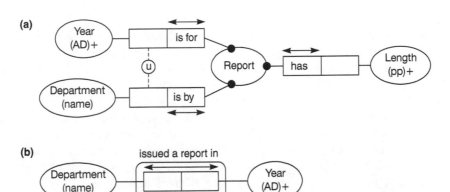

Figure 12.22 Since a report is a physical object, is (a) more natural than (b)?

First, let's consider choosing between nesting and coreferencing. Both these approaches always have the same relational mapping, no matter what the situation. Choose what seems most "natural". If in thinking about the real world, you first "see" a relationship and later want to talk about it, then nesting is probably the best choice. On this basis, more people would probably nest Enrollment rather than coreference it.

On the other hand, it often seems unnatural to think of a visible object in the real world as an objectified relationship. For example, consider Table 12.3, which provides details about the length of various annual reports by departments within a company.

Because you can hold a report (or at least a copy of a report) in your hand, it is natural to think of it first as an object and later ask yourself how to identify it. In this case we use both the year and department to coreference it, as in Figure 12.22(a). The nested approach in Figure 12.22(b) treats a report as a relationship between Year and Department. I find this unnatural, although some modelers still prefer to do it this way. Since both map the same way, you may choose whichever suits your taste.

If at least one of the object types used for the composite identification is a value type, then coreferencing is often more natural than nesting. Recall the following

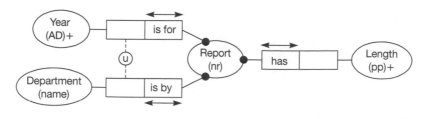

Figure 12.23 Annual reports are now identified by a report number.

coreferenced example: Subject (is offered by Department, has SubjectTitle). We could model this instead by objectifying the association Department offers a subject with SubjectTitle, but this seems unnatural (at least to me). As another example, consider the composite reference scheme Account (is at Branch, has AccountNr).

For efficiency, we sometimes introduce a new, simple identifier to replace a composite one, for example, Subject (code). In this case, the object type cannot remain nested, and if it was originally coreferenced, the former reference types become fact types. For example, in Figure 12.23 a simple report number is introduced to identify annual reports. We could use a plain serial number (e.g., 1, 2,...) or a coded number that humans can use to derive the semantics (e.g., "RES-99", "SAL-99",...).

Consider the relationship types Report is for Year; Report is by Department. These were reference types in Figure 12.22(a), but are now fact types. For example, two fact instances might be Report 'RES-99' is for Year 1999; Report 'RES-99' is by Department 'Research'. If the semantic basis of such introduced identifiers is unstable, then plain serial numbers might be preferred (e.g., suppose departments are often split, merged, or renamed). However, if the semantic basis is stable, such "information-bearing" identifiers can lead to efficiency gains by reducing the need to perform relational joins when information about the object is spread over many tables.

For example, suppose one table is used to store the data in Table 12.3 as well as an extra column for reportNr, and a separate table is used to store the $m{:}n$ fact type Employee (name) authored Report (nr). To find out who authored what reports, most users would be content with a listing of this second table, if meaningful report identifiers like "RES-99" are used, since this would be enough for them to work out the year and department. However, if plain serial numbers are used, most users would want the year and department listed too, requiring a join to the first table. As another example, consider the use of subject codes (e.g., "CS115") in listing results.

If a new identifier is introduced, the new schema is no longer strictly equivalent to the original one. For example, the schema in Figure 12.23 is stronger than the schemas in Figure 12.22. Any schema strengthening or weakening should result from a conscious decision of the modeler. However, shifting between a coreferenced and a nested approach (as in Figure 12.22) may be treated as an equivalence transformation. The general theorem, called **N/CR** (nest/coreference), is set out in Figure 12.24.

Here the objectified predicate R has n roles, where n is at least 2. In principle you could objectify a unary predicate, but this effectively amounts to a subtype, for which

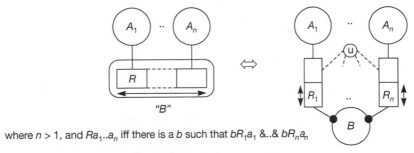

where $n > 1$, and $Ra_1..a_n$ iff there is a b such that bR_1a_1 &..& bR_na_n

Notes: A UC is understood to span the objectified predicate.
If B is independent, show it as *B !* in the coreferenced version.

Figure 12.24 N/CR: The nested version is equivalent to the coreferenced version.

we already have a more natural and more powerful notation. At any rate, coreferencing does not apply to such a case.

In Figure 12.24 the object types $A_1..A_n$ are not necessarily distinct. Though not shown in the figure, we assume the nested object type has at least one role attached. Recall that an object type is independent if the disjunction of its fact roles is optional. If independent, the object type must be explicitly marked so by appending "!" to its name.

For example, look back at Figure 12.21(b) and Figure 12.21(c), and suppose enrollments are recorded before any results are known. The mandatory role constraint must now be removed from the rating association, and the Enrollment object type renamed "Enrollment !". As we will see shortly, a more drastic change is needed to Figure 12.21(a) to maintain a flattened approach for this situation.

So long as the nested or coreferenced object type plays only one fact role, and this role is mandatory, we may transform to a single, flattened fact type. Recall the example in Figure 12.21. In such a case, the flattened approach is usually recommended since it gives a simpler diagram, is easier to verbalize, and sometimes avoids arbitrary decisions about which part of the predicate to objectify.

When a ternary or longer predicate has just one uniqueness constraint, and this spans all but one of its roles, the subpredicate spanned by this UC provides the best choice for objectifying. This was our choice in Figure 12.21. In principle, we could pick any subpredicate to objectify. For example, suppose in Figure 12.25(a) we objectify the subpredicate comprising the first and third roles, instead of the first two roles. This yields the awkward schema shown in Figure 12.25(b).

The external UC is needed to capture the UC in the flattened version (i.e., each student obtains at most one rating for each subject). Notice also that the UC on the outer predicate is compound. Although it maps to the same relational schema as the others, Figure 12.25(b) is harder for a human to understand.

If a ternary or longer predicate has overlapping UCs, then any objectification is best based on one of these. Each other UC in the flattened version is then captured by an external UC. See Figures 4.40 and 4.41 for an earlier example.

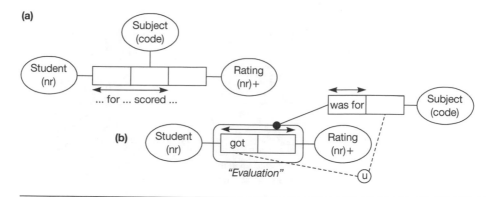

Figure 12.25 A poor choice for nesting (the UC spans other roles).

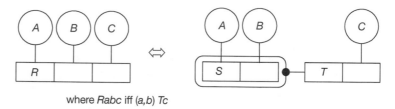

where *Rabc* iff *(a,b) Tc*

Corollaries: A UC exactly spans the *A, B* roles of *R* iff a simple UC spans the first role of *T*.
A binary UC over the *A, C* (or *B, C*) roles of *R* is equivalent to an external UC over
the *A, C* (or *B, C*) roles, respectively, in the nested version.

Figure 12.26 N/F: The nested version is equivalent to the flattened version.

In the case of overlapping UCs, there is more than one "natural" choice of a
subpredicate to objectify. This is also true if a ternary or longer predicate has a single
UC spanning all its roles, for example: Lecturer visits Country in Year. Here we could
objectify any of three role pairs: roles 1 and 2; roles 1 and 3; or roles 2 and 3. Unless
there are additional facts about the subpredicates, the flattened fact type provides the
simpler approach.

Figure 12.26 shows the ternary version of the **N/F** (nest/flatten) equivalence theorem. Here *A, B,* and *C* need not be distinct. A spanning UC over the roles in the nested
object type *S* is assumed. Typically a UC spans the *A, B* roles in *R;* this is equivalent to
a UC over the first role of *T.* For equivalence, the predicates must be formally related by
the condition shown in the **where** clause.

In Figure 12.26, if a UC spans all the roles of *R,* then a UC spans both roles of *T.* We
do not bother stating this corollary in the figure, since each predicate has an implied
UC spanning its full length. Recall that, for generality, schemas used to depict theorems may omit constraints that are not relevant to the transformation.

Our equivalence theorems state formal connections between predicates in the different versions, but do not specify how predicate names used in one schema might help to

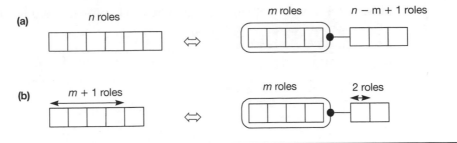

Figure 12.27 (a) Nesting ternaries and beyond; (b) nesting on a UC.

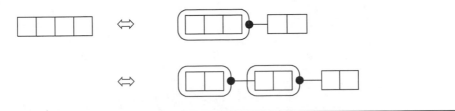

Figure 12.28 Binarizing a quaternary by nesting.

choose the different predicate names used in the other. A CASE tool could generate suggested names, but humans can often provide more natural ones (cf. generation of table names in relational mapping). In choosing identifiers, we should ensure that their background meaning agrees with the formal connection required by the transformation rule. This still leaves a lot of possibilities. In Figure 12.25(a), for example, instead of "... for ... scored ..." we might use "... enrolled in ... obtaining ...".

Note that since nesting can always be replaced by coreferencing, we could specify **CR/F** (coreference/flatten) equivalence theorems analogous to any N/F theorem. For example, consider transforming between the schemas in Figure 12.21(a) and Figure 12.21(b). To save space, however, we limit our unflattening discussion to nesting.

The ternary nest/flatten equivalence may be generalized to flattened fact types of any arity above 2. Note that nesting always introduces an extra role (to be played by the objectified association). If we objectify m roles of an n-ary predicate, the outer predicate will have $n - m + 1$ roles. This is shown in Figure 12.27(a), where other object types and role connectors are omitted for simplicity.

Recall that each UC of an elementary predicate must span at least all but one of its roles. If a UC exactly spans all but one role of a predicate, and we objectify on this UC, the outer predicate in the nested version has two roles, with a simple UC on its first role (Figure 12.27(b)).

Note that with long predicates, nesting may be applied more than once. A simple example is shown in Figure 12.28, where a quaternary is binarized in two stages. For simplicity other object types and role links are omitted. We saw earlier how unaries may be converted into binaries. Nesting or coreferencing may be used to convert ternary or longer predicates into binaries. So, in principle, any application may be modeled with

Table 12.4 Enrollments may be recorded before ratings are finalized.

Result:

studentNr	subject	rating
1001	CS100	?
1002	CS100	?
1002	CS114	5

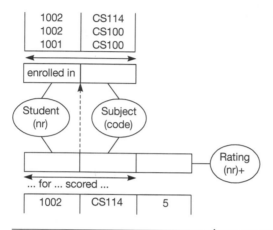

Figure 12.29 Modeling Table 12.4 with flat fact types.

binaries only. However, nonbinary predicates often enable an application to be modeled in a more natural and convenient way.

In our examples so far, the objectified association played just a single, mandatory role. In this case, flattening is generally preferable. But what if this role is optional? For example, suppose we modify our earlier Table 12.2 by allowing null values in the rating column (see Table 12.4). In this population, no ratings appear for the subject CS100. Perhaps the final exam for this subject is still to be held, or marking for it has not finished. In this UoD, it is possible to record the fact that a person enrolls in a subject before knowing what rating the student gets for that subject.

Since null values are not allowed at the conceptual level, we cannot model this as a single ternary. We may, however, use two fact types, one for enrollments and one for ratings. Figure 12.29 shows this flattened approach, together with the sample population.

The *pair-subset constraint* in Figure 12.29 indicates that students can score ratings only in subjects in which they enrolled. If this figure is part of a model with other roles for Student and Subject, the roles in the binary fact type may be optional; if not, they should be marked mandatory. This UoD can also be modeled using a nested or coreferenced object type. The nested version is shown in Figure 12.30, including the sample population. The role played by the objectified association is now *optional*. The objectified predicate corresponds to the binary predicate in Figure 12.29.

If no other role is played by Enrollment in the global schema, it is independent, as shown by the appended "!". This is not unusual with nesting. Any independent object

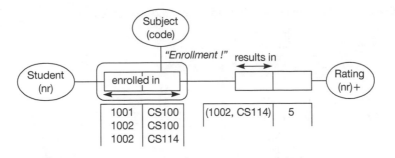

Figure 12.30 Modeling Table 12.4 with a nested approach.

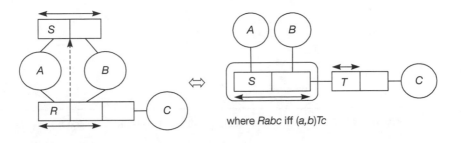

where *Rabc* iff (*a,b*)*Tc*

Figure 12.31 Another nest/flatten equivalence.

type, whether simple, nested, or coreferenced, should be explicitly declared independent by appending "!" after its name.

When two or more flat fact types are involved, the equivalence between nested and flattened versions is called **N/Fm** (nest/flatten into many fact types). The subset pattern illustrated by our example is only one of many cases for this theorem, but since it is the most common case we set it out in Figure 12.31.

We generally favor the nested version in this case, since it is more compact, and it Rmaps directly to just one table. In contrast, if the flattened version is passed to our standard Rmap procedure, two tables result. Nevertheless, the flattened approach is quite natural and it verbalizes easily. If you prefer the flattened approach for these reasons, it would be nice if your CASE tool displayed it this way, but gave you the option of having it mapped it to a single table in the same way as the nested version. However, such flexibility is typically not provided by current CASE tools. So the nested approach is generally preferable for this case.

In the flattened version in Figure 12.31, the *S* predicate is compatible with the subpredicate comprising the first two roles of *R* (they are played by the same object types *A* and *B*). It is this compatibility that enables the nesting to occur. For this subset case, any (*a, b*) pair in the population of either must belong to the population of *S*. So we objectify *S,* and add an optional connection to *C* to handle the *R* facts.

Recall that in our CSDP, whenever different predicates have compatible role sequences (of two or more roles) we should ask ourselves to what extent the populations

Table 12.5 Student assignment and exam marks.

Subject:	CS102		CS115	
StudentNr	Assignt	Exam	Assignt	Exam
1001	17	65	15	58
1002	20	79	20	67
1003	15	60	12	55

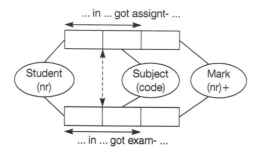

Figure 12.32 A conceptual schema for Table 12.5 (flattened version).

of these (sub-)predicates must overlap. If a set-comparison (subset, equality, or exclusion) constraint exists between them, it must be declared.

The kind of nesting transformation that may now occur depends partly on what kind of set-comparison constraint exists (if any) and on whether other roles occur in the full predicates. Let's look at some more examples before summarizing the overall procedure.

Consider the output report shown in Table 12.5. This may be modeled with two flat fact types, as shown in Figure 12.32. Notice the *equality constraint* between the two role pairs. An assignment mark is recorded for a student in a subject if and only if an exam mark is recorded for that student in that subject.

The compatible subpredicates might be read as did assignment in; did exam in. Since the populations of these must be equal, we may objectify their conjunction: did assignment and exam in. The nested version uses the wording was assessed in (see Figure 12.33). The specific marks are catered to by attaching two specific predicates as shown. Because of the equality constraint, these are both mandatory.

When passed to the standard Rmap procedure, the schema in Figure 12.32 maps to two tables, whereas the nested version in Figure 12.33 maps to a single table. For this reason, as well as compactness, the nested version is generally preferred whenever two or more functional roles are attached to the objectified predicate.

A more general N/Fm equivalence result is shown in Figure 12.34. This may be generalized further to n predicates ($n \geq 2$) and compatible subpredicates of any arity above 1. The object types $A..D$ need not be distinct. So long as (sub-)predicates are compatible, nesting may always be performed by objectifying their *disjunction*.

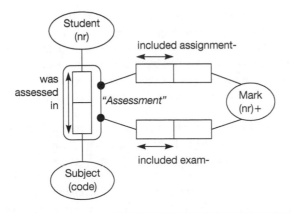

Figure 12.33 Another schema for Table 12.5 (nested version).

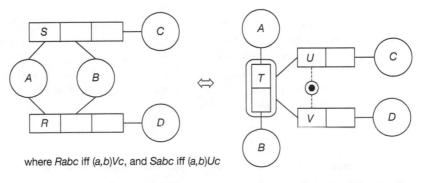

where *Rabc* iff (*a,b*)V*c*, and *Sabc* iff (*a,b*)U*c*

Corollaries: A binary UC over *S[a,b]* is equivalent to a UC on the first role of *U,* and a binary UC over *R[a,b]* is equivalent to a UC on the first role of *V*.
A pair-subset constraint from *R[a,b]* to *S[a,b]* makes U mandatory.
A pair-equality constraint between *R[a,b]* and *S[a,b]* makes *U* and *V* mandatory.
A pair-exclusion constraint between *R[a,b]* and *S[a,b]* adds an exclusion constraint between the attached roles in the nested version.

Figure 12.34 A more general nest/flatten equivalence.

Since the predicate *T* in Figure 12.34 is a logical disjunction, it may be verbalized using the word "or" to connect our verbalizations of the compatible (sub-)predicates. In terms of populations, the objectified relation *T* in Figure 12.34 is formed by taking the *union* of the compatible (sub-)relations. In relational notation: $T = R[a,b] \cup S[a,b]$.

Suppose we remove the equality constraint in Figure 12.32. If no other set-comparison constraint exists, we can nest this by replacing the two mandatory role constraints in Figure 12.33 with a disjunctive mandatory role constraint; each assessment included an assignment or exam mark (or both). The binary uniqueness constraints in the flattened version correspond to the simple UCs in the nested version (see first corollary in Figure 12.34).

In Figure 12.34, adding a pair-subset constraint from the first two roles of *R* to the first two roles of *S* is equivalent to adding a subset constraint from the first role of *V* to the first role of *U*. In the context of the disjunctive mandatory constraint, this means that *U* becomes mandatory (see second corollary). In terms of populations, it also means that the *T* relation becomes *S[a,b]*, since if one set is a subset of a second, then their union is just the second set. Compare this with the result in Figure 12.31.

A subset constraint in both directions is an equality constraint. So adding an equality constraint between *R[a,b]* and *S[a,b]* in Figure 12.34 makes both *U* and *V* mandatory in the nested version. The schema equivalence between Figures 12.32 and 12.33 provides an example.

If an exclusion constraint exists between *R[a,b]* and *S[a,b]* in Figure 12.34, and we decide to nest, we must add an exclusion constraint between the attached roles in the nested version. For example, suppose that for any given subject, a student can be awarded either an actual grade or a notional grade, but not both (a notional grade might be awarded on the basis of performance in a similar subject from another university). As an exercise, schematize this in both flat and nested versions.

A relation is said to be *partial* if it is a projection of a longer relation; otherwise it is said to be *whole*. Sometimes we run into a case where a whole relation must be a subset of another. Consider Table 12.6, for instance.

Here "?" is an ordinary null value. In this UoD, we want to know what subjects students have passed, but are not interested in their actual ratings. Figure 12.35 schematizes this using a flattened approach.

Table 12.6 Student enrollments and passes (if known).

Student	Subjects enrolled in	Subjects passed
3001	CS100, CS114, MP105	CS100, CS114
3002	CS114, MP105	CS114
3003	CS100, CS114	?

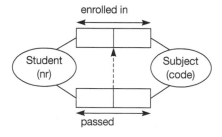

Figure 12.35 A schema for Table 12.6 (flat version).

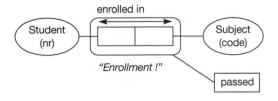

Figure 12.36 Another schema for Table 12.6 (nested version).

We can nest this by objectifying enrollment, and then using a unary to indicate which enrollments resulted in a pass (see Figure 12.36). By default, the flat version maps to two relational tables, while the nested version maps to one. So the nested version is usually preferred in such a case. You can decide for yourself whether to take an open- or closed-world approach when mapping the unary.

The **overlap algorithm** in Figure 12.37 summarizes the main cases of the N/Fm equivalence. This shows how to nest when two or more fact types include compatible role sequences, each with at least two roles. For simplicity, the diagram shows just two predicates with compatible role pairs (shaded). The predicates may have additional roles.

Let P and Q be the compatible (sub-)predicates. The nesting action depends on the amount of overlap allowed between the populations of P and Q. In any given case, this overlap condition is specified by replacing the pair connection marked "?" by a pair-subset (either direction), pair-equality, or pair-exclusion constraint, or by no constraint (proper overlap is possible).

In the figure, a subset constraint upwards from P to Q is denoted "↑", a downwards subset constraint is shown as "↓", and an equality constraint appears as "↕". Recall that a predicate is partial if it is embedded in a longer predicate.

The five cases are based on which set-comparison constraint is explicitly *displayed*. An equality constraint must be specified if it exists. Hence, in this context, display of a subset constraint is taken to imply that an equality constraint does not exist. In any situation, exactly one of the five cases listed will apply.

As one example of the "↑" case, consider the transformation from Figure 12.29 to Figure 12.30. Here Q is the whole enrollment predicate, while P is the partial predicate comprising the first two roles of the fact type Student for Subject scored Rating.

As an example of the "↑" case where Q is partial, replace the enrollment predicate in Figure 12.29 by the ternary Student enrolled in Subject on Date. The nested version in Figure 12.30 must now be modified by adding the mandatory binary Enrollment occurred on Date. As an example when both P and Q are whole, consider the transformation of Figure 12.35 to Figure 12.36.

As an example of the "↕" case, consider the reshaping of Figure 12.32 to Figure 12.33. Here both P and Q are partial, and their conjunction is reworded as "was assessed in". As an example of the "↕" case where neither P nor Q is partial, remove the mark information from Figure 12.32 to give two binaries: Student did assignment in Subject; Student did exam in Subject. The equality constraint enables these to be

Overlap algorithm:

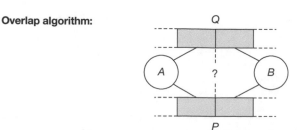

case ? constraint **of**

↑:   -- *P*'s population must be a subset of *Q*'s, but need not equal *Q*'s
          objectify *Q;*
          if *Q* is partial   **then** attach rest of its predicate via mandatory extra role;
          if *P* is partial   **then** attach rest of its predicate via optional extra role
                                              else attach optional unary "is-*P*"

↓:   reverse of previous case

↕:   -- *P*'s population must equal *Q*'s
          if *P* or *Q* is partial
                 then   objectify the single predicate "*P* and *Q*";
                                      attach rest of their predicates via mandatory extra role(s)
                 else   replace both by the single predicate "*P* and *Q*"

⊗:   -- *P's* population is mutually exclusive with *Q*'s
          objectify "*P* or *Q*";
          if *P* is partial   **then** attach rest of its predicate via extra role
                                              else attach as unary "is-*P*";
          similarly for *Q;*
          mark the attached roles as exclusive and disjunctively mandatory

  :   -- no constraint; proper overlap is possible
          as for ⊗ but omit exclusion constraint
end

Figure 12.37 Overlap algorithm for nesting when compatible subpredicates exist.

replaced by a single binary: Student did assignment and exam in Subject (or Student was assessed in Subject). Derivation rules may be specified for the former binaries if desired.

As an example of the "⊗" case where both *P* and *Q* are partial, recall this exclusive disjunction instance of Figure 12.34: Student for Subject obtained actual Grade; Student for Subject obtained notional Grade. This may be modeled by objectifying Student was assessed in Subject, and attaching the mandatory, exclusive disjunction resulted in actual Grade; resulted in notional Grade.

As an example where both *P* and *Q* are whole, consider the exclusive disjunction Student passed Subject; Student failed Subject. Suppose we objectify the disjunction of these predicates (i.e., Student passed or failed Subject) as Student was assessed in Subject. This Assessment object type may now be classified by attaching a mandatory disjunction of the following unaries: is a pass; is a fail. As an exercise, draw these examples.

While the mutual exclusion case may be transformed by nesting in this way, this is rarely the best modeling alternative. Sometimes the flat version is preferable, and sometimes a predicate generalization transformation is more appropriate. For instance, the pass/fail example just cited may be modeled instead using the ternary Student in Subject obtained Result {'pass','fail'}. And the nested solution to the actual/notional grade example may be transformed using PSG2 to replace the exclusive disjunction by has Grade; is of GradeType {'actual', ' notional'}.

In the final case of the overlap algorithm, no set-comparison constraint applies between P and Q, so their populations may properly overlap. For example, suppose that for any given student and subject we might have a predicted grade or an actual grade, or both. This may be modeled by two flat fact types: Student for Subject has predicted Grade; Student for Subject has actual Grade.

We may nest this by objectifying Student is assessed for Subject and attaching the mandatory, inclusive disjunction has predicted Grade; has actual Grade. As with the previous mutual exclusion case, other modeling alternatives may be preferable.

If P and Q are keys (i.e., each is exactly spanned by a UC) and the standard Rmap procedure is used, applying the overlap algorithm to flattened cases before mapping will reduce the number of relational tables. In this situation, especially for the subset and equality cases, nesting (or the equivalent coreferenced solution) is generally preferred.

Exercise 12.3

1. Consider the fact type: City in Year has Population. Population figures are collated only once each year. Populations may go up, down, or remain the same.
   (a) Model this using a flattened approach.
   (b) Now use a nested approach.
   (c) Now use a coreferenced approach.
   (d) Which solution do you prefer?
   (e) Use a nested approach that objectifies the association between City and Population. State whether this is better or worse than your solution to (b).

2. Consider the fact type "Flower blooms in City in Month." Note that flowers may bloom for more than one month in the same city.
   (a) Model this as a flat fact type.
   (b) Show three alternative nested solutions.

3. Schematize the following table using (a) flat, (b) nested, and (c) coreferenced approaches. Which do you find the most natural?

Software title	ReleaseNr	Size (Mb)
DataModeler	1	3
DataModeler	2	5
DataModeler	3	5
WordLight	1	5
...	...	...

4. Suppose employees are identified by their surname and initials, and each works for exactly one Department. In principle, we could model this using the ternary fact type Surname and Initials belong to an employee who works for Department.
    (a) Draw the flat fact type. Is this natural?
    (b) Nest this instead. Is this natural?
    (c) Now use coreferencing. Is this natural?
    (d) We now decide to primarily identify employees by an employee number, but still require that surname and initials provide an alternative identifier. Model this.

5. The following conceptual schema refers to the recent Olympic Games.

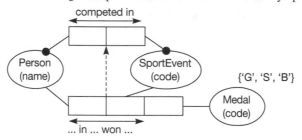

    (a) Rmap this.
    (b) Transform the conceptual schema by nesting.
    (c) Rmap your solution to (b).
    (d) Which conceptual schema do you prefer?

6. The following is an extract from a yearly report giving test results of reaction time (in milliseconds) and resting heart rate (in beats per minute) for members of a health club. As the table indicates, the club may gain or lose members during the year.

Month	Member	Reaction time	Heart rate
Jan	Jones, E	250	80
	Matthews, S	320	120
	Robinson, S	300	100
Feb	Jones E	250	75
	Matthews, S	300	100
Mar	Anderson, P	250	80
	Matthews, S	280	85
...	...	...	...

    (a) Schematize this using two flat ternaries.
    (b) Transform this by nesting.
    (c) Which schema do you prefer?

7. The following table indicates the rooms and times for lectures in various subjects. Schematize this using (a) flat and (b) coreferenced approaches.

Subject	Time	Room
CS213	Mon 3 p.m.	B19
CS213	Wed 9 a.m.	A01
CS213	Wed 10 a.m.	A01
EN100	Mon 3 p.m.	F23
EN100	Tue 3 p.m.	G24
...	...	...

8. The following output report indicates the performance of students in subjects in a given semester. Once a student has failed a subject in the semester, the subject cannot be passed by
the student in that semester. As students pass or fail subjects, these results are recorded. In
certain states it is possible that a student might have neither passed nor failed a subject taken
(e.g., the MP104 exam may yet to be held).

Student	Subjects taken	Subjects passed	Subjects failed
Adams AB	CS100, CS114, MP104	CS100, CS114	?
Brown SS	CS114, MP102	CS114	?
Casey J	CS100, CS114	?	CS100, CS114

(a) Schematize this UoD using three binaries.
(b) Transform this by nesting, with two attached unaries.
(c) Transform the two unaries into a binary.
(d) For this UoD is it possible that the null value for Adams AB might be updated to an actual value? What about the null value for Casey J?

9. The following table is an extract from an output report concerning the finals of a recent judo
competition. For each weight division, the four clubs that made it to the finals are recorded,
together with the results for first and second places. For a given weight division a club can
obtain at most one place. No ties are possible.

Event	Finalists	Winner	Runner-up
Lightweight	Budokan, Judokai, Kodokan, Zendokan	Kodokan	Judokai
Middleweight	Budokan, Judokai, Kodokan, Zendokan	Kodokan	Zendokan
Heavyweight	Budokan, Kanodojo, Kodokan, Mifunekan	Mifunekan	Kodokan

(a) An information modeler schematizes this UoD in terms of three fact types: Club is
finalist in Event; Club wins Event; Club is second in Event. Set out this conceptual
schema including all constraints.
(b) Transform the winner and second-place predicates into a single ternary.
(c) Transform this schema into an equivalent nested version.
(d) Assuming complete information is needed, show an alternative nested solution, by assigning the places "3A" and "3B" to the clubs that didn't get first or second in the event.
(e) Transform this to a flattened fact type.
(f) Which solution do you prefer?

10. The following examples are extracts of output reports from an information system about
media channels. Each channel (TV or radio) has a unique, identifying call sign. Some radio
channels broadcast using FM (frequency modulation), while others use AM (amplitude
modulation). All TV channels are rated in the range 1..7 in three categories on two surveys.
Channels are either commercial (com) or owned by the government (govt). All commercial
radio channels have their audience composition assessed (see the sample pie charts). The
mark "−" means "inapplicable because of other data".

   Schematize this, including uniqueness, mandatory role, value, subtype, and frequency
constraints. Provide meaningful names and definitions for each subtype. If a fact type is derived, omit it from the diagram but provide a derivation rule. Do not nest. Minimize the
number of fact types in your schema (if necessary, use transformations).

TV channels:

Call sign	Ownership	Ownership details		
		Company	% share	Head office
ATQ8	com	MediaCo	100	Brisbane
CTQ3	com	MediaCo	50	Brisbane
		TVbaron	50	Sydney
TVQ3	govt	–	–	–

Radio channels:

Call sign	Ownership	Ownership details			Modu-lation	Music played
		Company	% share	Head office		
4BZ	com	MediaCo	100	Brisbane	FM	rock country
RB3	govt	–	–	–	AM	–
STR5	com	MediaCo	30	Brisbane	AM	country
		OzRadio	70	Cairns		
4AA	govt	–	–	–	FM	–

TV survey ratings:

Channel	Survey	Category			Totals
		News	Drama	Sports	
ATQ8	A	5	3	3	
	B	4	4	3	22
CTQ3	A	5	3	4	
	B	5	4	5	26
TVQ3	A	3	4	4	
	B	2	4	5	22

Audience compositon of commercial radio channels:

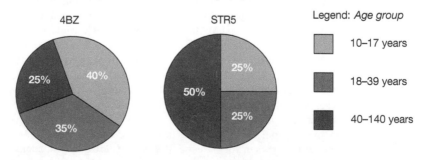

12.4   Other Transformations

The previous two sections covered the most useful conceptual schema transformations. In this section, several other transformations of lesser importance are considered briefly.

Recall PSG2, our second predicate specialization/generalization theorem (Figure 12.16). This may be generalized further by removing constraints. First note that removing the UC on A's role in R corresponds to removing the UCs on A's roles in each of the S_i predicates (see Figure 12.38). In the absence of additional internal UCs, the R and S_i binaries will be many:many. As an example, let A = Car, B = Status {'company', 'private'}, C = Employee, T = has, R = is used by, S_1 = is provided for, and S_2 = is privately used by. Allow the same employee to use many company cars and many private cars and vice versa.

Now suppose the equality constraint is weakened to an upward subset constraint. The T predicate must be retained since there may be instances of A that do not play R, and hence T will not in general be derivable from the S_i. Moreover, subtypes must now be introduced for the specialized predicates (Figure 12.39). The exclusion constraint over the subtype roles is omitted since it is implied by the subtype definitions.

For example, consider the car UoD just discussed, where some cars might not yet be used. In this case the subtypes are CompanyCar and PrivateCar. Cases that require one of these more general forms of PSG2 usually invoke some of the corollaries stated for

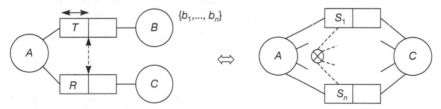

Each S_i corresponds to R where T is restricted to $B = b_i$

Figure 12.38 Another PSG2 case: R may be specialized into $S_1..S_n$ by absorbing B.

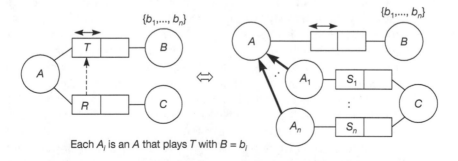

Each A_i is an A that plays T with $B = b_i$

Figure 12.39 Another PSG2 case: R is specialized into $S_1..S_n$, but B is not absorbed,

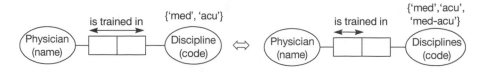

Figure 12.40 An example of value concatenation/separation.

the original version of the theorem (Figure 12.16). For example, suppose each employee uses at most one company car and at most one private car. An external UC is now required between the Status and Employee roles in the left-hand version, and a simple UC must be applied to each role of Employee in the right-hand version. As an exercise, draw both schema versions for this UoD, and prove that a frequency constraint of ≤ 2 is implied on the role played by Employee in the left-hand version.

If an object type in an *m:n* binary has two values, the fact type can be converted to a functional one by converting the object type to one that allows concatenated values. A simple example is shown in Figure 12.40. The transformation from left to right is called *value concatenation,* and the inverse transform is *value separation.* In this example, a physician may be trained in medicine or acupuncture or both. Allowing the "both" case to be recorded as a concatenated value (med-acu) is a "quick and dirty" way of effectively creating a set object type (in this case, Disciplines).

Appropriate translation rules are needed to license the transformation (e.g., Physician is trained in Discipline 'med' **iff** Physician is trained in Disciplines **in** {'med', 'med-acu'}). Moreover, the open/closed-world approach adopted should be the same for both. For example, if the left-hand version has a closed-world interpretation, then the code 'med' in the right-hand version means "medicine only".

Although sometimes used as a quick fix, this kind of transformation rapidly becomes unwieldy as the number of atomic values increases, since a list of *n* atomic values leads to $2^n - 1$ concatenated values (e.g., if we added herbalism and physiotherapy to give four atomic disciplines, we now have 15 concatenated disciplines). In such cases, if functional predicates are required, it is better to replace the binary with *n* unaries, one for each value, before mapping. Alternatively, if the target system supports set-valued fields (e.g., a nested relational or an object-oriented database), a mapping to a set-valued structure is possible.

In the presence of a pair-subset constraint, a binary may be *contracted* to a unary, or conversely, the unary may be *expanded* to a binary (see Figure 12.41). Note that the UC on the first role of *R* is implied by the other constraints (as an exercise, prove this). As an example of the left-hand schema, consider the fact types (*S* listed first) Politician is a member of Party; Politician is a minister in Party. Since you can be a minister only in your own party, a pair-subset constraint runs from the minister to the member fact type. In the right-hand version, the minister fact type is contracted to the unary Politician is a minister. Here a minister's party can be derived using the rule Politician is a minister in Party **iff** Politician is a member of Party **and** is a minister.

In this case, contraction is usually preferred to expansion. However, if the binary to be contracted is 1:1, its second uniqueness constraint needs to be captured as a textual

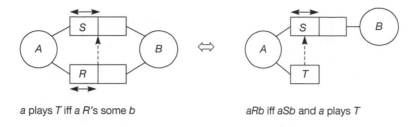

a plays *T* iff *a R*'s some *b*   *aRb* iff *aSb* and *a* plays *T*

Figure 12.41 Binary-unary contraction and unary-binary expansion.

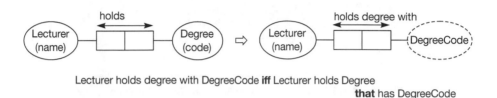

Lecturer holds degree with DegreeCode **iff** Lecturer holds Degree
that has DegreeCode

Figure 12.42 A simple case of entity type elimination/introduction.

constraint in the unary version. This may be enough reason to prefer the binary version. For example, suppose the following fact types appear in the position of *S* and *R* in Figure 12.41: Politician is a member of / includes Party; Politician leads Party.

Since each party has at most one leader, there is an extra UC on the lower binary, making it 1:1. Now suppose we contract this binary to the unary Politician is a leader. The extra UC in the binary version appears in the unary version as a textual constraint: **each** Party includes **at most one** Politician **who** is a leader.

In previous sections we have seen how object types can be absorbed in order to specialize predicates, and how nested and coreferenced object types may be removed by flattening. Apart from these cases, modelers sometimes eliminate an entity type from a fact type, phrasing the association in terms of the object type(s) formerly used to reference the entity type (usually, however, it is more convenient not to do this).

Figure 12.42 provides an example with a simple reference scheme. Transforming from the left-hand to right-hand version *eliminates* the entity type Degree. This weakens the schema, since the entity type and its reference scheme are lost. The translation defines the right-hand predicate in terms of the left. This is an implication rather than an equivalence. The reverse transformation from right to left *introduces* an entity type. In almost all cases, the left-hand version is preferred because of its richer formal semantics.

This transformation is sometimes performed with a coreferenced object type to which another object type is functionally related. Figure 12.43 provides an example. Here a room is identified by combining its local room number and building. Note the equality constraint; this is implied if the office roles of Employee are mandatory.

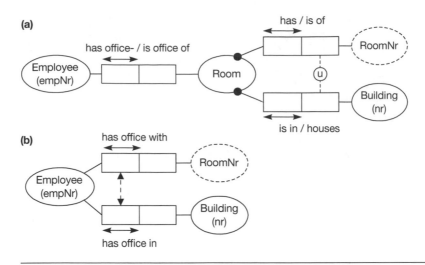

Figure 12.43 A functional coreferenced case; (a) is generally preferable.

Figure 12.43(a) is generally preferable to Figure 12.43(b) for two reasons. First, it facilitates schema changes that add other facts about rooms (e.g., Room has Size(sq_m)). Second, it is natural to think in terms of rooms, and the composite identification scheme is clearly displayed. In general, don't eliminate an entity type unless you feel that no further details will be recorded for it, and that no clarity is lost by its removal.

If you do decide to eliminate a compositely identified entity type, ensure that it is the target of only *functional* predicates. For example, consider the fact type Employee has office- Room. Suppose we now make this *m:n* to cater to some unusual case where an employee may have more than one office. For example, if an employee has to move his or her office from one building to another, the employee may be assigned an office in each building to facilitate working efficiently in both places until the move is completed. It would now be wrong to eliminate Room as in Figure 12.43(b), since the two associations are now *m:n,* losing the information about which room number goes with which building.

That covers the main conceptual schema transformations of practical relevance in information modeling. Other transformations exist, but are used so rarely that they are ignored here. Some transformations that deal with compound (nonelementary) fact types are discussed later in the context of denormalization and nonrelational mappings.

Exercise 12.4

1. (a) Each employee uses one or two phones, and each phone is used by an employee. Each phone is classified as a work phone or home phone. No employee can have two phones with the same classification. Schematize this using the entity types Employee, Phone, PhoneType.

(b) Provide an alternative schema, by absorbing PhoneType.

(c) Now suppose that some phones might not be used by any employee. Modify your answer to (a) accordingly.

(d) Provide an alternative schema by specializing the uses fact type.

2. (a) Consider the fact types Person is of Sex {'m', 'f'}; Person is parent of Person. Each person's sex is recorded. Parents of the same child must differ in sex. Some people might not be recorded as a parent or child. Schematize this.

(b) Set out an alternative schema, by specializing the parent fact type.

3. (a) Each person has at least one PersonType {'lecturer', 'student'}. It is possible that a lecturer is also a student. Assume all persons are identified by a person#. Schematize this in terms of a many:many fact type.

(b) Transform this to a schema comprising one functional fact type.

(c) Provide an alternative schema using unaries.

(d) People may now be classified as any or all of the following: lecturer, student, driver. How would you best model this?

4. (a) Consider the fact types Employee works for Department; Employee heads Department. Each employee works for exactly one department and heads at most one department (the department he or she works for). Each department has workers and at most one head. Schematize this using the two fact types given.

(b) Set out an alternative schema that contracts the heads fact type to a unary.

(c) Which schema is preferable? Discuss.

5. The following table indicates where certain objects are placed in three-dimensional space (x, y, z are the Cartesian coordinates). Only one object can occupy the same position at any given time.

Object	x	y	z
A	3	1	0
B	3	1	2
C	0	1	2

(a) Schematize this in terms of three binaries.

(b) Set out an alternative schema using Position as an entity type.

(c) Set out an alternative schema using AxisType {'x', 'y', 'z'} as an object type. Why is this alternative schema inferior?

12.5 Conceptual Schema Optimization

The previous three sections discussed how to transform conceptual schemas to equivalent, or at least acceptable, alternatives. *Conceptual schema optimization* involves transforming a conceptual schema into an alternative conceptual schema that maps to a more efficient (ideally, the most efficient) implementation. Section 12.1 presented a simple example of this. Guidelines for performing such optimizations are now discussed.

Four **main factors** to consider when optimizing a conceptual schema are the *target system*, the *query pattern*, the *update pattern*, and *clarity*. The target system is the

DBMS used for implementation. Here we assume it is a centralized relational system. The query pattern includes the kinds of questions that the system is expected to answer, together with statistical information about the expected frequency and priority of these questions. The update pattern includes the kinds, frequencies, and priorities of the expected insertions, deletions, and modifications to the database tables.

Response times for queries are usually more vital than for updates, so as a first criterion, we might try to minimize the response times of the "focused queries" (i.e., those queries with high priority or frequency). Clarity here refers to the ease with which the modeler can fully grasp the semantics conveyed by the schema.

Before the optimization procedure is executed, the global conceptual schema should be completed and validated. Any mapping choices (e.g., for 1:1 cases or subtypes) should also be declared. The procedure is then run on the whole schema. The complete optimization procedure for ORM schemas is somewhat complex, so only an overview of its main components is given here.

Although the default procedure could be executed without human intervention, better results may often be obtained by allowing modelers to override a suggested transformation when their additional insights reveal other factors that make the transformation counterproductive.

Several optimization strategies were introduced earlier in the chapter. Overall, the procedure comprises two main stages:

- Transform to reduce the number of mapped tables (steps 1–2)
- Transform to simplify individual tables (steps 3–5)

Since slow queries tend to involve joins or subqueries, a default strategy is to try to reduce the number of focused queries that involve joins or subqueries. Steps 1–2 of the optimization procedure do this for the main case (two or more tables involved), by transforming to reduce the number of tables involved in these queries. Since updates that require checking constraints between tables also tend to be expensive, this strategy usually improves update performance as well.

Recall that a composite key in a predicate amounts to a UC spanning two or more roles. Since the mapping algorithm maps predicates with composite keys to separate tables, a basic strategy is to reduce the number of (relevant) compositely keyed fact types in the conceptual schema. There are two main situations with the potential for achieving this: compatible keys that may be unified and nonfunctional roles that may be replaced by functional roles. Let's consider these in turn.

Step 1 aims to unify compatible, composite keys (see Figure 12.44). As preparation, step 1.1 includes two moves. As an example of its second move, consider a schema with fact types Company in State has staff of Sex {'m', 'f' } in Quantity; Company in State has budget of MoneyAmt. Compatible keys based on Company-State are formed by absorbing Sex to specialize the quaternary into two ternaries: Company in State has male staff in Quantity; Company in State has female staff in Quantity.

Steps 1.2 and 1.3 ensure that each pattern involving n compatible, composite keys is replaced by a single predicate ($n \geq 2$). The basic patterns for these steps are shown in Figure 12.44. For simplicity, Figure 12.44(a) shows only two predicates, and both cases

1.1 Flatten any objectified predicate that plays just a single, mandatory role;
    if   another compatible, composite key can be formed by absorbing a low
                cardinality object type into a predicate with a key of arity ≥ 3
    then do so.

1.2 **if** n nonfunctional, whole predicates form compatible, composite, exclusive
              keys and are incompatible with all other (sub-)predicates (see (a))
    then generalize them to a single longer predicate by extracting an object
              type of cardinality n (see Figure 12.11; transform to the left);

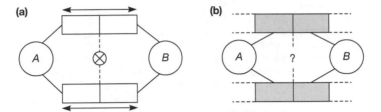

1.3 Apply the overlap algorithm to any pattern of compatible, composite keys
    (see (b) and Figure 12.37).
    Sometimes the $\otimes$ and no-constraint cases are best left as is.

Figure 12.44 Optimization step 1: unifying compatible, composite keys.

show compatible role pairs. Several examples were discussed in previous sections. Whereas the original pattern maps to n tables, the nested version maps to just one table.

As discussed earlier, if nesting leads to a loss of clarity in the conceptual schema, the modeler may prefer not to nest. Ideally, the modeler may then choose whether to have nesting performed automatically as an invisible, preprocessing stage to Rmap. Recall also that any nested object type may be recast as a coreferenced object type if this is felt to be more natural.

Step 2 examines *object types with both a functional and a nonfunctional role,* and typically attempts to replace the latter by functional roles that can be grouped into the same table as the former.

Figure 12.45 sets out the first stage: step 2.1. Most of step 2.1 amounts to predicate specialization using enumerated object types or frequency constraints. Several examples were discussed earlier. The predicate generalization case with the restricted UC is rare; for an example, recall Figure 12.12.

Step 2.2 completes the optimization strategy to reduce the number of mapped tables (see Figure 12.46).

The first case of step 2.2 for the pattern in Figure 12.46(a) uses PSG3 with its second corollary (see Figure 12.20). The second case for the pattern in Figure 12.46(a) is extremely rare and was ignored in earlier transformations. As an example, consider the fact type Official holds Position {'president', 'secretary', 'treasurer'}. Assuming each position is held by only one official, we may transform to three unaries: Official is president; Official is secretary; Official is treasurer; we also need to add the textual constraint that the population of each unary has a maximum cardinality of 1.

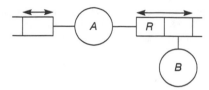

2.1   For each case where an object type A has simple and binary keys attached, where the other role of the binary key is played by B (see above):

if R is a binary
then if B has values $b_1,\ldots, b_n$ (and n is small)
    then specialize R to n unaries **or** replace B by B' $\{b_1, b_2, \text{both}\}$ (if $n = 2$)
      making the key(s) simple
    else if A's role in R has a frequency constraint n or $\leq n$ (and n is small)
      then specialize R into n exclusive binaries simply keyed on A
      else if A has just one functional role
        and the predicates are compatible, pair-exclusive binaries
        then generalize both to a single ternary with a restricted UC
else -- R is a ternary
    if B has values $b_1,\ldots, b_n$ (and n is small)
    then absorb B, specializing R into n binaries simply keyed on A.

Figure 12.45 Optimization step 2.1.

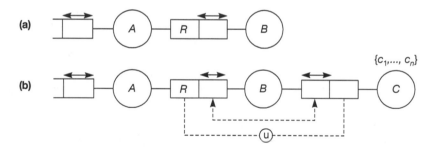

$\{c_1,\ldots, c_n\}$

2.2   For each case where an object type A has a functional role attached, as well as a 1:n binary predicate R connected to object type B:

if B has no other functional roles (see (a) above)
then if A's role in R has a frequency constraint of n, or $\leq n$ (and n is small)
    then specialize R into n 1:1 binaries with B's roles mutually exclusive
    else if B has values $b_1,\ldots, b_n$ (and n is small)
      then consider specializing R into n unaries
    else if B has exactly one more functional predicate, linked to C $\{c_1,\ldots, c_n\}$
      and an equality constraint spans B's functional roles
      and an external UC spans B's co-roles (see (b) above)
      then specialize R into n 1:1 binaries with B's roles exclusive,
        by absorbing C (this is PSG2 with corollary 2; see Figure 12.16).

Figure 12.46 Optimization step 2.2.

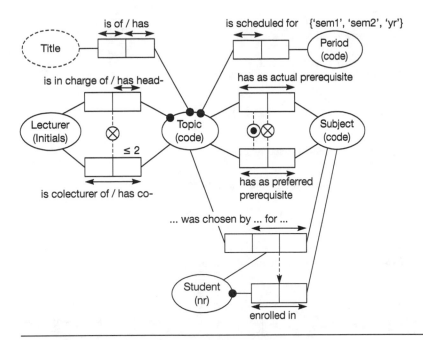

Figure 12.47 This suboptimal schema maps to six tables.

The final stage of step 2.2 (the pattern in Figure 12.46(b)) uses PSG2 and its second corollary. As an example, consider the main and backup driver UoD of Figure 12.15, and add the functional fact type Car is of CarModel. Specializing the drives predicate enables all the information to be mapped to a single Car table, instead of a Driver and a Car table. As an exercise, draw the schemas and perform the mappings.

Before going on to step 3, let's consolidate the first two steps by considering an example for which substantial optimization is possible. Figure 12.47 depicts a conceptual schema for postgraduate coursework in a computer science department. This UoD was first introduced in Exercise 4.2. The pair-subset constraint reflects the fact that after students enroll in a subject they choose a topic for it. Each topic has a lecturer in charge and at most two (other) colecturers. As an exercise, map the schema in Figure 12.47 to a relational schema, then check your solution with the one in Figure 12.48.

If you did this correctly, you should have obtained six tables. Notice the inter-table constraints. The "•" superimposed on "⊗" in the relational schema denotes a partition of PGtopic.topic (i.e., PGtopic.topic is the disjoint union of AcPrereq.topic and PrefPrereq.topic). The ordinary "⊗" indicates that the topic-lecturer pairs in ColecturedBy and PGtopic are exclusive. The other constraints are straightforward.

Suppose a focused query for this application is the following: list all topics (code and title) together with their main lecturers, colecturers, actual prerequisites, and preferred prerequisites. Let another focused query be the following: list students, the subjects in which they are enrolled, and the topics chosen by them (if any) for those subjects. With the relational schema of Figure 12.48, the first query involves a join of four

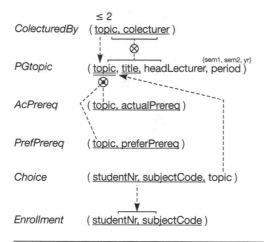

Figure 12.48 The relational schema mapped from Figure 12.47.

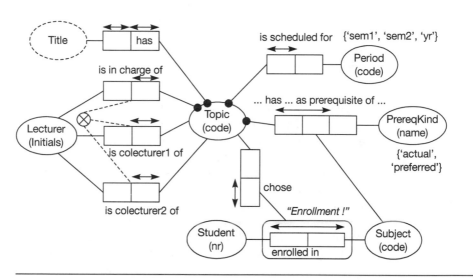

Figure 12.49 The conceptual schema obtained by optimizing Figure 12.47.

tables, and the second query involves a composite outer join of two tables. So these queries will be slow to run.

Applying optimization steps 1 and 2 to the conceptual schema of Figure 12.47 results in three main changes as shown in Figure 12.49. Step 1.2 generalizes the two prerequisite binaries to a ternary by extracting the object type PrereqKind { 'actual', 'preferred' }. Step 1.3 uses the overlap algorithm to nest the enrollment and topic fact types. Step 2.1 specializes the colecturer predicate into two exclusive binaries simply keyed

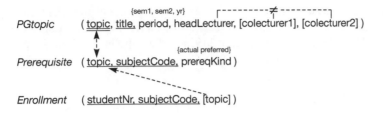

Figure 12.50 The relational schema mapped from Figure 12.49.

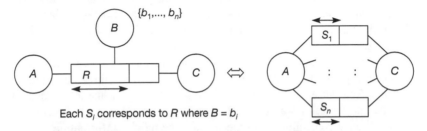

Each S_i corresponds to R where $B = b_i$

3   For the ternary pattern above, if focused queries on R require comparisions between different tuples, and the values $b_1,..., b_n$ are few and fairly stable, then absorb B, specializing R into n functional binaries.

Figure 12.51 Optimization step 3: the table width guideline (TWG).

on Topic. If we also demand that if a topic has colecturer2, it must have a colecturer1, then this may be added as a subset constraint.

As an exercise, Rmap this, then check your solution with that shown in Figure 12.50. The optimized relational schema has just three tables: one for the ternary, one for the nesting, and one for the five functional binaries of Topic. The "≠" symbol means that on the same row any non-null values for headLecturer, colecturer1, and colecturer2 must differ. This relational schema leads to much faster execution of the focused queries as well as simpler constraint enforcement on updates.

We now consider the final steps (3, 4, 5) in the optimization procedure. Unlike the previous steps, these do not reduce the number of tables. Step 3 is set out in Figure 12.51. This aims to reduce self-joins and is called the *table width guideline* (TWG) since it indicates when a wider table (more columns) may be preferable. The schema equivalence illustrated was considered earlier. If the object type A plays a functional role, the transformation to binaries would have already occurred in the last phase of step 2.1. Even if A has no functional role, the specialization into binaries may still be worthwhile if it avoids self-joins in focused queries.

As an example of step 3, suppose we wish to examine how full-time university fees varied for various degrees over the triennium 1991–1993. Assume we model this conceptually as the ternary Degree in Year had fulltime fee of MoneyAmt. Let us agree that a uniqueness constraint spans the first two roles, a frequency constraint of 3 applies to the first role, and a value constraint of {1991..1993} applies to Year. Suppose we map this to the following relational schema:

$$\begin{array}{cc} 3 & \{1991..1993\} \end{array}$$
FTfee (degree, yr, fee)

A fragment of a sample population for this table is shown in Figure 12.52. Let a sample focused query be "How much did the BSc full-time fee increase over the triennium?" Answer this query yourself by inspecting the table.

In arriving at the answer ($300), you compared values from two different rows from the same table. To perform this query in a relational database language requires joining the table to itself (a self-join). An SQL version of the query is included in Figure 12.52.

Such joins can be avoided by first transforming the schema via TWG. Absorbing the object type Year into the ternary specializes it to the three conceptual binaries Degree had 1991 fulltime fee of MoneyAmt; Degree had 1992 fulltime fee of MoneyAmt; Degree had 1993 fulltime fee of MoneyAmt. Here the roles of Degree are functional and linked by an equality constraint. If, in the global schema, fee information is mandatory for Degree, these roles are mandatory (which implies the equality constraint). If Degree has no other functional roles, these three conceptual binaries map to a single relational table:

FTfee (degree, fee91, fee92, fee93)

If Degree had other functional roles, the optimization would have been performed at step 2.1, with the extra functional fact types mapping to the same table. Figure 12.53 illustrates how the wider table enables the query to be performed simply by comparing values on the same row.

FTfee:

degree	yr	fee
BSc	1991	2000
BSc	1992	2000
BSc	1993	2300
MBA	1991	3000
MBA	1992	3300
MBA	1993	3700

How much did the BSc fee increase over the three years?

SQL code for query: **select** New.fee − Old.fee
                              from   FTfee **as** Old **cross join** FTfee **as** New
                              where Old.yr = 1991 **and** Old.degree = 'BSc' **and**
                                           New.Yr = 1993 **and** New.degree = 'BSc'

Figure 12.52 This query requires a self-join, since it compares different rows.

FTfee:	degree	fee91	fee92	fee93
	BSc	2000	2000	2300
	MBA	3000	3300	3700

How much did the BSc fee increase over the three years?

SQL code for query:
```
select  fee93 − fee91
from    FTfee
where   degree = 'BSc'
```

Figure 12.53 The transformed schema leads to a more efficient query.

This example was trivial and clear-cut, but life is not always so simple. If Year plays other roles in the global schema, the restriction to 1991..1993 would probably not apply to it. However, so long as the fee years have this restriction (effectively forming a subtype FeeYear) the transformation may still be performed. If the year range is large, the number of extra columns generated by the transformation may be too high.

For example, suppose we must record fees for the period 1951..2000. Specializing the ternary would generate 50 binaries and lead to a relational table with 51 columns: *FTfee*(degree, fee1951, .., fee2000). Such a large number of binaries would clutter the conceptual schema (though a flexible CASE tool could be set to display the ternary with the optimization hidden in the mapping). The very wide relational table would also be awkward to view (lots of horizontal scrolling) and to print. For these reasons, once the *cardinality* of the value constraint exceeds a reasonable number (e.g., 5), the ternary fact type might well be preferred.

The *stability* of the value constraint is also important. In many cases such a constraint is known to be stable (e.g., {'m', 'f'} for sexcode). Sometimes, however, the value constraint changes with time. For example, suppose fees are to be recorded for all years from 1991 to the current year, or for just the most recent triennium. The binary approach requires changes to the fact types and relational columns each year. In this case the ternary approach might be preferred since no structural change is needed (the year changes are made only to rows of data, not the table structure itself). The wording of optimization step 3 reflects this trade-off between query efficiency and the ease of table display and schema evolution. Although default choices can be built into an automated optimizer, interaction with human modelers is advisable to ensure the best trade-off.

The final steps (4 and 5) of the optimization procedure deal with exclusive roles (see Figure 12.54).

Step 4 is straightforward. Recall that different unaries attached to the same object type map to different columns of the same table. If these unaries are exclusive, we may replace them all by a functional binary that maps to just one column. Moreover, the transformation of the exclusion constraint to a uniqueness constraint enables it to be simply enforced by the primary key constraint of the table. For an example of this predicate generalization process, review Figure 12.9, where three exclusive unaries

4   Generalize each group of n exclusive unaries ($n \geq 2$) to a functional binary
by extracting an object type with n values.

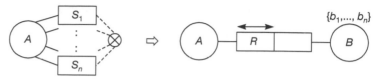

5   **if** A plays exclusive, functional roles in n 1:m predicates with C,
and C has no other functional role

then   replace these n predicates by two binaries, by extracting $B\{b_1,..., b_n\}$
as per the LHS of PSG2.

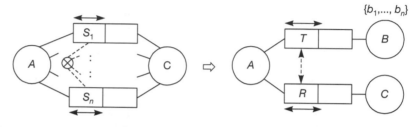

Figure 12.54 Optimization steps 4 and 5: further aspects of exclusive roles.

(Employee is a manager; Employee is a clerk; Employee is a secretary) are replaced by the functional binary Employee has Rank {'M', 'C', 'S'}.

Step 5 helps us decide when to favor predicate generalization in applying theorem PSG2. This is illustrated, along with several other optimizations, within our next example. Consider the conceptual schema shown in Figure 12.55. The interpredicate uniqueness constraint asserts that a team may have only one player of each sex. This conceptual schema maps to seven tables. As an exercise, you might like to check this for yourself, then optimize the conceptual schema before reading on.

The overlap algorithm (step 1.3) applied to the bottom ternaries of Figure 12.55 generates the intermediate, nested subschema shown in Figure 12.56. This is then transformed (step 5) to the nested pattern included in the optimized conceptual schema (Figure 12.57). This modification to the nesting does not change the number of tables, but it does simplify the constraint pattern that has to be enforced.

At the final stage of step 2.1, the subtype PlayingCountry is seen in Figure 12.55 to have a functional role attached (via its supertype) and a role within a composite UC, so the two-valued UniformItem is absorbed to specialize the ternary into two functional binaries. Note the constraint pattern arising from the application of corollaries.

At the first stage of step 2.2, the frequency constraint on the supplies predicate is used to specialize it into two functional binaries. The second half of step 2.2 is used to absorb the object type Sex, specializing the team membership predicate into binaries in which Team now has functional roles. Hence, these may be mapped to the same table

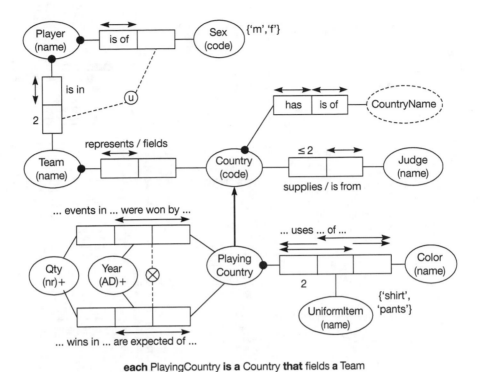

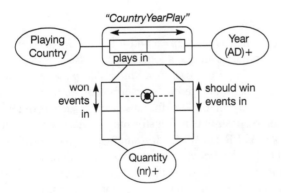

each PlayingCountry **is a** Country **that** fields a Team

Figure 12.55 This unoptimized conceptual schema maps to seven tables.

Figure 12.56 An intermediate transform of the bottom-left ternaries of Figure 12.55.

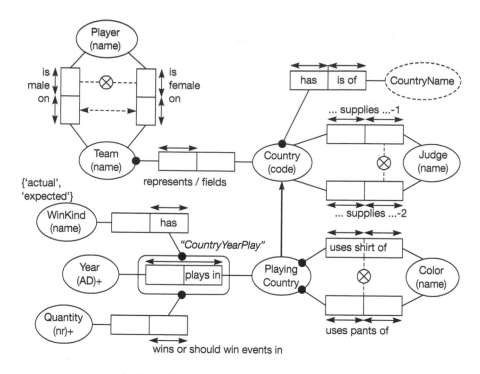

Figure 12.57 This optimized conceptual schema maps to three tables.

as Team's other functional fact type. Steps 3 and 4 are not invoked by this example. Step 5 transformed the original nesting to another, as discussed earlier.

This completes the basic optimization procedure. The generation of all the constraints in the optimized version is rigorously determined by the underlying transformation theorems and their corollaries. In the absence of such formal grounding, it would be easy to lose some constraints in transforming such a schema. Although UML and commercial versions of ER are useful for summarizing schemas, they typically lack the required detail (e.g., disjunctive mandatory or pair-exclusion constraints) to illustrate many complex transformations, unless supplemented by textual constraints.

The optimized conceptual schema maps to just three tables, as shown in Figure 12.58, thus reducing the number of tables by four.

Exclusion between column sets is shown by "⊗". The weaker constraint of exclusion between values on the same row is shown by "≠". Pairing attributes in the same square brackets entails that any qualification applies to each, and that if one is null, so is the other (this latter constraint is implied for the color attributes by their qualification).

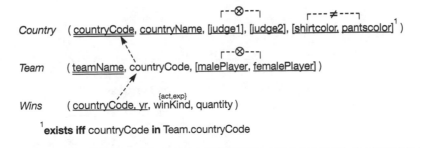

Figure 12.58 The relational schema mapped from Figure 12.57.

The schema optimization procedure discussed here does not include decisions about how subtypes and symmetric 1:1 fact types should be mapped, since these do not change the conceptual schema itself. As discussed in Chapter 10, however, these mapping choices can have a significant impact on the efficiency of the relational schema obtained.

Recall also that the optimization procedure assumes the target system is a relational DBMS, at least in the sense that each entry in a table column is either an atomic value or a null value. If multivalued fields are permitted (as in SQL:1999), other designs may be used to avoid table joins, leading to further possible optimizations (see Section 12.7).

Exercise 12.5

1. Consider a conceptual schema in which the only fact type associated with Department (code) is Department at Level {UG, PG} has students in Quantity. Here "UG", "PG" abbreviate "undergraduate", "postgraduate". The role played by Department has a frequency constraint of 2. Let a focused query be "What is the ratio of postgraduate to undergraduate enrollments for the department of computer science?"
   (a) Draw the conceptual fact type, and Rmap it.
   (b) Optimize the conceptual (sub-)schema, and Rmap it.
   (c) Although primarily identified by its code (e.g., "CS"), each department also has a unique name (e.g., "Computer Science"), which is now mandatorily recorded. The enrollment figures are now optional, but if any figures are recorded, both UG and PG figures are required. Draw the new conceptual schema and Rmap it.
   (d) Optimize the new conceptual schema, and Rmap it.

2. The following conceptual schema deals with applicants for positions as astronauts. Applicants are given ability tests (C = cognitive, A = affective, P = psychomotor), and their performance on various tasks is also measured.
   (a) Rmap this.
   (b) Optimize the conceptual schema.
   (c) Rmap your optimized conceptual schema.

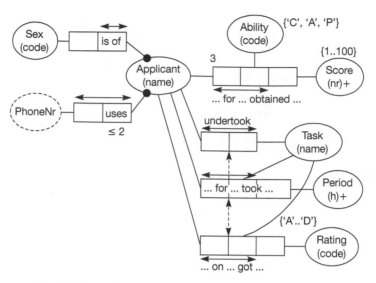

3. Consider the following conceptual schema. Assume that the Project-Programmer-Class subschema may be treated simply in snapshot fashion (i.e., only current data for these fact types are recorded).
   (a) Rmap this.
   (b) Optimize the conceptual schema.
   (c) Rmap your answer to (b).

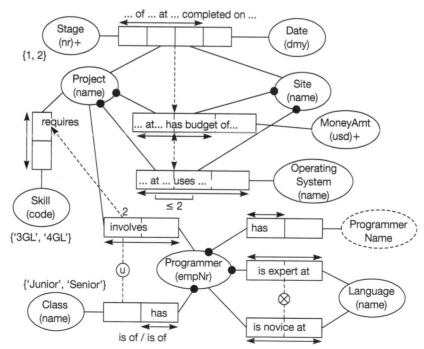

(d) As indicated in the original conceptual schema, each project must normally have a junior and senior programmer. However, suppose now that while, or after, working on a project, a programmer may be promoted or even demoted in class (junior, senior). Discuss briefly how you would deal with this situation from a practical business standpoint, and what changes, if any, you would suggest for the original and optimized conceptual schemas.

12.6   Normalization

The process of mapping from a conceptual schema expressed in elementary fact types to a relational schema involving table types is one of **deconceptualization.** This approach facilitates sound design primarily because it emphasizes working from examples, using natural language, and thinking in terms of the real-world objects being modeled.

The advantages of using *elementary facts* are clear: working in simple units helps get each one correct; constraints are easier to express and check; null values are avoided; redundancy control is facilitated; the schema is easier to modify (one fact type at a time); and the same conceptual schema may be mapped to different logical data models (hence decisions about how to group fact types together may be delayed till mapping).

Nowadays, many database designers do a conceptual design first, whether it be in ORM, ER, or UML notation, and then apply a mapping procedure to it. In the past, in place of conceptual modeling, many relational database designers used a technique known as **normalization.** Some still use this, even if only to refine the logical design mapped from the conceptual one. If an ORM conceptual schema is correct, then the table design resulting from Rmap is already fully normalized, so ORM modelers don't actually need to learn about normalization to get their designs correct. However, a brief look at normalization is worthwhile, partly to consolidate aspects of good design and partly to facilitate communication with those who use the normalization approach.

There are two techniques for normalization: *synthesis* and *decomposition* (sometimes called "analysis"). Each operates only at the relational level and begins with the complete set of relational attributes as well as a set of dependencies on these, such as functional dependencies (FDs). Herein lie the fundamental weaknesses of the normalization approach, if it is not used in combination with a conceptual modeling approach.

In any realistic application it is too easy to get an incorrect model if we begin by simply writing down a list of attributes and dependencies, since the advantages and safeguards of conceptual modeling are removed (e.g., validation by verbalization and population). Moreover, the set of dependencies is usually very limited (in some cases, only FDs are specified!) so that many of the application's constraints are simply ignored.

Another problem with normalization is that it can't change the set of attributes. Hence, apart from ignoring transformations that involve other kinds of constraints, normalization misses semantic optimization opportunities that might arise by allowing transformations to change attributes. For example, normalization is unable to transform {dept → location, (dept, sex) → nrStaff} into {dept → location, dept → nrMales, dept → nrFemales}. Compare this with the ORM schema optimization approach just discussed.

Considerations such as these indicate that use of normalization alone is inadequate as a design method. Nevertheless, the use of normalization as a check on our conceptual modeling may at times be helpful. On the positive side, by limiting their scope to a small but important class of constraints, and ignoring semantic transformations, normalization theorists have been able to rigorously prove several interesting results.

The output of both the synthesis and decomposition techniques is a set of table schemes, each of which is guaranteed to be in a particular "normal form". We will have a closer look at normal forms presently. The synthesis algorithm basically groups attributes into tables by finding a minimum, reduced, annular cover for the original dependencies. Redundant FDs (e.g., transitive FDs) are removed, redundant source attributes (those on the left of an "→") are removed, and FDs with the same source attribute are placed in the same table. With respect to its specified class of dependencies and attributes, the synthesis algorithm guarantees a design with the minimum number of tables, where each table is in elementary key normal form (see later for a definition of this concept).

For example, given the FDs {empNr → sex, empNr → birthdate, empNr → job, job → salary, empNr → salary}, synthesis generates two tables: *R1* (empNr, sex, birthdate, job); *R2* (job, salary). While this example is trivial, for more complex cases the execution of the synthesis algorithm is arduous and is best relegated to a computer. It should be apparent that the derived fact type checks in the CSDP, and the basic fact type grouping in Rmap, have a close correspondence to the synthesis method.

Unlike synthesis, the decomposition approach to normalization is an iterative one, progressively splitting badly designed tables into smaller ones until finally they are free of certain update anomalies, and it provides no guarantee of minimality of number of tables. However, the decomposition approach is more well known, and some modelers find its principles useful for correcting poor relational designs.

Although the synthesis approach is technically more interesting, a proper treatment of it requires a level of mathematical sophistication beyond that assumed for the readers of this book. Hence the rest of this section focuses on the decomposition approach, with some comparisons to ORM. To assist the reader who may read this section out of sequence, some basic concepts treated earlier are briefly reviewed.

A relational schema obtained by Rmapping it from a correct ORM conceptual schema is already fully normalized. Suppose, however, that some error was made in either the conceptualization or the mapping, or that the relational schema was designed directly without using a conceptual schema. It is now possible that some of the table designs might be unsafe because some conceptual constraint is not enforced. If a conceptual constraint may be violated when a table is updated by inserting, deleting, or modifying a row, the table design is said to contain an update anomaly.

Constraints on conceptual reference types are the responsibility of humans. Only people can ensure that primary reference schemes actually do provide a correct 1:1-into map from real-world entities to data values (or data tuples). Special care is required when an entity type plays just one fact role, this role is not functional, and an instance of this entity type changes its primary identifier.

For example, suppose City occurs only in the *m:n* fact type RussianTour (nr) visits City (name). In the early 1990s, the city then known as "Leningrad" reverted to its original name "St. Petersburg". As an exercise, discuss some problems arising if only some instances of "Leningrad" are renamed.

Assuming primary reference schemes are already enforced, the information system itself should normally enforce all the fact type constraints. So all constraints on (and between) conceptual fact types should be captured in the relational schema. The normalization procedure ensures that most of these constraints are so captured. In particular, it aims to remove any chance of redundancy (repetition of an elementary fact). If a fact were duplicated in the database, when the fact changed it would be necessary to update every instance of it, otherwise the database would become inconsistent.

Starting with a possibly bad table design, the normalization procedure applies rules to successively refine it into higher "normal forms" until it is fully normalized. Let's confine our attention to the normal forms that focus on eliminating problems with a table by splitting it into smaller ones. There are many such normal forms. In increasing order of acceptability, the main ones are first normal form (1NF), second normal form (2NF), third normal form (3NF), elementary key normal form (EKNF), Boyce/Codd normal form (BCNF), fourth normal form (4NF), fifth normal form (5NF), and domain key normal form (DKNF). We'll discuss each of these in turn.

The first three forms were originally proposed by E. F. Codd, who founded the relational model of data. The other forms were introduced later to cater to additional cases. These improvements were due to the work of several researchers including E.F. Codd, R. Boyce, R. Fagin, A. Aho, C. Beeri, and J. Ullman. Other normal forms have also been proposed (e.g., horizontal normal form and nested normal form), but are not discussed here.

A table is normalized, or in **first normal form** (1NF), if and only if its attributes are single valued and fixed. In other words, a 1NF table has a fixed number of columns, and each entry in a row-column position is a simple value (possibly null). For example, consider the output report shown as Table 12.7. While the first two columns store only atomic values, the Cars column stores sets of values, and the Results column holds sets of (subject, rating) pairs. To model this in a relational database, we need to flatten the

Table 12.7 A nested structure.

StudentNr	Sex	Cars	Results	
			Subject	Rating
1001	F	ABC123 PKJ155	CS100 CS114 PD102	6 7 6
1002	M		CS100 MA104	6 5

structure out into three tables: *Student*(studentNr, sex); *Drives*(studentNr, car); and *Scores* (studentNr, subject, rating). Hence, 1NF relations are often called *flat relations*.

However, it is possible to model the structure directly by using a relation that is not in first normal form. For example, we might use the following *nested relation* scheme:

Student (studentNr, sex, *Car* (regNr), *Result* (subject, rating))

Here an entry in the third column is itself a relation (in this case, a set of car registration numbers). Similarly, each entry in the Result column is a relation (with subject and rating attributes). Since the logical data model underlying this approach allows relations to be nested inside relations, it is called the *nested relational model*.

Since the table is not in 1NF, it is not a relational table (i.e., it does not conform to the relational model of data). The table is said to be in *non-first normal form* (NFNF or NF²). Although pure nested relational systems have yet to make any significant commercial impact, many of the major relational DBMSs have evolved into object-relational systems with support for NF² tables, as discussed in the next section. While tables not in 1NF might be in some other exotic "normal form", it is common practice to refer to them as being "unnormalized".

Set-valued fields like Cars in Table 12.7 are sometimes called "repeating attributes", and fields like Results that hold sets of grouped values are sometimes called "repeating groups". This term may be used to include the notion of repeating attributes by allowing degenerate groups with one value. Using this older, if somewhat misleading, terminology, we may say that 1NF tables have no repeating groups.

Another example of an unnormalized table is the "variant record type" used in languages such as Pascal and Modula. Here different "rows" in the same record type may contain different fields. For instance, a record type about colored geometric figures may include common fields for figureId, color, and shape (circle, rhombus, triangle, etc.), but have different remaining fields depending on the shape (e.g., radius for circle; side and angle for rhombus; three sides for triangle). Although this provides one way to implement a restricted notion of subtypes, the record structure used is completely unnormalized.

Recall that a *key* of a table is a set of one or more attributes spanned by an explicit uniqueness constraint. Here "explicit" excludes any UCs that are implied by shorter UCs inside them, so keys are spanned by "minimal" UCs. For a given relation, an attribute is a *key attribute* if and only if it belongs to some key (primary or secondary) of the relation. A *nonkey* attribute is neither a key nor a part of a composite key.

Given attributes X and Y of a relation, X *functionally determines* Y if and only if Y is a function of X (i.e., given any possible population of the table, for each value of X there is only one value for Y). We write this $X \rightarrow Y$ and say that Y is *functionally dependent* on X. Attributes X and Y may be composite.

A table is in **second normal form** (2NF) if and only if it is in 1NF and every nonkey attribute is (functionally) dependent on the whole of a key (not just a part of it). If a table is normalized, it is in at least 1NF. Since any table in a higher normal form is also in all lower normal forms, let us use the term "hNF" to describe the highest normal form of a table. Consider Table 12.8. Its hNF = 1 since height, a nonkey attribute, is

Table 12.8 This table is in 1NF but not 2NF.

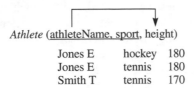

Athlete (athleteName, sport, height)

Jones E	hockey	180
Jones E	tennis	180
Smith T	tennis	170

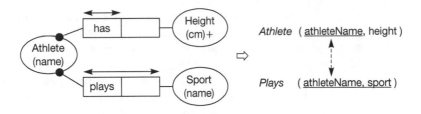

Figure 12.59 Conceptual and relational schemas for Table 12.8.

functionally dependent on athletename, which is just part of the composite key. This FD is shown as an arrow above the table.

Notice the redundancy: the fact that Jones E has a height of 180 cm has been recorded twice. To avoid redundancy we must split the original Athlete table into two smaller ones, as shown in Figure 12.59.

This figure shows both the conceptual and relational schemas for the example (assuming the information is mandatory for athletes). If you verbalized Table 12.8 correctly in terms of elementary facts, you would obtain this conceptual schema directly, and the relational schema would follow automatically using Rmap.

You would have to be a real novice to verbalize Table 12.8 in terms of a ternary, but suppose you did. The checks provided in the CSDP, especially steps 4 and 5, prompt you to discover the functional fact type Athlete has Height. On seeing this, you would know to split the ternary into two binaries.

If you were careless enough in applying the CSDP, you could end up with the ternary in your relational schema. At this stage you could look for an FD coming from only part of a key and use the 2NF normalization rule to at last correct your error. Even at this level you should think in terms of the functional fact type behind the FD.

Recall that if fact types are elementary, all FDs are implied by UCs. This property is preserved by Rmap, since it groups together only functional fact types with a common key. So if we find an FD in a relational schema that is not implied by a UC, we must have gone wrong earlier. Since UCs imply FDs, every nonkey attribute is functionally dependent on any key of the relation. Note that to determine the hNF of a relation we need to be told what the relevant dependencies are (e.g., keys and FDs) or have a significant population from which these may be deduced.

Although normalization to 2NF overcomes the redundancy problem in the original Athlete table, this reduces the efficiency of those queries that now have to access both the new tables. For example, if we want the name and height of all the hockey players, the 2NF design means that two tables must be searched and their athleteName fields matched. This kind of efficiency loss, which is common to each normalization refinement (each involves splitting), is usually more than offset by the higher degree of data integrity resulting from the elimination of redundancy.

For example, if we need to change the height of Jones E to 182 cm and record this change on only the first row of the original Athlete table, we now have two different values for the height. With more serious examples (e.g., defense, medical, business), such inconsistencies could prove disastrous.

As discussed in the next section, we may sometimes denormalize by introducing controlled redundancy to speed up queries. Although the redundancy is then safe, control of the redundancy is more expensive to enforce than in fully normalized tables, where redundancy is eliminated simply by enforcing primary key constraints. In short, normalization tends to make updates more efficient (by making constraints easier to enforce) while slowing down queries that now require additional table joins.

Given attributes X and Y (possibly composite), if $X \rightarrow Y$, then an update of X entails a possible update of Y. Within a relation, a set of attributes is *mutually independent* if and only if none of the attributes is (functionally) dependent on any of the others. In this case the attributes may be updated independently of one another.

A table is in **third normal form** (3NF) if and only if it is in 2NF and its *nonkey attributes are mutually independent*. Hence, in a 3NF table no FD can be transitively implied by two FDs, one of which is an FD between two nonkey attributes.

Consider Table 12.9. Its hNF = 2, since building depends on department, and these are both nonkey attributes. Note that building is transitively dependent on the key (surname determines department, and department determines building).

Table 12.9 exhibits redundancy: the fact that the CS department is located in building 69 is shown twice. To avoid this redundancy, the fact type underlying the FD between the nonkey attributes is split off to another table. This results in two 3NF tables: *WorksFor*(surname, department); *LocatedIn*(department, building). You may recall that this example was discussed in detail in Section 5.3, to illustrate the logical derivation check at step 5 of the CSDP. If this CSDP step has been carried out properly, FDs from one nonkey attribute to another cannot arise in any tables obtained from Rmap.

Moreover, the logical derivation check in the CSDP requires the following rule: Lecturer works in Building **iff** Lecturer works for **a** Department **that** is located in Building. If the

Table 12.9 This table is in 2NF but not 3NF.

Lecturer (surname, department, building)

Halpin	CS	69
Okimura	JA	1
Orlowska	CS	69
Wang	CN	1

"only if" part of the "iff" in this biconditional is not satisfied, then the two-table design loses information. For example, suppose in Table 12.9 that Wang does not work for any department (e.g., Wang might be a visiting lecturer who works in some general office). The last row of this table now becomes the tuple (Wang, ?, 1).

The original work on normalization assumed that nulls do not occur, but this assumption is often false. If we agree with Codd (1990, p. 201) that nulls should be ignored when applying rules about FDs, then the FDs shown above Table 12.9 still exist; but it is wrong to now simply decompose this table into two, so this normalization step can be unsafe. Clearly, the easiest and safest way to deal with such issues is at the conceptual level.

Codd's original definitions of 2NF and 3NF used "key" in the sense of primary key, so attributes of alternate keys were regarded as nonkey attributes. However, nowadays an attribute is termed a key attribute if it belongs to *some* key (primary or alternate), so a nonkey attribute belongs to *no* key.

Hence, in one sense the definition of 3NF does allow transitive dependencies if the intermediate attribute is a key. Consider the table scheme *Employee*(empNr, empName, sex). It has two keys. You might argue that the FD empNr → sex is transitively implied by the FDs empNr → empName; empName → sex. However, the relation is still in 3NF as there is no FD between nonkey attributes.

Let X and Y be attributes (possibly composite) of the same table. A functional dependency $X → Y$ is *trivial* if and only if X contains Y. A functional dependency $X → Y$ is *full* (rather than partial) if and only if there is no FD from just part of X to Y. A full, nontrivial FD is said to be an *elementary FD*. We avoid displaying nonelementary FDs because they are obviously implied by the elementary FDs.

A key is an *elementary key* if there is an elementary FD from it to some attribute in the table. An attribute is an elementary key attribute just in case it belongs to some elementary key. We may now define the next strongest normal form, which was proposed as an improvement on 3NF (Zaniolo 1982).

A table is in **elementary key normal form** (EKNF) if and only if all its elementary FDs begin at whole keys or end at elementary key attributes. In other words, for every full, nontrivial FD of the form $X → Y$, either X is a key or Y is (part of) an elementary key. If the primary key of a table includes all its columns, the table is automatically in EKNF since it has no elementary FDs; for example: *Enrollment*(studentNr, subjectCode).

Suppose that students also have a unique name, and we store their names in the same table (see Table 12.10). This table has two composite keys: (studentNr, subjectCode); (studentName, subjectCode). The primary key is indicated by a double underline; since its attributes are not adjacent, arrow tips are added to show this is a single, composite key rather than two simple key constraints. The secondary key is indicated by a single underline.

Since Table 12.10 has no nonkey attributes, it is automatically in 3NF. However, it has obvious problems (e.g., the fact that student 1001 is named 'Adams F' is duplicated). One way of spotting this bad design is to note that the table is not in EKNF. There is an FD from studentNr to studentName, and another FD from studentName to

Table 12.10 This table is in 3NF but not EKNF.

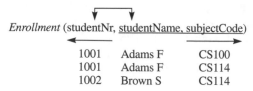

Enrollment (studentNr, <u>studentName, subjectCode</u>)

1001	Adams F	CS100
1001	Adams F	CS114
1002	Brown S	CS114

Table 12.11 This table is in EKNF but not BCNF.

Result (studentNr, <u>studentName, subjectCode</u>, rating)

1001	Adams F	CS100	6
1001	Adams F	CS114	7
1002	Brown S	CS114	7

studentNr (depicted by arrows above the table). These elementary FDs come from parts of keys rather than whole keys, and these FDs do not end at elementary attributes, since neither of the composite keys is elementary. So the table is not in EKNF.

The redundancy problem can be avoided by splitting the table into two EKNF tables: *Student*(<u>studentNr</u>, studentName); *Enrollment*(<u>studentNr, subjectCode</u>). The two FDs missed in the original table scheme are now captured by key constraints in the Student table. The same design is automatically obtained by Rmapping the correct conceptual schema, which has two elementary fact types: Student has StudentName; Student enrolled in Subject.

The next normal form is named after Raymond Boyce and Edgar Codd, who proposed it as an improvement on the old 3NF. An equivalent definition was given earlier by Heath (1971). A table is in **Boyce-Codd normal form** (BCNF) if and only if *all its elementary FDs begin at whole keys* (i.e., given any full, nontrivial FD $X \to Y$, it must be that X is a key). The only time that a relation can be in 3NF (or EKNF) but not in BCNF is when it has at least two candidate keys that overlap (Vincent and Srinivasan 1994).

As an example, consider Table 12.11. This is like the previous table, except that subject ratings are recorded for each student. The keys are now elementary, since they functionally determine the rating attribute. Since the FDs between studentNr and studentName now end at elementary attributes, the table is in EKNF. But the table has the same redundancy as the previous table.

One way to spot this problem is to note that it is not in BCNF, since the FDs shown above the table do not start at whole keys. For instance, the functional dependency studentNr $\to$ studentName exists, but studentNr is only part of the (studentNr, subjectCode) key.

The redundancy problem can be avoided by splitting the table into two BCNF tables: *Student*(<u>studentNr</u>, studentName); *Scored*(<u>studentNr, subjectCode</u>, rating). As an exercise, show how this design follows immediately from a correct conceptual schema.

The principle underlying the refinement to second and third normal forms has been nicely summarized by Kent (1983) as follows: "A nonkey field must provide a fact about the key, the whole key, and nothing but the key". This should be refined by replacing "the key" by "a key" and treated as a description of BCNF rather than 3NF.

In the previous two examples, a table with overlapping keys had to be split. Sometimes overlapping keys are permitted. Recall the example from Chapter 4 where students are assigned unique positions in subjects, with no ties. This leads to the BCNF table scheme

PlacedAt (<u>StudentNr, subjectCode</u>, position)

The previous normal forms considered only functional dependencies. The next normal form is due to Ronald Fagin (1977) and considers *multivalued dependencies* (MVDs). For a given relation with attributes X, Y, and Z (possibly composite), X *multidetermines* Y (written as $X \twoheadrightarrow Y$) if and only if the *set* of Y values is a function of X only (independent of the value of Z). In this case, Y is said to be multivalued dependent, or multidependent, on X; in such a case Z will also be multidependent on X. A functional dependency is a special case of an MVD, namely, when the set of dependent values is a unit set. An MVD $X \twoheadrightarrow Y$ is trivial if X includes Y, or X and Y together include all the attributes in the relation.

A relation is in **fourth normal form** (4NF) if and only if it is in BCNF and all its nontrivial dependencies are functional (single-valued) dependencies. So a 4NF relation cannot have any nontrivial MVDs that are not FDs. Basically, each nonfunctional MVD requires a separate table for itself.

Consider Table 12.12. It is in BCNF since it is "all-key". The table is not in 4NF since, for example, sport is multidependent (but not functionally dependent) on surname. A similar comment applies to language. These MVDs are depicted as double arrows above the table.

Semantically, the MVDs correspond to two *m:n* elementary fact types: Lecturer plays Sport; Lecturer speaks Language. So the table has redundancy problems. The facts that Halpin plays judo and speaks English are duplicated. To avoid this problem, the table is split into two 4NF tables: *Plays*(<u>surname, sport</u>); *Speaks*(<u>surname, language</u>).

Table 12.12 This table is in BCNF but not 4NF.

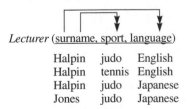

Lecturer (<u>surname, sport, language</u>)

Halpin	judo	English
Halpin	tennis	English
Halpin	judo	Japanese
Jones	judo	Japanese

Of course, this design may also be achieved by Rmapping the correct conceptual schema.

It can be shown that BCNF is equivalent to no redundancy when there are FDs, and 4NF is equivalent to no redundancy when there are FDs and MVDs (Vincent and Srinivasan 1993).

The next normal form is also due to Fagin (1979), and is based on *join dependencies* (JDs). A relation has a join dependency if it can be reconstructed without information loss by taking a join of some of its projections. If one of these projections is the table itself, this is a trivial join dependency.

A table is in **fifth normal form** (5NF) if and only if, for each nontrivial join dependency, each projection includes a key of the original table. A table is in **project-join normal form** (PJNF) just in case each JD is the result of the key constraints. The forms 5NF and PJNF are often treated as equivalent, but some subtle differences can be distinguished to show that PJNF is a stonger notion (Orlowska and Zhang 1992).

As an example of a key-based join dependency, *Employee*(empNr, birthdate, sex) is equivalent to the join of the projections *Emp1*(empNr, birthdate); *Emp2*(empNr, sex). The original table as well as the two smaller ones are all in 5NF. Since a relational schema is in a given normal form if its tables are all in that form, a relational schema that includes just the Emp1 and Emp2 tables is a 5NF schema. This illustrates that 5NF of itself does not guarantee that a schema is minimal with respect to number of tables.

Nontrivial join dependencies that are not key based are rare, so 4NF tables are almost always in 5NF as well. The theory underlying the test for 5NF was included in the projection-join check at CSDP step 4, so we confine ourselves here to a brief discussion. A classic example to discuss the notion is portrayed in Table 12.13. A small sample population is provided to show that the uniqueness constraint is the weakest possible (verify this for yourself).

Conceptually, this ternary fact type may be expressed as Agent sells CarType for Company. The fact types behind the three binary projections may be expressed as Agent sells Cartype; Agent represents Company; Company makes CarType. Assuming the population is significant, any attempt to split this ternary into two binaries will result in information loss. For example, from the facts that Smith is a representative for Foord and Foord makes a four-wheel drive (4WD), it does not follow that Smith sells a 4WD.

However, the population of the ternary (Table 12.13) does equal the join of the three binary projections (confirm this for yourself). So it is safe to split this particular table population into three binary table populations. But since database populations are

Table 12.13 Is this in 5NF?

Sells (agent, cartype, company)

Jones	sedan	Foord
Jones	4WD	Foord
Jones	sedan	Yotsubishi
Smith	sedan	Foord

continually updated, if we are to split the table scheme into three binary table schemes, we need to know that this join dependency applies to all possible populations. In other words, is the sample population significant in this regard? If it is, the following derivation rule applies:

Agent sells CarType for Company **iff**   Agent sells CarType **and**
                                            Agent represents Company **and**
                                            Company makes CarType

The only way to check that this is an actual business rule is to ask the domain expert. Let's suppose that it's *not* a rule. For example, it is now acceptable to delete just the first row of Table 12.13 (check for yourself that this deletion should be rejected if the rule did apply). In this case, the ternary fact type is elementary and should be left as it is. Let us define a table *scheme* (table type) to be in a given normal form if and only if all its possible populations (table instances) are in that form. If the derivation rule does not apply, the Sells table *scheme* is already in 5NF.

Now suppose the derivation rule *does* apply. This rule needs to be enforced, but the key constraint in the ternary fails to do this (e.g., it allows the first row to be deleted). To avoid this problem, the 4NF ternary should be split into three 5NF binaries: *Sells*(agent, carType); *Represents*(agent, company); *Makes*(company, carType). If desired, the original ternary may be defined as a view derived from the join of the new tables.

It has been argued (e.g., by Kent) that when schemes like the ternary in Table 12.13 are elementary, there is a kind of "unavoidable redundancy". For example, the "fact" that Jones sells sedans is repeated on rows 1 and 3. However, such "redundancy" is harmless because it is derived rather than stored. Although the tuple ('Jones', 'sedan') is stored twice, the fact that Jones sells sedans is not. This fact can only be obtained by using the derivation rule Agent sells CarType **iff** Agent sells CarType for Company.

The seven normal forms discussed so far are strictly ordered. Each higher normal form satisfies the lower forms. Recall that "⊂" denotes "is a proper subset of". Let "5NF-rels" denote the set of all possible relations in fifth normal form, and so on. The strict ordering may now be set out thus (in decreasing order of normality):

5NF-rels ⊂ 4NF-rels ⊂ BCNF-rels ⊂ EKNF-rels ⊂ 3NF-rels ⊂ 2NF-rels ⊂ 1NF-rels

Essentially, normalization through to fifth normal form simplifies table updates by ensuring that three kinds of dependencies (FDs, MVDs, and JDs) will automatically be enforced by key constraints (i.e., uniqueness constraints within each table). An FD is a special case of an MVD, which in turn is a special case of a JD. As noted by Fagin, BCNF ensures all FDs are implied by key constraints, 4NF ensures all MVDs are implied by key constraints, and 5NF ensures all JDs are implied by key constraints.

The last normal form we consider is **domain key normal form** (DKNF), which was introduced by Fagin (1981). A table scheme is said to be in DKNF if and only if all its constraints are expressible as domain dependencies or key dependencies. A domain dependency specifies a set of possible values for a given attribute. This basically declares a data type (e.g., varchar(20)) or a value constraint (e.g., {'M', 'F'}) for the attribute. A

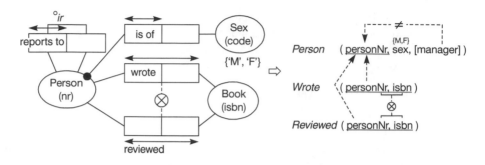

Figure 12.60 The relational schema is not in DKNF.

key dependency is a uniqueness constraint spanning one or more attributes in the table scheme. If all domains are infinite, any DKNF table scheme is also in 5NF.

For a relational database schema to be in DKNF, each of its table schemes should be in DKNF, and there should be either no intertable constraints or only "simple" intertable constraints that are easily enforced, such as inclusion dependencies (subset constraints).

DKNF designs are easy to understand, and their constraints can normally be efficiently enforced by a DBMS. Unfortunately, however, life is not so simple. Many other kinds of constraints often arise in practical applications and need to be enforced even though their inclusion in the relational schema violates DKNF.

As a simple example, Figure 12.60 shows a conceptual schema and its relational mapping. The table scheme Person is not in DKNF because it contains two constraints other than domain and key dependencies. First, the subset constraint from manager to personNr is an intratable inclusion dependency. Second, the "personNr ≠ manager" constraint enforces the irreflexive nature of the reporting association. The overall schema is not in DKNF because its Person scheme is not in DKNF and because of the intertable exclusion constraint (no Person wrote and reviewed the same Book).

Although the relational schema in Figure 12.60 is not in DKNF, each of its table schemes is in 5NF. The additional constraints are simply not included in the definition of 5NF, so they do not violate it. Any valid ORM schema, where each base fact type is elementary, will result in a 5NF relational schema if mapped according to our Rmap procedure.

As this example shows, ORM actually goes beyond 5NF by catering to other kinds of constraints. Although this rich support for expressing and mapping constraints may lead to schemas that violate DKNF, that's actually an advantage rather than a weakness, since such violations are needed to capture the relevant business rules.

It is very common to encounter cases where normalization to 5NF or DKNF fails to fully capture the relevant constraints. A modified version of an awkward but classic example is set out in Table 12.14. In this UoD, lecturers are assigned exactly one subject, and this is the only subject they may teach.

The null value indicates that Bloggs does not teach the assigned subject (e.g., because too few enrolled for it). For each subject they take, students have exactly one

Table 12.14 An unusual and awkward example.

Lecturer	Subject	Student
Halpin	CS113	Brown A
Rose	CS102	Brown A
Nijssen	CS113	Smith J
Rose	CS102	Smith J
Halpin	CS113	Wang J
Bloggs	CS226	?

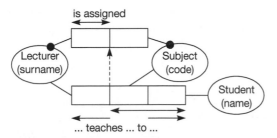

Figure 12.61 Is the ternary fact type elementary?

lecturer. The same subject may have many assigned lecturers. Because of its strange constraint pattern, this example is not easy to verbalize in elementary facts on a first attempt. You are invited to try this before reading on.

An initial conceptual schema based on one verbalization is depicted in Figure 12.61. If this is the global schema, the mandatory role constraints are implied by the pair-subset constraint. More importantly, the uniqueness constraint on the binary combined with the pair-subset constraint has other implications. Can you spot these?

The pair-subset constraint indicates that lecturers may teach only their assigned subjects, but the uniqueness constraint on the binary indicates that each lecturer is assigned at most one subject. Hence, lecturers may teach at most one subject. So there is an FD from the first role of the ternary to the second role. This implies the UC across the first and third roles. Moreover, since there is a third role in the ternary, the fact type now cannot be elementary. This is an example of the general rule set out in Figure 12.62. Two corollaries are included, one of which we will make use of in our example. You may wish to prove these corollaries as an exercise.

If a fact type is elementary, all its FDs are the result of its UCs. If another FD exists, then semantically underlying this FD is another fact type, which is the target of a pair-subset constraint from the original fact type. If this is expressed at the conceptual level, we know the original fact type is not elementary and should remove the relevant role (as in Figure 12.62).

The ternary in Figure 12.62 matches this pattern, but has an additional UC across its last two roles (for each subject, a student has only one lecturer). To preserve this

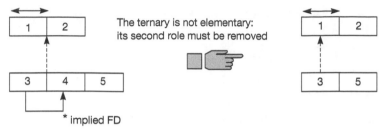

*The ternary is not elementary:
its second role must be removed*

* implied FD

Corollaries:

(1) A UC across roles 4 and 5 maps to an external UC between roles 2 and 5.

(2) A UC across roles 3 and 4 implies a simple UC on role 3 alone.

Figure 12.62   A basic splittability check.

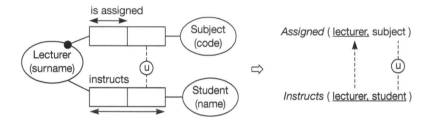

Figure 12.63   The corrected conceptual schema and its relational map.

constraint after removing the role, an external UC must be added between the subject and student roles in the new schema (see Figure 12.63).

The general requirement for this extra move is specified as corollary (1) in Figure 12.62. When the corrected conceptual schema is Rmapped, we obtain two table schemes with two intertable constraints (Figure 12.63).

Suppose that instead of dealing with Table 12.14 conceptually, we try to develop a relational schema for it by applying the normal form theory discussed earlier. We might begin with a single ternary: *Teaches*(lecturer, subject, [student]). Suppose that someone either tells us all the constraints or cleverly constructs a significant population from which the constraints can be deduced. We note that there are two composite "key" constraints over (lecturer, student) and (subject, student). Since student is an optional attribute, neither of these can be used as a primary key, so we know something is wrong (although the normal form theory discussed earlier ignored nulls). Indeed we know the table is not in BCNF since we are given the FD lecturer → subject, and lecturer is not a key.

At this stage we split the table into two: *Assigned*(lecturer, subject); *Instructs* (lecturer, student). These are the same two tables we arrived at by deconceptualization in Figure 12.63. However, the normal form theory discussed in this section tells us nothing about the two intertable constraints. We have to figure these out for ourselves.

Further normal forms could be invented to cater to further constraints, but surely it is better to focus on cleaning up design faults at the conceptual level where humans can more easily utilize their semantic understanding of the UoD.

As discussed in the next section, it is sometimes necessary to denormalize a relational schema in order to achieve acceptable performance. This is a possible option for the current example. Note that the intertable constraints are expensive to enforce, unlike key constraints. For example, enforcing the external uniqueness constraint effectively requires a table join each time a row is inserted into either table. Moreover, queries to list who teaches what to whom need a table join.

Another design is obtained by mapping the original conceptual schema (Figure 12.61). This gives two tables: *Teaches*(lecturer, subject, student); *Assigned*(lecturer, subject). A pair-subset constraint connects the tables; this implies the ternary's other key constraint on (lecturer, student), which may thus be omitted. Although the ternary is denormalized, it is safe since its problematic FD is enforced by the pair-subset constraint and the key constraint in the binary. We may now list who teaches what to whom, without a table join. If this is a focused query for the application, this design might be preferred.

To modify the example somewhat, suppose lecturers must teach the subject assigned to them (so the null value in Table 12.14 cannot occur). Figure 12.61 is changed to make both roles of Lecturer mandatory, with the subset constraint becoming an equality constraint. Figure 12.63 is changed to make both roles of Lecturer mandatory, and the relational subset constraint becomes an equality constraint.

If the normalized, two-table design has poor performance, we might choose a denormalized design with a single table that is their natural join: *Teaches*(lecturer, subject, student). With the subset constraint of Figure 12.61 replace d by an equality constraint, assignment facts can be retrieved by projecting on the first two roles of the ternary, but the uniqueness constraint on the assignment binary still needs to be catered to. In the denormalized ternary, this constraint cannot be enforced as a uniqueness constraint, so a separate constraint is required to enforce the FD lecturer → subject. So long as this additional constraint is enforced (e.g., as a user-defined constraint in SQL), the single-table design is safe. As before, the alternate key constraint is implied and hence omitted.

Advances in relational languages are making it easier to specify extra constraints such as FDs that are not key based; however, the overhead of enforcing such constraints needs to be factored in when choosing the final relational design. In general, we should first try a fully normalized design, using conceptual optimization where relevant to improve it. If performance is still unacceptable, controlled denormalization is an option.

Exercise 12.6

1. The conceptual schema for a given UoD is as shown. Some table schemes designed by novices for parts of this UoD are listed below. Indicate briefly, in terms of normalization theory, why each of these tables is not fully normalized.

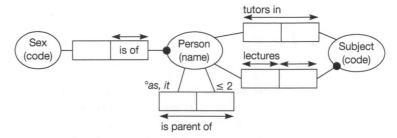

(a) *Parenthood* (<u>parentName</u>, sex, *Child*(childName, sex))
(b) *Teaches* (<u>person, subjectTutored</u>, [subjectLectured])
(c) *ParentOf* (<u>parent, child</u>, sexOfParent, sexOfChild)
(d) *Tutor* (<u>tutorName, subject</u>, [child])
(e) Use Rmap to generate a correct relational schema.

2. (a) The conceptual schema of Question 1 is incomplete with respect to real-world constraints. For example, parents of the same child must differ in sex, but this constraint is not captured. Replace the parent predicate with mother and father predicates, to develop a more complete schema that includes this constraint. (*Hint:* Include subtyping.)
   (b) Rmap your solution to (a).

3. Suppose that while developing a conceptual schema you specify the following fact type: Manager supervises Trainee on Project. Assume that no manager is a trainee, and that all objects are simply identified by name. The following constraint applies: no manager may supervise the same trainee on more than one project.
   (a) Draw this as a ternary fact type, including the constraint.
   (b) As part of the CSDP, you check whether there are any other functional fact types of interest between these object types. You now discover that each manager supervises at most one project. Add this binary fact type to your schema, then add any set-comparison constraint that you feel applies.
   (c) Is the ternary elementary? If not, explain why not, and correct the schema.
   (d) The following business rule is now added: each trainee on a given project has only one supervisor for that project. Add this constraint to your schema.
   (e) Rmap your answer to (d).
   (f) Because of poor performance, this relational schema is regarded as unsatisfactory. Using controlled denormalization, suggest an alternative relational schema.

12.7   Denormalization and Low-Level Optimization

Applying the conceptual optimization procedure followed by the Rmap procedure ensures a redundancy-free relational schema that should be reasonably efficient. To test the performance of this logical schema, it should be implemented as an internal schema on the target DBMS, using a realistic population. At this stage *indexes* should normally be created for all primary and foreign keys, as well as any other columns that play a significant role in focused queries.

For large tables, indexes can dramatically improve performance since they can normally be loaded, in part or whole, into main memory and their entries are sorted into structures that permit fast retrieval (e.g., binary trees). At times, indexes may slow down updates since they must be updated when relevant changes are made to the base tables; but even with updates, indexes can speed up many kinds of constraint checking (e.g., ensuring that primary keys are unique). There are many kinds of indexes (e.g., clustered, nonclustered), and indexing schemes often differ among vendors. Details on indexes for some popular DBMSs can be obtained from the references in the chapter notes.

To speed up certain complex queries, and sometimes to make a query execution possible, *working tables* may be used (e.g., to hold intermediate results, perhaps obtained by joining several tables, which might be reused several times before the base values are updated). These can be temporary tables that are dropped at the end of each session or "permanent temporary" tables that are reinitialized at the start of each session.

Different DBMSs offer other means of tuning the internal schema (e.g., clustering the storage of related data). In addition, since no query optimizer is perfect, the form of the actual query itself can impact (sometimes seriously) on the performance. With some older optimizers, merely changing the order in which tables are listed in a join condition can cause significant changes in the response time.

Sometimes it may help to temporarily deactivate constraint checking (e.g., when performing bulk updates by copying large volumes of prechecked data). Although most database applications can now be developed completely in 4GLs, it may still be necessary to write some of the modules in a 3GL (e.g., C) to speed up critical aspects or to achieve the desired control. For a few specific applications, a relational database system might not be capable of giving the desired performance, and a different kind of DBMS might be needed (e.g., a CAD package might be better implemented in an object-oriented or object-relational DBMS).

Since realistic applications typically require data updates by users to be performed via an external interface (e.g., screen forms) rather than directly on the base tables, it needs to be decided how much of the constraint checking will be done at the base table level and how much at the form level. With client-server networks we need to decide how much work is done at the client end and how much at the server end. With noncentralized database systems, great care is needed in deciding how to replicate data to reduce communication overhead. A proper discussion of these issues is beyond the scope of this book.

If the performance of the system is still unacceptable after the above internal schema optimization has been carried out, it may be necessary to *denormalize* the base relational schema. Typically this entails introducing *controlled redundancy* to reduce the number of table joins required for focused queries. This slows down updates (redundant facts must be kept consistent) and makes the system harder to work with, but it can dramatically reduce response times for queries. Any denormalization decisions should be carefully documented, and appropriate subset or equality constraints must be enforced to control the redundancy, unless the denormalized version is used only for queries, not for updates (e.g., a data warehouse).

As a simple example, consider the following relational subschema, which is extracted from our software retailer example.

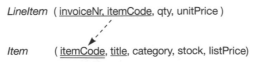

LineItem (<u>invoiceNr, itemCode</u>, qty, unitPrice)

Item   (<u>itemCode</u>, <u>title</u>, category, stock, listPrice)

Suppose we frequently need to list the line items, including item titles, for specified invoices. With the above schema, this requires a join of the two tables. If the tables are very large, accessing the second table simply to get the item title may slow things down too much. To avoid this, we might denormalize by inserting an extra copy of title in the LineItem table. This means the fact type Item has Title is now mapped to both tables. To control this *redundancy between tables,* we add a pair-subset constraint between the tables as shown:

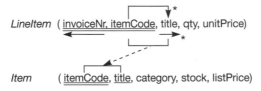

LineItem (<u>invoiceNr, itemCode</u>, title, qty, unitPrice)

Item   (<u>itemCode</u>, <u>title</u>, category, stock, listPrice)

The new LineItem table is denormalized to 1NF, since it includes the functional dependency itemCode → title, and itemCode is only part of its primary key. Although the constraint pattern is more complex, the query may now be performed by accessing just the LineItem table. The asterisked uniqueness constraint and FD are both implied by the other constraints (why?), so they need not be specified. The primary and alternate key constraints are inexpensive, but the pair-subset constraint may be expensive. It is not a foreign key constraint, but in SQL-92 it may be declared as the following assertion:

```
create assertion LineItem_itemCode_title_in_Item
    check (not exists
      (select * from LineItem
       where itemCode not in
         (select itemCode from Item
          where title = LineItem.title)))
```

If assertions are not supported, it may be coded with triggers. The subset constraint needs to be checked whenever items are deleted from or renamed (code or title) in the Item table, or inserted or renamed in the LineItem table. Since items are rarely deleted or renamed, the main overhead for the subset constraint involves validating insertions to the LineItem table. For some applications the additional update overhead may be a price well worth paying to improve the query performance.

The above example denormalized by storing item title facts twice in different tables. Another denormalization technique is to embed facts that functionally depend on a nonkey attribute, hence violating 3NF. For example, the conceptual schema in Figure 12.64(a) by defaults maps to the normalized relational schema in Figure 12.64(b).

The FD from roomNr to phoneNr is efficiently enforced by the primary key constraint in the Room table, but a query to list an employee's phone number requires a join. To speed up this query we could denormalize to 2NF by embedding the phone facts in the Employee table, as shown in Figure 12.64(c).

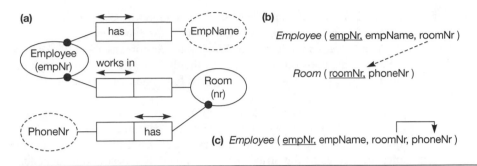

Figure 12.64 (a) A conceptual schema and its (b) normalized and (c) denormalized mapping.

Since many employees may share the same room, this denormalized schema is open to *redundancy within a table*. For example, if employees 1 and 2 share room 200, which has phoneNr 4251234567, then the fact that room 200 has this phone number is stored twice. To control this redundancy, we need to enforce the FD roomNr → phoneNr. Since this is no longer enforced by a key constraint, we need to specify it separately. In SQL-92 the following assertion may be used:

```
create assertion eachRoomHasAtMostOnePhoneNr
  check( not exists
    (select roomNr from Employee
     group by roomNr
     having count(distinct phoneNr) > 1))
```

If assertions are not supported (which is likely), the embedded FD can be enforced by insert and update triggers on the Employee table.

As you can see from these examples, denormalization can speed up queries but may slow down updates. So there is a trade-off in performance. In general, don't denormalize unless it is the only way to obtain the desired performance. If you do decide to denormalize, and your database will be used for updates, then make sure you control the denormalization by coding the relevant constraints.

Real-world applications sometimes use very poor database designs. In particular it is not uncommon for novice modelers to introduce uncontrolled redundancy (e.g., to ignore the pair-subset constraint and embedded FD in the above denormalized schemas). The next section discusses a reengineering example that illustrates, among other things, how such poor designs can be improved by applying conceptual modeling techniques.

If you are using an object-relational or object-oriented DBMS, you have the option of denormalizing to NF^2 by using complex types. For example, SQL:1999 allows array types and row types to be used as columns that may themselves be nested as components of array or row structures used for outer columns. Recall the Voter table example in Section 11.12. SQL:200n will probably add collections other than arrays (e.g., sets and multisets), and some DBMSs already support these. This gives you a far greater range of mapping choices, which need to be used judiciously.

As a simple example, Figure 12.65(a) models details about books in two normalized tables, using a position column to explicitly store each author's position in the book's author list. Up to 10 authors are allowed for a book, and some or all of these might not be recorded.

By using an array-valued column for the author list, the denormalized table scheme in Figure 12.65(b) allows all the details to be captured in one table. Although this solution might seem to be preferable, extra care is needed to enforce constraints. For example, the entries in the array must be unique. The best choice depends on the query/ update pattern for the application. For example, the normalized solution makes it easier to list all the books of a given author.

Considerable care is required in the use of collection types within table design, especially in constraint enforcement. I'll have a few more words to say about this in the next chapter. Given the current lack of a uniform approach to such object-relational extensions by commercial DBMSs, I'll say no more about object-relational mapping here. Some further discussion on this topic can be found in Chapter 12 of Muller (1999).

Besides denormalization, a technique known as *fragmentation* is commonly used to improve performance on very large tables. For example, a PhoneBook table for all of the United States would contain hundreds of millions of rows. To speed things up, we can partition this table into 50 smaller tables, one for each state (if needed, we could partition further into smaller regions). Each of these smaller tables has the same structure, with the name of the table providing the state information. If this process sounds familiar, it should be. It's simply an example of predicate specialization, as discussed early in the chapter. At any rate, if you want to query or update phone details about one state only, you can do this on the table for that state. This gives much better performance than trying to work with a table for the whole country.

If you need to work with multiple states at a time, you can create a view for it based on a union of the smaller tables. Some DBMSs enable good performance with such views. For example, if you include a column for the statecode in each table, and a check constraint to ensure the right statecode, SQL Server can use this information in the union view to consider only the base tables for the states mentioned in your query. For a good discussion of this technique, based on partitioning trades by month, see Seidman (2000).

Physical optimization techniques vary considerably among DBMSs. For example, Oracle supports *materialized views,* while Microsoft SQL Server supports *indexed*

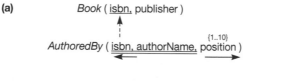

Figure 12.65 Modeling author lists with (a) normalized tables or (b) an NF² table.

views (Delaney 2000). Both of these techniques effectively compute base table joins before query time, so they can dramatically improve performance. Different systems support different kinds of indexing schemes (e.g., clustered, hash table), and Microsoft SQL Server even provides a tuning wizard to make the best index selection based on a significant sample of transactions. Detailed suggestions on physical optimization should be available in the online documentation for your specific DBMS.

Exercise 12.7

1. The following relational schema is used to store details about students and their results. A focused query is "List the studentNr and name of all students who enrolled in CS114". As there are over 50,000 students, and on average each enrolled in over 20 subjects, the tables are large. Denormalize the schema to improve the performance of the query, and discuss any possible disadvantages of this action.

   Student (<u>studentNr</u>, studentName, degree)

   Result (<u>studentNr, subjectCode</u>, [rating])

2. This question is based on an example from a colleague, Dr. Bob Colomb. A simpler version of the problem was discussed by Zaniolo in motivating EKNF and BCNF. As this problem involves some advanced ORM concepts, it should be considered a challenge.

   The application deals with a directory for making international direct-dial telephone calls. Suppose the following table scheme is used to store the data:

   PlaceCodes (<u>countryName, stateName, cityName</u>, <u>countryCode, areaCode</u>)

   The first key denotes the city (e.g., Australia, Queensland, Brisbane) and the second key gives the dial codes to phone that city (e.g., 61, 7). From a normalization point of view, the table has problems because there are some FDs that are not key based, in particular, countryName → countryCode. It is not the case, however, that countryCode → countryName (e.g., both Canada and the United States have the country code 1). Note also that three values are needed to identify a city (e.g., different countries could have states and cities with the same simple names).

   (a) Schematize this UoD, including derivation. Note that external uniqueness constraints may be declared across any join path. If any subset constraints apply (possibly from a join), specify them. Ensure that the fact types are all elementary.

   (b) Rmap your solution.

   (c) Discuss whether a denormalized relational schema may be more appropriate.

   (d) If you've gotten this far, take a break (fortunately, you don't run into problems like this very often!).

12.8   Reengineering

While conceptual modeling provides the best approach to developing new applications, it can also be used to remodel existing systems to better meet the application requirements. There are three main reasons for replacing or revising (perhaps drastically) an existing information system.

First, the current system might provide an *incorrect* model of the UoD, either by being *inaccurate* (wrong information) or *incomplete* (missing information). Such wrong or missing fact types, constraints, and derivation rules might arise because of bad modeling in the first place. For example, the schema might assert that planets orbit moons, allow people to have more than one birth date, or derive ages from a simple formula that ignores the extra day in leap years. Such errors can also arise because the model has not kept pace with changes in the UoD. For example, a system for recording academic results based on a seven-point numeric rating scale becomes outdated if the rating scheme is replaced by a five-point letter grade.

Second, the existing system might be *inefficient*. It might be too slow (e.g., too many table joins needed in queries), too large (e.g., too many null values gobbling up space), or difficult to evolve (e.g., outdated rules hard-wired into program code rather than modeled as data in tables). Perhaps the hardware platform itself is outmoded and needs to be replaced, or the external interface is awkward for users.

Finally the existing system might be *unclear.* This also makes it hard to maintain or evolve. Many legacy systems in place today were designed at the logical, or even internal, level and have no conceptual schema formulated for them. They may have been developed completely in 3GLs, with no underlying design method, have little or poor documentation, and be riddled with misleading or cryptic identifiers.

Often a combination of the three reasons leads to an information system that needs to be *reengineered,* or restructured, in order for its owner (e.g., a company) to remain competitive in today's marketplace. The company might even reengineer the very way it does business. Although the need for restructuring has sometimes been used as an excuse for retrenching, a creative response to this need can lead to major enhancements in the quality and efficiency of the business and its supporting information systems. Here we consider only the problem of reengineering a database system. This process may be divided into four stages, as shown in Figure 12.66.

The first stage, *conceptualization,* involves developing an initial conceptual schema of the application from the original database. This can be done simply by applying the

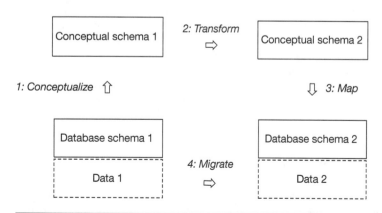

Figure 12.66 Four steps in reengineering a database.

CSDP to the database, treating it as a set of output reports. Most of the verbalization stage is usually straightforward since tables provide the easiest kind of output report to interpret. Usually at least an incomplete logical schema for the database is also available, and constraints in this schema (e.g., primary and foreign key constraints) can be used to help derive some of the constraints in a fairly automatic fashion.

If the database is not relational, some of the intertable connections may need to be verbalized as fact types. Often, additional constraints that have not been specified will be identified with the assistance of the domain expert.

The second stage, *transformation,* involves modifying the original conceptual schema to cater to changes in the UoD not modeled in the original database, and/or optimizing the conceptual schema as discussed in the previous sections.

The third stage, *mapping,* takes us down to the logical schema. If a relational database system is to be used, we may use the Rmap procedure for this.

The fourth stage, *data migration,* copies the facts stored in the original database to the new database. This involves conversion as well as copying since some of the fact types involved will now be grouped into different table structures (recall the patient data example in Section 12.1).

Stage 1 of this four-step process is sometimes called *reverse-engineering,* and stages 2 and 3 are sometimes collectively called *forward-engineering.* Much of the reengineering process can be automated, especially if a very detailed database schema is provided at stage 1. However, human interaction is also required to ensure a complete and elegant result. While our discussion is limited to the logical and conceptual levels, reengineering an application involves work at the external and internal levels as well.

The four basic reengineering stages are now illustrated with a worked example. As the main input to the process, Figure 12.67 shows a relational schema as well as two rows of data for each table (shown as tuples on the right to save space). Suppose this design is used to record details about a one-day computer conference, but its performance is poor mainly because of the number of table joins required for common queries.

Moreover, application developers find parts of the schema awkward or even unsafe. For example, the budget column in the Committee table applies to the committee as a whole, not to a particular chairperson of that committee (each committee has at most two chairpersons). It is suspected that this is not the only unnormalized feature of the tables.

Because of your expertise in conceptual modeling, you are hired to provide a conceptual model of the application, so that a clear and complete picture of the application is available. Moreover, you are asked to provide a new relational design that is both normalized and efficient, if this is possible.

In practice, reengineering usually requires dialogue with the domain expert to clarify the UoD, and especially to identify missing constraints. To help you try the reverse-engineering phase yourself, uniqueness, value, exclusion, and frequency constraints are depicted. However, other constraints are omitted (e.g., subset constraints and nonimplied functional dependencies due to denormalization). Some missing constraints are "obvious", and others may be identified from the brief description that follows.

Relational schema (some constraints missing)   **Sample data** (not significant)

	{Prog,Org}	
Committee	(<u>cteeCode</u>, chairPerson, [budget]) ≤ 2	('Prog', 'Adams, Prof. A.B.',?) ('Org', 'Bloggs, Dr F.', 10000)
Person	(<u>personName</u>, affiliation, [email])	('Adams, Prof. A.B.', 'MIT',?) ('Pi, Dr Q.T.', 'UQ','pi@uq.au')
Rated	{1..10} (<u>referee</u>, <u>paperNr</u>, rating)	('Adams, Prof. A.B.', 43,8) ('Pi, Dr Q.T.', 5,4)
Referees	(<u>personName</u>, <u>paperNr</u>)	('Adams, Prof. A.B.', 43) ('Knot, Prof. I.M.', 43)
	⊗	
Authored	(<u>personName</u>, <u>paperNr</u>, paperTitle)	('Sea, Ms A.B.', 5, 'EER models') ('Pi, Dr Q.T.', 43, 'ORM dialects')
Presents	(<u>author</u>, <u>paperNr</u>)	('Pi, Dr Q.T.', 43) ('Knot, Dr I.M.', 61)
Paper	{undec, accept, reject} (<u>paperNr</u>, paperTitle, status)	(5, 'EER models', 'undec') (43, 'ORM dialects', 'accept')
AcceptedPaper	(<u>paperNr</u>, [pageLength])	(43, 14) (75, ?)
AcPaperDiags	{tbl, fig} (<u>paperNr</u>, <u>diagramKind</u>, qty) 2	(43, 'tbl', 3) (43, 'fig', 5)
PaperSlot	{A,B} (<u>slotNr</u>, <u>stream</u>, <u>hr</u>, [bldgNr, roomNr], [paperNr])	(1, 'A', 9, 69, '110', 43) (2, 'B', 9, 50, '110', ?)
Room	{lab,lec,office} (<u>bldgNr</u>, <u>roomNr</u>, roomType, area)	(69, '110', 'lec', 100) (50, '110', 'lab', 120)
LabOrLecRm	(<u>bldgNr</u>, <u>roomNr</u>, [nrPCs], [nrSeats])	(69, '110' ,?, 350) (50, '110' ,40, ?)

Figure 12.67 The original database schema and some sample data.

As well, the sample rows of data enable you to apply CSDP step 1. These rows do not provide a significant, or even a legal, population (e.g., if the database were comprised of only these data, various subset constraints between the tables would be violated).

Abbreviated codes have the following meanings: Prog = Programming; Org = Organizing; undec = undecided; tab = table; fig = figure; lec = lecture; lab = laboratory. Authors submit papers that are then sent to referees to be rated. The method for determining which papers are accepted is not modeled here. Various statistics (number of pages, tables, and figures) may be kept about accepted papers, partly to help with publication of the conference proceedings. If statistics are kept for a paper, all three numbers must be recorded.

An accepted paper may be presented by one or more of its authors at the conference. Which authors present the paper might be unknown until some time after the paper is accepted.

The conference program includes slots to which accepted papers are eventually allocated. Each slot is of one-hour duration. Time is measured in military hours (e.g., 14 = 2 p.m.). To allow more papers on the same day, two streams (A and B) may be run in parallel (so two paper slots may have the same time).

A room directory is used to help assign slots to rooms; room area is in square meters. Only lecture rooms or laboratories may be used for paper presentations. The number of seats is recorded just for lecture rooms, and the number of PCs is recorded just for laboratories.

Before peeking at the solution provided, try to provide a conceptual schema for this application. Include all constraints (including those missing from the original relational schema). In performing this conceptualization, it will become apparent that some of the tables have redundancy problems. Which tables are these?

By now you should have completed your own reverse-engineering. Compare your solution with the one provided in Figure 12.68. Give yourself a pat on the back if you got all the constraints. It should be clear that the table grouping differs from what Rmap would generate if applied to the conceptual schema. To begin with, the two Committee fact types are wrongly grouped into the same table, even though one of them is nonfunctional.

As a result, the original Committee table is open to redundancy problems with facts of the type Committee has budget of MoneyAmt. Similarly, the Authored table exhibits redundancy problems by wrongly including facts of the type Paper has PaperTitle. So the original designer made a mess of things by denormalizing the relational schema in an uncontrolled way.

Although the conceptual schema looks fairly complicated, the conceptualization has actually clarified the UoD. For example, the semantics conveyed by the PaperSlot table are much easier to understand on the conceptual schema. Moreover, now that the detailed semantics are displayed graphically, we are in a better position to explore optimization possibilities in a controlled manner.

As the second phase of the reengineering, use the conceptual optimization procedure discussed in the previous section to transform the conceptual schema into one that Rmaps to a more efficient relational schema.

Compare your solution with that provided in Figure 12.69. The specialization of the chairperson and diagram predicates into functional binaries is straightforward (though care is needed to preserve all the constraints). In nesting the referee and author predicates, we could have gone further by uniting these exclusive but compatible predicates. However, although this additional move would lead to one less table, nesting these exclusive predicates would detract from the readability of the schema and lead to awkward constraint patterns.

Indeed, even the nesting in Figure 12.69 leads to awkward verbalization. The original flattening into four predicates seems to be more natural than the two nestings.

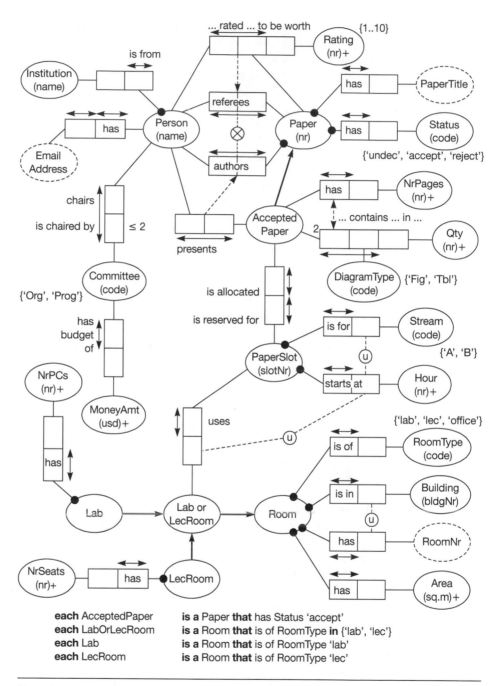

Figure 12.68 The conceptual schema resulting from reverse-engineering.

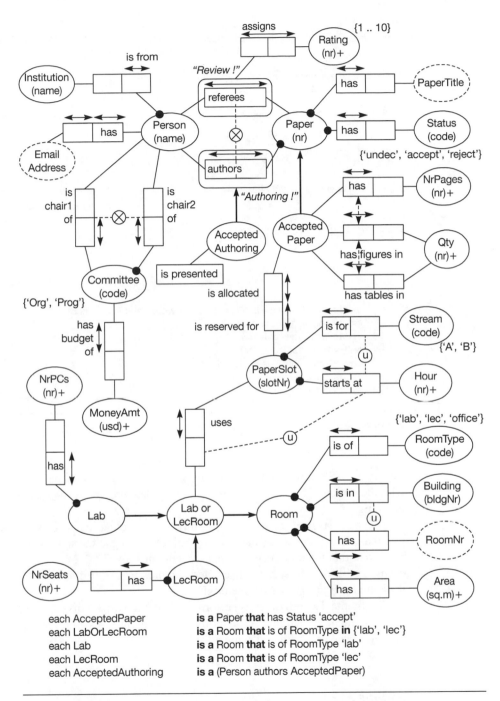

each AcceptedPaper   **is a** Paper **that** has Status 'accept'
each LabOrLecRoom   **is a** Room **that** is of RoomType **in** {'lab', 'lec'}
each Lab   **is a** Room **that** is of RoomType 'lab'
each LecRoom   **is a** Room **that** is of RoomType 'lec'
each AcceptedAuthoring   **is a** (Person authors AcceptedPaper)

Figure 12.69 The optimized conceptual schema.

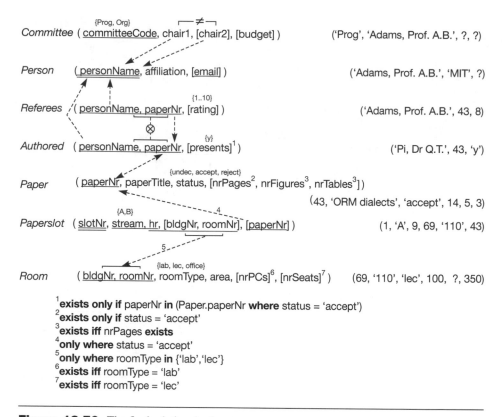

Figure 12.70 The final relational schema.

Ideally a CASE tool would allow the modeler to choose the flattened display for clarity, with the option of including the nesting as a hidden, preprocessing stage to the standard mapping.

The next stage is to map the optimized conceptual schema to a new relational schema. As an exercise, try this yourself before looking at the solution in Figure 12.70.

Notice that the final relational schema contains just 7 tables (compared with the 12 original tables), is fully normalized, and captures all the original constraints as well as those that were missing from the original.

Finally the data migration is performed. The main aspect of this conversion involves defining the new relation types in terms of the original ones. Once this is done, the data migration can be performed automatically. Figure 12.70 displays one row of converted data for each of the new tables.

Exercise 12.8

1. The following relational schema was designed to record details about academics and subjects, but its performance is poor, mainly because many joins are needed for common queries. Also, application developers find the Academic table and its qualified constraint to be

awkward to think about. This constraint says that on each row of the Academic table there is exactly one non-null value in the last three columns. The column "dept_where_lec" means the department (if any) where that academic is a lecturer, "dept_where_sen_lec" means the department (if any) where that academic is a senior lecturer, and "dept_where_prof" means the department (if any) where that academic is a professor.

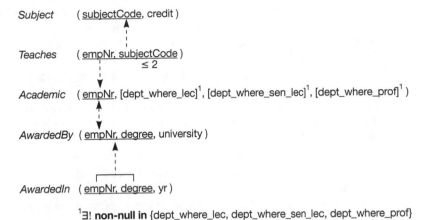

$^1\exists!$ **non-null in** {dept_where_lec, dept_where_sen_lec, dept_where_prof}

Here is one sample row from each table ("?" denotes a null value):

Subject: ('CS115', 8)
Teaches: (30572, 'CS115')
Academic: (30572, ?, 'Computer Science', ?)
AwardedBy: (30572, 'PhD', 'UQ')
AwardedIn: (30572, 'PhD', 1990)

Reengineer the model to improve its performance and clarity, using the following steps.
(a) Reverse-engineer the relational schema to an ORM schema. Include all constraints.
(b) Optimize the conceptual schema to prepare it for relational mapping.
(c) Forward-engineer your new conceptual schema by mapping it to a relational schema. Include all constraints.
(d) Populate the new relational schema with the sample data provided.

12.9   Summary

Conceptual schemas are *equivalent* iff they model the same UoD. Various *schema transformations* may be performed to reshape a conceptual schema into one that is either equivalent or an acceptable alternative. *Predicate specialization* fragments a predicate into two or more special cases, typically by *absorbing* an enumerated object type into it. For example, the association Person is of Sex {'M','F'} may be specialized into Person is male and Person is female by absorbing Sex.

The inverse transformation, *predicate generalization,* typically involves *extracting* an enumerated object type from a predicate. Predicate specialization/generalization (PSG) may also be performed by considering the *n* cases of a role with a frequency constraint of *n* or $1 - n$. For example, the association Person is a parent of Person with a frequency constraint of 2 on its last role may be specialized into Person is parent1 of Person and Person is parent2 of Person.

Nested object types may be interchanged with *coreferenced* object types, using the nest/coreference transformation (N/CR). Either representation may be replaced by *flattening* into one or more fact types. For example, consider the nesting (Student enrolled in Subject) results in Rating. If results are mandatory, this may be flattened into the ternary Student for Subject scored Rating. If results are optional, the flattened approach requires an extra binary (Student enrolled in Subject) targeted by a pair-subset constraint from the ternary.

The *overlap algorithm* indicates how nesting may be performed when compatible subpredicates exist, depending on the constraint between them (subset, equality, exclusion, and so on). See Figure 12.37. Various other schema transformations exist. Sometimes a transformation converts a graphical constraint to a textual constraint (or vice versa).

Although nested and coreferenced approaches have the same relational map, many other cases of equivalent conceptual schemas result in different relational schemas when subjected to the standard Rmap procedure. The process of transforming a conceptual schema into another that results in a more efficient relational map is called *conceptual schema optimization*.

Many optimization moves aim to reduce the number of relational tables, typically by specializing nonfunctional predicates into functional ones that can be grouped into the same table as another functional fact type, or by using nesting (or coreferencing) to unify compatible composite keys. This is particularly useful in reducing the number of table joins required for focused queries. Predicate specialization is sometimes used to enable comparisons between rows of the same table to be replaced by comparisons between columns on the same row, thus eliminating the need for a self-join to perform the query.

The Rmapping of a correctly designed conceptual schema automatically results in a safe, redundancy-free, relational schema where the number of tables has been reduced by grouping together functional fact types with the same key. In contrast to this deconceptualization approach, *normalization* provides a set of rules for achieving reasonable table designs by catering to low-level dependencies between attributes.

Normalization by *synthesis* inputs a set of attributes and some basic dependencies, and groups the attributes into tables, with the aim of minimizing the number of tables required to satisfy these dependencies. Normalization by *decomposition* applies rules to split a poorly designed table into two or more tables in an effort to ensure that some basic dependencies are implied by the table key constraints.

This decomposition approach recognizes a number of *normal forms*. A table is in *1NF* (first normal form) if it has a fixed number of columns, all of whose values are atomic. A nonkey attribute is neither a key nor a part of a key. In a *2NF* table, every nonkey attribute is functionally dependent on a whole key. In a *3NF* table there is no FD between nonkey attributes.

An FD $X \rightarrow Y$ is trivial if X contains Y, and full if the FD requires all of X, not just part of it. An elementary FD is full and nontrivial. An elementary key has an elementary FD to some other attribute. In an *EKNF* (elementary key NF) table, each elementary FD (if any) comes from a whole key or ends inside an elementary key. In a *BCNF* (Boyce-Codd NF) table, each elementary FD begins at a whole key.

A *multivalued dependency* (MVD) $X \twoheadrightarrow Y$ exists if the set of Y values in the table depends only on X. An MVD $X \twoheadrightarrow Y$ is trivial if X includes Y, or X and Y together include all the attributes in the table. A *4NF* table is a BCNF table where all its nontrivial dependencies are FDs. So each nonfunctional MVD requires a separate table for itself.

A table has a *join dependency* (JD) if it is equivalent to the join of some of its projections. If one of these projections is the table itself, the JD is trivial. A table is in *5NF* if, for each nontrivial JD, each projection includes a key of the original table.

These seven normal forms may be listed in increasing order of normality: 1NF, 2NF, 3NF, EKNF, BCNF, 4NF, 5NF. Higher-level forms satisfy all the lower forms. The 5NF form is often called "PJNF" (project-join NF) though some subtle differences exist between these notions.

If a fact type is elementary, all its FDs are the result of its UCs. If another FD exists, behind it is another fact type targeted by a tuple-subset constraint from the original fact type, which then requires role removal (see Figure 12.62).

A table is in *DKNF* (domain key normal form) if its only constraints are domain constraints and key constraints. A relational schema is in DKNF if all its tables are in DKNF and intertable constraints are either absent or simple (e.g., inclusion dependencies, which are typically foreign key constraints). In practice, more complex constraints often exist in the UoD being modeled, so DKNF is often inadequate for complete models. In general, normalization ignores various constraints that we have considered at both conceptual and relational levels.

Once conceptual optimization and mapping has been completed, the *internal schema should be tuned* (e.g., by adding indexes or working tables). Various choices are also made as to the best place to enforce constraints (e.g., at the base table level or the form level). If performance is still poor, it may be necessary to *denormalize* some of the base tables, via *controlled redundancy* to reduce the need for joins.

If an existing database application is unsatisfactory, it may be necessary to *reengineer* it. This remodeling may involve four main steps: conceptualize (or reverse-engineer) the existing database schema to a conceptual schema; optimize this by transformation; map it to the improved database schema; and migrate the original data in order to populate the new database.

Chapter Notes

Schema equivalence has been studied within the relational model (e.g., Kobayashi 1986, 1990), the ER model (e.g., D'Atri and Sacca 1984), EER models (e.g., Batini et al. 1992), and UML (e.g., Blaha and Premerlani 1998). To keep our treatment intuitive, some technical issues have been glossed over. More formal treatments of schema transformation in ORM may be found in Halpin (1989b, 1991b) and Halpin and Proper (1995a). For formal proofs of some conceptual schema equivalences, see Halpin (1989b).

Most work on schema optimization focuses on subconceptual levels. Date (2000) provides clear discussion of various optimization aspects at the relational level. For an approach to schema optimization that evaluates fitness functions on randomly generated, equivalent internal schemas, see van Bommel and van der Weide (1992).

A simple introduction to normalization is provided by Kent (1983). Classic papers include Codd (1970), Fagin (1977, 1979, 1981), Rissanen (1977), and Zaniolo (1982). In Fagin's original DKNF paper (Fagin 1981), the term "key" is used in the sense of "superkey", so a UC may be implied by a smaller UC within it. Fagin uses the terms "relation schema" and "database schema" for what we call a "table scheme" and "relational schema", respectively.

A general study of join dependencies (including functional and multivalued dependencies) is provided by Aho et al. (1979). For an early paper on deductive normal forms, see Thalheim (1984). For a very thorough analysis of normal forms, see Vincent (1994). An in-depth, formal treatment of normal forms and their relationship to ER modeling is given by Thalheim (1994). Chapters 11–12 of Date (2000) cover the main aspects of normalization and provide extensive references to the relevant literature.

13

Other Modeling Aspects and Trends

659

13.1   Introduction

Section 2.4 included an overview of the information systems life cycle. So far, we've focused on the stages of this cycle that deal with the conceptual and logical design of the data. We've seen how to perform conceptual data modeling using ORM, ER, or UML, and applied the Rmap algorithm to map a conceptual schema to a relational database schema. We've discussed how to query a relational schema using SQL, and applied conceptual schema transformations and lower-level optimizations to improve the efficiency of the implemented design.

This chapter discusses other aspects and recent trends related to modeling and querying information systems. We'll be covering a lot of ground, so the treatment of each topic is necessarily brief. You can use the references in the chapter notes to dive deeper into the areas examined.

Section 13.2 provides a brief introduction to data warehousing and online analytical processing. Section 13.3 discusses some very high level languages for querying information systems. Section 13.4 outlines some ways of performing schema abstraction, enabling the modeler to focus on various aspects of a schema by hiding other details. Section 13.5 presents an overview of process modeling and external schema design. Often, the design of external interfaces (e.g., screen forms) can be viewed in terms of operations on the major object types abstracted from the conceptual data model.

Section 13.6 examines the claim that relational databases should be replaced by object-oriented databases or other kinds of databases. It also mentions some other issues and recent trends, such as XML. Section 13.7 provides an introduction to metamodeling, in which conceptual schemas themselves may be treated as application models for which a conceptual metaschema is required. Section 13.8 furnishes a summary and additional notes, to complete this final chapter.

13.2   Data Warehousing and OLAP

Most commercial information systems are built to support heavy volumes of transactions by many users on a daily basis. Examples include banking, insurance, and order-processing systems. These *online transaction processing* (OLTP) systems typically require quick throughput for their largely predefined range of transactions, especially update transactions. To improve performance, historical data is often archived once it reaches a certain age, reducing the size of the data sets used for daily operations. A single organization may have several OLTP systems (e.g., purchasing, sales, inventory, customer records), possibly implemented using different kinds of DBMSs or other software applications, and the coupling between such systems may be weak or even nonexistent.

Over time, businesses became aware that the collective information contained in their various systems had great potential for analyzing market trends and improving their business processes. However, their OLTP systems were unsuitable for executives to perform this task, given the poor performance and complex interface for ad hoc analysis queries (e.g., aggregated multitable joins and nested correlated subqueries).

Moreover, insufficient integration or history made some queries simply impossible. Partly to address the problem of integrating data from prerelational systems for analysis purposes, IBM proposed the notion of an "information warehouse". Although performance problems delayed acceptance of this idea for some years, a later proposal for a "data warehouse" by Bill Inmon (1993) was enthusiastically embraced by the business community, and nowadays most large companies already have, or are building, a data warehouse.

A *data warehouse* is an enterprisewide, integrated, historical database of information extracted from individual data sources for the purpose of supporting analysis of the business by management. During analysis it is read-only. Since the patterns and trends sought from the analysis tend to evolve slowly, and some imprecision is acceptable, updates are performed in bulk according to an agreed schedule (e.g., weekly).

The construction of a data warehouse for a large enterprise can be a lengthy task. To exploit the benefits as soon as possible, the data warehouse is often built iteratively, one subject area at a time. As subject areas are added to the data warehouse, they may be used to load data marts. A *data mart* is a smaller "departmental warehouse" focused on one subject area, often containing more summarized and less detailed data than the data warehouse. For end users who perform their analysis within one subject area, a data mart provides a simpler model adapted to their needs, and the smaller data volume often leads to better performance. This overall approach is diagrammed in Figure 13.1.

Many different approaches to data warehousing exist. Sometimes, data marts are built first and used to incrementally construct the data warehouse. However, if an analytical query may span multiple subject areas, it is critical that an overall enterprise architecture be in place to make the appropriate connections.

It has been argued that the data warehouse should be implemented as a fully normalized relational model, based directly on the enterprise data model, with no summary data, postponing any denormalization and aggregation to the data marts loaded from

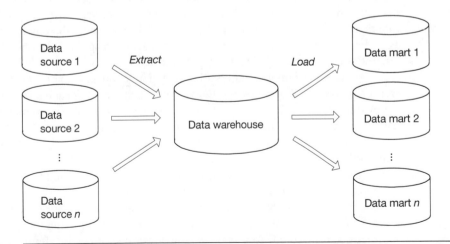

Figure 13.1 Data is extracted into the data warehouse, then loaded into data marts.

the warehouse (e.g., Moody and Kortink 2000). Current practice, however, usually does incorporate denormalized and summarized data in the data warehouse (Silverston et al. 1997).

Before extracting data to the data warehouse, the business analysis needs should be determined and the relevant data sources identified. The data sources may include operational databases as well as spreadsheets and legacy systems. Any details in the data sources irrelevant to the analysis needs should be removed. For example, the phone number and street address of a store are probably not of interest, but its city probably is. The remaining data now needs to be transformed to remove errors (applying integrity rules). For example, a sexcode field with lots of 'F' and 'M' entries might include a few instances of 'D', 'G', 'J', or 'N'. Assuming these are typographical errors, can you make a good guess as to the intended letter? (*Hint:* Look at the keyboard.)

We must also ensure that all facts of the same type are represented in the same way. As a trivial example, a customer's birth date might be recorded as a character string in a 'DOB' field in one source, and elsewhere in a 'birth date' column based on a date data type. Once the data is "cleansed", it is transformed into a uniform representation in the data warehouse (typically a relational database).

To facilitate the analysis of historical trends, appropriate temporal data should be included, at the desired granularity (e.g., daily, weekly, or monthly). For example, suppose an operational data source stores the fact type Employee manages Store. Over time, a store may have different managers. To retain history of these changes, when store management facts are loaded into the data warehouse, the load date may be inserted into the key, to populate the historical fact type Employee on Date managed Store. Temporal modeling in general is an interesting topic, but a full treatment of it is beyond the scope of this book.

To improve query performance, data marts (and usually the data warehouse) often contain derived data and denormalized structures. As a simple example of derived data, suppose an operational source stores the fact type Customer was born on Date. For demographical analysis, we may be interested in how product preferences are influenced by the age of customers. In this case it may be more appropriate in a data mart to store the age, or even just the age group, of the customer rather than their birth date, using a fact type such as Customer on Date belonged to AgeGroup. The snapshot dates are inserted when the fact type is incrementally updated.

A more typical example incorporating both derivation and denormalization is a data mart for analyzing sales trends. An ORM conceptual model of such a mart (simplified) is shown in Figure 13.2. In this UoD, the company makes sales from many stores, located in various cities within the same country (e.g., the USA).

A city is identified by combining its name and state (e.g., Portland, Oregon, differs from Portland, Maine). States are grouped into regions (e.g., Oregon and Washington belong to the Northwest region). Items sold have a unique code and title, and belong to a category (e.g., Developer Tools). A line item is identified by its line number on a given invoice, and records the sale of an item, as well as the quantity and unit price for that item. The line total for each line item is derived by multiplying the quantity by the unit price and then stored. To support sales analysis over time, the month number, quarter number, and year for each date is derived and stored. Although calendar years are used here, we could use fiscal years instead or as well.

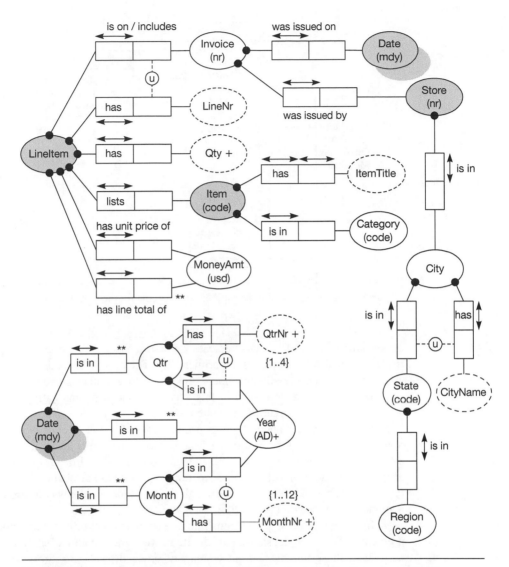

Figure 13.2 A conceptual schema for the Sales data mart (derivation rules omitted).

In Figure 13.2, fact types that are derived and stored are marked "**", but for simplicity the derivation rules are omitted. Using the default Rmap algorithm, this conceptual schema would map to the following six table schemes: *LineItem*(invoiceNr, lineNr, itemCode, qty, unitPrice, lineTotal); *Invoice*(invoiceNr, saleDate, storeNr); *Item*(itemCode, itemTitle, category); *Store*(storeNr, stateCode, cityName); *StateLocation*(stateCode, region); *TimeDimension*(saleDate, saleYear, QtrNr, MonthNr).

However, to improve query performance it is decided to denormalize the relational schema to four table schemes, as shown in Figure 13.3. The Item and TimeDimension tables are normalized, but the Sale and Store tables are not. The Sale table is

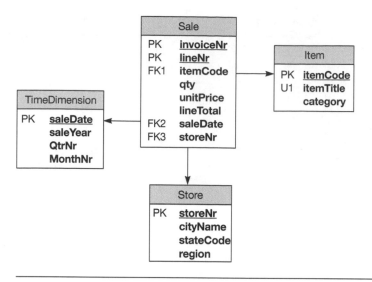

Figure 13.3 A denormalized, relational star schema for the model in Figure 13.2.

denormalized to 1NF, since saleDate and storeNr are functionally dependent on invoiceNr, which is just part of the primary key. The Store table is denormalized to 2NF since region is functionally dependent on stateCode, a nonkey attribute.

The decision to denormalize in this way is indicated by annotating the conceptual schema, as shown in Figure 13.2. Here the *key object types* are *shaded*. An object type is a key object type if and only if its primary identification scheme is used as the primary key of a table. Graphically, each key object type forms the root of a tree, where each node is an object type and each edge is a functional (*n:*1 or 1:1) predicate. For example, from the Store object type we run down functional chains to the leaf object types CityName and Region, gathering all the fact types on the way to group them into a single table based on the identifier for Store.

A functional chain stops if it runs into a key object type (or a leaf or a nonfunctional predicate). For example, starting at LineItem, we gather up all its functional fact types, as well as those for Invoice, but we cannot proceed past Date, Store, or Item, since these are key object types. This leads to the Sale table in Figure 13.3.

The denormalized Sale and Star tables contain embedded functional dependencies (e.g., stateCode → region), but there is no need to enforce these because they have already been enforced in the operational tables from which the data mart is derived. Since the operational tables are used for base updates, and not the data mart, it is acceptable to denormalize the data mart in this way. Reducing the number of tables eliminates the need for many joins, leading to faster queries.

The schema in Figure 13.3 is composed of a central table (Sale) linked by foreign key connections to outer tables (Item, Store, and TimeDimension). This is called a *star schema,* since the central table may be viewed as the center of a star pattern, with its outer tables becoming "points of the star". In data warehousing terminology, the *central table* is called a *fact table* and the outer tables are *dimension tables*. Since all tables contain facts, the term "fact table" is rather inappropriate here. Moreover, ORM uses the term "fact table" to mean an elementary fact table. To avoid confusion, I'll use the more descriptive "central table" instead of the more popular "fact table" in this context.

Some approaches require the primary key of the central table to include all the keys of its dimension tables. This would require the (invoiceNr, lineNr) key of the Sale table in Figure 13.3 to be expanded to the superkey (invoiceNr, lineNr, itemCode, saleDate, storeNr). From a purely logical standpoint this is not required, since joins can be made on nonkey attributes. If some dimension tables are themselves used as central tables for other stars, the overall schema is called a "snowflake schema". A set of star schemas with shared dimension tables is sometimes called a "galaxy".

Data warehouses and data marts are used for *online analytical processing* (OLAP) and *data mining*. The term "OLAP" was introduced by Edgar Codd to describe interactive analysis of dimensioned and aggregated data for decision support (Codd et al. 1993). Data mining involves deeper analysis of the data, typically using sophisticated statistical techniques and complex algorithms for detecting patterns. Nowadays, many tools for OLAP and data mining are in use. Either topic deserves a book in itself. The remainder of this section provides a brief overview of OLAP.

There are three main approaches to OLAP. Each uses base data as well as aggregated data (e.g., sales figures might be summed and grouped at various levels). *Multidimensional OLAP* (MOLAP) stores both base and aggregated data in multidimensional structures rather than tables. *Relational OLAP* (ROLAP) stores both base and aggregated data in relational tables. *Hybrid OLAP* (HOLAP) stores the base data in relational tables and the aggregated data in multidimensional structures. Some DBMSs, such as Microsoft SQL Server, support all three kinds of OLAP.

The multidimensional structures used for OLAP are popularly known as *cubes*. In geometry, a cube is a three-dimensional box structure. In OLAP theory, a cube can have as many dimensions as you like. Cubes provide an intuitive way to visualize and browse data, as well as fast access to aggregate information. Let's consider a simple example.

With reference to the star schema in Figure 13.3, suppose we wanted to list the number of units sold in the years 1997 through 1999 for each geographic region and each item category. As an exercise you might like to formulate the SQL query for this. You need to perform the natural join of the four tables; group by saleYear, region, and category; and compute sum(qty). An extract of a possible result is shown in Table 13.1, assuming only two categories (SW = software, HW = hardware) and four regions (N = North, S = South, E = East, W = West).

The fact type underlying this table is the quaternary in Year in Region items of Category sold in NrUnits. The full table display of the result would include 24 rows (8 for each year), only the first 9 rows being shown here. An alternative way of displaying the data using a cube is shown in Figure 13.4. Here the independent variables (year, region, and category) appear as the *dimensions* making up the edges of the cube, and the values for the dependent variable or *measure* (units sold) appear in the relevant cells. Only the software sales figures are shown here, in the 12 cells making up the front half of the

Table 13.1 Units sold.

Year	Region	Category	NrUnits
1997	N	SW	10,000
1997	N	HW	500
1997	S	SW	12,000
1997	S	HW	330
1997	E	SW	7,500
1997	E	HW	440
1997	W	SW	12,000
1997	W	HW	350
1998	N	SW	14,500
...	...	...	...

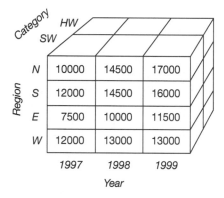

Figure 13.4 Cube depiction of units sold (only the software figures are shown here).

cube. You can imagine seeing the hardware sales figures by rotating the cube to see its other side.

OLAP cubes can be much more complex than this example. For any set of independent dimensions, there may be more than one measure (e.g., units sold and revenue). These different measures are often collectively referred to as the *Measures dimension.* Moreover, each independent dimension typically has a *hierarchy of levels.* For example, a Location dimension might have regions at its top level, composed of states at the second level, with cities at the third level, and stores at the fourth level. Similarly a Time dimension may be decomposed into Years, then Quarters, then Months, then Days. Finally the Item dimension may be decomposed into categories, then items.

So our data mart example can be used to construct a cube with three independent, hierarchical dimensions (Location, Time, and Item) and one dependent dimension for the UnitsSold and Revenue measures. The neat thing about the cube structure is that it enables aggregate values for the measures to be efficiently stored and accessed for all levels of the hierarchies. When analyzing a cube, you can choose to consolidate or *roll up* these aggregates (e.g., roll up sales figures for cities to regional sales figures). You can also do the opposite, *drilling down* to a finer level of granularity. Moreover, you can *slice and dice* the cube whichever way you like by taking a subcube of it (e.g., if you restrict the item category in Figure 13.4 to software, you get the front slice of the cube).

Because of such advantages, star schemas in data marts are often used to create a variety of cubes for easy analysis. SQL Server provides wizards to simplify the task of cube creation and also supports a Multidimensional Expression (MDX) language for querying cubes. For example, assume SalesCube is based on the hierarchical Location, Time, and Item dimensions discussed earlier. The following MDX query will result in a two-dimensional grid that lists the software units sold and revenue in Washington State in each of the first three quarters of 1999.

```
select { [Measures].[UnitsSold], [Measures].[Revenue] } on columns,
       { [Time].[1999].[Q1] : [Time].[1999].[Q3] } on rows
from   SalesCube
where ( [Item].[SW], [Location].[N].[WA] )
```

In MDX, braces are used to delimit sequences, and square brackets may be used to delimit identifiers or values. The dot notation is used to move down a hierarchy. Notice that Time is drilled down to quarters, and Location is drilled down to states. A colon ":" is used to indicate a range (like ".." in English). The result grid from the above query has two columns for units sold and revenue, and three rows for the first three quarters of 1999. A full coverage of MDX would require another chapter or two, so it is not pursued further here. An extensive treatment of MDX and OLAP for SQL Server is provided by Thomsen et al. (1999).

Different OLAP tools work differently. SQL:1999 now includes support for cubes and rollup, so hopefully some OLAP features will become more standardized in the future. MDX queries can be very complex, and Microsoft SQL Server provides a very high level language called *English Query* that can be used by end users to generate MDX queries. The topic of natural-language-based queries is discussed in the next section.

13.3   Conceptual Query Languages

An information system may be modeled at any of four levels: conceptual, logical, physical, and external. In principle, it may also be *queried* at any of these levels. In practice, however, although conceptual modeling is widely used, it is comparatively rare for systems to be queried at the conceptual level. Instead, queries are typically formulated either at the external level using forms, at the logical level using a language such as SQL, or at the physical level using a programming language. This section briefly indicates some problems with these lower-level approaches and explains how these problems are avoided by conceptual query languages, especially those based on ORM.

At the external level, Query By Form (QBF) enables users to enter queries directly on a screen form, by entering appropriate values or conditions in the form fields. This form-based interface is well suited to simple queries where the scope of the query is visible on a single form and no complex operations are involved. However, this cannot be used to express complicated queries. Moreover, saved QBF queries may rapidly become obsolete as the external interface evolves. For such reasons, QBF is too restrictive for serious work.

For relational databases, SQL and QBE (Query By Example) are more expressive. However, complex queries and even queries that are easy to express in natural language (e.g., who does not speak more than one language?) can be difficult for nontechnical users to express in these languages. Moreover, an SQL or QBE query often needs to be changed if the relevant part of the conceptual schema or internal schema is changed, even if the meaning of the query is unaltered. Finally, relational query optimizers ignore many semantic optimization opportunities arising from knowledge of constraints.

Logical query languages for postrelational DBMSs (e.g., object-oriented and object-relational) suffer similar problems. Their additional structures (e.g., sets, arrays, bags, and lists) often lead to greater complexity in both user formulation and system optimization. For example, OQL (Object Query Language) extends SQL with various functions for navigation as well as composing and flattening structures, thus forcing the user to deal directly with the way the information is stored internally (Cattell and Barry 2000). At the physical level, programming languages may be used to access the internal structures directly (e.g., using pointers and records), but this very low level approach to query formulation is totally unsuitable for end users.

Given the disadvantages of query formulation at the external, logical, or physical level, it is not surprising that many *conceptual query languages* have been proposed to allow users to formulate queries directly on the conceptual schema itself. Most of these language proposals are academic research topics, with at best prototype tool support, and typically based on ER schemas (e.g., ERQL, Super, Hybris) or deductive models (e.g., CBQL). By and large, these are challenging for naive users, and their use of attributes exposes their queries to instability, since attributes may evolve into entities or relationships as the application model evolves. References for these are included in the chapter notes.

Some commercial tools allow users to enter queries directly in English, then translate these into database queries in a language such as SQL or MDX. One early tool of this type was English Wizard. When I looked at it a few years ago, it suffered from problems with ambiguity and expressibility, as well as the correctness of its SQL generation. A Web search at the time of writing seems to indicate it has evolved into EasyAsk, which may have resolved some of these problems. The chapter notes include the Web site, so you can try it out for yourself. At any rate, most of the natural-language input tools I've looked at require you to spend considerable effort setting up a dictionary to relate conceptual terms to the underlying database structures, and most of them do an imperfect job at handling natural-language input. This is not really surprising, given the inherent ambiguity and complexity of natural language.

An interesting approach to address the ambiguity problem is taken by *English Query*, which comes with Microsoft SQL Server. When you enter a question in English, it's rephrased to indicate the interpretation taken. In some cases, more than one rephrasing may be given, and you can pick the one that conveys your intended meaning. There are of course limits on what kinds of questions can be understood, and you need to spend time setting up the connections between your semantic model and the database structures. For example, if you want to make a join between tables other than a foreign key to primary key reference, you need to explicitly add this beforehand. Also the SQL that's generated might not be as efficient as you might construct yourself.

However, once you've done all this work, you can make it possible for nontechnical end users to query the database in plain English. Although common, predictable queries are best made available through prewritten procedures, English Query is especially useful for ad hoc queries. For example, with reference to the data mart schema in the previous section, and assuming adequate setting up, the question "Which region has the most stores?" might generate the following SQL code:

```
select top 1 with ties dbo.Store.region as "Region", count(*) as "count"
from   dbo.Store
where dbo.Store.region is not null
group by dbo.Store.region
order by 2 desc
```

Besides returning the region(s) with the most stores, this query returns the number of stores in those regions, which we might not want. Moreover, the **where** clause and the **order by** clause are both redundant. But these are small issues for the nontechnical user who is incapable of formulating the SQL query. For OLAP applications, English Query can also be used to generate MDX queries. For example, referencing the SalesCube discussed in the previous section, the question "List the three items with the most unit sales" might result in the restatement "Show the 3 items with the highest total unit sales" and the following MDX query:

```
select { Measures.[UnitsSold] } on columns,
        topcount([Item].[ItemCode].members, 3, Measures.[UnitsSold] ) on rows
from [SalesCube]
```

As these examples illustrate, free input in natural language has a lot of potential for opening up databases to anybody who can write. As language recognition technology matures, it will also open up databases to anybody who can speak. However, we still have a long way to go before this becomes a totally reliable technology. In particular, it can be incredibly difficult to set up semantic dictionaries to always capture the intended interpretation of user questions.

These problems of ambiguity and onerous dictionary preparation can be eliminated in one stroke by taking a different approach: *conceptual-schema-based queries*. Here the user issues queries by selecting paths through the existing conceptual schema, rather than using free text input, so no ambiguity can arise. As discussed later, if an ORM conceptual schema is used, there is no need to predeclare any join paths, since ORM object types are the semantic domains on which all joins are based. Since ORM is attribute-free in its base conceptual model, it also avoids the instability problems of attribute-based queries, which require reformulation when attributes evolve into relationships (see later example). Moreover, ORM's sole data structure is the relationship type, providing a simple, sentence-based framework. For such reasons, I believe ORM conceptual query technology offers the greatest potential of any existing approach.

The first significant ORM-based query language was *RIDL* (Reference and Idea Language), a hybrid language with both declarative and procedural aspects (Meersman 1982a; Meersman et al. 1984). RIDL is a textual language for defining, populating, and querying models in NIAM, an early version of ORM from which all modern versions are derived. It was developed at the Control Data research laboratory at the University of Brussels and was the first truly conceptual query language ever implemented. Let's look at some RIDL examples. Consider a military conceptual schema with the following fact types: Officer has Rank; Officer was born in Year. In RIDL, these fact types would normally be declared as Officer having Rank; Officer born-in Year. To find which sergeants were born before 1950, the following RIDL query may be used:

```
LIST Officer (having Rank 'sergeant' AND born-in Year < 1950)
```

In RIDL, reserved words are in upper case. To illustrate the procedural side of RIDL, the following query lists pairs of officers of the same rank who were born before 1950:

```
FOR EACH o1, o2 IN Officer born-in Year < 1950 DO
    IF Rank OF o1 = Rank OF o2
        THEN LIST o1, o2
    END-IF
END-FOR
```

The original RIDL software mapped RIDL queries into internal statements that were directly executable on some early Control Data computers. RIDL was developed around the same time that SQL systems started to appear on the market. If you compare the above queries with equivalent SQL queries, you will see that RIDL was far ahead of its time. In later years, the data definition part of RIDL was implemented graphically in the RIDL* tool, but the query component was not supported. Another ORM query language is LISA-D (Language for Information Structure and Access and Descriptions). Although very expressive, it is technically challenging for end users and currently lacks tool support (ter Hofstede et al. 1996).

Like ORM, the OSM (Object-oriented Systems Modeling) approach avoids the use of attributes as a base construct. An academic prototype has been developed for the graphical query language OSM-QL based on this approach (Embley et al. 1996). For any given query, the user selects the relevant part of the conceptual schema, and then annotates the resulting subschema diagram with the relevant restrictions to formulate the query. Negation is handled by adding a frequency constraint of "0", and disjunction is introduced by means of a subtype-union operator. Projection is accomplished by clicking on the relevant object nodes and then on a mark-for-output button.

Another recent ORM query language is *ConQuer* (the name derives from "CONceptual QUERy"). ConQuer is more expressive than OSM-QL, easier for novice users, and its commercial tool transforms conceptual queries into SQL queries for a variety of back-end DBMSs. Moreover, the tool does not require the user to be familiar with the conceptual schema or the ORM diagram notation. The first version of ConQuer was released in InfoAssistant (Bloesch and Halpin 1996). Feedback from this release led to the redesign of both the language and the user interface for greater expressibility and usability, resulting in a tool called ActiveQuery (Bloesch and Halpin 1997). Typical queries can be constructed by just clicking on objects with the mouse and adding conditions. Owing to acquisitions, the ActiveQuery technology is now owned by Microsoft.

A basic understanding of the ConQuer technology will help provide insights into what a truly conceptual query environment can offer. The ConQuer language and its tool support were designed for expressibility, clarity, simplicity, semantic stability, and semantic relevance. These design principles were explained in Section 3.1. A ConQuer query can be applied only to an ORM schema. Using a software tool, an ORM schema may be entered directly, or instead reverse-engineered from an existing logical schema (e.g., a relational or object-relational schema). While reverse-engineering is automatic, some refinement by a human improves the readability (e.g., the default names generated for predicates are not always as natural as a human can supply).

Although ConQuer queries are based on ORM, users don't need to be familiar with ORM or its notation. A ConQuer query is set out in textual (outline) form (basically as a tree of predicates connecting objects) with the underlying constraints hidden, since they have no impact on the meaning of the query.

With ActiveQuery, a user can construct a query without any prior knowledge of the schema. On opening a model for browsing, the user is presented with an object pick list. When an object type is dragged to the query pane, another pane displays the roles played by that object in the model. The user drags over those relationships of interest. Clicking an object type within one of these relationships causes its roles to be displayed, and the user may drag over those of interest, and so on. In this way, users may quickly declare a query path through the information space, without any prior knowledge of the underlying data structures. Users may also initially drag across several object types. The structure of the underlying model is then used to automatically infer a reasonable path through the information space: this is called a *point-to-point query*.

Items to be displayed are indicated with a check mark "✓". These check marks may be toggled on/off as desired. The query path may be restricted in various ways by use of operators and conditions. As a simple example, suppose a company has branch offices in several cities around the world. Now consider the query "List each employee who lives in the city that is the location of branch 52". This may be set out in ConQuer thus:

```
Q1      ✓Employee
           └ lives in City
                 └ is location of Branch 52
```

This implicit form of the query may be expanded to reveal the reference schemes (e.g., EmpNr, BranchNr), and an equals sign may be included before "52". Since any ConQuer query corresponds to a qualified path through an ORM schema, where all the object types and predicates are well defined, the meaning of the query is essentially transparent. ActiveQuery also generates an English verbalization of the query in case there is any doubt. This ensures *semantic clarity*.

Since ORM conceptual object types are semantic domains, they act as semantic "glue" to connect the schema. This facilitates not only strong typing but also query navigation through the information space, enabling joins to be visualized in the most natural way (recall Section 4.4). The underlying ORM schema fragment for query Q1

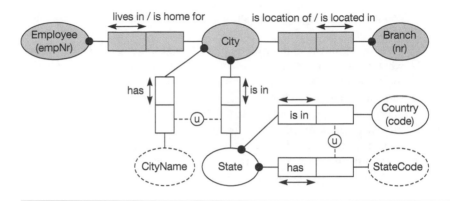

Figure 13.5 Only the shaded path is relevant to query Q1.

is shown in the shaded path within Figure 13.5, along with the identification scheme for City.

Notice how City is used as a join object type for this query. If attributes are used instead, the query formulation becomes more cumbersome. If composite attributes are allowed, we might use List Employee.empNr where Employee.city = Branch.city and Branch.branchNr = 52. If not, we might resort to List Employee.empNr where Employee.cityName = Branch.cityName and Employee.stateCode = Branch.stateCode and Employee.country = Branch.country and Branch.branchNr = 52. Apart from awkwardness, both of these attribute-based approaches violate the principle of *semantic relevance*. Since the identification scheme of City is not relevant to the question, the user should not be forced to deal explicitly with it.

Even if we had a tool that allowed us to formulate queries directly in ER or OO models, and this tool displayed the attributes of the current object type for possible assimilation into the query (similar to the way Active query displays the roles of the highlighted object type), this would not expose immediate connections in the way that ORM does. For example, inspecting Employee.city does not tell us that there is some connection to Branch.city. At the relational level, we have two tables *Employee*(empNr, countryCode, stateCode, cityName, ...) and *Branch*(branchNr, countryCode, stateCode, cityName, ...). Since there are no foreign key references to relate the city attributes in these tables, free text query tools rely on the join connection being explicitly entered into the dictionary beforehand, which is a risky assumption. The only way to automatically reveal all join possibilities is to use the domains themselves as a basis for connectedness, and this is one of the distinguishing features of ORM.

Because ConQuer queries are based on ORM, they continue to produce the desired result so long as their meaning endures. In other words, you never need to change a ConQuer query if the English meaning of the question still applies. In particular, ConQuer queries are not impacted by typical changes to an application, such as addition of new fact types or changes to constraints or the relative importance of some feature. This ensures *semantic independence* (i.e., the conceptual queries are independent of changes to underlying structures when those changes have no effect on meaning). This results in greater *semantic stability* than attribute-based approaches.

(a)

(b)

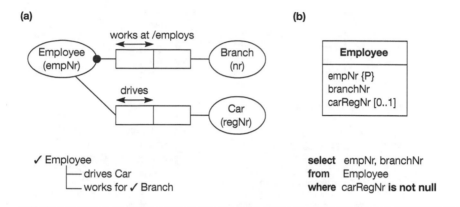

✓ Employee
— drives Car
— works for ✓ Branch

select empNr, branchNr
from Employee
where carRegNr **is not null**

Figure 13.6 Different queries to list the employee drivers and their branches.

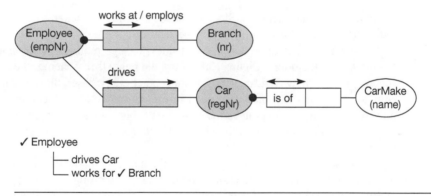

✓ Employee
— drives Car
— works for ✓ Branch

Figure 13.7 In ORM, the model change does not require a query change.

As a simple example, suppose that in our model each employee works at exactly one branch and drives at most one car. In the real world, an employee may drive many cars, but we decide to record at most one of these. Now suppose we want to list employee drivers and their branches. The ORM model and ConQuer query are shown in Figure 13.6(a). There is an implicit **and** between the two branches stemming from Employee. An equivalent UML model and SQL query are shown in Figure 13.6(b). Not only is this code subconceptual (null values are an implementation detail), but it is unstable, since a simple change to a conceptual constraint on the driving relationship requires the code to be changed as well.

For example, suppose we change our business rules to allow the recording of many cars for the same employee, and we also decide to record the make (e.g., Ford, Honda) of each car. From an ORM viewpoint, this new situation is depicted in Figure 13.7. The uniqueness constraint on the drives association is relaxed from *n:*1 to *m:n,* and a car-make fact type is added. These changes to the model have no impact on the ConQuer query, whose meaning relates just to the shaded fact types, not to their constraints, and

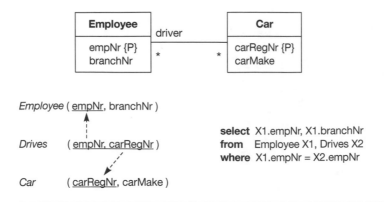

Figure 13.8 For attribute-based models, the model change requires a query change.

not to the additional fact type. Since the shaded portion is unchanged, the original ConQuer query means the same, so it may be reused.

For attribute-based approaches, the business change requires major changes to both the model and the query. Figure 13.8 shows the new UML schema, the new relational schema, and the new SQL query. Any conceptual query based directly on the UML or equivalent ER model would also need reformulation because facts about driving are now stored in an association rather than an attribute. In contrast, the ConQuer query stays valid; all that changes is the SQL code that gets automatically generated from the query.

An OO query approach is often more problematic than an ER or relational approach because there are many extra choices on how facts are grouped into structures, and the user is exposed to these structures in order to ask a question. Moreover, these structures may change drastically to maintain performance as the business application evolves.

In the real world, changes often occur to an application, requiring changes to the database structures. Even more work is required to modify the code for stored queries. If we are working at the logical level, the maintenance effort can be very significant. We can minimize the impact of change to both models and queries by working in ORM at the conceptual level and letting a tool look after the lower-level transformations.

The ActiveQuery tool generates *semantically optimized* SQL queries, wherever possible using knowledge of ORM constraints to produce more efficient code. For example, if the driving role were actually mandatory, the SQL generated by the previous ConQuer query would in both cases simplify to **select** empNr, branchNr **from** Employee. The tool can also generate different code for different back ends, to cater to their different support for the SQL standard, sometimes generating chains of queries over temporary tables to enable the query to run at all.

The simple examples above illustrate how ConQuer achieves semantic clarity, relevance, and stability. Let's look briefly at its semantic strength or expressibility. The language supports the usual comparators (=, <, **in, like**, etc.), logical operators (**and, or, not**), and bag functions (**count, sum**, etc.), as well as a modal operator (**possibly**) for conceptual left outer joins. Subtype/supertype connections appear as **is** predicates.

For example, assuming Manager is a subtype of Employee in the ORM model, the following query Q2 asks: List each manager and their cars (if any) where the managers do not work at branch 52.

Q2   ✓Manager
              └ **is** Employee
                      ├ **possibly** drives ✓Car
                      └ **not** works at Branch 52

The language is fully orthogonal and supports arbitrary correlation, using subscripted variables (e.g., $Person_1$, $Person_2$) when necessary to distinguish different instances of the same object type. As a simple correlation example, consider the query "Who supervises an employee who lives in the same city as the supervisor but was born in a different country from the supervisor?" Assuming appropriate birth and supervision fact types in the ORM model, query Q4 shows one way of expressing this in ConQuer.

Q4   ✓$Employee_1$
              ├ lives in $City_1$
              ├ was born in $Country_1$
              └ supervises $Employee_2$
                              ├ lives in $City_1$
                              └ was born in $Country_2$ < > $Country_1$

When an object type appears more than once, ActiveQuery automatically appends subscripts to distinguish the occurrences. You can equate instances by equating their subscripts (e.g., $City_1$). More generally, you can use comparators to compare instances (e.g., $Country_2$ < > $Country_1$). Try this in SQL. It's not that hard, but you have to admit it's easier in ConQuer!

As a final example, suppose the ORM model includes the *m:n* fact type Employee has Rating. Now consider the query "List each branch and those of its employees whose maximum individual rating exceeds the average of his or her branch (remember that an employee may have many ratings)". Query Q5 shows how to do this in ConQuer, illustrating the use of bag functions in **for** clauses.

Q5   ✓Branch
              └ employs ✓Employee
                      └ achieves Rating
                                      └ **max**(Rating) **for** Employee >
                                          avg(Rating) **for** Branch

At the relational level, two tables are used for the query: *Employee*(empNr, branchNr, ...); Achieves(empNr, rating). The SQL for this query is shown below. This is tricky, especially the final correlation between branch numbers, and even experienced SQL programmers might have difficulty with it. The equivalent ConQuer query, however, would be easy for most end users who had even minimal experience with the language. This gives some indication of the potential of a language such as ConQuer for empowering end users.

```
select max(X1.branchNr), X2.empNr
from   Employee as X1, Achieves as X2
```

```
where X1.empNr = X2.empNr
group by X2.empNr
having max(X2.rating) >
    (select avg(X4.rating)
     from Employee as X3, Achieves as X4
     where X3.empNr = X4.empNr
     and X3.branchNr = X1.branchNr)
```

Although ORM's graphical constraint notation is rich, it still needs to be supplemented by a textual language to provide a complete coverage of the kinds of constraints and derivation rules found in business applications. Although ORM's graphical constraints can be verbalized in FORML, as seen in earlier chapters, the ConQuer language is more general, can be used to define other business rules, and can be mapped automatically to SQL. Hence it could be used as a very high level language for capturing business rules in general, both derivation rules and constraints.

ActiveQuery allows you to define derived predicates and store these definitions. These derived predicates (or "macros") can then be used just like base predicates in other queries. A subtype may be thought of as a derived object type, with its definition provided by a ConQuer query. For example, the population of the subtype MalePatient can be obtained by executing the following ConQuer query: **find each** Patient **who** is of Sex 'M'. Given its generality, ConQuer can be easily adapted to provide a very high level language for specifying derivation rules.

A constraint may be viewed as a check that a query searching for a violation of the constraint returns the null set. Hence constraints may also be expressed in terms of queries. Various high-level constructs can be provided in the language to make it more natural than the **not exists check** query form provided in SQL. Although there is no room here to go into detail, it should be clear that this approach is quite powerful.

13.4   Schema Abstraction Mechanisms

At times we might feel almost swamped by the level of detail captured on an ORM conceptual schema diagram, or even on a UML, ER, or relational schema. Nevertheless, such detail is important when developing, transforming, or mapping schemas. The ORM notation has been crafted to facilitate these tasks. As we've seen, the diagrams may be verbalized naturally and populated with fact instances, their object-role-based notation allows many constraints to be expressed intuitively, and their object types reveal the semantic domains that glue the schema together. All of this helps the modeler to get a complete and correct picture, and to transform the model in a rigorous way with formal control of information loss or gain.

However, once a schema has been developed, we may at times wish to hide some of the information, in order to obtain a quick overview or to focus on some aspects. This is particularly the case if the schema is large and complex. Hence, there is a need for *abstraction mechanisms,* by which unwanted details may be removed from immediate consideration. This section outlines a few of the more useful ways of doing this. The chapter notes provide references for further study in this regard.

One obvious abstraction strategy is *modularization*. Here the complete schema is "divided up" into a number of conveniently sized modules or subschemas. One way to do this is to use different schemas for different modeling *perspectives*. For example, UML uses class and object diagrams for a data view, statecharts and activity diagrams for behavioral views, and so on. In addition you might use a purely conceptual model for analysis and annotated or modified conceptual models for a design view.

Within a given modeling perspective, the global model is still likely to be too large to conveniently inspect in one go, even though wall-sized schemas can be very useful at times for seeing far-reaching connections. One trivial way to divide a global schema diagram is to overlay a grid, to partition the schema into separate cells. However, it is typically much more useful to allow modules to overlap, so that, for example, the same object type might appear in more than one module. This technique also allows greater flexibility in basing modules on semantic groupings. One useful technique is to divide the global model into *reusable submodels* that can be imported into other models or projects at a later time. The most popular technique of all is to divide a given model into *pages*. Each page should be given a meaningful name and include a reasonable number of tightly coupled modeling elements.

Various means may be used to specify connections between modules, such as hyperlinks, annotations, and border overlaps (cf. a directory of road maps). Electronic browsing opens up greater possibilities than hard-copy browsing (e.g., scrolling, zooming in and out, hypertext navigation), but printed documentation on standard pages needs to be catered to as well.

With large applications, the original schema might be developed by different teams as separate modules that are later integrated. Additional care is then required for the *schema integration* process. In particular, global consistency must be ensured, either by agreeing on a uniform treatment of terminology, constraints, and rules or by specifying appropriate translations. Ideally, a basic architectural framework will be agreed upon early in the development, and all the modelers will attach the same meaning to words by resolving any synonym and homonym problems.

For example, if the same object type is called "Subject" in one module and "Course" in another, then one of these will be chosen as the standard term and the other term replaced by it. If different object types or nontrivial predicates in different modules are given the same name, one of these names must be changed.

Global identification schemes and constraints should be agreed upon, and where necessary contextual identification may be supported via subtyping, and textual constraints can be added to strengthen global constraints for a given context (e.g., restricted mandatory role and restricted uniqueness constraints). For some applications (e.g., federated databases), partial integration between relevant modules may be favored instead of global integration.

Another useful abstraction mechanism is provided by *constraint and rule toggles,* or *layering*. For instance, the display of one or more classes of constraints or derivation rules may be toggled off when they are not of immediate interest, in order to obtain a simpler picture. On an ORM schema, for example, we might toggle off value lists, ring constraints, frequency constraints, set-comparison constraints, textual constraints, and derivation rules in order to focus on uniqueness and mandatory role constraints. Each constraint class may be thought of as a constraint layer, with the modeler choosing which layers to view at any given time. An extreme option would be to toggle off all constraints.

Subtype display can be suppressed in many ways. We can hide the subtype defining rules or graphic constraints (e.g., exclusion and totality). We can hide just some of the subtypes, preferably indicating somehow that others exist (e.g., with an ellipsis or one of the UML annotations discussed in Chapter 9). We can also collapse subtypes into their top supertype. Depending on the model type, various other modeling elements can be hidden (e.g., reference schemes or attributes). When the additional layers of detail are needed, their display can be toggled on again. Although this layering concept can be adapted to hard copy (e.g., by using a series of overlaid transparencies or progressively detailed printouts), it should ideally be exploited interactively with a CASE tool.

Yet another abstraction mechanism is *object type zoom*. Here the modeler selects an object type of interest, in order to have the display focused on that object type and its immediate *neighborhood*. The object type is displayed with all its fact types. By specifying a *logical radius* for the zoom (e.g., in predicate units), the neighborhood may be expanded to include fact types of the object types in the first-level zoom, and so on. As discussed in the previous section, Active Query uses this mechanism to progressively open up the universe to the user, displaying a neighborhood of one-predicate radius for the currently highlighted object type.

A simple example will help illustrate some of the basic ways of abstracting. Figure 13.9 depicts an ORM schema for a small application. Here movies are identified by numbers, though the combination of their title and director is also unique. Some movies are based on another. For example, the Western *The Magnificent Seven* was based on an early Japanese movie *The Seven Samurai*.

When available, figures about the gross revenues of a movie are recorded, and the net profit too if this is known. The only people of interest in this application are movie directors and movie stars. We record their country of birth and, if known, their birth date. The country in which a movie was made is noted, as well as any export countries for it.

As a mental exercise, imagine toggling off the display of the constraint types on Figure 13.9 one at a time (ring, then set comparison, then mandatory role, then uniqueness) to visualize abstraction by peeling off constraint layers.

Figure 13.10 depicts a zoom on the object type Person, with a logical radius of 1, so that only the fact types directly connected to Person are shown. To highlight the zoom object type, a thicker line is used for it. Visualize for yourself a zoom on Country; this would display three fact types, one of which is also contained in the Person zoom.

Another abstraction mechanism that is especially useful with large ORM schemas is that of *refinement levels* based on *major object types*. This can be used in conjunction with *attribute abstraction* to provide an ER schema or UML class diagram.

When developing a conceptual schema, it is useful to treat all object types equally, since the relative importance of an object type is based on all the parts it plays in the global schema. Once the schema is complete, however, this information is available and can be used to determine which are the most important, or *major* object types. A procedure for deciding the major object types on ORM schemas was developed by

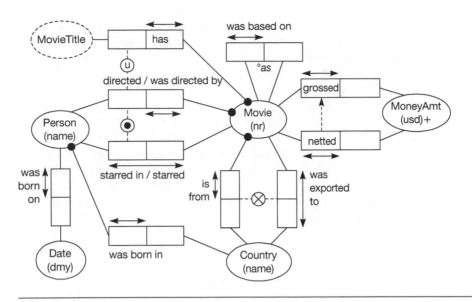

Figure 13.9 A small, but detailed conceptual schema.

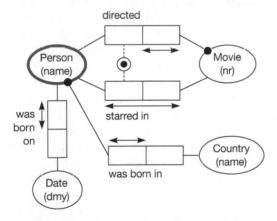

Figure 13.10 Zooming in on the Person object type.

Campbell and Halpin (1993) and used as a basis for generating default screen forms for the external user interface (since application screens basically enable users to perform operations on major objects).

Once the major object types are decided, an ORM diagram can be lifted to a higher level of abstraction. For example, we may choose to display only the *major fact types* (i.e., those fact types in which at least two roles are played by a major object type). With large applications, this diagram itself may be subjected to the same procedure, yielding a higher-level abstraction, and so on, until the top-level view of the model is obtained. So long as the fully detailed schema is accessible, this bottom-up abstraction may be reversed, allowing the top-level view to be successively refined down to the fully detailed bottom level.

The detailed schema diagram in Figure 13.9 has six object types: Movie, MovieTitle, Person, MoneyAmt, Country, and Date. Intuitively, these are not all equally important in this application. Which do you consider to be the major object types? Apart from using your intuition, you can make use of the constraint patterns to help you decide. In particular, mandatory role and uniqueness constraints are relevant. If an object type has an *explicit* mandatory role, it is major. Usually, an object type playing a functional role is also major, but this is not always the case (e.g., MovieTitle would still be a minor object type even if its role was functional; its role is still only implicitly mandatory).

There are some finer points to determining major object types, but this is enough to get the basic idea. Based on the previous reasoning, Figure 13.9 has only two major object types: Movie and Person. Figure 13.11 provides one overview of the application by displaying only the major fact types.

Instead of being hidden, minor fact types may if desired be viewed in terms of *attributes* of the major object types. Although this attribute viewpoint hides structural information (e.g., domains and certain constraints), the ER or UML diagram obtained provides a compact picture that is useful for quick overviews. Figure 13.12 shows a UML class diagram for the current example. Unlike most ER notations, UML allows the attribute domains to be specified if desired, and the missing constraints (here disjunctive mandatory, subset, exclusion, external uniqueness, and asymmetric constraints) could be documented in notes, although at the price of losing compactness.

Notice that country information is displayed here in terms of attributes (single- and multivalued) rather than as associations with a Country class. This is because Country is a minor object type in the original ORM schema. If instead Country played an explicit mandatory role, it would become major, and we would need to display it as a class. This is usually the case (e.g., we normally store both the code and name of countries).

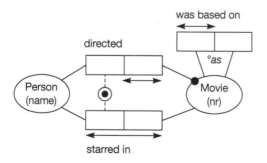

Figure 13.11 Only the major fact types are shown.

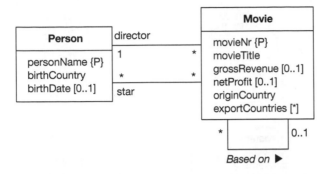

Figure 13.12 A UML class diagram abstracted from Figure 13.9.

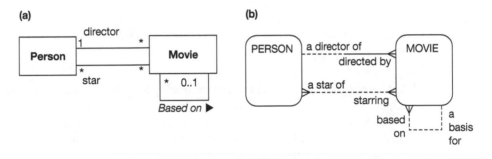

Figure 13.13 Attributes hidden in (a) UML class diagram and (b) Barker ER diagram.

More compact diagrams still can be obtained by hiding all the attributes. For example, Figure 13.13 shows the major fact types with all attributes hidden in both UML and Barker ER notations. Again, some ORM constraints are missing (disjunctive mandatory and asymmetric constraints). By using ORM to actually generate such diagrams, we can retain the benefits of ORM (e.g., for validation and completeness) and still have compact views when desired.

13.5   Process Modeling and External Design

We have seen how a data model may be specified at the conceptual level (e.g., with an ORM schema) and the logical level (e.g., with a relational schema). The overall information systems life cycle includes other tasks, as discussed in Chapter 2. For example, we need to specify what processes are to be performed on the data, and how the external interface should be constructed to facilitate these operations. This section provides a brief overview of these two tasks.

Process/behavior models specify the processes or activities of the application, how information flows occur, and how events trigger such actions. In practice, many

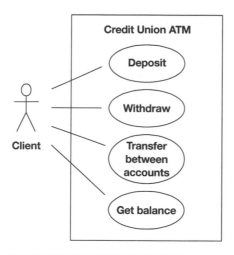

Figure 13.14 A use case diagram for an automated teller system.

different kinds of diagrams are used to specify these processes. For example, UML includes use case diagrams, sequence diagrams, collaboration diagrams, statecharts, and activity diagrams for this purpose. Other diagrams in popular use for process modeling include flowcharts, function trees, and data flow diagrams. We have space here to consider only some of these. Further details may be obtained from the chapter notes.

Suppose we are asked to design an information system for a credit union. As part of the requirements analysis phase, we determine that four main functions of the system are to enable clients to make deposits, withdrawals, transfers (e.g., from a savings account to a checking account), and obtain printouts of the account balances. In UML, each of these functions may be treated as a *use case* and included in a *use case diagram* to provide an overview of the processes supported by the system, as shown in Figure 13.14.

A use case is depicted as a named ellipse. The name may be written inside or below the ellipse. The system boundary is depicted as a named rectangle. An *actor* is a user type that participates in one or more use cases. A real-world object may be an instance of more than one actor (e.g., a person could be both a client and a clerk). Although not necessarily human, actors are standardly depicted as named "stick-man" figures. Actors may also be depicted as classes with the key word "«actor»". Lines drawn between actors and use cases indicate which actors participate in which use cases, and may be adorned with multiplicity constraints. In this simple example, there is only one actor (Client), and the participation associations may be marked 1 at the client end and * at the use case end.

Use case diagrams can be more complex. For example, a sales system would have many actors (e.g., Customer, SalesPerson, Supplier, ShippingClerk, SalesChief). Actors may be subtypes (e.g., SalesChief may be a subtype of SalesPerson). Use cases may include other use cases, or be extended to other use cases. Since use case diagrams tend to provide only high-level overviews of system processes, they are often supplemented by detailed descriptions of use cases (e.g., using textual descriptions or other diagrams). For example, a sequence diagram might be used to show the flow of messages between the client and the ATM, ordered by time. A detailed discussion of developing an ATM application using this approach is provided by Jacobson et al. (1999).

Of all the process modeling diagrams in UML, *activity diagrams* are the most intuitive for domain experts. Figure 13.15 shows a simple example based on our ATM example. An activity or action state is depicted as a named capsule. The Start and Stop actions are depicted as a solid dot and circled solid dot, respectively. Transitions between activities are shown as arrows, possibly annotated with guard conditions in square brackets. Each activity other than Start is assumed to be triggered by the completion of the previous activity and the satisfaction of the relevant guard condition (if any). If an activity has more than one possible outcome, a decision diamond is included with each outgoing branch labeled with the relevant condition. If an activity can be triggered by the completion of any one of many activities, the incoming transitions are

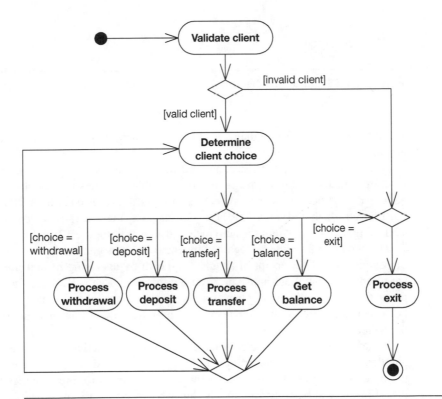

Figure 13.15 A top-level activity diagram for the ATM application.

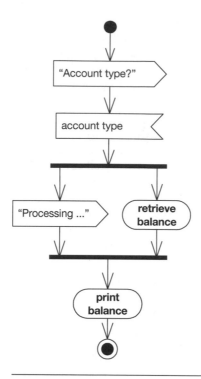

Figure 13.16 An activity diagram to refine the GetBalance activity.

first merged (using a merge diamond) so that each activity has only one input transition arrow.

An activity may itself be decomposed into an activity diagram to reveal the next level of refinement, and so on. Such decomposable activities may be distinguished by adding an icon in their lower-right corner to suggest the nested structure (OMG 1999), but I haven't bothered doing this here. For instance, the GetBalance activity in Figure 13.15 might be refined into the activity graph shown in Figure 13.16.

The sending of a signal is denoted by enclosing its signature in a convex pentagon or pencil shape. The receipt of a signal is shown by enclosing its signature in a concave pentagon. Although not typically used this way, I've used these shapes to show the activities of asking the client for the type of account for which a balance has been requested, recording their response, and telling them that their request is being processed.

If the completion of an activity triggers two or more activities that are executed in parallel, this is shown by inserting a fork, shown as a solid bar with one incoming and multiple outgoing transitions. If an activity requires two or more activities to be completed in order to be triggered, this is shown by inserting a join, shown as a solid bar with multiple incoming and one outgoing transition. As a trivial example, Figure 13.16 shows the system informing the client that his or her request is being processed at the same time as the balance is being retrieved. In an automated system, the message could have been sent before the retrieval. In a system with a human teller this is realistic, as a human teller often talks to the client while accessing the account records. As a more obvious example of parallel processing, driving a car often involves performing multiple actions at once (e.g., scanning the road ahead, turning the wheel, pressing the accelerator pedal).

The ATM example discussed here is based on a credit union that I used some years ago. In the ValidateClient process, the client inserted a credit card. The system checked whether the card was one of its own, and if so, accessed the client's identifier (client number) from the card. The same account could be used by many clients (e.g., a joint account for husband and wife), and each client had a distinct client number. In this way, the system could track which clients actually made the transactions.

Suppose we refine the ValidateClient process with an activity diagram or sequence diagram. Combining this with the detailed diagram for the GetBalance process, we see that the combined process of validating a client and printing a requested balance involves two input data flows (clientNr, accountType) from the Client and one output data flow (balance) to the client. If we consider the credit union's account database system to be separate from the ATM, it may be thought of as another actor that actually provides the balance details in response to a request (e.g., an SQL query) sent from the ATM. In a traditional data flow diagram, the various data flows could also be specified as labeled arrows connecting the processes with Client and an Accounts data store.

In such high-level views, little or no detail is provided on the structure of the data store or on how the process manages to find the relevant data. Since such details are so far undefined, diagrams like this fail to provide an adequate basis for modeling the data perspective. In spite of such informality, they can be of use in clarifying the UoD and for identifying functions to be included in the application's screen menus. Indeed, ordinary cartoons with intuitive icons can be quite useful for communication between modeler and domain expert in the early stages of requirements analysis.

In principle, a process model could be successively refined to elementary transactions that expose the underlying fact types. However, this approach is simply too time-consuming for data-intensive systems and is often too unstable, since business processes tend to change far more rapidly than the underlying data. To expedite the data modeling process, we should seed it with data use cases and apply a modeling procedure such as the ORM CSDP. If examples already exist, use these. If they don't, sit down with the domain expert and generate them. These could be in the form of tables, forms, graphs, or whatever. By now, you should have the verbalization skills to do CSDP step 1 properly on any of these varieties, and since clients find it easier to work at the instance level, this is the safest way to go. Moreover, by doing this you've already started prototyping external screens and reports the clients want.

Process models should be formally connected to the data models. This is best done after the conceptual and logical data models are determined. Although skilled modelers can refine process models into data models, this approach tends to be error-prone. For example, suppose we bypass conceptual data modeling, instead refining the process models discussed earlier for validating clients and getting balances into the following table scheme and SQL procedure. Here "&1" and "&2" are input parameters or

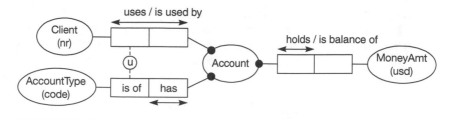

Figure 13.17 The primary reference scheme for accounts is unsafe.

placeholders. When the procedure is executed, actual values are input to these parameters.

D1:   *Account* (*clientNr, accountType,* balance)

P1:   **select** balance **from** Account
       where clientNr = &1
         and accountType = '&2'

Can you spot a potential problem with this design? It's easiest to see the problem if you do a conceptual schema for D1. This is depicted in Figure 13.17. Each account has one or more users, and has exactly one account type (e.g., L = loans, C = checking, S1 = main savings, S2 = other savings). That's fine. The problem lies in the primary reference scheme for Account. Although the combination of clientNr and accountType does identify an account, this should not be used for primary reference, since clientNr-accountType pairs do not relate to accounts in a 1:1 fashion.

For example, suppose my wife's clientNr is 1001, mine is 1002, and we share a main savings account (type = 'S1'). This joint account may now be referenced by (1001, 'S1') and by (1002, 'S1'). This will not do for primary reference. For instance, the Account table used for D1 will accept the population: {(1001, 'S1', 9000), (1002, 'S1', 0)}. But this means that the same account has two different balances, which is nonsense. The obvious solution is to introduce another primary identifier (e.g., accountNr), as shown in Figure 13.18. This figure also includes the new relational schema (D1') and the new procedure for computing the balance (P1').

This example is simplified (e.g., Exercise 6.4 discussed how balances might be derived from account transactions) but it does illustrate how conceptual modeling facilitates a correct data design, and that a detailed process specification is of no use unless the data structure on which the process operates is well defined.

In practice the use of accountNr for primary reference should be obvious by inspecting other data examples associated with this use case or a related one for the accounting system (e.g., a balance statement). As discussed in Section 5.4, a reference scheme within a given context might not be suitable for the global application. This is something to bear in mind when discussing data use cases with domain experts.

Although a rigorous process model is best built on top of a data model, an overview of the processes can be useful as a precursor to the data modeling, especially if the

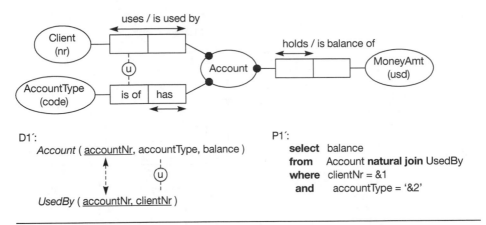

Figure 13.18 The primary reference scheme for accounts is now safe.

application is large or only vaguely understood. It is often helpful to get a clear picture of the functions of the application first.

Starting with the overall objectives, the main functions and processes of the application may be specified systematically, using a variety of diagrams. This kind of analysis helps us to divide the application into coherent modules of manageable size and facilitates the task of specifying information examples where none exist. At this point, CSDP step 1 may be applied to each module. Functional requirements may be laid out in top-down form using a *function tree*. For example, Figure 13.19 lists functions of a hospital information system. The four main functions are numbered 1..4. Each of these is refined or decomposed into a number of lower-level functions, numbered 1.1 and so on.

For example, function 3 is refined to functions 3.1 and 3.2. This may be refined further. For instance, function 3.1 is refined to functions 3.1.1, 3.1.2, and 3.1.3. To help fit the tree on a single sheet, this third level has been laid out vertically rather than horizontally. Tools such as the Org-Chart solution in Microsoft Visio allow very flexible layout of such diagrams. The other three main functions may be refined in a similar way. Other kinds of diagrams may be used to show dependencies between functions, and these can help in deciding how to group functions into processes.

One common way of specifying information flows between processes is by means of *data flow diagrams*. By decomposing the processes, a data flow diagram at one level may be refined into several lower-level diagrams, and so on. As a precursor to this refinement, we might specify a very high level view in the form of a *context diagram*. This provides an overview of the interaction between the information system and the environment, treats the system as a single process, and ignores any data stores.

A context diagram for the pharmacy module of our hospital application is shown in Figure 13.20. External agents appear as shadowed boxes. Material flows are not shown, but some data flows may be associated with material flows (e.g., drug supply details).

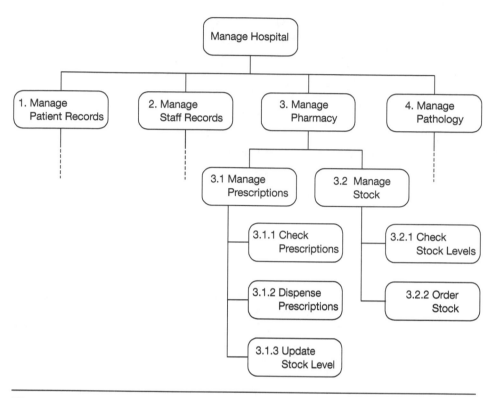

Figure 13.19 A function tree for a hospital information system.

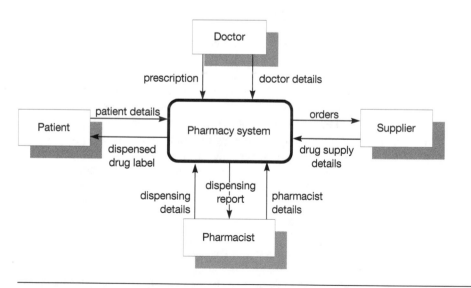

Figure 13.20 A context diagram for the pharmacy subsystem.

At a lower level of detail, Figure 13.21 shows a data flow diagram for a fragment of the pharmacy system. This could be further refined (e.g., decompose the order placement process into processes for computing totals, printing order forms, etc.). However, since such refinements are time-consuming, somewhat arbitrary, and lack the safeguards of population checks, there is usually little point in specifying low-level data flows.

In general then, once the requirements of the application are clear, and modules of manageable size are identified, modeling efforts are best focused on obtaining a set of information examples and applying the CSDP. Once the conceptual schema is specified, the logical schema is obtained by applying a mapping procedure, such as Rmap.

The external schemas may now be developed for the various categories of users. It is through the interaction of users with the external interface that the original functions specified in the requirements analysis phase are ultimately executed. Hence, it is important to design the external interface in a way that naturally reflects these functions.

Fundamentally, all that happens when users interact with an information system is that elementary facts are added, deleted, retrieved, or derived. In principle, we could specify the process perspective in terms of these two update and two query operations. But this is too fine a level of granularity for humans to work with efficiently.

We need a way of grouping these elementary operations into larger units. It is often natural to think of operations being performed on significant *objects,* like patients and stock items. The major object types abstracted from an ORM schema (see previous section) correspond closely to these object types, and hence provide a good basis for defining operations. The more important classes or entity types in UML class diagrams or ER diagrams provide another good choice for this.

A generic set of external update operations may now be generated with three varieties: add object, delete object, modify object. Some generic query operations may be generated (e.g., list all facts about an object), but specific queries require an appropriate selection of the relevant fact types (stored or derived).

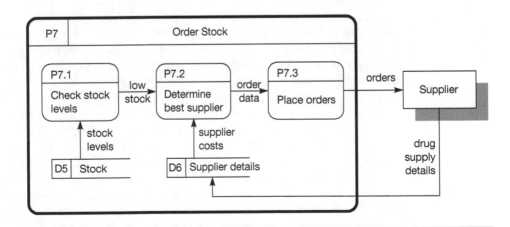

Figure 13.21 A data flow diagram for part of the pharmacy subsystem.

Users perform such operations through an *external interface,* typically *screen* forms or menus. For each screen, we need to consider *content* (which fact types and operations to include), *format* (how the screen is displayed), and *use* (how the operations are invoked by the user). As discussed, default decisions about screen content may be based on operations on the major object types. For example, if Patient is a major object type for the hospital system, a screen is required for it with at least the following operations: add Patient, modify Patient, delete Patient, show Patient.

Unlike conceptual and logical tables, forms may overlap in their content. This redundancy at the external level conveniently allows users to perform an operation whenever relevant, without having to switch screens. For example, consider the *m:n* fact type Doctor treated Patient. When working with a Doctor screen, we might query which patients were treated by that doctor. When at a Patient screen, we might query which doctors treated that patient. In the conceptual and logical schemas, facts of this type are stored only once. So long as the external screens have been properly set up as views of the underlying data structures, this overlap is safe. For further discussion on the use of ORM schemas to generate screen forms and transactions, see Campbell and Halpin (1993).

Although there is only one (global) conceptual schema for an application, there may be many external schemas. Different user groups might have different *authorization* levels that can be specified in *access rights tables.* This may be done at the conceptual level (e.g., for each fact type, which groups have read, add, delete rights) or at the logical level (e.g., for each table or column, which groups have read, insert, delete, update rights).

Regarding access to options on screen forms, it is generally best to display to users only those options that they are authorized to select. As usual, access rights to screen options may be soft-coded as data in tables rather than hard-coded in procedures. This avoids having to recompile the forms when access rights are changed, and simplifies reuse of common code. As part of the overall security, passwords are required, and users are given the power to change their passwords.

Apart from access rights, users might also differ in their *ability* level. Designing application screens to optimize the way various users can perform their tasks is a very important aspect of *human-computer interface* (HCI) design. Many kinds of interfaces can be used. For example, dialogue with the user may use natural language, short questions, command lines, menus, forms, tables, diagrams, images, or sound. Input devices include keyboard, mouse, joystick, pen, and microphone.

In general the user interface should be *easy to learn* and *easy to use.* To achieve this, the interface should be consistent, simple, efficient, and adapted to the user. Let's examine each of these in turn. *Consistency* of interface implies that all the components use the same basic conventions for display format and operations. This promotes positive transfer (learning how to use one screen helps you with the others) and avoids negative transfer. Consistency may be achieved at different levels: within the one screen, within the application, among applications from the same company, with external standards. For example, many windows applications are being developed nowadays in conformity with Microsoft's user interface guidelines (see chapter notes).

Simplicity of interface implies it is intuitive to use, with minimal effort on the part of users. Each screen should provide the right amount of relevant information (e.g., limit the number of menu options seen at once). Don't clutter the screen. If you wish to allow many operations directly from the one screen, remove all but the main options from the permanent screen display, allowing the user to toggle the extra options on as required. For example, use pull-down menus, pop-up windows (e.g., for lookup codes), and status line help (and pop-up detailed help). Facilitate navigation within and between screens (e.g., use arrow keys for movement) and allow windows and menus to be cascaded or tiled.

Efficiency of interface entails that options may be selected quickly and intuitively. A *graphical user interface* (GUI) provides a more intuitive means of operation, especially where graphics or sophisticated layouts are involved; here it is important that "what you see is what you get" (WYSIWYG). However, key-based shortcuts (e.g., hot keys) are sometimes faster and should be provided for the experienced user.

Menu design has a major impact on efficiency. Menus come in various shapes and sizes (full-screen, pull-down, pop-up, ring, button bars, etc.). They provide most if not all of the application's operations. Options on the same menu should be semantically related. Navigation between menus or screens requires planning—especially for Web-based applications that use hyperlinks to navigate from one place to another. Some possible navigation patterns are shown in Figure 13.22. Hyperlink access is typically cyclic.

In addition, the following principles should be observed. Order menu options in decreasing frequency of use. Vary color and fonts, but don't overdo it. For options either use intuitive icons, or terse, clear textual descriptions that are mostly in lower casc. Allow selection of options by mouse clicks or hot keys, and support undo.

Adapt the interface to the user by showing only what is relevant to that user and adopting most of the following suggestions. Provide simple procedures for casual users and shortcuts for experienced users. Let users configure the environment to their own taste. Provide levels of context-sensitive help: short messages on status lines and detailed help in pop-up windows. Trap errors as soon as possible, and give short and long error messages. Provide online tutorials, user manuals, technical support, and training courses.

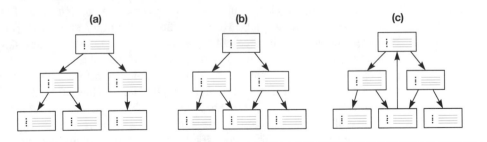

Figure 13.22 Some ways of navigating between menus or screens: (a) tree, (b) acyclic network, and (c) cyclic network.

If you use some software packages that you find particularly intuitive, have a close look at the interface design and see if you can adapt its good features to your own (so long as you don't violate any copyright in doing so!). Once you develop your prototype interface, test it on typical users and use their feedback and suggestions to finesse it.

That's a quick run through several topics that could easily fill a book on their own. Indeed, whole books are devoted to interface design, and many other schemes exist for modeling processes, including some very technical approaches that attempt to formally integrate these models with data models. Some interesting work in this regard is referenced in the chapter notes. Various methods and tools are also in common use for associated tasks such as project management (e.g., Gantt charts and PERT charts), testing, performance measures, documentation, and versioning.

13.6   Postrelational Databases and Other Trends

A conceptual schema may be mapped to various logical data models. The Rmap procedure discussed in Chapter 10 assumes that the application platform is a centralized, relational DBMS. It is a fairly simple task to specify other procedures for mapping to a hierarchic or network DBMS. However, it is being increasingly argued that the hierarchic, network, and even relational database systems are out-of-date and should be replaced by something better (e.g., object-oriented or deductive database systems). Moreover, there is a growing trend for databases to include special support for nontraditional kinds of data (e.g., spatial data, images, and sounds) and for databases to be decentralized in one way or another. This section outlines some issues behind these movements and some other recent trends in database research.

Although based on a data model introduced by Codd in 1970, relational DBMSs have only recently become dominant in the commercial marketplace. Traditional systems based on the hierarchic or even the network data model are still in use. While purely relational DBMSs suit most business applications, they may be unsuitable for complex applications such as CASE (computer-aided software engineering) tools, computer-aided design tools (e.g., VLSI design, mechanical engineering, architecture), document processing, spatial databases, expert systems, scientific databases (e.g., genetic engineering), and communications management. Note that most of these applications involve complex objects. Moreover, these account for at most 10 percent of database applications. For the other 90 percent, a relational DBMS is quite satisfactory.

Many reasons are cited for dissatisfaction with purely relational DBMSs for complex applications. They may be too slow—they don't perform well with complex objects mainly because they require too many table joins. They often model objects in an unnatural way (e.g., information about a single object such as a person may be spread over several tables—this gets worse with complex objects). They are dependent on value-based identifiers. They don't facilitate reuse (e.g., they have no direct support for subtyping). They require access to a procedural language for difficult tasks (e.g., special rules, behavior, and recursion), which leads to an "impedance mismatch" with the declarative, set-based, relational query language. They might not support BLOBs (binary large objects) such as images (icons, pictures, maps, etc.), sound tracks, video, and so on.

Over the last two decades, a lot of research has been aimed at developing a next generation of DBMS to overcome such deficiencies. Some of the new kinds of databases that have emerged are object databases, object-relational databases, deductive databases, spatial databases, and temporal databases. We'll briefly examine each of these in turn. At this stage, the only serious competitors to relational DBMSs for mainstream use are object databases and object-relational databases.

Object Orientation

An *object database* (ODB), or *object-oriented database* (OODB), incorporates various object-oriented features. Historically, ODB research drew upon related developments in four areas: programming languages, semantic data models, logical data models, and artificial intelligence. With programming languages, the need was seen for user-definable abstract data types and for persistent data. The object-oriented programming paradigm began with Simula (1967) and Smalltalk (1972). Nowadays many object-oriented programming languages exist (e.g., Eiffel), and many traditional programming languages have been given object-oriented extensions (e.g., C++ and C#).

Some object-oriented features were taken from semantic data modeling, which as we know models reality in terms of objects and their relationships, and includes notions such as subtyping (e.g., ORM, UML, and extended ER). Various ideas were also borrowed from work on logical data models (network, hierarchic, relational, and especially the nested relational model). Finally, some concepts were adapted from artificial intelligence, where structures such as frames are used for knowledge representation.

What features must a DBMS have to count as "object-oriented"? There is no commonly agreed-upon answer. A classic paper ("The OODBMS Manifesto") on this issue was presented at the first international conference on object-oriented and deductive databases (Atkinson et al. 1989). To distinguish ODBMSs from OO programming languages, five essential features of a DBMS were identified; then object-oriented features were added, of which eight were considered essential and five optional (see Table 13.2). Let's look briefly at the essential object-oriented features in this proposal.

Table 13.2 Feature list in "The OODBMS Manifesto" (Atkinson et al. 1989).

DBMS features	Essential OO features	Optional OO features
Persistence	Complex objects	Multiple inheritance
Secondary storage	Object identity	Type checking and inferencing
Concurrency	Encapsulation	Distribution
Recovery	Types or classes	Design transactions
Ad hoc query facility	Inheritance	Versions
	Overriding and late binding	
	Computationally complete	
	Extensibility	

Complex objects are built from simpler ones by constructors. The manifesto proposed that these constructors should include at least set, list, and tuple, and that these be orthogonal (they can be applied in any order, recursively). For example, one object might be a list of sets of sets of tuples. Constructors are not orthogonal in the relational model (only sets of tuples of atomic values are allowed) or the nested relational models (e.g., the top-level construct must be a set). The notion of complex objects is considered important since it allows us to model a complex structure in a direct, natural way.

The basic idea behind *object identity* is that objects should be identified by system-generated object identifiers (oids) rather than by the values of their properties. This is in sharp contrast to the relational model, where for instance tuples are identified by the value of their primary key.

Among other things, oids can help keep track of objects whose external, value-based identification may change with time. This may occur because of simple renaming. For example, television channel 0 becomes channel 10, or a woman changes her surname on marriage. More drastically, the reference scheme itself may change (e.g., a student identified by a student number becomes an employee identified by an employee number).

Object identifiers in the OO sense partly overcome this problem since they are rigid identifiers (i.e., they refer to the same object throughout time). They are system generated, nonreusable, immutable, and typically hidden. In ODB systems they might be implemented as surrogates (logical identifiers or autoincremented counters, mapped by index to physical addresses), as typed surrogates (which makes migration between types awkward), or as structured addresses.

Encapsulation involves bundling the operations and data of an object together, with normal access to the object being through its operational interface, with implementation details hidden. For example, hiring, firing, and promoting employees are regarded as operations on Employee and are encapsulated with it. Implementations of operations are often called "methods".

Encapsulation includes the idea that, as in a conceptual schema, objects should be classified in terms of *types* or *classes*. Moreover, some form of *inheritance* mechanism should be provided (e.g., so that a subtype may inherit the data and operational aspects of its supertype(s)). A subtype may have a specialized version of a function with the same name of one its supertype functions. In this case, the specialized version will typically *override* the more general version when the operation on the subtype is invoked. For example, the display procedure for a colored, equilateral triangle may differ from the general display procedure for a polygon. Various overriding options are possible.

The requirement for *computational completeness* means that any computable function can be expressed in the data manipulation language (if necessary, by calling programming languages). The *extensibility* requirement means that users may define their own types, and the system should support them just like its built-in types.

Partly in response to "The OODB Manifesto", a group of academic and industrial researchers proposed an alternative "Third Generation DBMS Manifesto" (Stonebraker et al. 1990). Here they referred to hierarchic and network systems as first generation and relational systems as second generation. Under this scheme, the third-generation DBMSs are the next generation. They specified three basic tenets and 13 detailed propositions to be adhered to by the next-generation DBMSs (see Table 13.3). This proposal essentially argued for extending existing relational systems with object-oriented features, and effectively laid the groundwork for today's object-relational database systems, which we'll discuss shortly.

Although supporting several of the object-oriented features, the group argued against implementing them in such a way as to negate key advances made by the relational approach. For example, all facts in a relational system are stored in tables. In contrast, some facts in hierarchic, network, and object database systems may be specified as links between structures, requiring navigation paths to be specified when the data is accessed. Hence OO queries typically require specification of access paths. Although path expressions are often more compact than relational queries, their reliance on existing navigation links can make it difficult to perform ad hoc queries efficiently.

Table 13.3 Next-generation DBMS features proposed by Stonebraker et al. (1990).

Basic tenets	*Detailed propositions*
1. Besides traditional data management services, next-generation DBMSs will provide support for richer object structures and rules.	1.1 Next-generation DBMSs must have a rich type system. 1.2 Inheritance is a good idea. 1.3 Functions, including database procedures, methods, and encapsulation, are a good idea. 1.4 Unique identifiers (uids) for records should be assigned by the DBMS only if a user-defined primary key is not available. 1.5 Rules (triggers, constraints) will become a major feature in future systems. They should not be associated with a specific function or collection.
2. Next-generation DBMSs must subsume previous-generation DBMSs.	2.1 Essentially all programmatic access to a database should be through a nonprocedural, high-level access language. 2.2 There should be at least two ways to specify collections, one using enumeration of members and one using the query language to specify membership. 2.3 Updatable views are essential. 2.4 Performance indicators have almost nothing to do with data models and must not appear in them.
3. Next-generation DBMSs must be open to other subsystems.	3.1 Next-generation DBMSs must be accessible from multiple high-level languages. 3.2 Persistent X for a variety of Xs is a good idea. They will all be supported on top of a single DBMS by compiler extensions and a (more or less) complex run-time system. 3.3 For better or worse, SQL is intergalactic dataspeak. 3.4 Queries and their results should be the lowest level of communication between a client and a server.

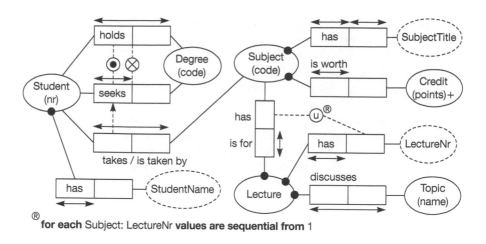

Figure 13.23 An ORM schema about university records.

As an example, consider the UoD schematized in Figure 13.23. Students either hold a degree or are currently seeking one (or both). The exclusion constraint forbids students from reenrolling in a degree that they already hold. Subjects are recorded only for current students, as shown by the subset constraint. Since this is not an equality constraint, students may enroll in a degree before choosing subjects. This aspect of the schema may alternatively be modeled by introducing the subtype CurrentStudent, to which the optional takes role is attached, using the definition **each** CurrentStudent **is a** Student **who** seeks **some** Degree.

Each subject is identified by its subject code, but also has a unique title. For some subjects, a lecture plan may be available. This lists the topics discussed in the various lectures. For example, lecture 10 for CS114 might discuss the following topics: relational projection, relational selection, and natural joins. The ® rule qualifies (and implies) the external uniqueness constraint, requiring lectures to be numbered from 1 for each subject.

The conceptual schema of Figure 13.23 might be specified in an ODB schema roughly as follows, using a syntax based on the Object Definition Language (ODL), as specified in Cattell and Barry (2000).

```
class Student {
    attribute unsigned long studentNr;
    attribute string studentName;
    attribute set<string> degreesHeld;
    attribute string currentDegree; };

class CurrentStudent extends Student {
    relationship set<Subject> takes
        inverse Subject::is_taken_by; };

class Subject {
    attribute string subjectCode;
```

```
        attribute string title;
        attribute unsigned short credit;
        relationship set<CurrentStudent> is_taken_by
            inverse CurrentStudent::takes;
        relationship list<Lecture> has
            inverse Lecture::is_for; };

class Lecture {
    attribute unsigned short lectureNr;
    relationship Subject is_for
        inverse Subject::has;
    attribute set<string> topics; };
```

Although readable, this OO schema is incomplete, and needs additional code for the extra constraints in the conceptual schema. We could display this on a UML class diagram, with the extra constraints in notes (e.g., disjunctive mandatory, pair-exclusion, and subset constraints). In general, OO schemas are best developed as abstractions of ORM schemas.

Notice that the OO classes correspond to the major object types abstracted from the conceptual schema. Hence, they provide a useful basis for building screen forms for the application. Encapsulation involves adding generic operations as well as type-specific operations (e.g., a graduate operation might be added to Student).

One problem with the ODB approach is that it mixes too many levels together—an OO schema includes conceptual, logical, and internal elements. It also involves redundant specification of associations. For example, consider the fact type Student takes Subject. In the OO schema this is specified twice: once on CurrentStudent and again on Subject.

In specifying the OO schema, inverses were used to declare bidirectional object links between CurrentStudent and Subject, as well as between Subject and Lecture. This enables queries in either direction to be specified using path expressions. This versatility is lost if the link is made unidirectional. Notice that no such navigational problem can exist in the relational model, although of course many queries will require joins. While joins might slow things down, there is no restriction on their use, since they do not require links to be set up beforehand. In contrast, the ODB approach obtains its efficiency by "hard-wiring" in the links to be used in queries. This makes it difficult to optimize ad hoc queries.

The problem of relying on predeclared access paths in the model itself to achieve efficiency is exacerbated when the schema evolves. We may then have to reset navigation pathways to optimize them for the new situation rather than simply relying on the system optimizer to do the job, as in current relational systems.

This is not to say that ODBs are a bad idea or that complex objects should not be modeled as such at the implementation level. Many complex structures are awkward to model in relational terms. However, we ought to be able to specify such structures in a clean way, without resorting to low-level mechanisms.

Unlike ODBs, relational databases are based on a single data model formally based on predicate logic. Moreover, relational DBMSs are now dominant, and many are being extended to address several of the deficiencies mentioned earlier. Such extended relational database systems are usually called *object-relational database* (ORDB) systems.

These are essentially relational DBMSs extended by adding support for many OO features, such as extra data types (spatial, image, video, text, etc.), constructors (arrays, sets, etc.), and inheritance. Some of the major commercial systems support extended data types by allowing modules to be plugged in. Such modules may be developed by the vendor or a third party. IBM calls these modules "relational extenders", Informix calls them "datablades", and Oracle calls them "data cartridges".

The SQL:1999 standard has also been significantly extended to include several object-oriented features (e.g., user-defined types and functions, encapsulation, support for oids, subtyping, triggered actions, and computational completeness) as well as deductive features (e.g., recursive union).

Given the massive installed base of relational DBMSs, the ongoing extensions to these products, the cost of porting applications to a new data model, and the widespread adoption of the SQL standard, it may well be that the next generation of DBMSs will evolve out of current relational products. Just as Hinduism absorbed features from other religions that threatened its existence, the relational model can probably absorb the interesting features of the object-oriented faith without being replaced by it.

It's debatable whether all the transformations taking place in SQL-based DBMSs are actually desirable. While the use of extended data types (spatial, video, etc.) is clearly a step forward, the use of constructors (sets, etc.) is questionable in many cases, since they can make it harder to design efficient databases for ad hoc queries and updates, and they complicate the task of writing good optimizers. For a detailed critique of the way in which many OO features have been grafted onto the relational model, see Date (2000) and Date and Darwen (1998). At any rate, relational and object-relational systems currently dominate commercially, and other contenders such as object database systems are so far struggling to gain any significant market share.

Although object-relational systems may well dominate the market for the near future, they may be "overkill" for some specialized or small applications. And there are things that even SQL:1999 can't do (e.g., it doesn't allow triggers on views) or does awkwardly (e.g., recursion).

SQL:1999 includes array collections, and SQL:200n is likely to add other collection types such as sets, multisets, and lists. One challenge then is to model such collections and provide mapping algorithms to implement them efficiently. Various constructors (e.g., for sets, bags, sequences, and schemas) have been added to some versions of ORM and ER. In addition, both ORM and UML allow some kinds of collections to be expressed as mapping annotations on the conceptual schema.

As a simple example, consider Figure 13.24. Here, constructors are shown as frames around the component object type, with their structure type named. For example, "seq" abbreviates "unique sequence" (i.e., an ordered set where each element appears at most once in the sequence). Some other modeling notations use different shapes for different kinds of collections (sets, sequences, unique sequences, bags, etc.).

Figure 13.24 indicates that a subject may have a unique sequence of lectures, each of which discusses a set of topics. The leftmost UC says each subject includes at most one sequence of lectures. Since sequences have internal order, there is no need for explicit lecture numbers, as used in Figure 13.23. If we wish to indicate that topics are also ordered within a lecture, the structure over Topic would be changed to a sequence.

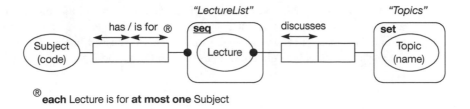

® **each** Lecture is for **at most one** Subject

Figure 13.24 Unique sequence and set constructors (not recommended).

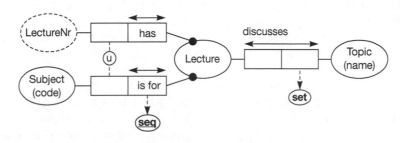

Figure 13.25 Annotations for mapping to collection types.

Although direct portrayal of complex object types may appeal, this practice needs great care. The associations in Figure 13.24 are not elementary, so the schema is not an ORM schema in the standard sense. Such diagrams may help with the following tasks: direct modeling of complex objects (especially unnamed structures), making schemas more compact, and visualizing mapping to object schemas or object-relational schemas.

On the downside, it is much easier to make mistakes when modeling complex object types directly. In particular, some constraints are harder to see, or even express, unless the elementary fact types are shown as well. For example, the ® rule in Figure 13.24 might easily be missed. Populating complex associations is also awkward, making validation more difficult. For example, try populating Figure 13.24.

Some empirical research has also revealed a tendency among modelers to "overuse" constructors, when simpler solutions without constructors actually exist. Clearly, if constructors are to be used at all in conceptual design, the design procedure needs to be augmented to control their use. In my opinion, it's best to avoid constructors completely when doing conceptual analysis. If you do want to use constructors at the logical design stage, you can annotate the conceptual schema with mapping directives to provide a view for this purpose. For example, Figure 13.25 indicates that some roles are to be mapped to collections contained within the object type that plays the other role. The sequence mapping needs extra annotation to use LectureNr to order the sequence.

This example is complicated by the composite reference scheme for Lecture. As a simpler example, consider the paper-authoring example from Section 9.7. Here the ternary Paper was authored by Person in Position can be reformulated in a design view as the binary Paper was authored by Person, annotated to map the author role to a unique sequence. The UML version of this was discussed in Section 9.7. A detailed discussion of mapping collection types in both ORM and UML can be found in Halpin (2000b).

Other Recent Trends

Deductive databases offer elegant and powerful ways of managing complex data in a declarative way, especially for information that is derived by use of recursion. Deductive systems typically provide a declarative query language such as a logic programming language (e.g., Prolog). This gives them a strong rule enforcement mechanism with built-in backtracking and excellent support for recursive rules. For example, the ancestor relation can be derived from a base parent relation and the following two rules: X is an ancestor of Y **if** X is a parent of Y (basis clause); X is an ancestor of Y **if** X is a parent of Z **and** Z is an ancestor of Y (recursive clause).

In contrast, SQL-92 cannot express recursive queries at all. SQL:1999 introduced a recursive union operator, but its syntax is more complex and its execution does not enjoy built-in backtracking. Despite their elegance, however, deductive database systems have major problems to be solved (especially in the performance area) and in the short term are unlikely to achieve more than a niche market.

Although purely deductive databases are not popular, there is a growing need to enforce many event-condition-action (ECA) rules. For example, on the event that client X requests an upgrade to class 'B' on flight Y, if the condition that X.rating = 'premier' and count(vacant B seats on flight Y) > 0 is satisfied, then perform the action: upgrade client X to class 'B' on flight Y. Most relational DBMSs effectively support ECA rules by using triggers or procedures, and triggers are now included in the SQL:1999 standard.

Two specialized database varieties that have recently become popular are spatial databases and temporal databases. *Spatial databases* require efficient management of spatial data, such as maps (roads, land, etc.), two-dimensional designs (circuits, town planning, etc.), and three-dimensional designs (visualization of medical operations, molecular structures, flight paths, etc.). They provide built-in support for spatial data types (points, lines, polygons, etc.), spatial operators (overlap, contains, intersect, etc.), and spatial indexes (R-trees, quad trees, etc.). This allows efficient formulation and processing of spatial queries such as "How many houses are there within 5 km of the proposed shopping center? Which flights fly over the greater LA area? Which figures are similar to Figure 37?"

Previously, special systems were used for spatial data while a relational DBMS was used for alphanumeric data. The current trend is to manage both standard and spatial data in the one system. A typical application of a geographic information system (GIS) might proceed as follows: standard data on traffic accidents is entered; the road maps are displayed that highlight the accident sites; this is now used to determine regions where extra precautions need to be taken (e.g., radar traps).

Historically, GIS vendors adopted three main approaches: hybrid (georelational— objects in a spatial file store are given identifiers that can be referenced in relational tables); integrated (spatial and nonspatial data are stored in relational tables); and object-oriented (all data is stored in an ODB). More recently, many spatial database applications as well as other applications using nonstandard data have been implemented using object-relational technology.

Although time has only one dimension, unlike space's three dimensions, the efficient management of *temporal information* is no easy task. If historical rather than snapshot records need to be maintained about objects, time will feature largely in the modeling. An exercise question is included at the end of this section to help you appreciate how this complicates even a basic application.

A variety of approaches may be adopted for modeling time. In some cases we simply include object types such as Time and Period on the conceptual schema and map these like other object types. Distinctions may be needed between *transaction time* (when the system records a fact) and *valid time* (when the fact is true in the UoD being modeled). Often we need to make use of temporal relations (such as before and after) and temporal operations (e.g., to compute an interval between two time points). Sometimes, an ordinary relational database does not allow the model to be implemented efficiently. For such applications, special DBMSs known as "temporal database systems" are sometimes used; these provide in-built support for automatic timestamping and the various temporal operators. The SQL standard currently includes only basic support for temporal data. A major extension to SQL:1999 to handle temporal information, called "Part 7/Temporal", is planned for release around 2003. For a thorough discussion of developing time-oriented applications in SQL, see Snodgrass (2000).

Most work on temporal databases focuses on maintaining relevant histories of application objects through time, with the assumption that the conceptual schema itself is fixed. Moving up one level, the problem becomes more complicated if we allow the conceptual schema itself to change with time. This is one aspect of the schema evolution problem.

Moving up another level, we might allow the conceptual metaschema itself to change with time (e.g., we might decide at a later stage to allow constructors for complex object types in our conceptual schema language). The management of such higher-order evolution has been addressed in recent research on evolving information systems. This topic provides one motivation for the next section on metamodeling.

Apart from the kind of database used, the size and spread of databases has seen a continued upward trend. Many databases are becoming very large, with users at many different sites. For this situation we need to decide whether the overall system will be centralized, distributed, or federated.

In a *centralized* system, the database and management is controlled at a single site. Any site may send update and query requests to the central site, and results are sent back. If the sites are far apart, the communication times involved in such transactions can be very significant.

To reduce the communication overhead, a *distributed* database system allows the data to be spread across various sites, with most of the data relevant to a given site stored locally at that site. In the simplest case, the population of a schema might be partitioned (e.g., each branch of a bank stores data about its clients only). Typically, however, there is a need to replicate some data at more than one site, thus requiring measures to be enforced to control the redundancy. As you might guess, optimizing the performance of a distributed system requires attention to a whole new batch of problems. The research literature on distributed databases is vast, and many commercial systems already provide distributed capabilities, to varying extents.

More recently, the notion of *federated* databases has arisen to deal with situations where there is a need for data sharing between several existing database systems, possibly heterogeneous (e.g., some relational, some hierarchic, and so on). In this framework, each individual system maintains its local autonomy and communicates with other sites on a needs basis. As the heterogeneity problem requires translation between different data models, the control of federated systems is nontrivial. The size of the problem can be reduced by supporting only partial integration; any two sites need only share the common data relevant to both of them, rather than all their data.

Different solutions have arisen to address the problems of communicating between different database systems, possibly of different types. For a long time, SQL has been used as a common language between relational DBMSs. In today's world of e-commerce, the variety of systems that need to exchange data has grown significantly. At the time of writing, the most promising solution to this problem appears to be the use of *eXtensible Markup Language* (XML) for communicating structured information between different systems. XML is a low-level, hierarchically structured, textual language that allows the specification of both schema and data.

Like SQL, XML is good for communication between computer systems, but is not high level enough for humans to easily visualize and model their application domain. Hence an XML schema is best developed by first modeling in a high level-language such as ORM, ER, or UML, then mapping the model to XML.

One of the most exciting, and perhaps almost frightening, trends in modern computing has been the recent progress in artificial intelligence. If you'd like an insight into where computer science may well go in the next 50 years, have a read of Denning and Metcalfe (1997). For a radical view of where AI may take us in the next 100 years, see Kurzweil (1999)—I don't agree with his materialist philosophy, so I disagree with many of his projections, but they are worth thinking about. The chapter notes provide some further discussion and references for the topics covered in this section.

13.7   Metamodeling

Modeling involves making models of application domains. *Metamodeling* involves making models of models—this time the applications being modeled are themselves models. Just as recursion is one of the most elegant and powerful concepts in logic, metamodeling is one of the most beautiful and powerful notions in conceptual modeling. This section uses a simple example to convey the basic idea.

A database holds fact instances from an application, while its conceptual schema models the *structure* of the application. Figure 13.26 recalls our basic view of an

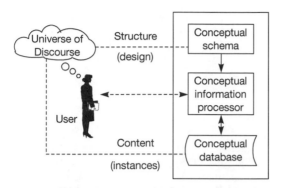

Figure 13.26 The database must conform to the structure of the conceptual schema.

Table 13.4 One report extracted from a movie database.

MovieNr	Title	Director	Stars
1	Wilderness	Tony O'Connor	
2	Sleepy in Seattle	Anne Withanee	Ima Dozer
			Anne Withanee
3	Wilderness	Anne Withanee	Paul Bunyip

information system, where the information processor ensures that the database conforms to the rules laid down in the conceptual schema. Essentially a DBMS is a system for managing various database applications; for each application it checks that each database state agrees with the structure specified in the conceptual schema for that application.

Among other things, a conceptual modeling tool is a system for managing conceptual schemas. Each valid schema diagram in this book may be thought of as an output report from this system. The trick then is to treat a schema as a database instance of this higher-level system. So long as we can verbalize the diagrams into elementary facts, we can use the CSDP to develop a conceptual schema for such conceptual schemas. We would then have a conceptual *metaschema* (schema about schemas).

Suppose that Table 13.4 is part of an output report from a movie database. Other reports from the same application provide further information (e.g., people's birthplaces).

The conceptual subschema for this report is shown in Figure 13.27. The disjunctive mandatory role constraint on Person is shown explicitly since Person plays other roles in the global schema (e.g., as in Figure 13.9).

In this case, the information system architecure in Figure 13.26 still applies, but the user is an information modeler, the database holds a conceptual schema, the UoD is about conceptual schemas, and the conceptual information processor ensures that only

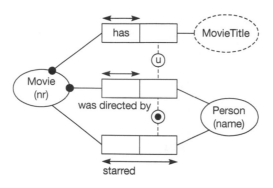

Figure 13.27 A conceptual schema for Table 13.4.

valid conceptual schemas are placed in the database by checking that they satisfy the structure specified in the meta conceptual schema.

Rather than developing a complete metaschema for ORM conceptual schemas, let's confine our discussion here to simple examples like Figure 13.27, ignoring nesting, subtyping, derivation, and all constraints other than uniqueness and mandatory role constraints. If you've never done metamodeling before, it seems a bit strange at first. As a challenge, see if you can perform CSDP step 1 using Figure 13.27 as a sample report.

Metamodeling is like ordinary modeling, except the kind of information to be modeled is structural. You might begin by describing Figure 13.27 roughly. For example: "It has two entity types (Movie and Person) and one value type (MovieTitle). The first role of the 'was directed by' predicate is mandatory and has a uniqueness constraint", and so on. This verbalization conveys the information, but we need to express it in terms of elementary facts. For example, using "OTkind" to mean "kind of object type", we might say: "The ObjectType named 'Movie' is of OTkind named 'Entity'".

In previous chapters we saw that the same UoD may be modeled in different ways. This applies here too, since there are many different ways in which the information in Figure 13.27 can be verbalized as elementary facts. For example, consider the information that both roles of the predicate called "starred" are spanned by the same uniqueness constraint. How would you say this in elementary facts?

With diagrammatic applications like this, you often find that you want to talk about an object (such as a constraint) but it *hasn't got a name* on the diagram. You would naturally identify it to somebody next to you by *pointing* to it, but this won't help you convey the information over the telephone to someone.

In such cases it is often convenient to introduce an artificial name, or *surrogate,* to identify the object. This is done in Figure 13.28, where each constraint has been given an identifying constraint number. For convenience, I've also introduced role numbers and predicate numbers (though we could have identified roles by their positions in predicates and predicates by their names). If names are used to identify predicates, in general, we need to expand them with the OT names (e.g., to distinguish "Movie starred Person" from "Play starred Person").

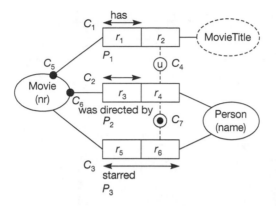

Figure 13.28 Surrogates are added to identify constraints, roles, and predicates.

The metaschema shown in Figure 13.29 is only one of many possible solutions. As an aid to understanding, it is populated with the database, or set of facts, that corresponds to the conceptual schema shown in Figure 13.28. Here, "UI", "UE", and "MR" abbreviate "uniqueness internal", "uniqueness external", and "mandatory role", respectively. Recall that other constraints are ignored in this discussion. For simplicity, only one name is stored for each predicate, and nesting is ignored. This solution also ignores the implicit reference types implied by reference modes. If you developed an alternative metaschema, don't forget to do a population check.

The metaschema actually contains features not present in our original example (e.g., value constraints and subtyping). So it is not rich enough to capture itself. As a nontrivial exercise you may wish to extend the metaschema until it can capture any ORM schema. For instance you can capture subtype links by adding the fact type ObjectType is a subtype of ObjectType. To test a full ORM metaschema, you should be able to populate it with itself.

Metamodeling is not restricted to conceptual schemas. Any well-defined formalism can be metamodeled. Apart from being used to manage a given formalism, metamodels can also be developed to allow translation between different formalisms (e.g., ER, ORM, and UML). This is sometimes referred to as metametamodeling.

Because of ORM's greater expressive power, it is reasonably straightforward to capture data models in UML or ER within an ORM framework. Though less convenient, it is possible to work in the other direction as well. To begin with, UML's graphic constraint notation can be supplemented by textual constraints in a language of choice (e.g., OCL). Moreover, the UML metamodel itself has built-in extensibility that allows many constraints specific to ORM to be captured within a UML-based repository.

For example, the ORM model in Figure 13.30(a) contains four constraints $C_1..C_4$. While the uniqueness constraints are easily expressed in UML as multiplicity constraints, the subset and exclusion constraints have no graphic counterpart in UML. The UML metamodel fragment shown in Figure 13.30(b) extends the standard UML metamodel with constraintNr, constraintType, and elementNr attributes, and SetCompConstraint as a subtype along with the argLength attribute. The full UML

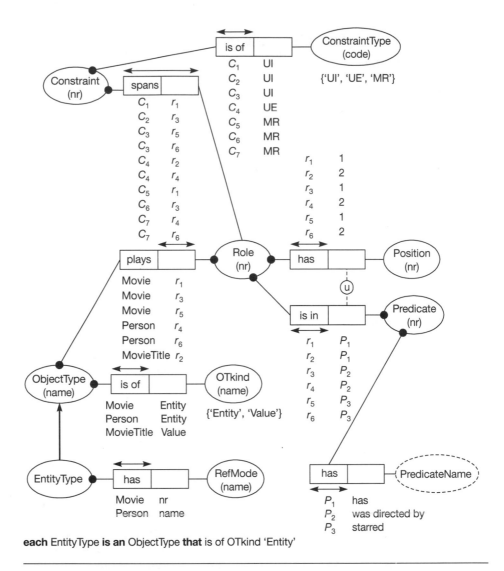

Figure 13.29 A conceptual metaschema, populated with the schema of Figure 13.28.

metamodel is vast, so I've included only the fragment relevant to the example. The attribute constraintType stores the type of constraint (subset, exclusion, mandatory, etc.). SetCompConstraint denotes set-comparison constraint (subset, equality, or exclusion), and argLength is the argument length or number of roles (association ends) at each end of the constraint.

The four ORM constraints may now be stored as the object relation shown in Table 13.5. The subset (SS) and exclusion (X) constraints have their argument length recorded. The actual arguments of these two constraints may now be derived by "dividing" the role lists by this number. Thus, the arguments of the subset constraint are the

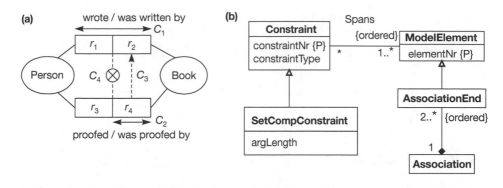

Figure 13.30 Modeling ORM constraints in an extended UML metamodel fragment.

Table 13.5 Metatable for storing ORM constraints.

Constraint:	constraintNr	constraintType	roles	argLength
	C_1	UI	r_1, r_2	
	C_2	UI	r_4	
	C_3	SS	r_4, r_2	1
	C_4	X	r_1, r_2, r_3, r_4	2

simple roles r_4 and r_2, whereas the arguments of the exclusion constraint are the role pairs (r_1, r_2) and (r_3, r_4). The constraint type may now be used to determine the appropriate semantics.

Though this simple example illustrates the basic idea, transforming the complete ORM metamodel into UML is complex. For example, as the UML metamodel fragment indicates, UML associations must have at least two roles (association ends), so rather artificial constructs must be introduced for dealing with unaries.

A taste of metamodeling can really whet one's appetite, but I'm afraid this is as far as we go in this book. I hope you have gained some insights into the science and art of conceptual modeling by reading this book, and that you share my belief that modeling the real world is one of the most challenging, important, and satisfying things that humans can do.

Exercise 13.7

1. Devise a conceptual metaschema (in ORM, UML, or ER) to store simple SQL schemas where each table has at most one primary key (possibly none). A primary key may be composite (multicolumn), but each foreign key references a simple (single-column) primary key. Tables are identified by simple names. Columns are ordered by position, and may be optional or mandatory. Each column in a primary key is mandatory, but it is possible that all columns in a keyless table are optional. Ignore domains and all other constraints (e.g.,

uniqueness constraints on column sets other than primary keys). For example, your meta-schema should be able to store the following schema:

Employee (<u>empNr</u>, empName, salary, [taxPaid])

Drives (<u>empNr, carRegNr</u>)

2. Map your answer to Question 1 to a relational schema.

13.8   Summary

Online transaction processing (OLTP) systems are used for typical database applications involving frequent updates and queries. A *data warehouse* is updated only on a scheduled basis from online sources and is used in read-only mode for enterprisewide analysis of trends by management. *Data marts* are departmental subsets derived from the data warehouse but focused on a single subject area. Data marts are often denormalized for performance reasons and are often based on a *star schema* structure with one central "fact" table, referenced by dimension tables. Data warehouses and data marts are used for online analytical processing (OLAP) and data mining. Often a star schema is used to construct a multidimensional structure, or *cube,* containing base and aggregated measures that can be accessed across various dimensions, including time.

Just as information systems can be modeled at different levels, so they can be queried at different levels. Conceptual query languages allow queries to be formulated either in natural language (e.g., English Query) or by selecting and constraining paths on a conceptual schema (e.g., ConQuer). Conceptual query tools automatically transform these high-level queries into queries in a lower-level language such as SQL. Conceptual queries based on an attribute-free model such as ORM are far more stable when the schema evolves.

With large, complex schemas there is a need for *abstraction mechanisms* to hide details that are not of immediate relevance. Modularization divides the global schema into conveniently sized subschemas. Constraint layers and textual rules may be toggled off and on as desired. We may zoom in on, or out from, a selected object type, specifying how much of its neighborhood is to be displayed.

Major object types may be identified by their importance in the global schema (e.g., having an explicit mandatory role), and the display suppressed for "minor" fact types (without two roles played by major object types). This view may be refined further by focusing on its major fact types, and so on. Such bottom-up abstraction may be reversed to give top-down refinement.

Minor fact types may also be displayed in terms of attributes of major object types. In this case, ER diagrams and UML class diagrams may be generated as abstractions of ORM diagrams. While such abstractions are good for compact overviews, detailed ORM diagrams are best for developing, transforming, and evolving conceptual schemas.

Although the data model is the foundation of any information systems application, there is also a need to specify *process models* to indicate the permissible *operations* on the data, and to design the *external interface*. For such purposes, various diagrams and notations may be used to supplement data model diagrams.

In early stages, informal diagrams such as cartoons can help clarify the UoD, and *function trees* and UML *use case diagrams* are useful for providing overviews of the system requirements. Use cases may be refined somewhat using other kinds of diagrams such as UML activity diagrams and sequence diagrams. *Data flow diagrams* may also be used to picture information flows between processes, agents, and information stores. However, at some stage a formal connection needs to be made between processes and data. For this purpose, *data use cases* may be used to determine the data model to which processes may be bound (e.g., by defining *operations on the major object types*). This can also be used to generate the content (operations) of default screen forms for the external interface. Some default decisions can be made about the format and use of these screens.

Design of the *human-computer interface* (HCI) typically requires careful planning by humans. Access rights for different user groups need to be controlled. Users may also differ in their ability level. To make the *user interface* (UI) easy to learn and use, the interface should be consistent, simple, structured, efficient, and adapted to the user. In most cases a graphical user interface (GUI) is preferable. The *menu* design needs to provide efficient navigation, and various levels of online and offline help are required.

Relational DBMSs are suitable for about 90 percent of business applications, but may prove inefficient for structurally complex applications such as CASE tools and VLSI design. In the near future, such applications might best be implemented using either an *object-relational database* (ORDB) or an *object database* (ODB). In the long-term future, *deductive databases* might prove a viable option.

Apart from the usual DBMS features, ODB systems provide direct support for complex objects, object identity, encapsulation, object types and subtypes, overriding, and late binding, and are computationally complete and extensible. Object identifiers are basically rigid, system-generated surrogates that are hidden from the user. They avoid many of the problems associated with changing identifiers, but it is at least debatable whether they should be used when a stable primary key is available.

Object-oriented database schemas include a mix of conceptual, logical, and external levels. Elementary facts may be redundantly specified to provide two-way navigation between objects. Like ER and UML schemas, they are awkward to populate and do not facilitate the expression of many constraints. Hence, they are best developed after an ORM schema has already been constructed.

Object-relational systems support some object-oriented features, but provide these on top of the basic relational features. To facilitate mapping to ODBs or ORDBs, it is sometimes argued that we should model complex objects on conceptual schemas using constructors for collections (e.g., set, bag, sequence, schema). However, it may well be better to keep the conceptual schema in its elementary form, and later annotate it where necessary to provide mapping to collections.

Instead of being centralized, a database might be *distributed* or *federated*. This raises additional design and optimization problems (e.g., communication overhead, redundancy control, and translation). Further design problems may arise in the modeling of *temporal* or *spatial* data and in controlling the *evolution* of schemas.

By treating conceptual schemas as sample database states, the CSDP may be used to develop a conceptual *metaschema*. This may be used by a CASE tool to ensure that only valid conceptual schemas are entered. The activity of *metamodeling,* or making models of models, may be also used to clarify and translate between other formalisms.

Chapter Notes

The literature on data warehousing and OLAP is substantial. Date (2000, Chapter 21) provides a clear overview of decision support. Inmon (1993), Kimball (1996), and Silverston et al. (1997) provide practical advice on data warehousing. The sexcode example of data cleansing was suggested by Scot Becker—thanks, Scot! Thomsen et al. (1999) provide a thorough discussion of OLAP for SQL Server, including a detailed coverage of MDX.

A brief review of conceptual query prototypes, such as ERQL, Super, Hybris, and CBQL, is given in Bloesch and Halpin (1997). Some other graphical database query languages are surveyed in Ozsoyoglu and Wang (1993). English Wizard appears to have evolved into EasyAsk (see *www.easyask.com*). For details on English Query, see *www.microsoft.com/sql/eq*.

The RIDL language was originally used in conjunction with Control Data's IAST tool for NIAM, which was the first true CASE tool for information modeling (Meersman and Van Assche 1983). A full description of the RIDL language is given in Meersman et al. (1984), and further discussions of RIDL may be found in Meersman (1982a, 1982b) and Verheijen and van Bekkum (1982). For further discussion of ConQuer, see Bloesch and Halpin (1996, 1997) and Halpin (1998a).

For more details about schema abstraction within ORM, see Campbell and Halpin (1994a) and Campbell et al. (1996) and their various references. A procedure for generating default external forms from major object types is discussed in Campbell and Halpin (1993).

McLeod (2000) offers useful suggestions for extending use cases and activity diagrams in UML. For practical advice on traditional ways to model the process aspects on information systems, see Barker and Longman (1992) and Barker (1990). Some promising ways to integrate data and process are discussed by Shoval and Kabeli (2000). Extensive discussions of HCI design are provided by Shneiderman (1992) and Dix et al. (1993). Microsoft Windows user interface guidelines can be accessed at the following URL: *http://msdn.microsoft. com/library/books/winguide/ welcome.htm*.

The OODB "manifesto" is stated in Atkinson et al. (1989), and an alternative, extended relational "manifesto" is proposed by Stonebraker et al. (1990). Two good papers on object identity are provided by Khoshaflan and Copeland (1990) and the ever lucid Kent (1991). One of the best books on object-oriented databases is Cattell (1991); it includes an excellent, annotated bibliography (pp. 273–310). Cattell and Barry (2000) provide a thorough coverage of the ODMG 3.0 standard. Date (2000, Chapters 24 and 25) provides a critique of object databases and object-relational databases. An alternative foundation for object-relational databases is provided by the "Third Manifesto" of Date and Darwen (1998).

Date (2000, Chapters 20, 22, and 23) gives a clear overview of distributed, temporal, and deductive databases. There is a vast literature on temporal databases and the impact of time in information systems. A classic survey of the area is given by Snodgrass (1990). For a survey of temporal issues within the context of fact-based modeling, see Petrounias and Loucopoulos (1994). An advanced and extensive treatment of evolutionary aspects of information systems is given by Proper (1994). A thorough treatment of developing temporal databases in SQL is provided by Snodgrass (2000).

Two useful books on XML are Pardi (1999) and Finkelstein and Aiken (2000). The latest official news on XML standards is accessible from the Web site *www.w3.org*.

Metamodels for ORM and Barker ER are discussed in Halpin (2000d, 2000e). NIST (1993) includes a metamodel for IDEF1X. A metamodel for UML is contained in OMG (1999). The UML metamodel is large and currently has many errors. As a final exercise, see if you can find them!

An overly optimistic (or pessimistic, depending on which way you look at it) account of the future of artificial intelligence can be found in Kurzweil (1999). A more balanced account of the expected future of computing over the next 50 years is given in Denning and Metcalfe (1997).

ORM Glossary

This glossary lists key terms and symbols used in Object-Role Modeling and briefly explains their meaning. A concise explanation of other technical terms may be found in the chapter summaries. Further details on technical terms may be accessed by using the index.

Arity: Number of roles in a relationship (unary = 1, binary = 2, ternary = 3, etc.).

Association: Relationship type, usually involving at least two roles.

Base fact type: Fact type that is primitive (not derived from others).

Compositely identified object type: Either a coreferenced object type or a nested entity type.

Compound fact type: Fact type that is equivalent to a conjunction of smaller fact types.

Conceptual schema: Conceptual model of the UoD structure; design that specifies what states and transitions are possible; declaration of elementary fact types, constraints, and derivation rules.

Conceptual schema design procedure (CSDP):
0   Divide the UoD into manageable subsections
1   Transform familiar examples into elementary facts, and apply quality checks
2   Draw the fact types, and apply a population check
3   Check for entity types that should be combined, and note arithmetic derivations
4   Add uniqueness constraints, and check arity of fact types
5   Add mandatory role constraints, and check for logical derivations
6   Add value, set-comparison (subset, equality, exclusion), and subtype constraints

7   Add other constraints and perform final checks
8   Integrate the subschemas into a global conceptual schema

Constraint: Restriction on possible states (static constraint) or transitions (dynamic constraint).

Coreferenced object: Object that is identified by means of two or more reference types in combination. Hence its identification scheme involves an external uniqueness constraint.

Database: Variable set of related fact instances.

Derivation rule: Rule that declares how one fact type may be derived from others.

Derived fact type: Fact type that is derived from other fact types using a derivation rule.

Elementary fact: Assertion that an object has a property, or that one or more objects participate in a relationship, where the fact cannot be split into simpler facts with the same object types without information loss.

Entity: Object that is referenced by relating it to other objects (e.g., the Country that has CountryCode 'AU'); not a value. Typically, an entity may undergo changes over time. An entity is either atomic or nested (i.e., an objectified relationship). At the top level, entities are partitioned into primitive entity types, from which subtypes may be defined.

Fact: Sentence not used for primary reference. It may be elementary or compound.

Fact role: Role in a fact type.

Fact type: Kind of fact, including object terms and predicate.

Flatten: Restate without nesting.

Functional fact type: Fact type with a functional role.

Functional role: Role with a simple uniqueness constraint.

Generalization: Forming a more general case from one or more specific types; the inverse of specialization.

Independent entity: Entity that may exist without participating in any fact. The disjunction of fact roles played by an independent entity type is optional.

Instance: An individual occurrence (one specific member of a type).

Mandatory role: Role that must be played by all instances in the population of the object type playing the role; also called a total role.

Nesting: Relationship that plays some role (also called an objectified relationship).

Object: Thing of interest. An object may be an entity or a value.

Object-Role Modeling (ORM): Conceptual modeling method that pictures an application domain in terms of objects playing roles. It provides graphical and textual languages for verbalizing information as well as a design procedure.

Population: Set of instances present in a particular state of the database.

Predicate: Proposition with object holes in it (e.g., "... works for ...").

Reference: Relationship used as the primary way to reference or identify an object (or to provide part of the identification).

Reference mode: Mode or manner in which a single value references an entity; used to abbreviate simple reference schemes, for example, (code), (kg).

Reference role: Role in a reference type.

Relationship: Property or association involving one or more objects. If we talk about a relationship (i.e., the relationship itself plays some role), it then becomes an object as well, called an objectified relationship, objectified association, or nesting.

Rmap: Relational mapping procedure.

Role: Part played by an object in a relationship (possibly unary).

Specialization: Forming special cases from a more general type; the inverse of generalization.

Subtype: Object type that is contained in another object type. Subtypes must be well defined in terms of relationships played by their supertype(s). Subtypes with the same top supertype may overlap.

Type: Set of possible instances.

Uniqueness constraint (UC): Repetition is not allowed in the role or role sequence spanned by the constraint. A uniqueness constraint on a single predicate is an internal UC, and a uniqueness constraint over roles from different predicates is an external UC.

Universe of discourse (UoD): Application domain (the aspects of the world that we want to talk about).

Value: Unchangeable object that is identified by a constant. In this book, a value is either a character string or a number. Sometimes called a label.

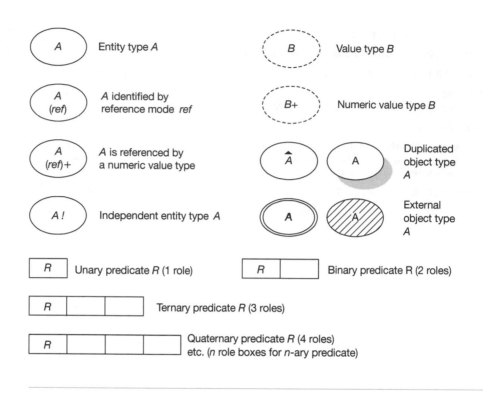

A	Entity type A	
A (ref)	A identified by reference mode *ref*	
A (ref)+	A is referenced by a numeric value type	
A !	Independent entity type A	
B	Value type B	
B+	Numeric value type B	
Â / A	Duplicated object type A	
A (doubled) / A (hatched)	External object type A	

R	Unary predicate R (1 role)
R □	Binary predicate R (2 roles)
R □ □	Ternary predicate R (3 roles)
R □ □ □	Quaternary predicate R (4 roles) etc. (*n* role boxes for *n*-ary predicate)

Internal uniqueness constraints:

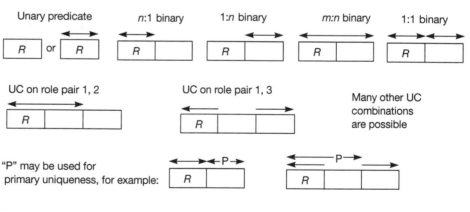

Unary predicate   *n*:1 binary   1:*n* binary   *m*:*n* binary   1:1 binary

UC on role pair 1, 2

UC on role pair 1, 3

Many other UC combinations are possible

"P" may be used for primary uniqueness, for example:

External uniqueness constraint:

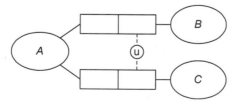

Each *bc* pair relates to only one *a*

External uniqueness constraints may apply over *n* roles (*n* > 1)

Ⓟ may be used to denote primary reference

Role played only by *A*   Role mandatory for population of *A*

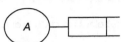   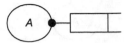   or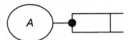

Inclusive-or constraint:
Disjunction of roles is mandatory
for population of *A*; that is,
each *a* in pop(*A*) plays
at least one of roles $r_1 .. r_n$

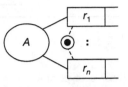   or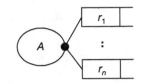

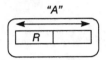

Objectified association (nested entity type):
Relationship type *R* is objectified as entity type *A*

Nesting may be applied to two or more roles with a spanning UC

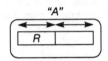

Nesting may also be applied
to 1:1 relationships

Value constraints indicate possible values or value ranges or both

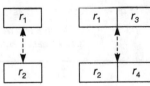

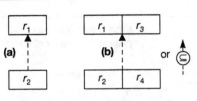

Subset constraints:

(a) Each object that plays r_2 also plays r_1

(b) Each object pair playing r_2, r_4 also plays r_1, r_3

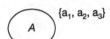   or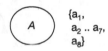

Equality constraints:

Populations must be equal

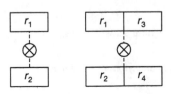

Exclusion constraints:

Populations must be mutually exclusive

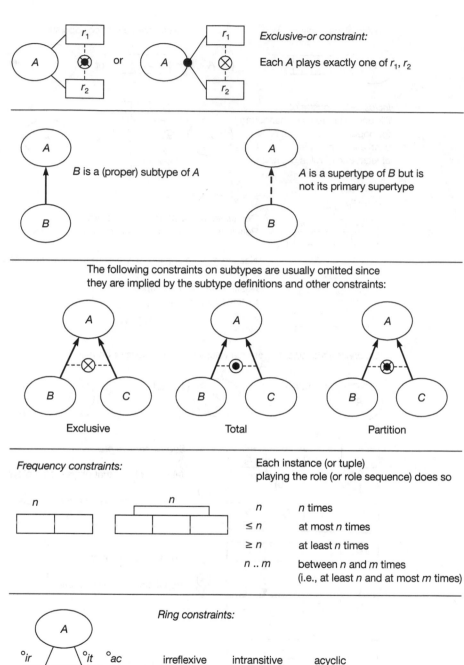

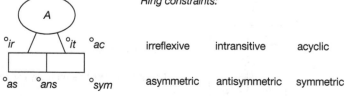

Exclusive-or constraint:

Each *A* plays exactly one of r_1, r_2

B is a (proper) subtype of *A*

A is a supertype of *B* but is not its primary supertype

The following constraints on subtypes are usually omitted since they are implied by the subtype definitions and other constraints:

Exclusive   Total   Partition

Frequency constraints:

Each instance (or tuple) playing the role (or role sequence) does so

n	n times
$\leq n$	at most n times
$\geq n$	at least n times
$n .. m$	between n and m times (i.e., at least n and at most m times)

Ring constraints:

°*ir*   °*it*   °*ac*   irreflexive   intransitive   acyclic

°*as*   °*ans*   °*sym*   asymmetric   antisymmetric   symmetric

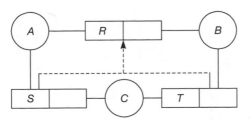

A join-subset constraint.

Each *ab* pair in the conceptual join of *S* and *T* is also in *R*

Any set-comparison constraint may be specified between compatible role paths

---

$*$ derived
fact type

$**$derived and stored

(R) extra rule applies

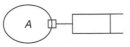

$\# < n$

Cardinality of any population of *A* must be less than *n*

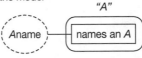

Relative closure:
  If *a* plays the role in the real world,
  this is known in the model

"A"

Aname — names an A

Entity type *A*
in FCO-IM

A simple example of constraint verbalization:

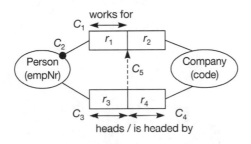

works for

heads / is headed by

C_1:   **each** Person works for **at most one** Company
C_2:   **each** Person works for **at least one** Company
C_3:   **each** Person heads **at most one** Company
C_4:   **each** Company is headed by **at most one** Person
C_5:   **each** Person **who** heads **a** Company **also** works for **that** Company

The absence of a UC on role r_2 may be verbalized as

        it is possible that more than one Person works for **the same** Company

ER Glossary

This glossary lists the symbols used in the Barker ER notation, the Information Engineering notation for ER, and the IDEF1X notation, as discussed in Chapter 8.

Barker ER notation

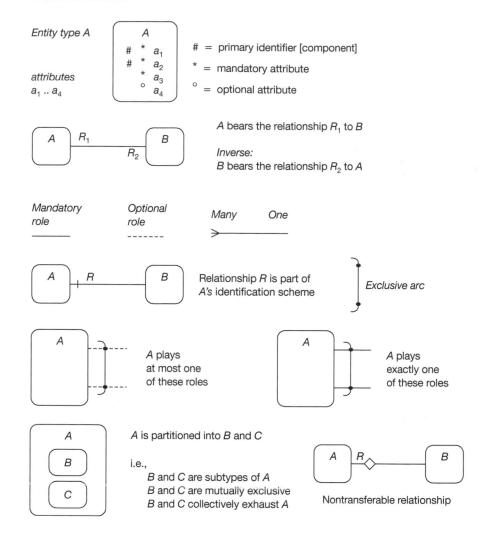

Information Engineering notation

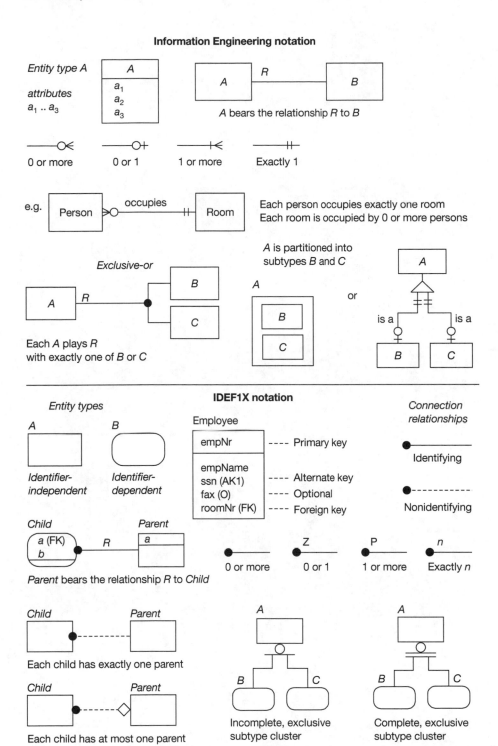

Entity type A

attributes
$a_1 .. a_3$

A bears the relationship R to B

0 or more   0 or 1   1 or more   Exactly 1

e.g. Person occupies Room   Each person occupies exactly one room
Each room is occupied by 0 or more persons

Exclusive-or

Each *A* plays *R*
with exactly one of *B* or *C*

A is partitioned into
subtypes *B* and *C*

or

is a   is a

IDEF1X notation

Entity types   *Connection relationships*

A   B

Employee

empNr ---- Primary key

empName
ssn (AK1) ---- Alternate key
fax (O) ---- Optional
roomNr (FK) ---- Foreign key

Identifying

Nonidentifying

*Identifier-
independent*   *Identifier-
dependent*

Child   *Parent*

a (FK)
b   R   a

Parent bears the relationship R to Child

0 or more   Z 0 or 1   P 1 or more   n Exactly n

Child   *Parent*

Each child has exactly one parent

Child   *Parent*

Each child has at most one parent

Incomplete, exclusive
subtype cluster

Complete, exclusive
subtype cluster

UML Glossary

This glossary lists key terms and symbols used in UML data models (*class diagrams*), as discussed in Chapter 9. In addition, Section 7.4 mentions UML statecharts, and Section 13.5 briefly discusses UML use cases and activity diagrams. UML also includes interaction diagrams (sequence, collaboration) and implementation diagrams (component, deployment).

Aggregate: Class that is the "whole" in a whole-part relationship.

Association: Relationship type, involving two or more association roles.

Association class: An association that is also a class; an objectified association in ORM.

Association end: Corresponds to a role in ORM.

Attribute: Property of an object; either single valued or multivalued.

Changeability: How an attribute or role value may change: changeable, frozen, addOnly.

Class: Type of object (cf. ORM entity type).

Composition (composite aggregation): Each part belongs to at most one whole.

Data value: Scalar constant; data type instance; self-identifying (cf. ORM value).

Derived element: An attribute or association that is computed or inferred from others.

Generalization: Forming a more general class (a superclass) from one or more classes.

Link: Relationship instance—a fact or reference in ORM.

Multiplicity: Number of instances to which the same object may relate in an attribute or association.

Object: A thing that may typically change its state; a class instance; identified by an oid (cf. ORM entity instance).

Oid: Object identifier; system-generated constant that references an object.

Ordered constraint: Annotation to map role to an ordered set.

Qualified association: Association where one class relates to another via a qualifier.

Shared aggregation: A part may belong to more than one whole.

Specialization: Forming one or more specific classes (subclasses) from a more general class.

State: The properties of an object at a point in time.

Subset constraint: Restricts the population of one association to be a subset of another.

Xor constraint: Exclusive-or constraint between roles (association ends).

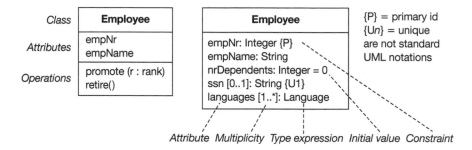

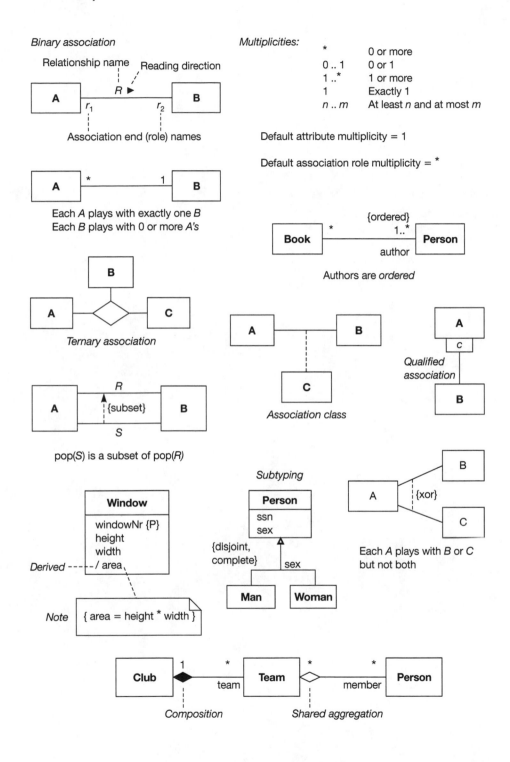

Binary association

Relationship name   Reading direction

A —— R ▶ —— B
r_1 r_2

Association end (role) names

Multiplicities:

*	0 or more
0 .. 1	0 or 1
1 ..*	1 or more
1	Exactly 1
$n .. m$	At least n and at most m

Default attribute multiplicity = 1

Default association role multiplicity = *

A —— * —— 1 —— B

Each *A* plays with exactly one *B*
Each *B* plays with 0 or more *A's*

{ordered}

Book —— * —— 1..* —— Person
author

Authors are *ordered*

Ternary association

Qualified association

Association class

R
A {subset} B
S

pop(*S*) is a subset of pop(*R*)

Subtyping

Person
ssn
sex

{disjoint, complete}   sex

Man   **Woman**

A {xor} B / C

Each *A* plays with *B* or *C* but not both

Window
windowNr {P}
height
width
Derived ---- / area

Note   { area = height * width }

Club —1—— *—— Team ——* —— *—— Person
team   member

Composition   *Shared aggregation*

Bibliography

Entries marked with an asterisk "*" are accessible online at *www.orm.net*.

Abrial, J.R. 1974. "Data Semantics". *Data Base Management*. J.W. Klimbie and K.L. Koffeman (eds.). Amsterdam: North-Holland, pp. 1–60.

Aho, A.V., C. Beeri, and J.D. Ullman. 1979. "The Theory of Joins in Relational Databases". *ACM Trans. on Database Systems,* vol. 4, no. 3, pp. 297–314.

ANSI. 1999. *Database Languages—SQL*. ANSI/ISO/IEC9075-1999. New York: American National Standards Institute. Published in five parts; can be purchased online at *www.ncits.org (www.cssinfo.com/features/ISO_IEC_9075.html)*.

Ascaris Software. 2000. FCO-IM Casetool. Details online at *www.fcoim.com*.

Atkinson, M., F. Bancilhon, D. DeWitt, K. Dittrick, D. Maier, and S. Zdonik. 1989. "The Object-Oriented Database System Manifesto". *Proc. DOOD-89: First Int. Conf. on Deductive and Object-Oriented Databases,* Kyoto. W. Kim, J-M. Nicolas, and S. Nishio (eds.). Amsterdam: Elsevier, pp. 40–57.

Bakema, G.P., J.P.C. Zwart, and H. van der Lek. 1994. "Fully Communication Oriented NIAM". *NIAM-ISDM 1994 Conf. Working Papers*. G.M. Nijssen and J. Sharp (eds.). Albuquerque, NM, pp. L1–35.

Barbier, F., B. Henderson-Sellers, A. Opdahl, and M. Gogolla. 2000. "The Whole-Part Relationship in UML: A New Approach". *Unified Modeling Language: Systems Analysis, Design and Development Issues*. K. Siau and T. Halpin (eds.). Hershey, PA: Idea Group Publishing Company.

Barker, R. 1990. *CASE*Method: Tasks and Deliverables*. Wokingham, England: Addison-Wesley.

Barker, R., and C. Longman. 1992. *CASE*Method: Function and Process Modelling.* Wokingham, England: Addison-Wesley.

Batini, C., S. Ceri, and S. Navathe. 1992. *Conceptual Database Design: An Entity-Relationship Approach.* Redwood City, CA: Benjamin/Cummings.

Bentley, J. 1998. "Little Languages". *More Programming Pearls.* J. Bentley (ed.). Reading, MA: Addison-Wesley.

Blaha, M., and W. Premerlani. 1998. *Object-Oriented Modeling and Design for Database Applications.* Englewood Cliffs, NJ: Prentice Hall.

Bloesch, A.C., and T.A. Halpin. 1996. "ConQuer: A Conceptual Query Language". *Proc. ER'96: 15th Int. Conf. on Conceptual Modeling.* Springer LNCS, no. 1157, pp. 121–33.*

Bloesch, A.C., and T.A. Halpin. 1997. "Conceptual Queries Using ConQuer-II". *Proc. ER'97: 16th Int. Conf. on Conceptual Modeling.* Springer LNCS, no. 1331, pp. 113–26.*

Booch, G., J. Rumbaugh, and I. Jacobson. 1999. *The Unified Modeling Language User Guide.* Reading, MA: Addison-Wesley.

Bruce, T. 1992. *Designing Quality Databases: Practical Information Management and IDEF1X.* New York: Dorset House.

Campbell, L., and T.A. Halpin. 1993. "Automated Support for Conceptual to External Mapping". *Proc. 4th Workshop on Next Generation CASE Tools.* S. Brinkkemper and F. Harmsen (eds.). Paris: Univ. Twente Memoranda Informatica 93-32, pp. 35–51.

Campbell, L., and T.A. Halpin. 1994a. "Abstraction Techniques for Conceptual Schemas". *Proc. 5th Australasian Database Conf.,* Christchurch (Jan.). Singapore: World Scientific.

Campbell, L., and T.A. Halpin. 1994b. "The Reverse Engineering of Relational Databases". *Proc. 5th Workshop on Next Generation CASE Tools,* Utrecht (June).

Campbell, L.J., T.A. Halpin, and H.A. Proper. 1996. "Conceptual Schemas with Abstractions: Making Flat Conceptual Schemas More Comprehensible". *Data and Knowledge Engineering,* vol. 20, no. 1, pp. 39–85.*

Cattell, R.G.G. 1991. *Object Data Management.* Reading, MA: Addison-Wesley.

Cattell, R.G.G., and D.K. Barry (eds.). 2000. *The Object Data Standard: ODMG 3.0.* San Francisco: Morgan Kaufmann.

Celko, J. 1999. *Data & Databases: Concepts in Practice.* San Francisco: Morgan Kaufmann.

Celko, J. 2000. *Joe Celko's SQL for Smarties: Advanced SQL Programming,* second edition. San Francisco: Morgan Kaufmann.

Chamberlin, D. 1998. *A Complete Guide to DB2 Universal Database.* San Francisco: Morgan Kaufmann.

Chamberlin, D., and R. Boyce. 1974. "SEQUEL: A Structured English Query Language". *Proc. 1974 ACM SIGMOD Workshop on Data Description, Access and Control,* Ann Arbor, MI.

Chawdhry, P.K. 1992. "NIAMEX—ANIAM Compiler and EXPRESS Pre-processor". *Proc. EXPRESS Users Group Conf.,* Oct.

Chen, P.P. 1976. "The Entity-Relationship Model—Toward a Unifed View of Data". *ACM Transactions on Database Systems,* vol. 1, no. 1, pp. 9–36.

Choobineh, J., M.V. Mannino, and V.P. Tseng. 1992. "A Form-Based Approach for Database Analysis and Design". *CACM,* vol. 35, no. 2, pp. 108–20.

Codd, E.F. 1969. "Derivability, Redundancy, and Consistency of Relations Stored in Large Data Banks". *IBM Research Report* RJ599. August 19.

Codd, E.F. 1970. "A Relational Model of Data for Large Shared Data Banks". *CACM,* vol. 13, no. 6, pp. 377–87.

Codd, E.F. 1990. *The Relational Model for Database Management: Version* 2. Reading, MA: Addison-Wesley.

Codd, E.F., S.B. Codd, and C.T. Salley. 1993. "Providing OLAP (On-line Analytical Processing) to User-Analysts: An IT Mandate". Arbor Software Corporation. Accessible at *www.arborsoft.com/essbase/wht_ppr/coddToc.html.*

Connolly, T., C. Begg, and A. Strachan. 1999. *Database Systems,* second edition. Reading, MA: Addison-Wesley.

Control Data. 1982. *IAST: Information Analysis Support Tools.* Reference Manual, Control Data
   Publication no. 60484610.

Creasy, P.N. 1989. "ENIAM—A More Complete Conceptual Schema Language". *Proc. 15th
   VLDB Conf.,* Amsterdam.

Czejdo, B., R. Elmasri, M. Rusinkiewicz, and D.W. Embley. 1990. "A Graphical Data Manipulation Language for an Extended Entity-Relationship Model". *IEEE Computer,* March,
   pp. 26–37.

Date, C.J. 1998. "The Birth of the Relational Model: Parts 1–3". *Intelligent Enterprise,* vol. 1,
   Oct–Dec. San Mateo, CA: Miller Freeman.

Date, C.J. 2000. *An Introduction to Database Systems,* vol. 1, seventh edition. Reading, MA:
   Addison-Wesley.

Date, C.J., and H. Darwen. 1997. *A Guide to the SQL Standard,* fourth edition. Reading, MA:
   Addison-Wesley.

Date, C.J., and H. Darwen. 1998. *Foundation for Object/Relational Databases: The Third Manifesto.* Reading, MA: Addison-Wesley.

D'Atri, A., and D. Sacca. 1984. "Equivalence and Mapping of Database Schemas". *Proc. 10th
   Int. Conf. on Very Large Databases,* VLDB, Singapore, pp. 187–95.

Delaney, K. 2000. "Introducing Indexed Views". *SQL Server Magazine,* no. 15, pp. 32–37. Duke
   Communications, *www.sqlmag.com.*

Denning, P.J., and R.M. Metcalfe (eds.). 1997. *Beyond Calculation: The Next Fifty Years of Computing.* New York: Springer-Verlag.

De Troyer, O. 1991. "The OO-Binary Relationship Model: A Truly Object-Oriented Conceptual
   Model". *Advanced Information Systems Engineering: Proc. CAiSE-91,* Springer-Verlag
   Lecture Notes in Comp. Science, no. 498, Trondheim.

De Troyer, O. 1993. *On Data Schema Transformation.* Ph.D. thesis, Katholieke Universiteit of
   Brabant, Tilburg.

De Troyer, O., and R. Meersman. 1995. "A Logic Framework for a Semantics of Object Oriented
   Data Modeling". *Proc. OOER'95: Object-Oriented and Entity-Relationship Modeling,*
   Springer Lecture Notes in Comp. Science, no. 1021, Gold Coast Australia, pp. 238–49.

Dc Troyer, O., R. Meersman, and P. Verlinden. 1988. "RIDL* on the CRIS Case: A Workbench
   for NIAM". *Computerized Assistance during the Information Systems Life Cycle: Proc.
   CRIS-88,* T.W. Olle, A.A. Verrijn-Stuart, and L. Bhabuta (eds.). Amsterdam: North-
   Holland.

Dix, A., J. Finlay, G. Abowd, and R. Beale. 1993. *Human-Computer Interaction.* New York:
   Prentice Hall.

Elmasri, R., and S. Navathe. 1994. *Fundamentals of Database Systems,* second edition. Redwood City, CA: Benjamin/Cummings.

Embley, D. 1998. *Object Database Management.* Reading, MA: Addison-Wesley.

Embley, D.W., B.D. Kurtz, and S.N. Woodfield. 1992. *Object-Oriented Systems Analysis.*
   Englewood Cliffs, NJ: Prentice Hall.

Embley, D.W., H.A. Wu, J.S. Pinkston, and B. Czejdo. 1996. "OSM-QL: A Calculus-Based
   Graphical Query Language". Tech. Report, Dept. of Comp. Science, Brigham Young
   Univ., Utah.

Evans, C. 1980. *The Mighty Micro.* London: Coronet Books.

Everest, G. 1976. "Basic Data Structure Models Explained with a Common Example". *Proc.
   Fifth Texas Conference on Computing Systems,* Austin, TX (Oct.). Long Beach, CA: IEEE
   Computer Society Publications, pp. 39–45.

Everest, G.C. 1994. "Experiences Teaching NIAM/OR Modeling". *Proc. 2nd NIAM-ISDM
   Conf.,* Albuquerque, NM.

Fagin, R. 1977. "Multivalued Dependencies and a New Normal Form for Relational Databases".
   ACM Trans. on Database Systems, vol. 2, no. 3.

Fagin, R. 1979. "Normal Forms and Relational Database Operators". *Proc. 1979 ACM SIGMOD
   Int. Conf. on Management of Data,* Boston.

Fagin, R. 1981. "A Normal Form for Relational Databases That Is Based on Domains and Keys". *ACM Trans. on Database Systems,* vol. 6, no. 3, pp. 387–415.

Falkenberg, E.D. 1976. "Concepts for Modelling Information". *Modelling in Database Management Systems.* G.M. Nijssen (ed.). Amsterdam: North-Holland Publishing.

Falkenberg, E.D., W. Hesse, P. Lindgreen, B.E. Nilson, J.L.H. Oei, C. Rolland, R.K. Stamper, F.J.M. Van Assche, A.A. Verrijn-Stuart, and K. Voss. 1998. *A Framework of Information System Concepts: The FRISCO Report* (Web edition), IFIP. Available online by anonymous *ftp://ftp.leidenuniv.nl/pub/rul/fri-full.zip.*

Falkenberg, E.D., and J.L.H. Oei. 1994. "Meta-model Hierarchies from an Object-Role Modeling Perspective". *Proc. First Int. Conf. on Object-Role Modeling (ORM-1),* Magnetic Island, Australia. T.A. Halpin and R.M. Meersman (eds.), pp. 218–27.

Fillmore, C.J. 1968. "The Case for Case". *Universals in Linguistic Theory.* E. Bach and R.T. Harms (eds.). New York: Holt, Rinehart, and Winston, pp. 1–88.

Finkelstein, C. 1989. *Introduction to Information Engineering.* Reading, MA: Addison-Wesley.

Finkelstein, C. 1992. *Information Engineering: Strategic Systems Development.* Reading, MA: Addison-Wesley.

Finkelstein, C. 1998. "Information Engineering Methodology". *Handbook on Architectures of Information Systems.* P. Bernus, K. Mertins, and G. Schmidt (eds.). Berlin: Springer-Verlag, pp. 405–27.

Finkelstein, C., and P. Aiken. 2000. *Building Corporate Portals with XML.* New York: McGraw-Hill.

Fowler, M., with K. Scott. 1997. *UML Distilled.* Reading, MA: Addison-Wesley.

Haack, S. 1978. *Philosophy of Logics.* London: Cambridge University Press.

Habrias, H. 1993. "Normalized Object Oriented Method". *Encyclopedia of Microcomputers,* vol. 12. New York: Marcel Dekker, pp. 271–85.

Halpin, T.A. 1989a. "Venn Diagrams and SQL Queries". *The Australian Computer Journal,* vol. 21, no. 1, pp. 27–32.

Halpin, T.A. 1989b. "A Logical Analysis of Information Systems: Static Aspects of the Data-Oriented Perspective". Ph.D. thesis, University of Queensland.

Halpin, T.A. 1989c. "Contextual Equivalence of Conceptual Schemas". *Proc. Advanced Database Systems Symposium.* Kyoto: Inform. Proc. Society of Japan, pp. 47–54.

Halpin, T.A. 1990a. "Conceptual Schemas and Relational Databases". *Databases in the 1990s: Proc. 1st Australian Database Conf.* B. Srinivasan and J. Zeleznikov (eds.). Singapore: World Scientific, pp. 45–56.

Halpin, T.A. 1990b. "Conceptual Schema Optimization". *Proc. 13th Australian Computer Science Conf.,* Monash University, Melbourne.

Halpin, T.A. 1991a. "Optimizing Global Conceptual Schemas". *Databases in the 1990s:2 —Proc. 2nd Australian Database Conf.* B. Srinivasan and J. Zeleznikov (eds.). Singapore: World Scientific.

Halpin, T.A. 1991b. "A Fact-Oriented Approach to Schema Transformation". *Proc. MFDBS-91 Int. Conf. on Mathematical Fundamentals of Database and Knowledge Base Systems.* Springer-Verlag Lec. Notes in Computer Science, no. 495, Rostock.

Halpin, T.A. 1991c. "WISE: A Workbench for Information System Engineering". *Proc. 2nd European Workshop on Next Generation of CASE Tools,* Trondheim. Revised and reprinted in the book *Next Generation CASE Tools,* IOS Press (1992).

Halpin, T.A. 1992. "Fact-Oriented Schema Optimization". *Proc. CISMOD-92* (Int. Conf. on Inform. Sys. & Management of Data), Indian Institute of Science, Bangalore, India, pp. 288–302.

Halpin, T.A. 1993. "What Is an Elementary Fact?" *Proc. 1st NIAM-ISDM Conf.,* Utrecht.*

Halpin. T.A. 1995. "Subtyping: Conceptual and Logical Issues". *Database Newsletter,* R.G. Ross (ed.), Database Research Group, Inc., vol. 23, no. 6, pp. 3–9.*

Halpin, T.A. 1996. "Business Rules and Object-Role Modeling". *Database Programming and Design,* vol. 9, no. 10 (Oct.), pp. 66–72.*

Halpin, T.A. 1998a. "Conceptual Queries". *Database Newsletter,* R.G. Ross (ed.), Database Research Group, Inc., vol. 26, no. 2 (Mar./Apr.).*

Halpin, T.A. 1998b. "Object-Role Modeling (ORM/NIAM)". *Handbook on Architectures of Information Systems.* Heidelberg: Springer, Ch. 4.*

Halpin, T.A. 1998–99. "UML Data Models from an ORM Perspective: Parts 1–10". *Journal of Conceptual Modeling.* Minneapolis, MN: InConcept.*

Halpin, T.A. 1999a. "Object Role Modeling: An Overview". *www.orm.net.**

Halpin, T.A. 1999b. "Data Modeling in UML and ORM Revisited". *Proc. EMMSAD'99: 4th IFIP WG8.1 Int. Workshop on Evaluation of Modeling Methods in Systems Analysis and Design,* Heidelberg, Germany (June).*

Halpin, T.A. 2000a. "Integrating Fact-Oriented Modeling with Object-Oriented Modeling". *Information Modeling for the New Millennium.* K. Siau and M. Rossi (eds.). Hershey, PA: Idea Group Publishing Company.

Halpin, T.A. 2000b. "Modeling Collections in UML and ORM". *Proc. EMMSAD'00: 5th IFIP WG8.1 Int. Workshop on Evaluation of Modeling Methods in Systems Analysis and Design,* Kista, Sweden.*

Halpin, T.A 2000c. "Supplementing UML with Concepts from ORM". *Unified Modeling Language: Systems Analysis, Design and Development Issues.* K. Siau and T. Halpin (eds.). Hershey, PA: Idea Group Publishing Company.

Halpin, T.A. 2000d. "An ORM Metamodel". *Journal of Conceptual Modeling,* no. 16. Minneapolis, MN: InConcept.*

Halpin, T.A. 2000e. "An ORM Metamodel of Barker ER". *Journal of Conceptual Modeling,* no. 17. Minneapolis, MN: InConcept.*

Halpin, T.A., and A.C. Bloesch. 1999. "Data Modeling in UML and ORM: A Comparison". *Journal of Database Management,* vol. 10, no. 4. Hershey, PA: Idea Group Publishing Company, pp. 4–13.*

Halpin, T.A., and R.A. Girle. 1981. *Deductive Logic,* second edition. Brisbane: Logiqpress.

Halpin, T.A., and J.I. McCormack. 1992. "Automated Validation of Conceptual Schema Constraints". *Advanced Inf. Systems Engineering: Proc. CAiSE-92.* P. Loucopoulos (ed.). Springer-Verlag LNCS, vol. 593, Manchester, pp. 445–62.

Halpin, T.A., and H.A. Proper. 1995a. "Database Schema Transformation and Optimization". *Proc. OOER'95.* M. Papazoglou (ed.). Springer LNCS, no. 1021, pp. 191–203.*

Halpin, T.A., and H.A. Proper. 1995b. "Subtyping and Polymorphism in Object-Role Modeling". *Data and Knowledge Engineering,* vol. 15, pp. 251–81.*

Halpin, T.A., and P.R. Ritson. 1992. "Fact-Oriented Modelling and Null Values". *Proc. 3rd Australian Database Conf.* B. Srinivasan and J. Zeleznikov (ed.). Singapore: World Scientific.

Halpin, T.A., and P.R. Ritson. 1996. "Entity Integrity Revisited". *The Australian Computer Journal,* vol. 28, no. 3, August, pp. 73–80.

Halpin, T.A., and D. Vermeir. 1997. "Default Reasoning in Information Systems". *Database Applications Semantics.* London: Chapman & Hall, pp. 423–41.

Harris, R.L. 1996. *Information Graphics: A Comprehensive Illustrated Reference.* Atlanta, GA: Management Graphics.

Hay, D.C. 1999a. "There Is No Object-Oriented Analysis". *DataToKnowledge Newsletter,* vol. 27, no. 1. Houston, TX: Business Rule Solutions, Inc.

Hay, D.C. 1999b. "Object Orientation and Information Engineering: UML". *The Data Administration Newsletter,* no. 9 (June), R.S. Reiner (ed.). Available online at *www.tdan.com.*

Heath, I.J. 1971. "Unacceptable File Operations in a Relational Database". *Proc. 1971 ACM SIGFIDET Workshop on Data Description, Assess and Control,* San Diego, CA.

Hohenstein, U., and G. Engels. 1991. "Formal Semantics of an Entity-Relationship-Based Query Language". *Entity-Relationship Approach: The Core of Conceptual Modelling (Proc. 9th ER Conf.),* H. Kangassalo (ed.). Amsterdam: Elsevier Science.

IEEE. 1999. *IEEE Standard for Conceptual Modeling Language Syntax and Semantics for IDEF1X$_{97}$ (IDEF$_{object}$).* IEEE Std 1320.2–1998. New York: IEEE.

Inmon, W.H. 1993. *Building the Data Warehouse.* New York: John Wiley & Sons.

Intellibase. 1990. *RIDL-M User's Guide.* Belgium: Intellibase N.V.

Jacobson, I., G. Booch, and J. Rumbaugh. 1999. *The Unified Software Development Process.* Reading, MA: Addison-Wesley.

Jarke M., J. Mylopoulos, J. Schmidt, and Y. Vassiliou. 1992. "DAIDA: An Environment for Evolving Information Systems". *ACM Transactions on Inform. Systems,* vol. 10, no. 1, pp. 1–50.

Kendall, K.E., and J.E. Kendall. 1988. *Systems Analysis and Design.* Englewood Cliffs, NJ: Prentice Hall.

Kennedy, P. 1993. *Preparing for the Twenty-First Century.* London: Harper Collins.

Kent, W. 1977. "Entities and Relationships in Information". *Proc. 1977 IFIP Working Conf. on Modelling in Data Base Management Systems,* Nice, France. G.M. Nijssen (ed.). Amsterdam: North-Holland Publishing, pp. 67–91.

Kent, W. 1978. *Data and Reality: Basic Assumptions in Data Processing Reconsidered.* Amsterdam: North-Holland Publishing.

Kent, W. 1983. "A Simple Guide to Five Normal Forms in Relational Database Theory". *CACM,* vol. 26, no. 2, pp. 120–25.

Kent, W. 1991. "A Rigorous Model of Object Reference, Identity, and Existence". *Journal of Object-Oriented Programming,* June, pp. 28–36.

Khoshaflan, S.N., and G.P. Copeland. 1990. "Object Identity". *Readings in Object-Oriented Database Systems.* S.B. Zdonik and D. Maier (eds.). San Francisco: Morgan Kaufmann, pp. 37–46.

Kimball, R. 1996. *The Data Warehouse Toolkit.* New York: John Wiley & Sons.

Kobayashi, I. 1986. "Losslessness and Semantic Correctness of Database Schema Transformation: Another Look at Schema Equivalence". *Information Systems,* vol. 11, no. 1. Tarrytown, NY: Pergamon Press, pp. 41–59.

Kobayashi, I. 1990. "Transformation and Equivalence among Predicate Systems". *Proc. French-Japanese Seminar on Deductive Databases and Artificial Intelligence,* INRIN, Sophia-Antipolis.

Kobryn, C. 1999. "UML 2001: A Standardization Odyssey". *Communications of the ACM,* vol. 42, no. 10, pp. 29–37.

Kurzweil, R. 1999. *The Age of Spiritual Machines.* London: Phoenix.

Levesque, H. 1984. "A Fundamental Trade-off in Knowledge Representation and Reasoning". *Proc. CSCSI-84,* London, Ontario, pp. 141–52.

Ling, T.W., F.W. Tompa, and T. Kameda. 1981. "An Improved Third Normal Form for Relational Databases". *ACM Trans. on Database Systems,* vol. 6, no. 2, pp. 329–46.

Loney, K., and G. Koch. 2000. *Oracle8i: The Complete Reference.* Berkeley, CA: Osborne/McGraw-Hill.

Mark, L. 1988. "The Binary Relationship Model". Tech. Report UMIACS–TR–88–67, University of Maryland.

Martin, J. 1993. *Principles of Object Oriented Analysis and Design.* Englewood Cliffs, NJ: Prentice Hall.

Martin, J., and J. Odell. 1998. *Object-Oriented Methods: A Foundation, UML Edition.* Englewood Cliffs, NJ: Prentice Hall.

Matthews, R.W., and W.C. McGee. 1990. "Data Modeling for Software Development". *IBM Systems Journal,* vol. 29, no. 2, pp. 228–35.

McCormack, J.I., T.A. Halpin, and P.R. Ritson. 1993. "Automated Mapping of Conceptual Schemas to Relational Schemas". *Advanced Info. Systems Engineering: Proc. CAiSE-93,* Paris (June). C. Rolland, F. Bodart, and C. Cauvet (eds.). Springer-Verlag LNCS, vol. 685, pp. 432–48.

McLeod, G. 2000. "Beyond Use Cases". *Proc. EMMSAD'00: 5th IFIP WG8.1 Int. Workshop on Evaluation of Modeling Methods in Systems Analysis and Design,* Kista, Sweden.

Meersman, R. 1982a. "The RIDL Conceptual Language". Research report, Int. Centre for Information Analysis Services, Control Data Belgium, Brussels.

Meersman, R. 1982b. "The High-Level End User". *Infotech State of the Art Report,* series 10, no. 7. Tarrytown, NY: Pergamon Press, pp. 535–53.

Meersman, R., O. De Troyer, and F. Ponsaert. 1984. *The RIDL User Guide.* Control Data Corp., Brussels.

Meersman, R., and F. Van Assche. 1983. "Modeling and Manipulating Production Databases in Terms of Semantic Nets". *Proc. 8th IJCAI Conference.* San Francisco: Morgan Kaufmann.

Melton, J., and A.R. Simon. 1993. *Understanding the New SQL: A Complete Guide.* San Francisco: Morgan Kaufmann.

Menzel, C., and R.J. Mayer. 1998. "The IDEF Family of Languages". *Handbook on Architectures of Information Systems.* P. Bernus, K. Mertins, and G. Schmidt (eds.). Berlin: Springer-Verlag, pp. 209–41.

Mok, W.Y., and D.W. Embley. 1996. "Transforming Conceptual Model to Object-Oriented Database Designs: Practicalities, Properties and Peculiarities". *Proc. ER'96: 15th Int. Conf. on Conceptual Modeling.* Springer LNCS, vol. 1157, pp. 309–24.

Moody, D., and M. Kortink. 2000. "From Enterprise Models to Dimensional Models: A Methodology for Data Warehouse and Data Mart Design". *Proc. DMDW'00: Int. Workshop on Design and Management of Data Warehouses,* Report 25, Swiss Life IT R&D, Zurich.

Muller, R.J. 1999. *Database Design for Smarties.* San Francisco: Morgan Kaufmann.

Mylopoulos, J. 1998. "Information Modelling in the Time of the Revolution". *Information Systems,* vol. 23, no. 3/4. Tarrytown, NY: Pergamon, pp. 127–55.

Nijssen, G.M. 1976. "A Gross Architecture for the Next Generation Database Management Systems". *Proc. 1976 IFIP Working Conf. on Modelling in Data Base Management Systems,* Freudenstadt, Germany. G.M. Nijssen (ed.). Amsterdam: North-Holland Publishing, pp. 1–24.

Nijssen, G.M. 1977. "Current Issues in Conceptual Schema Concepts". *Proc. 1977 IFIP Working Conf. on Modelling in Data Base Management Systems,* Nice, France. G.M. Nijssen (ed.). Amsterdam: North-Holland Publishing, pp. 31–66.

Nijssen, G.M. 1994. "A General Analysis Procedure: Recent Advances in Universal Informatics". *Proc. 2nd NIAM-ISDM Conf.,* Albuquerque, NM.

NIST. 1993. *Integration Definition for Information Modeling (IDEF1X).* FIPS Publication 184. National Institute of Standards and Technology. *www.sdct.itl.nist.gov/~ftp/idef1x.trf.*

Odell, J. 1998. *Advanced Object-Oriented Analysis and Design Using UML.* New York: Cambridge University Press and SIGS Books.

Olle, T.W., J. Hagelstein, I.G. Macdonald, C. Rolland, H.G. Sol, F.J.M. van Assche, and A.A. Verrijn-Stuart. 1991. *Information Systems Methodologies: A Framework for Understanding,* second edition. Reading, MA: Addison-Wesley.

OMG. 1999. *OMG Unified Modeling Language Specification,* version 1.3. UML Revision Task Force. Available online from *www.omg.org* and *http://uml.shl.com/artifacts.htm.*

Orlowska, M., and Y. Zhang. 1992. "Understanding the Fifth Normal Form (5NF)". *Australian Computer Science Communications,* vol. 14, pp. 631–39.

Ozsoyoglu, G., and H. Wang. 1993. "Example-Based Graphical Database Query Languages". *Computer,* vol. 26, no. 5, pp. 25–38.

Pardi, W.J. 1999. *XML in Action.* Redmond, WA: Microsoft Press.

Petrounias, I., and P. Loucopoulos. 1994. "Time Dimension in a Fact-Based Model". *Proc. ORM-1 Conference,* Dept. of Computer Science, University of Queensland.

Pohl, K. 1994. "The Three Dimensions of Requirements Engineering: A Framework and Its Applications". *Information Systems.* Tarrytown, NY: Pergamon, pp. 243–58.

Proper, H.A. 1994. "A Theory for Conceptual Modelling of Evolving Application Domains". Ph.D. thesis, University of Nijmegen.

Reiner, D. 1992. "Database Design Tools". *Conceptual Database Design.* C. Batini, S. Ceri, and S. Navathe (eds.). Redwood City, CA: Benjamin/Cummings, Chapter 15.

Rissanen, J. 1977. "Independent Components of Relations". *ACM Trans. on Database Systems,* vol. 2, no. 2, pp. 317–25.

Ritson, P.R., and T.A. Halpin. 1993a. "Mapping One-to-One Predicates to a Relational Schema". *Advances in Database Research: Proc. 4th Australian Database Conf.* M.E. Orlowska and M. Papazoglou (eds.). Singapore: World Scientific, pp. 68–84.

Ritson, P.R., and T.A. Halpin. 1993b. "Mapping Integrity Constraints to a Relational Schema". *Proc. 4th ACIS,* Brisbane (Sep.), pp. 381–400.

Rochfeld, A., J. Morejon, and P. Negros. 1991. "Inter-Relationship Links in E-R Model". *Entity Relationship Approach: The Core of Conceptual Modelling (Proc. 9th ER Conf.).* H. Kangassalo (ed.). Amsterdam: Elsevier Science.

Ross, R.G. 1998. *Business Rule Concepts.* Houston, TX: Business Rule Solutions, Inc.

Rumbaugh, J., I. Jacobson, and G. Booch. 1999. *The Unified Modeling Language Reference Manual.* Reading, MA: Addison-Wesley.

Seidman, C. 2000. "Creating Horizontally Partitioned Views". *SQL Server Magazine,* no. 14, pp. 51–53. Duke Communications, *www.sqlmag.com.*

Senko, M.E. 1975. "Information Systems: Records, Relations, Sets, Entities and Things". *Information Systems,* vol. 1, no. 1, Jan. 1975. Tarrytown, NY: Pergamon Press, pp. 3–13.

Shneiderman, B. 1992. *Designing the User Interface,* second edition. Reading, MA: Addison-Wesley.

Shoval, P., E. Gudes, and M. Goldstein. 1988. "GISD: A Graphical Interactive System for Conceptual Database Design". *Information Systems,* vol. 13, no. 1, pp. 81–95.

Shoval, P., and J. Kabeli. 2000. "Functional and Object-Oriented Analysis & Design of Information Systems—An Integrated Methodology". *Proc. EMMSAD'00: 5th IFIP WG8.1 Int. Workshop on Evaluation of Modeling Methods in Systems Analysis and Design,* Kista, Sweden.

Shoval, P., and N. Shreiber. 1993. "Database Reverse Engineering: From the Relational to the Binary Relational Model". *Data and Knowledge Engineering,* vol. 10, pp. 293–315.

Siau, K., and T. Halpin (eds.). 2000. *Unified Modeling Language: Systems Analysis, Design and Development Issues.* Hershey, PA: Idea Group Publishing Company.

Silverston, L., W.H. Inmon, and K. Graziano. 1997. *The Data Model Resource Book.* New York: John Wiley.

Snodgrass, R.T. 1990. "Temporal Databases: Status and Research Directions". *SIGMOD Record,* vol. 19, no. 4, pp. 83–89.

Snodgrass, R.T. 2000. *Developing Time-Oriented Database Applications in SQL.* San Francisco: Morgan Kaufmann.

Stonebraker, M., L. Rowe, B. Lindsay, J. Gray, M. Carey, M. Brodie, P. Bernstein, and D. Beech. 1990. "Third Generation Database System Manifesto". *ACM SIGMOD Record,* vol. 19, no. 3.

ter Hofstede, A.H.M. 1993. *Information Modelling in Data Intensive Domains.* Ph.D. thesis, University of Nijmegen.

ter Hofstede, A.H.M., H.A. Proper, and T.P. van der Weide. 1993. "Formal Definition of a Conceptual Language for the Description and Manipulation of Information Models". *Information Systems,* vol. 18, no. 7, pp. 489–523.

ter Hofstede, A.H.M., H.A. Proper, and T.P. van der Weide. 1994. "Fact Orientation in Complex Object Role Modeling Techniques". *Proc. 1st Int. Conf. on Object-Role Modeling (ORM-1),* Magnetic Island, Australia. T. Halpin and R. Meersman (eds.), pp. 45–59.

ter Hofstede, A.H.M., H.A. Proper, and T.P. van der Weide. 1996. "Query Formulation as an Information Retrieval Problem". *The Computer Journal,* vol. 39, no. 4, pp. 255–74.

Thalheim, B. 1984. "Deductive Basis of Relations". *Proc. MFSSS-84.* Lec. Notes in Computer Science, no. 215. Heidelberg: Springer-Verlag, pp. 226–30.

Thalheim, B. 1994. *Fundamentals of Entity-Relationship Modelling.* Heidelberg: Springer-Verlag.

Thomsen, E., G. Spofford, and D. Chase. 1999. *Microsoft OLAP Solutions.* New York: John Wiley.

van Bommel, P., and T.P. van der Weide. 1992. "Reducing the Search Space for Conceptual Schema Transformations". *Data and Knowledge Engineering,* vol. 8, pp. 269–92.

van Griethuysen, J.J. (ed.). 1982. *Concepts and Terminology for the Conceptual Schema and the Information Base*. ISO TC97/SC5/WG3. Eindhoven.

Verheijen, G.M.A., and J. van Bekkum. 1982. "NIAM: An Information Analysis Method". *Information Systems Design Methodologies: A Comparative Review. Proc. IFIP WG8.1 Working Conf.*, Noordwijkerhout, Netherlands: North-Holland Publishing, pp. 537–90.

Vermeir, D. 1983. "Semantic Hierarchies and Abstractions in Conceptual Schemata". *Information Systems,* vol. 8, no. 2, pp. 117–24.

Vincent, M.W. 1994. "Semantic Justification of Normal Forms in Relational Database Design". Ph.D. thesis, Monash University.

Vincent, M.W., and B. Srinivasan. 1993. "Redundancy and the Justification for Fourth Normal Form in Relational Databases". *Int. Journal of Foundations of Computer Science,* vol. 4, no. 4, pp. 355–65.

Vincent, M.W., and B. Srinivasan. 1994. "A Note on Relation Schemes Which Are in 3NF But Not in BCNF". *Information Processing Letters,* vol. 48, pp. 281–83.

Warmer, J., and A. Kleppe. 1999. *The Object Constraint Language: Precise Modeling with UML*. Reading, MA: Addison-Wesley.

Wintraecken, J.J.V.R. 1990. *The NIAM Information Analysis Method: Theory and Practice*. Deventer, Netherlands: Kluwer.

Zachman, J. 1987. "A Framework for Information Systems Architecture". *IBM Systems Journal,* vol. 26, no. 3, pp. 276–92.

Zaniolo, C. 1982. "A New Normal Form for the Design of Relational Database Schemas". *ACM Trans. on Database Systems,* vol. 7, no. 3, pp. 489–99.

Index

Symbols and Numbers

About the Author

Dr. Terry Halpin is program manager in the database modeling, enterprise framework, and tools unit at Microsoft Corporation. During a lengthy career as an academic in computer science, he also worked in industry on database modeling technology and as a data modeling consultant. His recent positions include head of database research at Asymetrix Corporation; research director at InfoModelers, Inc., which was acquired by Visio Corporation in February 1998; and director of database strategy at Visio Corporation, which was acquired by Microsoft Corporation in January 2000. His doctoral thesis provided the first full formalization of Object-Role Modeling (ORM/NIAM), and his publications include over ninety technical papers, as well as three previous books.